AF599087

EXPLORING WINE REGIONS

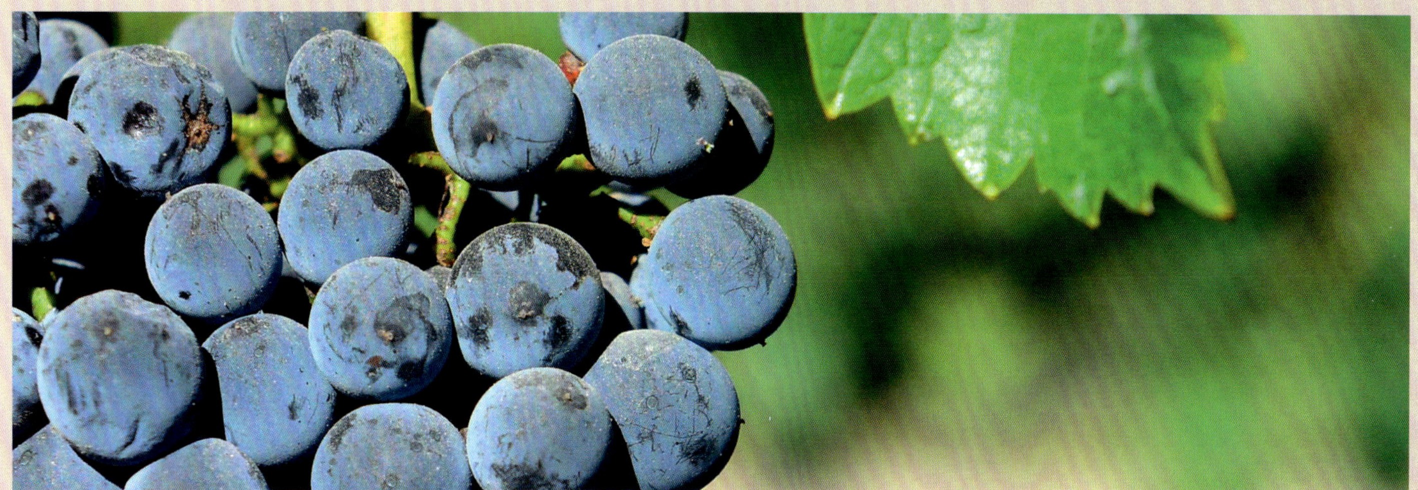

Argentina

Written & Photographed by

– Michael C. Higgins, PhD

International Wine Traveler & Photographer

The Forward by

– Paul Hobbs

World-Renowned Winemaker/Consultant

Leading Advocate for Argentina Wines

Published by

International Exploration Society

United States of America

On The Cover: 150-year-old Malbec Vines growing on the Mosso Estate in Luján de Cuyo

ExploringWineRegions.com

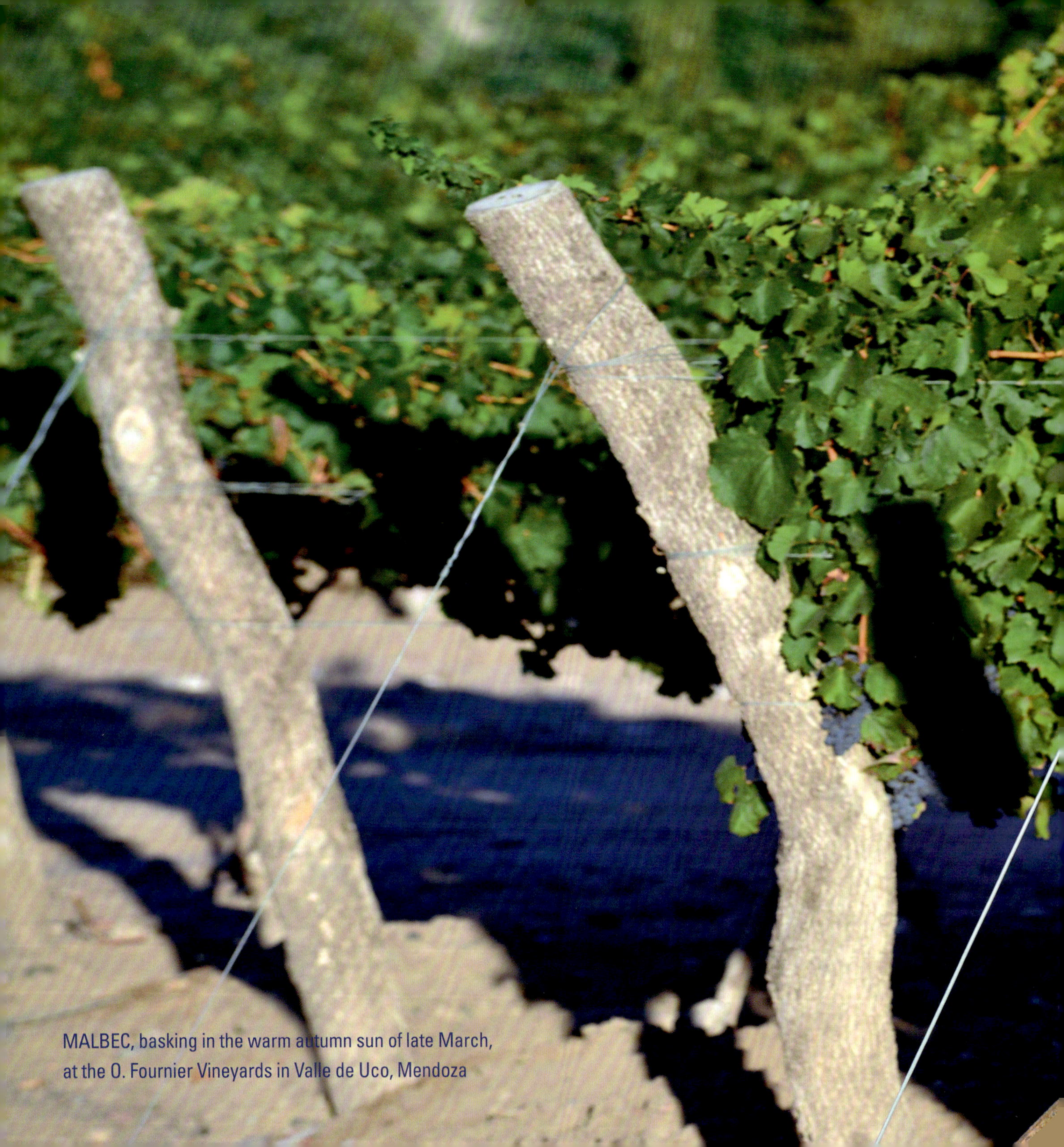

MALBEC, basking in the warm autumn sun of late March, at the O. Fournier Vineyards in Valle de Uco, Mendoza

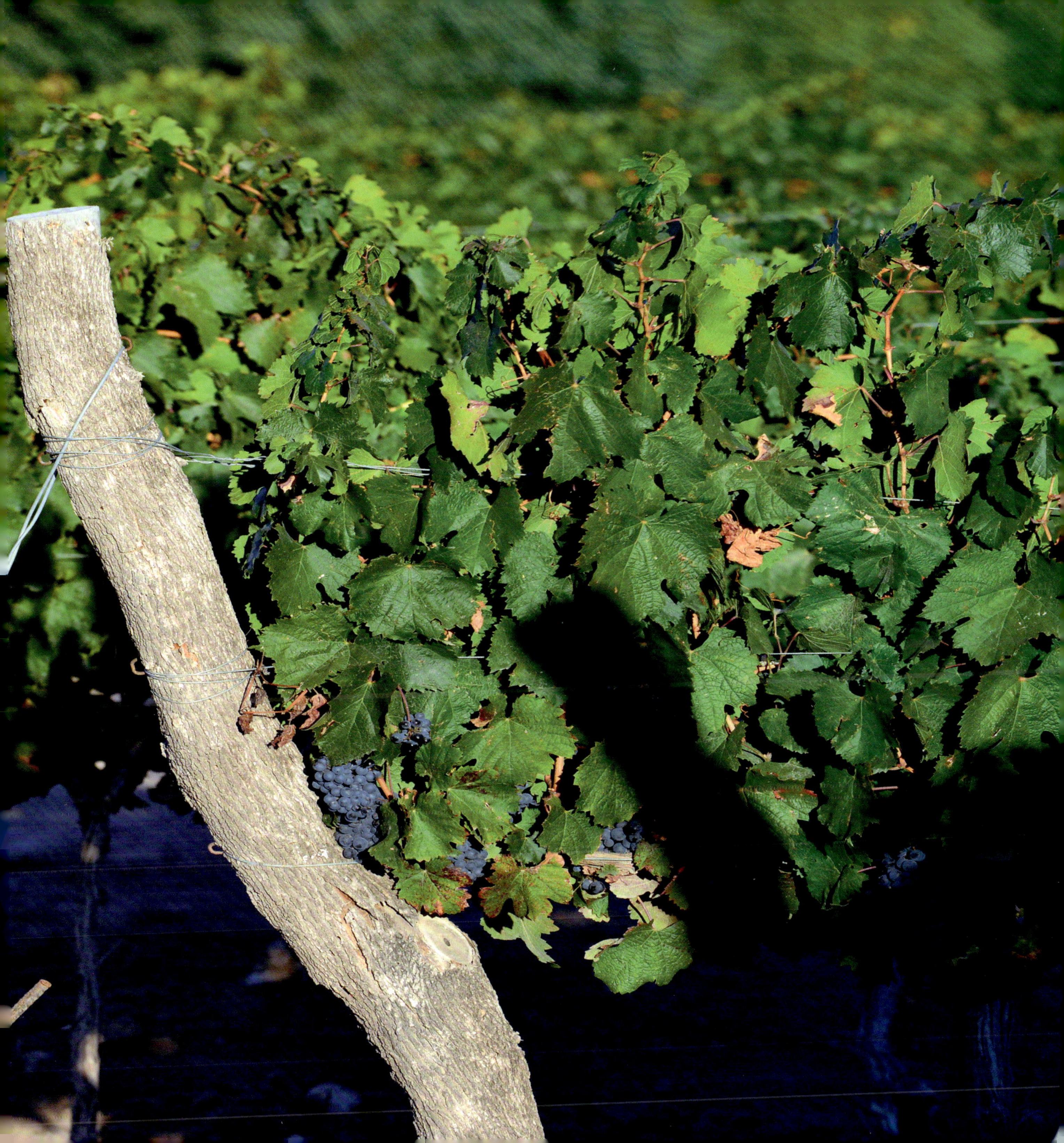

THE FOREWORD

Introducing You to the Magic of Argentina

By Paul Hobbs

Leading international winemaker and consultant in Argentina.
Forbes Magazine calls him the "Steve Jobs of Wine."

The history of wine in Argentina extends back over four hundred years, when vine cuttings brought from Spain were planted in the Mendoza province at the foothills of the Andes; but it is in the last two decades that Argentine wine has begun its ascension to excellence, gaining international recognition and helping to forge the future of winemaking throughout the world.

The recent success of these wines is driven by a progressive interest in quality at every level, from the vineyard, where the wine begins, to the last sip in your glass. This native passion makes the country one of the world's most vital and engaging wine regions to visit today.

You might travel to Mendoza, and the surrounding areas of Luján de Cuyo and Maipú, where vines were first planted, and where some of the country's most elegant wines are now made. You might go to the high altitude vineyards in Valle de Uco, where the cool weather produces wines of unsurpassed balance; to the northern province of Salta, where the finest Torrontés in the world are made; or to Patagonia in the south, where climactic extremes make for exceptionally aromatic Pinot Noir and Malbec.

During your travels, you will find that Argentineans know how to live well. Food and wine are inextricable components in a culture that values such pleasures as part of the fabric of daily life. The people are welcoming and gracious, with an infectious passion for wine and culture. Join them in taking the time to savour a classic Asado barbeque, or to watch a romantic Tango.

Here, old world winemaking techniques and values are harmoniously married with a distinctive new world vitality, and an enthusiasm for exploring the country's potential. High elevations, extreme temperatures, and arid conditions allow for an exacting approach in the vineyards, while dedication to quality promotes interest in discovering the best methods of winemaking. This combination produces complex, elegant Cabernet Franc, Malbecs, Pinot Noirs, Chardonnays and Cabernet Sauvignons, which compete with the best bottles from France and California, while authentically expressing their origin.

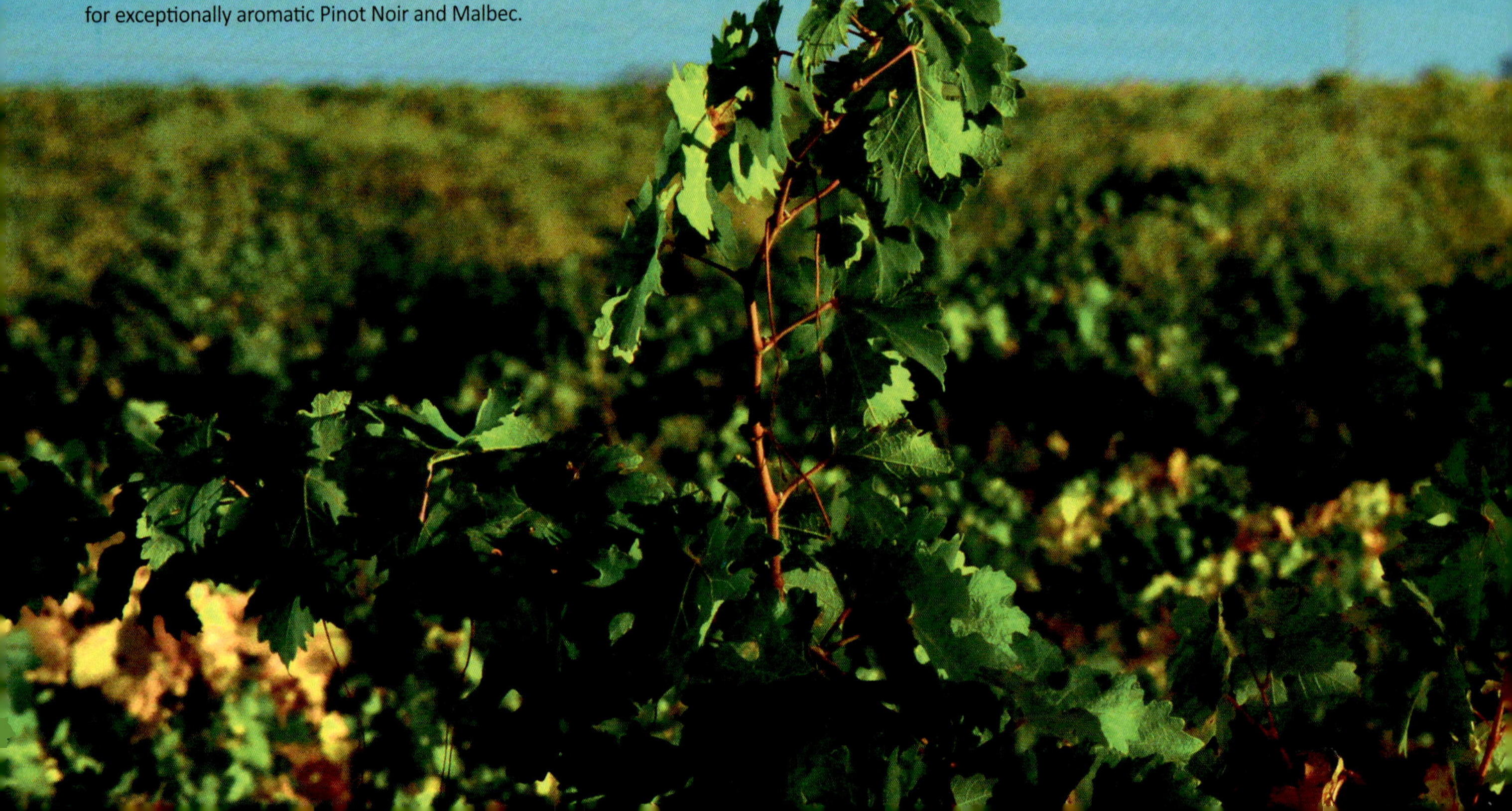

Exploring Wine Regions: Argentina will help to guide you in your explorations of one of the most exciting and beautiful wine regions in the world, whatever the duration of your journey. Thorough maps and abundant photographs serve to situate you in the place. In these maps, terroir is defined, appellations are distinguished, and consideration of sub-regions and micro-appellations provides you with the knowledge to plan as simple or extensive a trip as you desire.

Michael provides both technical information and a strong sense of the unique traits of the wine, landscape and culture of each individual region. Informative sections on the individuals who bring its wines to fruition tell a more personal story of the country, while a consideration of geology, landscape and culture will help to settle you in Argentina's historical context.

Although the book takes its shape from wine regions, the coverage of each place is enriched with extensive information about transportation, unique places to stay and restaurants to sample. Suggested activities such as horseback riding, hiking and rafting will further complement your journey.

With this book at your side, you will experience Argentina at its most memorable.

– Paul Hobbs
Mendoza, Argentina 2015
See profile on page 332

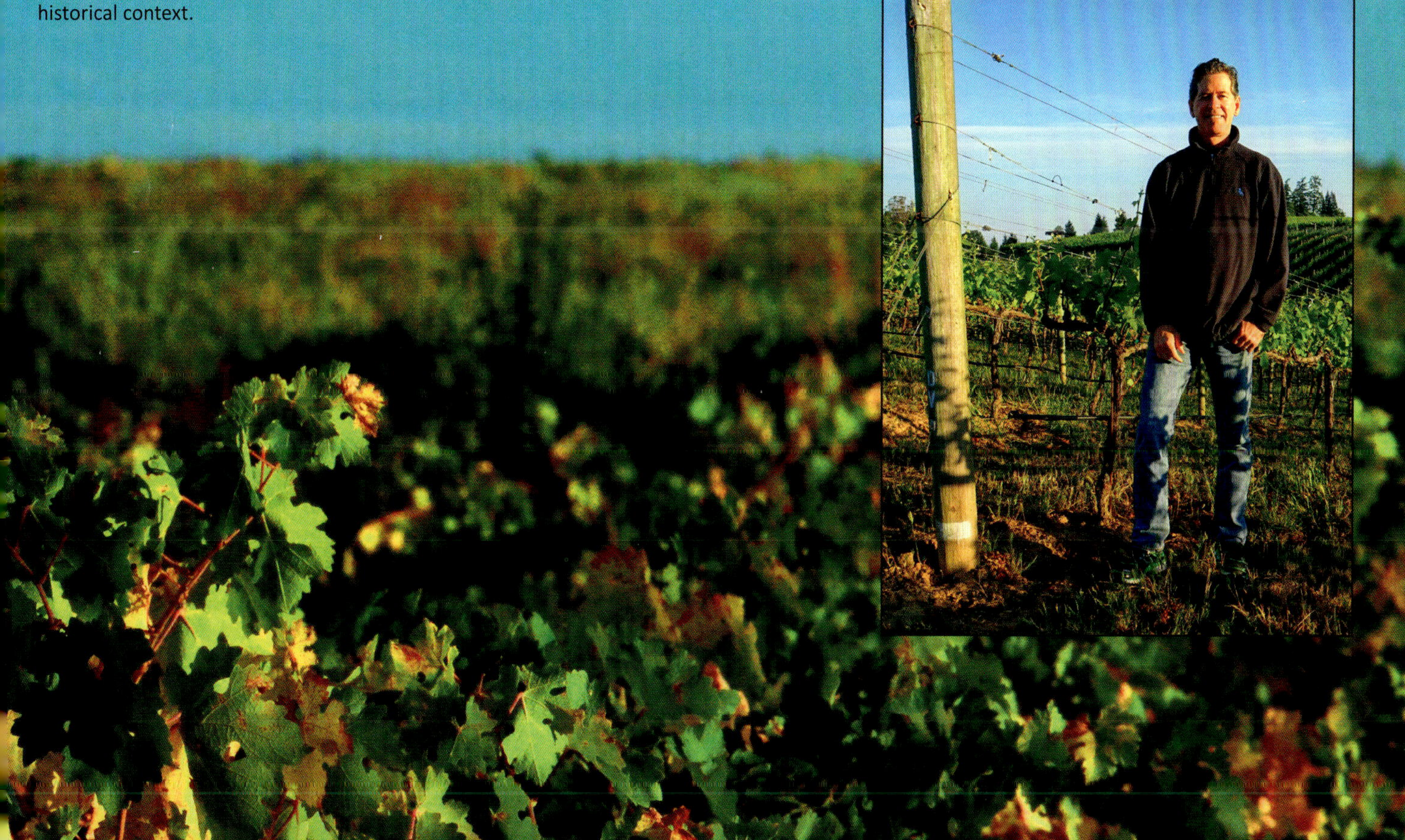

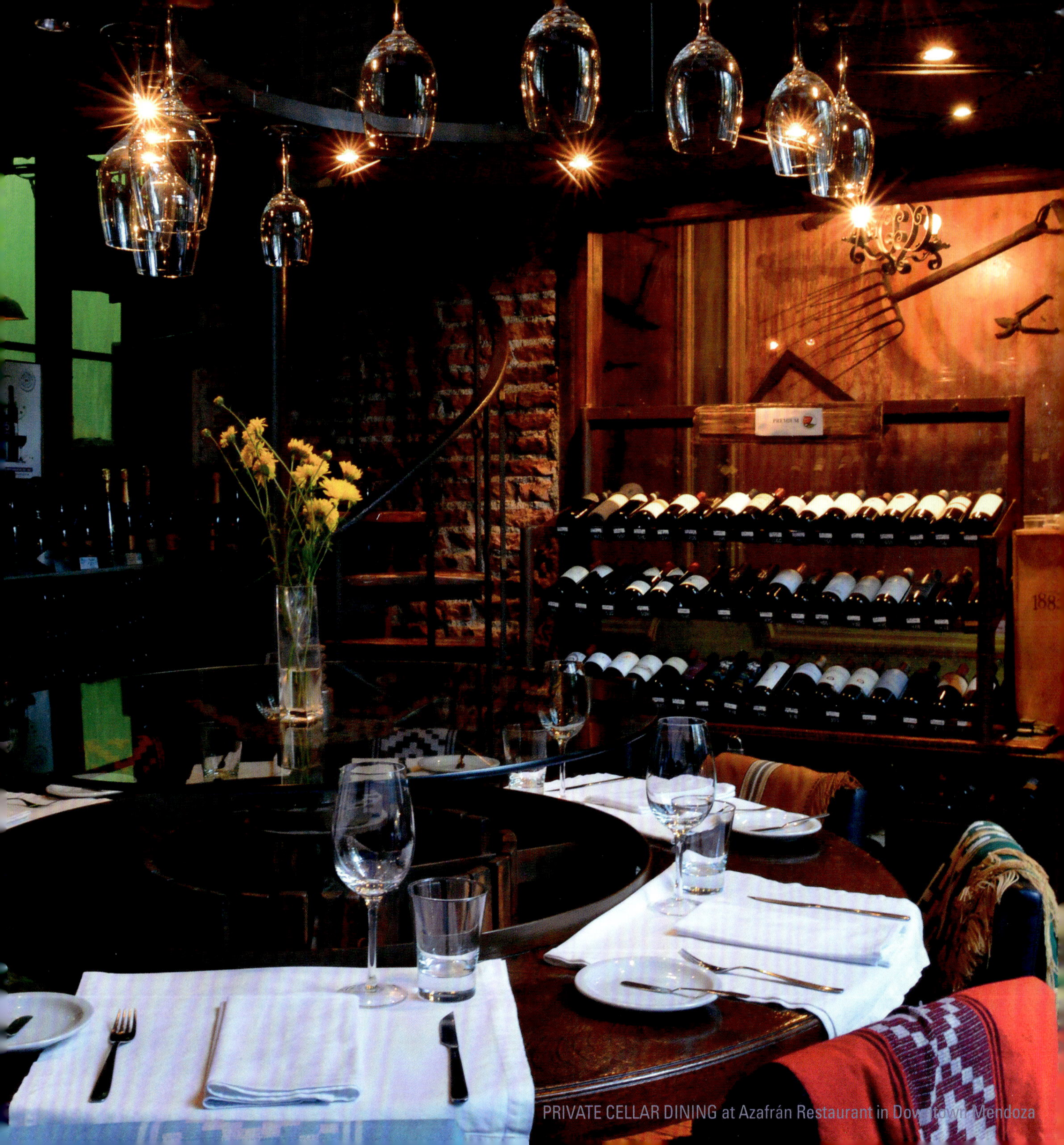

PRIVATE CELLAR DINING at Azafrán Restaurant in Downtown Mendoza

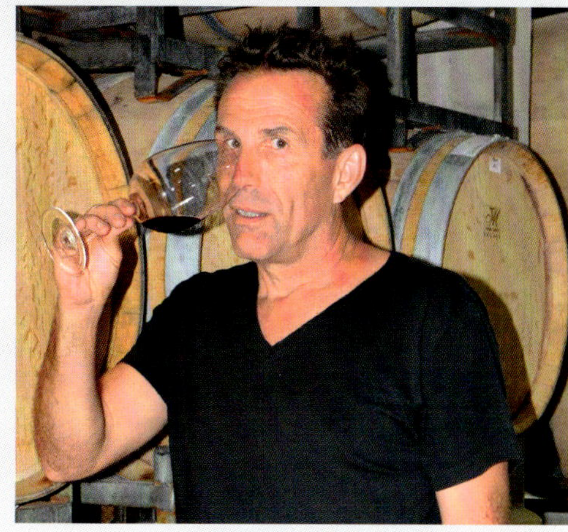

Michael C. Higgins, PhD
International Wine Traveler

I NEVER MET A MALBEC I DIDN'T LIKE

Restaurant after restaurant, I was finding myself ordering another Malbec from Argentina. Even though I did not know how to choose the better bottles, or just to know what would be good or not, I was always pleased with what I received... this Malbec wine I was finding is pretty good stuff! I was loving its big bold flavors with lots of ripe fruit. I love big wines, like Cabernet Sauvignon, yet with the Malbec I also got nice fruit flavors included. Now I found a wine with both! And I was finding my friends were loving it too. Even women who tended to like lighter and fruitier wines were being intrigued by the new Malbecs they were tasting.

So I found myself, restaurant after restaurant, always liking the Malbec... to the point that I started saying "I have never met a Malbec I didn't like." And it was true. But why?

– Is it that Argentina does not allow their wineries to export bad wine?
– Or, are the Argentine wineries only exporting their best stuff?
– Could it be that the Argentina terroir is so ideal for Malbec that it is impossible for them to produce a bad wine?
– Had I not developed a palate yet to distinguish the good from the not so good?
– Maybe it is because my dining tends to be at the better restaurants, and they are savvy for me in choosing the best of the Malbecs for their wine lists.
– Possibly it is a combination of all of the above?

The longer this was going on, the more I needed to know. Argentina has become famous for their Malbec in a way the French never achieved. There must be a secret, and I had to find out why.

I thought, well, five weeks in Argentina ought to get me started. Something will be discovered with such immersion. And why not do it during Harvest Season to see first-hand, and to experience hands-on, exactly what is the magic to their success!

So I started reaching out. Networking. Connecting with the winemakers and vintners who are at the forefront of making the best Malbecs in the world. An itinerary was created and off I went.

In this book, you will find that I have visited every place you read about. I do not use compilations from tourism brochures you so often find in travel books and guides. Everything I write is from my personal experiences and interactions. Plus, the photos are authentic and innocent from my camera and eye.

Get ready to be captivated by these real stories from my first-hand encounters. It's time to board!

I hope you thoroughly enjoy my journey, and yours.

Happy Tasting,

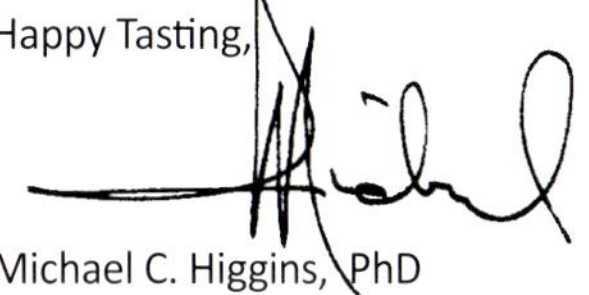

Michael C. Higgins, PhD

I am a lucky guy... 20 years as the Publisher of Flying Adventures magazine (a lifestyle travel magazine for people who own and travel on private airplanes, and of whom are food & wine connoisseurs), has led me to the most amazing wine experiences.

I have been fortunate to taste some of the best wines ever produced, have enjoyed dinners and detailed discussions with very famous winemakers and vintners in their homes, wineries, and at special wine events and auctions. I have made wine with them, made my own wine, have participated in blind tastings, food & wine pairings with celebrity chefs... and I have worked in the vineyards, pruned the vines, picked grapes (eating as I go of course), all of which reach the point that I know so much about wine that I know I know very little.

So what do I really know? I know I love wine, and I love travel! I know enough to know where to look, what to look for, what questions to ask, how to understand complex answers, and I have developed a palate to experience wine, and food, in an extraordinary way!

I am traveling the world Exploring Wine Regions, finding interesting and unusual wine experiences, an insiders concierge to share special and hard-to-find gems and travel experiences with you. Please enjoy with me.

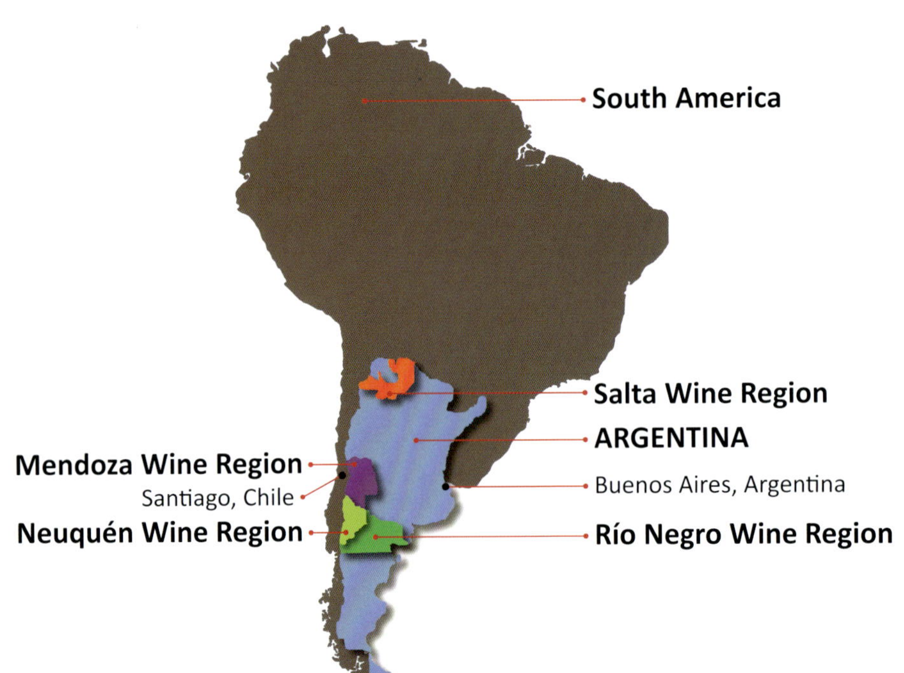

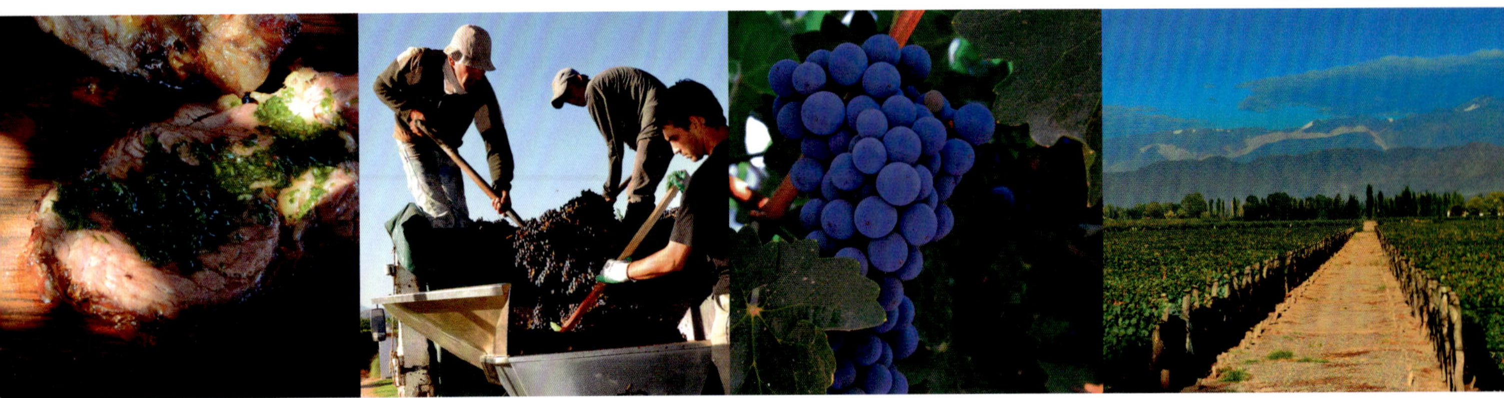

EXPLORING WINE REGIONS™ • 1ST EDITION

ISBN 978-0-9969660-1-6 - Printed Edition • ISBN 978-0-9969660-0-9 - Digital Edition

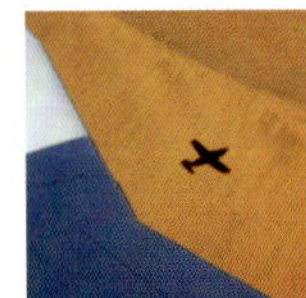

Published by: **International Exploration Society**

Box 93613 • Pasadena, CA 91109-3613 • USA • 626-618-4000

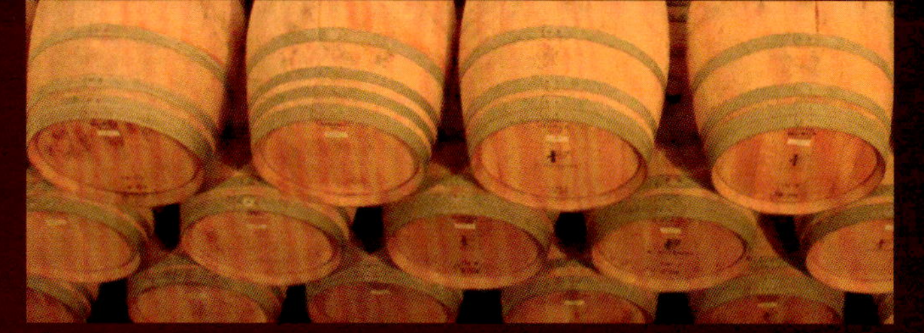

CONTENTS

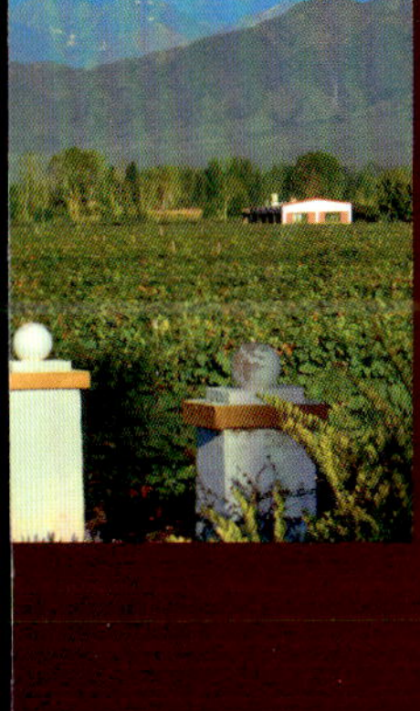

ARGENTINA **TERROIR**

A Unique Environment in the World of Grape Growing

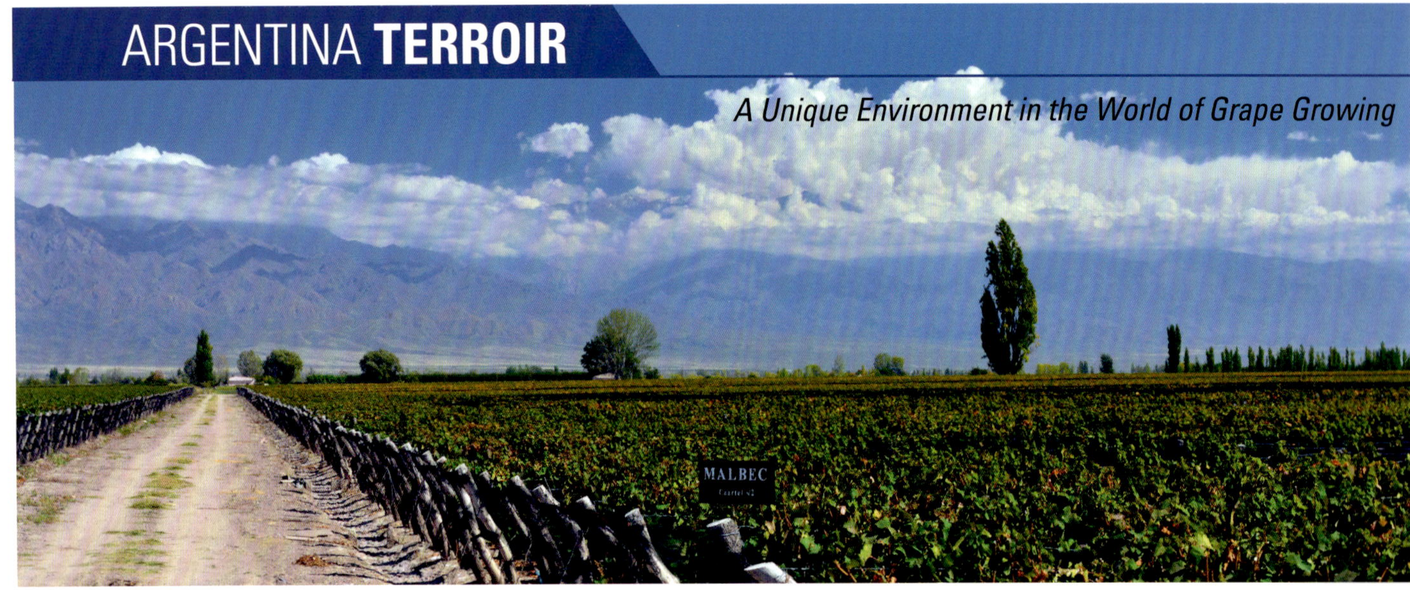

THE LAY OF THE LAND

Argentina, the second largest country in South America, is made up of three primary wine regions spanning the western edge of the country... **Salta** in the extreme northwest of Argentina, **Mendoza** is central and **Patagonia** to the south; all three regions running along the eastern edge of the Andes Mountains.

Salta and **Patagonia** are about 600 miles north and south of Mendoza, respectively. With mountainous roads, expect 15 hours or more for driving times from Mendoza. Flying your own private aircraft is the most efficient solution. Commercial airlines have no direct flights, so you must transfer through Buenos Aires, back and forth.

Salta is considered the highest altitude wine growing region in the world averaging 5,500 to 6,500 feet elevation in Cafayate, 7,500 feet in Molinos and exceeding 10,000 feet in Payogasta. Salta is growing an exciting newer varietal originating in Argentina: **Torrontés**. We will be exploring this new wine, nicknamed *The Liar* because of its beautiful floral sweet nose, then a surprise of a crisp dry finish on the mouth of apricot, peach and grapefruit.

Patagonia being so much farther south, the climate is significantly cooler (with an average annual temperature of 59°F), giving this region an ideal climate for growing **Pinot Noir** and **Chardonnay** grapes. Patagonia boasts having the southernmost vineyards in the world.

Mendoza is the primary wine producing region of Argentina, with more than 80% of the wines produced here and 400,000 acres of vineyards already planted. To put this in perspective, Napa Valley has only 45,000 acres of vineyards and Bordeaux, the largest wine region in France, and the origin of Malbec, has 300,000 acres of vineyards. Argentina is clearly on the path of becoming a major and significant wine producer in the world.

Malbec is Argentina's flagship wine, and the country has the largest Malbec acreage in the world. This grape originally comes from France, as a Bordeaux varietal. In 1852, Malbec was brought to Argentina by Michel Pouget, a French agronomist who was hired by the Argentine government. When phylloxera destroyed the French viticulture toward the end of the 19th century, Argentina became the only country to have the original Malbec vines of true French heritage.

Malbec more than adapted to Argentina's terroir, it thrived, and winemakers began to produce wines better than in its original land. Argentina is now the main producer of Malbec in the world, with 78,000 acres of vineyards planted across the country, far surpassing France with 13,000 acres.

Mendoza has 85% of all Malbec vineyards in Argentina, with 66,000 acres. San Juan ranks second with 7,000, followed by Patagonia with 2,200, Salta with 1,700 and La Rioja with 1,200.

In Mendoza, Luján de Cuyo trademarks their region as *Tierre Malbec*, and was the first Denomination of Origin of the Americas. Malbec from Luján de Cuyo has an intense, dark cherry red color, which may look almost black. It shows mineral expressions, with black fruit and sweet spices standing out.

In Mendoza's Valle de Uco, Malbecs from Tupungato, Tunuyán and San Carlos are more elegant and display distinctive spicy and floral notes. Valle de Uco is the "new frontier" where much of the growth in new wineries and tourism is occurring in Mendoza.

In the north, Salta (Cafayate and Catamarca) is a land of sun and high altitude. Malbec from this region expresses a different personality: aromas of very ripe red and black fruits, black pepper and paprika, with a very solid structure of solid, sweet tannins.

In the south, the climate in Patagonia (Neuquén and Río Negro) is slightly colder and altitudes are less extreme, which leads berries to retain acidity, yielding wines with notes of ripe black fruits in combination with a marked mineral tone.

A BEGINNING THOUGHT

I got to thinking... I wonder if Mendoza is the same distance south of the equator as Napa is north of the equator, or Bordeaux is north of the equator? It would make sense if it was true?

Indeed! The Mendoza wine regions span from 2,200 miles to 3,400 miles south of the equator, and the California wine regions span 2,300 to 2,600 miles north of the equator, and France from 3,000 to 3,300 miles north of the equator.

Mendoza's expansive wine regions encompass the distances north and south of the equator similar to California, France, Italy, Spain, Chile and Australia. It is an interesting tidbit of information to learn, knowing further what grapes favor in growing locations from the equator.

WHY ARGENTINA IS SPECIAL AND MALBEC IDYLLIC

There are many special characteristics about Mendoza's wine regions that all add up to a very unique and idyllic grape growing environment.

The day/night temperature range is tremendous! During the summer growing season, daytime temperature can reach 100 degrees and then it can cool into the 50s at night. Consistently, the temperatures are 90s day and 60s night, a minimum of a 30-degree spread.

This 30-plus degree range is very important for wine grapes, giving them naturally balanced acidity. Grapes already love the extreme wide temperature ranges from day to night (a characteristic of wine regions around the world), and in Mendoza, it is more extensive! Malbec in particular loves this extreme.

Add to this, the water for irrigation is none other than the fresh pure snow-melt from the Andes Mountain Range towering above these three wine regions. The soil is especially ideal for Malbec... calcareous, clay and sandy soils found at the foot of the Andes Mountains are where Malbec seems to thrive, and excel.

The altitude and climate are special as well. Mendoza is a desert. If it wasn't for the Andes producing water year-round, along with the rivers and canal system built throughout the region, there may be no life there, including people. Plus the pristine air quality breathes life into all inhabitants, vineyards and people alike.

This extreme dry climate, along with an unusually high elevation to wine growing distinctive to Argentina (average elevation is 3,000 feet above sea level), creates a consistent climate, primarily free of diseases and insects found in the wet, climate changing environments typical of wine regions. This produces a consistency from year to year, easy to be organic, and allows the winemaker to focus on the expression and style he or she desires to produce. Every year is a great year!

Add all these amazing components together... and you have not only a unique wine growing region like no other in the word, you truly have a special environment, ideal for Malbec, and an magnificent opportunity for you to explore and discover as you adventure in Argentina!

These geographic and climatic features make Argentine Malbec stand out particularly for the quality of their tannins: sweet, silky and mouth-filling. Malbec's most significant characteristic is its intense dark color. Its aromas evoke cherries, strawberries and plums; in some cases it is reminiscent of cooked fruit (like marmalade), depending on when and where the grapes were harvested. In the mouth, Malbec is warm, soft and sweet, with non-aggressive tannins. When it is aged in oak, it develops coffee, vanilla and chocolate aromas.

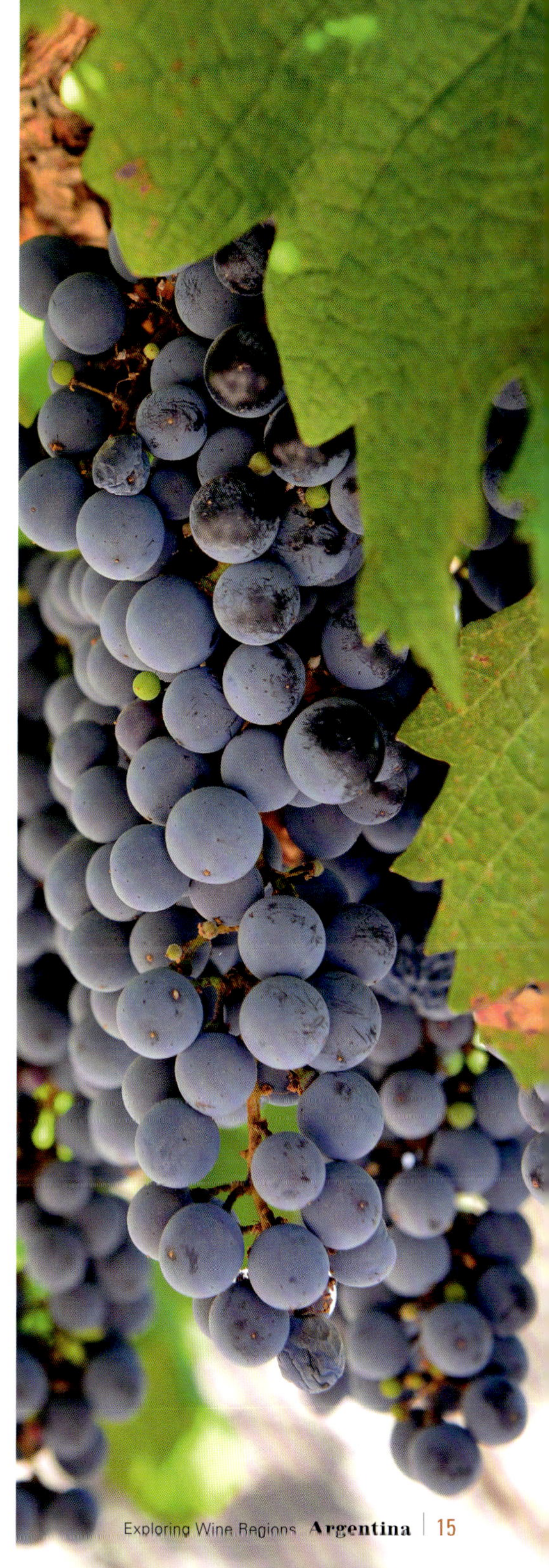

ABOVE THE ANDES

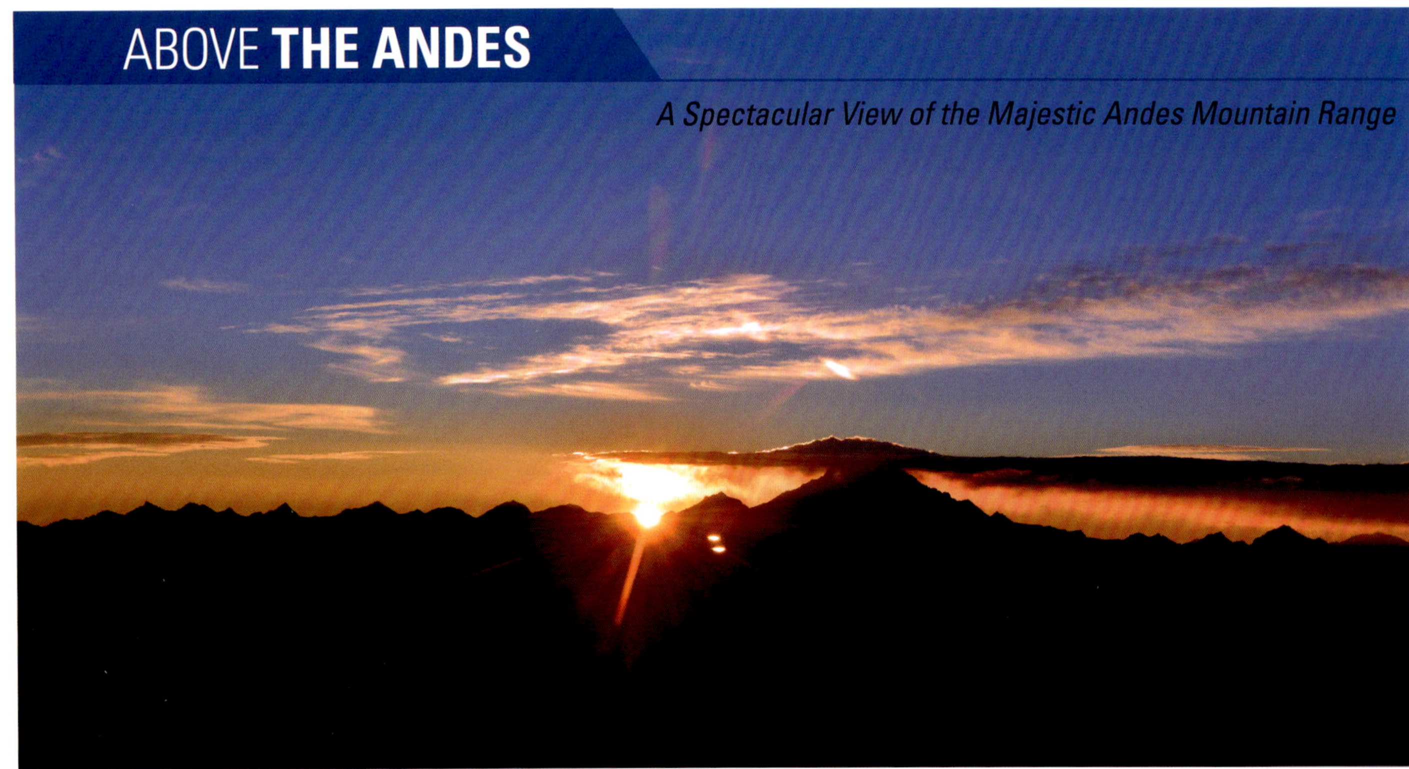

Get ready for a spectacular sight... The Andes Mountains, from the air, are impressive! In your own airplane or by commercial flight, you can witness this amazing geographic wonder and its many towering peaks and high plateaus.

The Andes Mountains are the world's highest mountain range outside of Asia, and are the longest continental mountain range in the world, spanning the western coast of South America, extending from north to south through seven countries... Venezuela, Colombia, Ecuador, Peru, Bolivia, Chile, and Argentina. The range is about 4,300 miles long, fluctuating from 120 to 430 miles wide, with an average height of about 13,000 feet.

The highest peak in the Andes is Mount Aconcagua (ä-kōn-kä-gwä), standing at 22,841 feet above sea level (pictured above). It is located in the province of Mendoza, Argentina, only 70 miles northwest of the city of Mendoza (and just nine miles from the international border with Chile). This makes for a spectacular entrance arriving Mendoza's Wine Regions.

If you are flying an unpressurized aircraft, you might need to navigate your west to east crossing at a breathable altitude at some point in your flight. You will see on the charts that there are many good locations to cross.

The peak of Chimborazo, in the Ecuadorean Andes, claims the farthest point from Earth's center than any other location on Earth due to the equatorial bulge resulting from Earth's rotation.

The world's highest volcanoes are in the Andes, including Ojos del Salado on the Chile-Argentina border which rises to 22,615 feet. Over 50 other Andean volcanoes rise above 19,685 feet!

The Altiplano Plateau, located in the very northwest of Argentina, northern Chile, western Bolivia and southern Peru, is the world's second-highest plateau, the most extensive area of high plateau on Earth, outside of Tibet.

Get ready for an adventure and exhilarating experience flying south... encountering the grandeur of the Andes Mountain Range. When on the ground in Mendoza enjoying the vineyards and wineries, raise your glass and take a look to the west, the Andes will always be standing there as a towering sculpture of magnificence!

ABOVE, first glimpse of the sun, rising over the Andes, almost kissing Mount Aconcagua's peak of 22,841 feet of towering magnificence - photographed flying over Chile looking east toward Argentina where this peak is located.

RIGHT PAGE, into the Andes, snow top peaks in February, summer in South America, just west of Valle de Uco, Mendoza Wine Region.

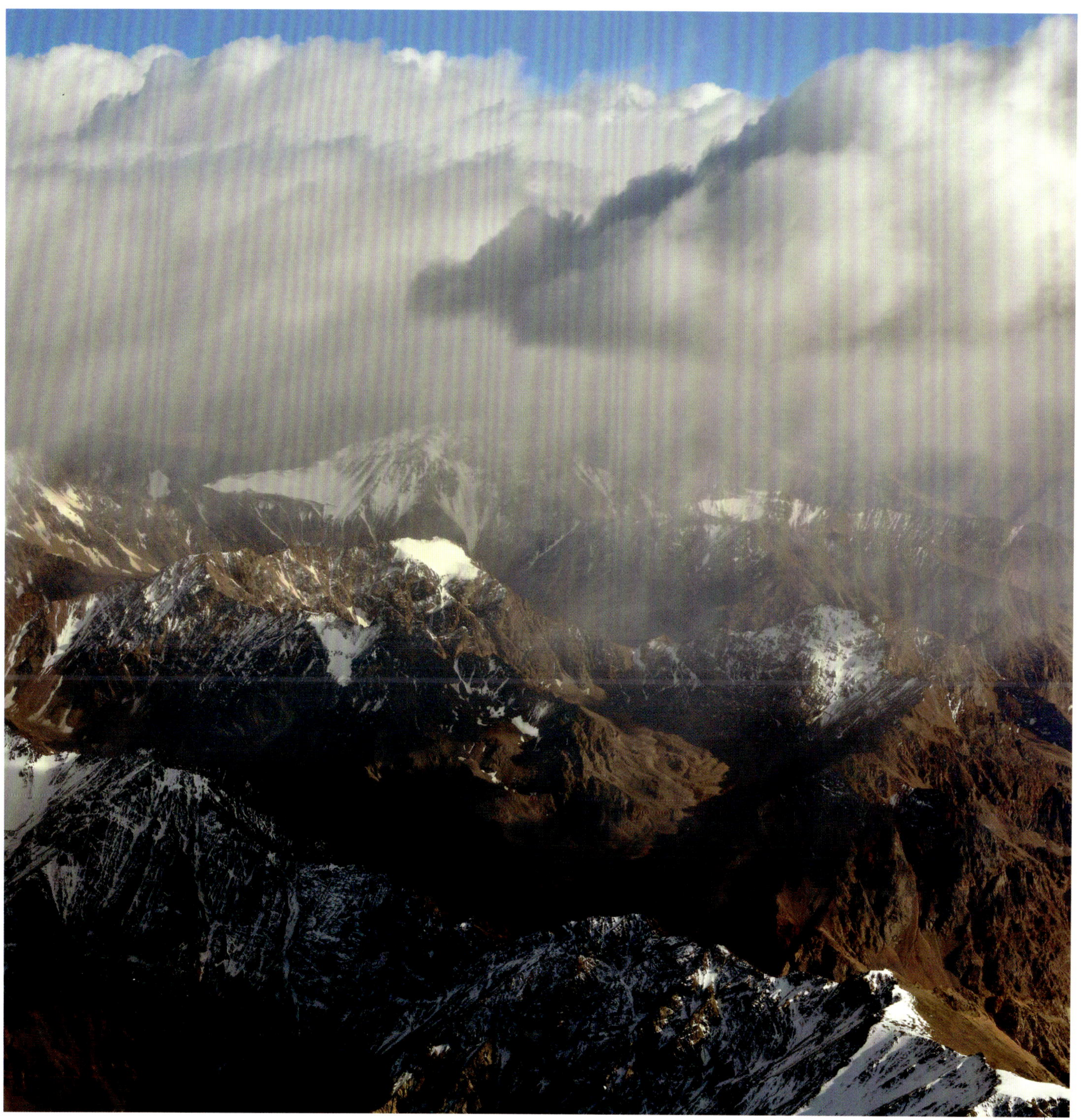

MENDOZA **DOWNTOWN**

The Capital of the Mendoza Wine Region

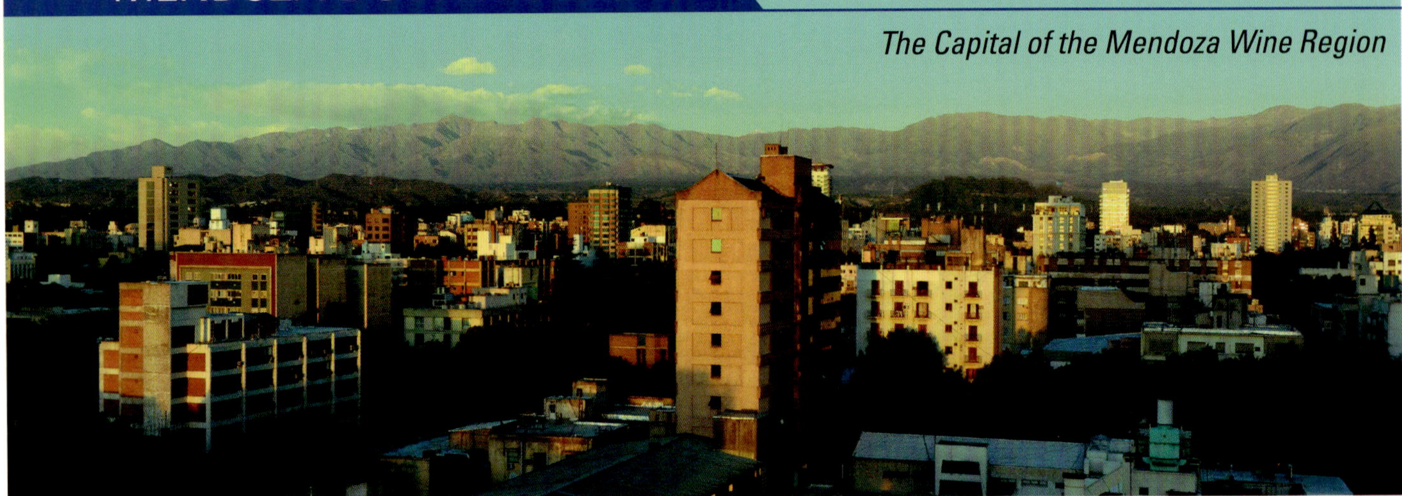

AN EXCITING CITY

OK, so you are headed to the Wine Regions, for vineyards, wineries and their amazing wines. I came here to discover why I never met a Malbec I didn't like. Before you venture out though, you really must experience the exciting city of Mendoza.

Mendoza is the capital of the Mendoza Wine Regions, of the Mendoza Province, with roughly two-thirds of the region's population living in the big city of a million people. Enjoying downtown is an easy stop, with the Mendoza Airport (MDZ) just 20 minutes from downtown, located on the northeast edge of the city.

The wineries are primarily located to the west, south and southwest of the city. Many wineries are so close that you could stay downtown in one of their magnificent hotels, enjoying the city at night, and be back in wineries the next day.

Mendoza has an interesting architectural and landscape infrastructure with a canal system running throughout the city. Remember, Mendoza is a desert. In order to bring fresh water from the Andes Mountains, the city has an elaborate infrastructure of waterways that line every street (left, right-side and cross-streets), located between the street curb and the sidewalk throughout the city. Trees are planted in these canals, which brings about a beautifully green tree-filled city.

Mendoza has five lush and monument-filled squares downtown. The largest, *Plaza Independencia* (encompassing four very large square blocks), founded in 1861 following the earthquake, now marking the center of the new city. Each of the other four squares is two blocks kitty-corner to the main square, each being an entire square block in size themselves.

Plaza Independencia is the city's most important square, meeting place and central hub. A craft fair is held Thursdays to Sundays, and there is often live music or street theater playing for free. Not a surprise to see Tango dancers practising their art, or showing off this dramatic and sexy dance. The Plaza is full of activity with couples and families all through the night with ornamental lamps providing light, magnificent fountains (pictured right), ambiance, and wrought-iron park benches, all under a mixture of pines, palms, poplars and beautiful flower beds.

The other squares represent... the two countries of original immigration, *Plaza Italia* and *Plaza España* (pictured right), Argentina's ally in the war for independence, *Plaza Chile,* and Argentina's General winning the battle for independence, *Plaza San Martín.* Each square has historical significance and monuments to learn from and discover.

This is a great walking city, with lots of outdoor dining and cafes, and many interesting shops and entertainment.

ABOVE, sunrise downtown, a view from the Sheraton; BELOW, love, and the Argentine entertainers.

RIGHT PAGE (clockwise), the magnificent fountains of Plaza Independencia; historic national bank building near Plaza San Martín; and Plaza España.

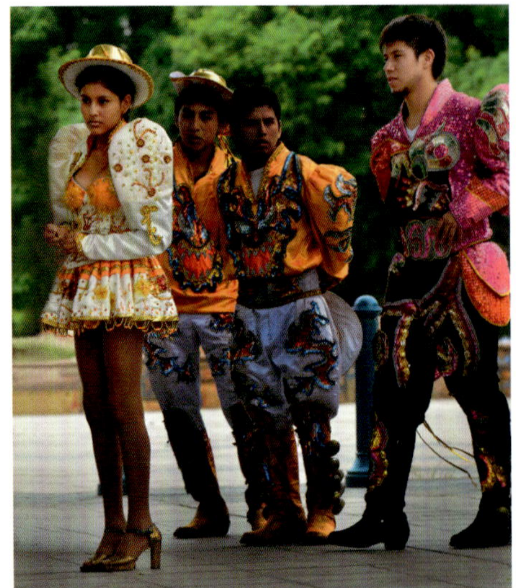

VIVIR EN LA NOCHE

One evening, as I was walking down the street near *Plaza Independencia*, at midnight, I was taken aback by how many children were on the streets, with their families. Little children, during the week, families out having dinner, enjoying the beautiful evening. Most Argentines generally have dinner at 11:00pm or midnight.

These people are: Living In The Night! Vivir en la noches, as you would say in Spanish. When in Rome (Argentina), do what the Argentine do... great food, superb wine, lively culture, and a beautiful evening, into the night!

LANGUAGE

Especially in the wineries, hotels, restaurants and shops, many people speak English. Original immigrants to Argentina came from Spain and Italy, making the primary languages spoken Spanish and Italian, and then English, in that order. Many people in Argentina are bilingual.

Mendoza has very much a European feel, which is influenced by their Italian and wine culture. It is a much cooler Latin American country, very much on the same latitude (except south) as the United States and Europe. You can't help but love the atmosphere, the culture and the people.

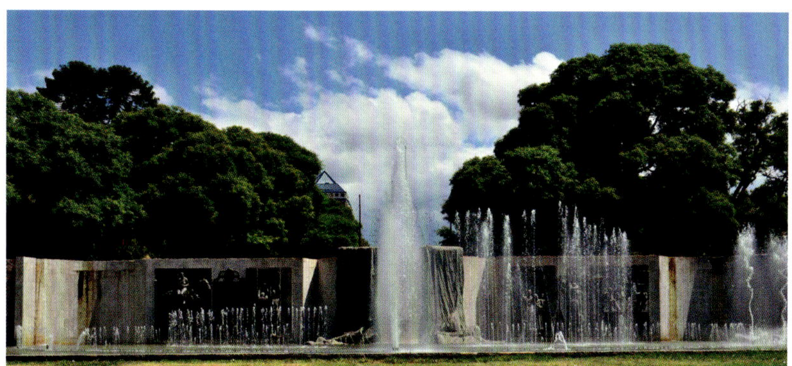

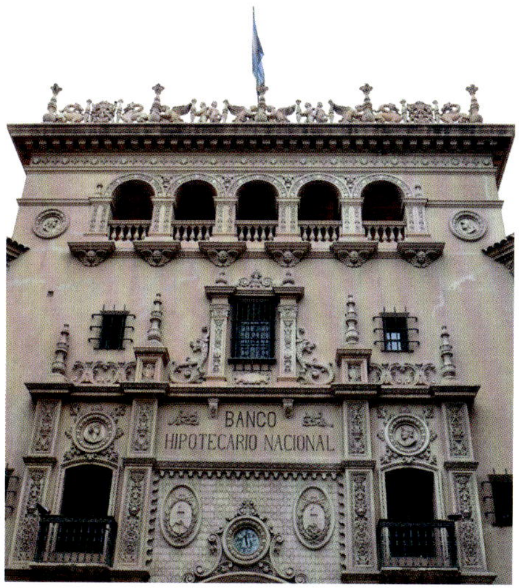

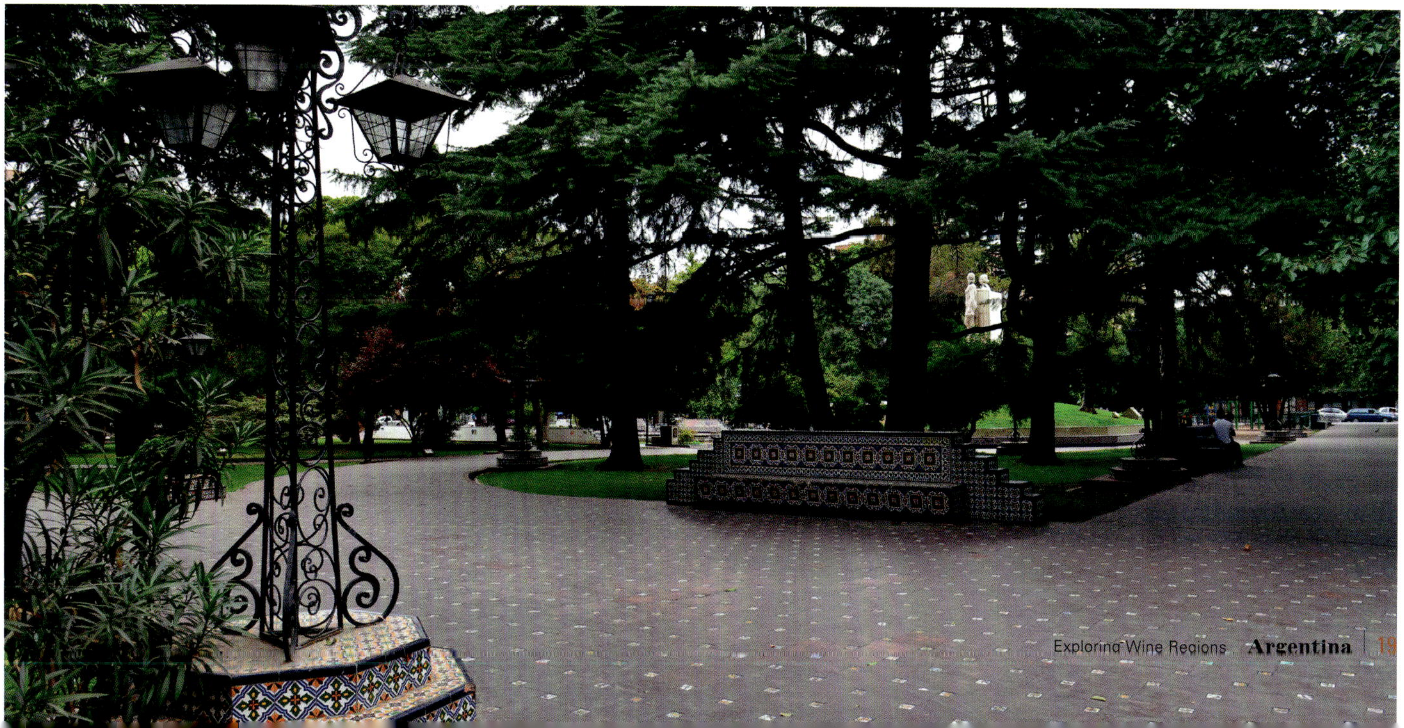

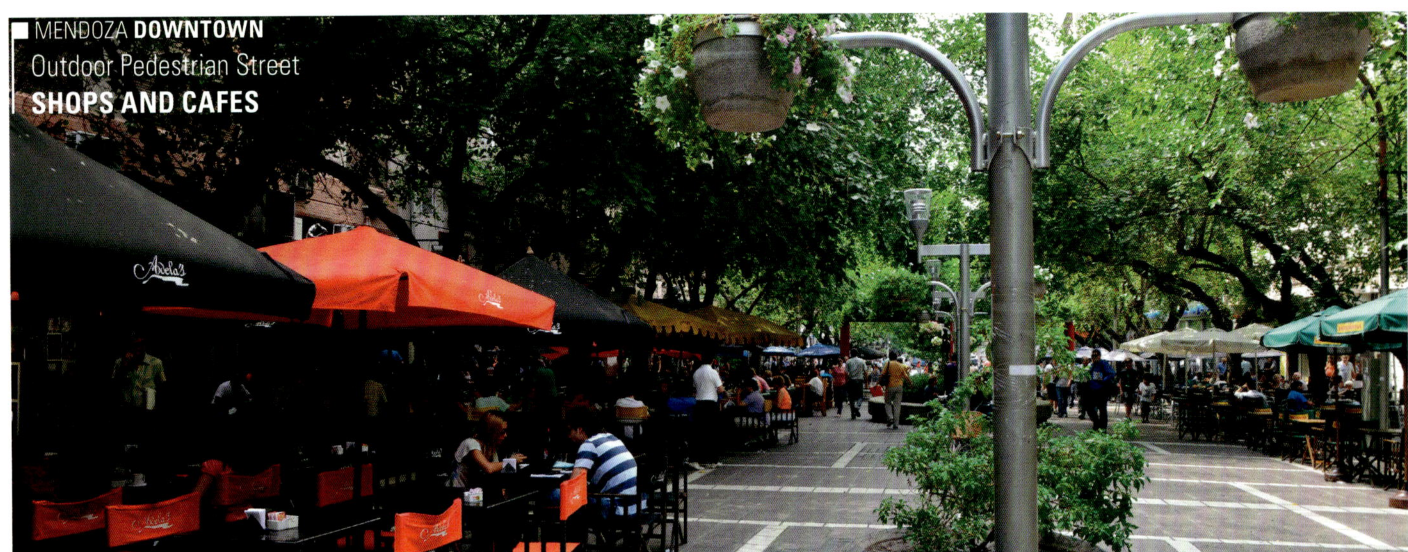

PEATONAL SARMIENTO

The Sarmiento Pedestrian Street (above) extends three blocks east from Plaza Independencia, into a lush tree-filled street lined with restaurants, cafes and retail shopping. Permanently closed to cars, this shaded walkway has transformed into a beautiful setting where you must spend some time... just hanging out, relaxing, enjoying a latte or lunch.

Arbors, gazebos, fountains, and several notable buildings such as the St. Nicholas Church, the Provincial Legislature and the Stock Exchange, have made this an important meeting point of workers, tourists and the young. Even Saturday morning downtown is an important venue for Mendocinos and tourists alike.

RESTAURANTS ON SARMIENTO

In the other direction, three blocks extending to the west of the Plaza Independencia, the street is lined with many restaurants of serious culinary exploits. Magnificent trees shade this outdoor and fine dining experience.

You really get the sense of the Italian influence in Mendoza when you stroll down this street. Almost every business is a restaurant, and most of them Italian. I was told half the original immigrants came from Italy. No wonder the Italian food is authentic, and delicioso!

ESTANCIA LA FLORENCIA

This large casual Italian restaurant on Sarmiento, two floors and outside dining, and is open a wider range of hours than most restaurants. Great Italian dishes with classic Argentine meats; they will tell you "a meal without meat isn't a meal." I recommend trying one of their steaks, the lomo being the most tender; or a half-grilled chicken served with a lemon slice. They serve SieteFincas wines, to be discovered later, but order a bottle now. Their Gran Secreto is an amazing reserve Malbec, and for only US $10.

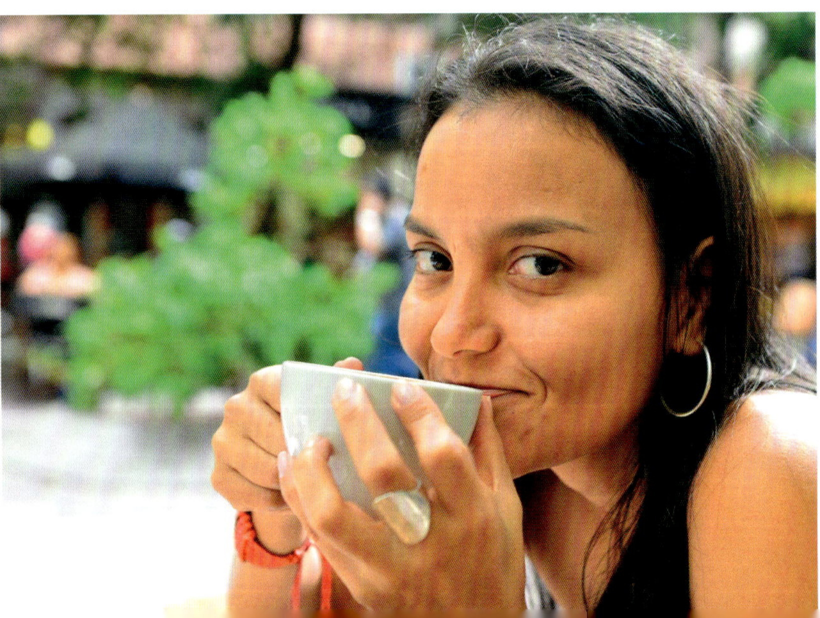

NO WINES BY THE GLASS

In Mendoza, the food and wine are not the only things exceptionally great, so are the low prices. When you can buy a great bottle of wine at a restaurant for only US $5 to US $10, there is no purpose for wines by the glass. So splurge!

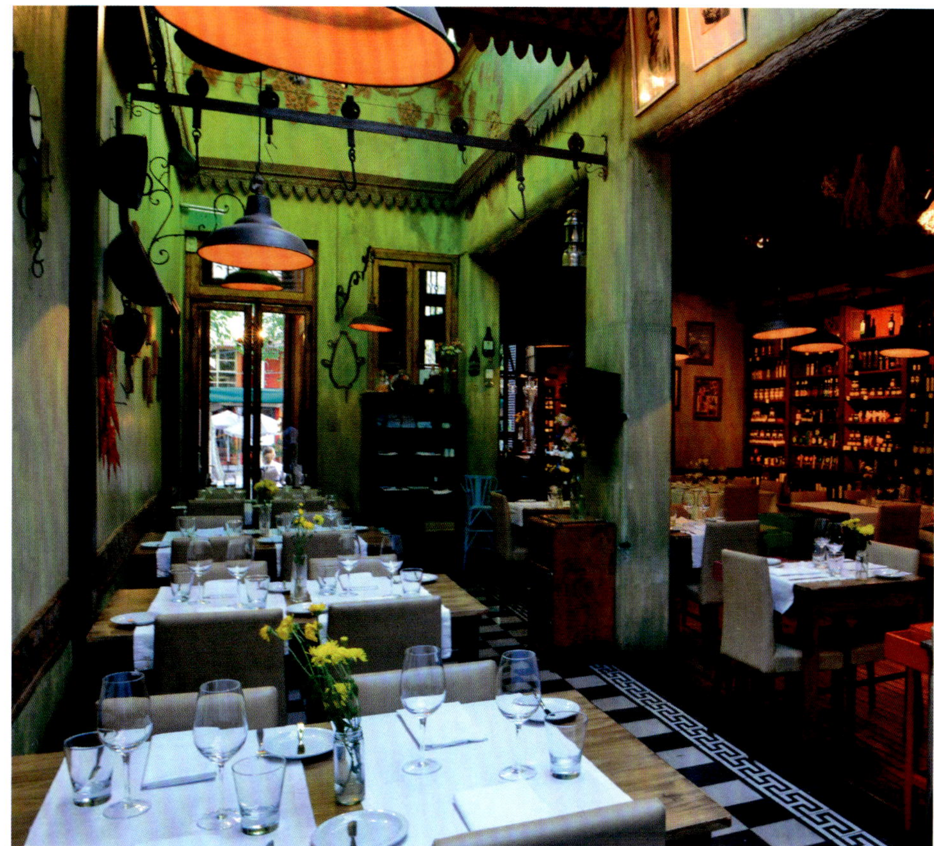

MENDOZA **DOWNTOWN**

Restaurant

AZAFRÁN RESTAURANTE

765 Sarmiento
(between Belgrano and Perú)

011 (+54 261) 429.4200
reservas@azafranresto.com

Reservations Highly Recommended

AzafranResto.com

English & Español

Baby Goat Ravioli...
with mushrooms and Parmesan cheese.
Paired with the 2010 Zuccardi {Serie A} Syrah.

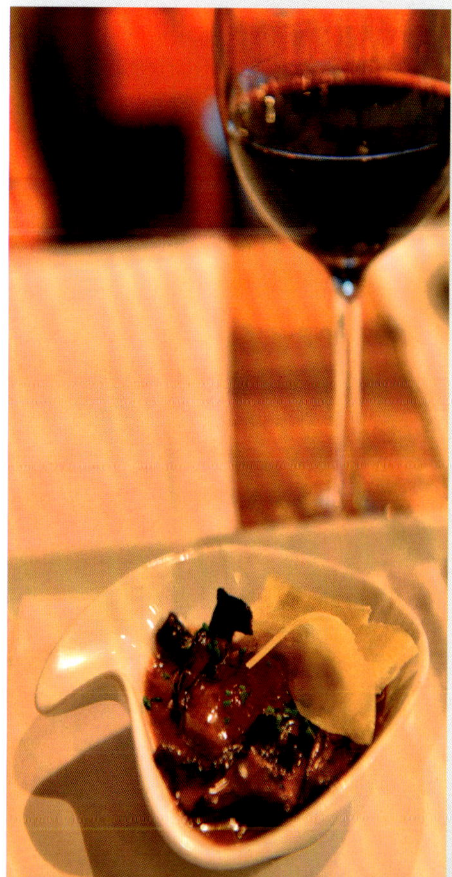

Azafrán Restaurante is a unique experience also on Sarmiento. This charming little restaurant is named after the highly prized and rare saffron spice, where Chef Pablo Ranea has created his cuisine to accompany Mendoza's fine wines.

It all begins in the cellar... In the very front of the restaurant, a beautifully decorated all-wood and climate-controlled wine cellar awaits your perusal (see photo page 10). You can also dine in the cellar with a small group of up to six people, warm blankets provided.

There is no wine list in this restaurant. You choose what you would like to drink first, from over 300 different and interesting Mendoza wine labels, yourself or with the expertise of their sommelier, who'll encourage you to match your food to your wine (not the other way around).

This makes so much sense to me. What I feel like drinking is generally more important than what I am eating, as long as what I am eating is fantastic! And Azafrán will deliver fantastic. The food is imaginative, with fresh ingredients and creatively presented.

The *Trío of Empanadas* is a unique twist on this typical Argentine appetizer... Sweetbread with mushroom, sausage with onion and black sausage with parmesan. Try the pairing option, select wines perfect for each.

The *Filet Mignon* is a tenderloin steak, with blue cheese and spinach, wrapped in Argentine dough. Sweet potato honey puree, and a roasted bell pepper sauce. Magnificent! Chef Ranea prepared this "work of art" for the 2013 World Malbec Day in New York City at The Met.

Dulce de Leche, a caramelized milk, is an Argentine love for breakfast, lunch and dinner. Not my cup of tea, until... the Azafrán Dulce de Leche Créme Brûlëe with blueberries and a Rice Pudding with cinnamon and biscotti. Delectable!

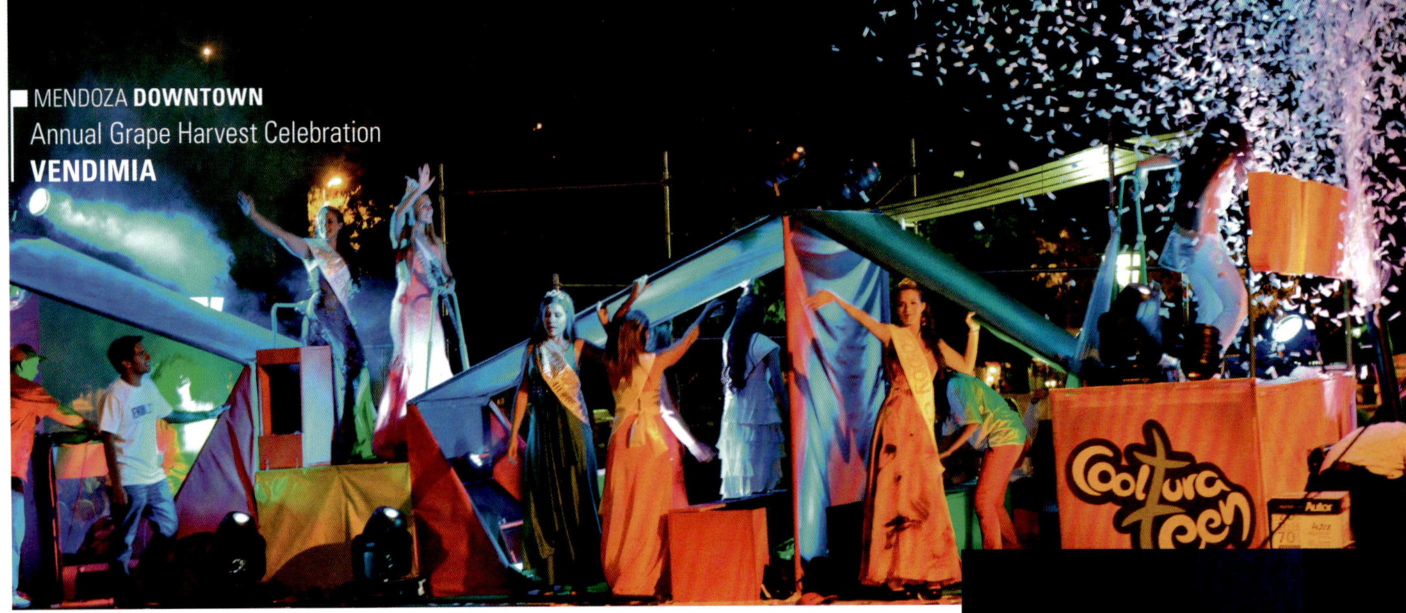

MENDOZA **DOWNTOWN**

Annual Grape Harvest Celebration

VENDIMIA

Planning a trip to Mendoza in March has many opportunities. March is summer in Argentina, the weather is gorgeous and the grapes are full on the vines. Harvest has already begun, and... Mendoza plans a very exciting party, in fact it is their biggest and most important party of the year – Fiesta de la Vendimia (National Grape Harvest Festival).

Held the first weekend of March, with most activities on Friday and Saturday, the Fiesta de la Vendimia brings the city alive to celebrate, with the local nectar flowing freely. An abundance of Malbec, traditional cuisine, folkloric song and dance, Tango!, parades day and night, and a beauty contest to select the "Queen of Vendimia." Plus, their delicious peaches are harvested this time of year too.

Activities take place province-wide in the months leading up to the main event with each of the 18 wine regions of Mendoza selecting a local contestant for the beauty pageant. Each of these wine regions builds elaborate floats and parade through the streets of Mendoza. It is a carnival-like atmosphere in the streets! Expect a parade Friday night meandering through downtown, ending at the Plaza Independencia, in front of the Park Hyatt Mendoza Hotel.

The Park Hyatt faces and overlooks the Plaza, and hosts a grand party in the hotel Friday night after the parade, with live music, dancing and many culinary treats!

On Saturday, the parading reconvenes during the day. Judges are out front of the Park Hyatt, where a private invite-only event takes place, and each of the regions proudly presents their candidate for Queen of Vendimia on their floats.

Needless to say, staying at the Park Hyatt is an excellent idea in order to get in on all the spectacular activities. Make your reservations early if you are serious.

Wine connoisseurs from around the world come to Mendoza for Vendimia and harvest. Artists throughout South America arrive in Mendoza during this time as well. Locals, both in the wine industry and not, come out in masses to celebrate the most important industry in their region... winemaking!

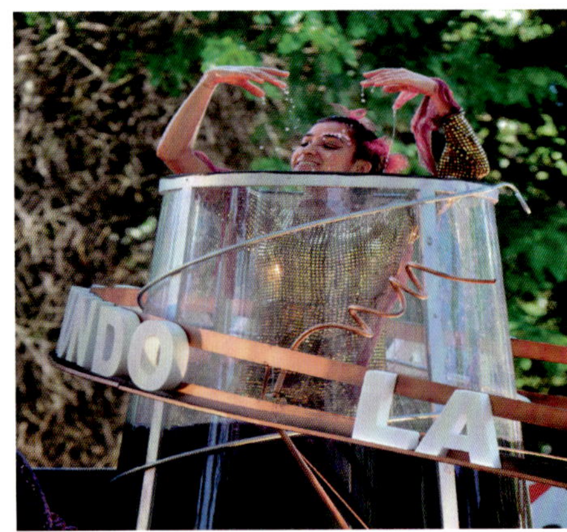

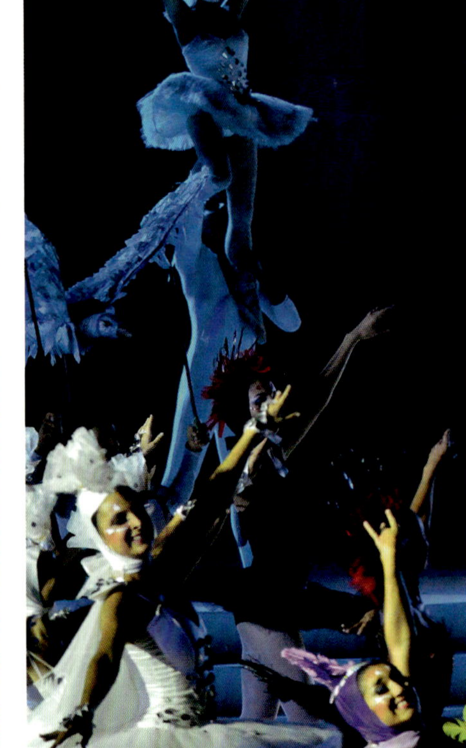

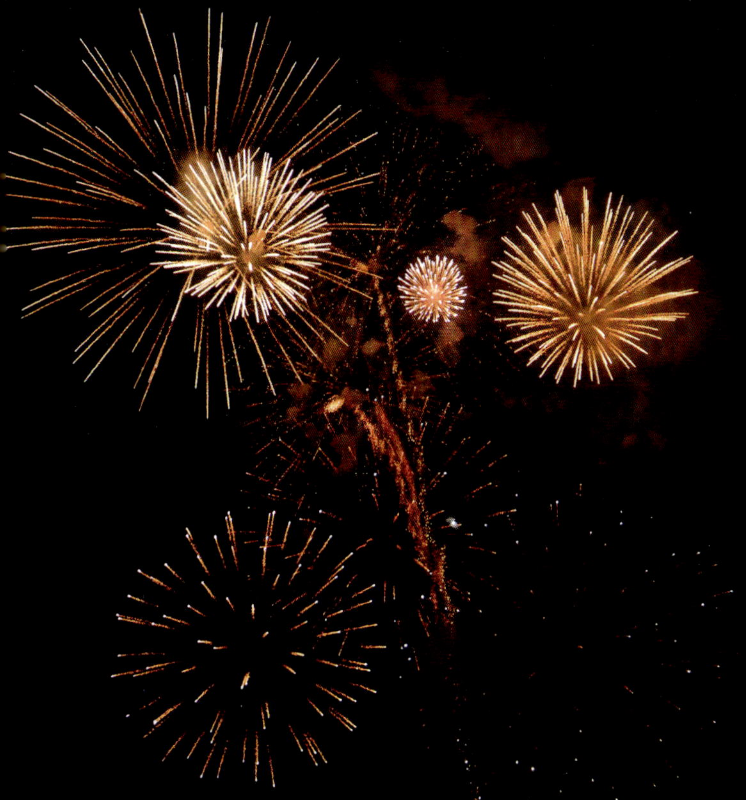

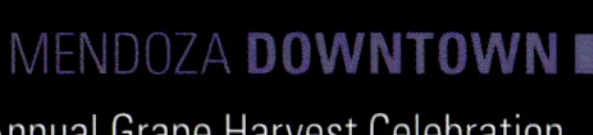

VENDIMIA CENTRAL EVENT

Saturday night is a very flashy, Vegas-style performance of music, theatre and dance. This main event fills 25,000 people into their outdoor theater to watch the performance, followed by the crowning of Queen of Vendimia.

The finale is a fireworks show beyond your imagination. I have seen many professional fireworks shows, yet this show reigns top, choreographed to perfection with the explosions in the sky. The music is as dramatic and as brilliant as the light-show above.

To obtain special seating, with transportation, seat cushions and box dinner and wine, contact the concierge at the Sheraton Mendoza Hotel.

The central event goes on for several nights following, just without the crowning of the queen, adding a lot more music, even famous musical artists!

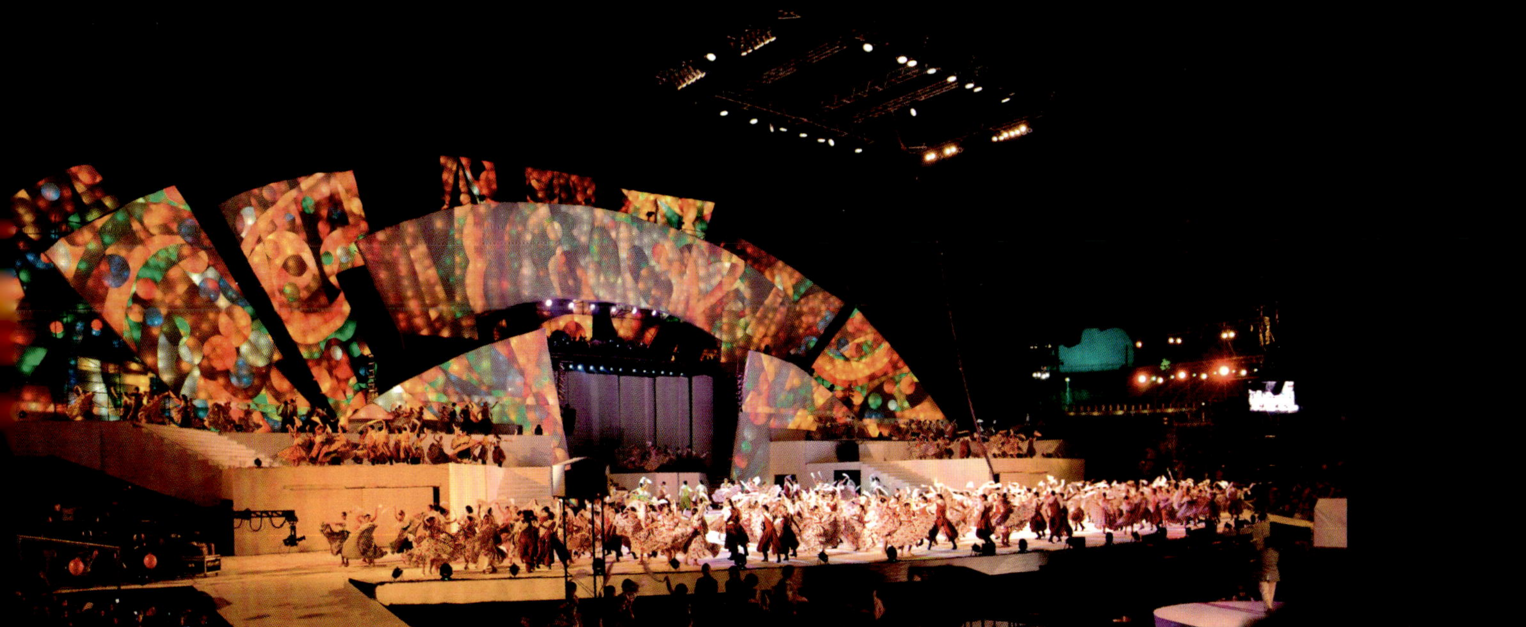

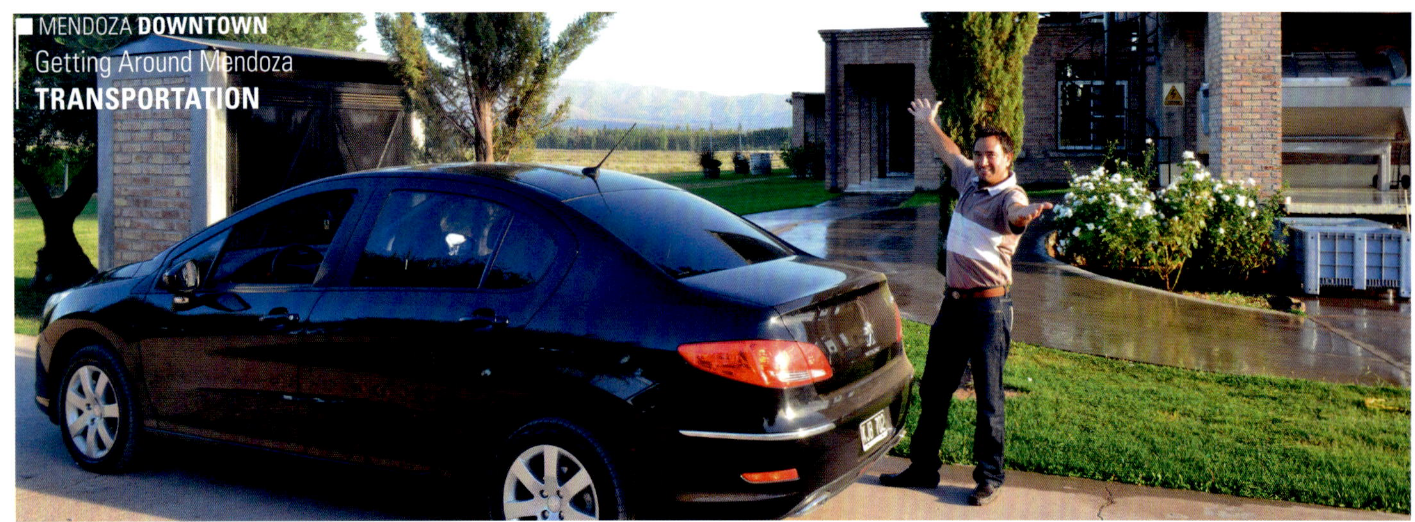

USE A PRIVATE DRIVER

While you are staying in downtown, you will not need a car. This is a great walking city. And, you could choose to continue staying downtown; many of the wineries are within day-trip distance. You could rent a car, which will cost about US $100 a day for a basic compact, or you could hire a private driver to take you where you want to go for roughly the same price.

I was referred to a very special private driver, Felipe Canedo. His company, Mendoza Transfer, has three private drivers, so he can be available on call and meet your needs.

Felipe speaks English fluently, and is a super nice guy to be your traveling chauffeur. He knows the right people in high places. He can get you into wineries and restaurants with very special treatment. I have very good contacts myself, however Felipe came to the rescue for me several times with who he knew.

Felipe will drive you in style, in a beautiful black Peugeot French sports car (photo above). Weekends, holidays, a midnight pickup at the airport, or 2:00am at a club, Felipe and his team are first-class and available.

Felipe Canedo - Mendoza Transfer
cell - 011 (+54 9 261) 569.4716
email - mendozatransfer@hotmail.com

WINE GELATO

A new twist on Italian Gelato, perfect for the Mendoza Wine Region, *Ferruccio Soppelsa* makes Gelato from Malbec and other wines. There are 17 locations, with seven in the city and one on Sarmiento (at Belgrano), since 1927.

- Vainilla al Malbec (Vanilla in Malbec)
- Melocoton al Syrah (Peach in Syrah)
- Maracuya al Sauvignon Blanc (Passion Fruit in Sauvignon Blanc)

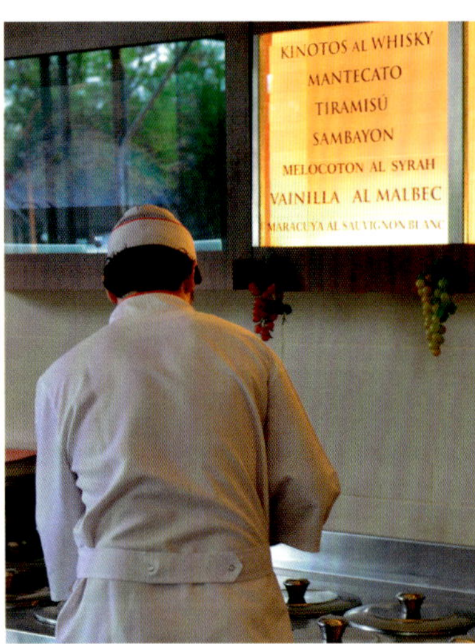

011 (+54 261) 422.9000
SoppelsaHelados.com

THE VINES OF MENDOZA

This is the best first and last stop when traveling to the Mendoza wine region. Why? Because you can taste from many of the wineries and decide ahead of time where you would like to visit based on your particular liking. And then before you leave, you can purchase wines you want that you did not acquire at the wineries directly.

Downtown Mendoza Tasting Room

Visiting The Vines of Mendoza's tasting room is like visiting the best Argentine boutique wineries without having to leave the city. It is the only place in Mendoza where wine enthusiasts can enjoy flights of the very best Argentine wines as well as taste hundreds of different wines by the glass. Each tasting includes an interesting discussion of the wines and their production with their wine experts.

Lounge & Wine Bar – in Park Hyatt

The Vines has a beautiful lounge in the Park Hyatt where they have selected a "Top 100" of the finest Argentine wines.

The Vines Of Mendoza
1194 Belgrano Ave
(one block from Sarmiento Ave)

US# 707.320.2699
AR# 011 (+54 261) 438.0021
wineshop@vinesofmendoza.com

VinesOfMendoza.com

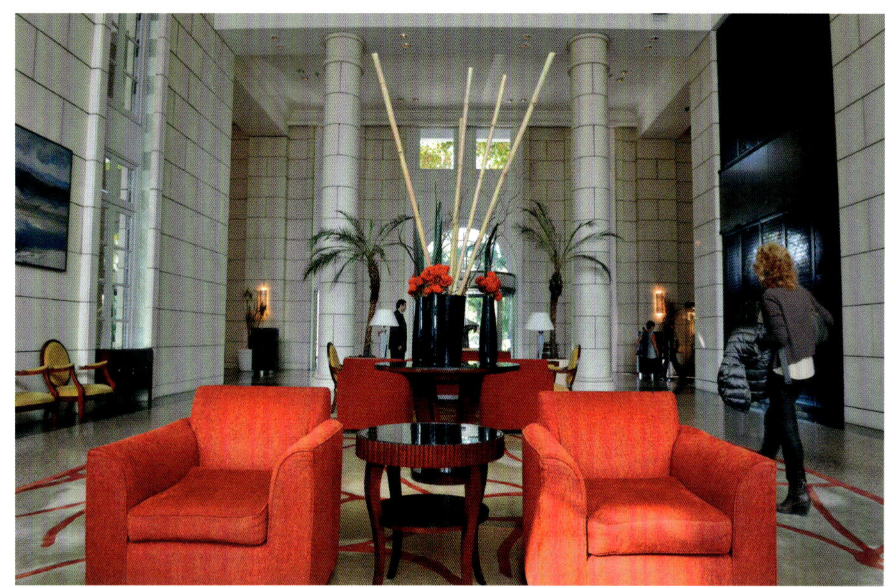

MENDOZA **DOWNTOWN**

Hotel • Spa • Casino

PARK HYATT MENDOZA

1124 Chile
(overlooking Plaza Independencia)

011 (+54 261) 441.1234
mendoza.park@hyatt.com

Uber Five-Star Property

Mendoza.Park.Hyatt.com

English & Español

PRESTIGIOUS LUXURY IN HISTORIC MAGNIFICENCE

The Park Hyatt Mendoza is a magnificent property. The architecture is a beautifully restored 19th-century Spanish colonial style with an ideal location... overlooking Plaza Independencia and adjacent to Sarmiento Avenue hosting numerous amazing restaurants.

Just standing in front of the hotel puts you in awe with its grandeur. Its prestigious nature makes you feel good standing in its presence! A historical landmark, a place in time, restored to today's opulent standards, with all the beauty and luxury to expect of a five-star hotel.

And more... we have all experienced the difference between five-star and what I call Uber Five-Star. At this Park Hyatt, expect uber. Attentiveness extraordinaire! The staff at this property have the attitude of over-and-above customer service. And you will feel it. Felicity.

The rooms are elegant and sleek, with minimalist design. Even a standard room is quite spacious with king-size beds (plush feather pillows and lavish duvet), sizable work desk (WiFi and USA outlets) and a large white marble bath, including a separate overhead shower.

You will find a gifts in your room when you arrive, culinary goodies brought to your room during your stay, and the availability of service is constant.

The Regency Casino Mendoza is located on premises in the back of the hotel. It's a large two-level casino with the usual gaming tables and slot machines. The Salon Prive is a private room for experts to play in a sophisticated environment.

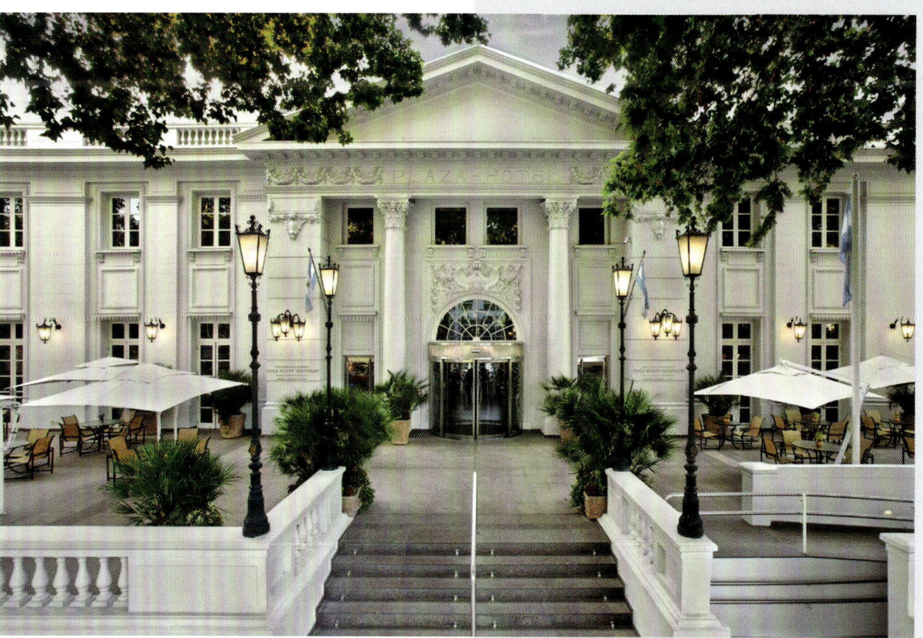

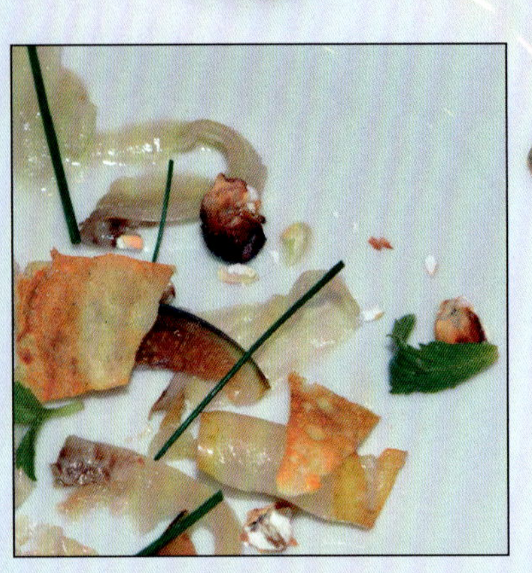

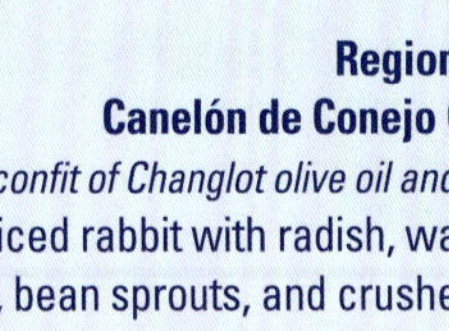

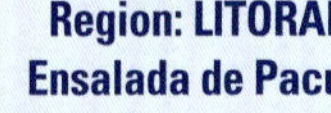

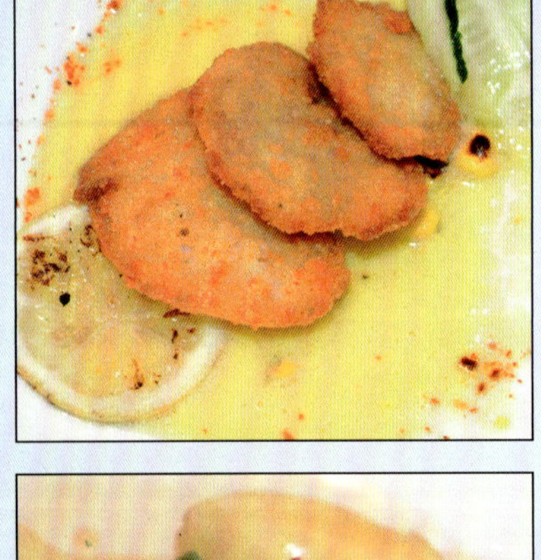

TASTING THE SEVEN REGIONS

TOP COUNTERCLOCKWISE

Region: PAMPA
Canelón de Conejo Confitado
Rabbit confit of Changlot olive oil and leek soup
Thinly sliced rabbit with radish, watercress, soy leafs, bean sprouts, and crushed pepper

Region: LITORAL
Ensalada de Pacu
Herbivorous freshwater fish native to South America
Filet of pacu salad (cured in salt and sugar for an entire day) with figs, dry corn, almonds, cheese and basil leaves

Region: MAR
Cachetes de Abadejo
Cheeks of the Atlantic Pollock fish
Fried Atlantic pollock cheeks with a side of warm sweet corn soup and zucchini slice

Region: METROPOLITANA
Tortellini de Rabo de Ternera
Tortellini of the Calf Tail with fresh herbs
Veal Tail Tortellini in juices of the calf tail boiled with the bones, vegetables and wine for 10 hours

Region: NOA
Helado de Miel de Cana
Cane honey ice cream
Cane syrup ice cream, crispy almonds and creamy caramel toffee

Region: PATAGONIA
Sorbet de Frutos Rojos
Red Berries Sorbet

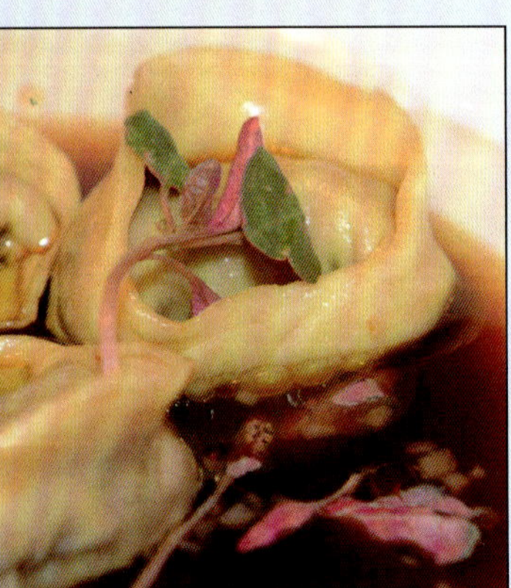

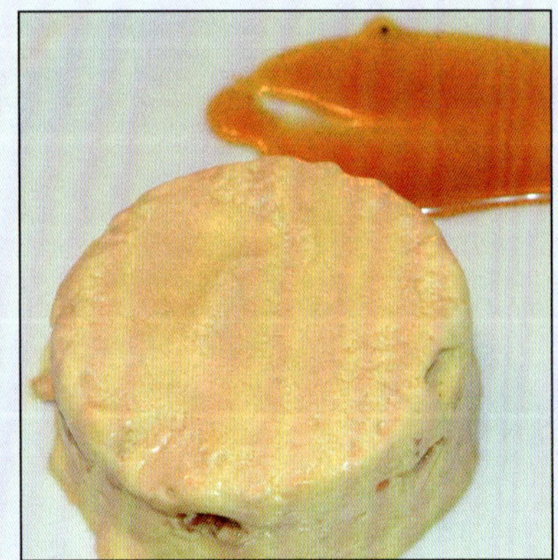

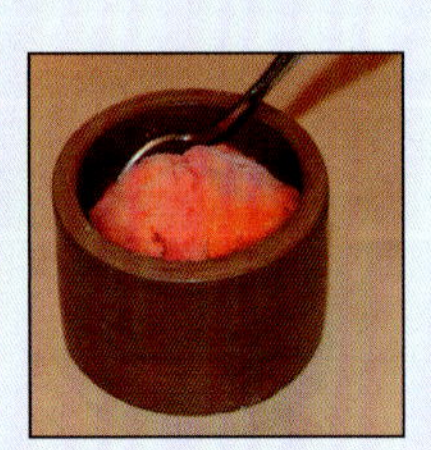

RIGHT PAGE (far right)

Region: CUYO
Chivo Asado en el Horno de Barro
Goat Roasted in a clay oven
Clay oven-roasted goat, grilled potatoes with butter and chilli, side of cooked creole sauce

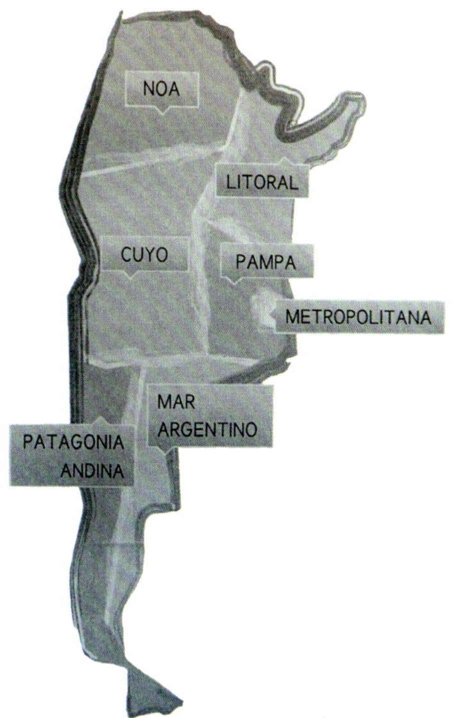

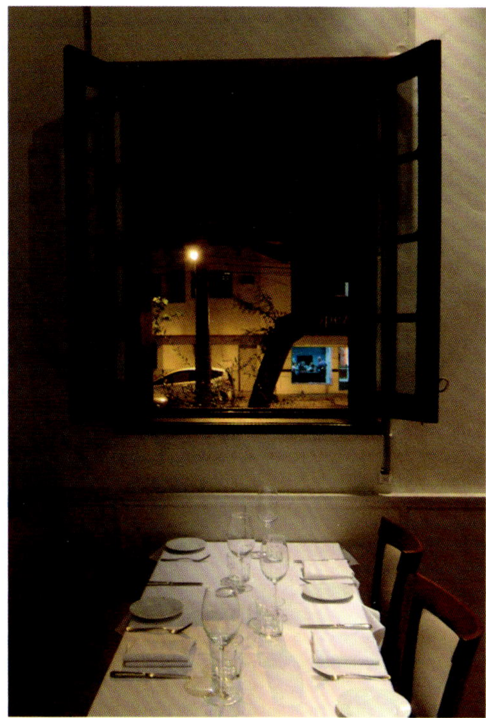

MENDOZA **DOWNTOWN**

Vinoteca • Restaurant

SIETE COCINAS

794 Bartolomé Mitre Ave
(corner of San Lorenzo)

011 (+54 261) 423.8823
restaurante@sietecocinas.com.ar

SieteCocinas.com.ar

English & Español
Open nightly at 9:00 pm

THE SEVEN KITCHENS OF ARGENTINA

Renowned Chef Pablo del Rio is one of Argentina's most innovative chefs and he has created a totally unique restaurant in downtown Mendoza called *Siete Cocinas*. Translated is *Seven Kitchens*.

Away from the typical Argentine Asado (barbeque meats), Pablo designed a menu of what is special about each region of Argentina. Seven Kitchens are the kitchens of these seven regions of Argentina. See map above for the seven regions.

Each region has its own style of food and Pablo brings out their uniqueness and then makes them special as he shows you the different culture and customs around his country.

For example, MAR (translated is sea) is the region of their southeast coast along the Atlantic Ocean where their diet is primary fish they obtain from their ocean... and Pablo's kitchen creates mouth-watering concepts in seafood dishes.

Then the region of CUYO (the wine region) is nestled against the Andes Mountains where goats are found climbing the cliffs, as goats do. If you would like to savor a clay oven roasted goat that will melt in your mouth, then you must visit Siete Cocinas and enjoy this treat.

You could focus on an a la carte choosing of a specific region you would like to experience, or... my recommendation is to taste the entire country, where you sit down and travel with Pablo at your table as he takes you through a seven-course journey of his country. I had the pleasure to experience this amazing *Tasting the Seven Regions* found on the page to the left. Enjoy!

Pablo is well connected in the world of winemakers and has an extensive collection of interesting Argentine wines to accompany your dinner. He tells you the winemaker behind the wine, its wine region and the specific terroir of the vines. They are special wines, by special people, from special places, paired with very special food.

Interesting menu concept, isn't it? Pablo del Rio is in demand for creating these unique menus, and just recently designed the menu for *The Bistró*, at *Casa de Uco Wine Resort & Spa*. A must-go resort in Valle de Uco found later in the book.

"My quest to communicate Argentina in all its aspects, brings me not only to design and enhance products and traditional cuisine, but also to try to understand and discover wine beyond the bottle.

There are certain wines that are special, for the soil where they are grown, for the vessel where they are stored or prepared, for the moment of the harvest, for the people who make them, or just for that simple selection of plants from a particular region. These wines have a concept, you might like them or not, but believe me they are different and unique."

MENDOZA **DOWNTOWN**

Hotel • Spa • Casino

SHERATON MENDOZA

1009 Primitivo de la Reta
(two blocks Plaza España)

011 (+54 261) 441.5500
reservas.mendoza@sheraton.com

Five-Star Property

Sheraton.com/Mendoza

English & Español

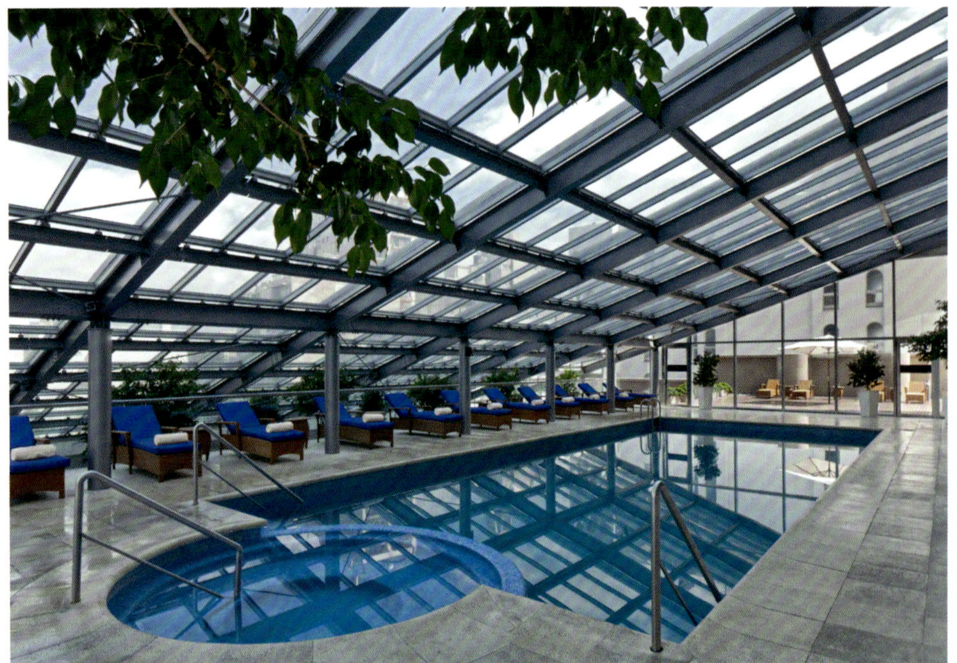

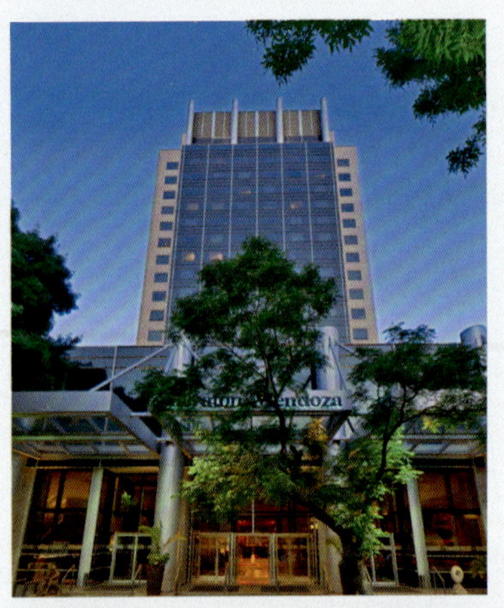

MODERN LUXURY IN DOWNTOWN MENDOZA

EL MIRADOR RESTAURANT & LOUNGE
Enjoy an elegant romantic evening at the El Mirador Restaurant with incredible views of the city from the 17th floor, the highest restaurant in all of Mendoza with 360° views of the city and Andes Mountains. International cuisine. Dinner from 4:00pm to midnight. Note: this is a very convenient opening time, five hours prior to most Argentine restaurants.

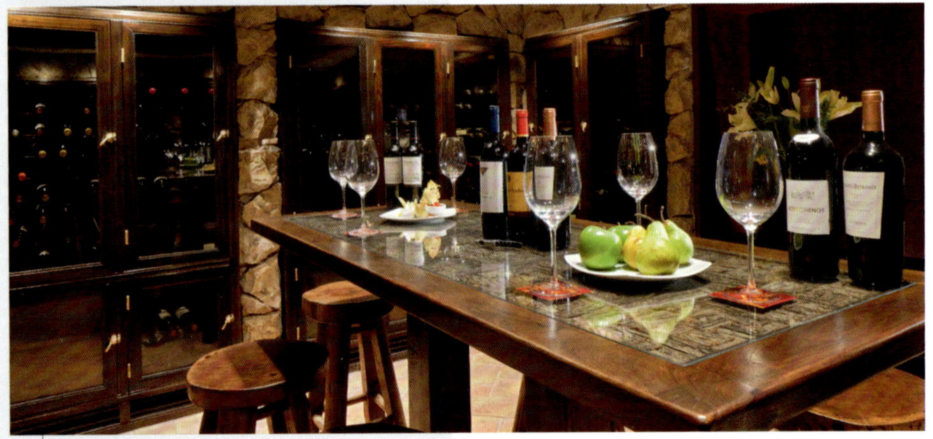

The Sheraton Mendoza Hotel is a new modern luxury hotel built in 2008 in the heart of downtown Mendoza, just two blocks from both Plaza España and the Sarmiento Pedestrian Street. This 17-story building has the super modern and luxury architecture you would expect of a new downtown five-star hotel.

What I found inviting and the perfect addition to a wine region adventure, is the Sheraton has wine tastings in their lobby most every night. Visiting wineries come to show off their wines so you can get a good idea what is out there before you leave the city headed to wineries. Also, most every night, the Sheraton's sommelier introduces interesting upscale wines from a sophisticated prospective in their stylish lounge.

The Sheraton has a spectacular heated indoor pool and jacuzzi, all encased in a huge glass atrium. It is bright, beautiful and the air is always nice and warm. Adjacent, are outside sun decks, a fitness center and sauna & steam rooms, plus a spa with an interesting wine treatment: Malbec grapes to exfoliate and scrub, combined with wine oils and hot stones massage.

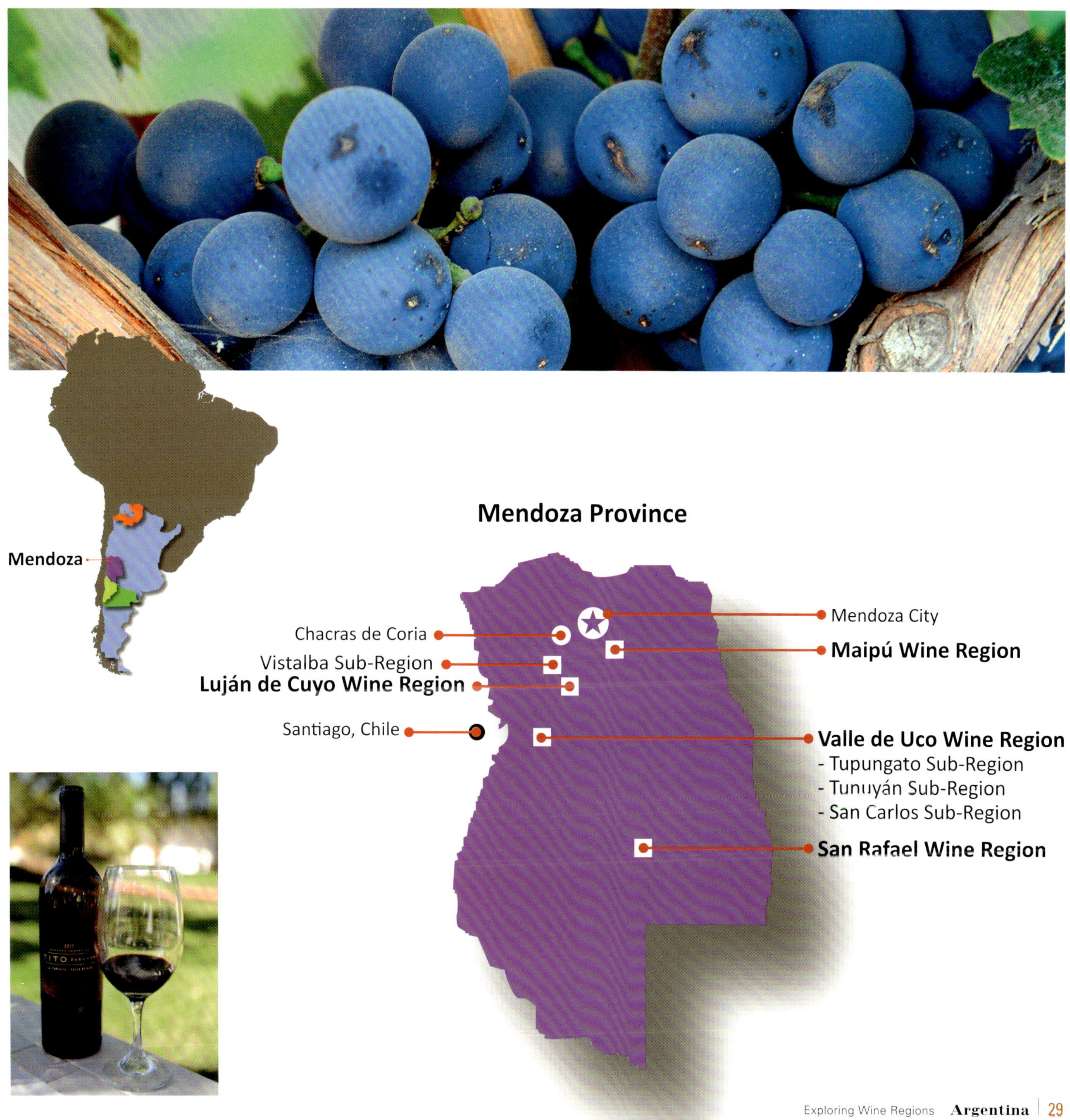
Mendoza
Mendoza Province
Mendoza City
Chacras de Coria
Maipú Wine Region
Vistalba Sub-Region
Luján de Cuyo Wine Region
Santiago, Chile
Valle de Uco Wine Region
- Tupungato Sub-Region
- Tunuyán Sub-Region
- San Carlos Sub-Region
San Rafael Wine Region

MENDOZA **LUJÁN DE CUYO**

Tierra Malbec

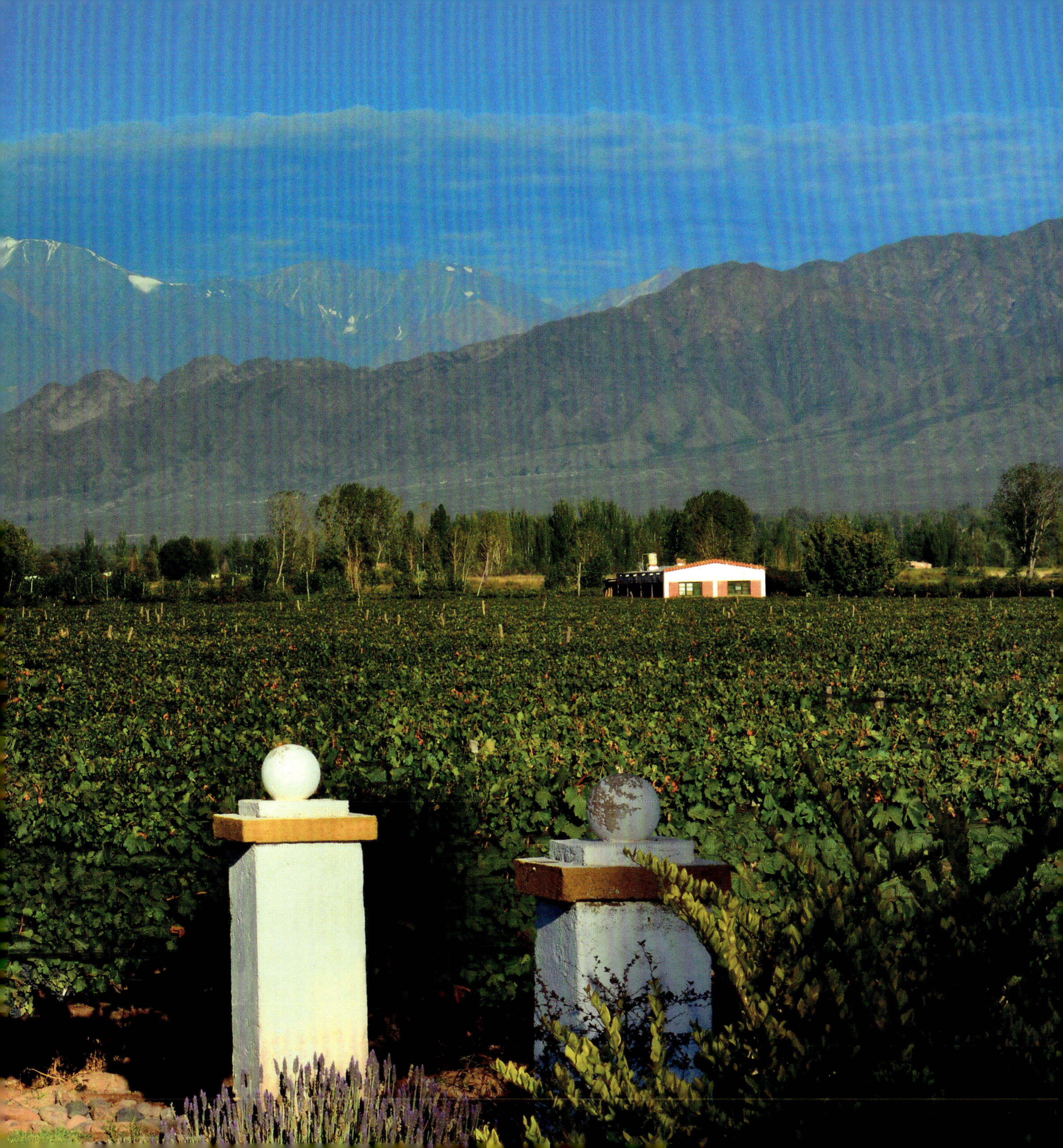

Vineyards (Viñedos)

BODEGA VIAMONTE

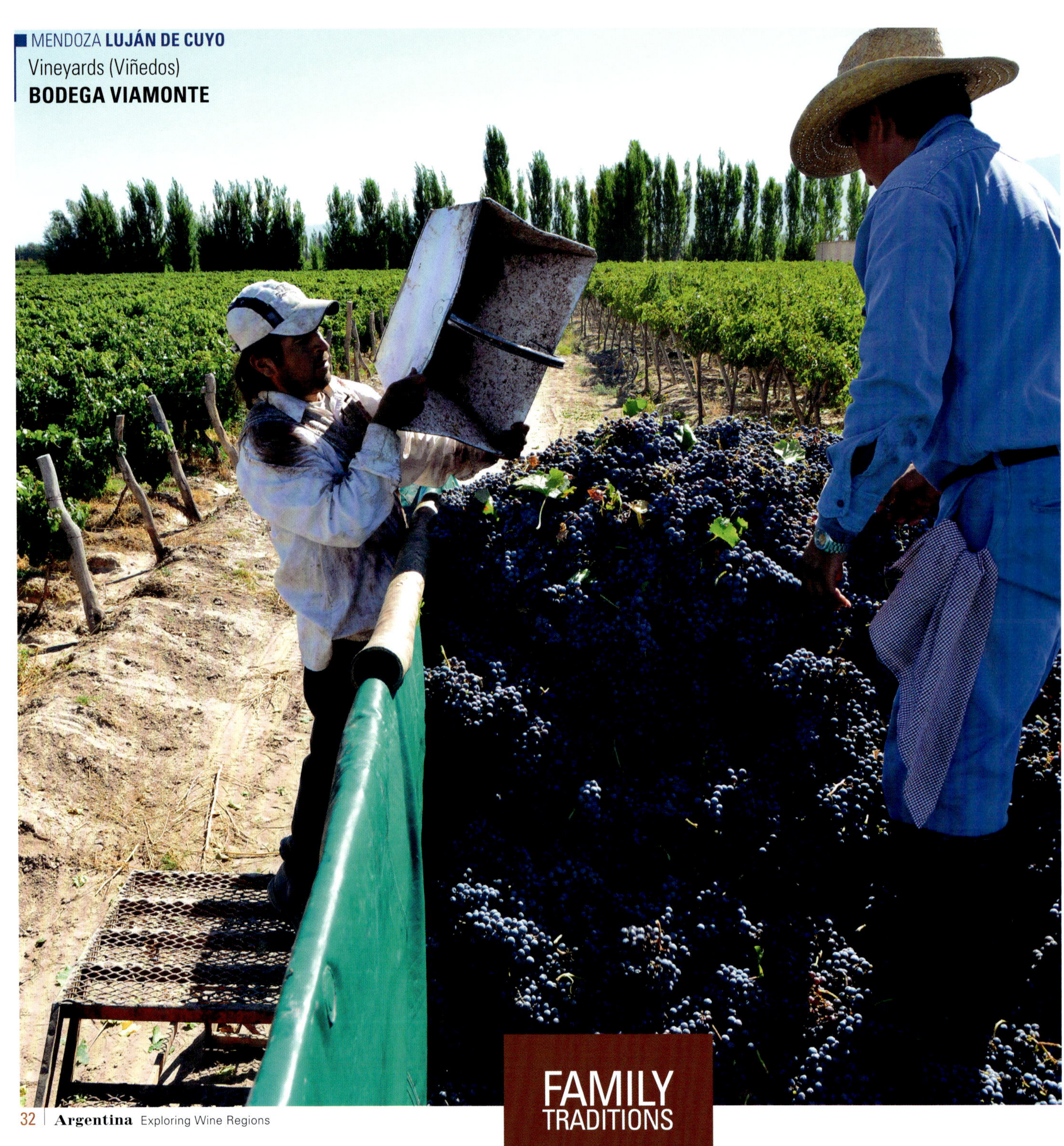

FAMILY TRADITIONS

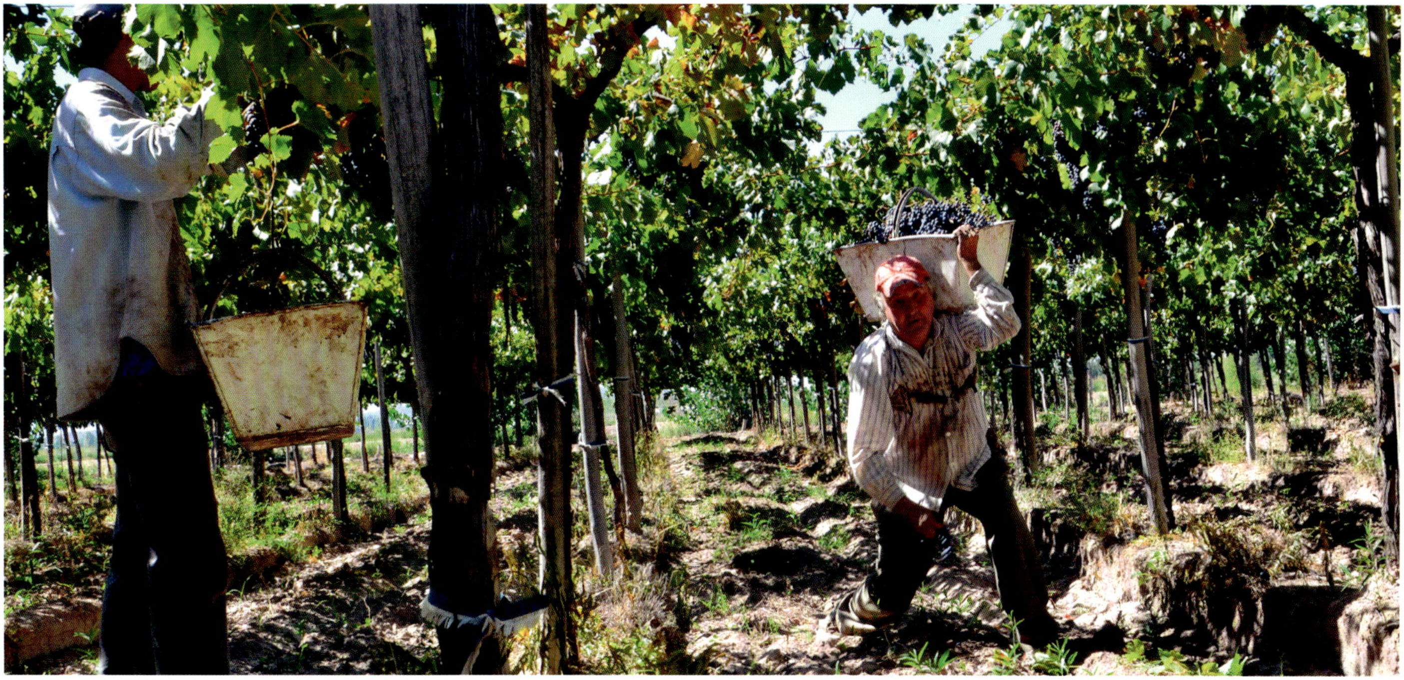

JUMPING IN

I figured the best way to get started understanding Mendoza wines is to just "jump in!" and get my feet wet, or should I say "my fingers purple."

Jumping into the back of a truck being filled with freshly picked grapes, climbing under the canopies of grape vines and experiencing the laborious hard work of a hand-picked harvesting. This is the way to learn. In the middle of it all, hands on, and conversing with seasoned experts...

Luján de Cuyo is where it all began in Argentina, a deep-rooted lineage of grape growing expertise for centuries. In 1993, Luján de Cuyo was established as Argentina's first official appellation, creating an atmosphere for a massive improvement to high-quality wines. Today Luján is considered the No. 1 location in the world for growing Malbec, and now has numerous awards, accolades and high scoring points.

Luján is located in the foothills of the Andes Mountains, just 30 minutes south of the city, right in the path of the Mendoza River, bringing fresh snow-melted water from the Andes on a year-round basis. The Inca Indians created an ingenious irrigation system in the 14th century, a channel they called Goazap Mayú, which fed the Luján properties and then eventually created the canal system in downtown Mendoza today.

The grapes are irrigated by flooding the vineyards. When it is time for a drink, the flood gates are opened and the vineyards are filled with water. This contrasts other severe dry climates where extreme water conservation occurs, and yet here, the Andes provide an endless supply of water.

The landscape is picture-perfect with lush green vineyards sitting at 3,000 feet elevation, crystal clear blue skies with bright sunshine, a dry and fresh climate, arid and rocky soils, with a spectacular backdrop of snow-capped mountain peaks.

If you only have time to visit one region in Mendoza, Luján is the place to experience Malbec and beauty at its very best.

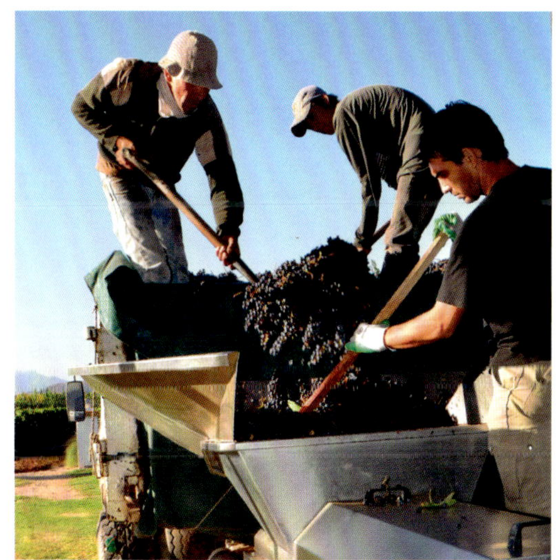

LEFT PAGE, a truck is filled with tons of grapes, handpicked by knowledgeable workers; ABOVE, whose discernment of grapes and gentler handling give advantages to producing finer premium wines.

From vineyard to truck to unloading in the winery, Merlot is harvested at Bodega Viamonte.

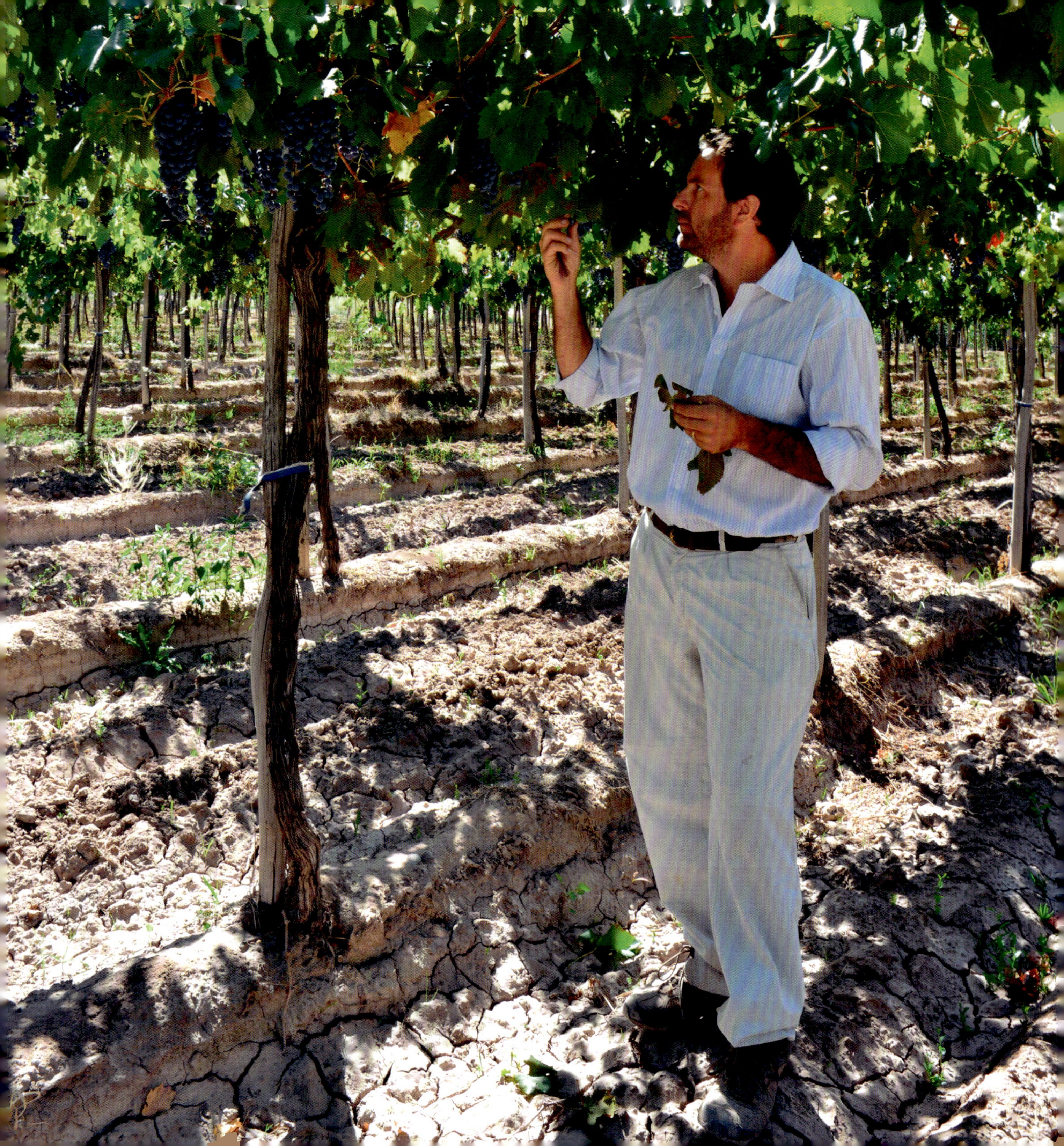

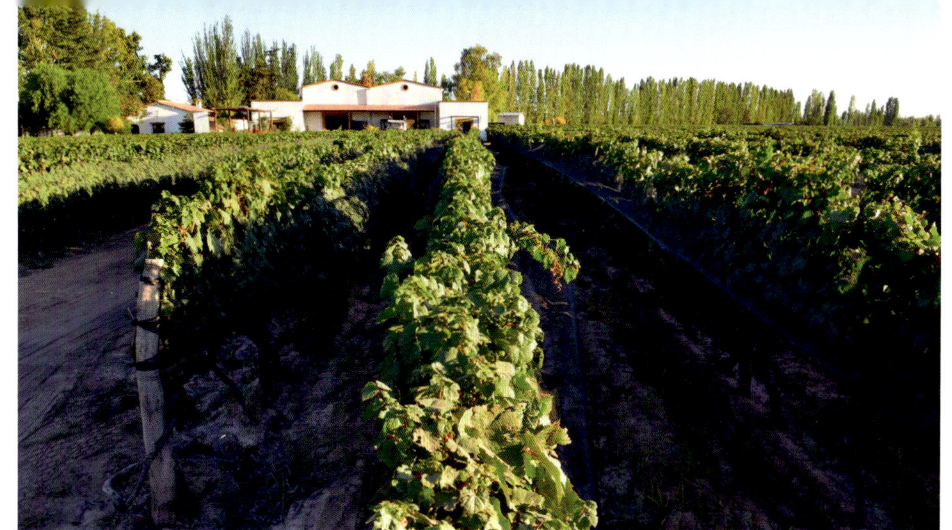

MENDOZA **LUJÁN DE CUYO**

Winery (Bodega)

BODEGA VIAMONTE

962 Viamonte
(Chacras de Coria, Luján de Cuyo)

011 (+54 9 261) 155.02851
informes@ViamonteWinery.com

ViamonteWinery.com

English & Español

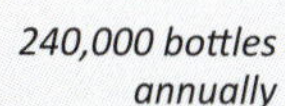

240,000 bottles annually

A FAMILY TRADITION, TODAY

For generations, the Celasso family has been growing grapes for some of the most notable wineries in Argentina. In 2007, brothers Martín and Nicolás, and their sister Andrea, united to create their own premium wines from their combined skills, great technology in the winery, and from very selective locations in their vineyards.

For example, my Favorite Pick is their *Malbec Reserva*, which comes from a very special vineyard with vines planted in 1912. The yield is lower, the quality higher and the color deeper. They get to choose the best of their best grapes, and in the winery ferment in small tanks and only age one year in French barrels so the wine is more fruit forward... and we get to experience the amazing flavors of this special and historical vineyard.

Martín Celasso (left), is an agricultural scientist and the Viticulturist and Enologist at Viamonte Winery (above). I learned a tremendous amount from Martín, and you will too if you stop by to visit with him (the winery is open every day, but by appointment only). This winery is worth a visit. The family is fun and knowledgable. You will learn a lot and have a great time. And you can purchase premium wines at great prices!

Martín is proud to be a part of the terroir and worldwide reputation of Luján de Cuyo. Not just because of the old vines planted by generations long ago, he sees it that Luján de Cuyo has the perfect soil. Perfect because the soil is very deep with more than six feet of clay and sand mix, followed by a rocky profile. This alluvial soil allows the water that the vines don't need to flow out to the underground rivers. In the chalkboard drawing (above) Martín illustrates this Luján de Cuyo terroir advantage.

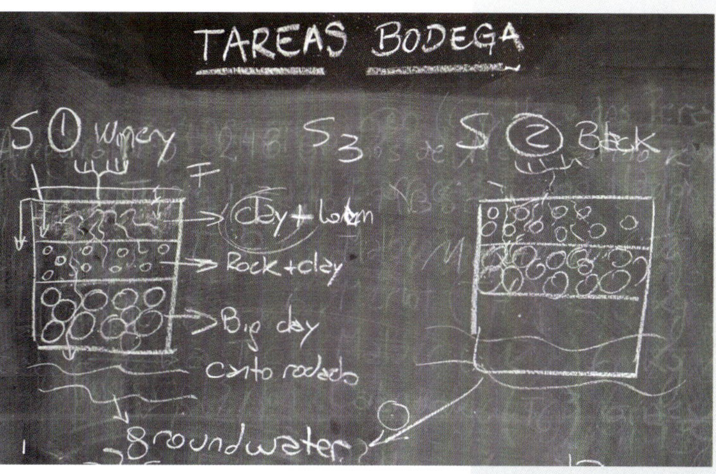

The weather is perfect too! During the day, the super clear sky provides a very high intensity of light and the photosynthesis process is optimum. During the night, the respiration process is minimum so the relation of photosynthesis/respiration is better for the vines and grapes. The Luján climate and soil, along with their unique vineyard locations, are all part of the terroir that gives their wines their distinctive character and expressions.

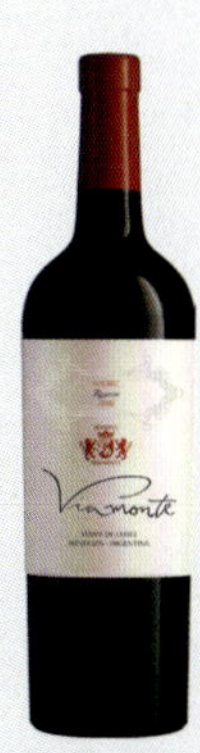

Michael's Favorite Pick
Viamonte Malbec Reserva
100% Malbec, Luján de Cuyo

Total Collection of Wines
Malbec
Malbec Rose
Malbec Reserva
Viamonte Blend
Cabernet Sauvignon
Merlot Reserva
Sauvignon Blanc

To get Viamonte wines in the USA
Direct from the Importer: CopaFina.com
at CopaFina.com/**viamonte**buywine.html

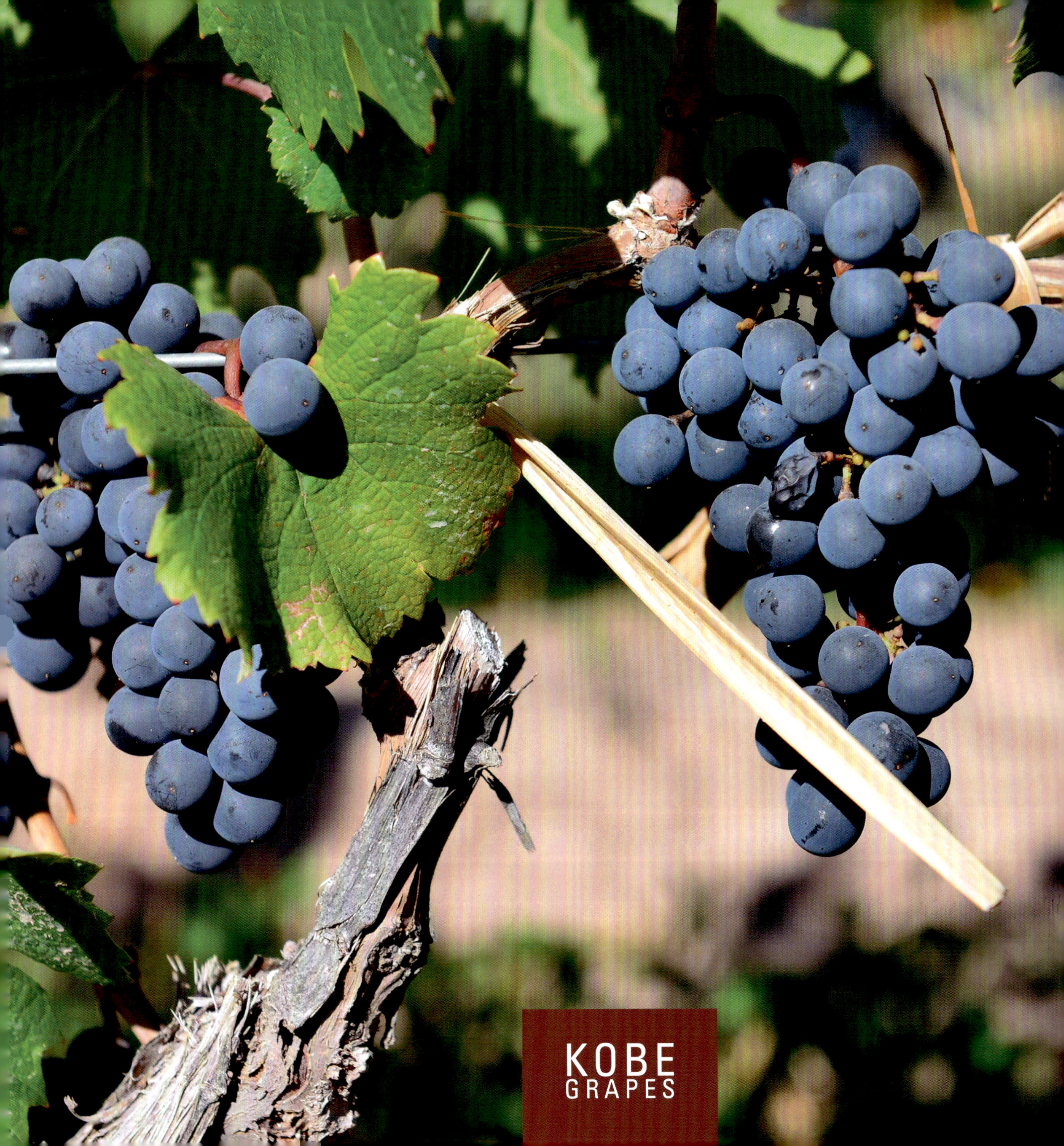
KOBE
GRAPES

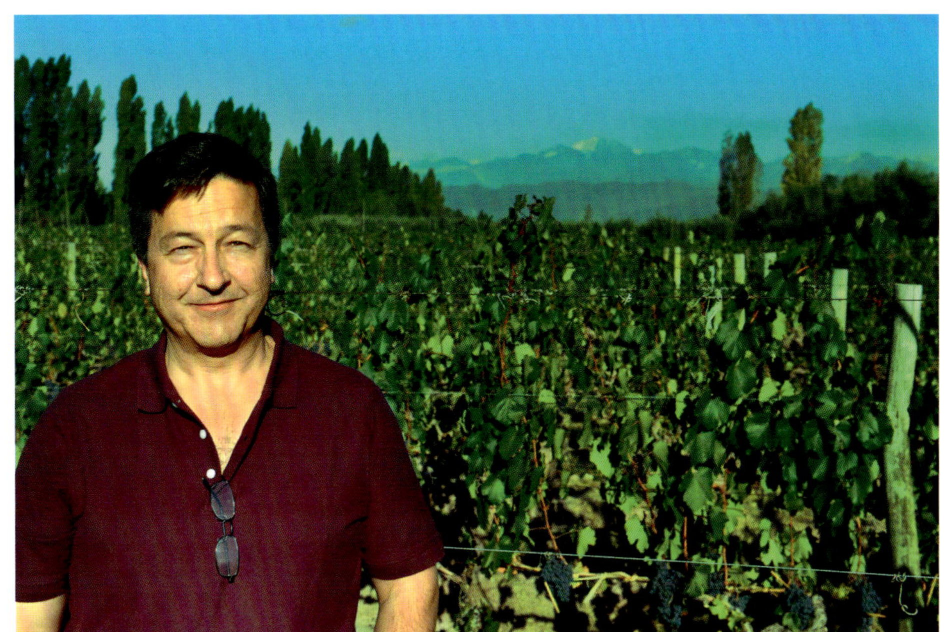

THE MAKING OF ARGENTINA'S HIGHEST SCORING WINE

In the land where you find the most flavorful beef in the world, Argentina... one also finds KOBE GRAPES!

Santiago Achaval loves his grapes like the Japanese love their cows. Truly! The love and care that are expressed in an Achaval vineyard is best described as "Kobe" style!

Not that long ago, Santiago Achaval was in California studying for an MBA in Finance from Stanford University, making trips to the Napa Valley and discovering how much he loved great wines. Upon returning to Argentina, he realized he had friends who shared the same love for wine, and in 1998 four of them formed Bodega Achaval-Ferrer, united by their passion to make great wines. And their focus, the best Malbec possible.

Just 12 years later, Achaval-Ferrer boasts four of the five highest rated wines in Argentina history, as judged by Wine Spectator, who awarded their 2010 Finca Bella Vista as one of the "Top 10" best wines in the world. Robert Parker, Wine Advocate, says they are the highest rated Argentine wines to date, giving their 2004 Finca Altamira Malbec a whopping 98 points!

Meet **Santiago Achaval**, above, standing in his Finca Bella Vista vineyard, with the prized Malbec grapes (close-up left) that honored him with the "Top 10" wine in the world.

To spend time with Santiago, as I did twice, and to walk with him through his vineyards, you suddenly feel the sensation of love and compassion he has for the grapes hanging beautifully from the vines. A tremendous amount of care goes into raising these most exquisite grapes, grapes I call: *Kobe Grapes*!

Achaval started by acquiring four impressively special vineyards, creating history right from the beginning, all adoring old vine Malbecs, one with 100-year-old vines. Each of these vineyards brings unique Malbec wines with their own personality expressive of its terroir.

Their four vineyard estates, Finca Bella Vista, 100-years-old vineyards (planted in 1910) at the winery in Luján de Cuyo, Finca Altamira (1900) and Finca Diamante (1900), both in the Uco Valley – these three vineyards are for single vineyard wines, and Finca Mirador (1921), in the village of Medrano, is used for their Quimera, a blend of the Bordeaux grapes, except Malbec leads the way in this Argentine style Bordeaux. Quimera is a Spanish translation of an illusionary dream, a foolish search, for the unattainable... their insatiable quest for perfection.

At first glance, a big noticeable difference at Achaval-Ferrer is the leaf thinning in the vineyards. It is significant. The grapes are fully exposed to the sun. Brilliant idea, yet uncommon. Take a look at the photos and you will see that the grape clusters are fully open to the elements. This creates thicker skins, which will produce bigger aromas and flavors. And the sun benefits the full ripening of the fruit. Most of the leaf pulling is done in the month of December, when the grapes are still green so the clusters stay completely exposed at they ripen.

Then, in January and February at the onset of ripening, they thin (remove) the grape clusters when the grapes start to change from green to purple. This is common practice, however at Achaval-Ferrer it is substantial. They reduce the crop yield from an average of 11 pounds per plant/vine to less than one pound per vine. To put this in perspective, this means it now takes three plants just to produce one bottle of wine.

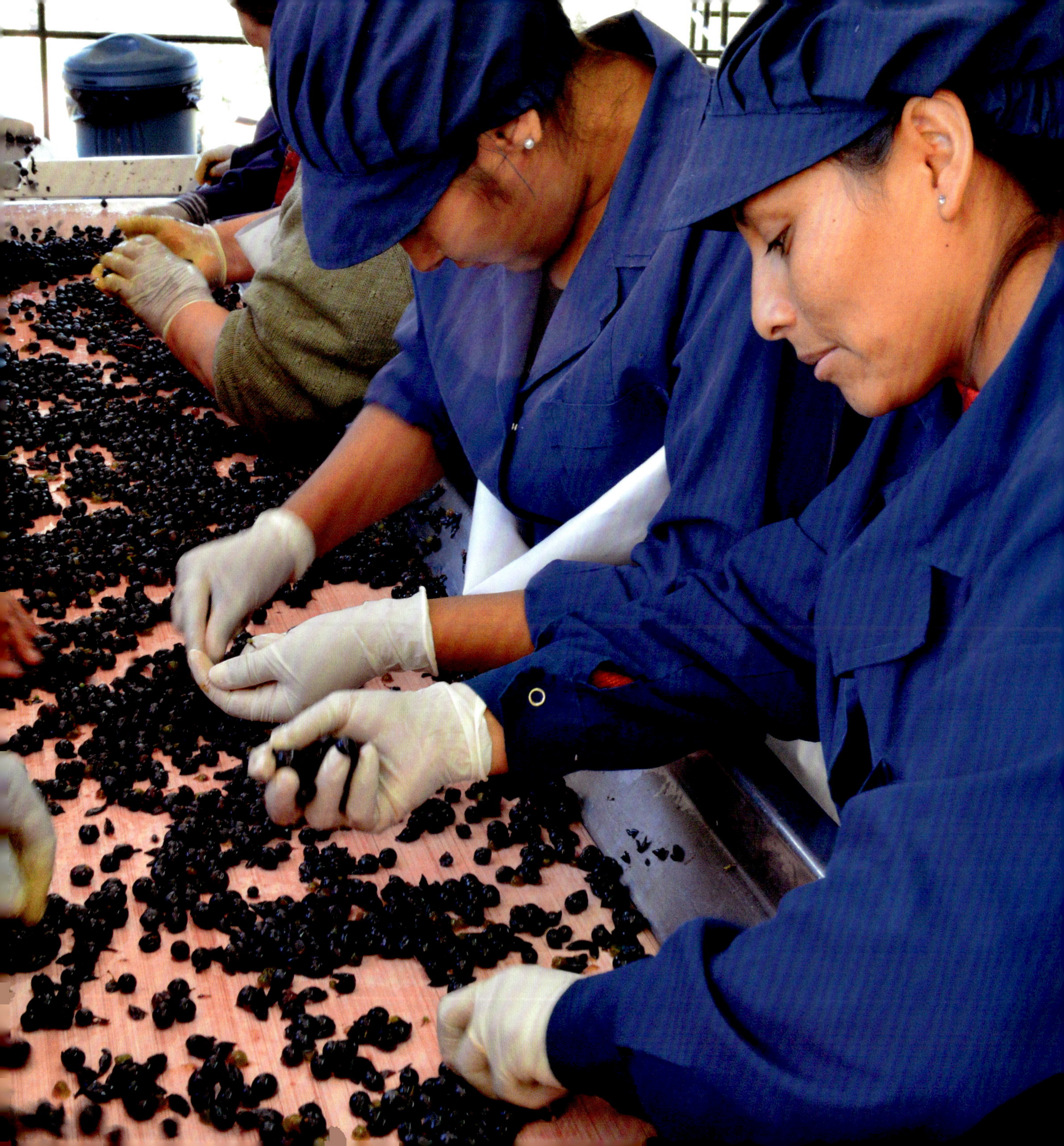

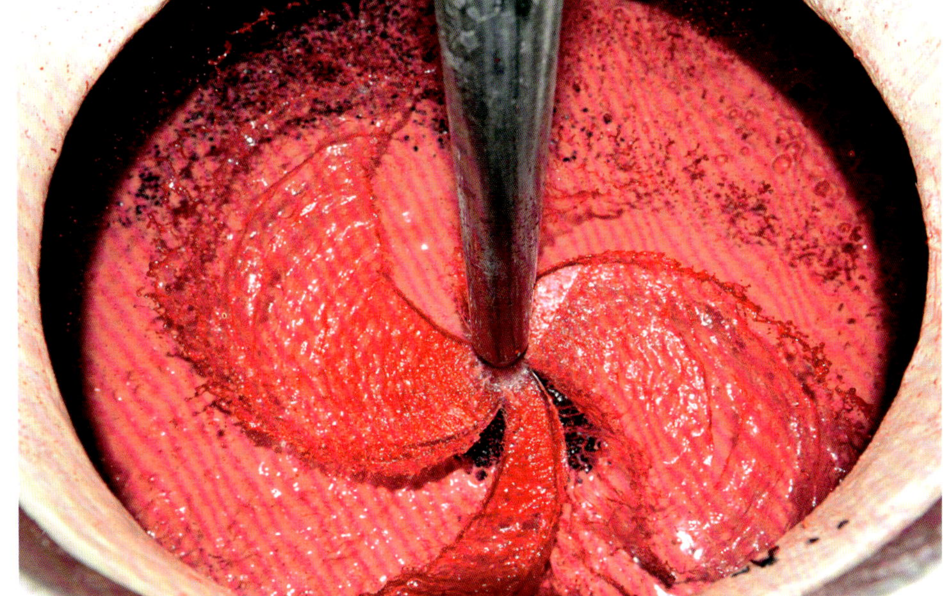

MENDOZA **LUJÁN DE CUYO**

Winery (Bodega)

ACHAVAL FERRER

2601 Calle Cobos
(Pedriel, Luján de Cuyo)

011 (+54 9 261) 155.35565
Winery@Achaval-Ferrer.com

Achaval-Ferrer.com

English & Español
240,000 bottles annually

Vintners generally boast about their extensive thinning to produce high-quality grapes when they are thinning to about three tons of harvested fruit per acre. This is considered extensive, and great fruit comes from this much thinning.

However, for Achaval Ferrar, their thinning goes as far as just .75 ton an acre. I want you to get the impact... that the remaining fruit on the vines are now getting all the love, they have unabstructed sunlight, and are now poised for an abundance of nutrition the vines and roots will focus upon them. As the harvest yield drops, the quality is optimized.

Further, Achaval reduces irrigation to half the normal irrigation levels for a month starting mid-December. This course of action is done at the moment to determine the grape size by the vine. By reducing irrigation, they decrease the grape diameter and increase the relationship of skin to pulp, trying to achieve more skin than pulp. This increases the wine's notable aromas and flavors.

Achaval loves low yields. It brings out the character and personality of what the root system has to say... the minerality, the complexity, the intensity, and the land's ability to express itself in the form of wine. This is the meticulous care that goes into creating a beautiful Kobe Grape.

In the winery, Achaval likes to keep it simple, low intervention so the grapes can fully express their vineyard in the bottle. After harvest, the de-stemming is fanatical. See the photo (left page) where beautiful and knowledgeable women sort through the grapes to perfection... not a single leaf, not a stem, not a bad berry is missed. Only perfect specimens continue on to fermentation.

To avoid damaging the grapes, Achaval refrains from the "push down" method during the fermentation. Instead of pushing down the skins into the juice, they delicately pump the fermenting juice out from under and over onto the floating pulp allowing ongoing skin to juice contact necessary for leaching the rich flavors and colors into the juice. It is a beautiful sight (photo above).

Achaval does not correct the acidity of his wines (natural high acidity), no cold soaks, no added enzymes, no commercial yeast (natural fermentation), no extended masuration (total contact with the skins is 10 days at the most), no racking the wine in and out of the barrel, and he does not filter the wine.

As you can see, Santiago Achaval is dedicated to producing wines that are quite expressive of their terroir. This is a small winery and each of their wines has a different expression of Malbec.

They offer individualized tours and tastings with an English-speaking wine expert. Reservations are required. You really must go to see and experience this winemaking at an ultimate level.

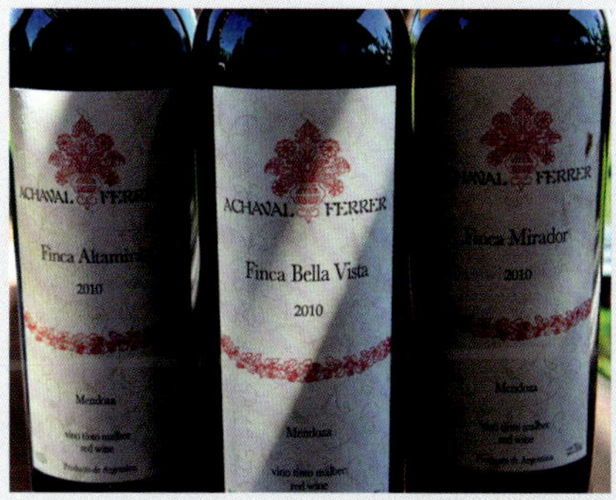

Michael's Favorite Pick
The Single Vineyard Malbec Trio
- Finca Bella Vista (Luján de Cuyo, Estate)
- Finca Mirador (Uco Valley, Tunuyán)
- Finca Altamira (Uco Valley, La Consulta)

This is a great experience to distinguished three different expressions of terrior in the same grape

Total Collection of Wines
Finca Bella Vista
Finca Mirador
Finca Altamira
Quimera (Argentine-Style Bordeaux)
Mendoza Malbec

To get Achaval Ferrer wines in the USA
Call TGIC Importers for nearest retailer
TGICImporters.com • 800-924-0030

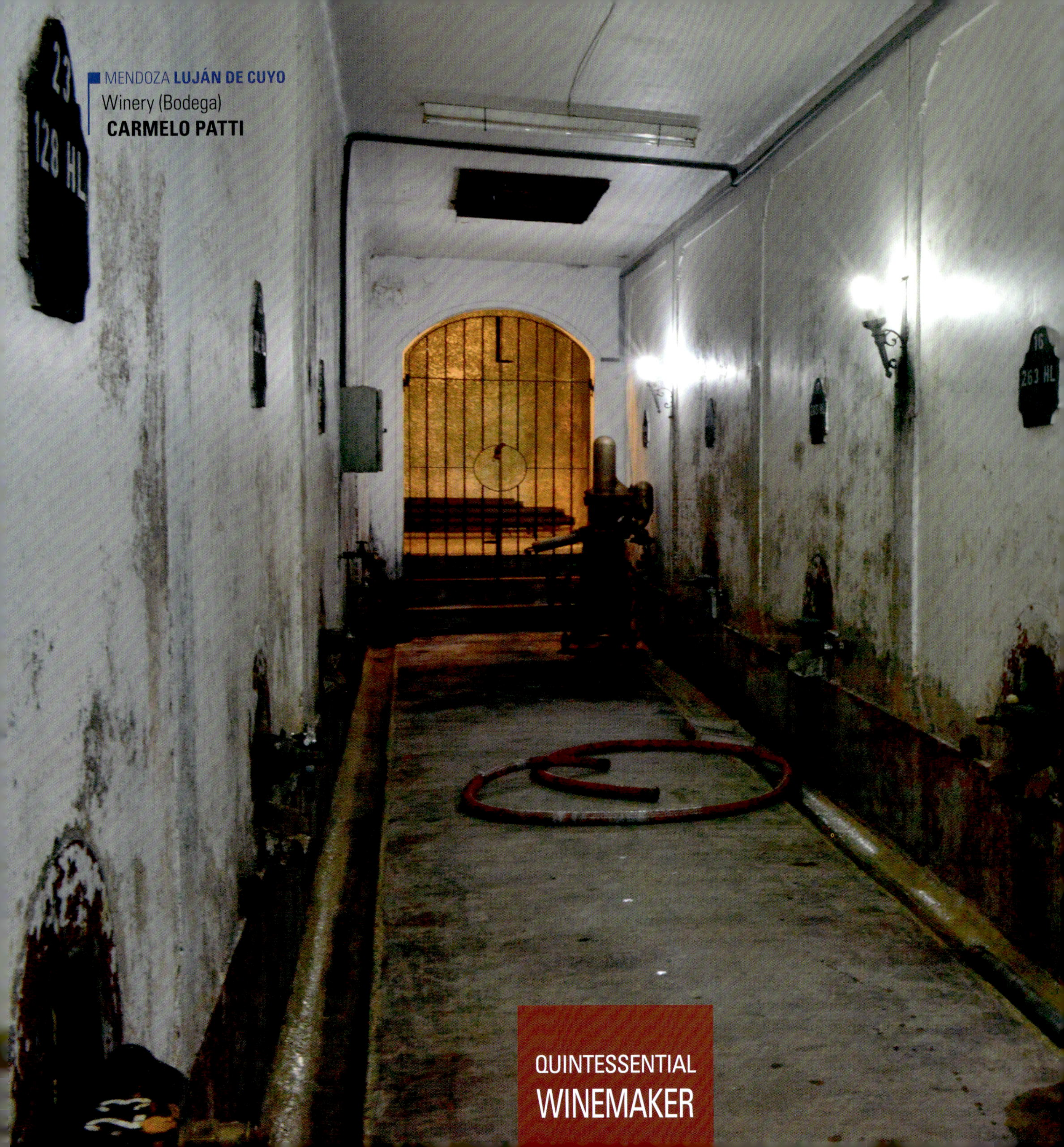

MENDOZA **LUJÁN DE CUYO**

Winery (Bodega)

CARMELO PATTI

QUINTESSENTIAL

WINEMAKER

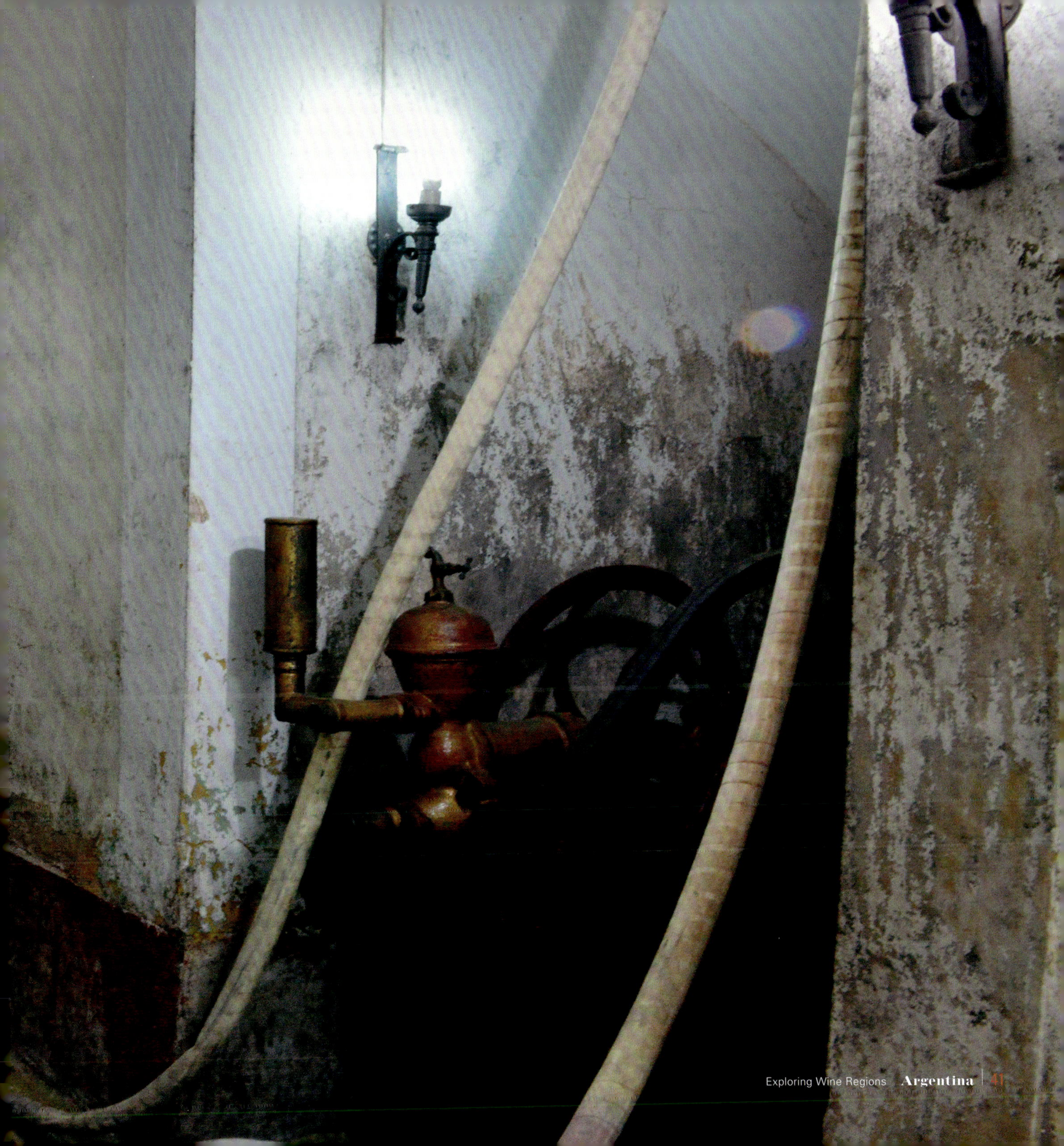

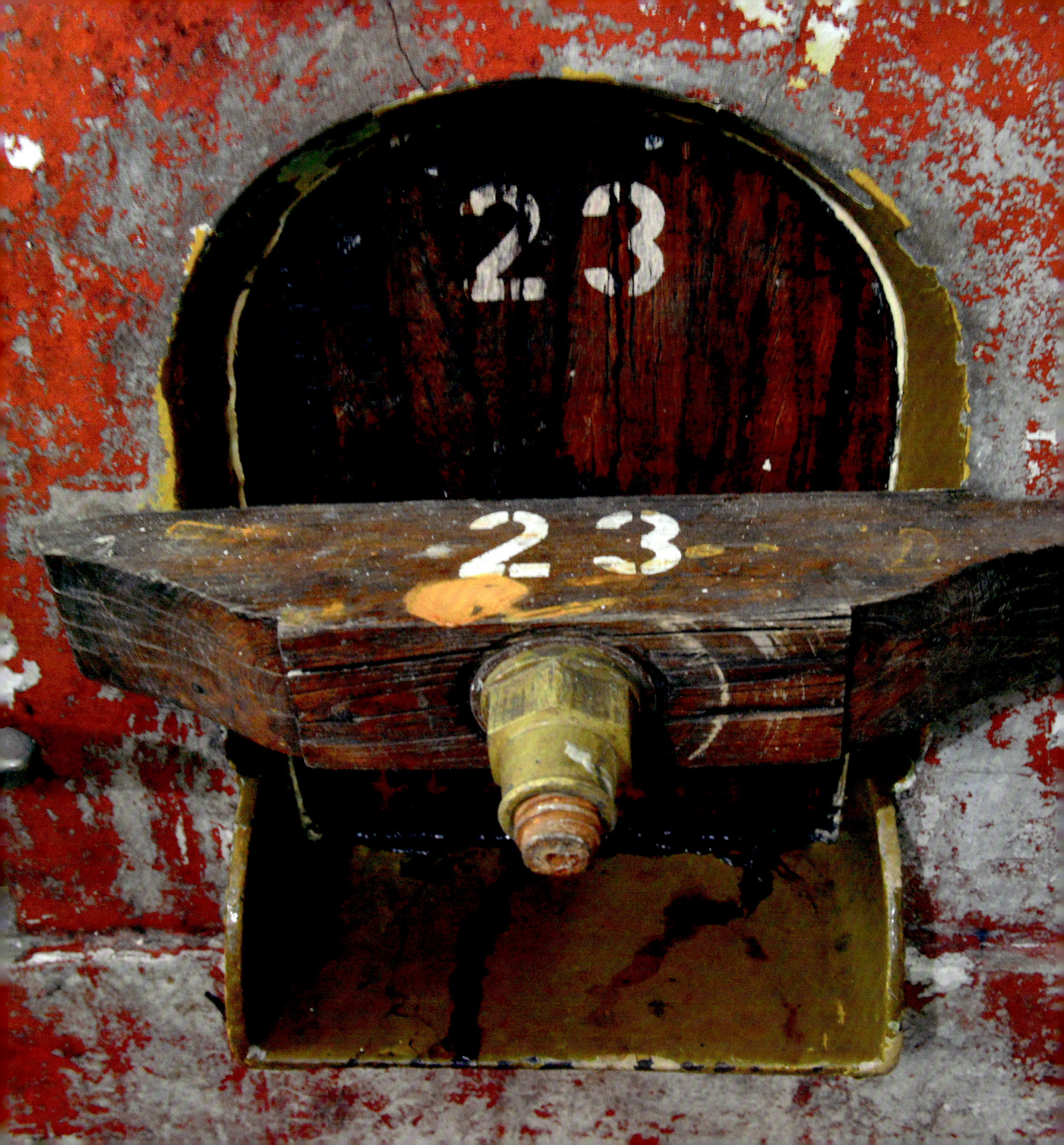
23
23

MENDOZA **LUJÁN DE CUYO**

Winery (Bodega)

CARMELO PATTI

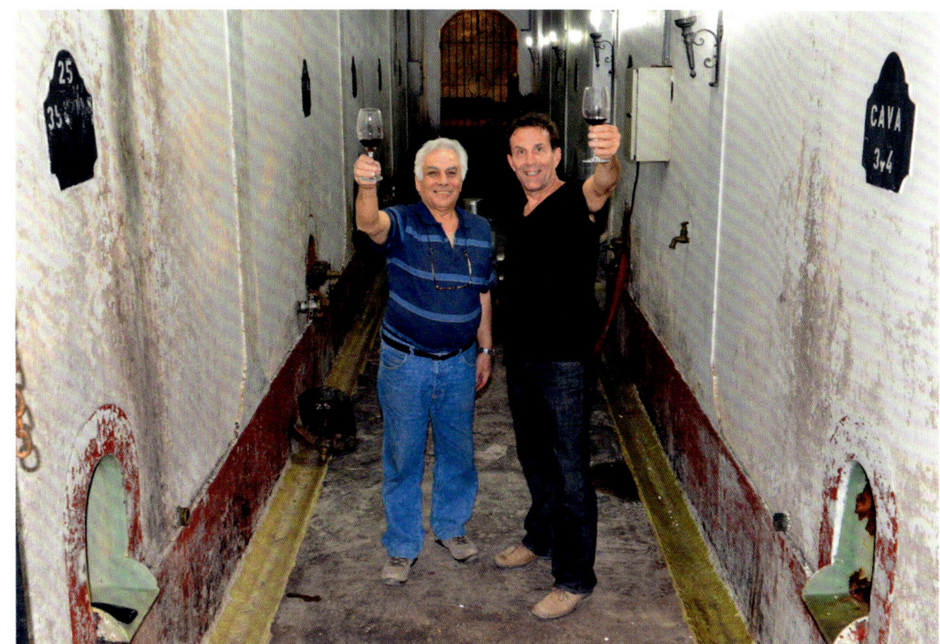

2614 San Martín
(Mayor Drummond, Luján de Cuyo)

011 (+54 261) 498.1379
carmelo_patti@hotmail.com
no website

Español Only
65,000 bottles annually

A VINTAGE IN TIME

Stepping into the Bodega of Carmelo Patti is like finding yourself in another place in time (see the photos on these four pages). Underground, castle lighting, concrete fermentation tanks built into the walls of the building, wooden vise doors to hold back the wine, wine-dripped stained walls, layers of paint colors showing the passage of time like dendrochronology... you can feel the ghosts of the wine's past vintages in this historic site for making wine, *today*.

Thirty-five vintages later, Patti continues to make his wine the old-fashioned way. No modernization here! Carmelo will tell you: "some people build architectural masterpieces, and some people make magnificent wine." This is a very small winery, a one-man show, where Patti runs every corner of his quirky operation. And there is no formal procedure, he makes great wine like he wants to make great wine, and until it is perfectly ready to drink, he won't sell it to you. Nor will he get on the phone and look for a sale. You want his great stuff, you will find him.

Carmelo ages his wine for a year in the old concrete tanks and at least another year in barrels (and he prefers American Oak) before the wine goes to bottle. Carmelo's winemaking style is equally as unique as his character, and he insists on holding onto all wine until he deems it "ready" for release, which generally means five years after harvest.

A bohemian enologist, Carmel Patti is something of a legend in Mendoza and has built his reputation on being the master of fine wines in the area. Originally brought to Argentina on a small boat from Sicily when he was one year old, Carmelo was a catalyst for the rebirth of fine wine production in Mendoza in the 80s and is to this day one of the most respected enologists in the country.

The Gran Assemblage is his masterpiece. It is a blend of his other wines and is a Bordeaux-style wine in the French tradition (lead with Cabernet Sauvignon, then Malbec, Merlot and Cabernet Franc), and is big and complex as you can imagine. This was an exciting difference to taste in the land of Argentina Malbecs.

When Carmelo is in his winery, he will welcome you with open arms. And I suggest you do not miss this extraordinary experience. Carmelo only speaks Spanish, but don't let that stop you from experiencing one of Mendoza's most interesting personalities.

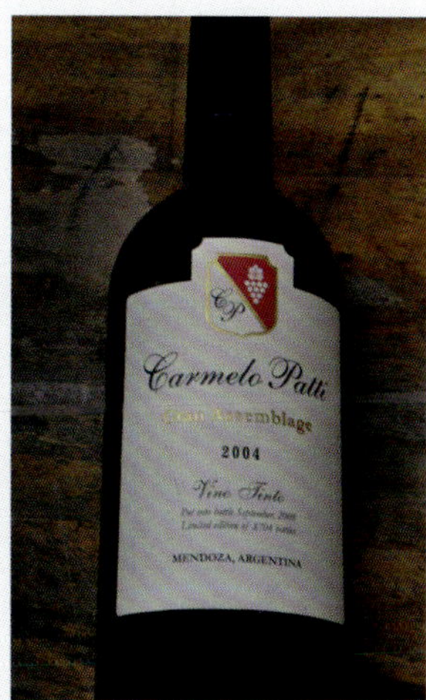

Michael's Favorite Pick
Carmelo Patti Gran Assemblage
Bordeaux Style: Cabernet Sauvignon, Malbec, Merlot and Cabernet Franc

Total Collection of Wines
Carmelo Patti Malbec
Carmelo Patti Cabernet Sauvignon
Carmelo Patti Extra Brut (Champagne)
Gran Assemblage (Bordeaux style)

To get Carmelo Patti wines in the USA
SouthernWineGroup.com ships direct

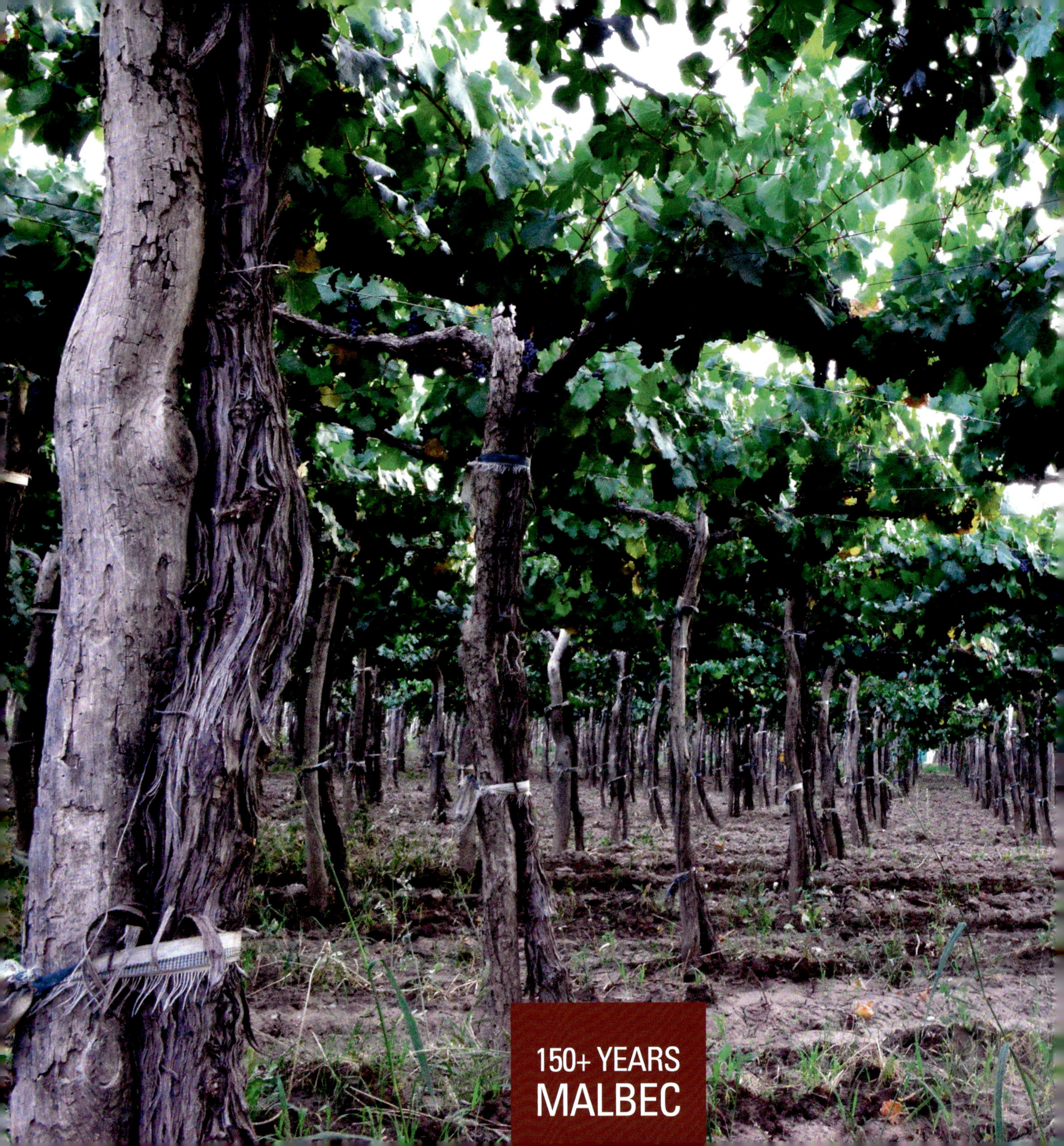
150+ YEARS
MALBEC

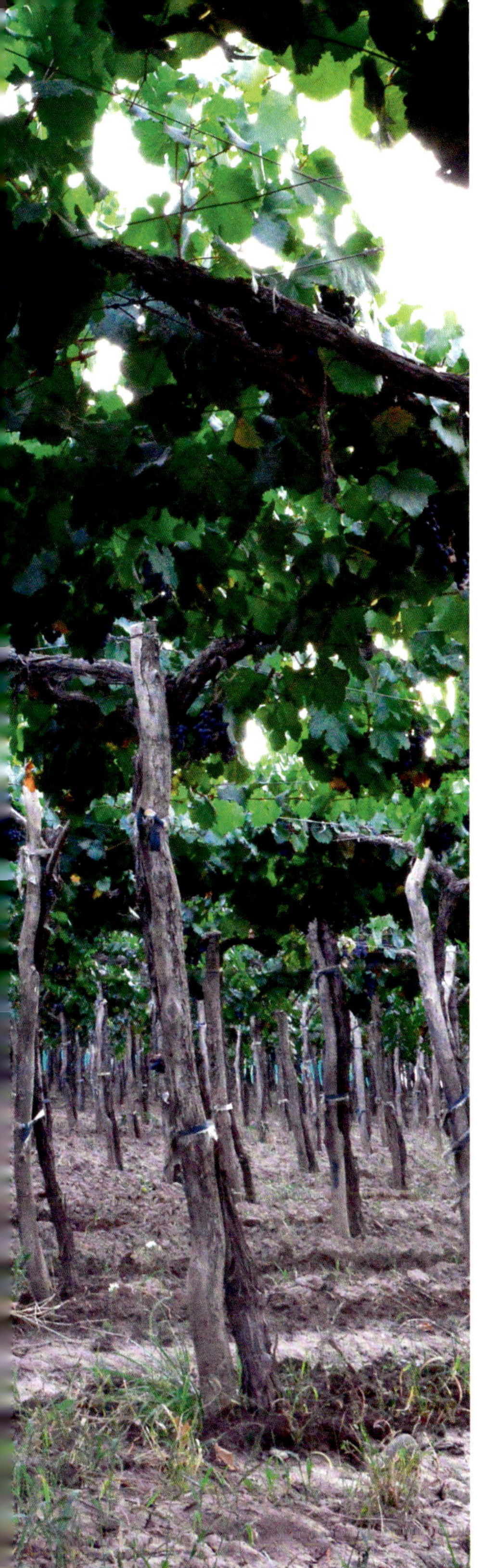

MENDOZA **LUJÁN DE CUYO**
Winery (Bodega)
FAMIGLIA MOSSO

AGED PERFECTION

It all began in 1860 when Francesco Mosso departed Turin, Italy for Argentina, acquiring a winery in Luján de Cuyo and started producing a Turin-style Vermouth, which became famous and gave immense prestige to the Mosso name. Vermouth is a fortified wine flavored with various botanicals, and originated in Turin.

Fifty years later, his sons Juan and Antonio built a large winery and estate vineyards to grow and produced wines from the "French grapes" known to us today as Malbec. Their wines were distributed throughout Argentina. Today these Famiglia Mosso Old Labels are exhibited in the museum Piazzale dei Cappuccini, in Turin, Italy.

Now, more than 150 years later, great-grandsons Pablo and Ernesto Mosso recharged the family heritage in a new way... cultivating the old vines from the estate property into the absolute finest premium Malbec. They sacrifice nothing and meticulously care for the vineyard; using an Agronomist Juan Giugno who implements a strict quality control regimen throughout the winemaking.

No more volume wine for Mosso. A very limited production of only a 1,000 cases annually of super-premium wine. I came to Argentina to discover amazing Malbec. Well, here at Mosso, I found it!

Famiglia Mosso wines are exclusive, limited in production, and can only be found in very nice restaurants in the United States. They do not have a winery to visit. This is a very small boutique operation. My suggestion is to buy a couple of bottles from their importer (below right) and see if you become as enamored with this wine, as I am. And, if you really are into their wine, send them an email and tell them. They will be happy to hear from you and to welcome you to a private vineyard visit; and enjoy some empanadas with their wine.

596 España
Mendoza - Vineyards in Luján de Cuyo

011 (+54 261) 499.0721
trade@MossoWines.com

MossoWines.com

English, Español & Italiano
12,000 bottles produced annually

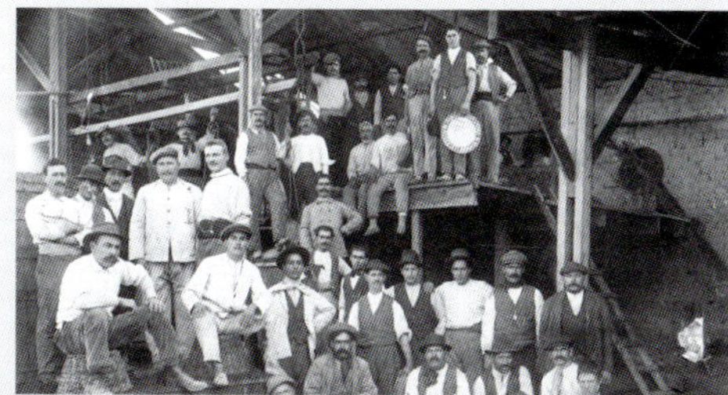

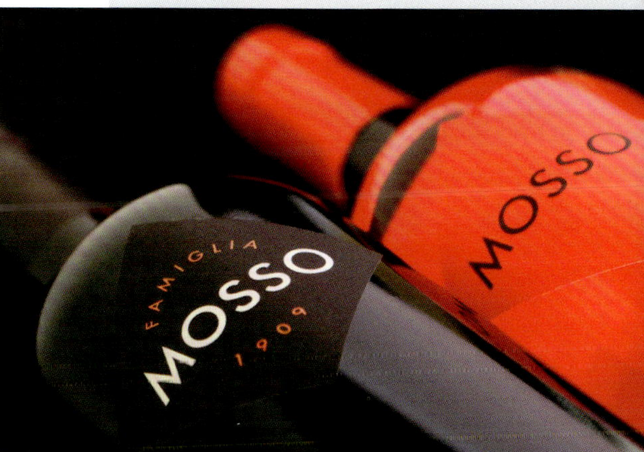

Michael's Favorite Pick
Mosso Malbec

Total Collection of Wines
Mosso Malbec
Mosso Blend

To get Mosso wines in the USA
Direct from the Importer: CopaFina.com
at CopaFina.com/**mosso**buywine.html

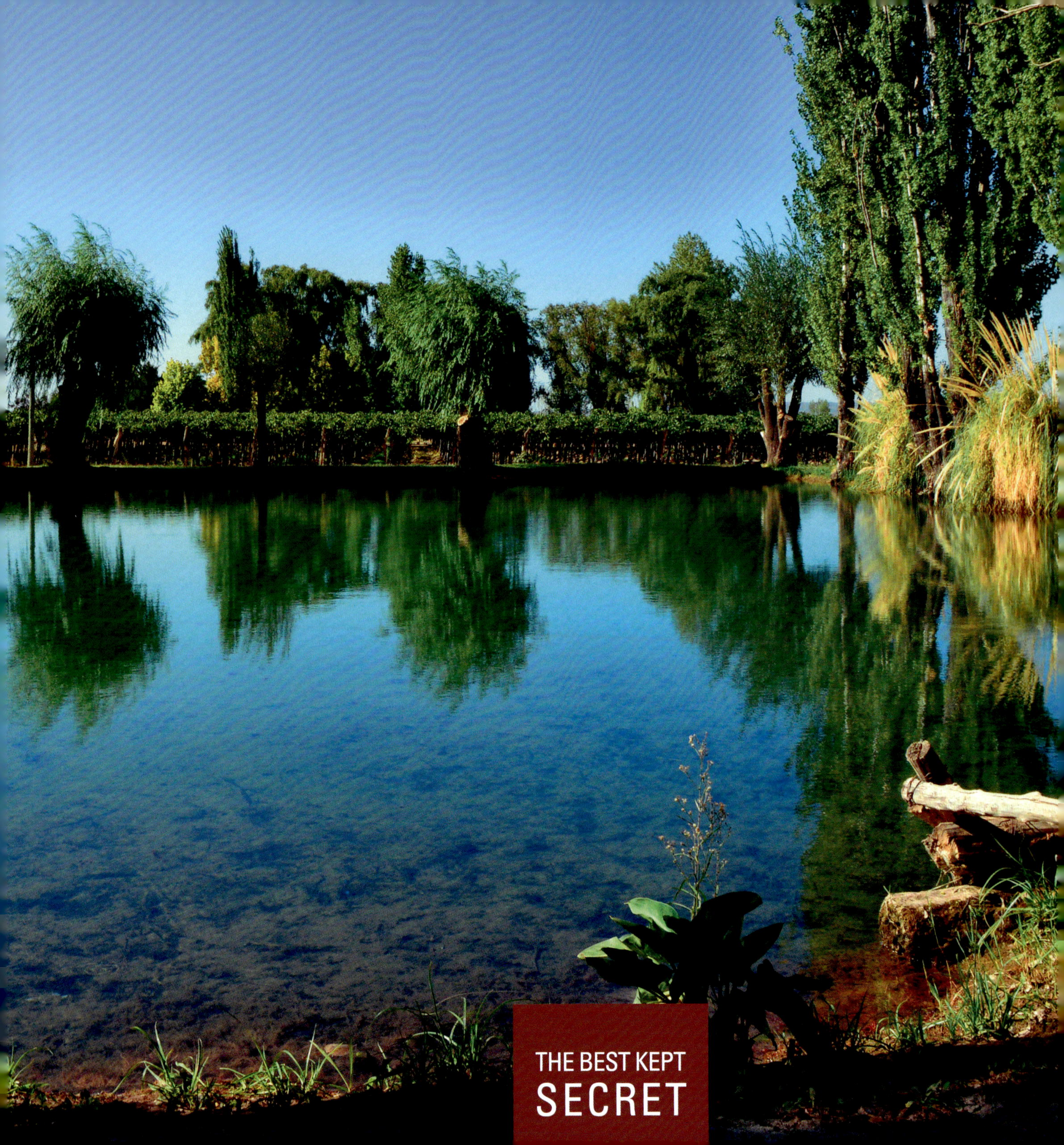
THE BEST KEPT
SECRET

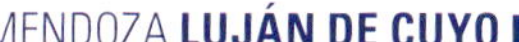

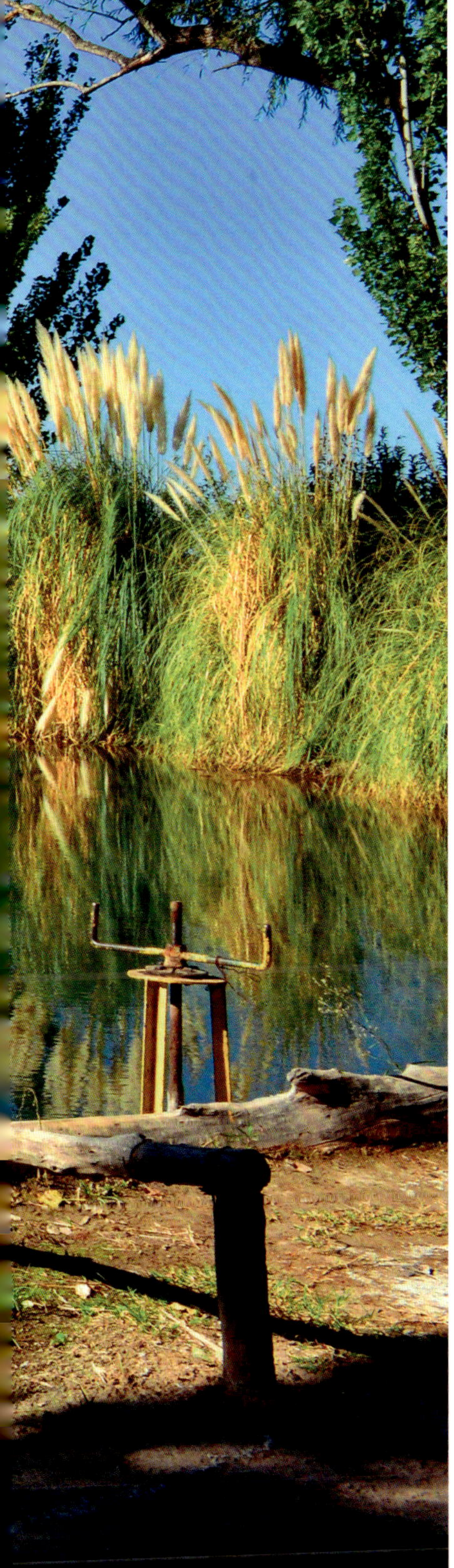

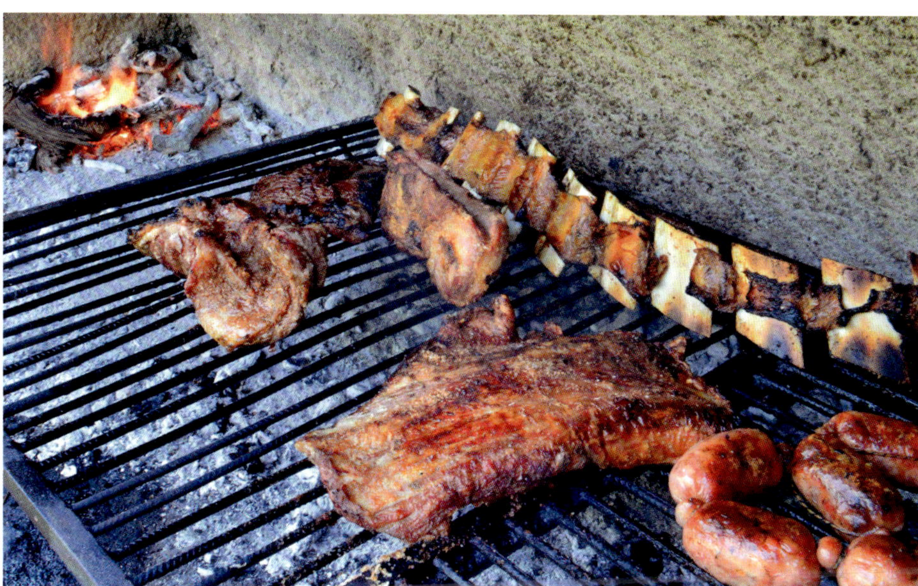

UNIQUE BBQ PICNIC IN A PARK VINEYARD EXPERIENCE

Siete Fincas does not have a winery to visit. They use multiple wineries conveniently located near the vineyards where they source their fruit. This provides short distances from vineyard harvest to winery crush. Afterwards, the wines are brought to their central facility for aging.

Siete Fincas has a large 75-acre Finca (vineyard property) in Luján de Cuyo that has been in the family for three generations. This property is beautiful, has a grass park setting with grand Alamos trees and a freshwater lake from the Andes used as a reservoir for irrigating the vines (photo left page). All with the magnificent backdrop of the Andes Mountains.

As a special experience unique to most anything else you will find in Mendoza, or the world for that matter... Siete Fincas will host you for an afternoon in their Finca. You can walk the vineyards, see real live vineyard activities as they happen and have stimulating conversations with the experts who care for the vines and create the wines. And, have a BBQ picnic, a classic Argentine Asado, prepared on their outdoor Parilla and paired with their outstanding wines.

Now... this is the way to do a wine tasting! Siete Fincas has 14 different wines and developing several more interesting wines as I write. This is a magical way to spend an afternoon discovering the wines you want to buy and take home.

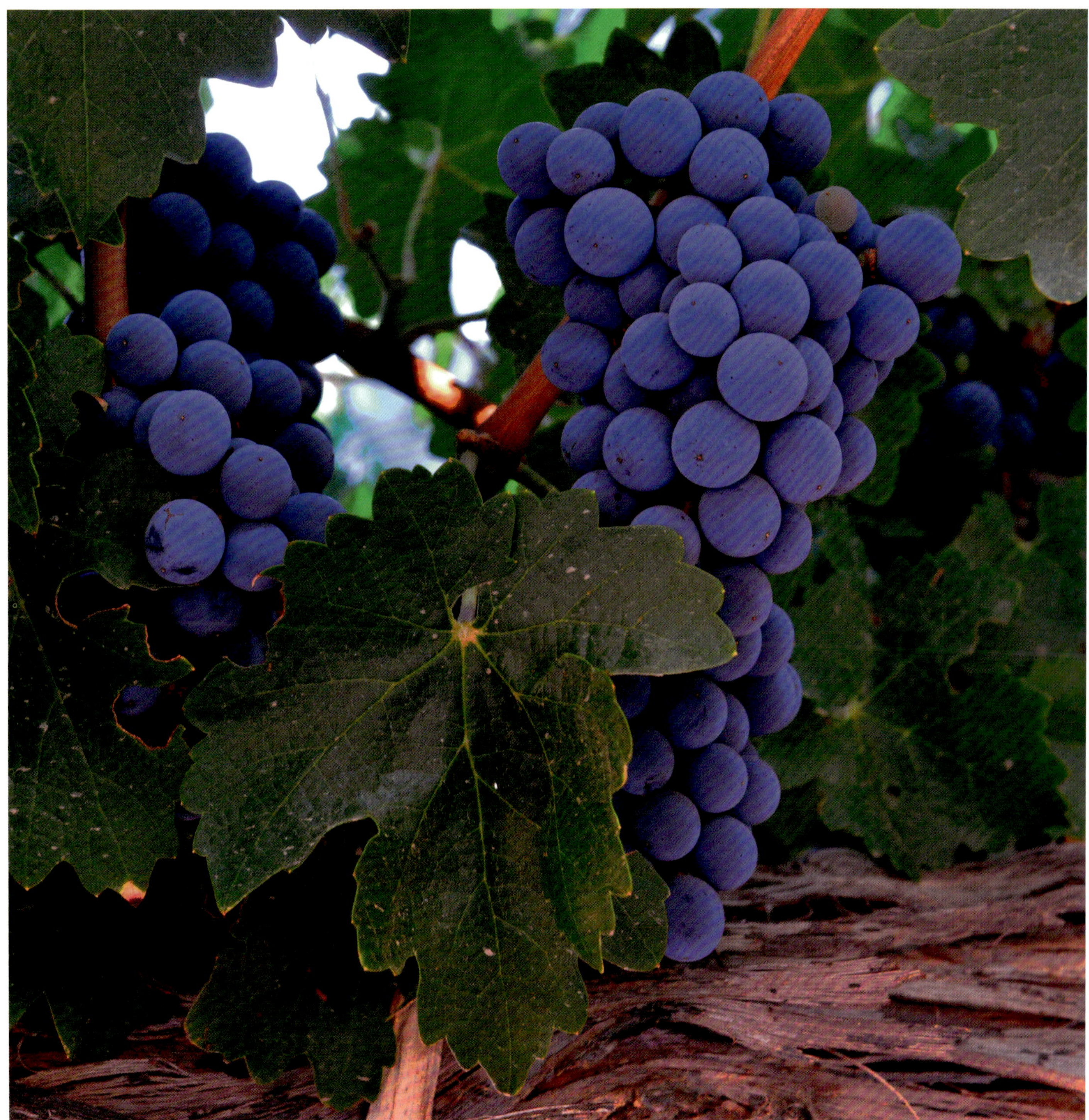

NO SECRET HERE

It is no secret, Edgardo Stallocca (photo right), founder of Siete Fincas in 2000, had a vision... to create wines people want, with good quality at a good price. And this he has done. Edgardo has a lineup of quite the variety of most wines we come to enjoy. A few surprises for me though...

The Siete Fincas Cabernet Sauvignon got my attention. I did not expect to taste great Cabernet in Argentina. I am from California, the land of great Cabernet. I knew they grew Cabernet Sauvignon in Mendoza, however, I did not expect this fantastic quality. I like his Cabernet over his Malbec. And the real secret as I see it, the *Secreto*, his wine which means "secret," is his Cabernet Sauvignon blended with his very best Malbec, Cabernet Franc and a touch of Petit Verdot.

And the grand secret, *Gran Secreto*, is 100% very selective Malbec from his estate vineyards in Luján de Cuyo, which his grandfather planted in 1904 (photo left page). This is an ultra-elegant big wine, with intense colors and rich flavors.

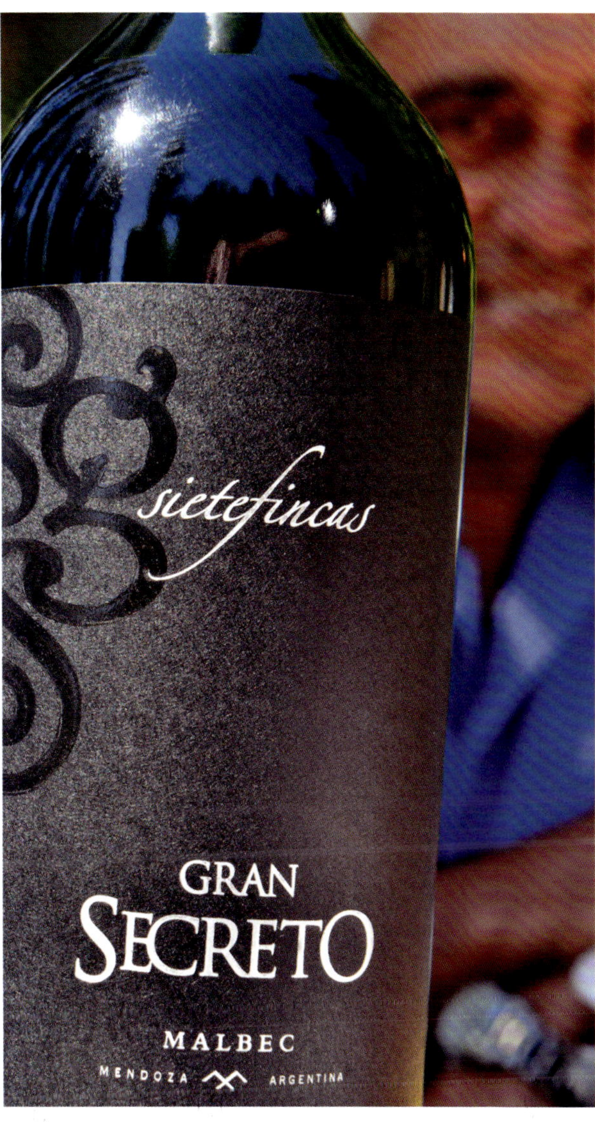

The next surprise is the *Dulce Natural*. A sparkling Torrontés. Torrontés is a unique grape to Argentina, grown in the far northwest of the country on some of the highest vineyard elevations in the world. This contrasting floral sweet and dry wine makes for an unbelievable sparkling wine delight. I need say nothing more than sharing these tasting notes prepared by a good friend of mine...

"The Siete Fincas Dulce Natural is a sweet sparkling Torrontés which greets you with rich aromas of baked apple and key lime pie, with aromatic notes of meyer lemon and gardenia. Medium bodied and friendly, balanced notes of mandarin orange, candied lychee, and dried apricots meet light notes of minerality on a pleasingly sweet finish."

Now isn't that mouth-watering? I can tell you it is everything that is special and more.

Siete Fincas is building a Visitor Center in Chacras de Coria, Luján de Cuyo which opens in 2015. This will be a place to come to discover more of these secrets and mingle with winemakers and chefs.

MENDOZA **LUJÁN DE CUYO**

Winery (Bodega)

SIETE FINCAS

3405 Viamonte
(Chacras de Coria, Luján de Cuyo)

011 (+54 261) 496.1070
comercial@SieteFincas.com

SieteFincas.com

English & Español & Italiano
100,000 bottles produced annually

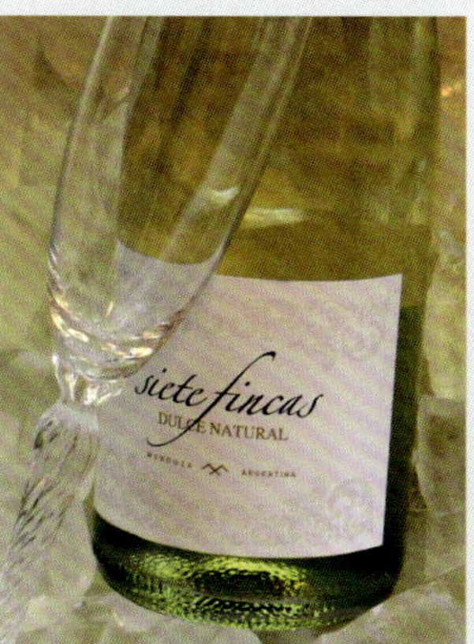

Michael's Favorite Pick
Dulce Natural (Sparkling Torrontés)

Total Collection of Wines

Reserve Reds
Secreto and Gran Secreto

Reds
Malbec, Cabernet Sauvignon, Merlot, Syrah, and Malbec Rosé

Whites
Chardonnay, Sauvignon Blanc, Sauvignon Blanc Dolce, and Torrontés

Sparklings
Extra Brut, Brut Rosé, and Dulce Natural (Sparkling Torrontés)

To get Siete Fincas wines in the USA
Direct from the Importer: CopaFina.com
at CopaFina.com/**sietefincas**buywine.html

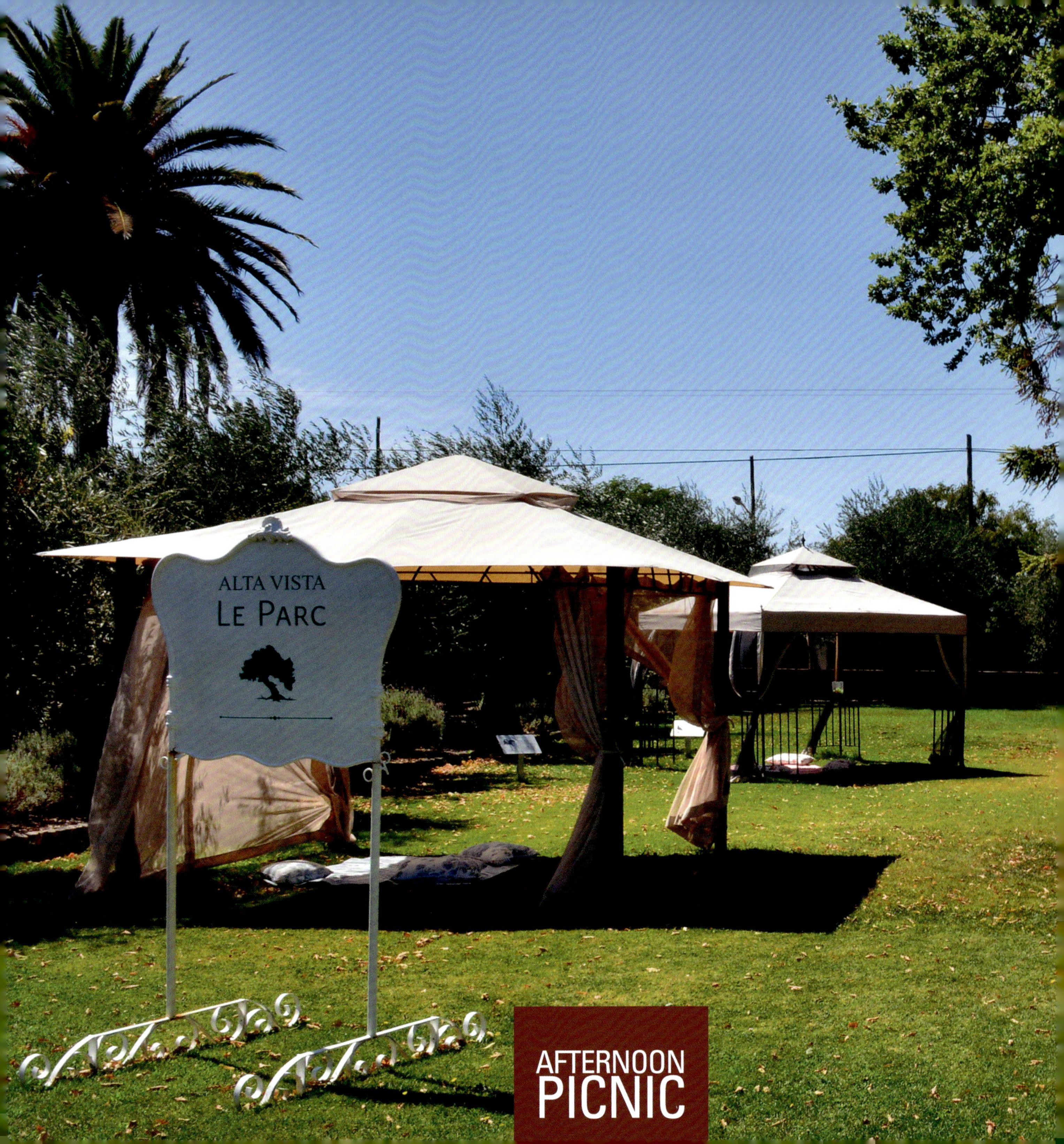

AFTERNOON PICNIC

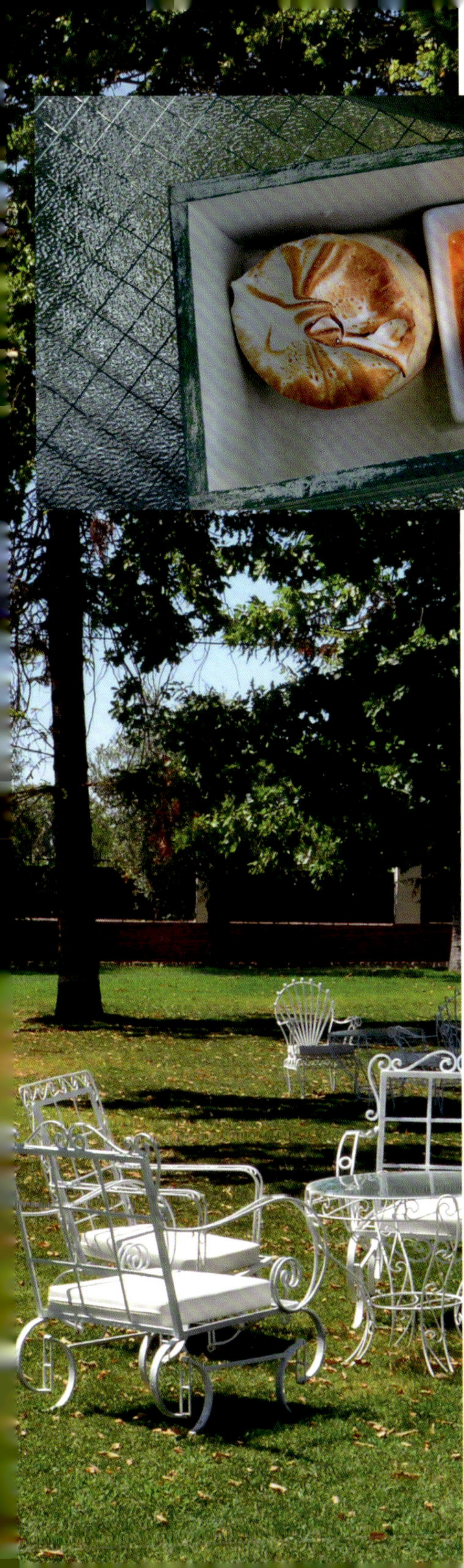

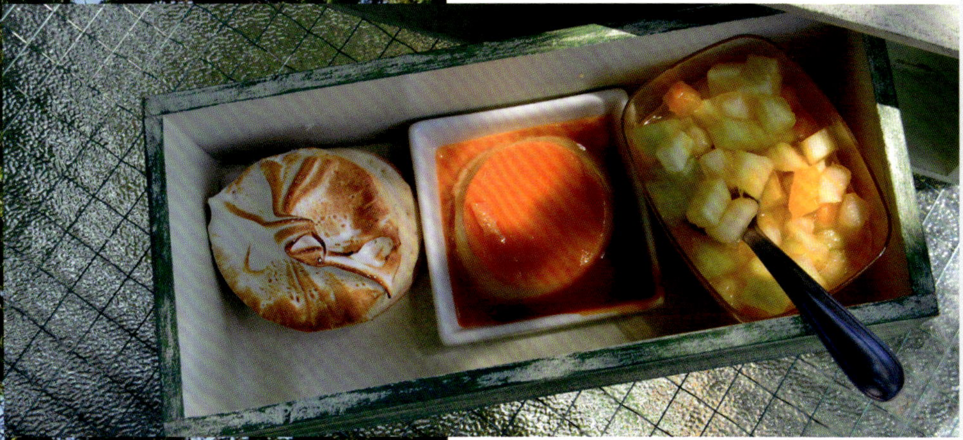

MENDOZA **LUJÁN DE CUYO**
Winery (Bodega)
ALTA VISTA

3972 Alzaga
(Chacras de Coria, Luján de Cuyo)

011 (+54 261) 496.4684
info@AltaVistaWines.com

AltaVistaWines.com

English & Español
1.6 million bottles produced annually

AN AFTERNOON IN THE PARK

Le Parc... a magical afternoon, a gourmet picnic, a pairing with delicious wines, a romantic escape, a nap, a kiss, a peaceful delight under the shade of a canopy, and an enjoyment of a beautiful afternoon in Le Parc. Only at Alta Vista winery, on their 62-acre square historic estate.

In the heart of Chacras de Coria, full of hundred-year-old olive trees, the Alta Visa winery is a circa 1899 adobe brick buildings of sun-dried earth and straw, fully restored with cutting-edge technology for today's modern vineyard management and winemaking techniques.

A French-owned winery, the d'Aulan family produces wines all over the world, from France (their origin) to unique wine regions like Hungary and Argentina, where they created Alta Vista in 1998, in the search of the greatest qualities of two emblematic varieties: Malbec and Torrontés. The result is the perfect combination of French savoir faire and Argentinian passion.

I did not do a winery tour or wine tasting, although I heard it is a fantastic experience. For me, it was a beautiful afternoon in Le Parc where I enjoyed two glasses of their Atemporal Blend. I chose the Atemporal (meaning timeless) because it is a blend of Bordeaux grapes produced by a French winemaking family. I wanted to see the French influence on an Argentine-style Bordeaux (the leading grape is Malbec), versus Cabernet Sauvignon as they would in France. Atemporal, rich and elegant.

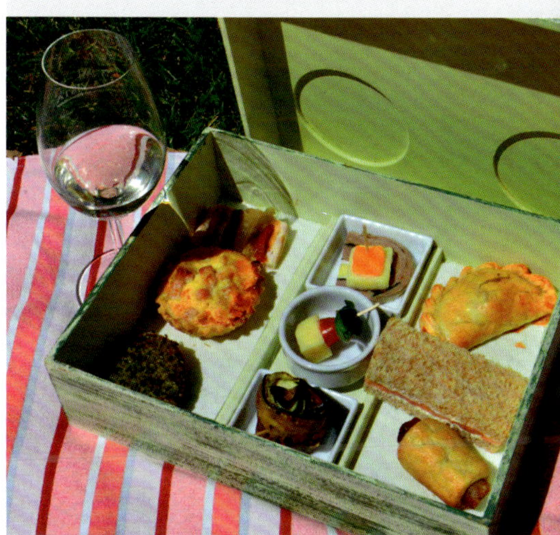

Michael's Favorite Pick
Atemporal Blend (an Argentine Bordeaux)

Total Collection of Wines
Alto
Single Vineyard
Terroir Selection
Atemporal Blend
Atemporal Sparkling
Premium
Premium Extra Brut
Alta Vista Rosé
Classic

To get Alta Vista wines in the USA
Contact the Importer: KobrandWineAndSpirits.com
914.253.7700

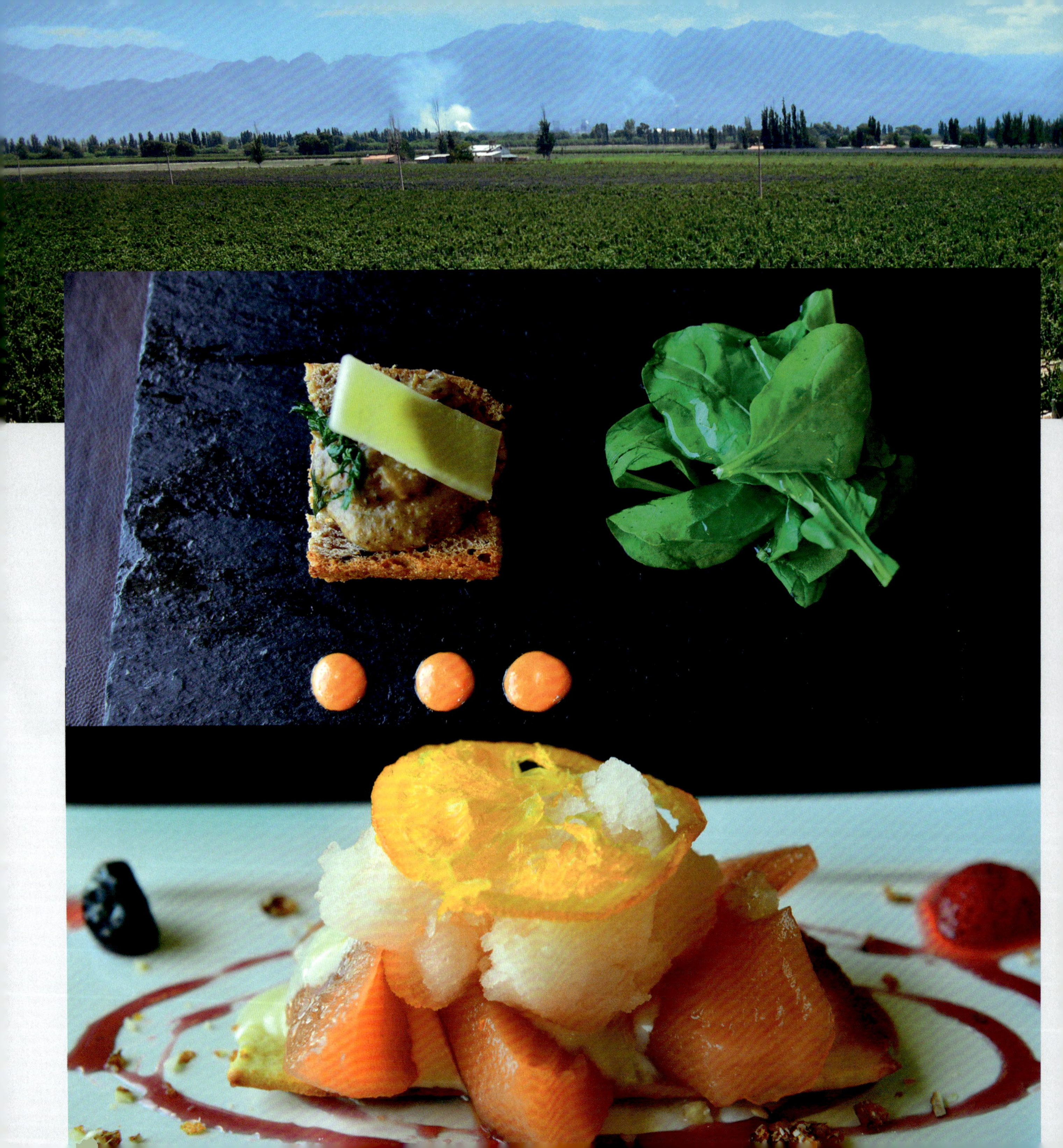

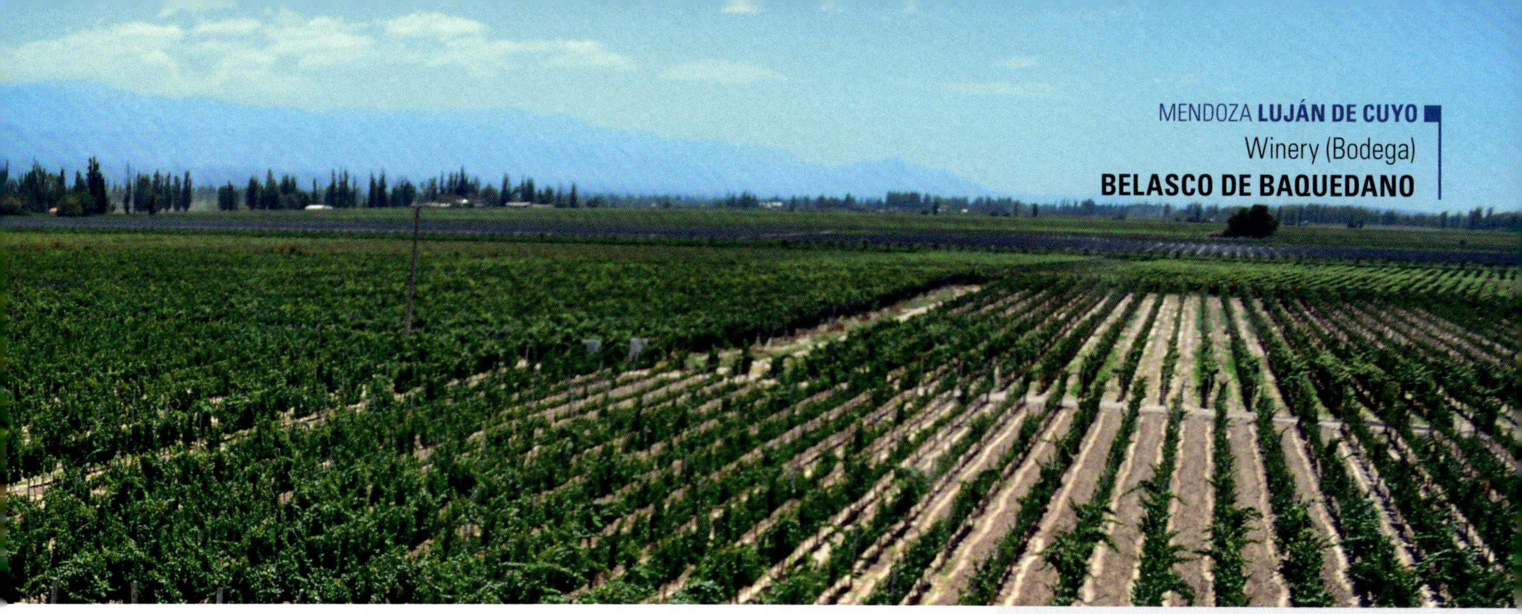

MENDOZA **LUJÁN DE CUYO**
Winery (Bodega)
BELASCO DE BAQUEDANO

A GOURMET VIEW

Attracted by the food, little did I know that this was a 100% Malbec winery, and all vineyards on this 222 estate acres are 100-plus-year-old vines flourishing around this restaurant, all part of the amazing view, all part of the dining wine pairing experience.

I particularly enjoyed Swinto, a meticulous selection of their best clusters from 100-year-old vines to capture the greatest expression of the Malbec grape. It is their biggest wine, and much fruitier to go with it. This wine is their highest scoring wine as well, 93 points by Robert Parker. A real treat, and paired with the grilled sirloin.

The meal... well, just look at the photographs. Gourmet expression in every sense. Five-Course pre-designed spectacular menu, each course paired with one of their Malbec wines.

ABOVE, view from the restaurant.

LEFT PAGE TOP, black olive focaccia with roasted eggplant pâté, Andean grilled goat cheese, selection of green leaves and roasted red pepper emulsion.

LEFT PAGE BOTTOM, apple shortbread marinated in Rosa de Argentina Malbec and quince jelly, with sweet orange English cream, grapefruit granita and seasonal red fruit syrup.

BELOW, grilled sirloin of beef on roasted onion cream, carrots glazed with black pepper syrup, buttered potatoes with fresh chives and plum coulis marinated in Swinto.

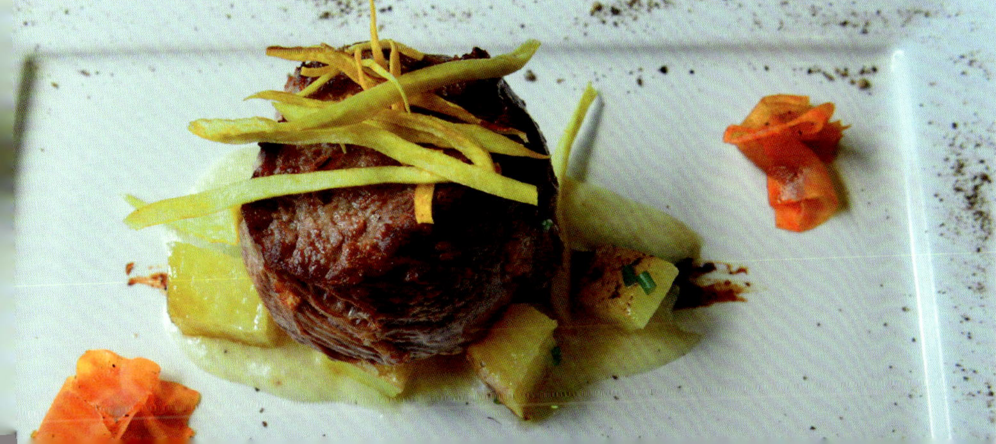

8260 Cobos
(Luján de Cuyo)

011 (+54 261) 524.7864
turismo@GrupoLaNavarra.com

BelascoMalbec.com

English & Español
100,000 bottles produced annually

Michael's Favorite Pick
Swinto (Old Vine Malbec)

Total Collection of Malbec Wines
Swinto (Old Vine Malbec)
AR Guentota (Malbec)
LLAMA (Malbec Roble)
Rosa (Malbec Rosé)
Antracita (Late Harvest Malbec)

To get Belacso wines in the USA
Contact the Importer: CabernetCorp.com

MENDOZA **CHACRAS DE CORIA**

A Quaint Village in the Luján de Cuyo Wine Region

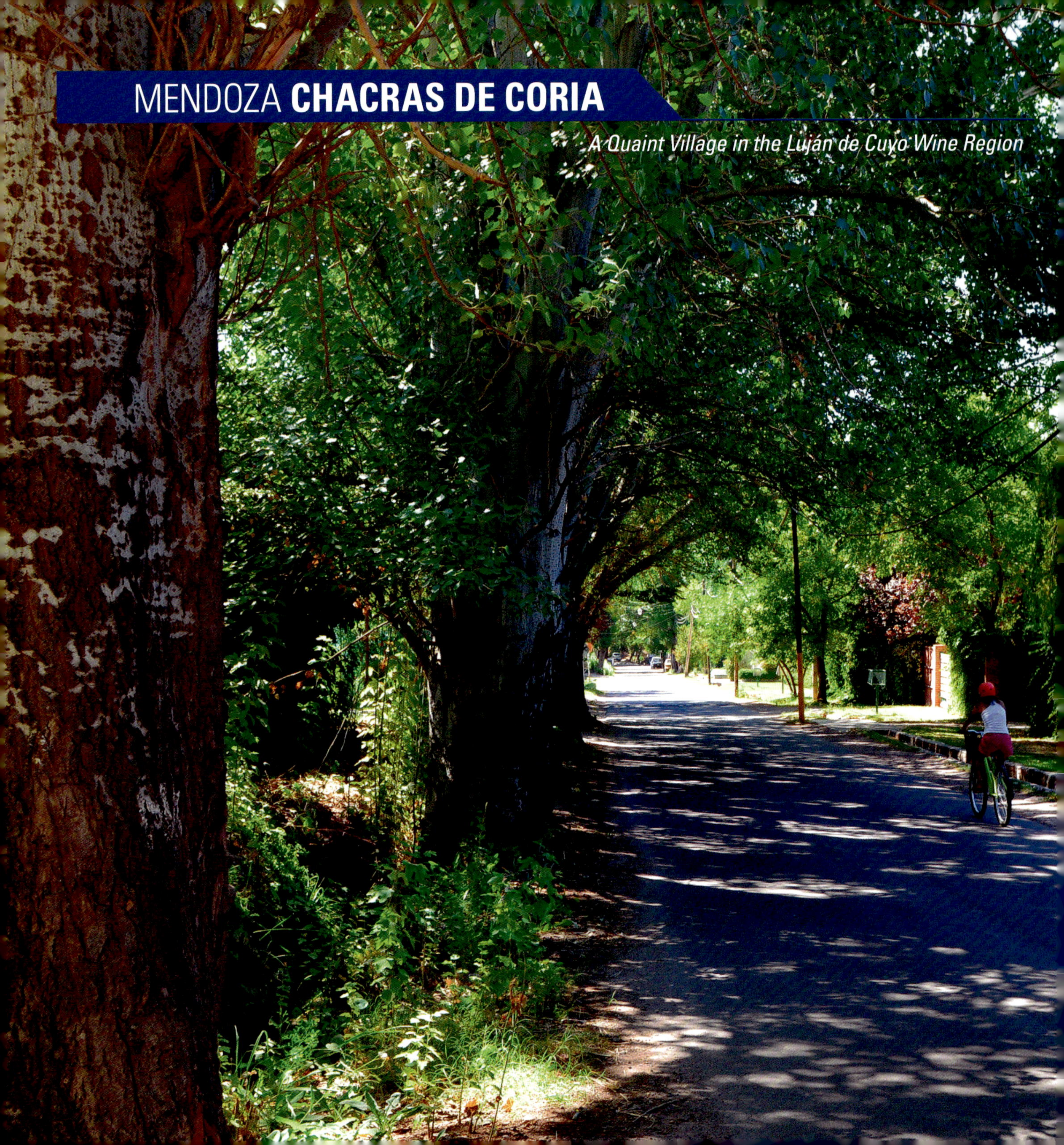

THE LITTLE VILLAGE OF CHACRAS DE CORIA

Chacras de Coria is a cute little town just a few miles outside the city of Mendoza, in Luján de Cuyo. It is an upscale neighborhood where you will find many beautiful homes of residences and visitors nestled along quiet tree-lined streets, as seen in the photo to the left. Architectural styles range from large traditional houses to ultra-modern homes and exquisite mansions.

In the center of Chacras de Coria is the main square called *Plaza Gerónimo Espejo*, which still holds its traditional function of "town centre" for all daily needs... the butcher, the baker, and various convenience stores, Internet café, bistros, and several exceptionally great restaurants, for example Nadia O.F., awarded the No. 1 restaurant in all of Argentina (see pages 64-65).

Plaza Gerónimo Espejo is a must-go spot to visit on Sundays. You will find artists, artisans and antique dealers selling their crafts. There is much entertainment to enjoy: performers playing music, doing puppet shows, providing pony rides and a variety of other entertainment enjoyed by visitors and residents alike.

The name Chacras de Coria originated in 1615 when Don Bohorquez de Coria was granted this track of land, and settled the place, creating small chacras (farms). Soon they were known by the locals as the "Chacras de don Coria," a name that stuck.

Facing Chacras square is the architectural beauty of Nuestra Señora del Perpetuo Socorro Church, built in 1935, standing out amidst the landscape. Sunday mass is heard both inside and outside the church as numerous people congregate on the beautiful grounds in front of the church. Check out the magnificent stone altar carved in the Mendocino-Colonial style. Visitors are invited.

You can still find a few old chacras, boutique vineyards and small family wineries left in Chacras de Coria; one of which is now a boutique hotel *Finca Adalgisa*, just nine blocks from the square, nestled amongst their own vineyards and fruit trees (pages 58-63). Plus, Chacras de Coria is in Luján de Cuyo with the many spectacular wineries I have been sharing with you. Also, you will find museums like the Museum of Emiliano Guiñazu and Casa de Fader.

Renting a bike is a fantastic experience to pedal the neighborhoods, visit the wineries, and enjoy the shops and restaurants. Baccus Biking is two blocks from Chacras square and they provide maps to easily navigate the area, with a wine route. Take off on your own or they can provide an experienced guide. And when finished, they will come get your bike(s) wherever you are... no need to bring it back.

Baccus Vineyards Biking
5727 Loria

011 (+54 261) 496.1975
info@BaccusBiking.com.ar

BaccusBiking.com.ar
English & Español

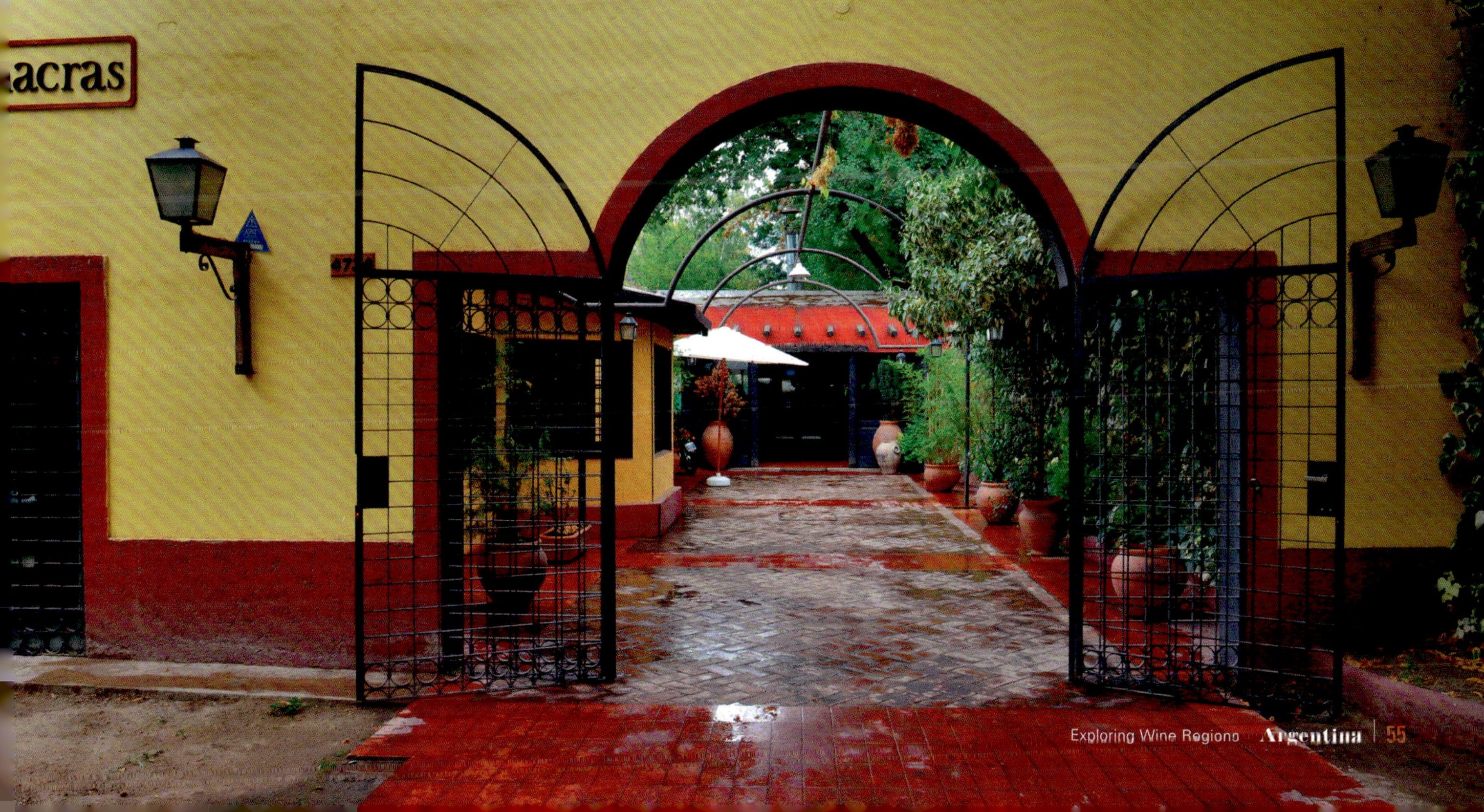

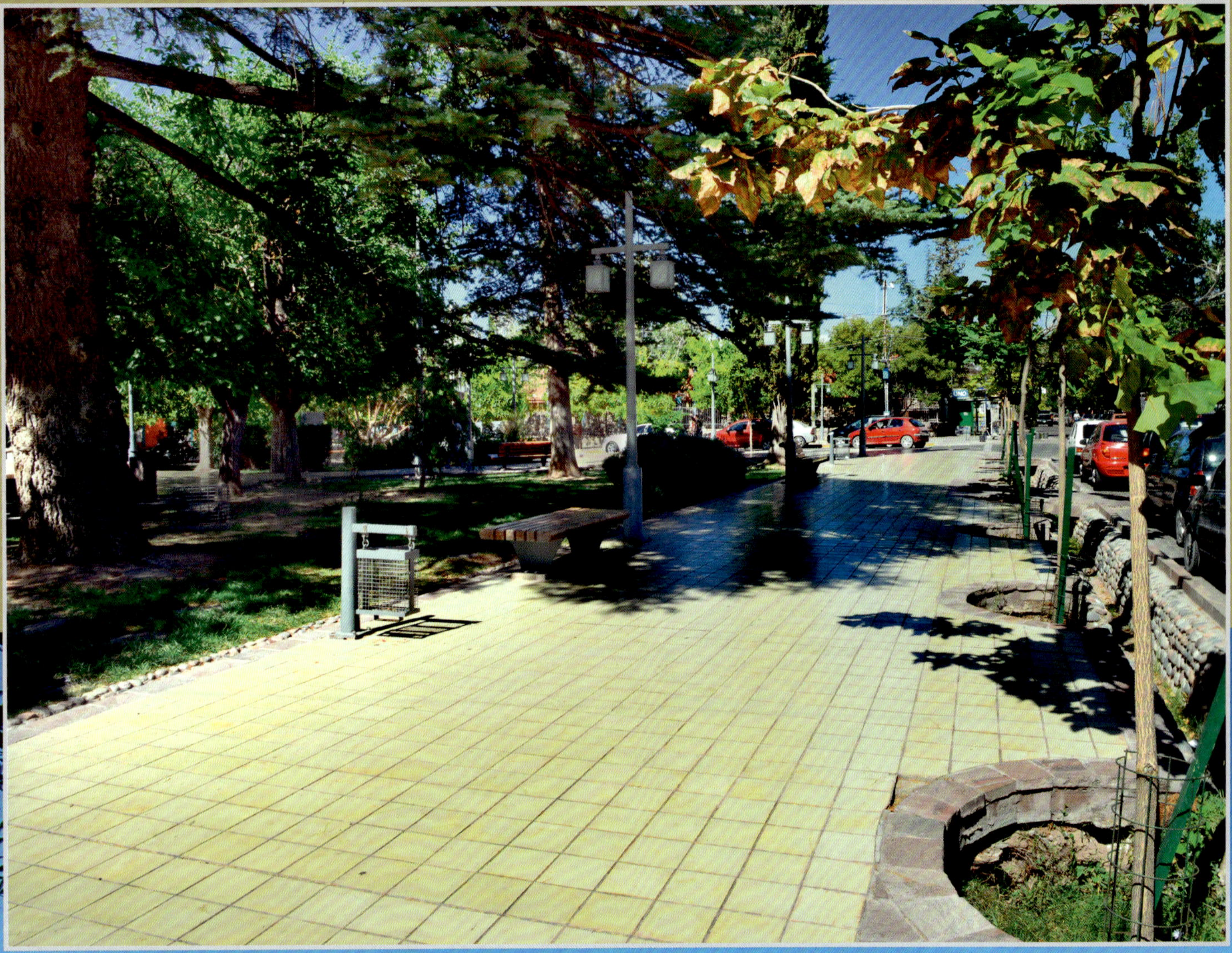

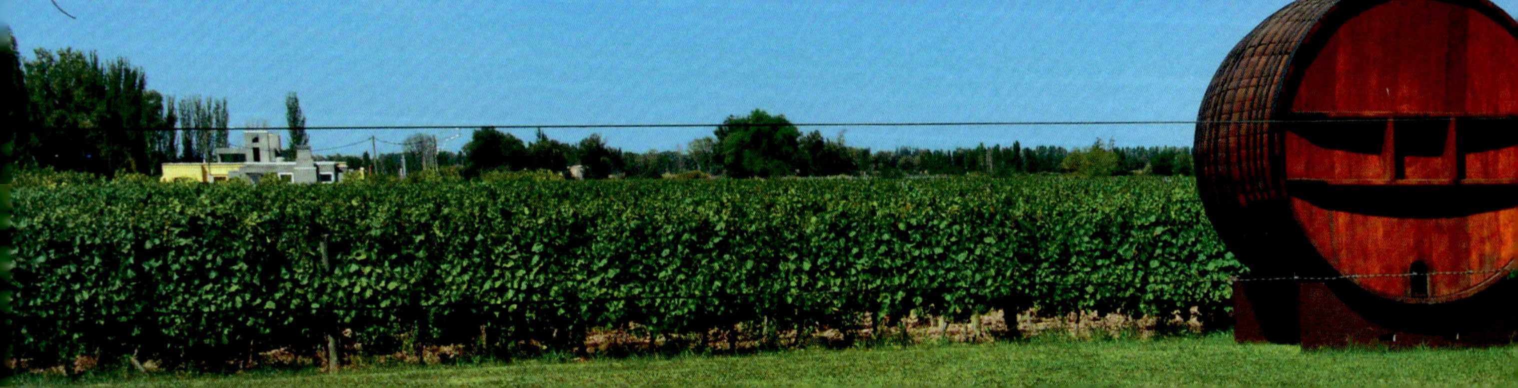

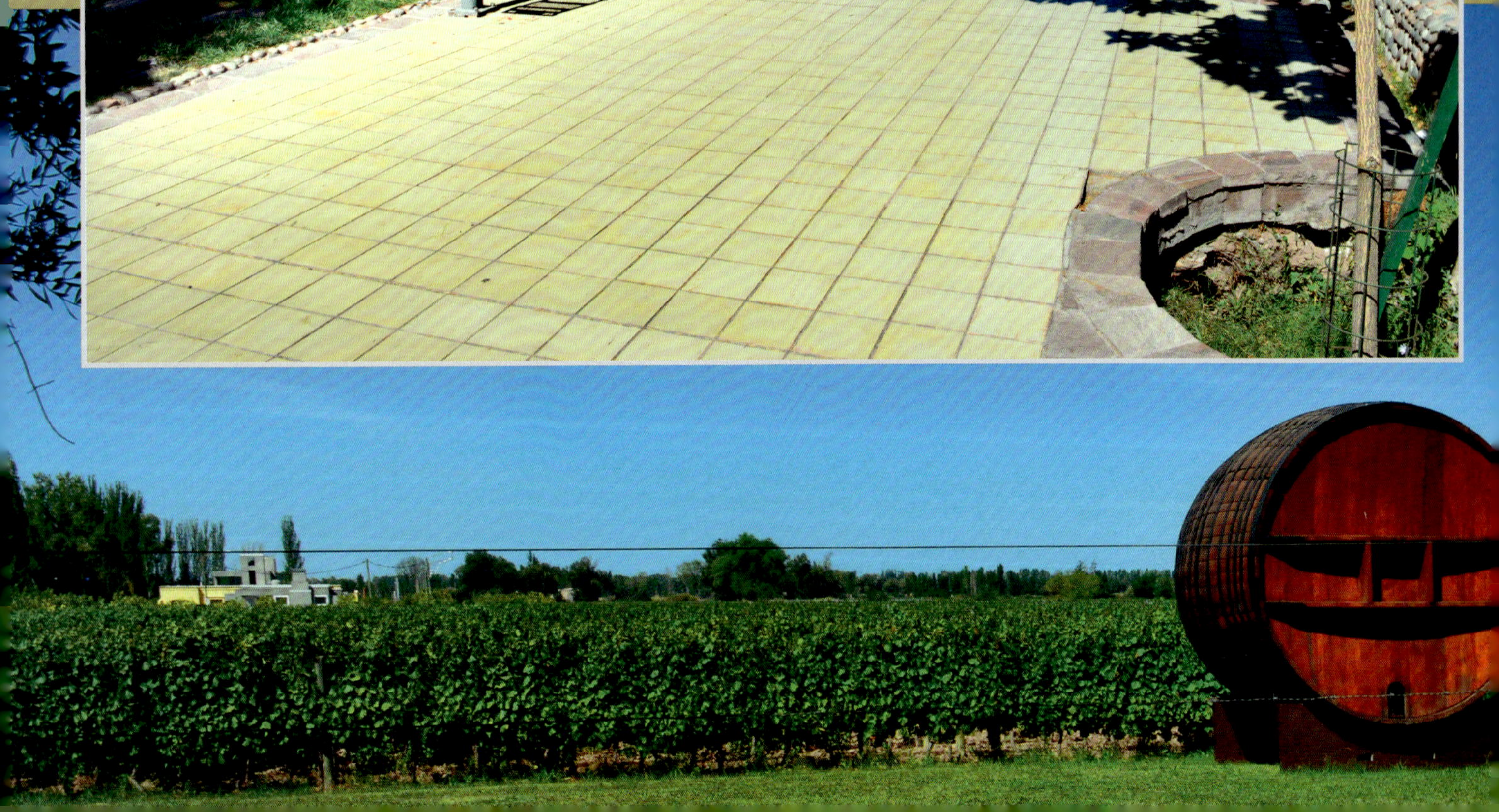

THE WINERIES OF CHACRAS

There are a small number of wineries still located in the town of Chacras de Coria. These are interesting wineries worth visiting, and all reachable by bike. I was able to find 10 wineries. Below are the ones mentioned in greater detail.

Alta Vista **Page 50**
(10 blocks from the square)

Bodega Viamonte **Page 32**
(17 blocks from the square)

Carmelo Patti **Page 40**
(11 blocks from the square)

Famiglia Mosso **Page 44**
(by private appointment)

Finca Adalgisa **Page 62**
(nine blocks from the square)

Siete Fincas **Page 46**
(visitors center 12 blocks from the square)

RESTAURANTS OF CHACRAS

Chacras de Coria has become a destination for fine dining. The choices are unique. Here are a few I discovered.

Alta Vista **Page 52**
- Picnic in Le Parc
(10 blocks from the square)

Finca Adalgisa **Page 60**
- Spectacular Cooking Class/Experience
(nine blocks from the square)

Nadia O.F. **Page 64**
- No. 1 Restaurant in Argentina
(three blocks from the square)

Siete Fincas **Page 46**
- BBQ/Wine Tasting in the Vineyard
(pre-arranged event in Luján de Cuyo)

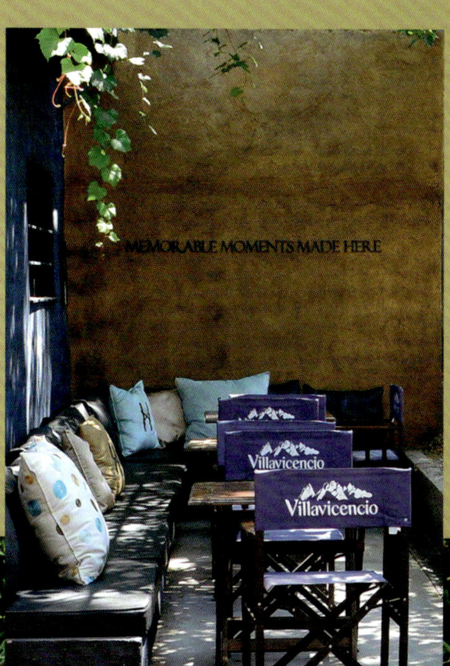

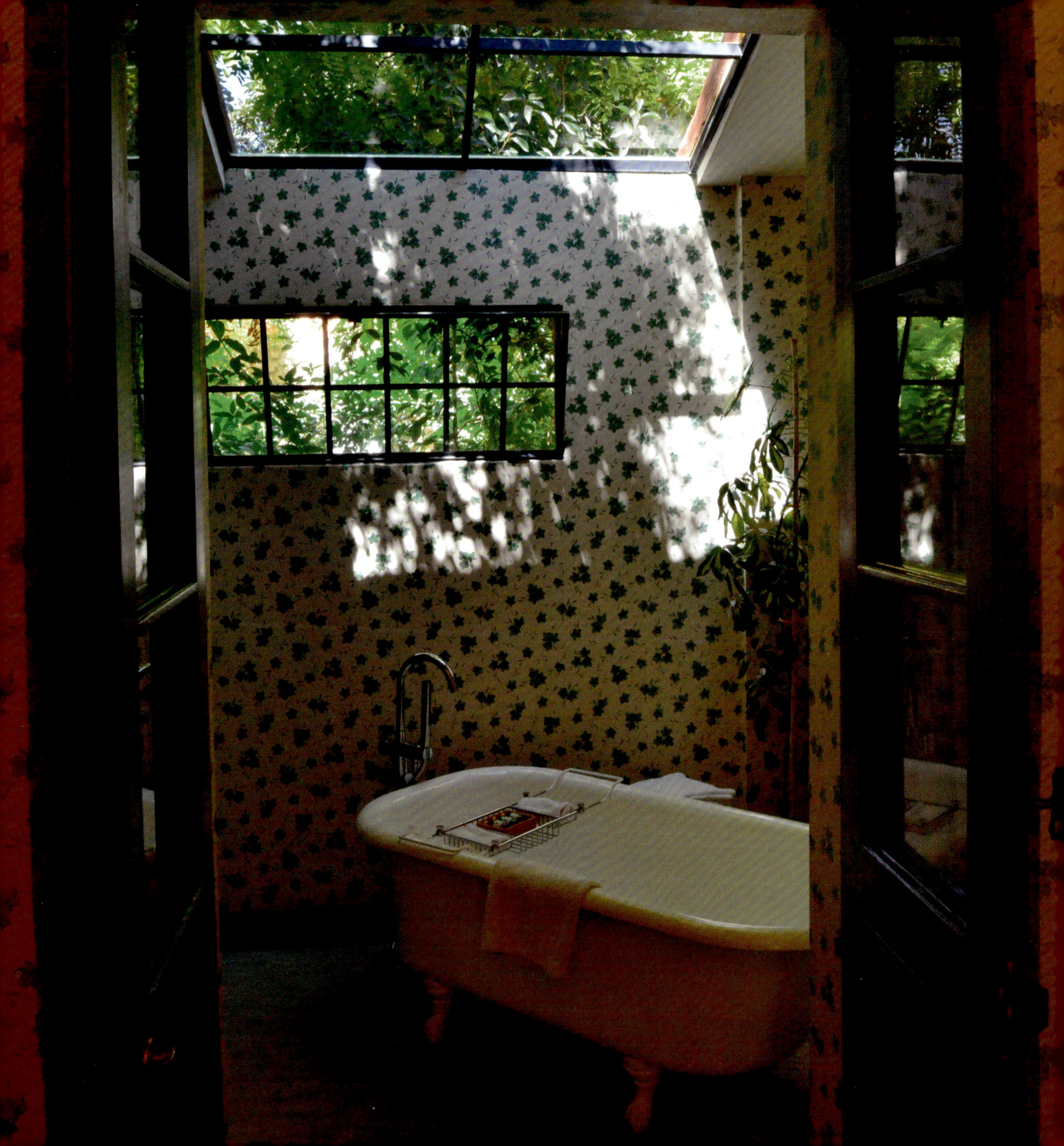

A BOUTIQUE HOTEL IN THE HEART OF CHACRAS DE CORIA, IN THE LUJÁN DE CUYO WINE REGION

This delightful property is the perfect place to hang your hat while exploring the Luján de Cuyo wine region...

The historic buildings have been beautifully restored and provide the kind of luxury accommodations and services of a five-star international hotel company, yet this small family-run business welcomes you to their home in a laid-back, informal and relaxed environment where they have lived for three generations – and still live on the property today!

Nestled in the middle of five acres of Malbec vineyards, from the beginning of your stay you are already amidst the vines and grapes, with a working winery on the property that produces a spectacular Malbec. You must enjoy the wine experience on the back patio of the winery in the evenings.

Enjoy their pool, vineyard-side! Eleven uniquely designed rooms in historic buildings. Enjoy a full breakfast in the morning among ponds, fountains and lush landscape. In the evening, you are very close to the notable restaurants of Chacras de Coria. One evening, you must experience the cooking class. It is like none other!

If you love to read history, democracy and Argentina's quest to build a society after gaining independence, the Finca Adalgisa Library will fascinate you. It is an in-depth collection written by Argentina's finest intellectuals who were trying to imagine a modern state. Finca Adalgisa's founder was a politician who served as a Senator, Member of Parliament and State Attorney. In this role, he was very interested in how to build a democracy and has assembled this amazing collection of literary works.

MENDOZA **LUJÁN DE CUYO**

Hotel • Vineyard • Winery

FINCA ADALGISA

2222 Pueyrredon
(Chacras de Coria, Luján de Cuyo)

011 (+54 261) 486.0713
info@FincaAdalgisa.com.ar

FincaAdalgisa.com.ar

English & Español
11 beautifully restored historic rooms

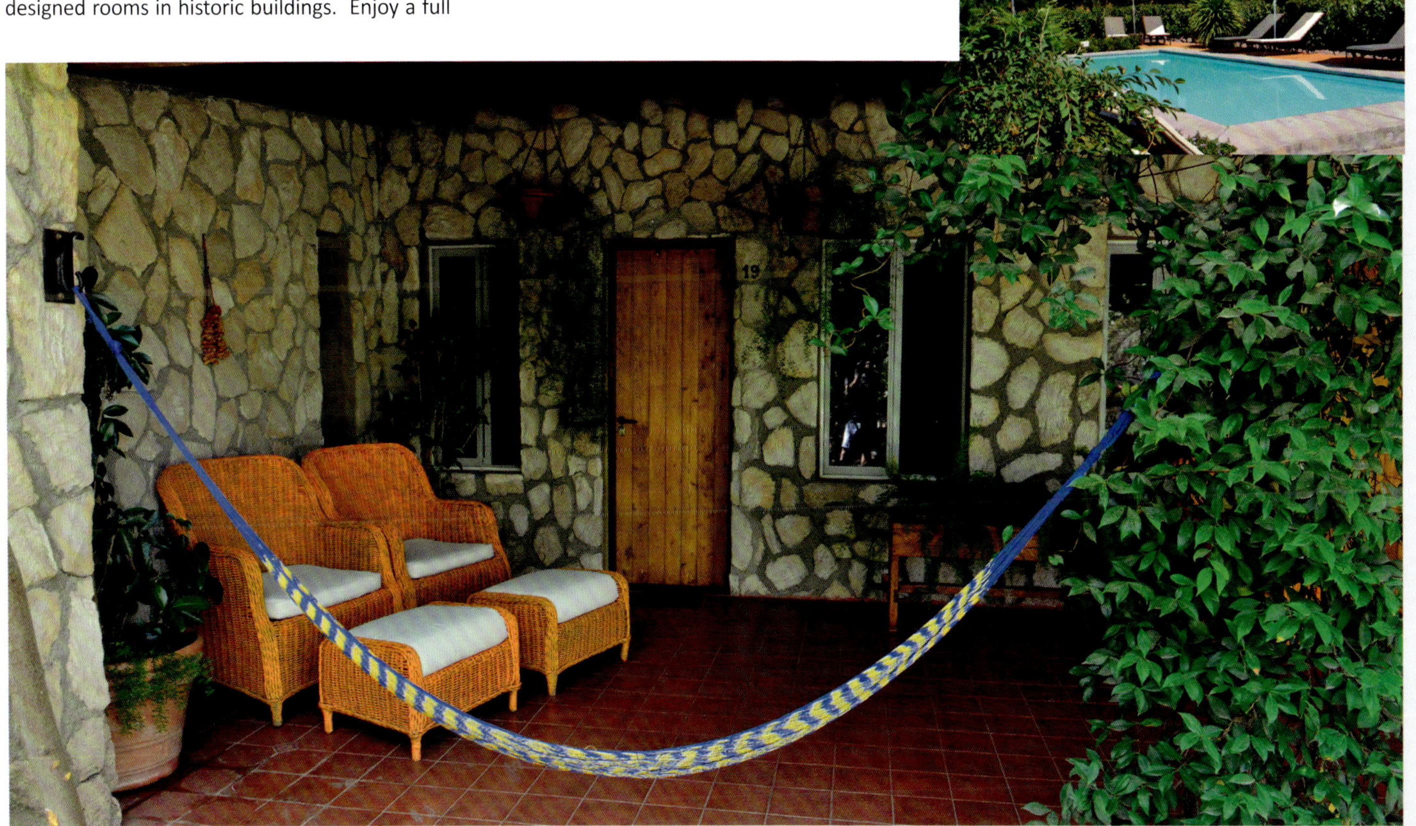

LEFT, folding empanadas and baking in clay oven.
BELOW, mixing sugar into fruit and the finale of Baked Fruite.
LOWER RIGHT, Ojo De Bife, topped with special Chimichurri Sauce.

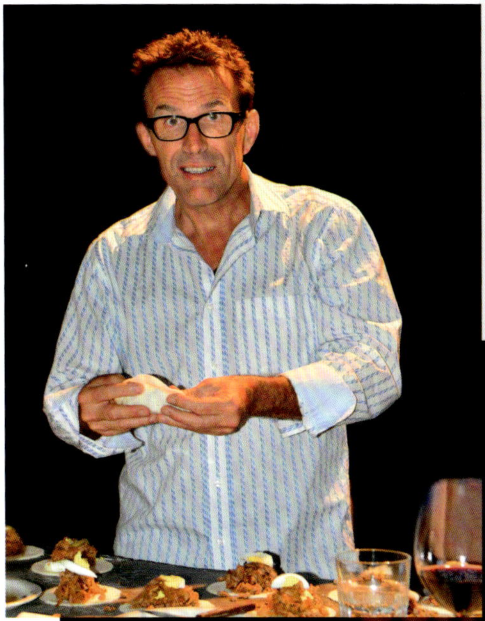

COOKING CLASS
EXTRAORDINAIRE

WITH
CHRISTINA BRINO

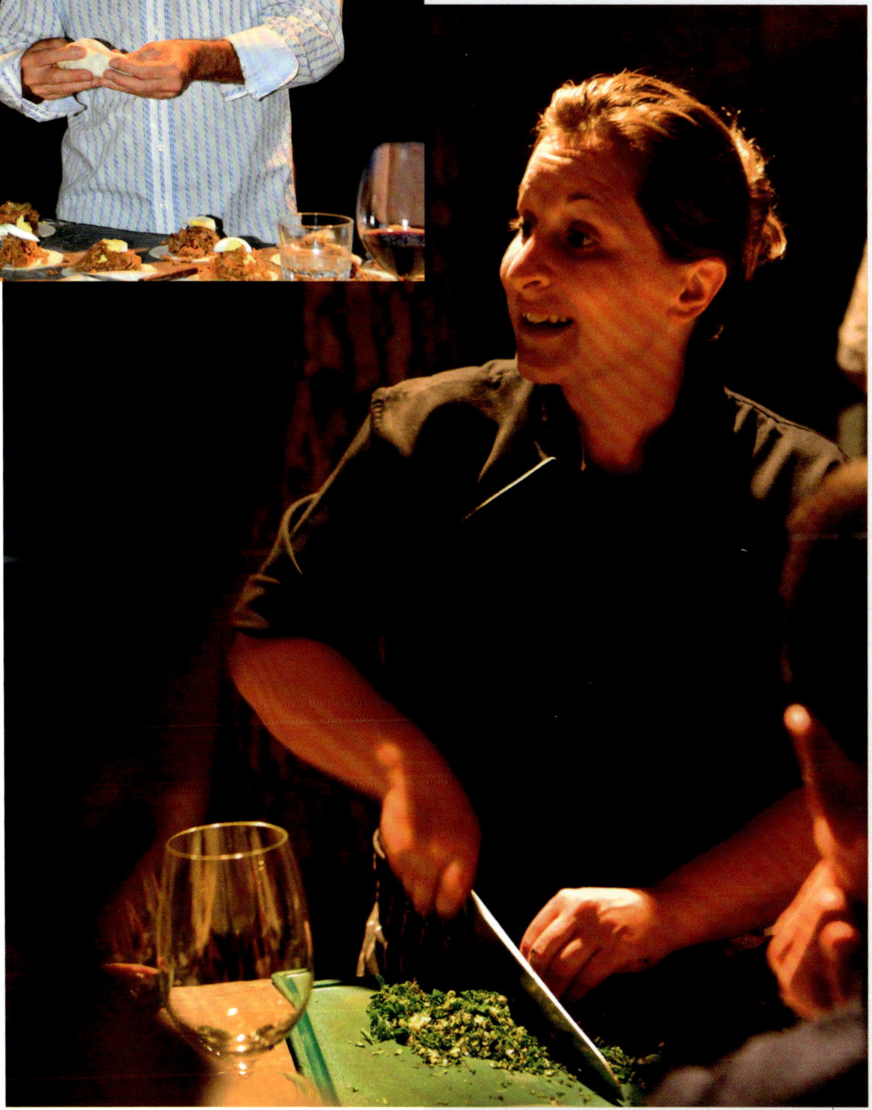

This is a cooking class and a feast! Come with a big appetite and a desire to learn traditional foods of Mendoza. Christina is uniquely talented, has extraordinary recipes, is very entertaining as she teaches you, hands on, the art of making...

- **Empanadas Mendocinas**
  This classic appetizer is stuffed with meat, herbs and vegetables, and then baked in the clay oven.

- **Ojo De Bife**
  Huge and thick cut of ribeye steak, potatoes and grilled tomatoes, topped with Chimichurri Sauce cooked over an open fire parrilla.

- **Baked Fruite with Ice Cream Crisp**
  Dessert of caramelized fruit from the clay oven, topped off with herbs from the Finca.

Christina will teach you to make everything from scratch. Even the empanada dough. The Chimichurri Sauce, with Christina's wonderful recipe using fresh herbs and Arauca olive oil (all grown on the Finca), will give you a whole new appreciation for delicious mouth-watering steaks!

This all takes place outdoors, underneath a grand old walnut tree, tasting Adalgisa wines and enjoying the results of the magnificent meal.

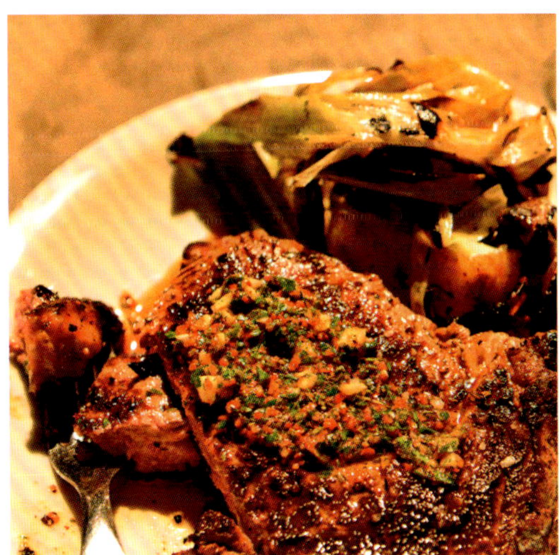

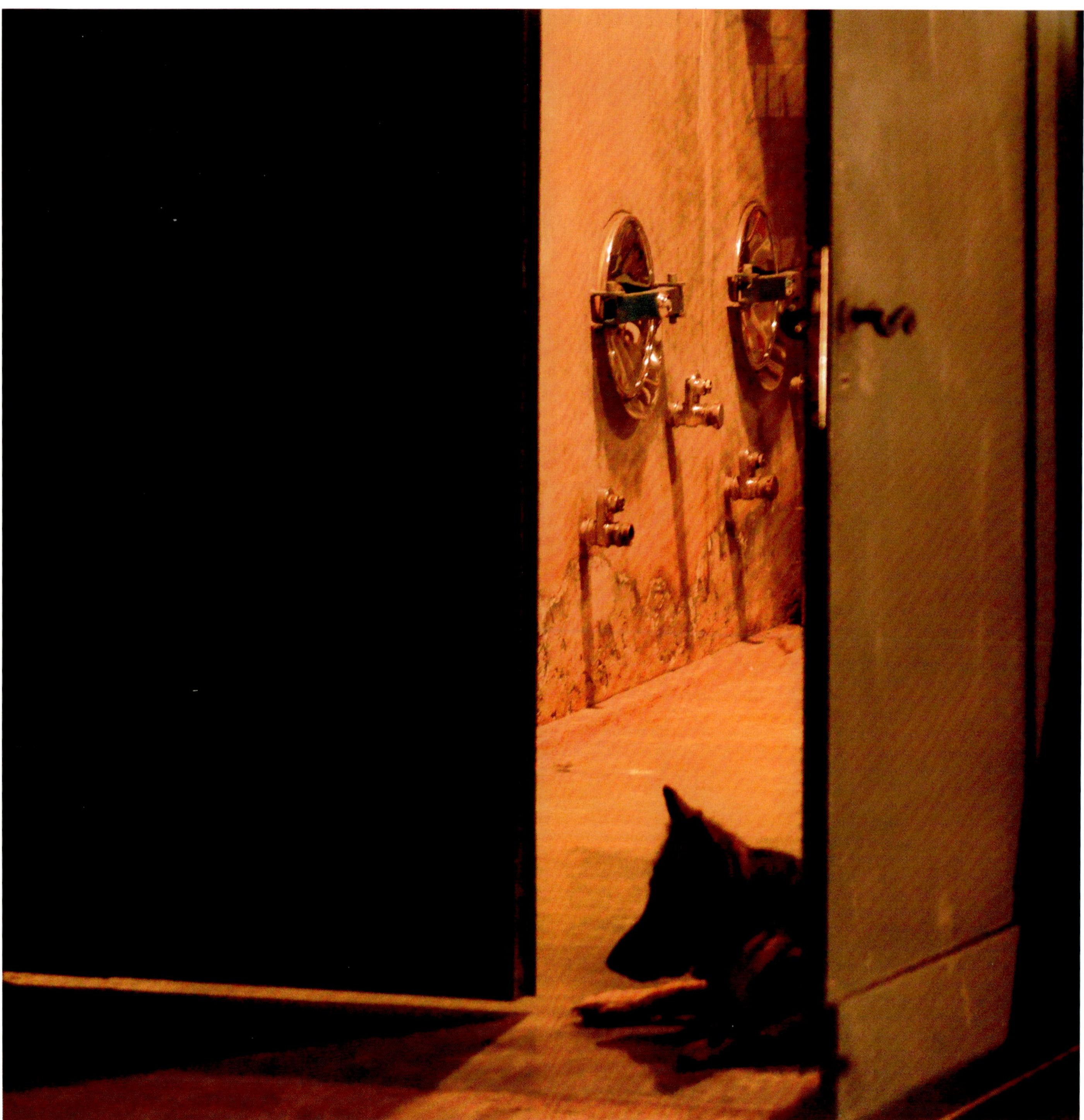

MALBEC VINEYARDS, SURROUNDING THE HOTEL

The Finca Adalgisa property is five acres of prime real estate in downtown Chacras de Coria planted with fruit trees and Malbec vines, nearly 100 years old (c. 1916). The family has been farming here for three generations.

If you are going to explore the Luján de Cuyo wine region, what better way to do this than to stay in the middle of a vineyard with a working winery.

And if you are not staying there, you must stop by one evening and taste their wines, sit out on the patio and enjoy the view of the vineyards and savor some fresh empanadas. Also, watch the horse plowing and flood irrigation through the canal system. This single-vineyard estate Malbec is rich and delicate with deep black fruit and long finish. Expect fantastic wines, as their winemaker is the famous Carmello Patti (pages 40-43). They also source fruit from Salta for a very nice Torrontés.

Only 5,000 bottles of this spectacular Malbec are produced annually. The wine is only available at the winery and through the hotel. Special arrangements though have been made to have wine shipped to the USA, and purchase two cases, gets the shipping included for free. Email them at info@AdalgisaWines.com for the details.

Finca Adalgisa is deeply involved with their local Chacras community. Every harvest, for example, they invite third-graders from the local school to visit them to learn about the winemaking process. The Adalgisa agronomist teaches them the different parts of the plant and how the vines produce grapes. The kids get to pick grapes and they are shown the tricks of the harvest. They get involved with the de-stemming of the clusters and selecting the best grapes to be made into wine. In the end, all the kids are treated to a delicious lunch of grilled sausages.

Yes, you do see a handsome German Shepherd lying in the doorway of the winery. Vinko is considered the boss around this finca. He adopted himself to the property by jumping over the wall of the estate and charming himself into the heart of Gabriela Furlotti, the current owner of the hotel and winery. Not to mention there were two very cute female German Shepherds living here too. Today he is a gentleman farmer and looks after the property and precious wine.

What a beautiful way to start your day in wine country... a full breakfast on the patio of the hotel... and a stroll through the vineyards of Finca Adalgisa... now ready to take on your wine discovery day...

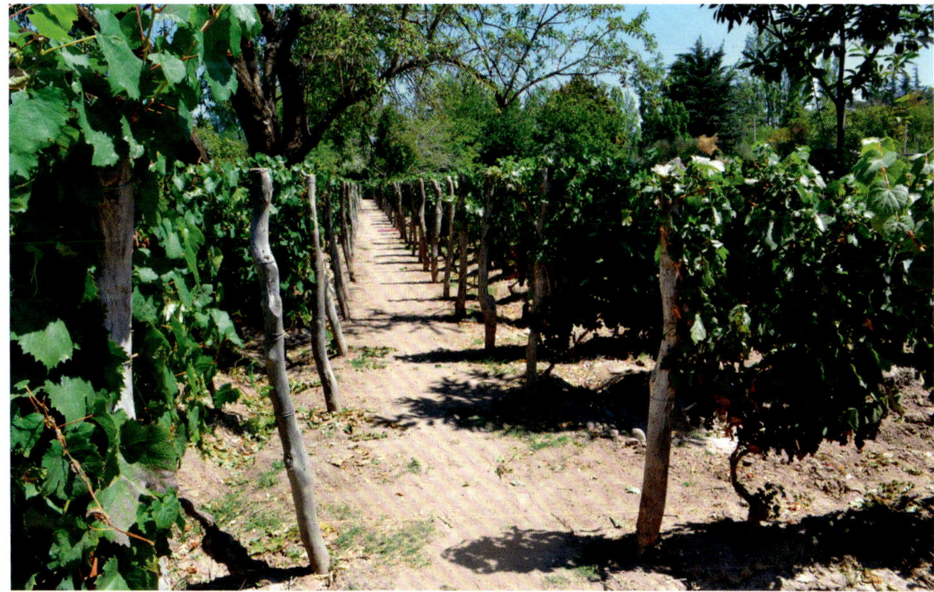

MENDOZA **LUJÁN DE CUYO**

Hotel • Vineyard • Winery

FINCA ADALGISA

2222 Pueyrredon
(Chacras de Coria, Luján de Cuyo)

011 (+54 261) 486.0713
info@AdalgisaWines.com

AdalgisaWines.com

English & Español
5,000 bottles produced annually

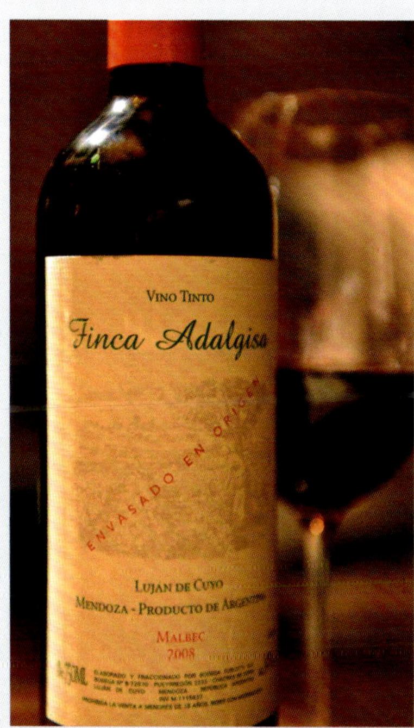

Michael's Favorite Pick
Estate Malbec

Total Collection of Wines
Estate Malbec
Salta Torrontés

To get Finca Adalgisa wines in the USA
Contact the winery direct:
info@AdalgisaWines.com

SELECTED NUMBER ONE RESTAURANT IN ALL OF ARGENTINA

On my last day in Argentina, at the last hour, I get an invitation to visit the famous restaurant: *Nadia O.F.* And not just a special invitation, an extraordinary invitation to arrive before the restaurant opens and to cook with Nadia herself in the backyard behind her restaurant (see photos to the right). The restaurant is in an old home in Chacras de Coria, only a few blocks from the central square.

This is not Buenos Aires where you might expect the country's No. 1 restaurant. *Nadia O.F.* is located inside of an old restored house in Chacras de Coria, in the Luján de Cuyo wine region, just outside the city of Mendoza. Owner and Chef, Nadia Harón, showed me some of her secrets to success.

We started by breaking bread... a glass of wine and we literally made bread together. She practiced bread chemistry every day for three months to perfect her delicacy. Passion, attention to detail and perfection! This is what reflects in everything Nadia creates at her restaurant.

Born in Sebastián, Spain, Nadia began buying cook books at age eight while her friends got kids stuff. College went a different direction with a degree in chemistry, and working as a chemist for a large pharmaceutical company. It did not take long for Nadia to realize that her skills in chemistry were better suited for her love of gastronomic ingredients. Today, chemistry is well incorporated in her creative and scientific gourmet pleasures.

There is no menu in her restaurant, so to speak. Nadia decides what's for dinner. She changes her six-course meals weekly. Sometimes daily, depending on what she finds interesting or fresh at the market. It is a seasonal Spanish Argentine event. It is like joining Nadia for a home-cooked meal, although in this case an extraordinary culinary experience.

And no wine list either! Nadia is married to the president of the O.Fournier Winery, and each course is appropriately paired with one of his wines. It is truly a family affair in this home of Nadia O.F.

LOWER LEFT TO RIGHT across the bottom

Crema de Lentejas
Cream of Lentils
Lentil creme, mushroom confit and truffle oil, with sweet onion skin
Wine Pairing: Torrontés

Salmorejo con Crujiente de Berenjena
Crispy Eggplant Gazpacho
Thick tomato gazpacho with crispy eggplant slices, egg yolk and crunchy olive paste
Wine Pairing: Tempranillo/Malbec

Risotto Mar y Montaña
Sea & Mountain Risotto
Trebolgiano Cheese, Soft-Boiled Egg and Lupkfish Caviar
Wine pairing: Malbec

Torre de Masa Philo
Phyllo Tower (very thin pastry sheets)
Dulce de Leche (sweet thick creamy milk) and Caramel Nest
Wine pairing: Chardonnay

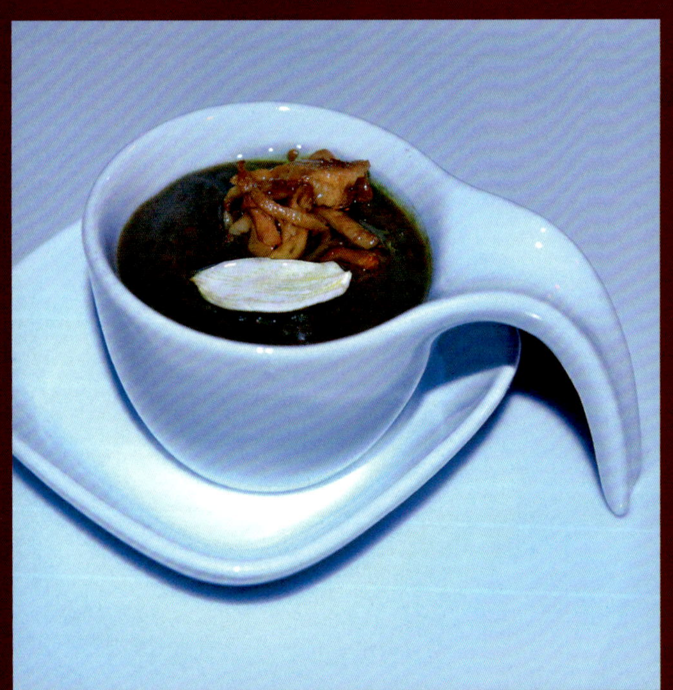

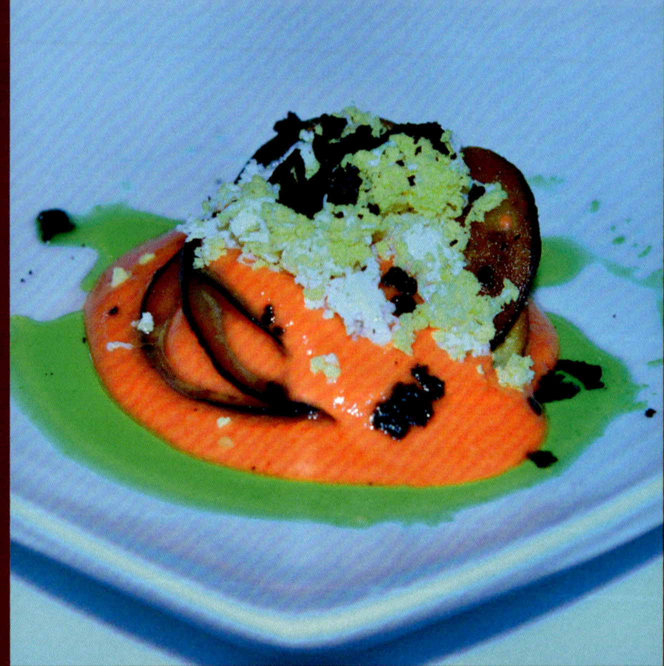

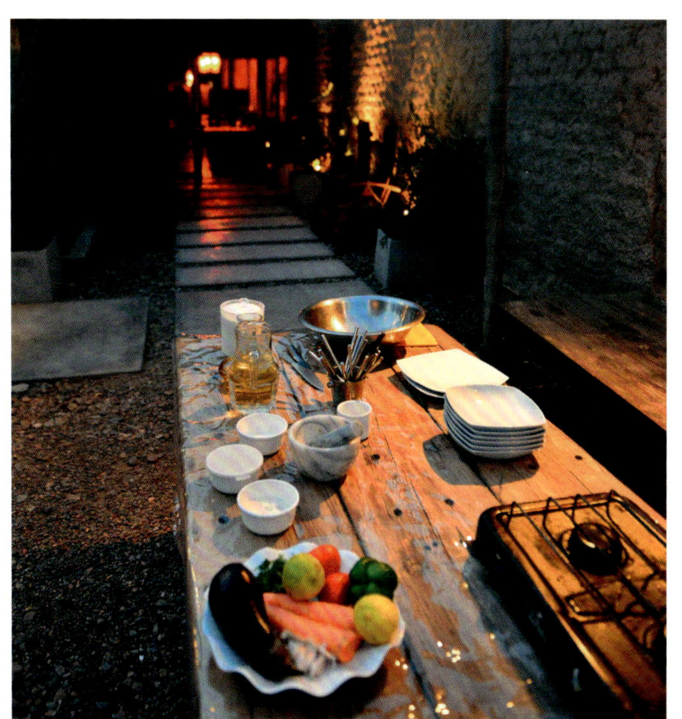

MENDOZA **LUJÁN DE CUYO**

Hotel • Vineyard • Winery

NADIA O.F.

6055 Italia
(Chacras de Coria, Luján de Cuyo)

011 (+54 261) 496 1731
reservas@NadiaOF.com

Reservations
Highly Recommended

NadiaOF.com

English & Español
Open nightly at 8:30 pm

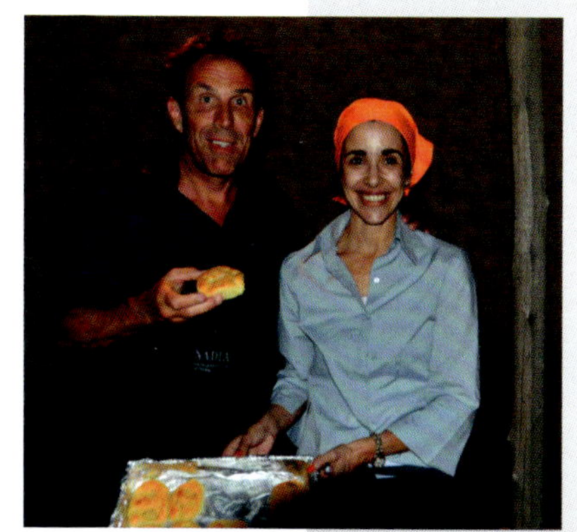

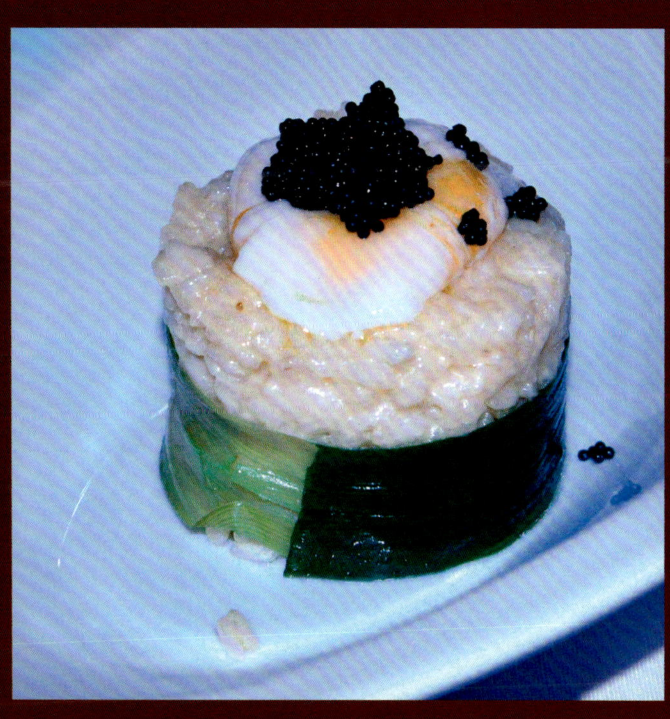

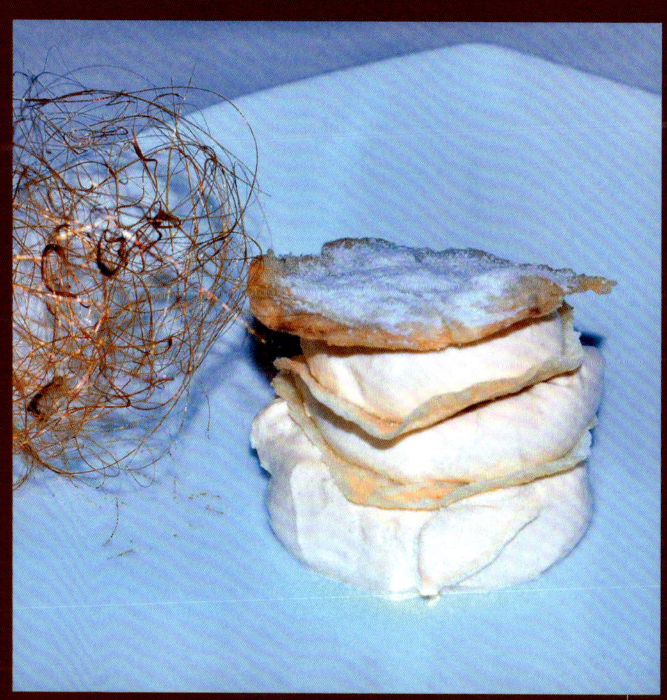

MENDOZA **VISTALBA**

A Micro Sub-Region of Luján de Cuyo Specializing in Malbec

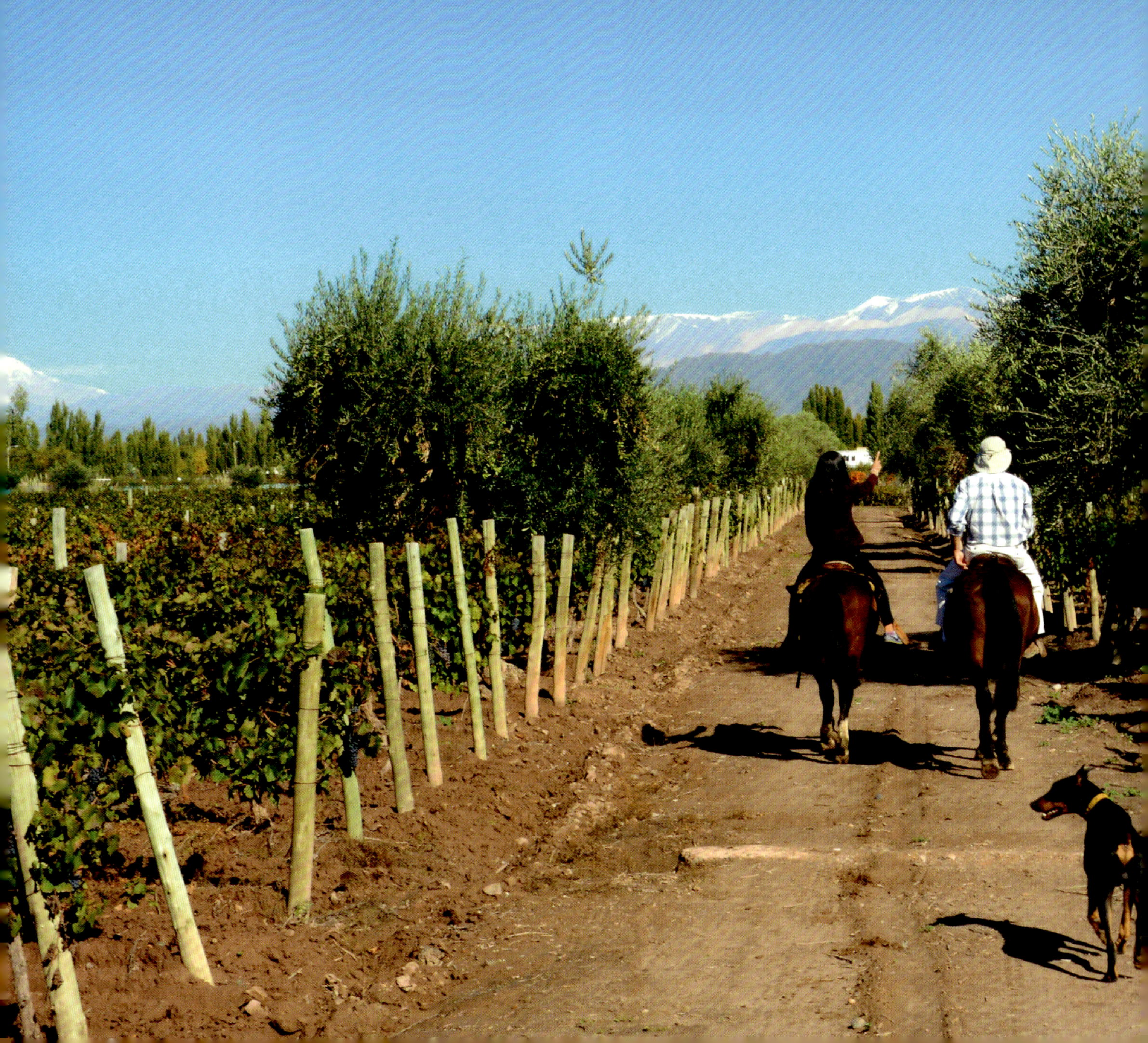

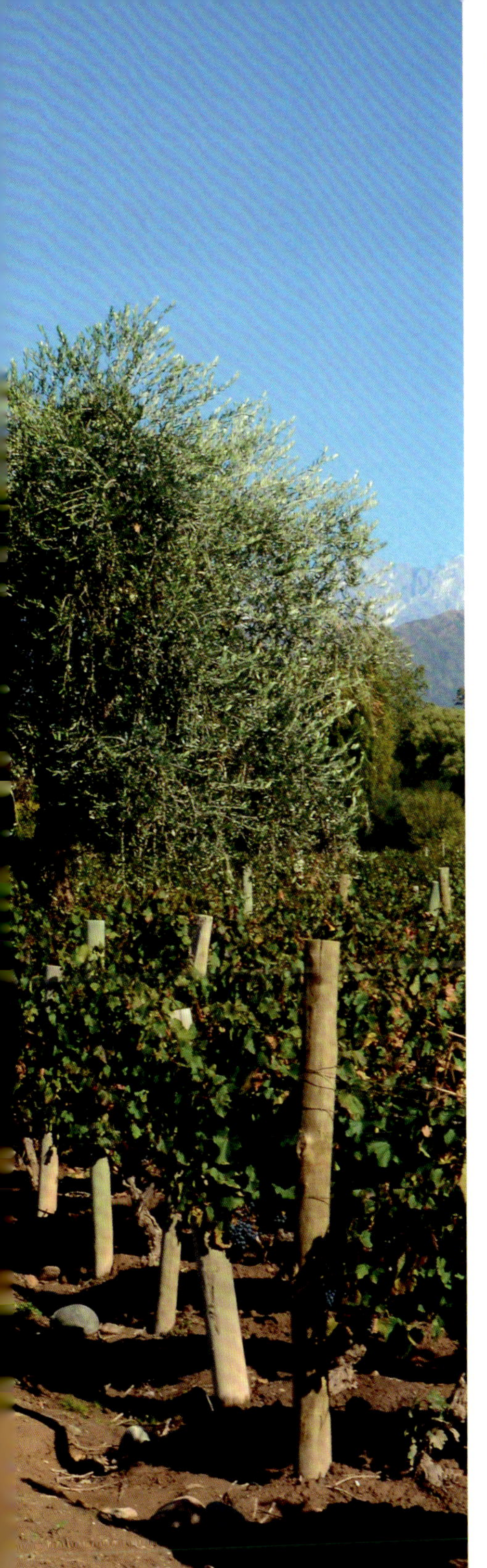

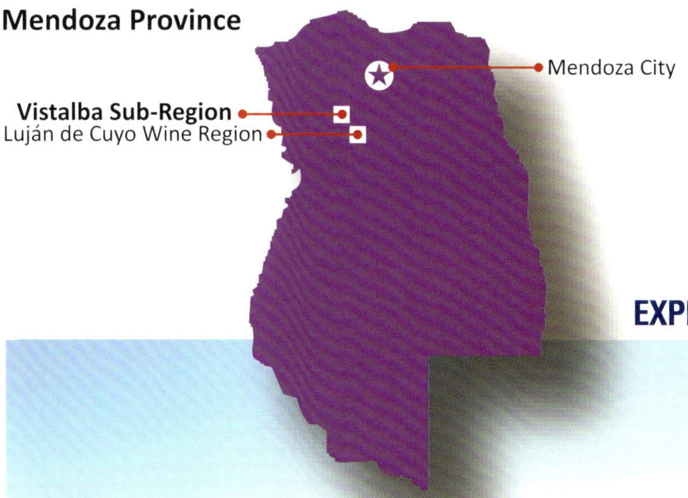

Mendoza Province

Mendoza City

Vistalba Sub-Region

Luján de Cuyo Wine Region

EXPLORING VISTALBA

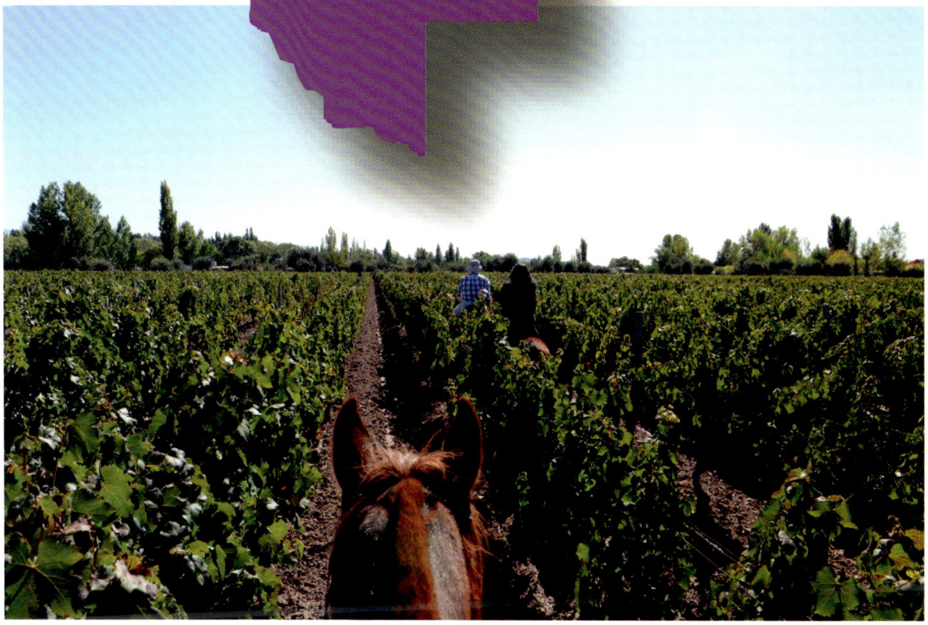

Adjacent to Chacras de Corea is a special little sub-region of Luján de Cuyo called Vistalba. Sitting in the foothills of the Andes, Vistalba enjoys the mountainous terroir of 3,300-foot elevation that contributes significantly to the style of wine produced here. And, being just north of the Mendoza River, this region receives plenty of pure Andean melt water for irrigation. Malbec is Vistalba's key grape varietal; with Chardonnay and Cabernet Sauvignon vines also planted here.

Vistalba, which means "view of the dawn" in Spanish, benefits from a position that is slightly higher in elevation than the surrounding region, giving it the advantage of increased exposure to sunlight and better air circulation, having the warm sunny days followed by significantly cooler nights that balances the development of essential sugars and acids so valuable in producing premium grapes.

The soil in Vistalba is alluvial, with sandy topsoil over a stone and a clay-dominated base. This composition allows for very good drainage and is therefore excellent for quality-driven viticulture here. Vines are forced to grow deep-root systems to access the water lower in the ground, and are stronger and healthier for it.

The flood irrigation employed extensively throughout Vistalba has also brought deposits from the river into the vineyards, and this is said to be one of the key reasons for the high levels of minerality evident in the region's wines.

Top-level premium wine producers have established vineyards and wineries in this Vistalba region. We are going to explore two of them... Nieto Senetiner and Bodega Vistalba.

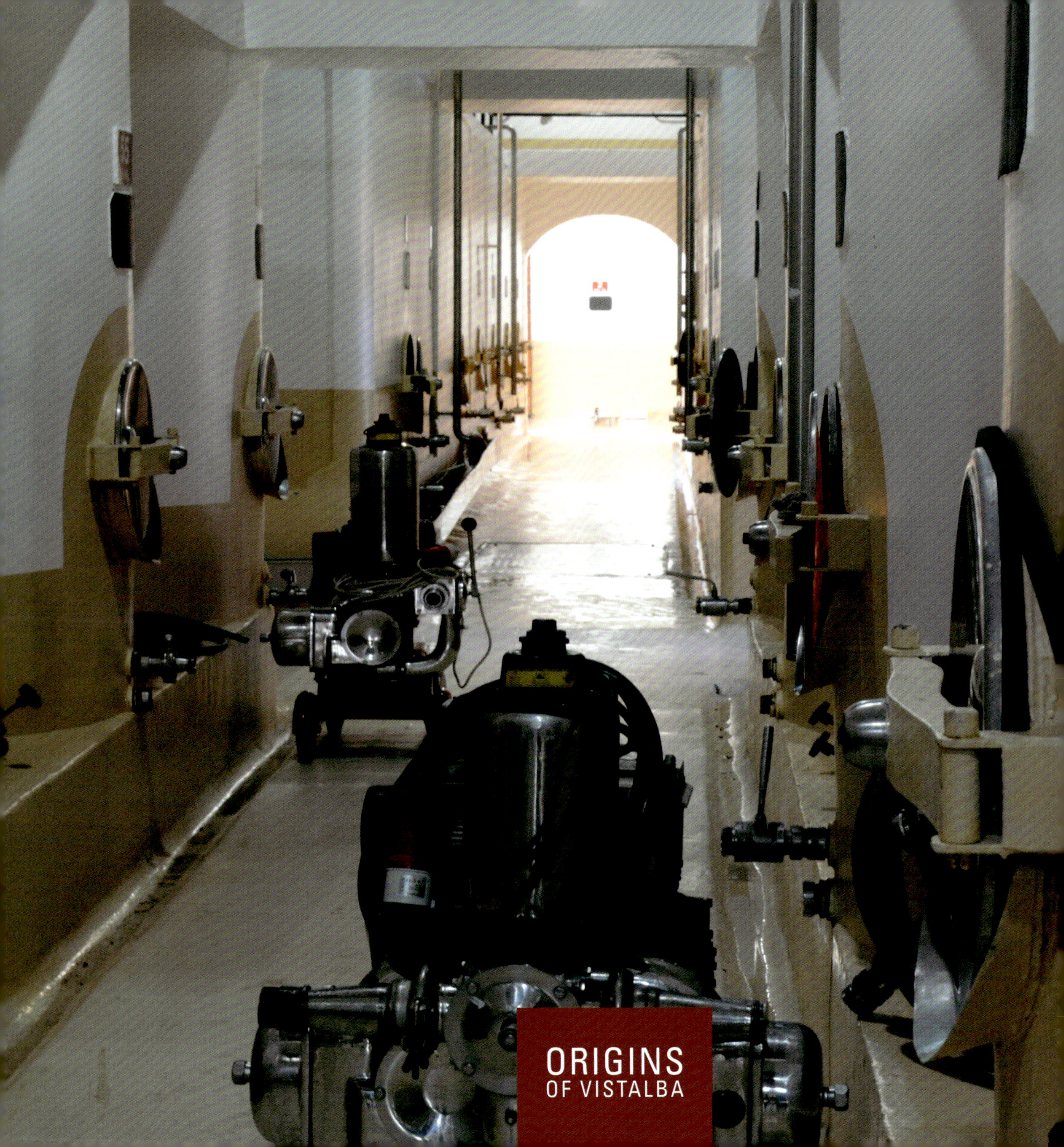
ORIGINS
OF VISTALBA

Winery (Bodega)

NIETO SENETINER

It all began in 1888 when Italian wine-loving immigrants were arriving in Mendoza, and one particular family discovered this special little area within Luján de Cuyo and started planting the first vineyards in what is known today as Vistalba. Over the next century, several families cultivated this special land into its acclaimed terroir of today's Nieto Senetiner vineyards.

When the Nieto and Senetiner families bought the property in 1969, they began an expansion and branding growth of premium wines that brought a new vision to what was possible here. In 1998, Molinos Río de la Plata, Argentina's largest food products company, purchased Nieto Senetiner, providing huge resources to modernize the winery with the latest of today's winemaking technology.

For example, the winery has converted to 100% concrete fermentation tanks (photo left page), no more stainless, with a three-story tier system for managing the winemaking process using as much gentle gravity flow as possible.

Inside their Vistalba winery is state-of-the-art. The concrete vats are small volume pools for small batch fermentation to pay extra special attention to the treatment of the grapes as micro-harvests in the vineyards to achieve the best quality from the incoming grape. And they are obsessed with cleanliness as you see in the photos.

Their winemaker, Roberto González (photo right), is detailed in every respect concerning the winemaking process, using cutting-edge equipment, technology and craftsmanship to optimize quality and to produce the finest wines... and, at the same time, he will tell you "making wine is like painting, it is art."

Each of Nieto's wineries receives a classification specific to quality standards based on performance of kilograms of grapes (translated into numbers of bunches) per plant and standardizes price for each segment of wine. It is an equation of quality wine grapes = quality / price per bottle. In Vistalba, they have their best grape classifications and therefore their most exclusive wines are made in this winery.

"**The Soils of Vistalba** are glacier soils and very poor. The organic compounds are around 0.7%. The drainage is very good. The composition is a combination of sand and clay in the first 40 to 50cm, and the rest is gravel. The irrigation comes from the Mendoza River from snow and glacier melting from the Andes Mountains.

Our vineyards are 67 years old planted by Italian immigrants after World War II. The area is next to hills that makes the vineyards cool down in the afternoon, causing cooler nights of 14.5°C average temperature. We do spur pruning, extensively separated, so the bunches receive very good sunlight.

The density of plantation is 5,500 plants per hectare, with 1 to 1.2 kg per plant to give very thick skins and a good concentration of tannins. Finally, the wines achieved are very intense with nice black fruit and spices, with a good concentration of tannins and soft finish."

*– **Tomás Hughes,** Agronomist, Nieto Senetiner*

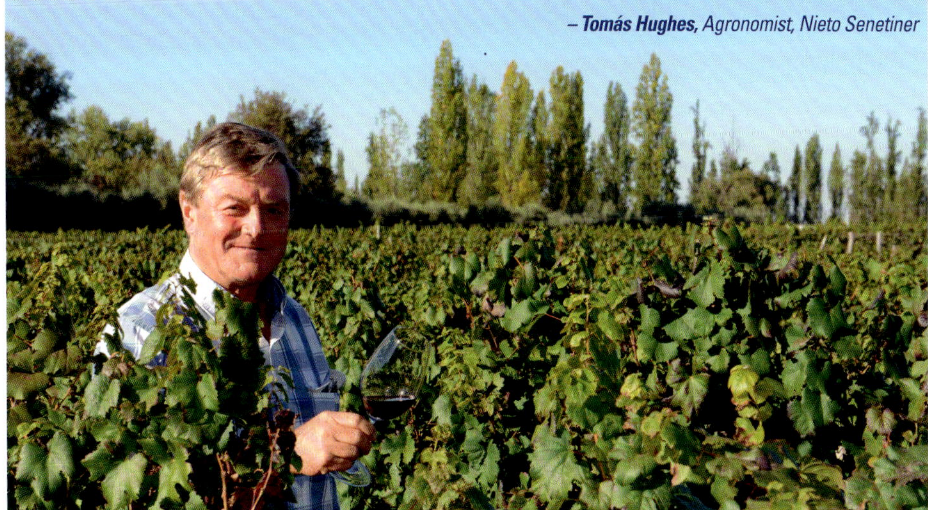

"**As a Winemaker,** I express: an identity or personality in the wines and uniqueness, expressing a unique and unrepeatable being, there is no two alike in the world, which reflects the thinking and culture of the place.

As an Academic, I have committed as president of the Argentina Academy of Vine and Wine, to defend handling of the current rational biotechnological process without losing the notion of importance of the culture of our place that comes from over 400 years of history, which were enriched by the various European immigration waves.

I bring the Greco-Roman evangelizing culture of the Mediterranean... the French, which gave the French varieties; and Italy, which provided education and a teacher education model for winemaking."

*– **Roberto González,** Winemaker, Nieto Senetiner*
President, Argentina Academy of Vine and Wine

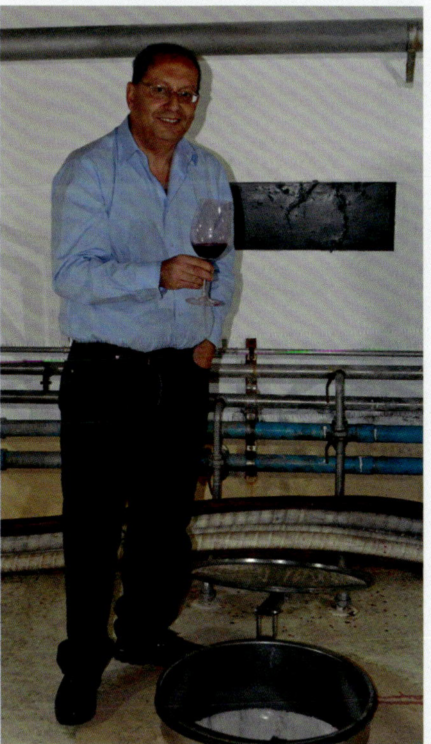

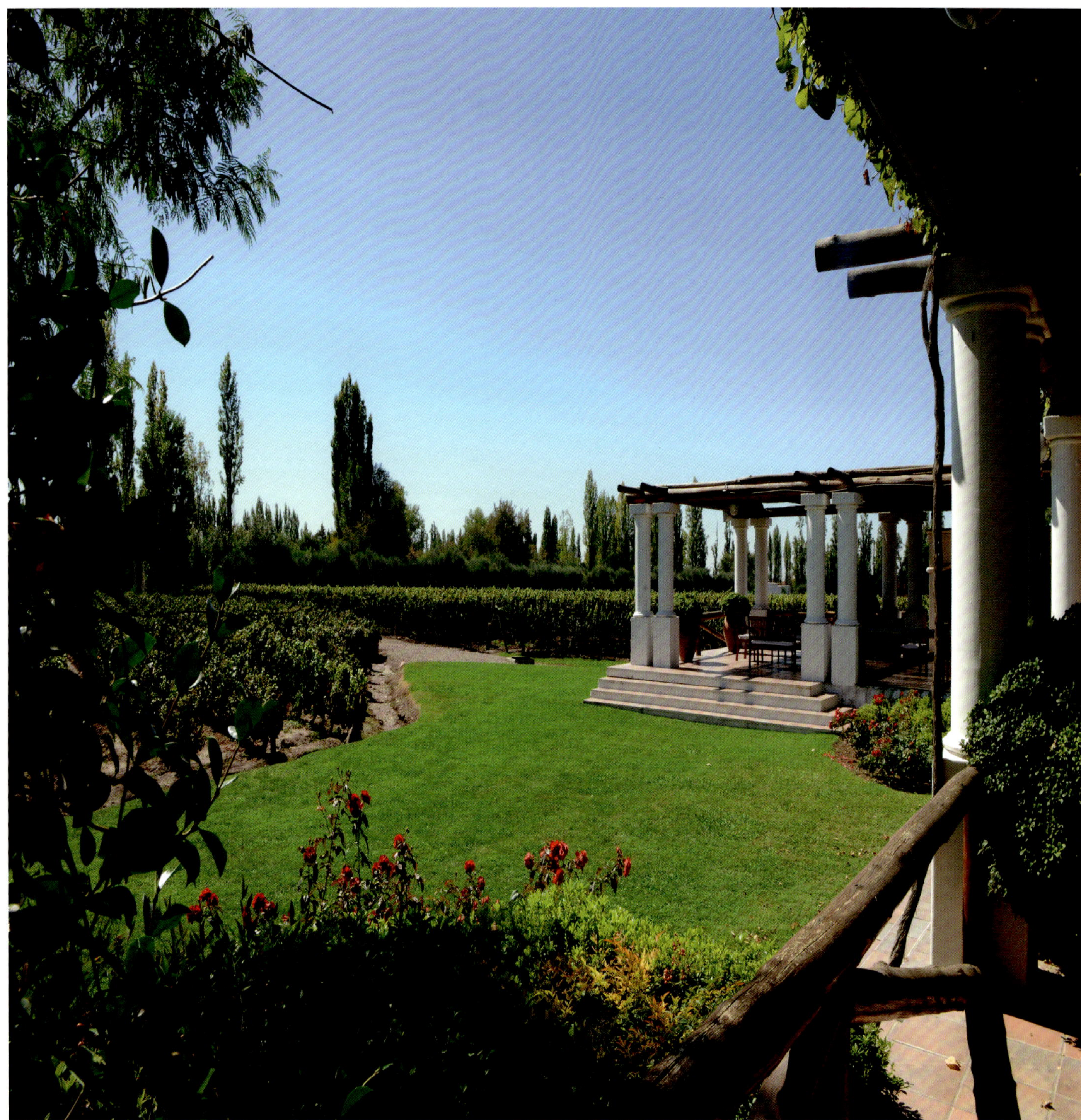

THE NIETO ASADO WINE PAIRING EXPERIENCE

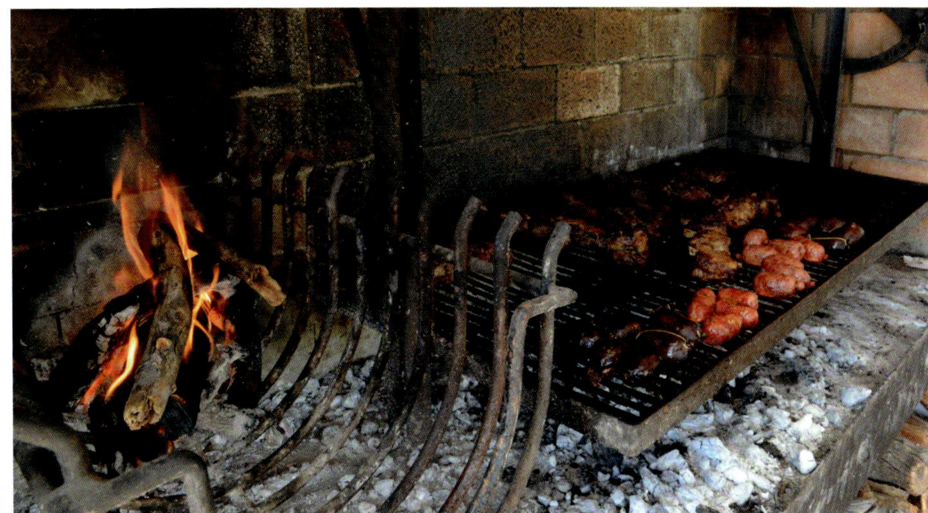

Nieteo Senetiner has a beautiful property in Vistalba. Nestled within their prized Vistalba vineyards is their winery and entertainment area.

The traditional colonial-style architecture is restored meticulously to its 1884 construction. A grand outside patio (photo left page) and barbeque (photo above) are ready for you to enjoy a beautiful day of some of the best wine and barbeque you can experience in Argentina.

And not just a food and wine tasting, Nieto puts on a traditional Argentine Asado (BBQ) to pair with their wines for an afternoon of total enjoyment.

Of course you can just visit the winery, and no reservations are required. Open seven days.

I suggest you make reservations for one of the **Special Nieto Senetiner Experiences**...

- *Lunch at the Winery Estate*
- *Wine Tastings in their Vineyards*
- *Horseback Riding the Vineyards and Vistalba*

Each of these includes winery tours and tastings. And only a 24-hour advanced notice is required. 261.496.9099 or turismo@nietosenetiner.com.ar

Nieto Senetiner has six brands: Cadus, Don Nicanor, Nieto Senetiner, Emilia, Benjamin, and Espumantes for sparklings, each of which has an extensive selection of wines.

Cadus are their first-level, super-premium wines. It is a single-vineyard focus specializing in Malbec, with one Bonarda. This is the agronomist's ultimate expression of the vineyard, where Tomás Hughes defines the bottle of wine through his meticulous attention in the vineyard, and low grape yield of only half litre per plant (17 ounces) to produce extremely high-quality juice.

Cadus Malbec Blend (of their single vineyards) combines the best attributes of each elevation: 950, 1,050 and 1,150 meters. Each height brings different elements to blend, for example: 950m (body & fruit) brings higher fat content and glycerol to create a well rounded wine. 1,050m (color) provides intense purple and blue, sometimes black. 1,150m (acidity) cuts acidity and brings freshness and minerality.

Don Nicanor are their super-premium blended wines, where winemaker Roberto González is the artist, the chef in the winery, creating his ultimate expression from a complete palate of vineyards, maceration, fermentation and aging processes, oaks and other creative and technological tools.

Nieto Senetiner are their second-level premium wines with an unusual Malbec DOC wine that represents the typical expression of their soil, climate and culture. The DOC (Controlled Origin Denomination) certifies the grapes coming from a particular area and produced under special quality standards. Its color is very intense purplish red, changing to blue. The nose has red fruits of plum and black fruits of blackberries, combined with subtle vanilla notes from aging in the wood of French oak barrels. Enjoy!

Winery (Bodega)

NIETO SENETINER

2275 Vieytes (Carrodilla)
(Vistalba, Luján de Cuyo)

011 (+54 261) 496.9000
Turismo@NietoSenetiner.com.ar

NietoSenetiner.com

English & Español

26,000,000 total bottles annually
3,000,000 bottles of Premium Wines

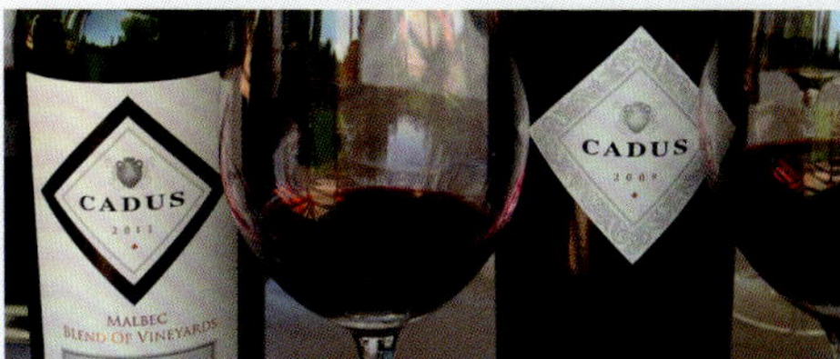

Michael's Favorite Pick
Cadus - Malbec Blend of Vineyards

Collection of Nieto Senetiner Wines
Six Different Brands - 48 Different Wines

First Level - **Cadus Single-Vineyard** - (4 tons / hectare)
Grand Vin - (Malbec, Cabernet Sauvignon, Bonarda)
Malbec - Finca Las Tortugas
Bonarda - Finca Las Tortugas
Malbec - Finca Villa Blanca
Malbec - Finca Las Torcazas
Malbec Blend of Vineyards (All Three Fincas)

Second Level - **Don Nicanor** - (8 tons / hectare)
Blend (Malbec, Cabernet Sauvignon, Merlot)
Malbec
Bonarda
Barrel Select (Malbec)
Cabernet Sauvignon
Chardonnay/Viognier

Second Level - **Nieto Senetiner** - (8 tons / hectare)
Malbec DOC (Vistalba)
Controlled Origin Denomination, distinction certifies the wine comes from a particular area produced under special quality standards

To get Nieto Senetiner wines in the USA
Contact the Importer: FoleyFamilyWines.com

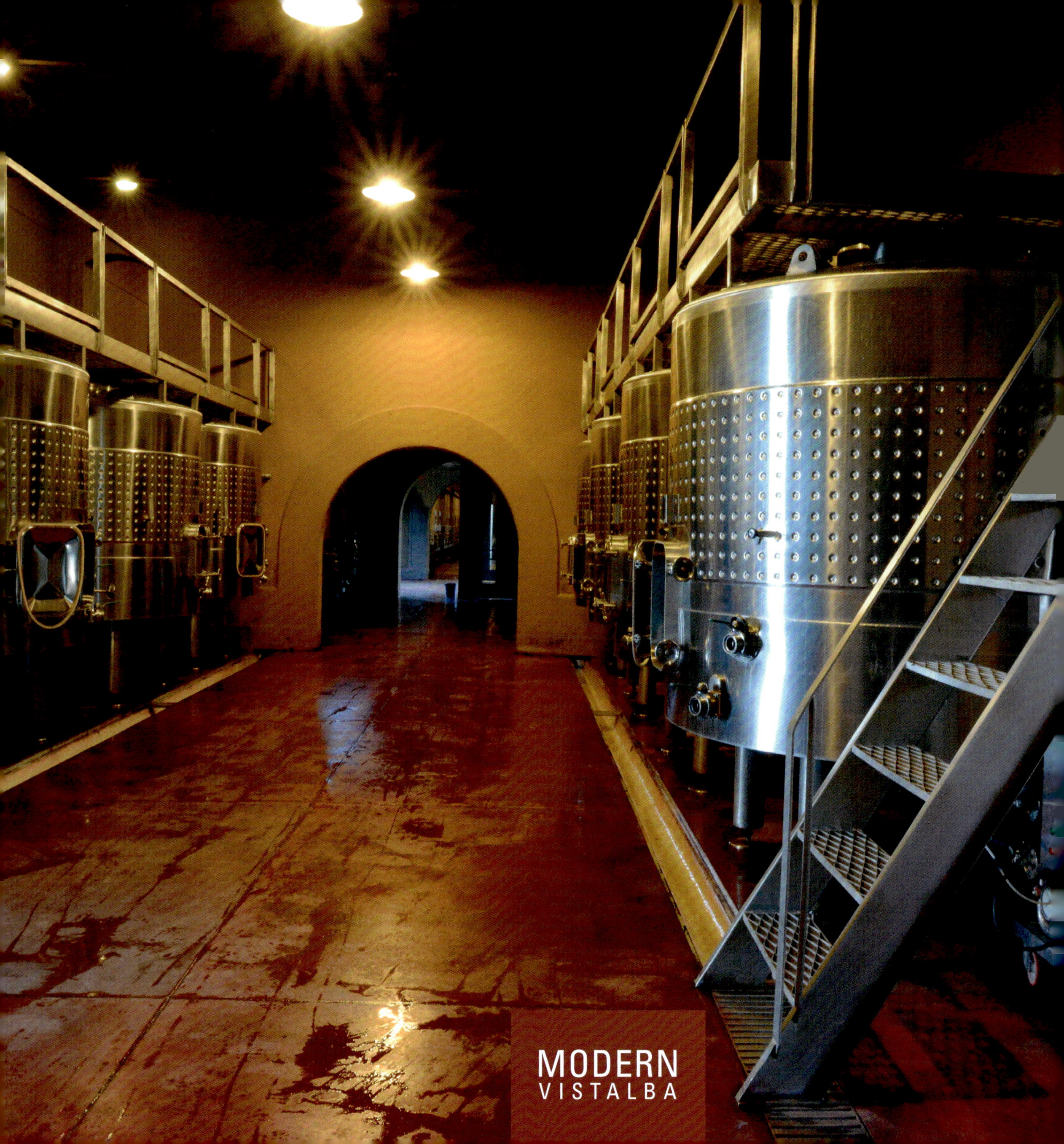
MODERN
VISTALBA

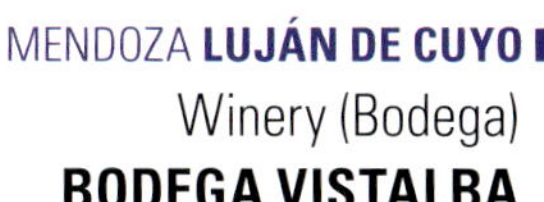

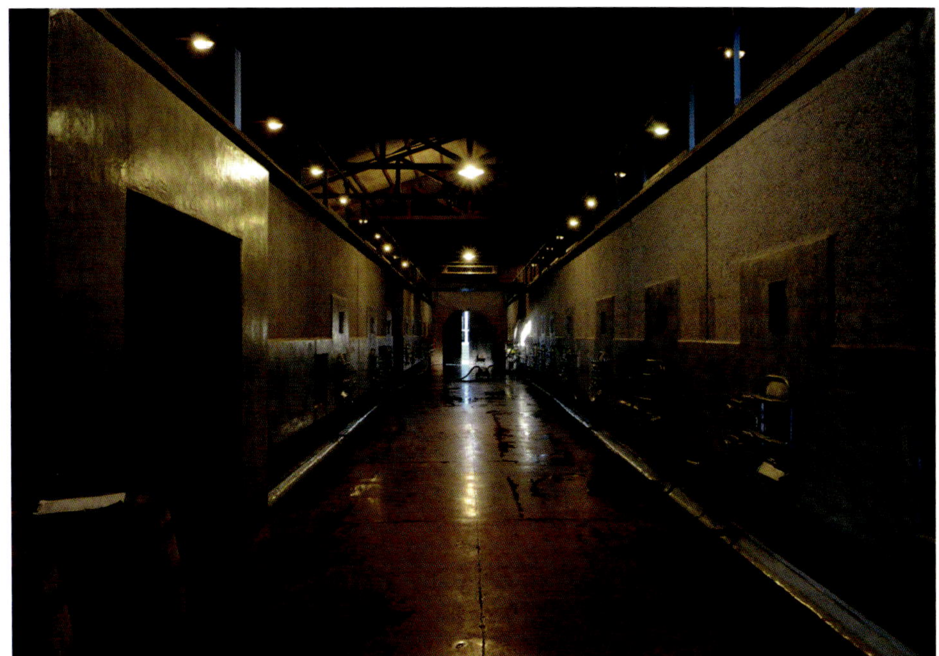

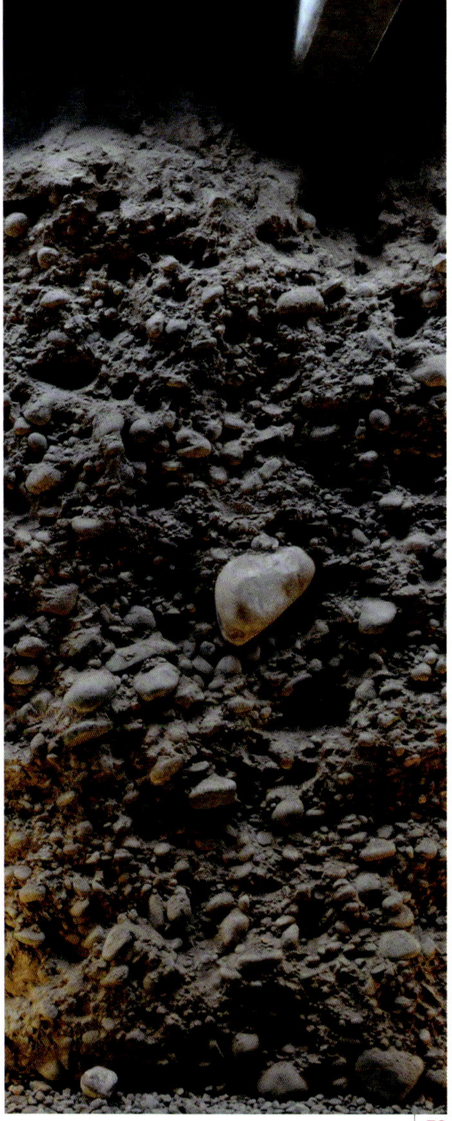

PREMIUM BLENDED WINES

Built in the 21st century (2002), Bodega Vistalba had the opportunity of incorporating modern technologies and innovations into all aspects of their winery from design-up of this state-of-the-art facility.

Carlos Pulenta, the visionary behind the Bodega Vistalba, grew up in the vineyards working aside his father and uncle in the wine business all his life. Sixty years ago his father and uncle found this special property in Vistalba and planted 131 acres of vines, of which 70% are still active today, producing the old-vine qualities for their super-premium wines. Carlos learned tremendously from his family making history as pioneers in the Mendoza wine industry with such notable wineries as Peñaflor and Trapiche.

Although an Italian descendant (his great-great-grandfather immigrated from Italy with the Gallo family), Carlos's vision with Bodega Vistalba is to create sophisticated blends in the French Bordeaux style of big wines with long aging potential. Malbec is their primary grape, with Cabernet Sauvignon and Bonarda used for blending perfection.

The winery is completely gravity fed. No pumps are used for the most gentle handling of the grapes, their juice and ultimately the wines. The grapes are harvested manually, stems and berries are meticulously sorted twice, and their temperature reduced in a cooling tunnel to 15°F. The grapes are gently placed in concrete fermentation tanks (photo above), where, after three to four days of cold maceration, fermentation begins, vinified using natural yeasts.

These concrete tanks were designed by Carlos himself, where inside the tank walls there are water pipes that circulate water to control temperatures, with advantages of thermal inertia and micro-oxygenation, all done by computer. In addition, two large French wooden barrels are used for their optimum selected grapes destined to their top blend, Corte A.

Tours are extensive, informative and interesting. Their underground wine cellars (photo next page) also include a tasting room where the dug-out dirt remains exposed as one of the walls, so you can see the content of the alluvial soil (photo right). Guides are extremely knowledgable. My experience might be the most knowledgable guide experience I have ever encountered, as this young woman was extremely qualified, being that she grew up in her parent's French Chateau in Bordeaux, France.

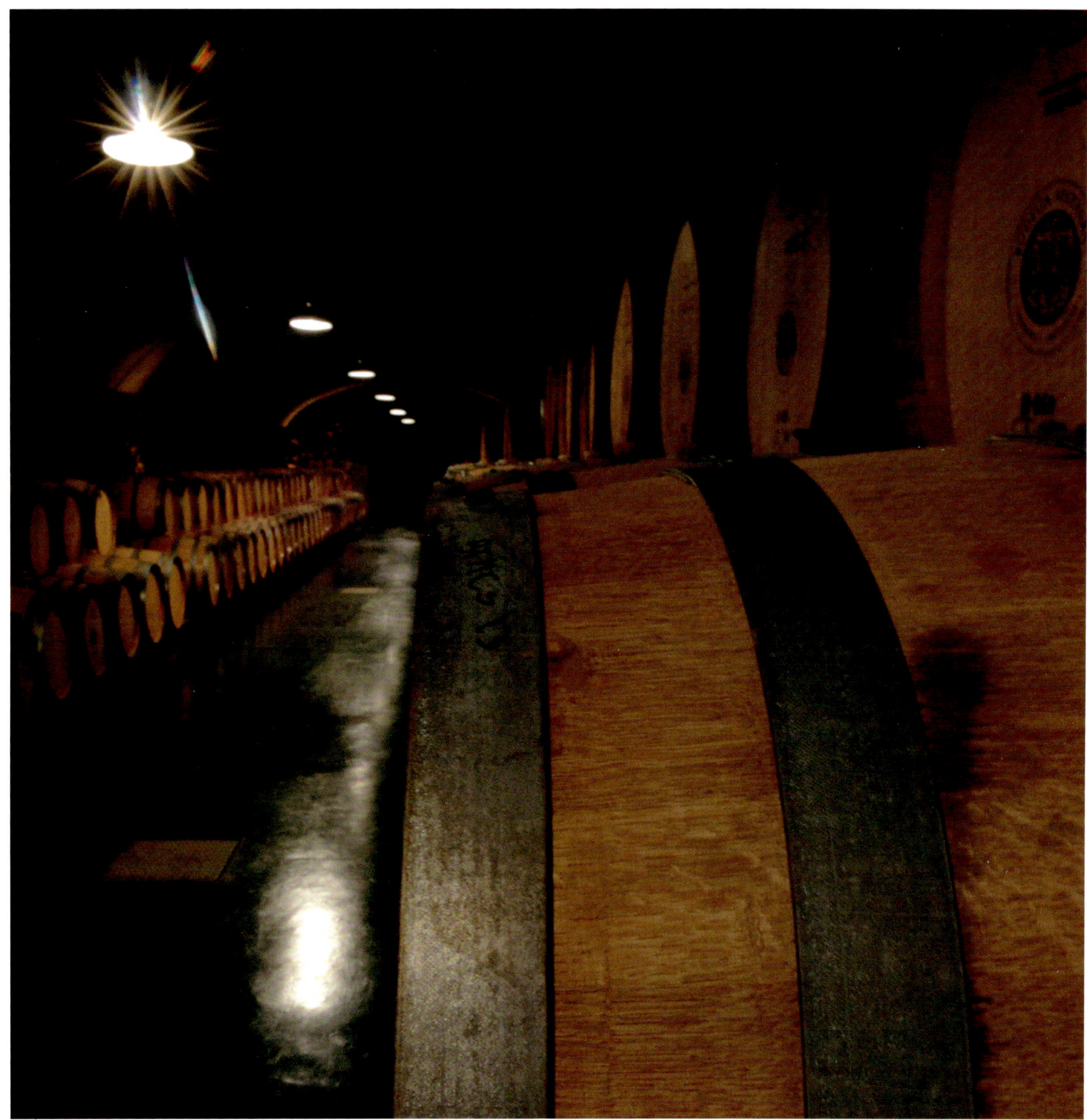

FRENCH-INSPIRED BLENDS

As I mentioned previously, the focus of Bodega Vistalba is Bordeaux-style blends, with Malbec as the primary grape. They name their wines after the Spanish word for blend: Corte A, Corte B and Corte C. The wines are selected based on structure and density, with the Corte A being their biggest among the three, followed by Corte B, then the most accessible style, Corte C.

The distinct Corte blends are the result of the best grapes of each harvest and differ from vintage to vintage. Malbec is always primary with Cabernet Sauvignon and Bonarda as the secondary blends.

Each blend is distinct and different.

Corte A: Primarily Malbec, with small amounts of Cabernet and Bonarda, it is a characteristically intense, complex and well-structured blend. It is 100% aged in French oak barrels for 18 months and in bottles for 12 months before release.

Corte B: This typically lush, well-rounded blend with velvety tannins is 100% aged in French oak barrels for 12 months and in bottle for 10 months.

Corte C: This ripe, juicy blend is created for more immediate consumption, 20% is aged in French oak barrels for 12 months and six months in bottle.

Bodega Vistalba is a very special project and a personal undertaking of Carlos Pulenta to create top-level, sophisticated blends. To achieve this, Carlos involves members of his family, advisors, enologists, and a highly esteemed group of people who know his vineyards to produce his super-premium wines.

Bodega Vistalba also has a line of reserve and classic *non-blended* wines called **Tomero**, named after the person who manages the distribution of water from the rivers through the canals and into the vineyards.

I am a purist that loves single varietal wines, and these wines are special. I particularly enjoyed the Petit Verdot Reserva, not often found, and will capture your attention in their wines.

Finally, they also have a series of sparkling wines called Progenie. My favorite, **Progenie I**, is as beautiful as it tastes, with its distinguishing metal label on the bottle (photo right).

In the end, Bodega Vistalba is the only winery allowed to use the appellation Vistalba on their label. I hope you visit and enjoy this special place.

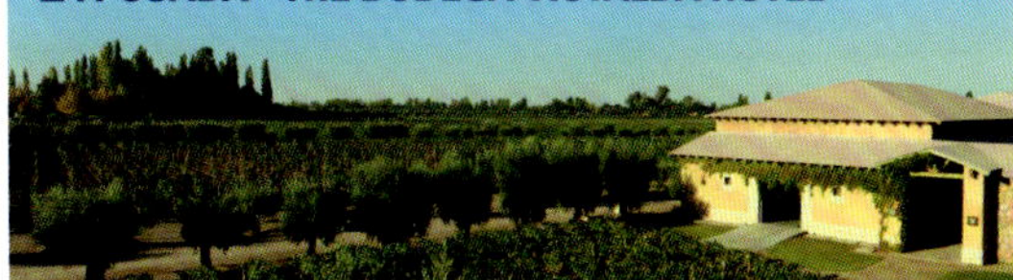

La Posada Vistalba has just two rooms, above their winery, spacious with views of the Andes, vineyards and the winery... with the modern convenience of WiFi, TV and refrigerator. Breakfast included.

Staying at their inn is an opportunity to discover the spirit of the winery and their people, up close and personal. During your visit, they will show you the winemaking process from the beginning... they will walk you through the vineyards so you get to know the journey of the grape, experiencing the elaborate winemaking process from vineyard to winery to bottle... all aspects of production, live, at Bodega Vistalba while you are there. To complete the visit, there is nothing better than tasting their wines with the winery's enologist in the underground wine cellar.

Their **Wine Bar** offers the opportunity of learning about their wines while paired with local produce, such as olives, cheeses and other organic produce from their own orchards.

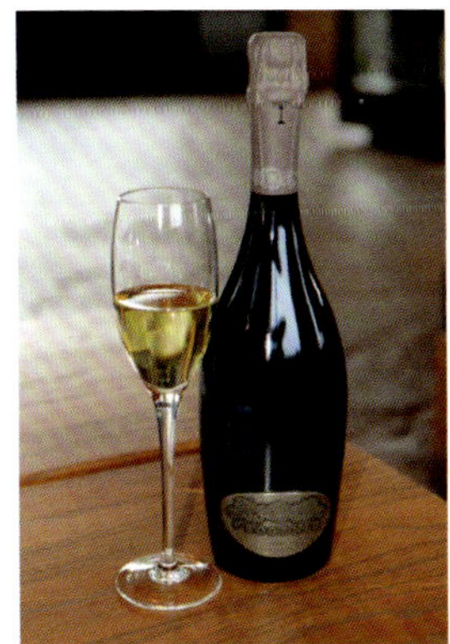

Winery (Bodega)

BODEGA VISTALBA

3531 Roque Sáenz Peña
(Vistalba, Luján de Cuyo)

011 (+54 261) 498.9400
info@BodegaVistalba.com

BodegaVistalba.com

English, Español & Français
300,000 total bottles annually

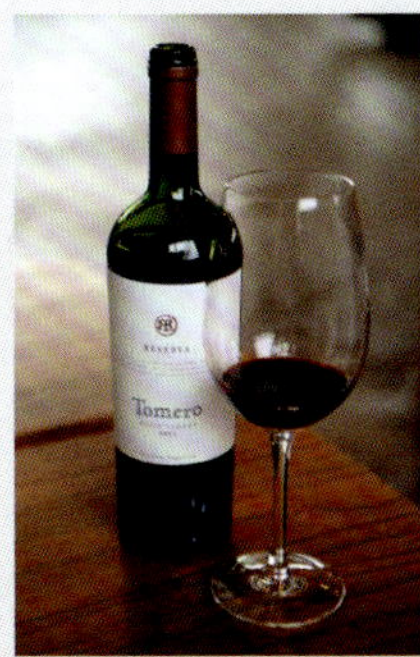

Michael's Favorite Pick
Petit Verdot - *Reserva*

Collection of Wines
Corte A - (Intense and Complex)
Corte B - (Lush and Velvety)
Corte C - (Ripe and Fruity)

Tomero - (8 tons / hectare)
Malbec - *Grand Reserva*
Petit Verdot - *Reserva*
Pinot Noir - *Reserva*
Semillon - *Reserva*
Syrah - *Reserva*
Malbec - *Clásico*
Cabernet Sauvignon - *Clásico*
Chardonnay - *Clásico*
Torrontés - *Clásico*
Malbec Rosé Dulce Natural - *Clásico*
Sauvignon Blanc - *Clásico*

Progenie - (Sparkling Wines)
Progenie I, II, III

To get Bodega Vistalba wines in the USA
Contact the Importer: BlendsInc.com

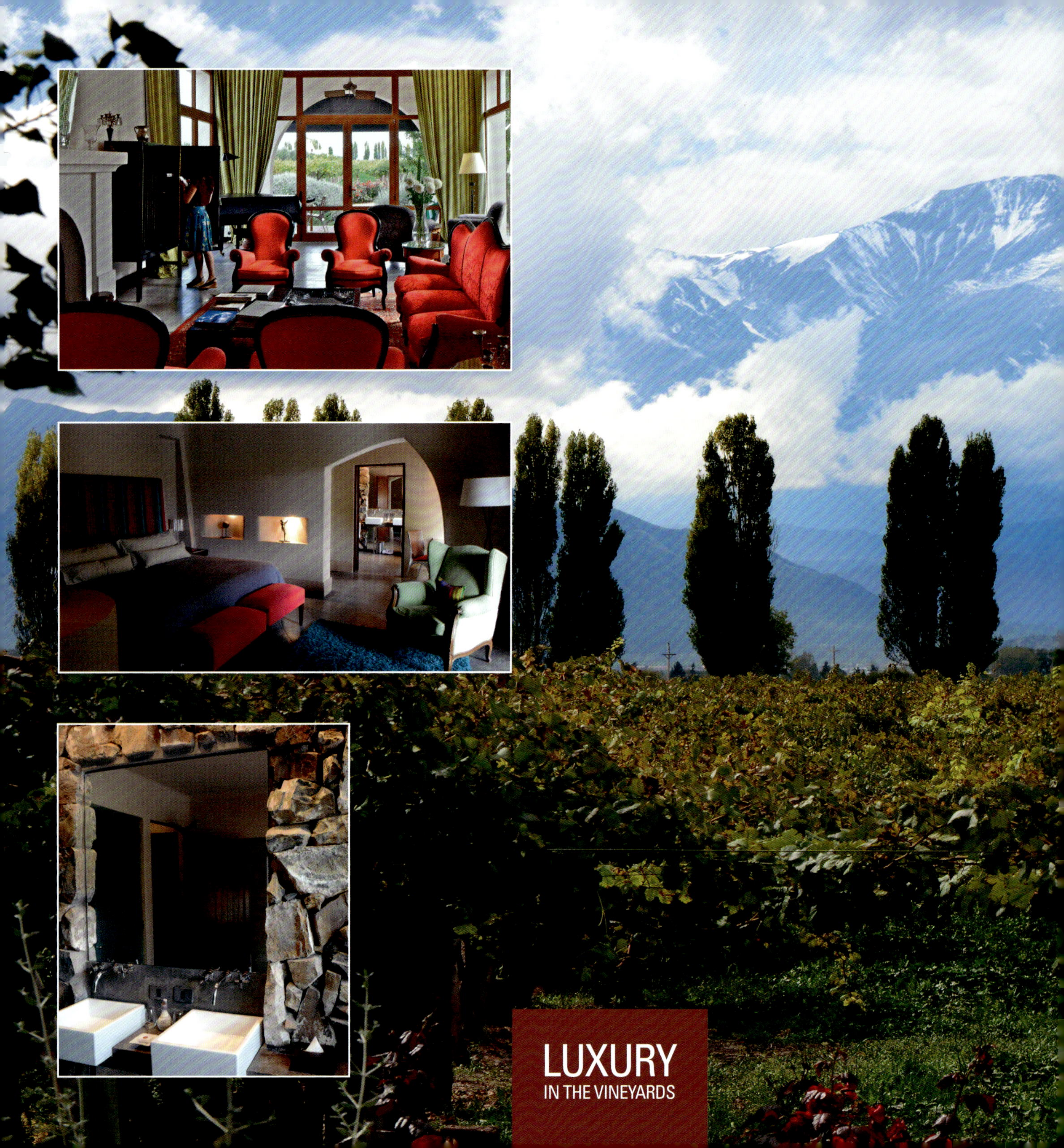

LUXURY
IN THE VINEYARDS

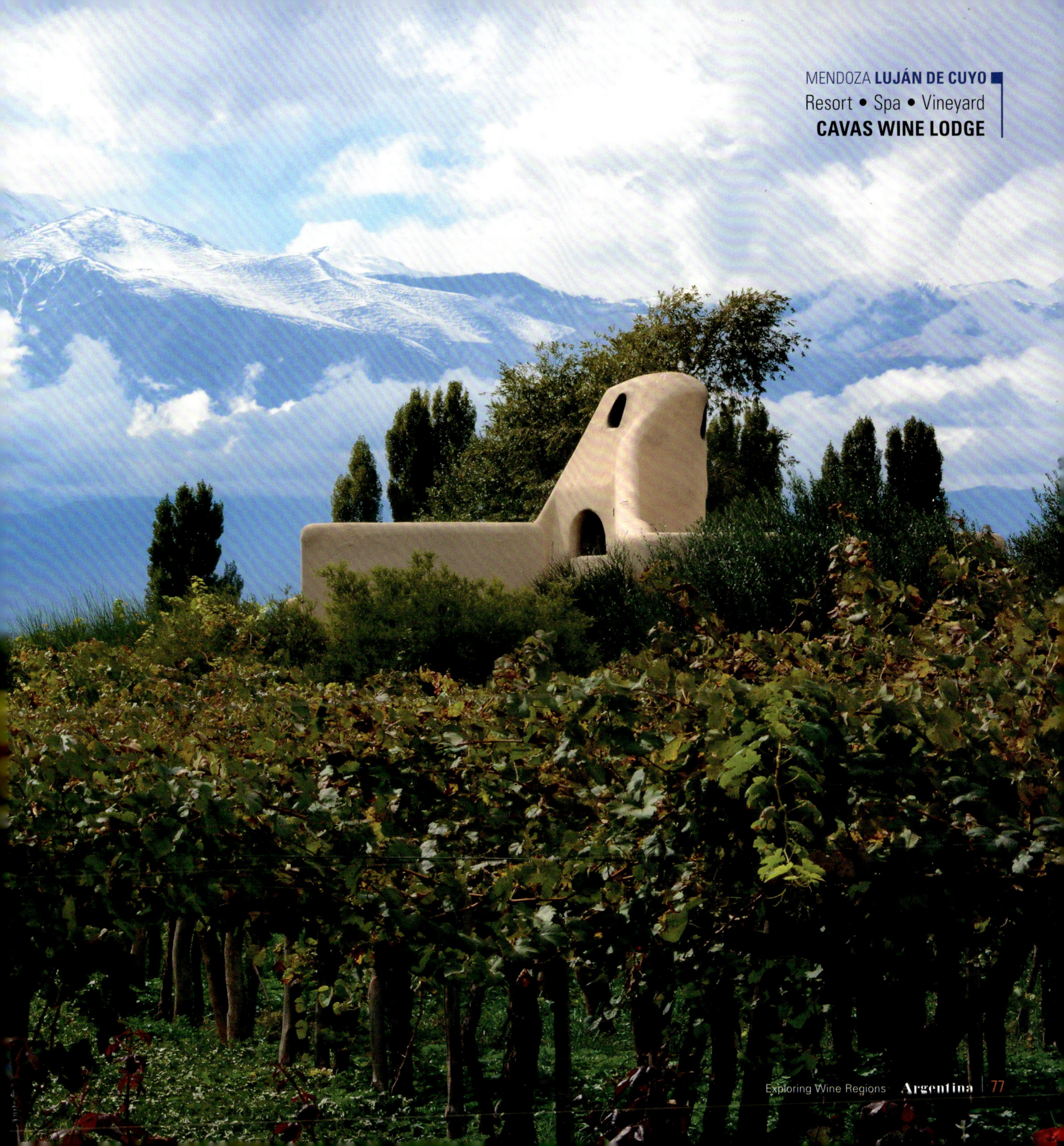

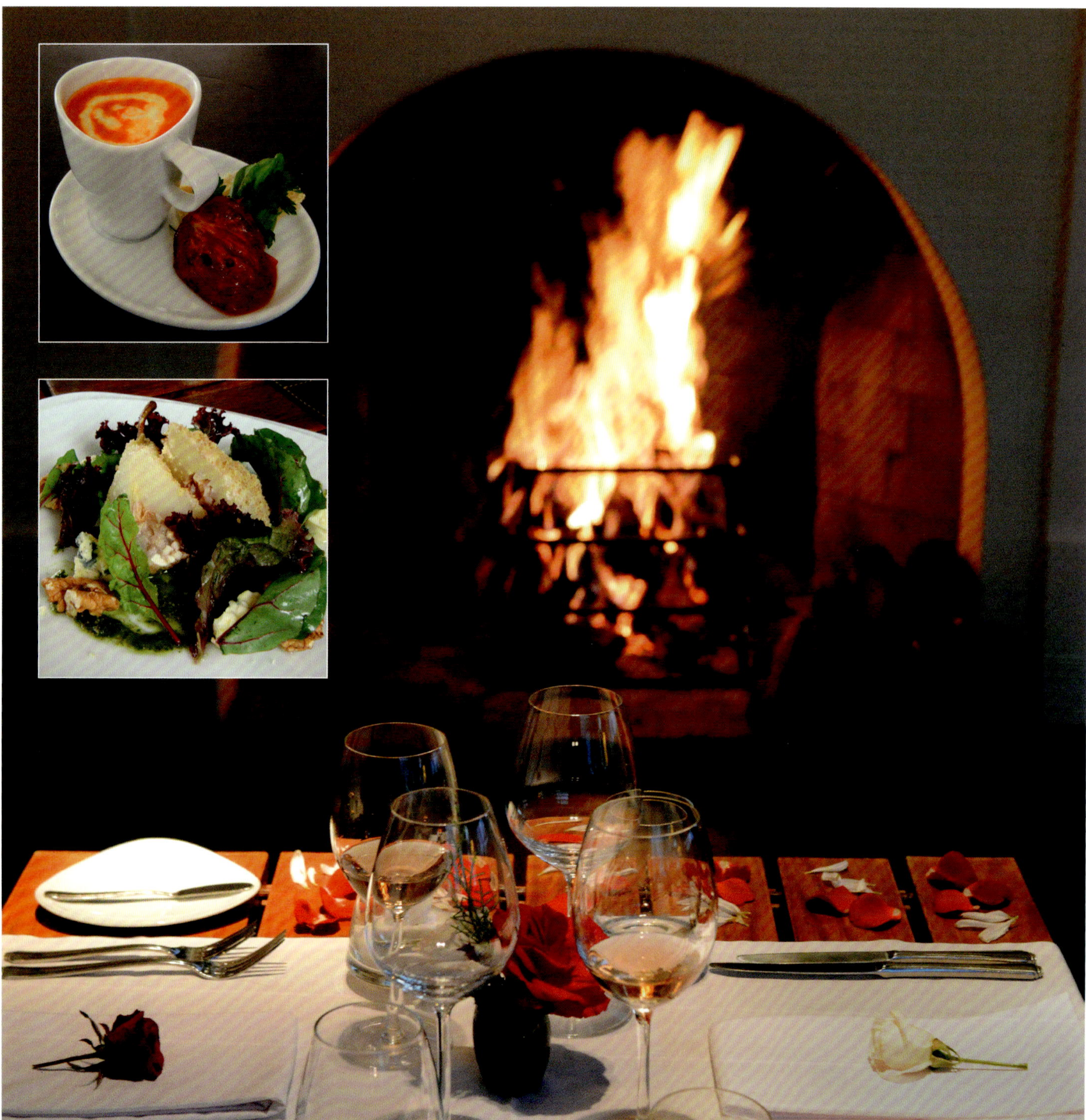

UNIQUE VILLAS

Imagine 55 acres of vineyards with private villas secluded with westerly views of the Andes and all the luxuries you would expect of a five-star hotel... in a casual environment of natural building materials and textiles (photos on previous spread).

Indoors... separate living room, bedroom, office, walk-in closet, wood-burning fireplace, king bed with Egyptian cotton, spa-style bathroom, dual vanities, separate shower and vintage soaking tub.

Outdoors... outdoor shower and garden, plunge pool, wood-burning fireplace, and very private.

Upstairs... rooftop terrace with mattress and wood burning fireplace. They will serve you dinner or make bedding for an overnight under the stars.

Service... nightly turndown, morning wake-up, breakfast, twice daily housekeeping and an attention to pleasing your every desire.

This place is so nice you will not want to venture out to wineries. I didn't. I stayed in and enjoyed the property, wine spa treatments and delicious culinary experiences.

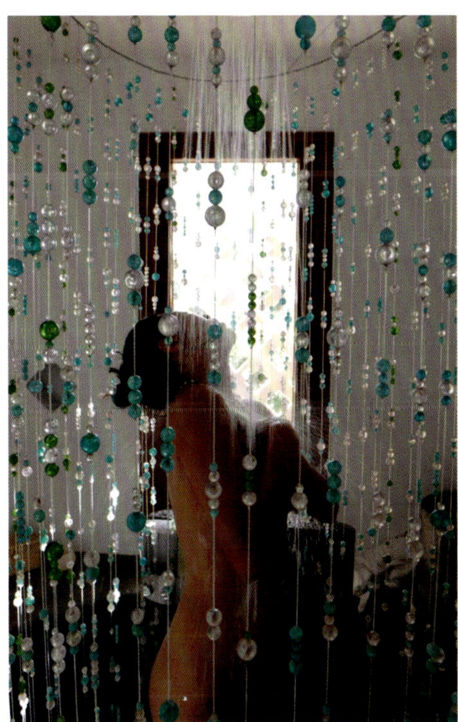

WINE THERAPY SPA

Expand your wine experience by using the latest discoveries in vine and grape seed extracts on your body. Rich in polyphenols, these extracts combat the free radicals responsible for 80% of aging. The **Cavas Wine Spa** offers a sequence of comprehensive treatments to fully gain the therapeutic effects.

It begins with a **Crushed Malbec Scrub** of grape seeds and essential oils derived from organic crops to free the skin of dead skin cells. Next is the **Bonarda Red Wine Bath** to stimulate the circulatory system by soaking in bubbling water enriched with red vine extracts and organic essential oils. Next is the **Torrontés Wine Wrap** of wine yeast and organic essential oils to strengthen immune defenses. And lastly is a choice of either a **Revitalizing or Relaxing Massage** using grape seed oil and organic essential oils conducive to your choice.

FRESH & ORGANIC FOODS

The **Cavas Wine Restaurant** is also a special experience... with both a gourmet chef and a focus on organically grown foods that are harvested in ways that are ecologically sound. This offers a seasonally fresh menu changing frequently to show off the finest local ingredients obtainable.

LEFT PAGE, try the healthy **Sopa de Día** tomato soup with red bell peppers and brix cheese, and **Ensalada de Queso Azul** blue cheese salad with crusted pears, nuts and arugula.

Plus, enjoy cooking lessons with their chef and sommelier pairing foods with top wines from their underground cellar of 250 carefully selected wines from the Mendoza region.

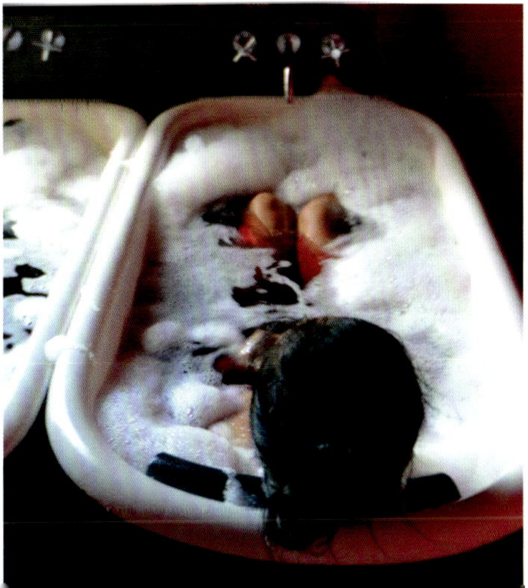

MENDOZA **LUJÁN DE CUYO**

Resort Spa • Spa • Vineyard

CAVAS WINE LODGE

Costa Flores s/n (2.2 km)
(Alto Agrelo, Luján de Cuyo)

011 (+54 261) 479.0200
reservas@CavasWineLodge.com

CavasWineLodge.com

English & Español
7,000 total bottles annually

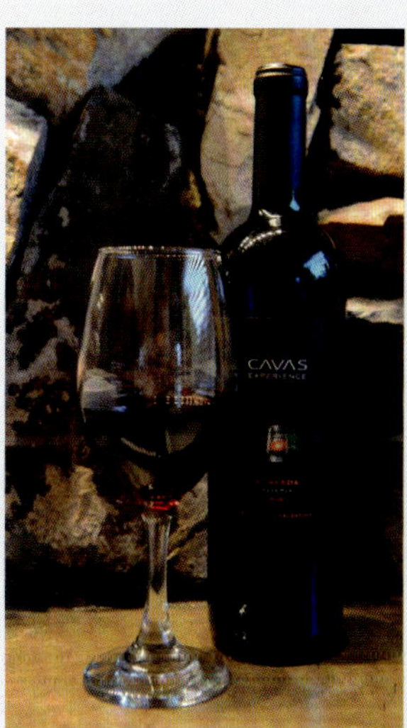

Michael's Favorite Pick
Bonarda Reserva

Total Collection of Wines
Bonarda Reserva
Bonarda Gran Reserva
Blend Reserva (Malbec, Cabernet Sauvignon, Bonarda)
Malbec Gran Reserva
19 Escalones Sauvignon Blanc
Cecilia's Becquignol Rosè

To get Cavas wines in the USA
Contact the winery direct:
reservas@CavasWineLodge.com

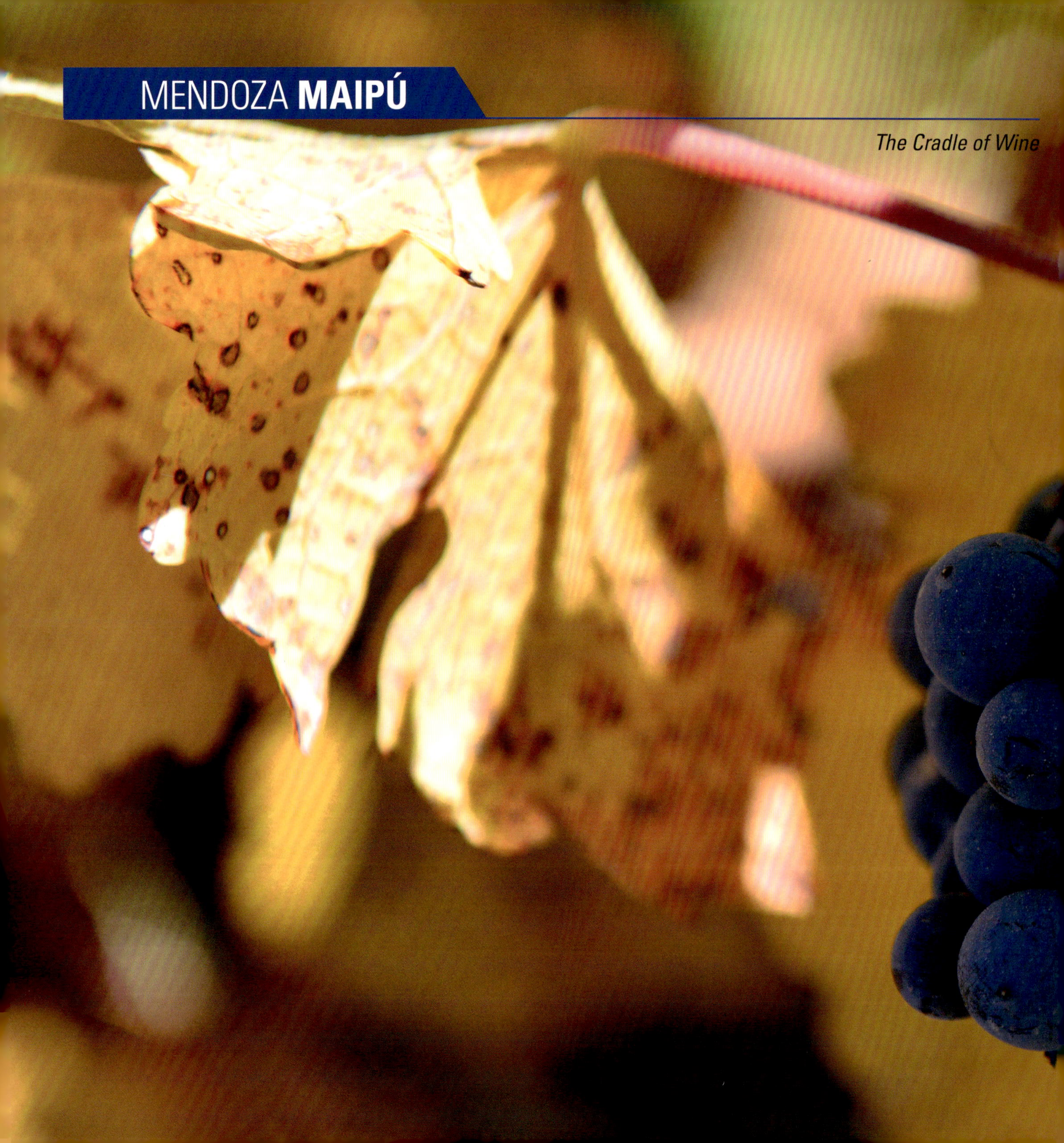
MENDOZA MAIPÚ
The Cradle of Wine

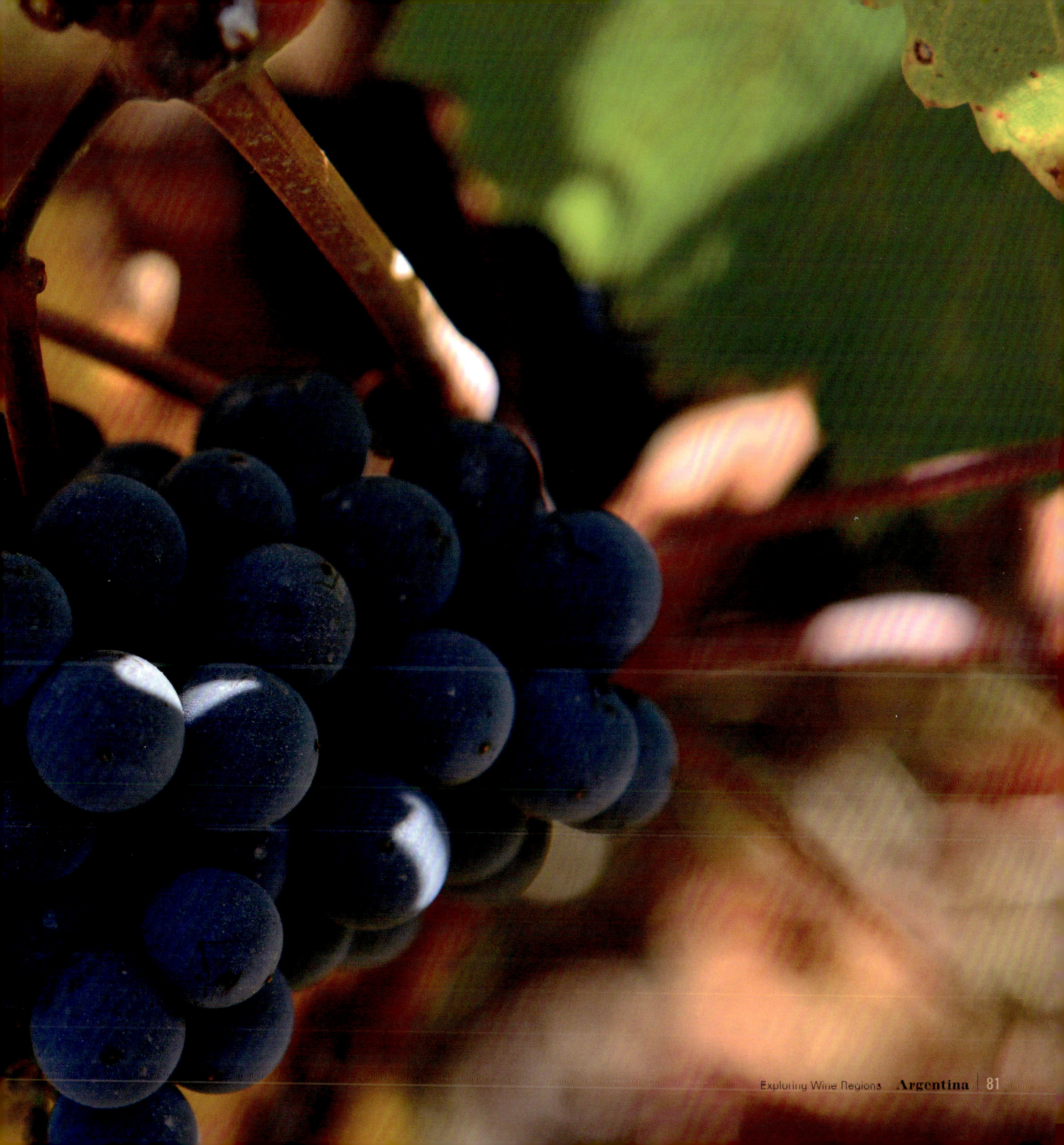

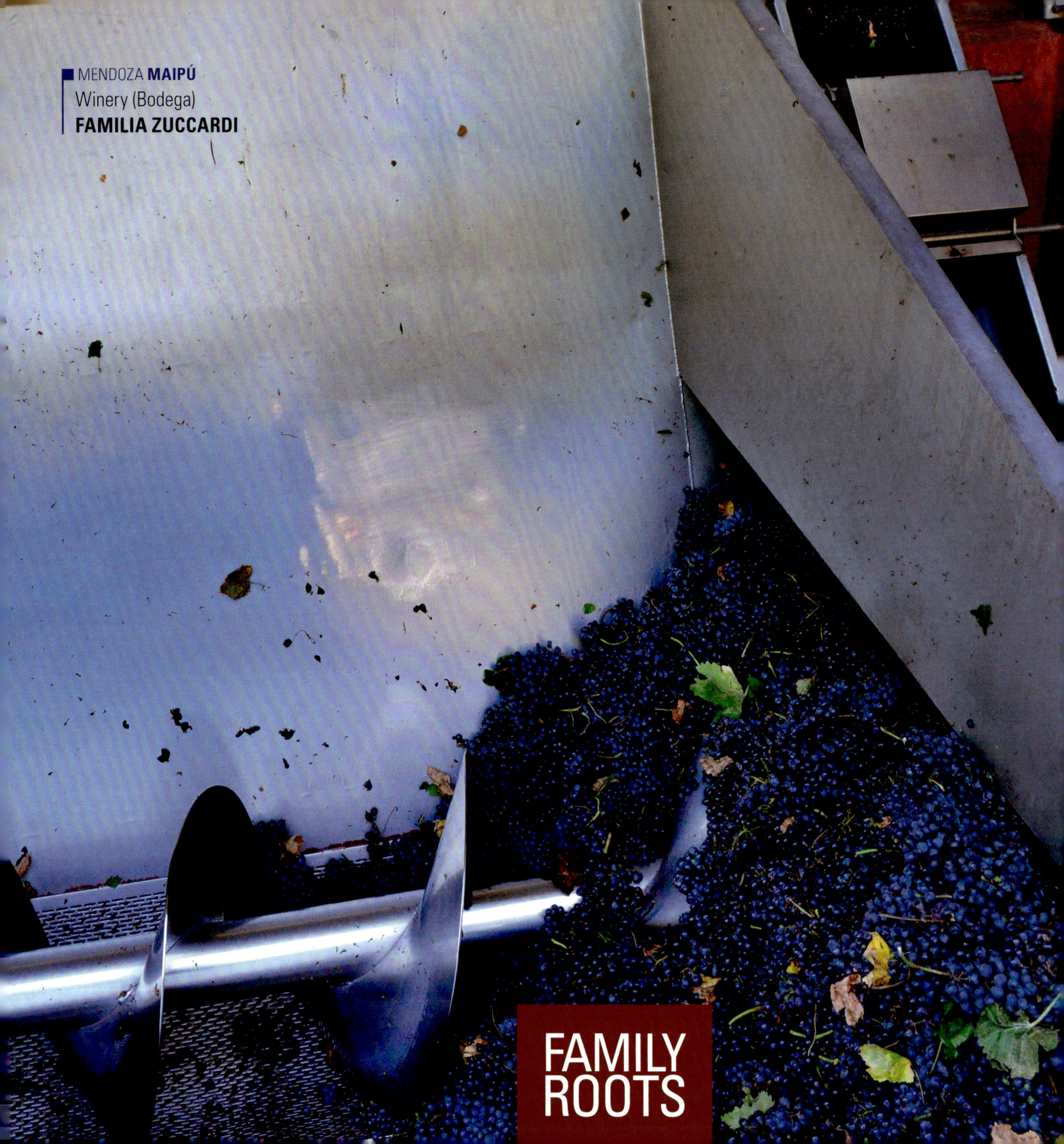
MENDOZA MAIPÚ
Winery (Bodega)
FAMILIA ZUCCARDI
FAMILY ROOTS

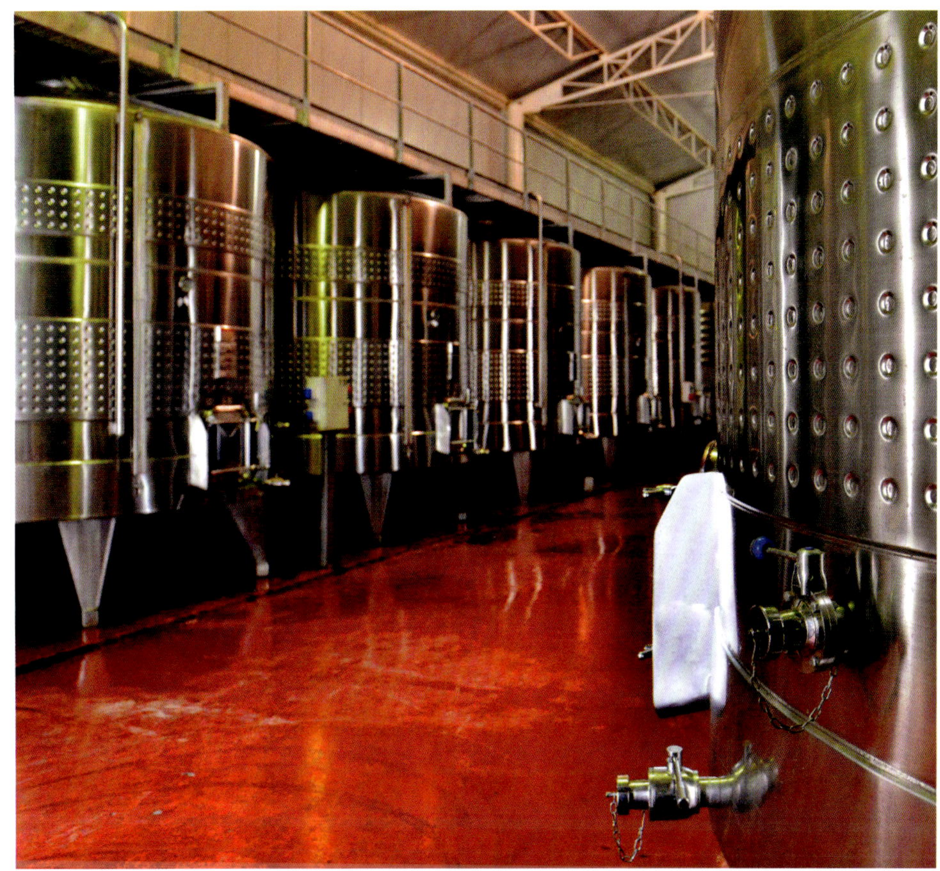

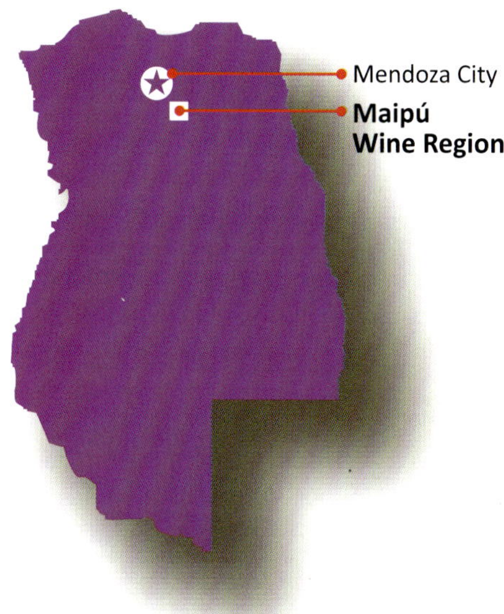

HISTORY MADE IN MAIPÚ

Maipú is directly south and only a few minutes from the city of Mendoza. It is to the east of Luján de Cuyo, farther away from the Andes Mountains, at lower elevation and a warmer climate with deep rocky clay soils, perfect for red varietals.

Maipú has the attraction of the big Diurnal Shifts, the large temperature variation from the highs of the day to the cools of nights, ideal for grapes.

Maipú calls themselves "The Cradle of Wine" because they are very proud of their rich history as the designated location for European immigrants to continue their important tradition of winemaking. The land proved to be ideal in climate and soil for these winemakers who were tenacious and dedicated to making a success of this region.

Bautista Gerónimo Gargantini and Don Juan Giol were the most illustrious vintners cultivating this wine region. Their bodega, *La Colina de Oro* (The Hill of Gold), opened in 1896 and quickly became the largest winery in the word, and responsible for producing more than half of the wine in Argentina.

Today, Maipú commemorates these two pioneers and their winery in the city's central Metropolitan Park. Gargantini and Giol's two mansions are named *Patrimonio Cultura de la Provincia de Mendoza* and are open for visitors in the Park. The *Wine and Grape Harvest Museum* is one of the treasures in Maipú celebrating Argentina's national beverage.

Maipú was only a one-day adventure for me on this trip. There is so much to see and discover here that I am looking forward to further exploring the history and wines of Maipú.

So, if you are only going to make one stop in Maipú, I suggest Familia Zuccardi, another long-established family winery. Zuccardi produces a large number of varietals and a range of wine qualities, ideal to learn about the local wines. Further, they have an extensive tour, a grape picking program during the harvest season, and a comprehensive food and wine pairing experience in their restaurant. This is a great educational way to start out your Mendoza wine region experience.

LEFT PAGE, fresh-picked grapes are dumped into this receiving hopper with screw augur moving grapes to the lift conveyer on their way to destemming. ABOVE, after crushing the grapes, the juice is pumped into these huge 50,000-liter fermentation and cooling tanks at the Zuccardi Winery in Maipu.

Modern technology assists and enhances the winemaking process today, even in such old family wineries as Familia Zuccardi.

MENDOZA **MAIPÚ**

Winery (Bodega)

FAMILIA ZUCCARDI

33 Ruta Provincial
(Miapú)

011 (+54 261) 441.0000
info@FamiliaZuccardi.com

FamiliaZuccardi.com

English, Español, Português
12,000,000 bottles produced annually

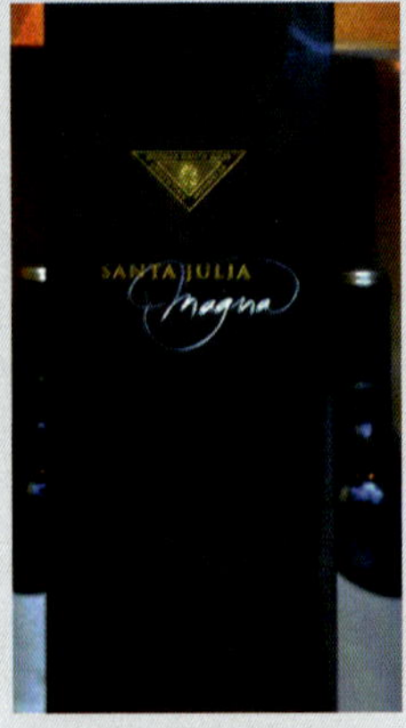

Michael's Favorite Pick
Santa Julia Magna - Malbec

Collection of Santa Julia Wines
The Santa Julia brand has 49 different wines
SantaJulia.com.ar

Their Top Seven High-End Wines

Santa Julia Magna
Malbec
Cabernet Sauvignon
Corte (a special blend of Cabernet Sauvignon, Malbec, Syrah)

Santa Julia Alambrado
Malbec
Cabernet Sauvignon
Chardonnay
Sauvignon Blanc

To get Santa Julia wines in the USA
Retailer: The Fresh Market
Online: SpecsOnline.com

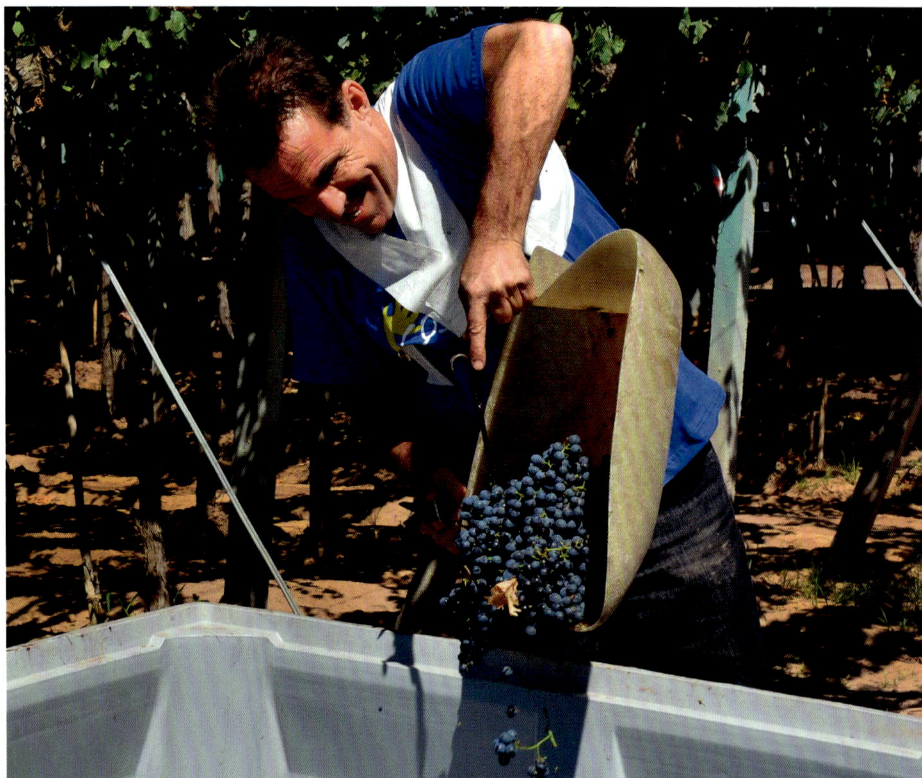

LET'S HARVEST TOGETHER

Familia Zuccardi offers you the opportunity to participate in harvesting grapes (photo above), and olive harvesting too. These are seasonal events. There is nothing like hands-on learning, understanding the tools and equipment, and how the perfect harvest occurs. These are followed by lunch and wine (or olive oil) tastings.

Grape harvesting is... February 15 to April 15
Olive harvesting is... May to July

Zuccardi offers many special and unique activities at their property... a picnic in their beautiful gardens under the shade of olive trees, an afternoon tea, cooking classes with their five-star chef, hands-on pruning of the vines, extensive winery tours, an interesting art gallery, and more. So many ways to enjoy and learn the secrets of winemaking. And they have two very nice restaurants on the premises as well.

FULL RANGE OF WINES

Familia Zuccardi has four brands: Zuccardi, Santa Julia, Malamado (fortified wines), and Aceite de Oliva (varietal olive oils), each of which has an extensive selection of wines. I am aware of at least 65 different wines. What is great about Zuccardi wines is the great price for quality. And even at the top end of their wines, the price is good.

Zuccardi Zeta is their super-premium wine. Why have an "A" wine, when you are a Zuccardi? Zeta is a beautiful blend of Malbec, Cabernet and Tempranillo, with 40 days in concrete tanks, extensive oak and bottle aging. At less than US $40!

Zuccardi Q (for Quality) is their second highest, offering four distinct premium wines, and yet the price is under US $20 imported to the USA.

Santa Julia Magna and ***Alambrado*** are the high-end wines in the Santa Julia brand. These wines have less oak influence, allowing much greater fruitiness, which I particularly find attractive for Malbec.

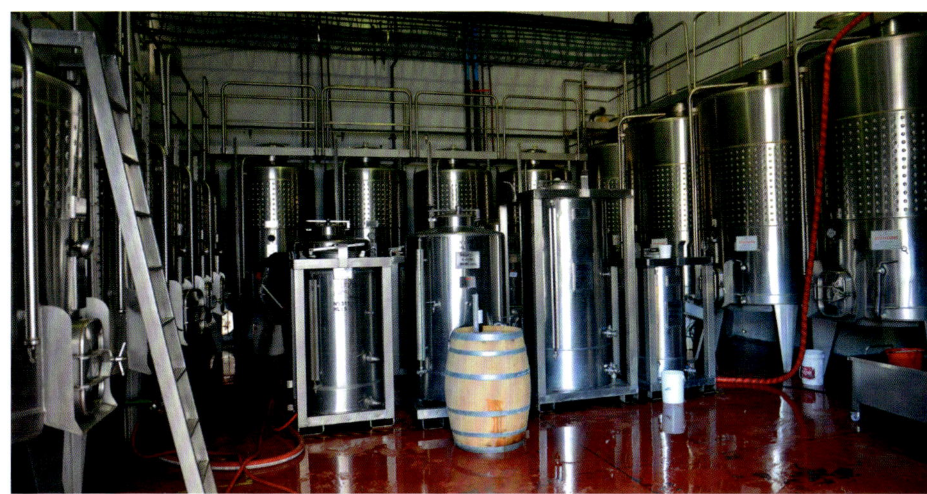

MENDOZA **MAIPÚ**

Winery (Bodega)

FAMILIA ZUCCARDI

33 Ruta Provincial
(Miapú)

011 (+54 261) 441.0000
info@FamiliaZuccardi.com

FamiliaZuccardi.com

English, Español, Português
12,000,000 bottles produced annually

GREAT WINE GREAT EDUCATION SUPER-GREAT EXPERIENCE

Familia Zuccardi is the perfect winery to begin your wine experience in Mendoza. This is a huge winery with 50 years of experience producing a wide variety of wines, and they have numerous educational experiences!

Familia Zuccardi was started by Alberto Zuccardi, an engineer, who in 1950 began an irrigation company experimenting with innovative methods of irrigating vineyards. To illustrate and prove his concepts, Zuccardi planted a vineyard in the bare desert of Maipù in 1963 to show his prospective customers his new systems... which resulted in the arid, infertile soil being transformed into a flourishing vineyard, impressing new customers.

Now, with thriving vineyards, he decided to build a winery and start making his own wine. Zuccardi continued introducing innovation to Argentina with the Italian Pergolas Trellising System for better canopy management and fruit ripeness.

Zuccardi has always maintained an experimental area in his winery, where several dozen new wines, varietals and techniques are always under development. Furthermore, Familia Zuccardi has five separate wineries, each operated autonomously with completely different teams. This is how Zuccardi can create super-premium wines alongside mass-market wines. Each winery has a different philosophy and objective, using different winemakers and grapes from their own select vineyards, to produce the different brands.

To further enhance their premium brands, small lot wines and their experiments, Familia Zuccardi has a small tank room to ferment and cold stabilize as little as 500 gallons (photo above). Innovation runs at the core of Zuccardi and it would not be unusual for you to run into more than one of the Zuccardis as they are restlessly running around the wineries and vineyards. They have very approachable and passionate personalities. Three generations are now active in various parts of this family operation.

Tours at Zuccardi are more than just another tank and barrel room viewing, Zuccardi offers extensive learning experiences, and the guides are extremely knowledgable and bilingual. My guide was a sommelier with an MBA in wine business management. This is no ordinary winery or educational experience.

They offer very interesting vineyard tours... you could walk, cycle or drive in an antique car through the vineyards; or fly, yes flying over them in an aerostat balloon. And the tours are deeply educational. For example, they will teach you how to recognize grape varietals by their unique leave designs, distinguish the taste of the different grapes, learn about the canopy systems they designed throughout their properties, and proper grape harvesting techniques.

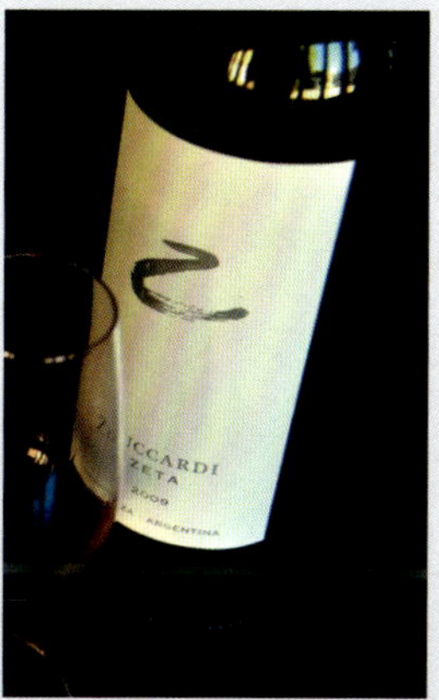

Michael's Favorite Pick
Familia Zuccardi - Zeta

Collection of Familia Zuccardi Wines
The Familia Zuccardi brand has 16 different Wines
ZuccardiWines.com

Their Top Five Super-Premium Wines

Zuccardi Zeta
Zeta (a special blend of Malbec, Cabernet Sauvignon, Tempranillo)

Zuccardi Q
Malbec
Tempranillo
Cabernet Sauvignon
Chardonnay

To get Zuccardi wines in the USA
Retailer: Whole Foods Market

Winery Restaurant

FAMILIA ZUCCARDI CASA DEL VISTANTE

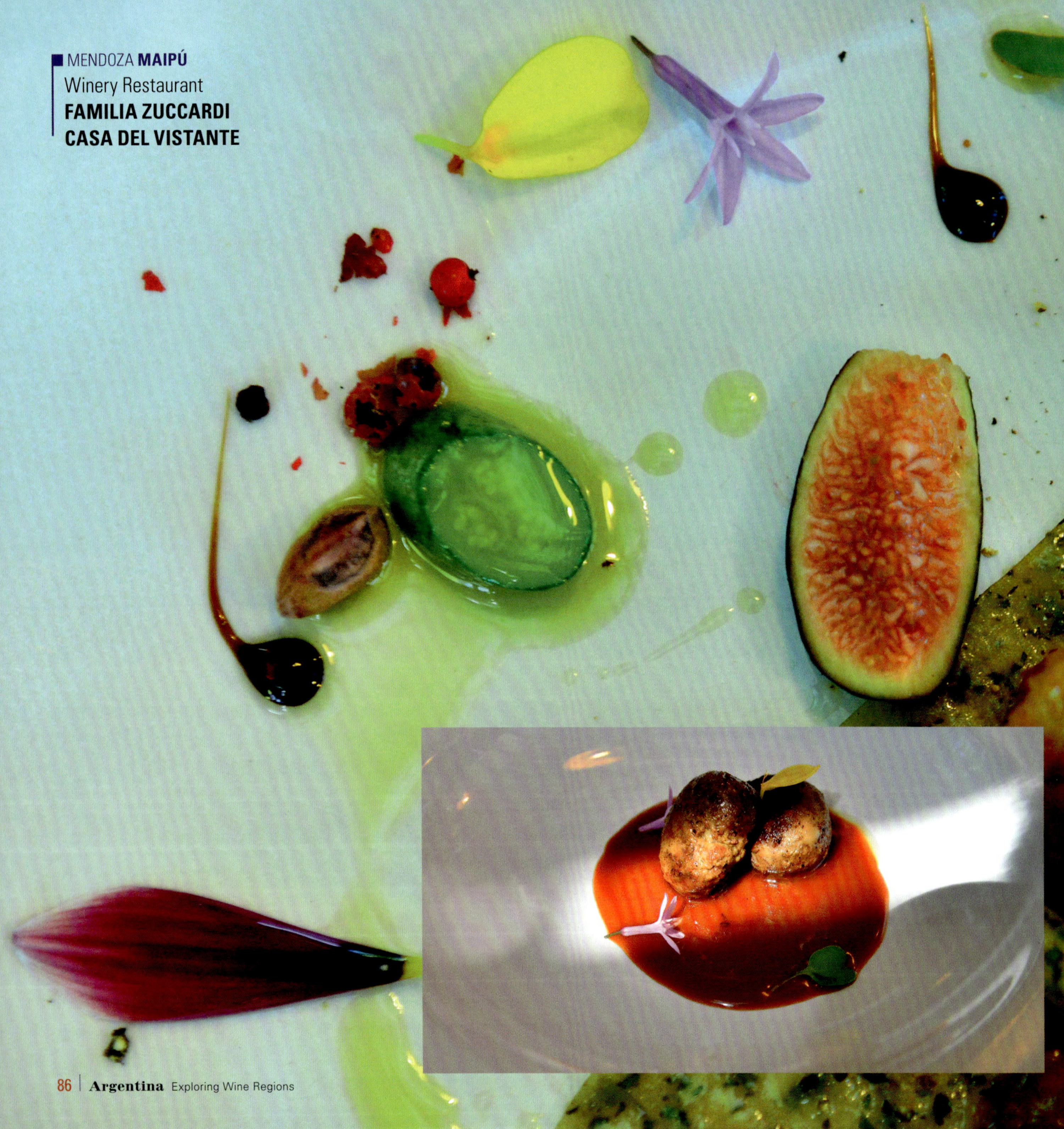

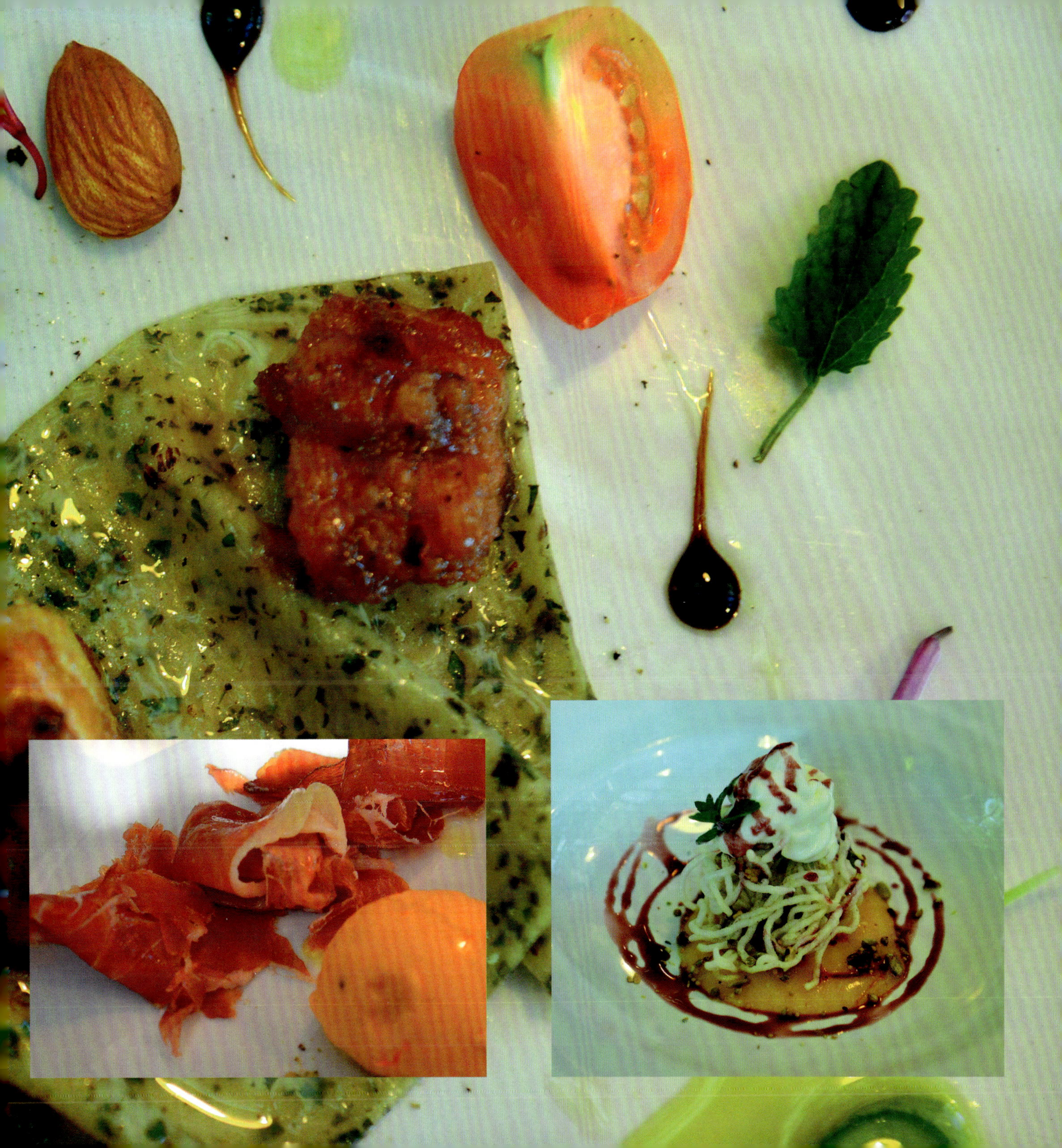

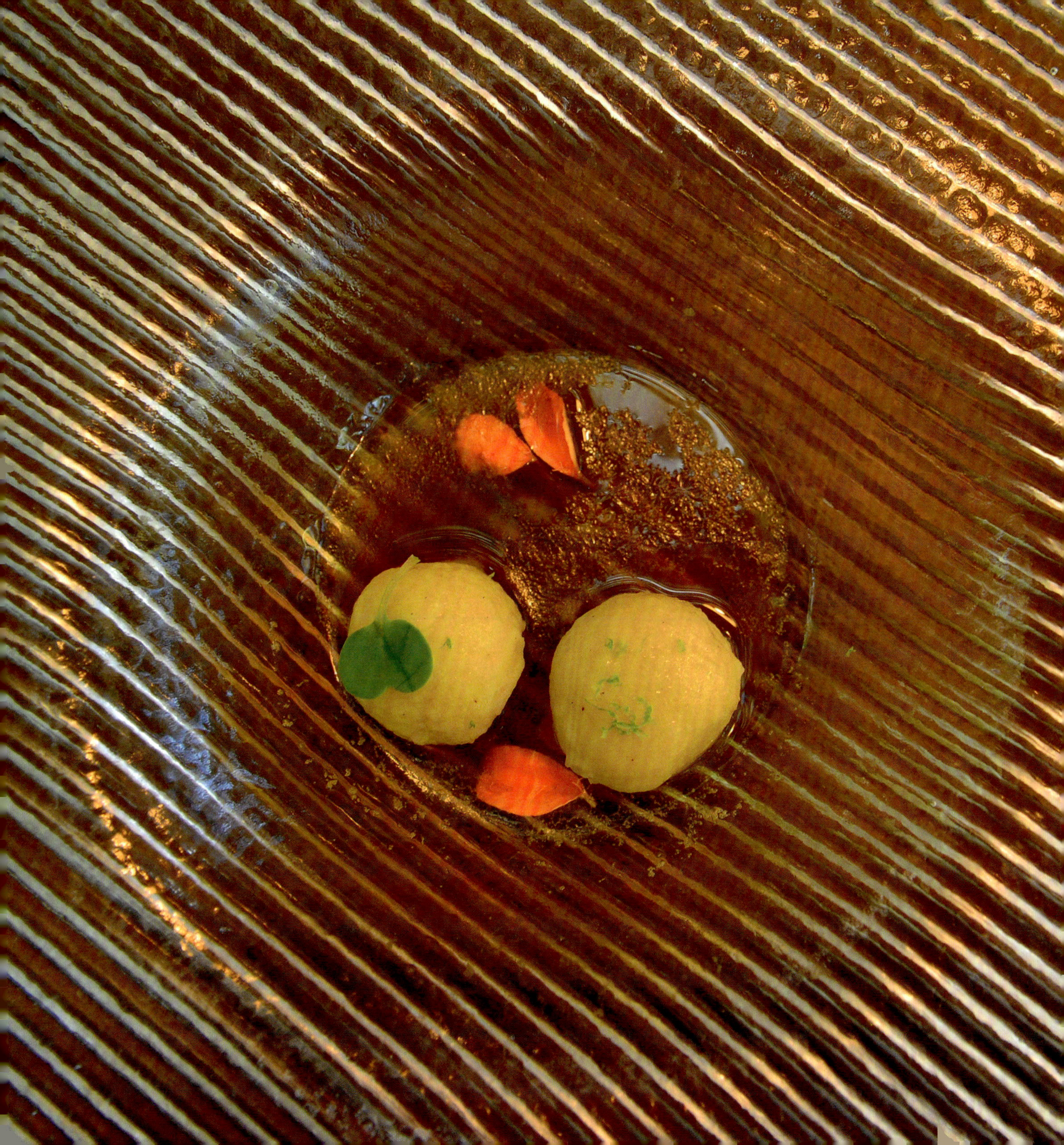

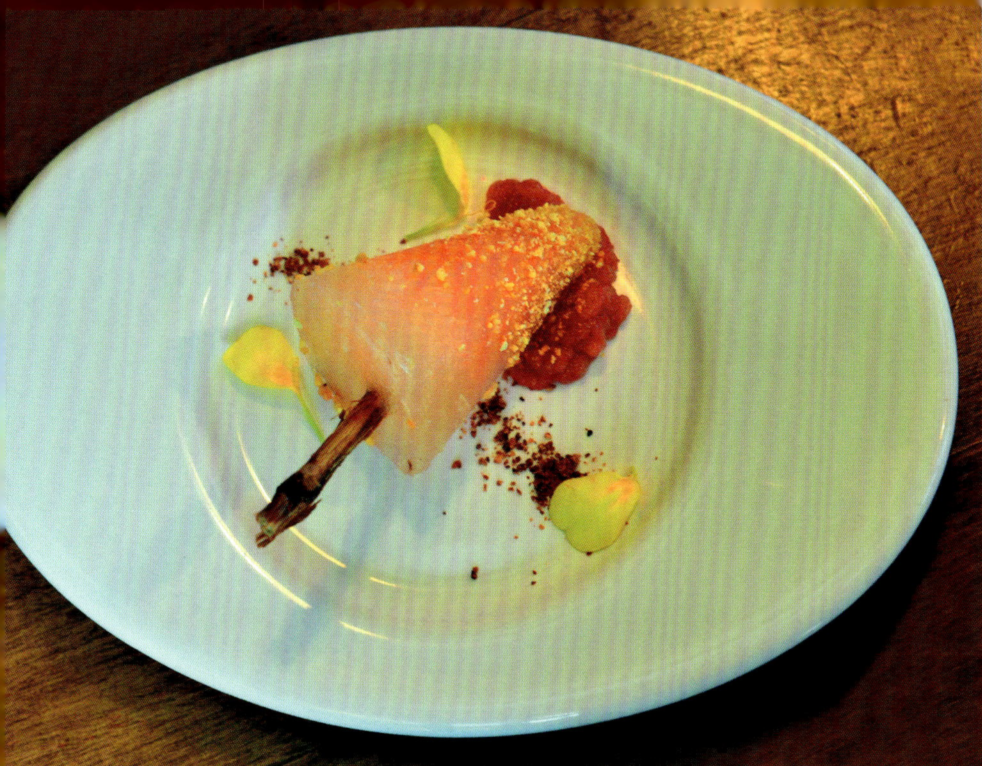

MENDOZA **MAIPÚ**

Winery Restaurant

FAMILIA ZUCCARDI
CASA DEL VISTANTE

33 Ruta Provincial
(Miapú)

011 (+54 261) 441.0000
reservas@FamiliaZuccardi.com

CasaDelVisitante.com

English, Español, Português

12 COURSE • 5 STAR • FOOD & WINE PAIRING • EXTRAORDINAIRE

Take in the photographs on these four pages, read the captions, they say it all... gourmet, unique, creative, decadent... designed by one of Argentina's top chefs, Matías Aldasoro.

Casa del Visitante is a five-star restaurant nestled in the Zuccardi vineyards, each table with views of the Andes Mountains.

Aldasoro and Zuccardi have prepared a comprehensive 12-course food & wine pairing experience in their restaurant. Complete with a sommelier, you will distinguish the masterful art of pairing wines in a detail that you may have never experienced before. With the depth and diversity of the Zuccardi wines, each course is impeccably paired. What I am trying to tell you is this is an experience you do not want to miss.

Also, ***Casa del Visitante*** offers a traditional Argentine menu of empanadas, barbecue, salads, and grilled vegetables.

Or, simply enjoy a relaxing afternoon on the vine-covered patio with a glass of wine.

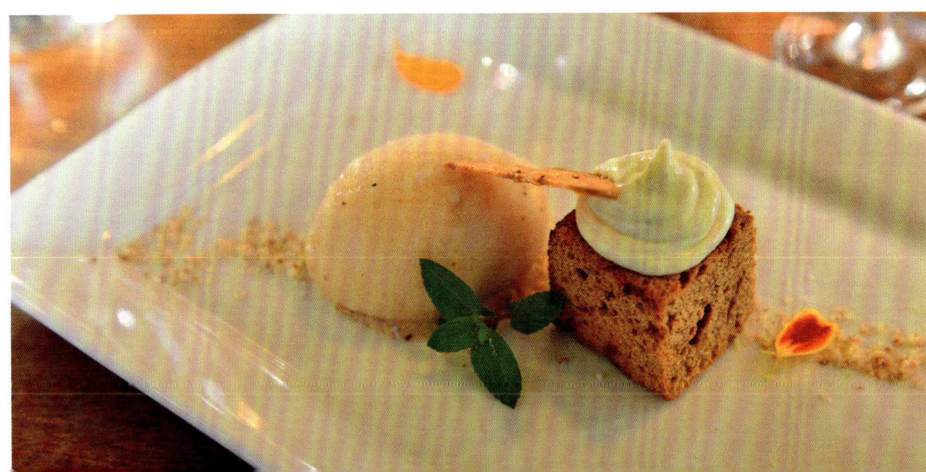

PREVIOUS PAGES 86-87
Fresh Pasta of Lemon Balm & Mint,
with caramelized sweetbreads,
fruits, nuts and edible flowers
Wine Pairing: Zuccardi Serie A Syrah

INSET PHOTOS LEFT TO RIGHT
Lamb Kidneys
with toffee sauce
Wine Pairing: Santa Julia Extra Brut

Salmorejo Ice Cream
with acorn ham and yolk
Wine Pairing: Santa Julia Extra Brut

Crunch Rice Tuille
with coconut foam and peach sauce
Wine Pairing: Santa Julia Tardio

THESE PAGES 88-89 - CLOCKWISE
Lemon Gnocchi
filled with trout and bull's tail au jus
Wine Pairing: Alambrado Sauvignon Blanc

Frozen Grapefruit & Thyme Lollipop
with strawberry and chilli gelée,
on a dried grape vine stick.
Wine Pairing: Santa Julia Tardio

Spiced Bread
topped with blue cheese purée,
with pear & nutmeg ice cream
Wine Pairing: Malamado Viognier

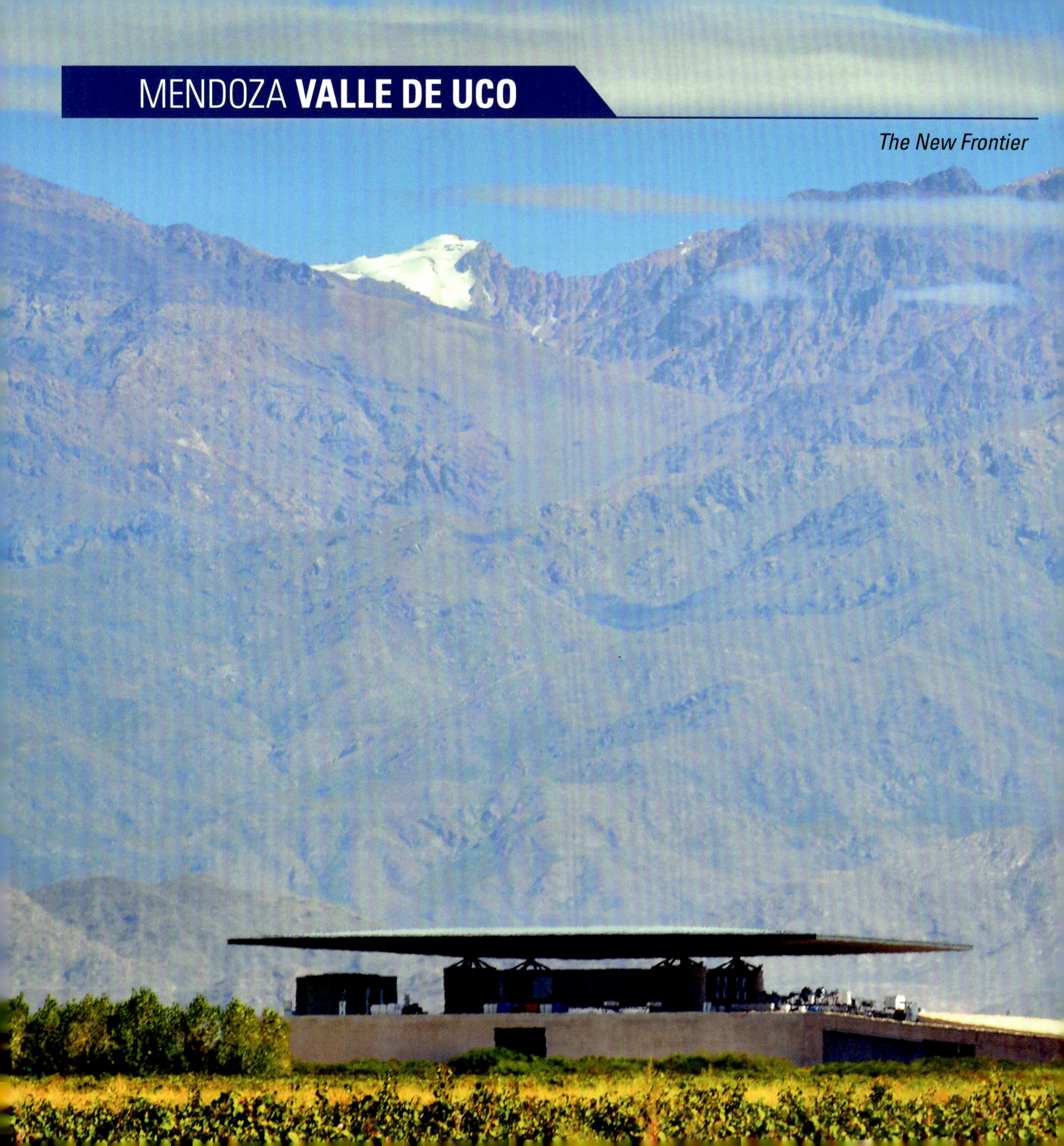

MENDOZA **VALLE DE UCO**

The New Frontier

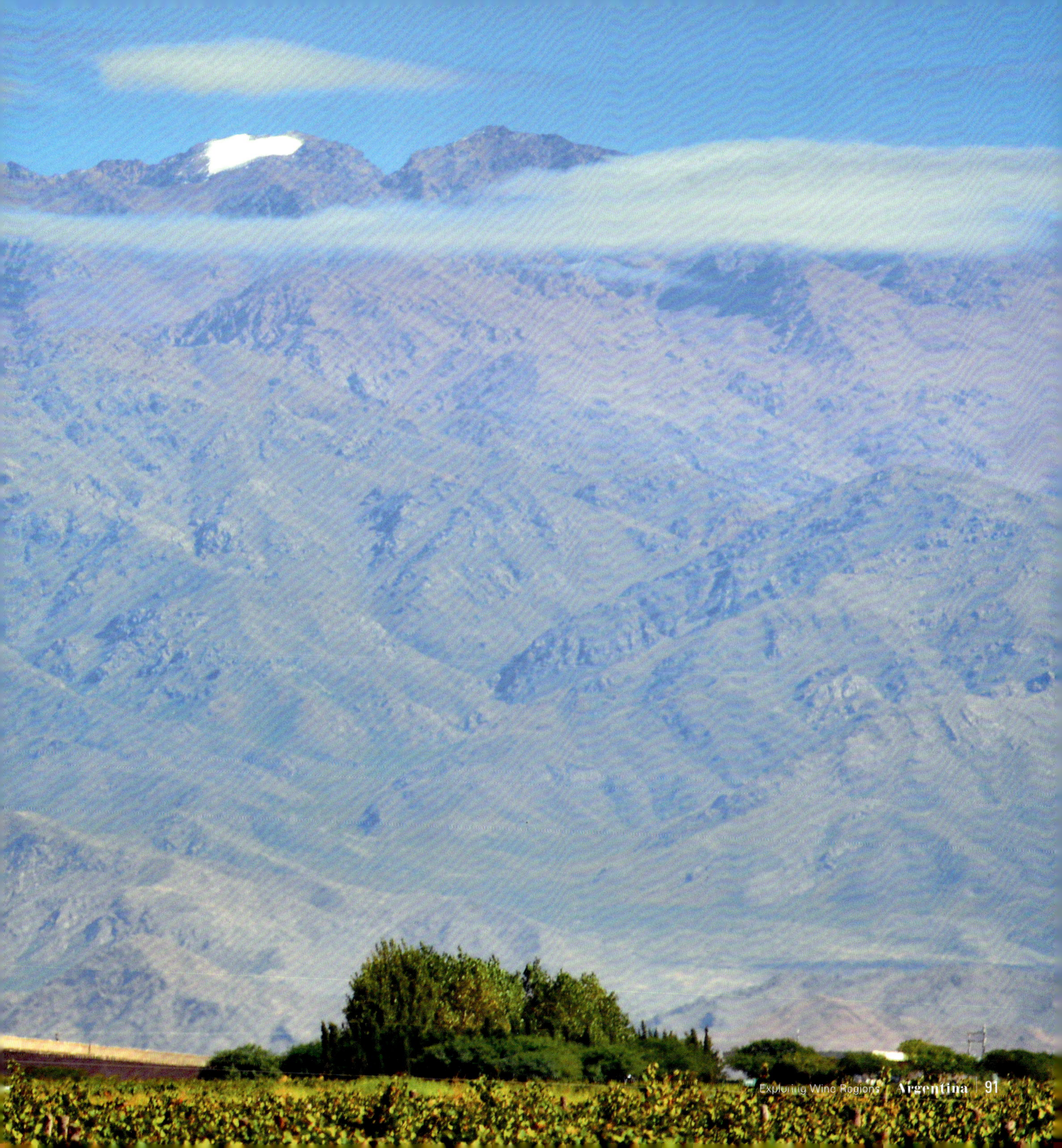

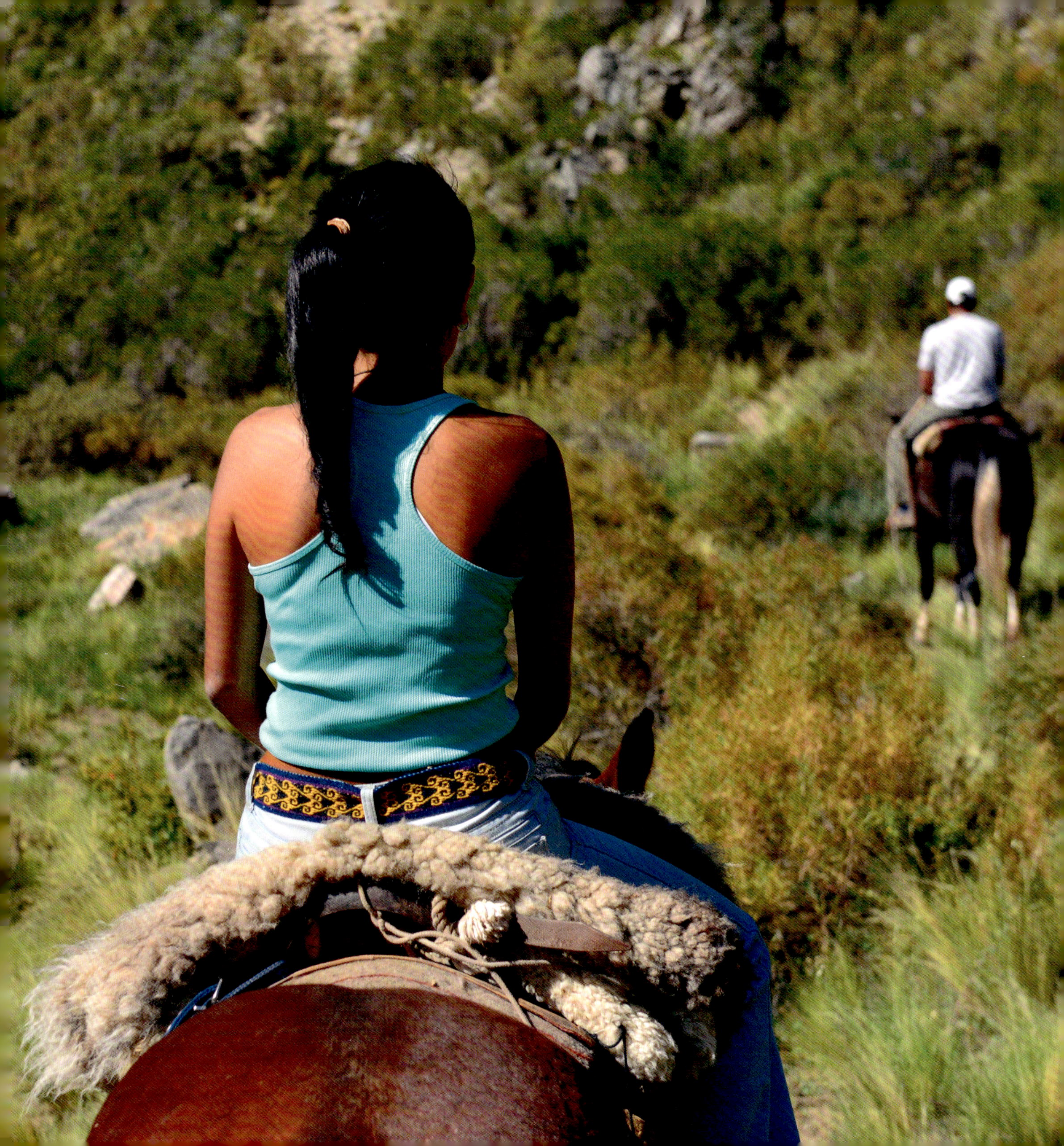

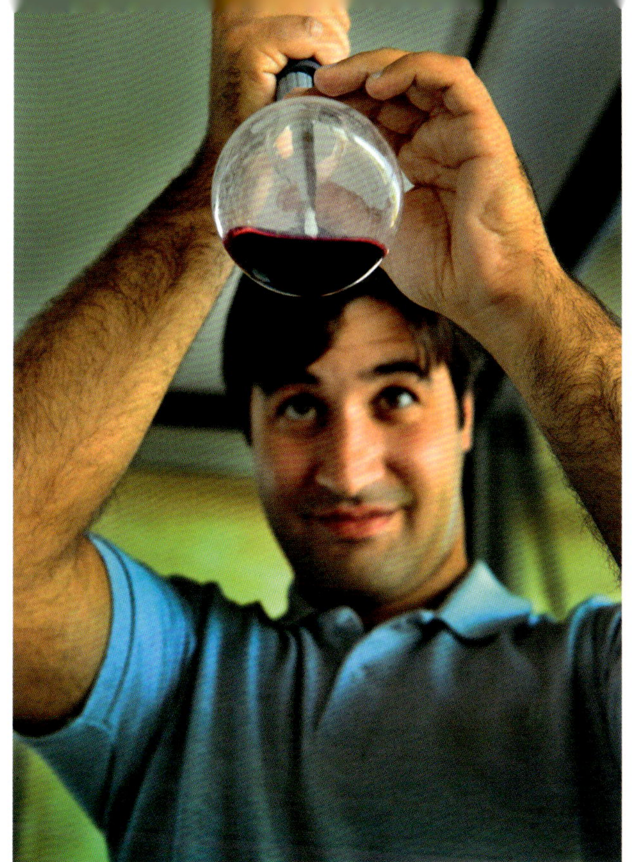

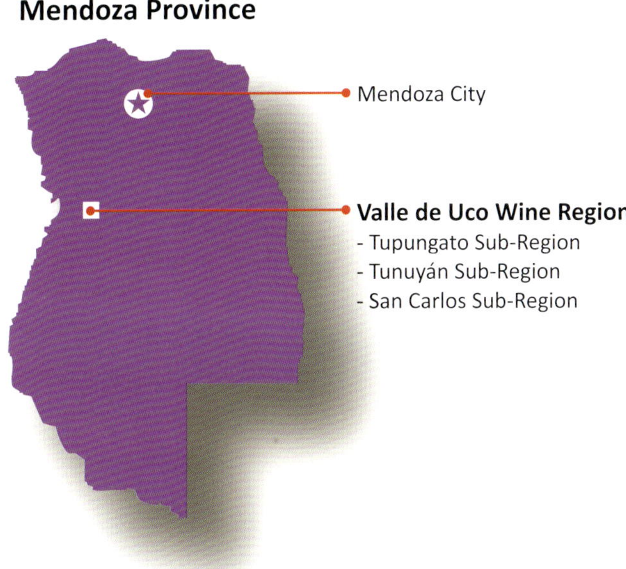

MENDOZA'S NEW FRONTIER

It is like the Gold Rush of California – winemakers have struck "gold" and are claiming stakes in Valle de Uco with a newly discovered terroir that many are considering to be the best-of-the-best of Mendoza's Wine Regions.

Nestled in the base of the Andes Mountains, about an hour's drive southwest of Mendoza city, Valle de Uco is at an even higher elevation than the famed Luján de Cuyo, ranging from 3,000 to 5,000 feet elevations with its rock, sand and clay soils, extreme day/night temperature ranges, pristine air quality, and fresh snow-melt Andes water entering the valley through its magnificent rivers. Add to this a long growing season, with harvest late into the fall (primarily April) with fruit hanging on the vines through a beautiful palette of yellow, orange and red autumn leaf transformation.

This special micro-climate is producing an elegance to wine that has grabbed the attention of top winemakers around the world. From its Mendoza neighbors of Santiago Achaval and Sebastian Zuccardi, to Napa Valley's Paul Hobbs, to the far distances of Bordeaux's famous Barons de Rothschild and Michel Rolland... all of these notable winemakers have now established themselves in Valle de Uco and are investing in the future of this new frontier.

Plus, new and innovative vintners are arriving too, planting vineyards and building state-of-the-art wineries at a rapid pace, using the latest viticultural and winemaking technology. And, the few old established families of the valley, who already knew, are now seizing this opportunity to expand and explore new styles of wines and fame.

It is not just a new elegant style to Malbec, Uco is producing Cabernet Sauvignon that rivals Napa and Bordeaux, in a new Argentine style that will make you smile. It is not about asking for a Malbec from Argentina anymore. It is now a distinction of choosing, for example, a Zuccardi Altamira, a distinct Malbec from a micro-region of the La Consulta sub-appellation in the valley of Uco.

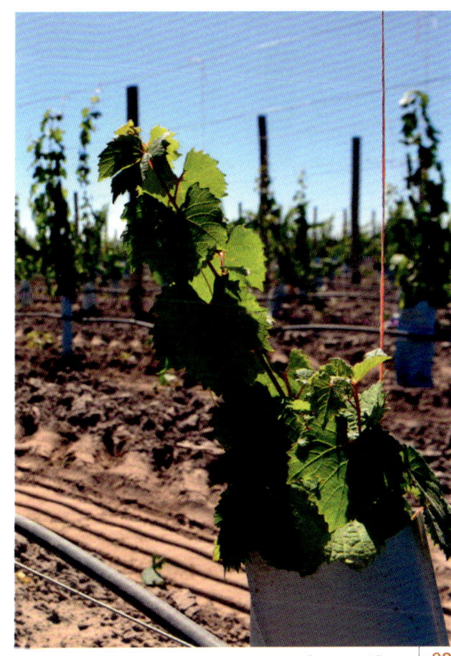

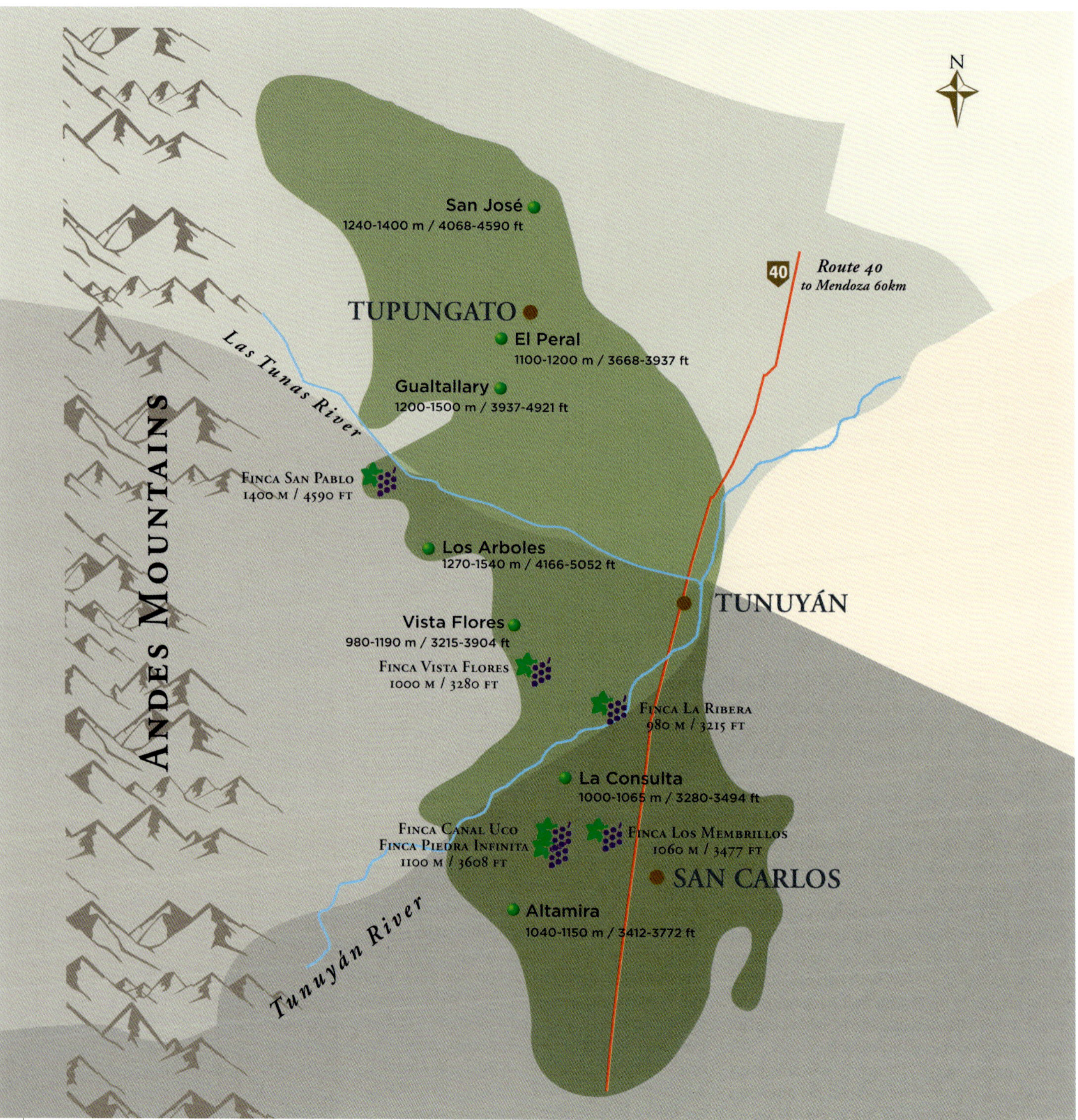
N
San José
1240-1400 m / 4068-4590 ft
Route 40
to Mendoza 60km
40
TUPUNGATO
El Peral
1100-1200 m / 3668-3937 ft
Gualtallary
1200-1500 m / 3937-4921 ft
Las Tunas River
Finca San Pablo
1400 m / 4590 ft
Los Arboles
1270-1540 m / 4166-5052 ft
TUNUYÁN
Andes Mountains
Vista Flores
980-1190 m / 3215-3904 ft
Finca Vista Flores
1000 m / 3280 ft
Finca La Ribera
980 m / 3215 ft
La Consulta
1000-1065 m / 3280-3494 ft
Finca Canal Uco
Finca Piedra Infinita
1100 m / 3608 ft
Finca Los Membrillos
1060 m / 3477 ft
SAN CARLOS
Altamira
1040-1150 m / 3412-3772 ft
Tunuyán River

HIGHER GROUND

Adjacent to the Andes Mountains, Valle de Uco takes on three different sub-regions divided distinctly by two rivers flowing from the mountains, the Tunuyán and Las Tunas Rivers. These rivers, as we will discuss later, are the source of the contents of the soils found in this valley, as the rivers have brought them from deep in the mountains for centuries through their year-round flow of glacier and snow melt.

The three sub-regions of Valle de Uco are **Tupungato** in the north, defined by being north of the Las Tunas River. **Tunuyán** in the center, defined by the Las Tunas River to the north and Tunuyán River to the south. The southern region is **San Carlos**, defined as being south of the Tunuyán River. The map to the left will give you a clear picture.

I particularly like this map, provided by Familia Zuccardi, as it shows both the three sub-regions and their dividing rivers. The map also shows where Zuccardi has planted vineyards throughout Valle de Uco over the past decade in what today has become landmarks for the most spectacular sub-appellations where winemakers are producing their finest wines.

Within each sub-region, sub-appellations are being established to identify further qualities and uniqueness of the terroir; defining unique flavor profiles in the resulting wines from each place. In Tupungato, **Gualtallary** is the main sub-appellation where elevations are reaching 3,900 to 4,900 feet, with soils formed from the sediments of the Las Tunas River basin and other streams in the foothills. In Tunuyán, **Vista Flores**, the main sub-appellation rising from 2,600 to 3,300 feet, has soils coming from the sediments of the streams and alluvial cones near the Andes. In San Carlos, **La Consulta** is the main sub-appellation with its soil containing lots of rocks and pebbles dragged by the river when it emerged from the Andes mountains 200 million years ago.

Further, **Altamira** is the most northern part of the **La Consulta** sub-appellation and has become notable terroir for Malbec. This is the location of Achaval-Ferrer's vineyard that awarded them with the highest scoring wine ever for Argentina... 98 points for their Finca Altamira Malbec.

Because of the distinguishing qualities of these sub-appellations, vintners are beginning to put these identifying marks on their bottles to acknowledge their unique qualities. This is what you want to look for in choosing your better wines.

Tupungato is the largest town in Valle de Uco, with a population of 43,000, followed by Tunuyán and San Carlos, populations 42,000 and 4,000, respectively. Outside these busy towns, the area has small rural villages, and is mostly agriculture (of wine grapes, peaches, olives, etc.) with some very noteworthy wineries, delicious restaurants and beautiful hotels.

In the pages that follow, I have organized Valle de Uco by these three sub-regions, starting from the south, moving north. Most of the growth, wineries, restaurants and hotels are located in the central region of Tunuyán.

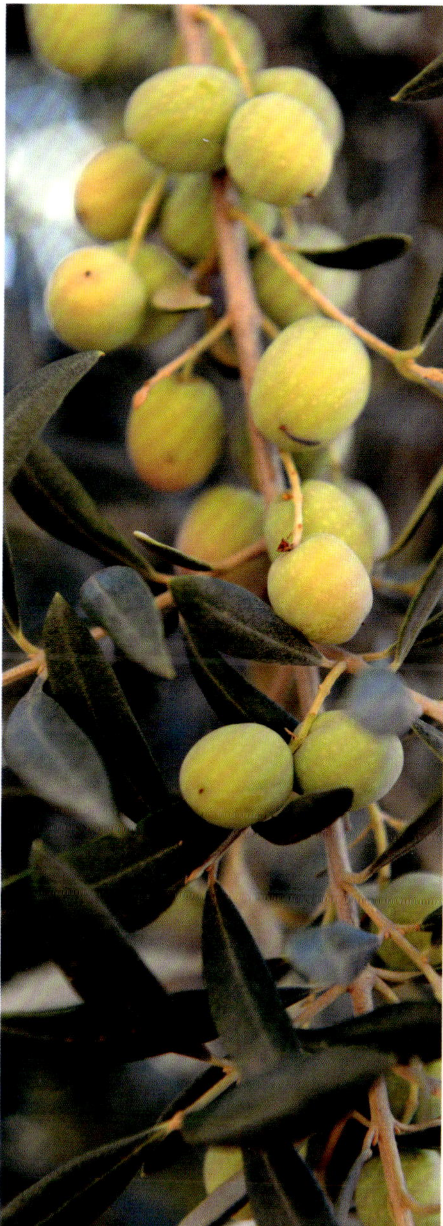

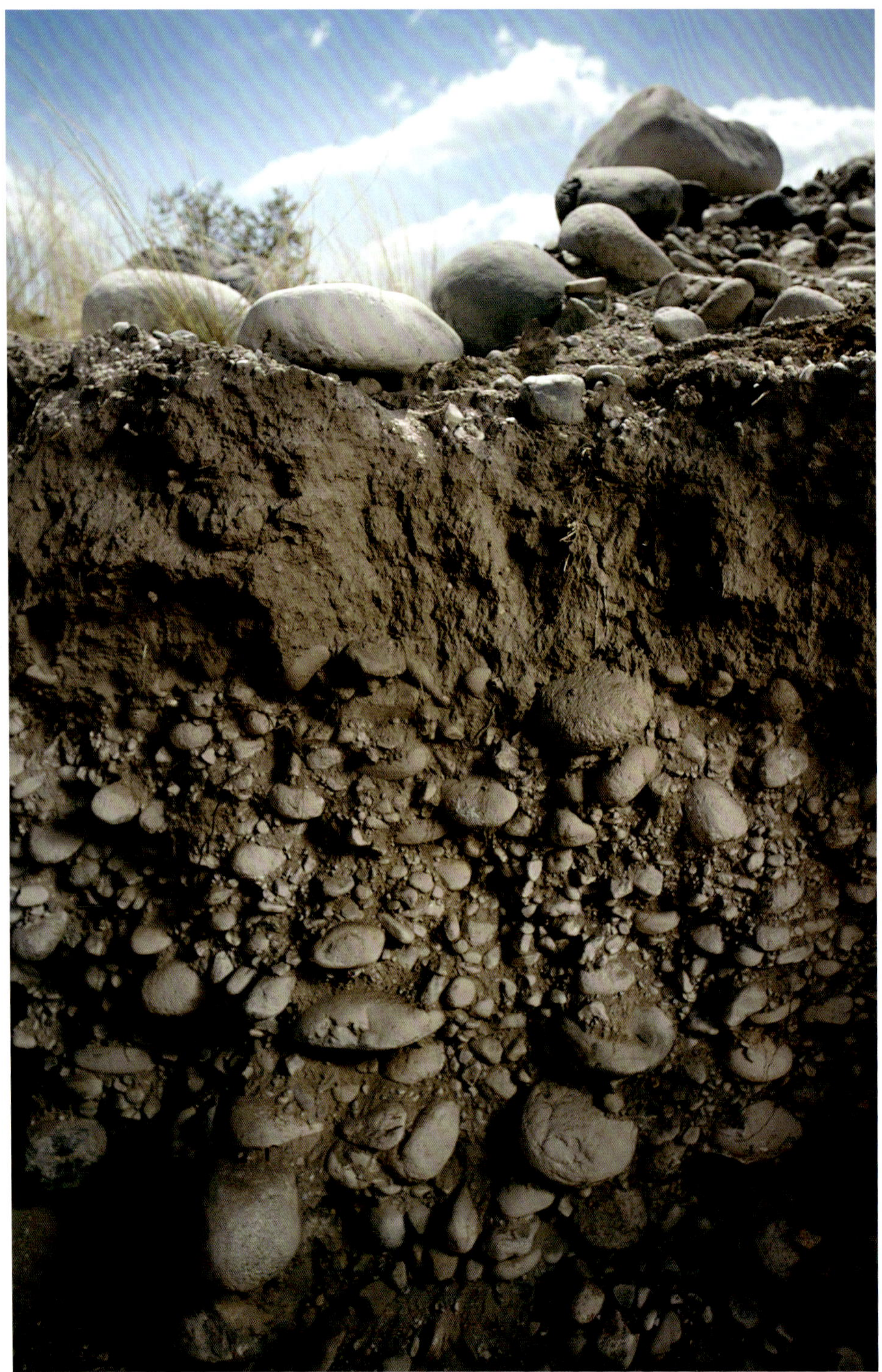

THE AGRONOMIST VIEW UNDERGROUND

After digging more than 500 calicatas in Valle de Uco, Agronomist Martin Di Stefano, is getting a clear picture of the underground. Calicatas are holes dug as test pits to explore the minerals in the subsoil.

Calicatas in vineyards are generally dug four to six feet deep, three feet wide and 20 feet long - think of this size fitting in-between a vineyard row.

Agronomists are the scientists educated in agricultural engineering to study the soil integrated with climate, weather, plant genetics, physiology, and soil science.

Di Stefano is Zuccardi's agronomist for their Valle de Uco vineyards, where he regularly digs holes in the middle of their vineyards to see how the roots are growing, the moisture, the structure of the soil, and ultimately identifying the unique environments as micro-vineyards. This leads to harvesting and then processing the grapes in smaller batches from specific sections of their vineyards.

With all that being said, you can imagine that Di Stefano would have a very difficult time characterizing sub-regions as having similar characteristics. Tupungato, Tunuyán and San Carlos are too big and heterogeneous. Even their sub-appellations, although much smaller areas, are very complex and have many different terroirs inside of them. To Di Stephano, even a single vineyard has dramatically different soil characteristics from one side to another.

What is most exciting to me seeing all this, is that we have come a long way from a generic "Argentina Malbec" to vintners distinguishing the quality characteristics in the bottle and on the label. For all too long, Malbec from Argentina, has been labeled simply "Argentina Malbec." In recent years through the fame of Mendoza, the Malbecs have become labeled "Mendoza Malbec" for good marketing purposes. In addition, winemakers are further labeling Valle de Uco. And now we are coming to a new era of distinction with sub-appellations and creating special wines from unique vineyards.

MENDOZA **SAN CARLOS**

*Including the Sub-Appellations of **La Consulta** and **Altamira** in This Sub-Region of **Southern Valle de Uco***

Trying to give us some generic description of the underground, Di Stefano takes on defining some of the common characteristics of five of the Valle de Uco sub-appellations...

Altamira (San Carlos sub-region) has very unique characteristics in its soil. All the area is inside the alluvial cone of the Tunuyan river. It is a typical alluvial soil, with at least two layers. The topsoil is a sandy loamy soil, and the depth of that layer is normally less than three feet. The subsoil is the layer of rounded edge stones. The stone is mainly granite, and is always covered with calcium carbonate (lime). In the matrix between the rocks we find an amount of clay near to 5%. This clay helps keep the moisture and make the roots go to the interface with the stones. It's easy to find very large rocks. The altitude of the place is about 3,600 feet above sea level. This terroir gives the wine a very unique mineral character. The typical Malbec from Altamira is long and vertical, with good structure. Not very concentrated, and with a chalky note.

Although **La Consulta** (San Carlos) is very close to Altamira, and both places have the same geological origin, the soil is very different. While Altamira is in the top of the alluvial cone, La Consulta is in the bottom. So, the soil is deeper and it is more difficult to find rocks. The rocks are there, however deeper. The soil is typically sandy, and we find the lime mixed up in the sand. The altitude is a little lower, around 3,300 feet. And because of this, the microclimate of La Consulta is warmer than Altamira. The wine in this area normally shows very soft and rounded tannins. In the mouth, it is wider than Altamira's wine, because of the temperature and the soil depth. And the expression of the fruit is also different. It is more common to find black fruit in La Consulta's wine.

Gualtallary (Tupungato) is a very complex zone. It is a big district, with different terroirs in it. The main factor here is the altitude. We start from 3,900 feet up to 5,100 feet. This is the place where the higher vineyards are planted at this latitude. The soil is also alluvial, and there are some units with the typical two-layers configuration. The topsoil is always sandy. This is a very sandy area, because there were also sediments carried by the wind (at that altitude, the zonda wind is very strong). And in the topsoil we find different expressions of the calcaire. In some places there is a hard and compacted layer of lime and clay called "caliche" in Spanish, and in others the lime is covering the rounded edge stones, like in Altamira. The difference is that there are not big rocks here. The river that formed this alluvial movement (Las Tunas river) hasn't had the energy enough to move very big rocks. The wine coming from Gualtallary shows the identities of high altitude: higher acidity, red fruit, some vegetal character, and the mineral texture coming from the lime.

San Pablo (Tunuyán) is another very similar region. While Gualtallary lies on the left bank of Las Tunas river, San Pablo is on the right. The altitude is around 4,600 feet, and the soil is less sandy, and we don't find the caliche, but the typical two-layer soil with stones covered with lime.

Vista Flores (Tunuyán) is also a very big and complex zone. There are many Vista Flores. There is a zone very close to the left bank of Tunuyan river, with typical fluvial soil (perfect rounded and small stones, with no lime cover, and sandy and silty topsoils); there is the "medium" Vista Flores, with deep sandy soils, and there is the higher part, where we begin to find some little stones mixed up in the soil. These stones don't have the edges rounded, the erosion of the water during the carriage was weaker. Just a few spots have calcareous stones. Once again, the wines will show these differences.

As you can see, Valle de Uco is a very interesting wine region to explore. Clearly a must-go place for wine lovers. An education in the finer aspects of winemaking. And the future vision of quality winemaking in Argentina.

By the way, *above the ground* Valle de Uco is a spectacularly beautiful landscape as well.

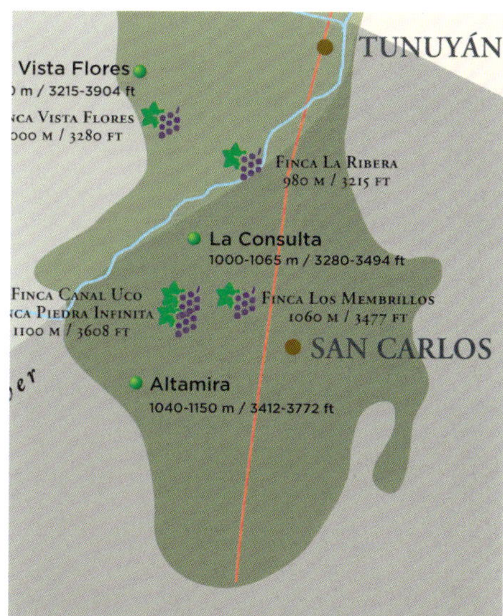

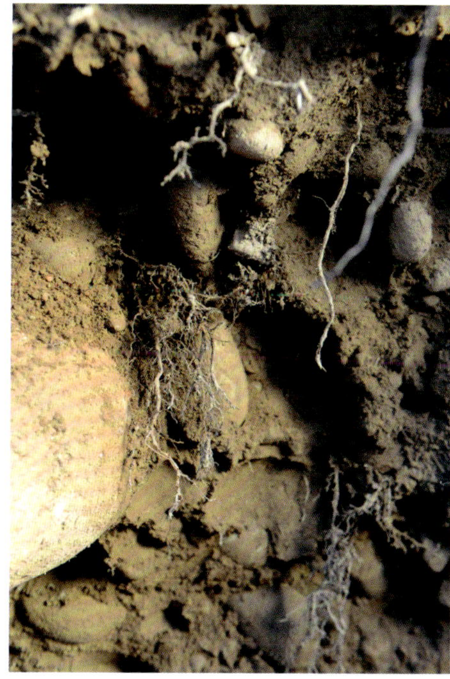

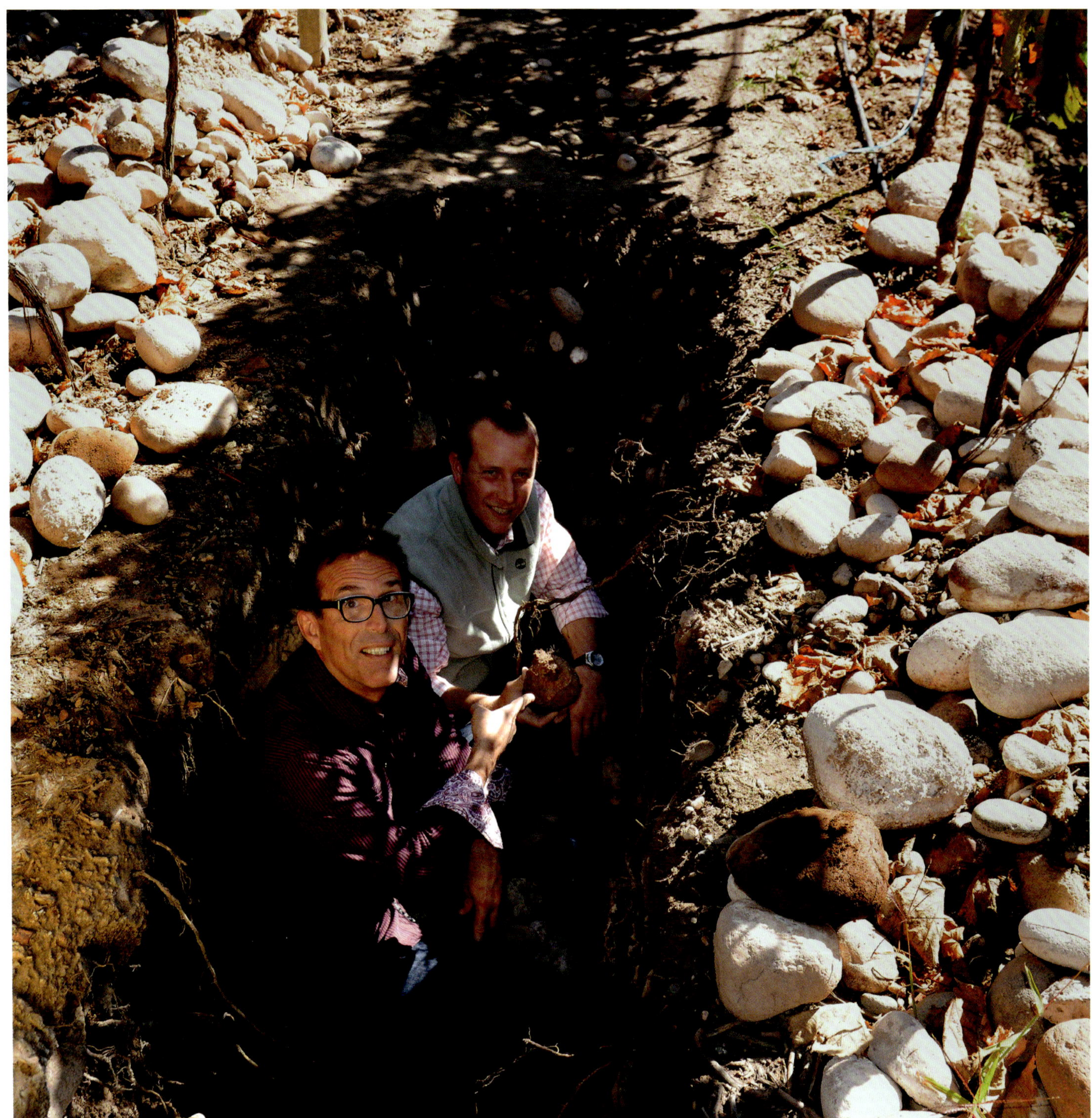

REVEALING ALTAMIRA

My turn to dig in the soil (photo left page). In the Zuccardi *Finca Canal Uco* vineyard in Altamira, I uncovered what makes the soil here so special, and an epiphany into the magic of Altamira wines.

As discussed in the previous pages, Altamira is located beside the Tunuyán River, along the south, downhill banks of the river as it enters the valley. The Tunuyán River is the largest river flowing into Valle de Uco and begins deep in the Andes Mountains from numerous streams surrounding Tupungato Mountain (elevation 21,555') on the Chile and Argentina border. Due to the size and strength of this river, numerous rocks and limestone have been brought into the valley. With Altamira and La Consulta, located on the downhill slope of the river, this area has been filled with these rocks and lime over the past 200 million years.

Lime is a magic ingredient to amazing Malbec. Malbec roots seek out the lime, wrap themselves around the lime-coated rocks and dig for any lime found in the soil, absorbing its nutrients, and creating a flavor profile in Malbec like none other.

I was very inspired about Valle de Uco and the future of Argentine wines when I met Sebastian Zuccardi, grandson of the founder of the prominent Familia Zuccardi Winery in Maipù.

Ten years ago when Sebastian joined in the family business, he had his sights on Valle de Uco. He noticed that the grapes his family was buying from different growers in this area were different and some things were special about the quality of the wines... finesse, freshness and better color.

Then, in 2005 he decided to plant their very first vineyard in the Vista Flores sub-appellation of Tunuyán, and continued to expand to the other sub-regions in Valle de Uco. La Consulta was becoming well-known with its many old vineyards, so Zuccardi put his focus on this area and began to produce what was at that time their most premium wine yet, the Zuccardi Zeta.

In 2007, he discovered Altamira, this very small section of the La Consulta sub-appellation, and began planting, studying the soils, the micro-climate, and how to choose and manage the different varieties in each place. Seeing the big rocks in Altamira covered with lime got his attention. And with the knowledge he gained, he pushed the limits of what is possible and continued to higher and higher ground, taking them to planting their San Pablo vineyards in Tunuyán.

Now, the Zuccardi wines have expanded to five super-premium labels being produced in Valle de Uco, and the building of a winery and restaurant (open August 2015) on their property in Altamira.

And they are still learning and searching!

LEFT PAGE, Agronomist Martin Di Stefano and Michael Higgins inside a calicata in the Zuccardi *Finca Canal Uco* vineyard in Altamira, the same vineyard also pictured below.

LEFT TO RIGHT BELOW, **First Calicata** has *Calcareous Clay* soil, the deeper soil found in Altamira. The topsoil layer is around three feet deep, and the texture of the soil is sandy-loamy, with a higher amount of clay (close to 10%-15%). **Second Calicata**, less than 100 feet from the first calicatas, has *Supercalcareous* soil, with no topsoil, and the fine soil layer is very thin (around eight inches). Under that, the rounded edge stones are covered with a very strong layer of lime. **Third Vineyard** with blue tape separates the two Calicatas soil differences for unique picking and processing of the grapes.

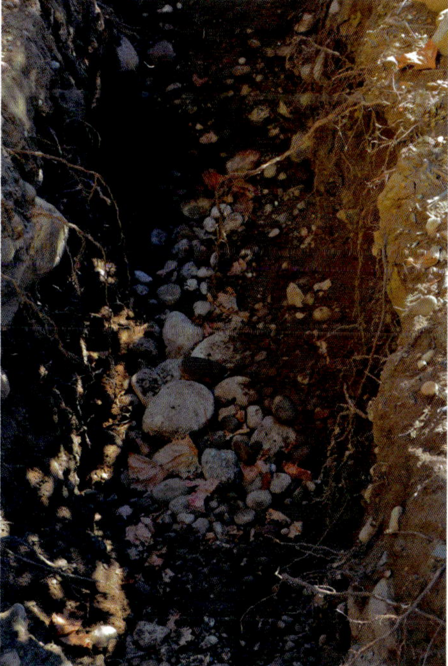

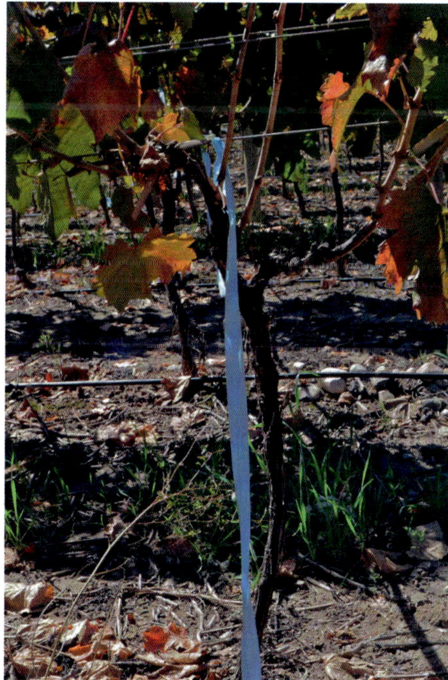

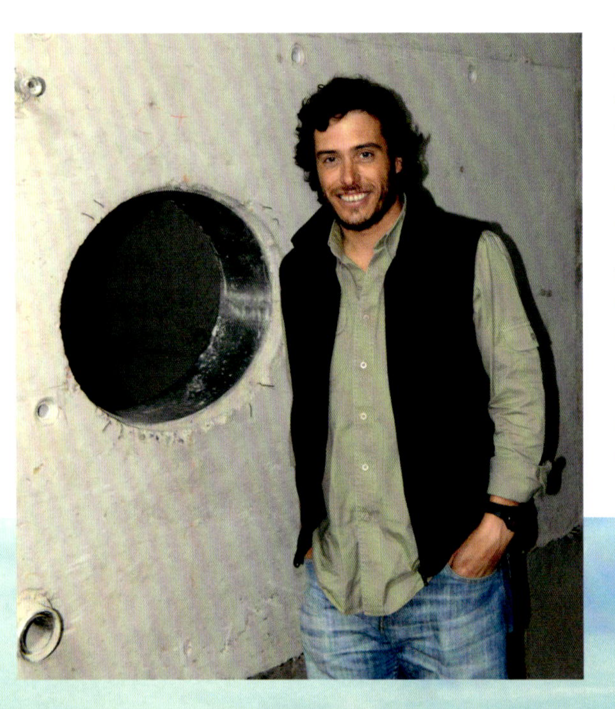

Building a new winery within their prized Altamira Vineyards (photo below) came with more than just the education and experience of discovering this terroir, it includes the many years of experimenting and winemaking expertise that allows Zuccardi to build a unique winery to produce the ultimate qualities in their wines... a 100% all natural concrete winery!

Sebastian Zuccardi (pictured left underground the construction of his new winery), decided to build a complete different kind of winery due to a series of practical advantages and also some important philosophical aspects to the material concrete.

Zuccardi once bought concrete tanks for his Maipù R&D facility for economic reasons. Two of the tanks did not have epoxy, and from the experimentation with all natural concrete, he realized that in order for him to create wines that express their place, such as Valle de Uco, he needed natural materials that strongly respect the place's identity. Zuccardi discovered several advantages to achieve this through concrete versus stainless steel.

Temperature: concrete walls (seven inches) are thicker than those of stainless steel tanks. This not only allows reducing energy consumption, it also allows dynamic fermentation with much softer temperature changes, which is key when working with native yeast.

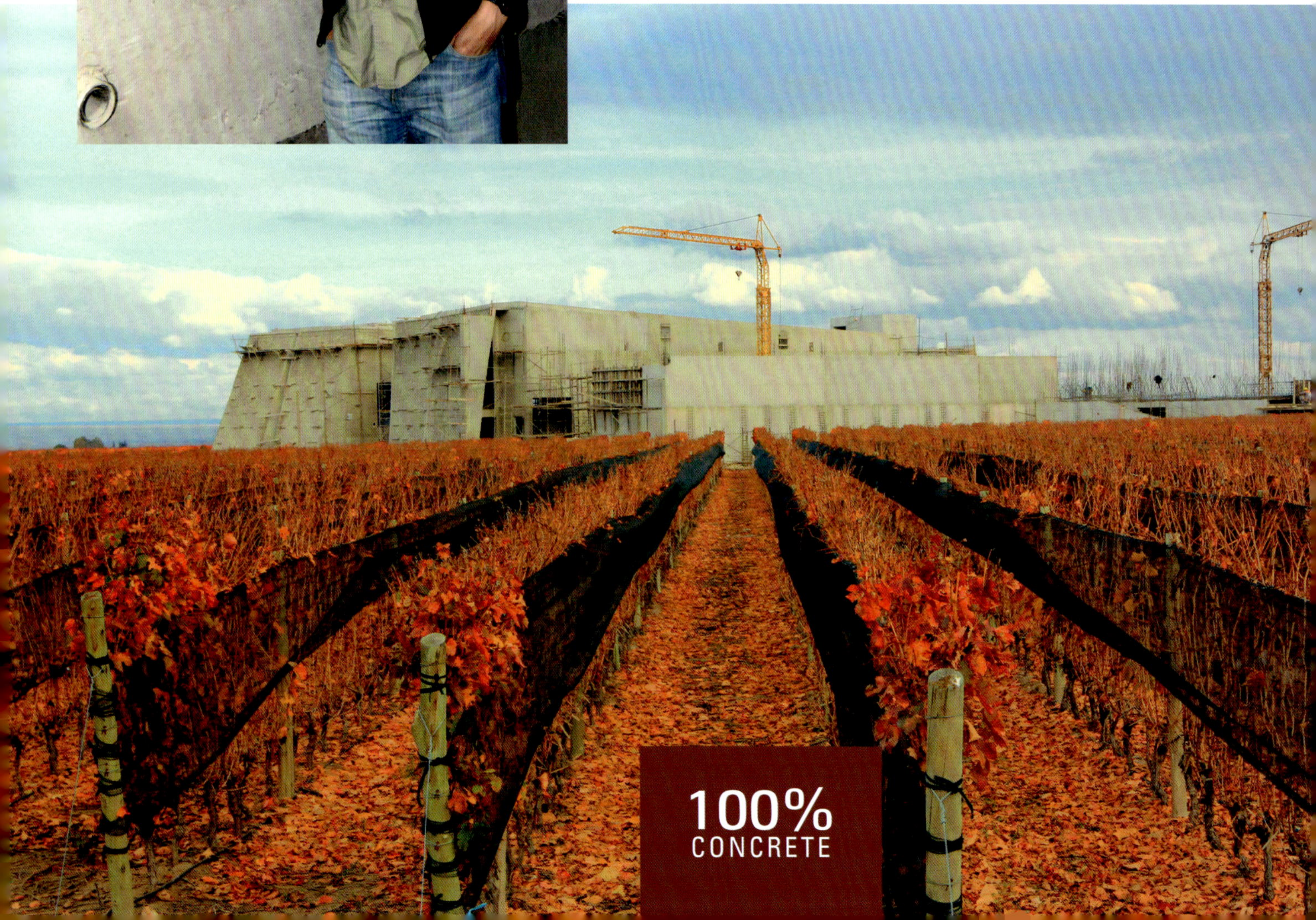

100%
CONCRETE

Micro-Oxygenation: since concrete is a natural and porous material, micro-oxygenation is produced through its walls, which allows the entrance of oxygen during fermentation. This is important for yeasts and also a key process for wine aging since in its micro-oxygenation it allows a development of the wine in the vats, avoiding using barrels that might add oxygen as well as aromas and flavors of the wood. This is key in the style of wines Zuccardi is looking for today. For this process to take place, it is fundamental to avoid the use of epoxy, since fermenting on vats with epoxy would be the same as doing it in a glass container.

Limpidity: since concrete is a natural element and has no electric load, turbidity is lower during fermentation and aging. A natural process takes place and wines are preserved better.

Cleanliness is one of the great doubts about concrete. In Zuccardi's experience, it is just a matter of punctuality to clean and take care of them. He only works with pressurized hot water and a brush, and so far they have never had any problems.

Troncoconical Vats: the shape of the vats is something Zuccardi has worked on extensively. He first bought square vats, however quickly realized round vats would be better since they would not have corners and would be easier to work on. What more strongly drove this change was considering that there are no pure square forms in nature, and through round shapes there is a higher respect for the movements produced in the liquid. Once he achieved round vats, Zuccardi still wanted to go further and that is how he developed the troncoconical vats. Their cone-shape is aimed so that during vinification, every time the hat opens it would have a soft and natural pressure process. See the troncoconical vats photo below.

Today, at the Zuccardi Altamira Winery, they only work with concrete vats without epoxy, with rounded shapes, avoiding corners. Plus, the entire winery is made of concrete, not just the vats, as you can see from the photos, concrete is everywhere, inside, outside, walls, floors, ceilings... it is a landmark of the beauty of concrete.

Remember Zuccardi's extensive soil classifications from the calicata diggings? This results in micro-harvesting in various quantities, creating the need for a great variety of vat sizes and shapes to separate the grapes. They now have egg-shaped vats of 1,000 and 2,000 liters, amphoras vats of 3,000 liters, and troncoconical vats of 5,000 and 7,500 liters.

There is no doubt that what determines the quality of Zuccardi's wines are a combination of the special vineyards and their unique terroir, along with the curved concrete vats to care for and maintain their identities.

And so we did a tasting. The entire lineup of Zuccardi's Valle de Uco wines. In a word... spectacular! How do I choose a favorite among all these amazing wines? In the end, two wines stood out, nose and mouth delighted, a familiar friend, of expressions and personality discovered in the calicatas earlier in the day. It was the Altamira terroir that caught my attention, Sebastian pointed out, knowing exactly what he created in these two bottles. The common denominator of the *Aluvional* and *Tito* wines was the place, exactly as Sebastian intended... to create wines that express their place.

Deep red/purple colors, rich black fruit and berry flavors, and a particular minerality and spiciness that defines what has become my terroir of choice. So I picked my favorite as 100% Malbec, the purist that I am... *Aluvional, La Consulta*.

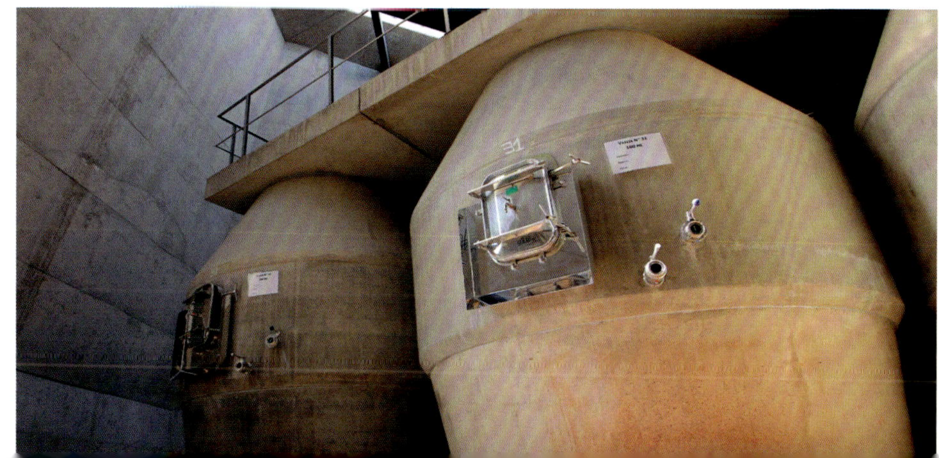

MENDOZA **VALLE DE UCO** SAN CARLOS

Winery (Bodega)

FAMILIA ZUCCARDI

GPS: 33°46'21.4"S 69°09'26.6"W
(Altamira, **San Carlos,** Valle de Uco)

011 (+54 261) 441.0000
info@ZuccardiWines.com

ZuccardiWines.com

English, Español, Português
12,000,000 bottles produced annually

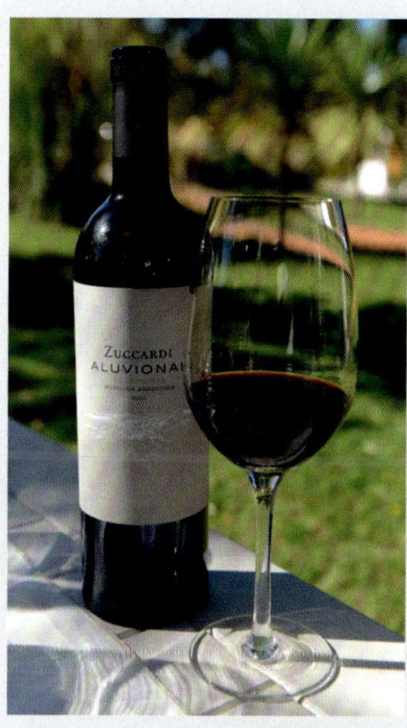

Michael's Favorite Pick
Aluvional - La Consulta (Malbec)

The Zuccardi Wines of Valle de Uco
Aluvional - La Consulta (Malbec)
Aluvional - El Peral (Malbec)
Zuccardi Zeta (83% Malbec, 17% Cabernet)
Tito Zuccardi (83% Malbec, 10% Cabernet, 7% Caladoc)
Emma Zuccardi (100% Bonarda)

To get Zuccardi wines in the USA
Retailer: Whole Foods Market

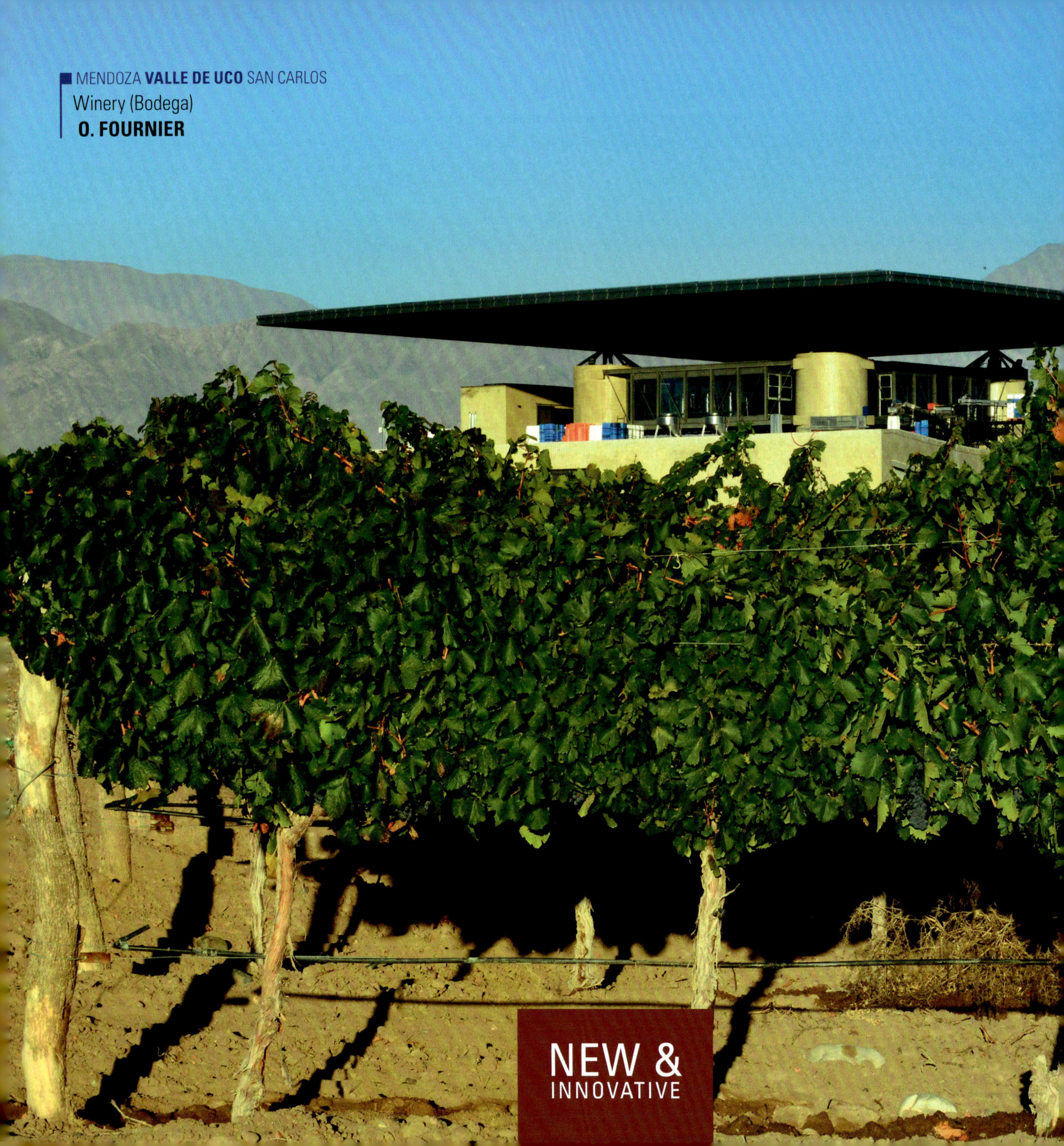
MENDOZA VALLE DE UCO SAN CARLOS
Winery (Bodega)
O. FOURNIER
NEW &
INNOVATIVE

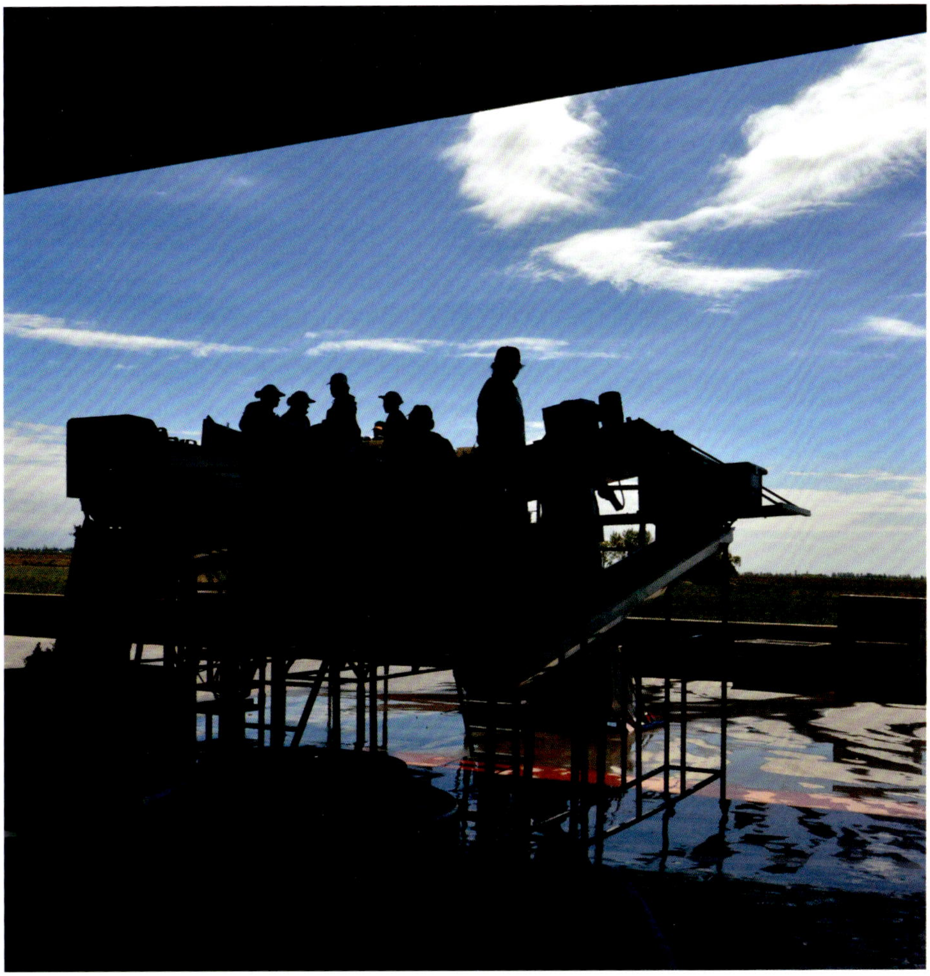

Winery (Bodega)

O. FOURNIER

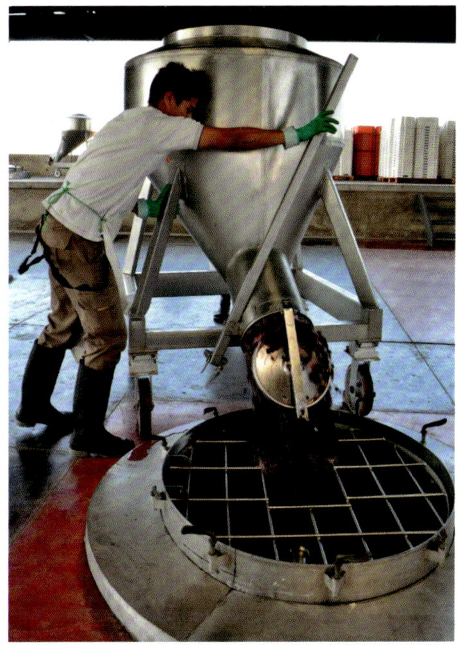

LEFT PAGE, Bodega O. Fournier rising from the deliciously ripe vineyards. ABOVE, hand sorting, washing and gravity transport of the grapes gently to fermentation tanks.

NEW WORLD WINERY

At the southernmost end of this 25- by 45-mile Uco Valley is the ultimate in innovative wineries. O. Fournier is an architectural masterpiece... from its spectacular exterior design that won an architectural gold medal, to an infrastructure designed to gently handle the grapes and wines as they transition through the winery and to ease the workflow for their employees. The result... wines that are winning the "Top 100 Wines of the Year" award on multiple occasions, plus achieving scores as high as 94 points.

Picture naturally breathtaking snow-capped Andes Mountains as a backdrop for a strikingly modern, minimalist structure, that rises from rich green vineyards. A stark design, insisting on your curiosity. A helicopter landing pad over a winery, you wonder? It's the winery's outdoor roof, designed with the aerodynamics of an aircraft wing to create airflow below, keeping the grapes and workers cool.

Innovation in the winery is everywhere. The entire wine-making process uses primarily gravity. From sorting downward to fermentation, to aging, to bottling... they minimize pumps to maximize gentleness with the grapes, juice and wine. An extensive laboratory overlooks the winery and is part of their commitment to excellence and ongoing improvements. This lab includes micro-vinification to experiment with small batches to understand their single terroir characteristics. The winery even has a built-in canal system within the concrete floors to capture water used in meticulously cleaning the environment. Above the aging cellar grows rosemary to naturally hydrate the cellar in this dry desert environment.

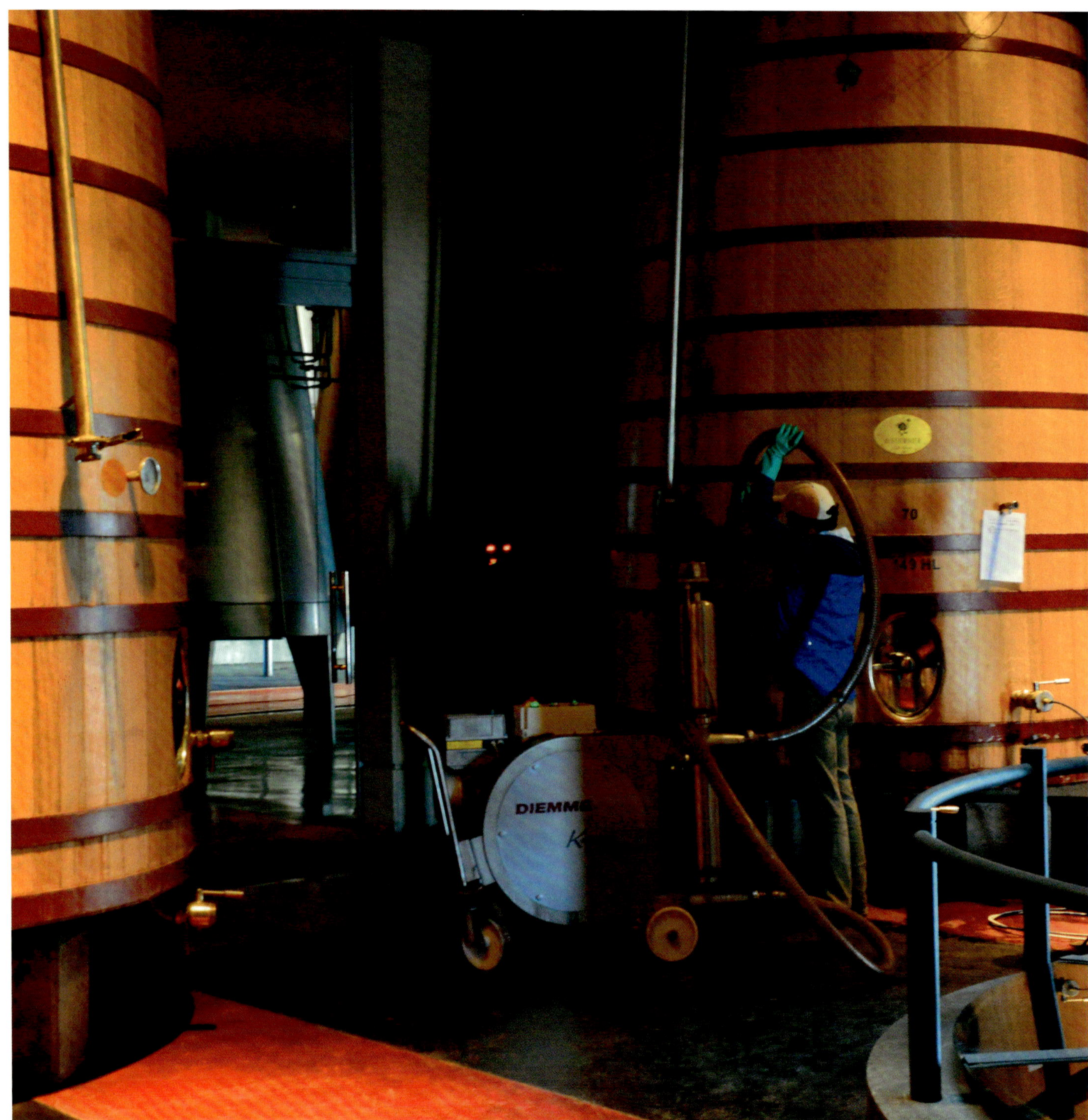
70
149 HL

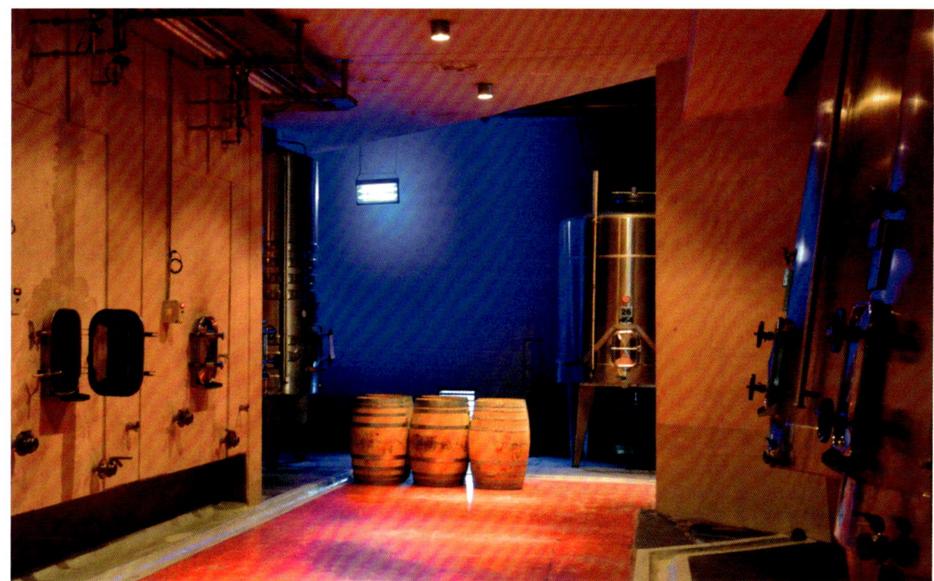

MENDOZA **VALLE DE UCO** SAN CARLOS

Winery (Bodega)

O. FOURNIER

5567 Calle Los Indios
(La Consulta, **San Carlos,** Valle de Uco)

011 (+54 262) 245.1579
reservas@OFournier.com

OFournier.com

English, Español, Português
1,000,000 bottles produced annually

O. Fournier's visionary José Manuel Ortega Gil-Fournier is an interesting worldly entrepreneur, born in Spain, educated at Notre Dame in USA, worked as an investment banker with Goldman Sachs in London and Banco Santander in Madrid... then put up all his savings, mortgaged his house and took out five personal loans and headed to Argentina to embark on this new and innovative venture... O. Fournier.

Ortega brought his sister and brother-in-law with him from Spain to manage the development of the vineyards and winery. And his wife, a culinary expert, to create the winery's five-star restaurant. O. Fournier is a family-run business, whose financially leveraged risks have turned into much fame and success with the wines' high scores and winery's design awards.

To give you an idea of the magnitude of this young business, the winery has the capacity of 1.2 million liters of juice in stainless, oak and cement vats at any one time, and has a massive underground cellar holding up to 2,800 oak barrels of aging wine (see magnificent cellar photo next page). O. Fournier is now producing one million bottles of wine annually and exporting to 42 countries. Plus, expanding the vineyard and winery operations to Chile and Spain.

Not surprising from Ortega's heritage, the primary grape grown on the estate is Tempranillo, a native Spanish black grape varietal used to make full-bodied red wines. When you arrive at the winery, the Tempranillo is distinct in its wild untrellised growth, similar to what you might see in Zinfandel vineyards. The estate also grows Malbec, Syrah and Cabernet Sauvignon.

O. Fournier produces four different levels of wine: *O. Fournier, Alfa Crux, B Crux, and Urban*. The *O. Fournier* is a special barrel selection of the *Alfa Crux*, only 200 to 300 cases selling for about US $100 a bottle with scores as high as 94 points. Depending on the year it could be a Malbec, Syrah, Cabernet, or even a blend.

The *Alfa Crux* is their premium line. Available as a 100% Malbec or as a Tempranillo/Malbec blend. Hitting 93 points and under US $40, this is my favorite.

Urban is their low-end wine; however, they get scores of 90 points at times for bottles in this line and you can buy them for under US $10. If you like a more fruitier Malbec derived from less oak time, this is a great find.

To best get to know their wines, enjoy the six-course gourmet wine pairing menu in their restaurant, designed to show off the wines in a laid-back environment with spectacular views of the Andes.

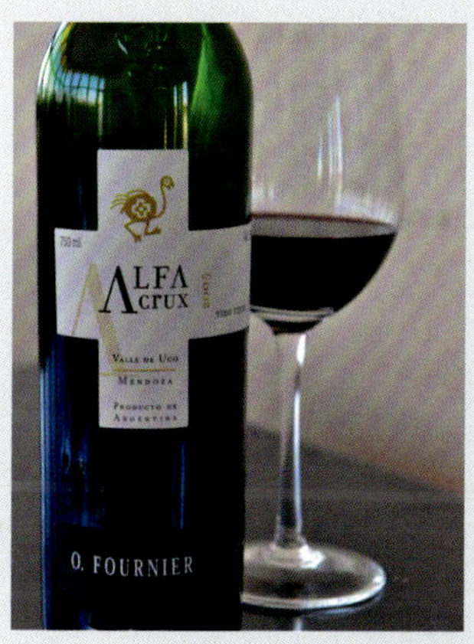

Michael's Favorite Pick
Alfa Crux, Malbec

Total Collection of Wines

O. Fournier
O. Fournier - 2008 is Malbec

Alfa Crux
Malbec
Blend - Tempranillo Malbec

B Crux
Blend - Tempranillo Malbec
Sauvignon Blanc

To get O. Fournier wines in the USA
National Online Retailer: SpecsOnline.com
Or email: Liz.Mathews@TheVintnerGroup.com

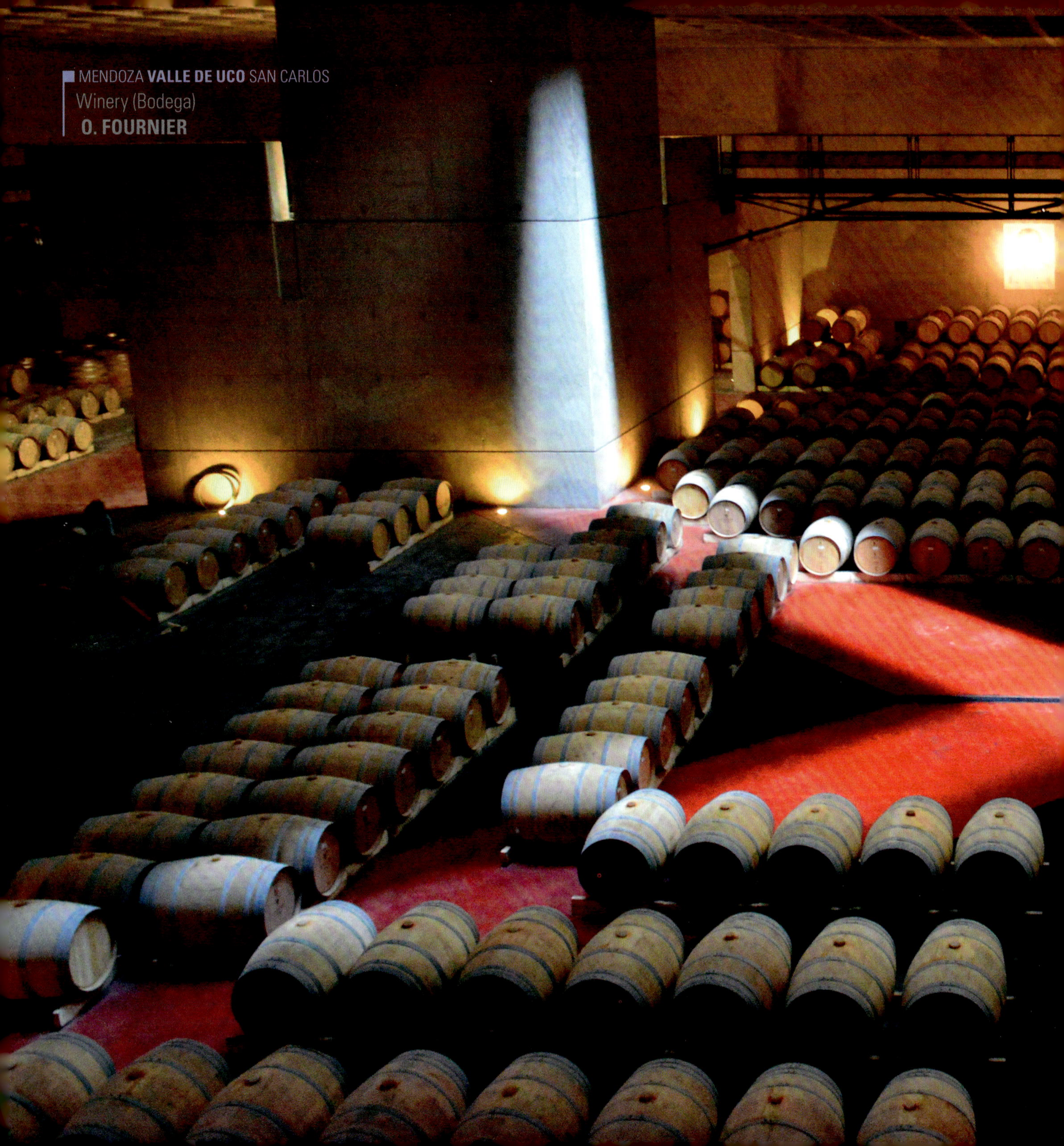
MENDOZA **VALLE DE UCO** SAN CARLOS
Winery (Bodega)
O. FOURNIER

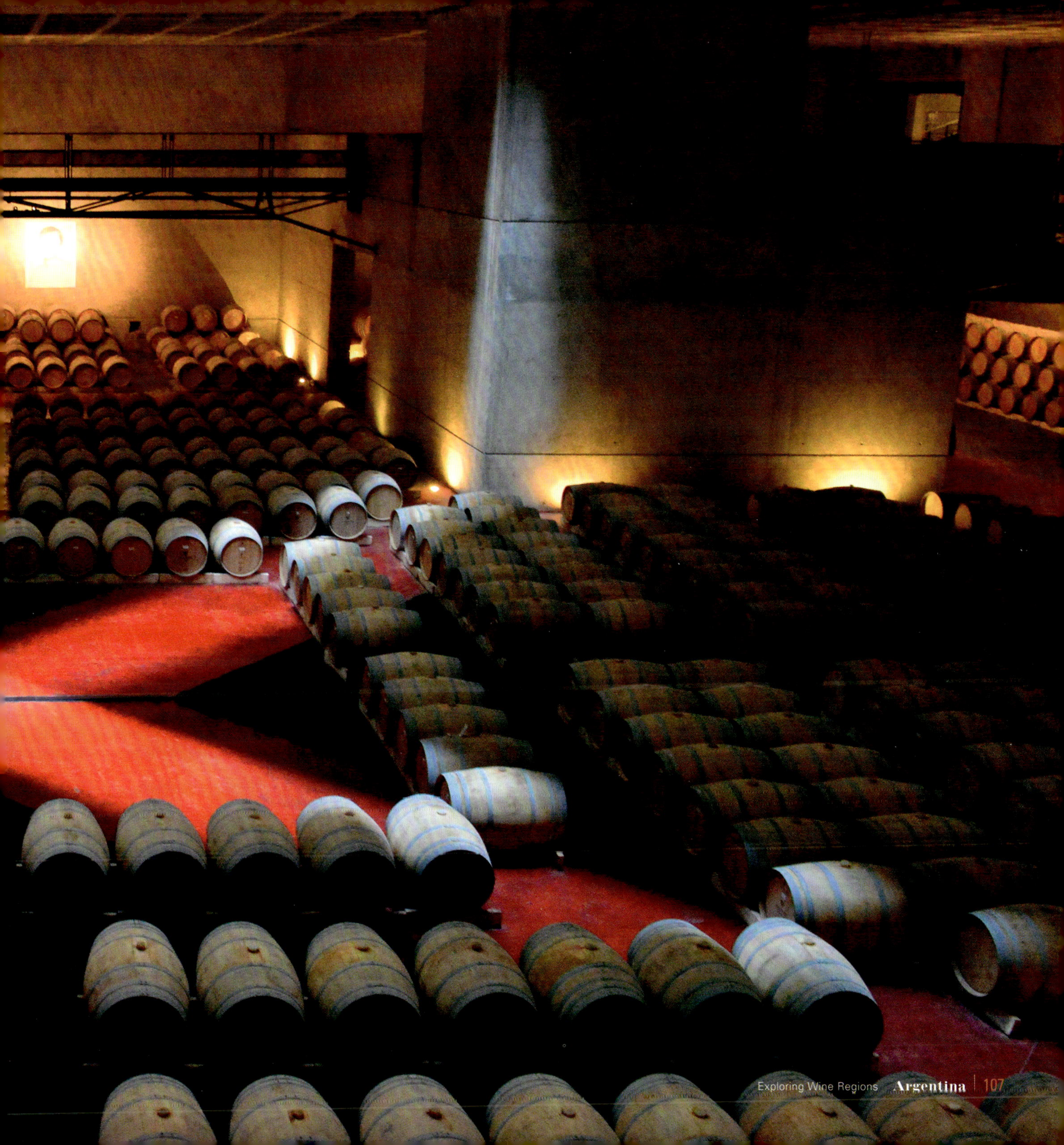

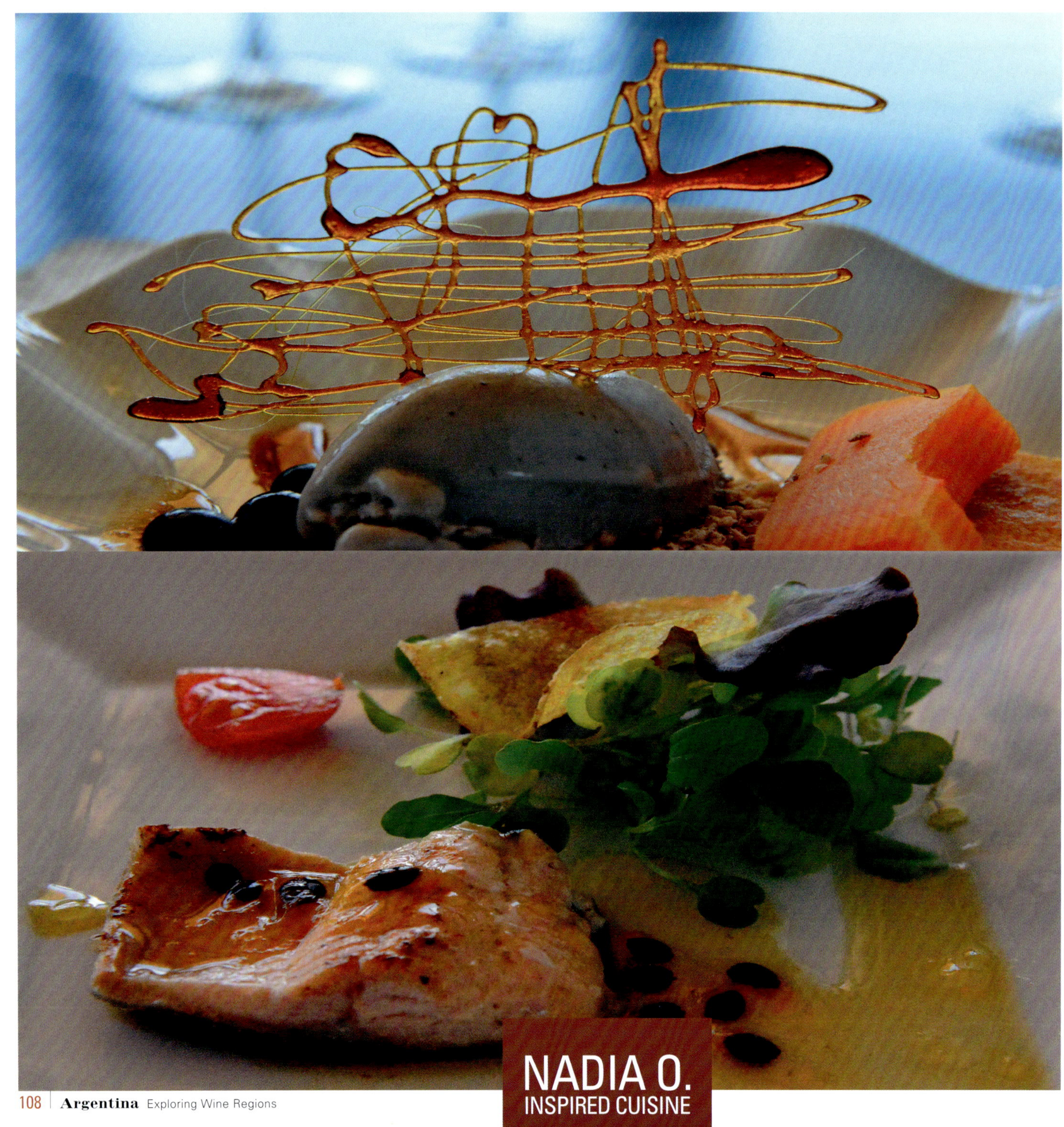

NADIA O.
INSPIRED CUISINE

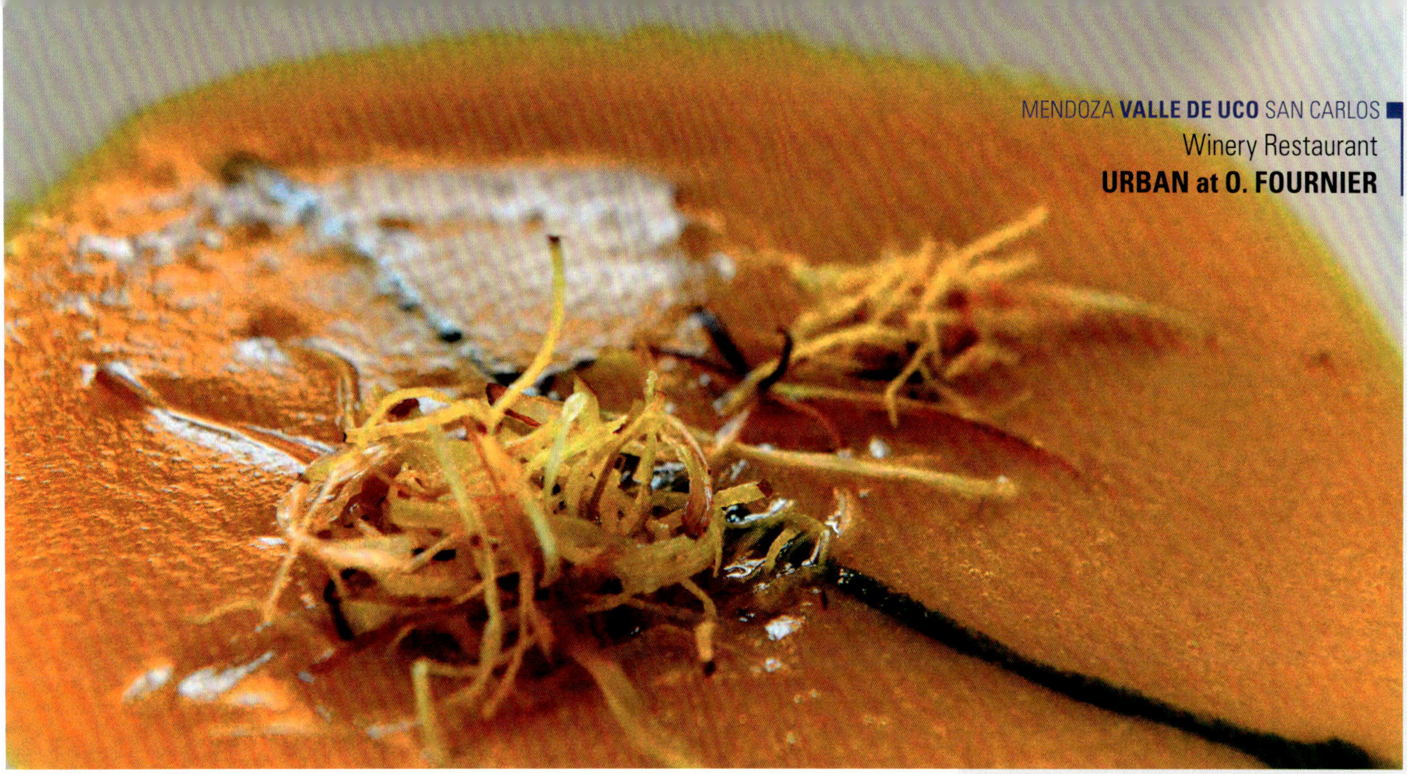

Winery Restaurant

URBAN at O. FOURNIER

WORLD'S GREATEST WINERY RESTAURANT

...and so Urban, O. Fournier's restaurant, wins the award from Wine Access magazine. For me, it would be a tall order to be the world's greatest winery restaurant... not just exquisite food, it must be paired properly with the winery's wines, plus the ambiance, service, and environment must make me feel at home.

This is the best way to taste a winery's wines, paired with food. And add a relaxing and inspiring environment to get to know the wines.

Cube minimalist structure and decor, with wall-to-wall, floor-to-ceiling glass windows, every table looks out across the lake front, through vineyards, allowing the Andes Mountains to be admired. It's a casual, non-rushed environment to enjoy the view as much as the culinary experience. On warm days, you can sit outside on the desk, lakeside.

The food is seasonally inspired by local ingredients changing the six-course fixed menu weekly. Big flavors of Argentine and Mediterranean-Spanish cuisine pair well with the winery's big red wines showcasing the Alfa Crux, B Crux and Urban wines.

All this should be of no surprise; the Executive Chef is Nadia Haron Ortega, the winery president's wife, her other restaurant being the famed Nadia O.F. that was awarded ***Best Restaurant in Argentina*** by the Argentine Academy of Gastronomy in 2011 (see review on page 64).

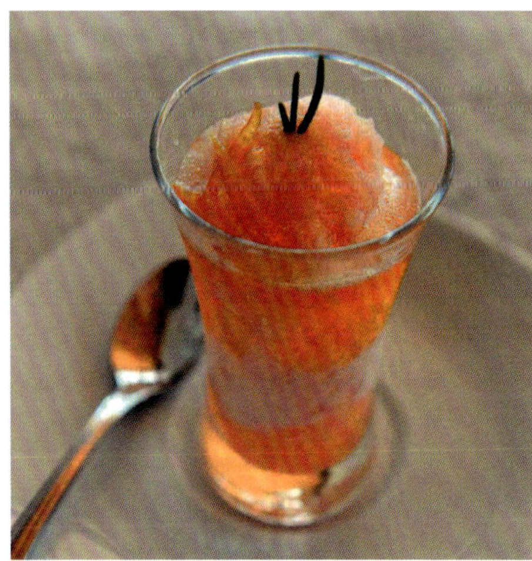

011 (+54 261) 467.1021

turismo@OFournier.com

Reservations Required

OFournier.com

TOP LEFT PAGE to BOTTOM RIGHT

Cubo de Calabaza en Almibar
Cubed Pumpkin in Syrup
Caramelized pumpkin cube on breton dough, grape ice cream and caramel

Trucha Grillada
Grilled Trout
Grilled trout with passion fruit sauce and green salad

Sopa de Zapallo
Pumpkin Soup
Pumpkin, sweet potato and ginger soup with crispy leeks

Sorbete de Pomelo
Grapefruit Sorbet
Grapefruit sorbet with rosemary honey sauce

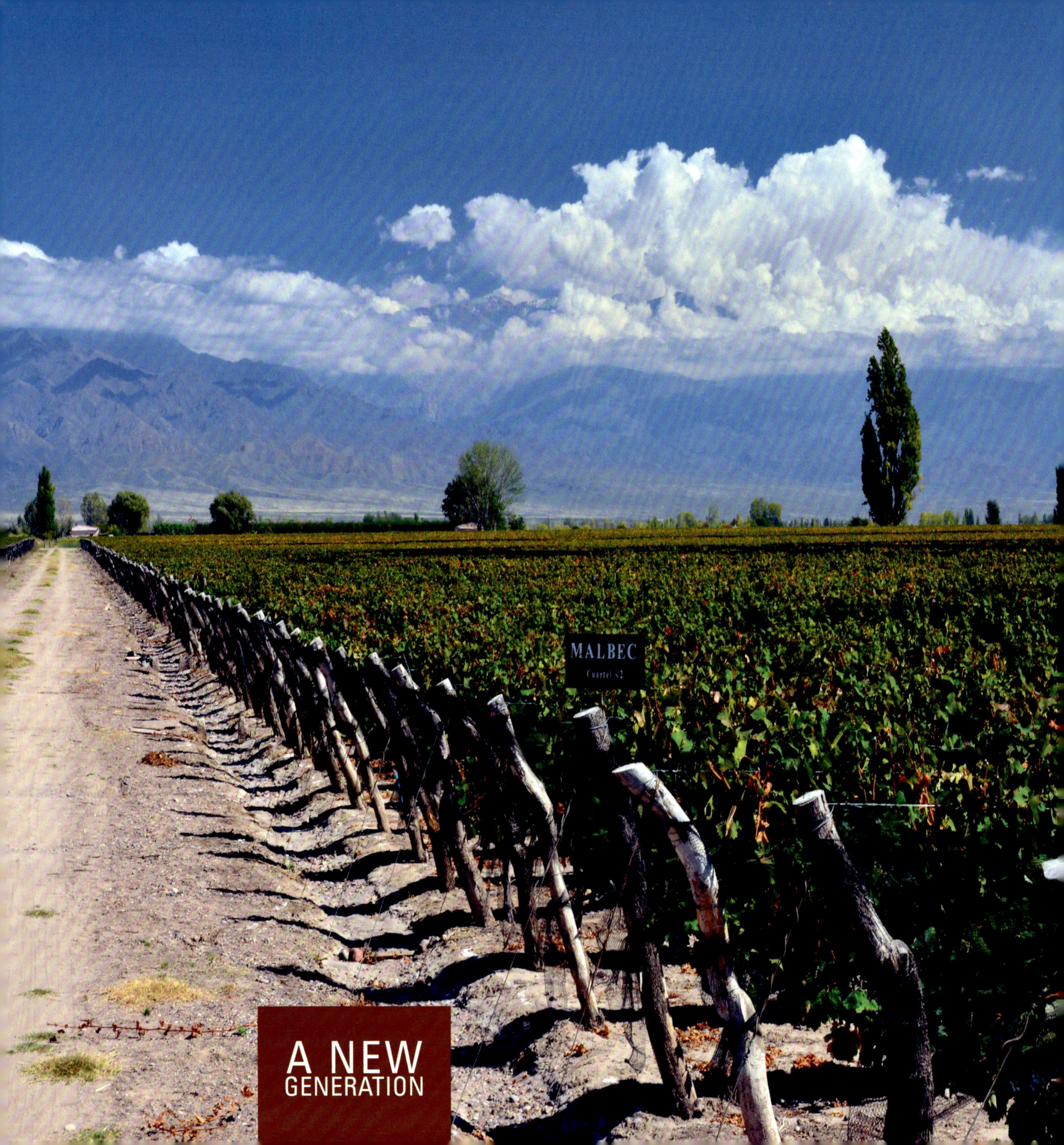

A NEW GENERATION

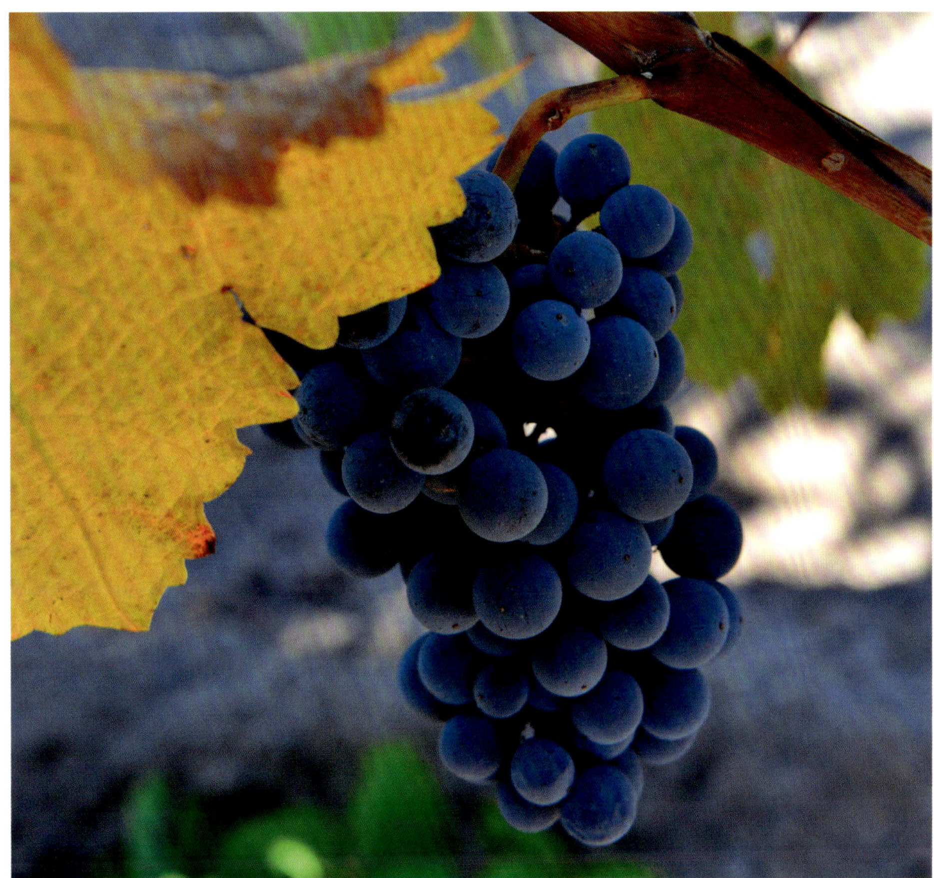

A HANDCRAFTED DREAM

For generations, the Bianchetti family has been growing grapes in Valle de Uco. They have always known how good the region is for wine grapes. And so do others... the Bianchetti family has been selling their grapes to notable wineries for decades. Maybe this is how the word got out that this valley is gold?

In the early 20th century, Isidro Ernesto Bianchetti immigrated to Argentina from Italy, where he and his father worked on the land with castrated bulls called oxen, or bueyes in Spanish (there was no machinery back then). Working hard, saving money, buying land in Valle de Uco, and planting vineyards are what he did with all his spare time and money.

Decades later, grandson Jesús Bianchetti had a dream, inspired by the enterprising spirit of his grandfather, to now produce their own wines from certain special sections in their vineyards. He saw using the very best grapes from the family's numerous vineyards, cultivating them for the highest quality output, pruning extensively to one bottle per plant... all to achieve the greatest concentration of aroma and color, with soft tannins.

Today, Bueyes is the name of Bianchetti's wines, a tribute to the hardworking animals and the efforts and sacrifices of past generations. These are very small handcrafted wines, made to perfection.

Their Malbec is special. Deep dark purple color with lots of big rich fruit and soft tannins. The salt and BBQ in meat brings out the fruit and diminish the tannins in this big wine.

You must try their sparkling Malbec. An Extra Brut Malbec Rosé. Berries on the nose with a very dry delicate fruit taste. This is a different experience that must go with any Malbec adventure.

Winery (Bodega)

BUEYES WINES

La Consulta • **San Carlos**

011 (+54 261) 558.9196
info@BueyesWines.com.ar

BueyesWines.com.ar

Español
35,000 bottles produced annually

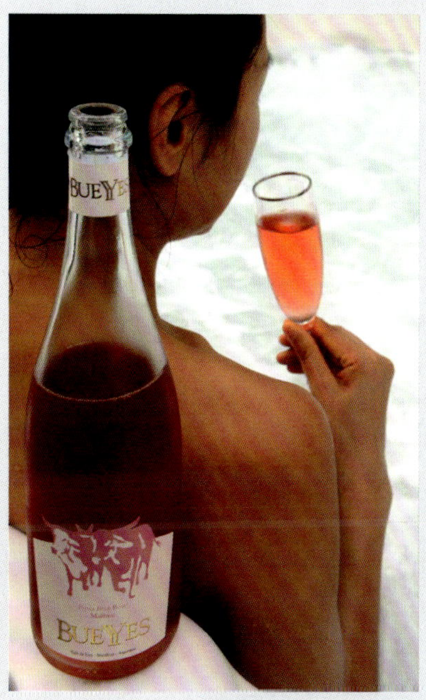

Michael's Favorite Pick
Malbec Extra Brut Rosé
A Refreshing Spa Experience!

Total Collection of Wines
Malbec
Malbec Extra Brut Rosé (sparkling)
Cabernet Sauvignon
Blend Gran Reserva
Torrontés
Syrah

To get Bueyes wines in the USA
Direct from the Importer: CopaFina.com
at CopaFina.com/**bueyes**buywine.html

Extreme Adventure

LAGUNA DEL DIAMANTE

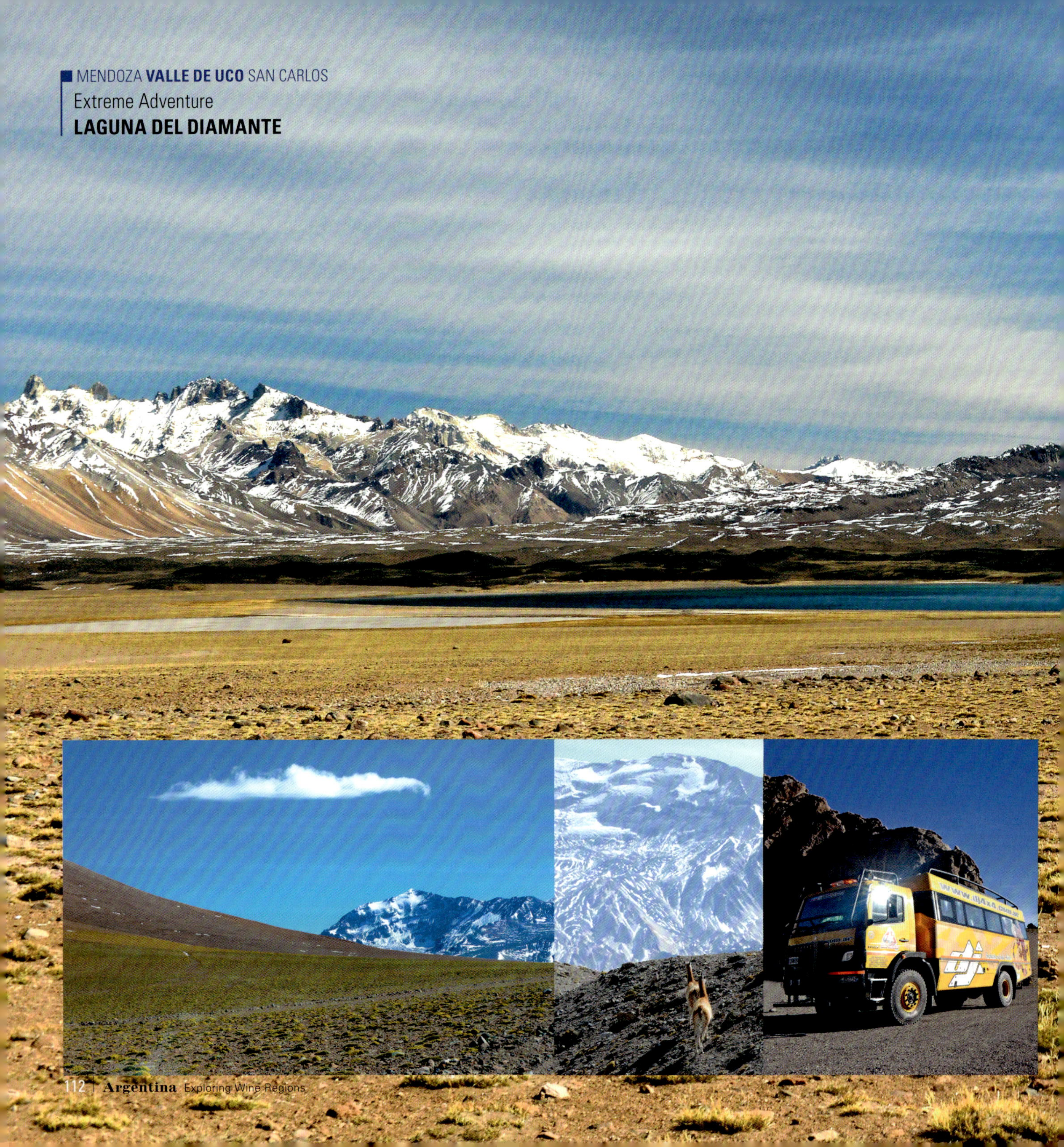

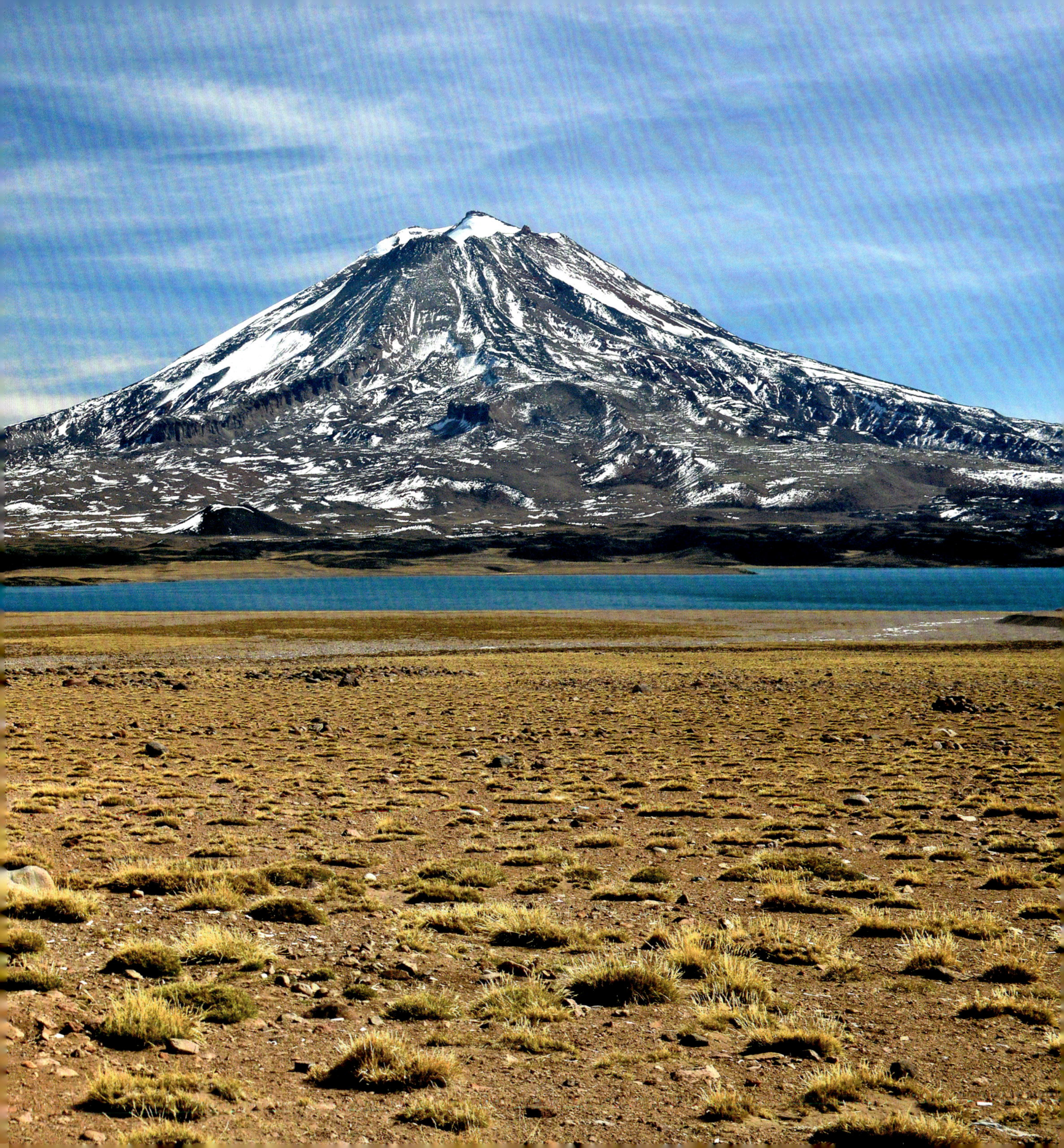

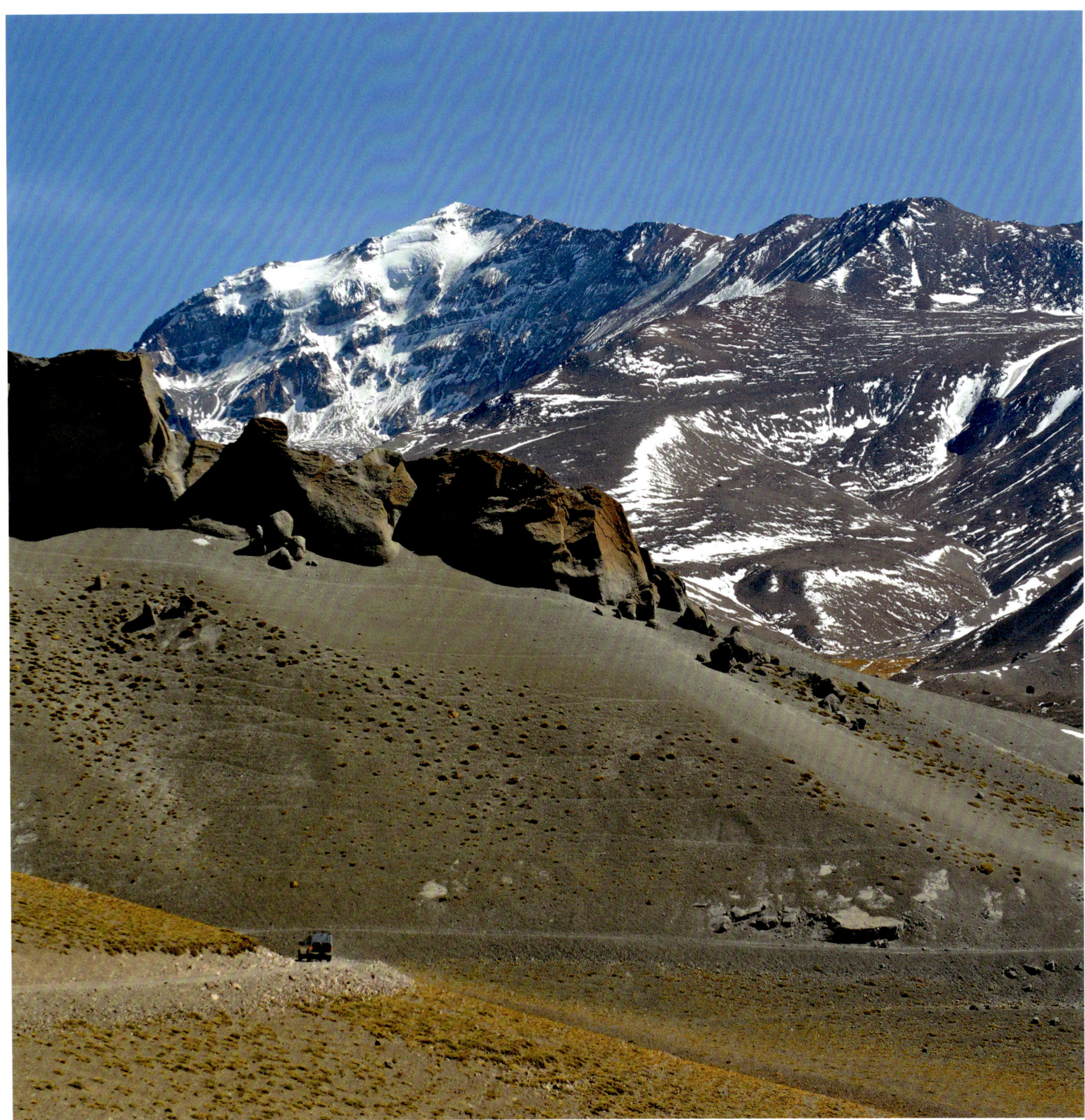

GETTING THERE IS HALF THE FUN

THE JOURNEY IS THE ADVENTURE... meandering canyons and driving over high plateaus that exceed 10,000 feet elevations, with cold winds requiring heavy jackets in the summer, traversable only January throught mid-April, this is an extreme environment where the journey is the most exhilarating part of getting to **Laguna del Diamante** (Spanish for: lake of the diamond).

These are extreme conditions where life barely exists. Only the strong and adaptable survive. The views are breathtaking so a few stops along the way are necessary to take it all in. You must go in a well-equipped off-road vehicle. I went with DJ Servicios in their Monster 4x4 Mercedes-Benz (photo previous spread); they specialize in transportation to areas of difficult access like mining and industrial personnel. They do group trips to Laguna del Diamante and include a knowledgable guide.

Laguna del Diamante (elevation 10,827') is located in the south part of San Carlos Region deep into the Andes Mountains on the border between Argentina and Chile. It is an all-day trip to Laguna del Diamante, which is highlighted by the towering Maipo Volcano reflected majestically in the lake (photo previous spread). The volcano and its reflection in the lake form a diamond-shape image, which gives the lake its name.

Maipo Volcano (elevation is 17,270') is a half million years old stratovolcano located within the **Diamante Caldera**. It rises 6,230 feet above the floor of the caldera. Immediately to the east of the peak is Laguna del Diamante as the picturesque lake that formed when lava flows blocked drainage channels from the caldera in 1826. Maipo retains a symmetrical, conical volcanic shape, unlike many of the other nearby peaks, making it the best known peak in the entire region.

Interestingly, the effects on vegetation, clumps of grasses usually take the form of circles or semicircles. Animal and plant species that live here are of particular interest, with a remarkable adaptation to high altitude life. This reserve protects herds of guanacos (llama family), red foxes, cauquén (sheldgoose), a species of duck that feeds on plants and seeds, and several species of mountain mice that take refuge in burrows to avoid predators such as the eagle and red fox. The lake surprisingly has no native fish.

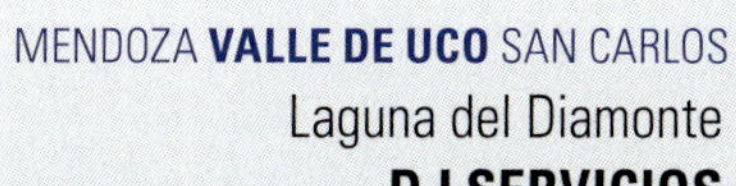

MENDOZA **VALLE DE UCO** SAN CARLOS

Laguna del Diamonte

DJ SERVICIOS

San Carlos • **San Carlos**

011 (+54 260) 446.4526

info@DJ4x4.com.ar

DJ4x4.com.ar

English & Español

Get yourself a jacket and camera, and prepare yourself to experience a breathtaking day of what will feel like you are visiting another planet. San Carlos is not just another great wine region... being contiguous with the Andes Mountains gives you direct access to the many wonders of the world's second highest mountain range on the planet.

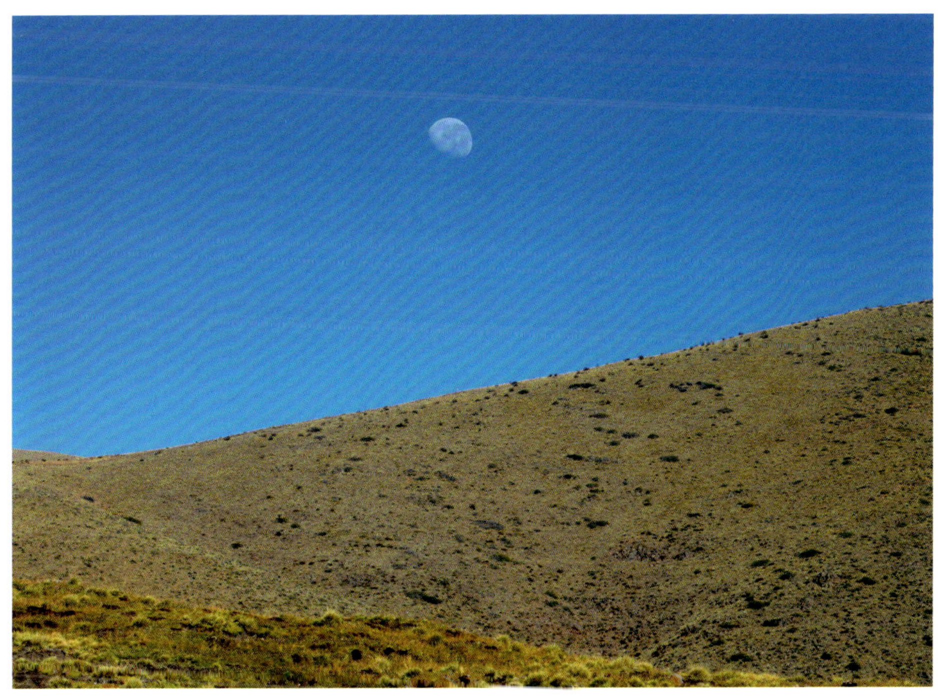

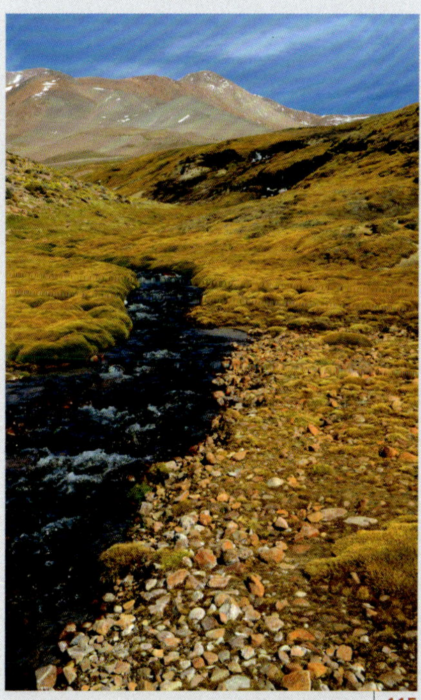

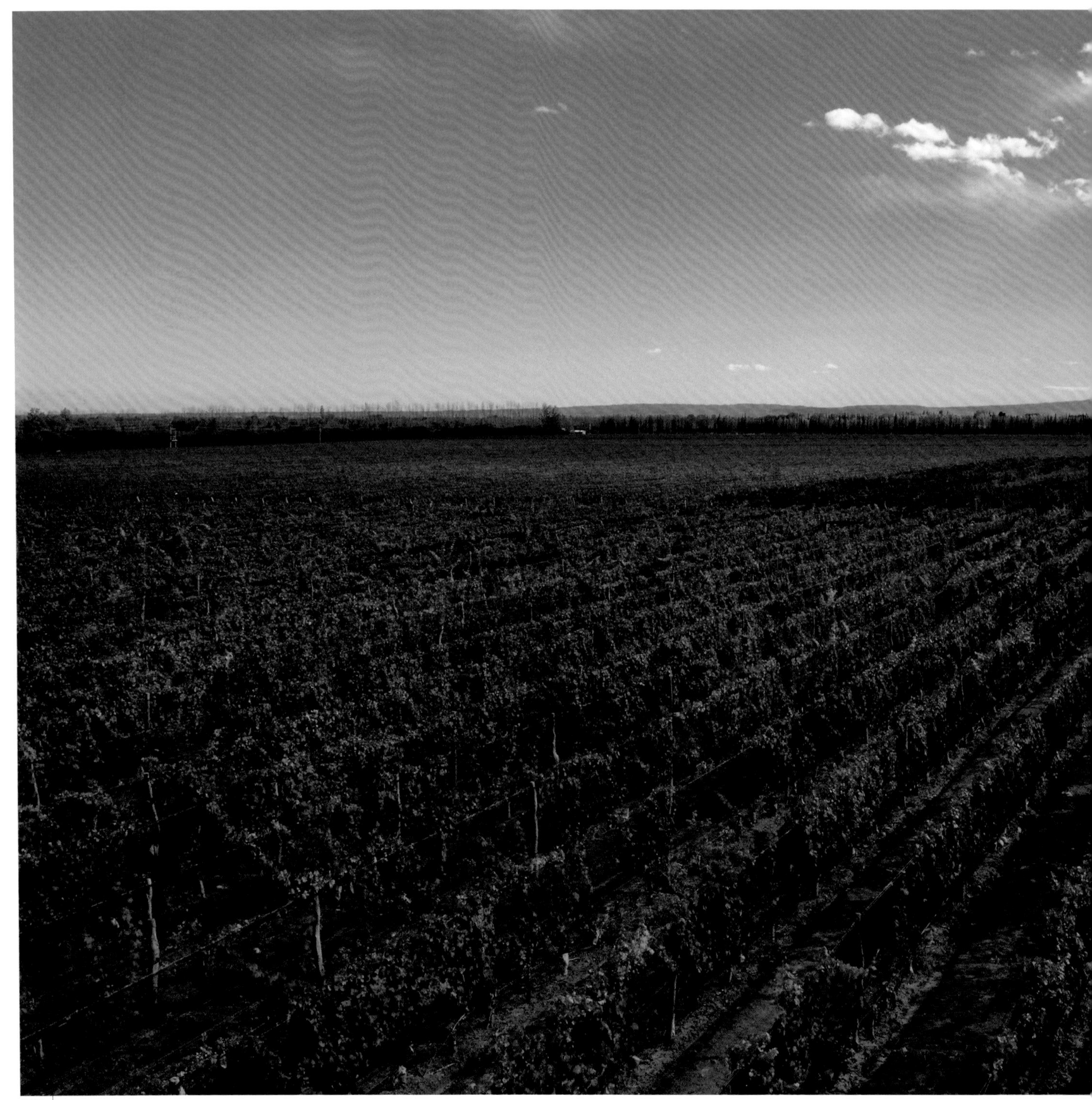

MENDOZA **TUNUYÁN**

*Including the Sub-Appellation of **Vista Flores** in This Sub-Region of **Central Valle de Uco***

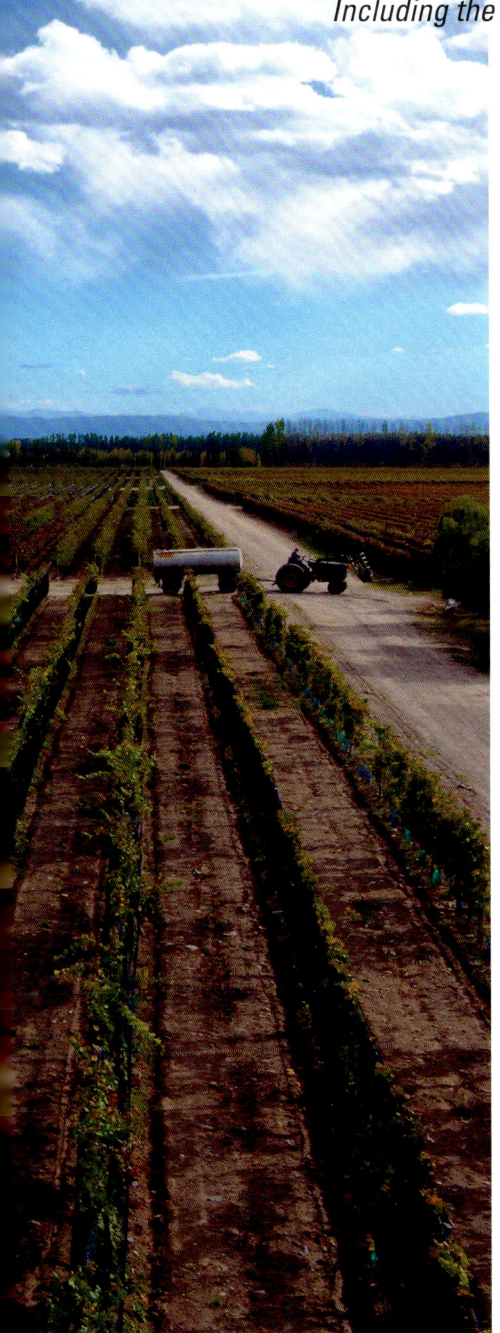

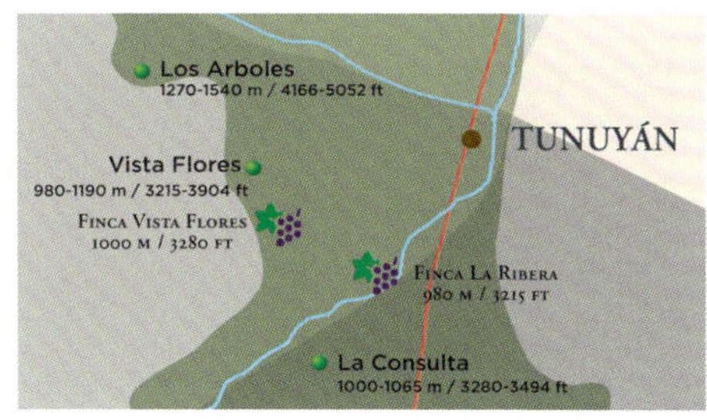

EXPLORING TUNUYÁN

Valle de Uco's central wine sub-region is Tunuyán, and the town of Tunuyán is the major city (pop 42,000) along Ruta 40 in this valley. This national Route 40 highway spans Argentina longitudinally (over 3,000 miles), connecting, in this case, downtown Mendoza with Valle de Uco. Roads lead from Tunuyán to the west, southwest and northwest providing access as the main artery to the entire Valle de Uco's three wine sub-regions.

The town of Tunuyán is where the valley's two main rivers merge (Tunuyán and Las Tunas) as they leave the valley after feeding the vineyards from their Andes snowmelt supply that makes it possible to grow grapes here. From the town of Tunuyán, the Tunuyán sub-region fans out to the west in roughly a 30° angle towards the mountains, defining this sub-region by these two rivers.

Vista Flores is Tunuyán's most famous sub-appellation, with awards being won for the wines produced here, because of its special terroir and masterful winemakers making it happen.

Bodega Antucura, for example, was given 95 points by Decanter Magazine for their *2012 Antucura Malbec*, and awarded the No. 2 Argentine Malbec of the Year for this wine produced from their estate vineyards in Vista Flores. The following year, a Gold Medal and another 95 points for their *2013 Antucura Cabernet Sauvignon.* Both wines are under US $20 in the USA. Casa Antucura is their hotel where you can stay in the heart of Vista Flores.

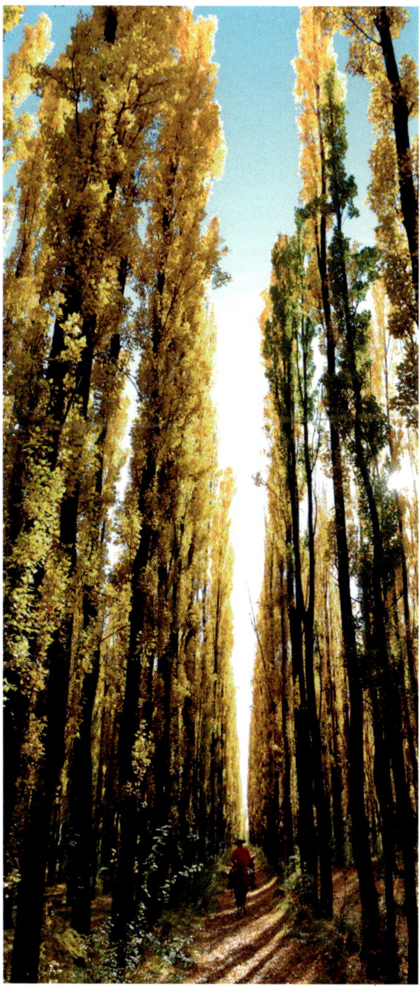

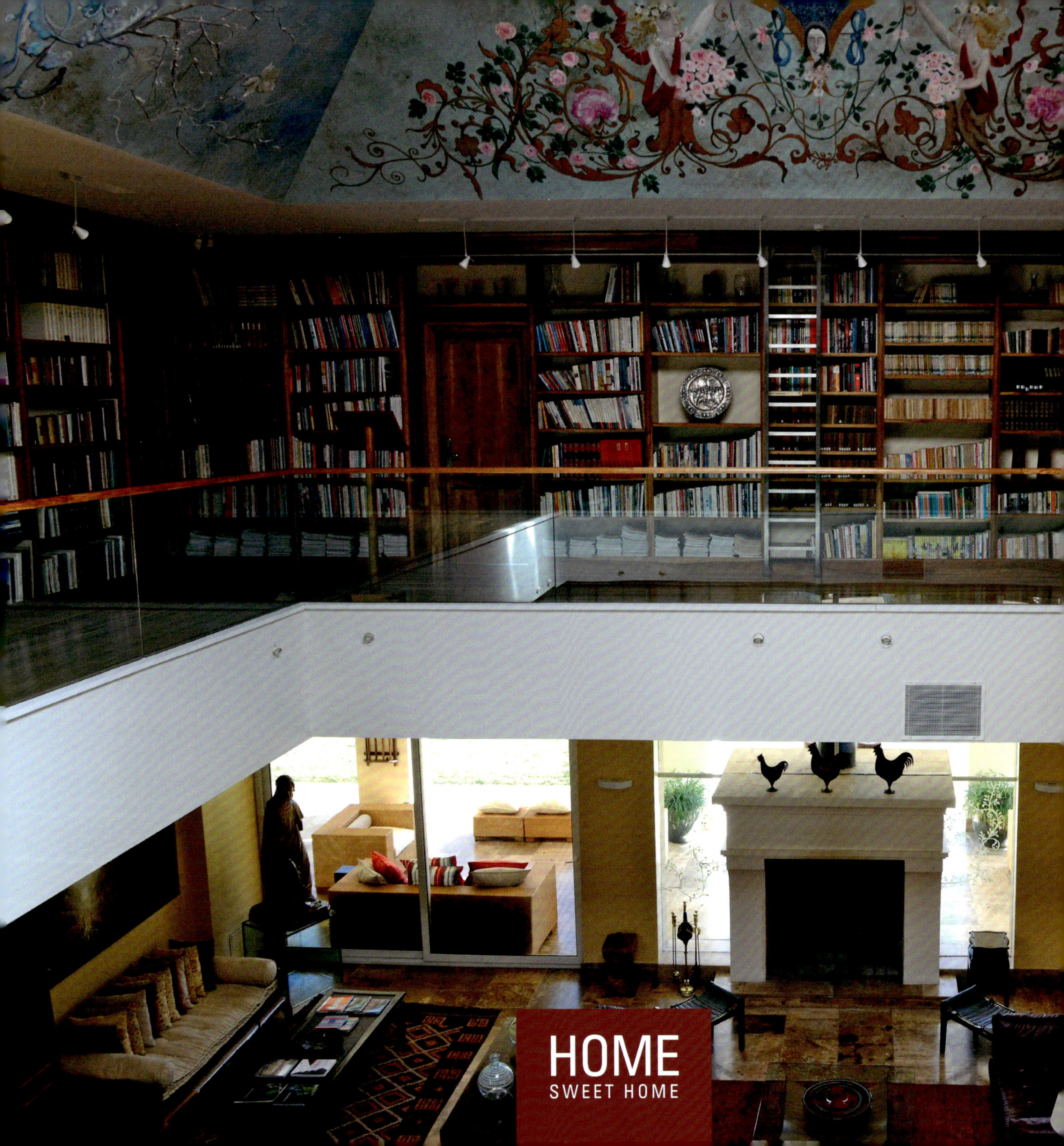
HOME
SWEET HOME

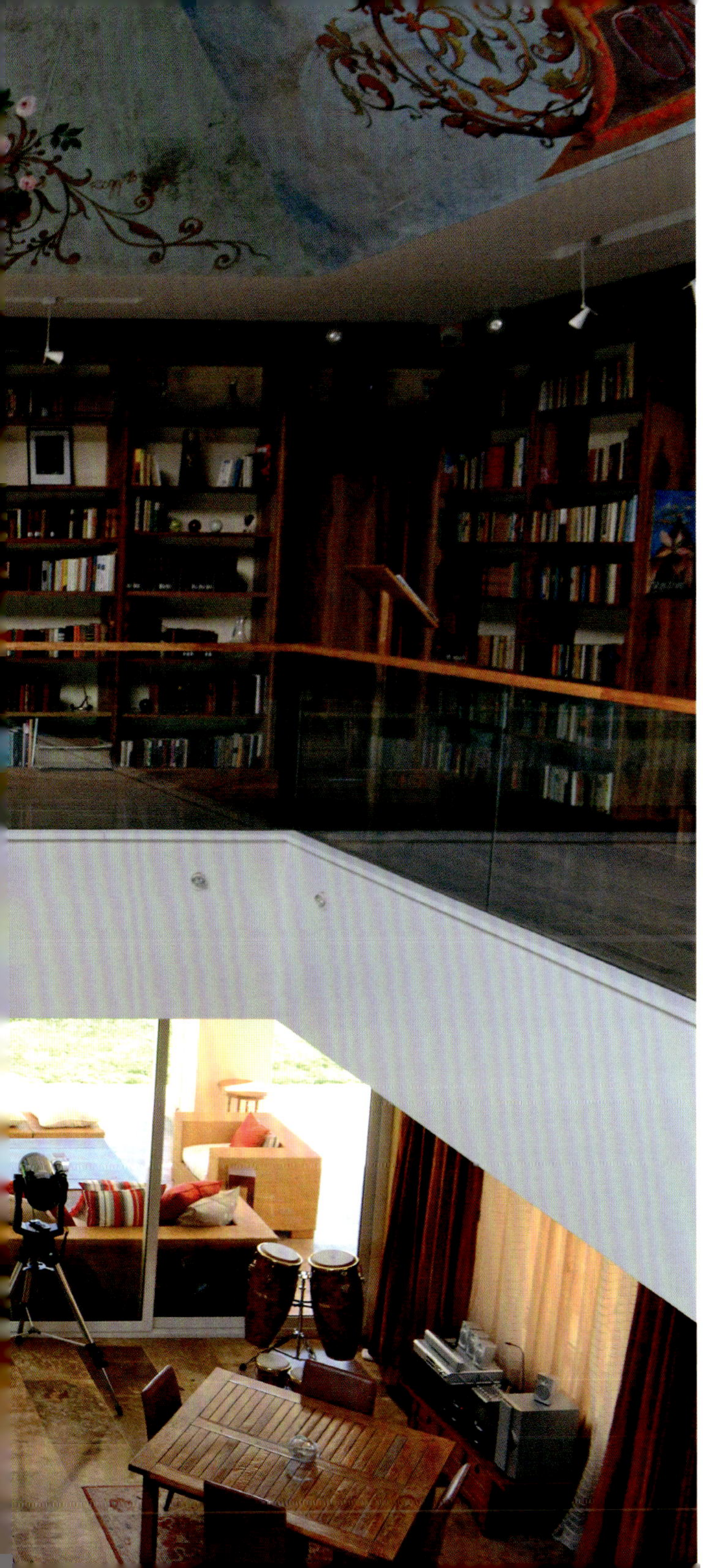

MI CASA, ES SU CASA

Make yourself at home in this beautiful and very private eight-bedroom home in the heart of Vista Flores, Tunuyán. This two-story home (photo below) is located in the middle of a private estate vineyard, with winery, lake, fruit trees, original art sculptures, hundreds of roses and numerous mature trees... all to create a very special environment like none other you will experience in Argentina.

Downstairs is an elegantly appointed living area, open to the second-floor library (photo left) and its massive dome ceiling – a hand-painted, fresco mural of the four seasons. The library surrounds the entire second floor with an 8,000-book collection of valuable and interesting literature from around the world, on most every topic, and in various languages... an exploration in which you can enjoy during your stay. Off the library are the eight private rooms overlooking their spectacular landscape.

The library is one of the most remarkable works of art at Casa Antucura. For the owner of this estate, Anne-Caroline Biancheri, the inspiration for the library was simple. Anne-Caroline is a Literary Editor, for this is her first office, she loves books and has always been surrounded by them. She will tell you... *"In Casa Antucura, books are the soul of the place. I have no special book, I have special moments in which I enjoy different books. Just like wine!"*

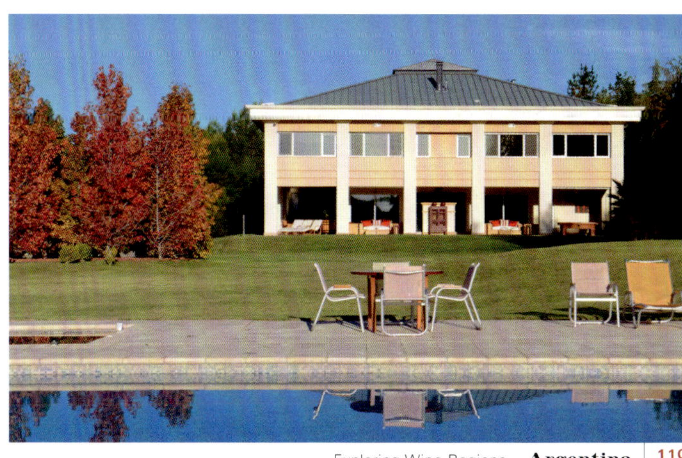

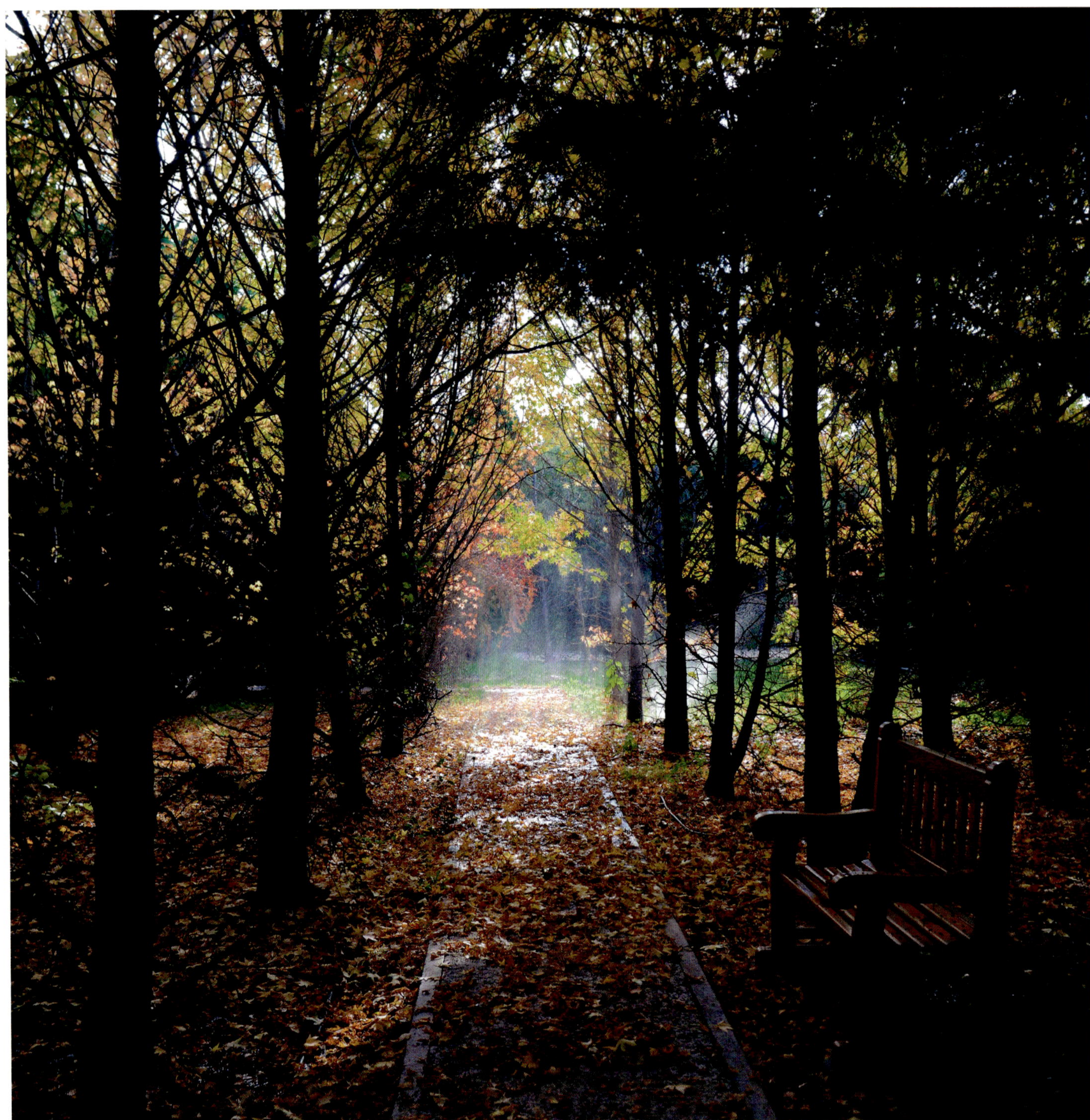

Casa Antucura (meaning "Stone of the Sun" in Pehuenches, the ancient language of the first inhabitants of the area) was originally designed as a private residence. Today, Anne-Caroline welcomes guests from around the world, taking care of every detail in providing a very high-level of accommodation service.

Each of the eight rooms are completely unique, designed with individual themes of ultra-modern decorative details including regional art of the highest level. Each room has the luxuries of home and with private baths, plus views from their two-story vantage.

I stayed for a week, and felt I was at home. This was an experience analogous to living in an estate, with staff and personal chef. A relaxing home, in an environment of art and luxuries. With my extended time exploring Mendoza and Valle de Uco, this was the perfect place, right environment, home away from home.

Outside, is a spacious patio (photo below right) with very comfortable furniture inviting a quiet, relaxing afternoon gazing out across the park-like setting. Have lunch on the patio, as I did. Read a book from the amazing library. Visit with friends. Enjoy a glass of one of their Antucura wines.

The setting is deliberately designed to relax your mind and allow you to make contact with nature and the colors of the different seasons. Stroll for hours through the dense foliage and open vineyards. Pick fruit from the orchards, visit the activity in the winery, or enjoy the pool, hot tub and bar.

Casa Antucura is a very special place, especially when you make it your home for a little while.

MENDOZA **VALLE DE UCO** TUNUYÁN

Hotel • Vineyards • Winery

CASA ANTUCURA

3 km Calle Barrandica s/n
(Vista Flores, **Tunuyán,** Valle de Uco)

011 (+54 9 261) 339.1440
reserva@CasaAntucura.com

CasaAntucura.com

English & Español
No Children

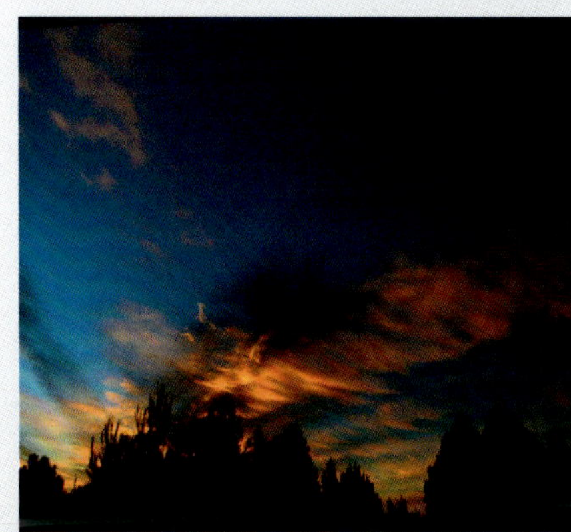

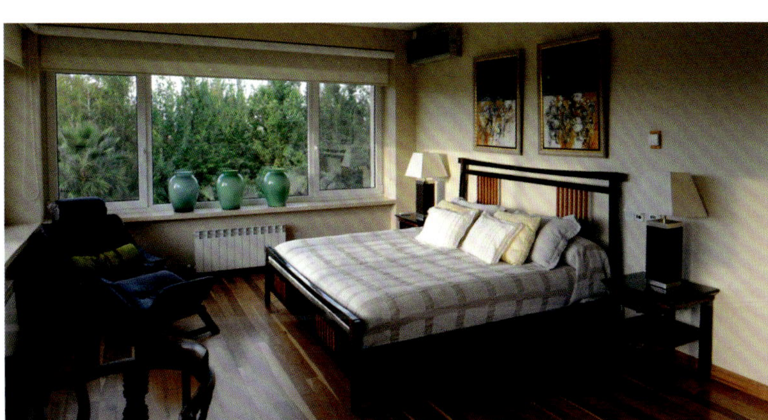

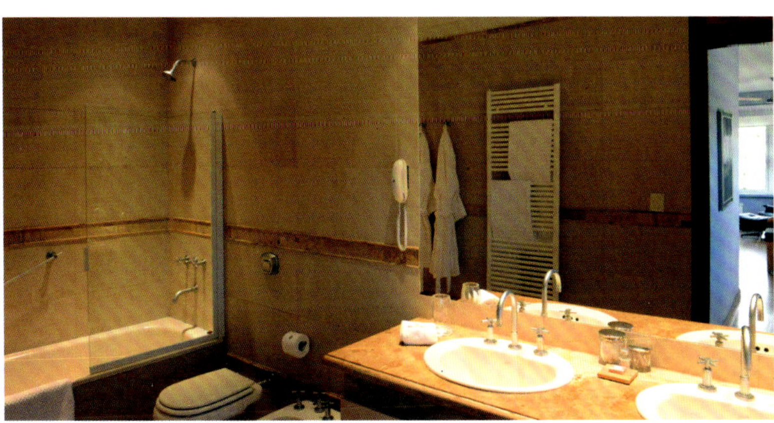

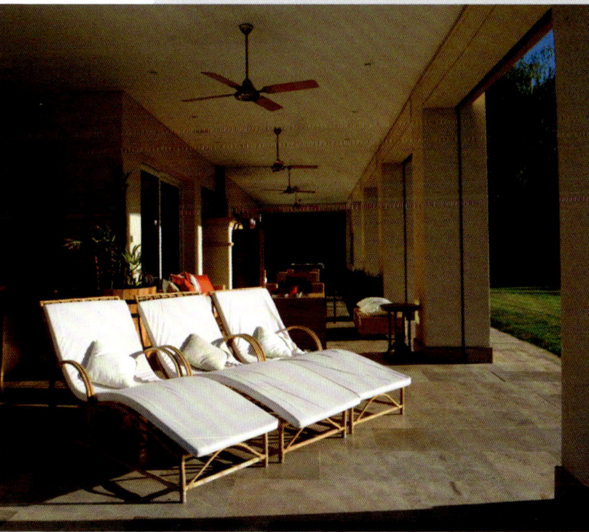

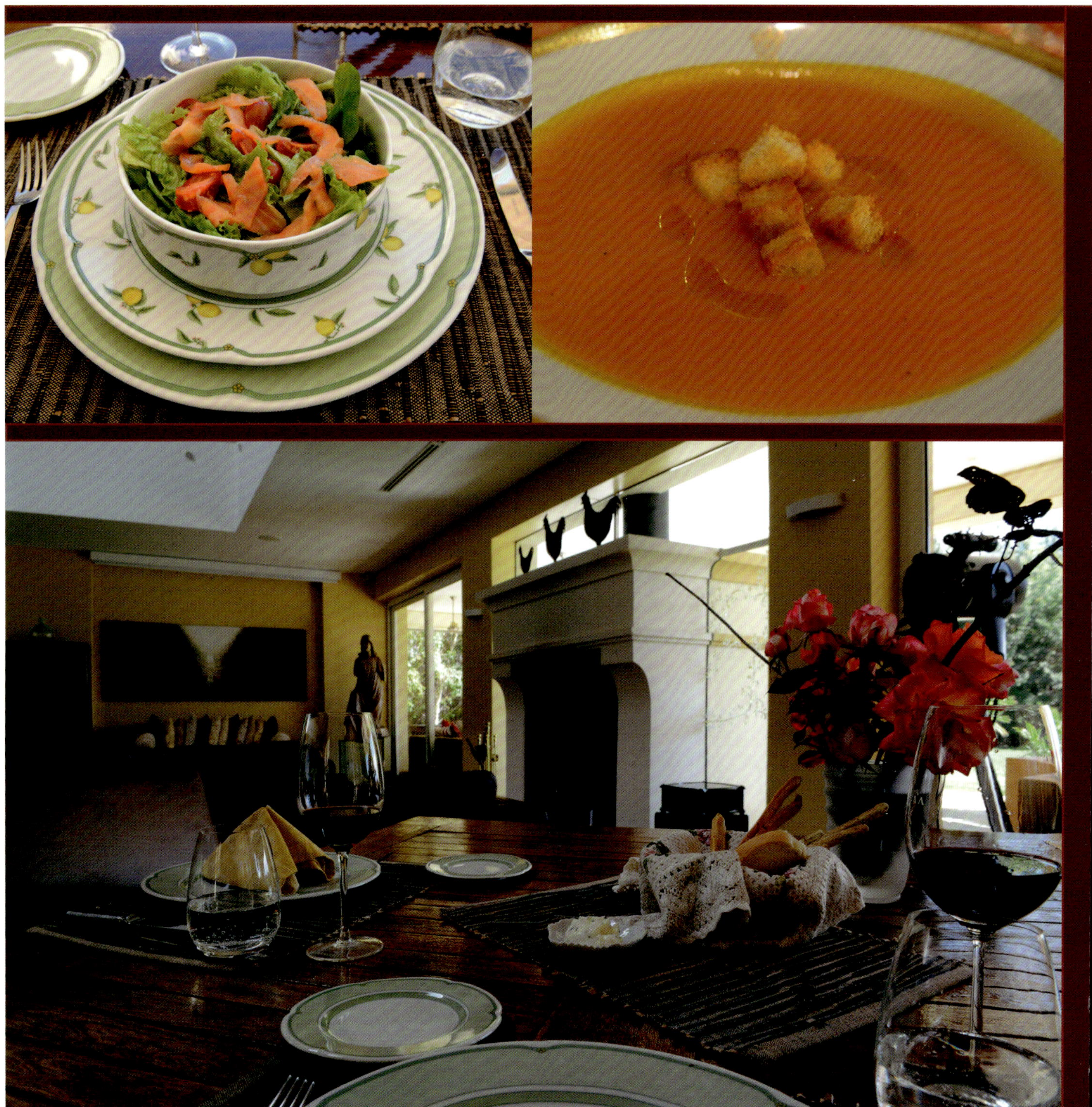

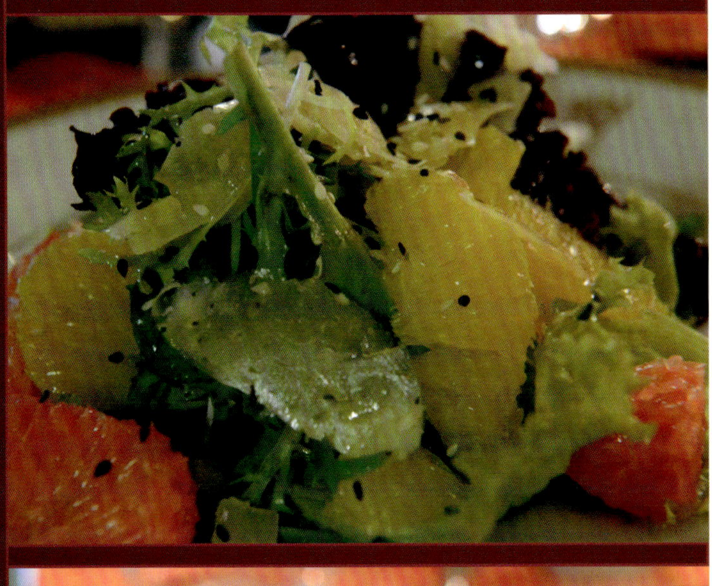

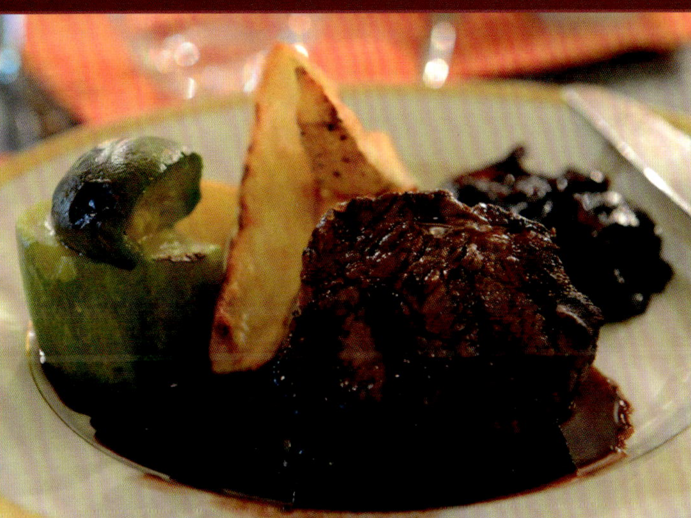

FRENCH CUISINE NOUVEAU ARGENTINA

Exquisite china, homemade cooking, personal service, and a unique menu created by the chef nightly... as you would expect in the home of a French estate, with a professional chef.

The photography on these two pages should say it all.

Joie de Vivre as the French express their *joy of living*, and as you will experience dining in the Casa Antucura living room (photo left page). Antucura wines are decanted for you in beautiful crystal at your private table. No menu! You will discuss a few delicious meal choices the chef has gathered from ingredients for the day.

The cuisine of Casa Antucura reflects the aromas, flavors and natural products of the region with a French influence of rich tastes and subtle nuances, prepared with elegant simplicity that goes perfectly with their wines.

You will feel at home. Staff and chef customize your experience. And you can choose your time for dinner, different from the late evening dining typical of Argentina.

Breakfast, lunch and dinner – private, only for guests of the house.

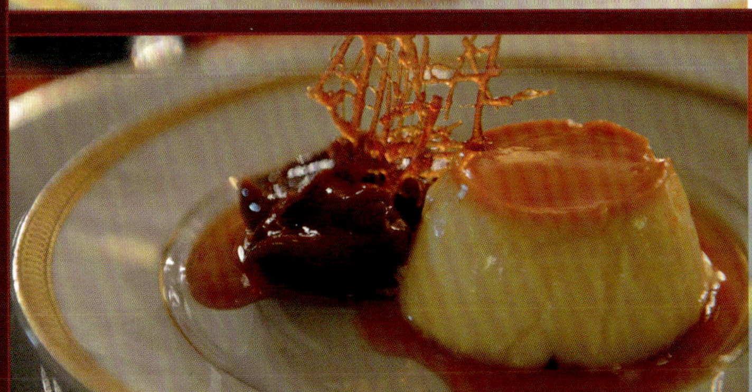

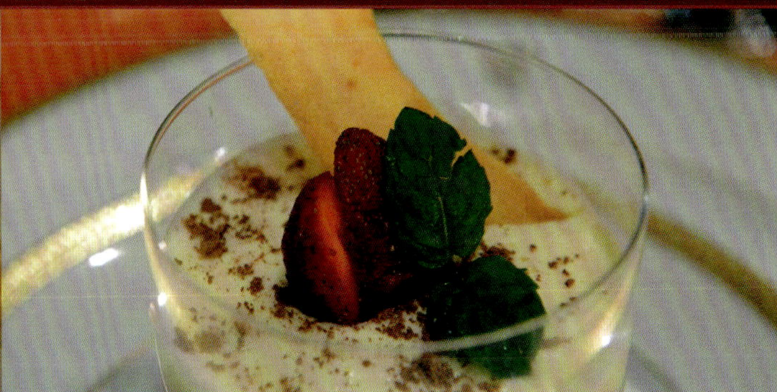

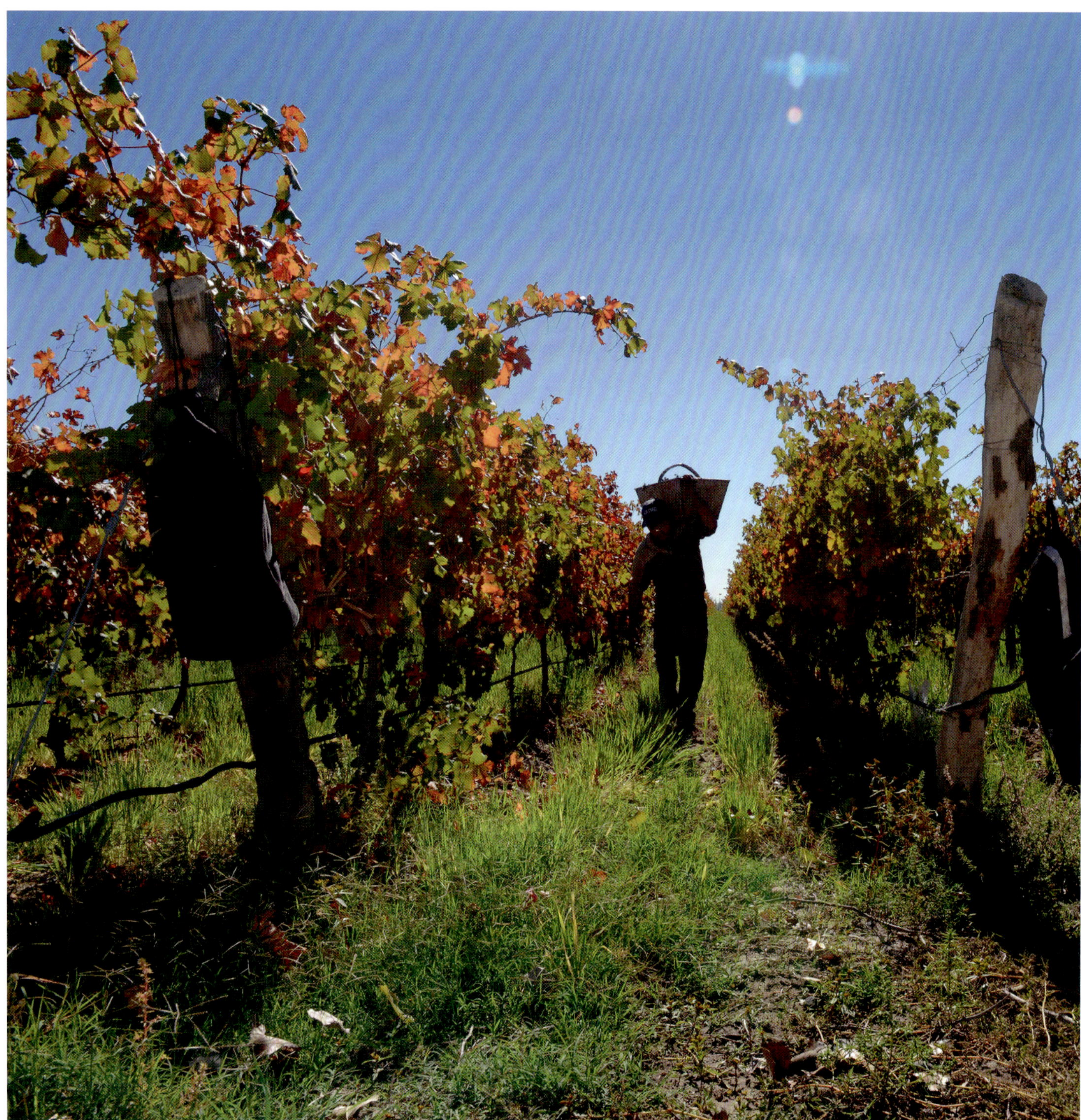

MAGNIFICENT BORDEAUX

What else would you expect from an all French owner, winemaker (Hervé Chagneau) and notable winemaker consultant (Michel Rolland), team... to create a Bordeaux-style wine in Argentina. Primarily Cabernet Sauvignon, blended with Malbec and Merlot, like the French would do in Bordeaux. Don't be uninterested... this is a magnificent wine! The Antucura Blend Selection was a particularly special treat for me, *every night*. By choice.

And, Hervé is bringing home the awards...

2012 Antucura Malbec

- 95 points by Decanter Magazine
- No. 2 Argentine Malbec of The Year

2013 Antucura Cabernet Sauvignon

- 95 points by Decanter Magazine
- Gold Medal, Decanter's World Wine Award

Plus, both these wines are under US $20 in the USA!

The Bodega Antucura magic begins with special vines purchased in Pomerol France, plus high density planting and meticulous harvesting, resulting in the most perfect berries possible for making their wines. Hervé (photo below) chooses the best 30% of the vineyard, hand-picks each block in a morning (photo left), transfers the fresh bunches to a refrigerated container to preserve freshness, double sorting to choose only the perfect berries (photo below left) to then conducts dozens of micro-vinifications off distinctly sandy, clay, and gravel blocks. Hervé spends weeks playing with the assemblage to create his final blends.

The results are wines worth noticing. A great synergy of blending the attributes of the Andes terroir with classic French winemaking to make wines with the luscious elegance shared by both Pomerol France and the prestigious micro sub-appellation of Vista Flores, Argentina.

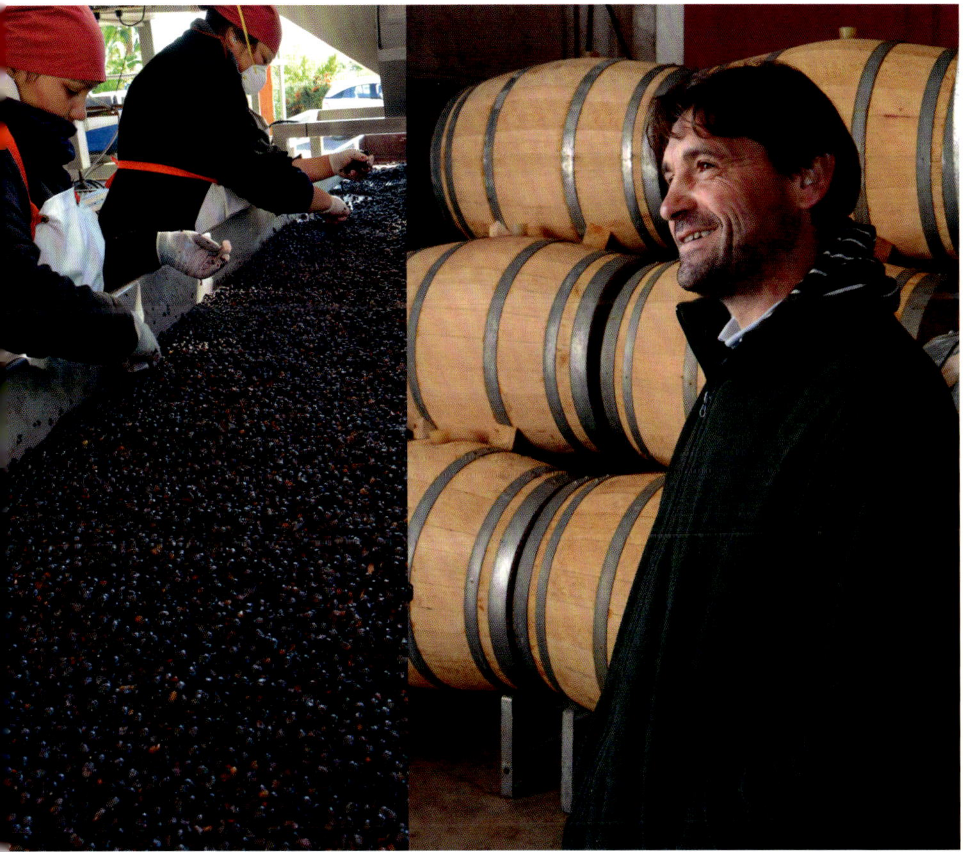

MENDOZA **VALLE DE UCO** TUNUYÁN

Vineyards (Viñedos) • Winery (Bodega)

BODEGA ANTUCURA

3 km Calle Barrandica s/n
(Vista Flores, **Tunuyán,** Valle de Uco)

011 (+54 261) 524.2069
info@Antucura.com

BodegaAntucura.com

English, Español & Français
200,000 bottles produced annually

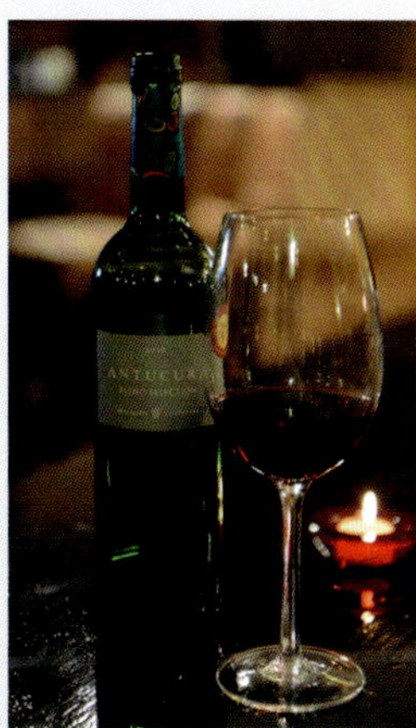

Michael's Favorite Pick
Antucura Blend Selection

Total Collection of Wines
Antucura

Gran Vin (Merlot/Cabernet Sauvignon)
Blend Selection (Cabernet Sauvignon/Malbec/ Merlot)
Calcura (Cabernet Sauvignon/ Merlot /Malbec)
Malbec (100% Malbec)
Cabernet Sauvignon (100% Cabernet)

Barrandica

Barrandica Blend Selection (Malbec/Merlot/Syrah/ Cabernet Franc/Petit Verdot/Cabernet Sauvignon)
Malbec Selection
Cabernet Sauvignon
Pinot Noir

To get Antucura wines in the USA
Nationwide Distributors: SouthernStarz.com

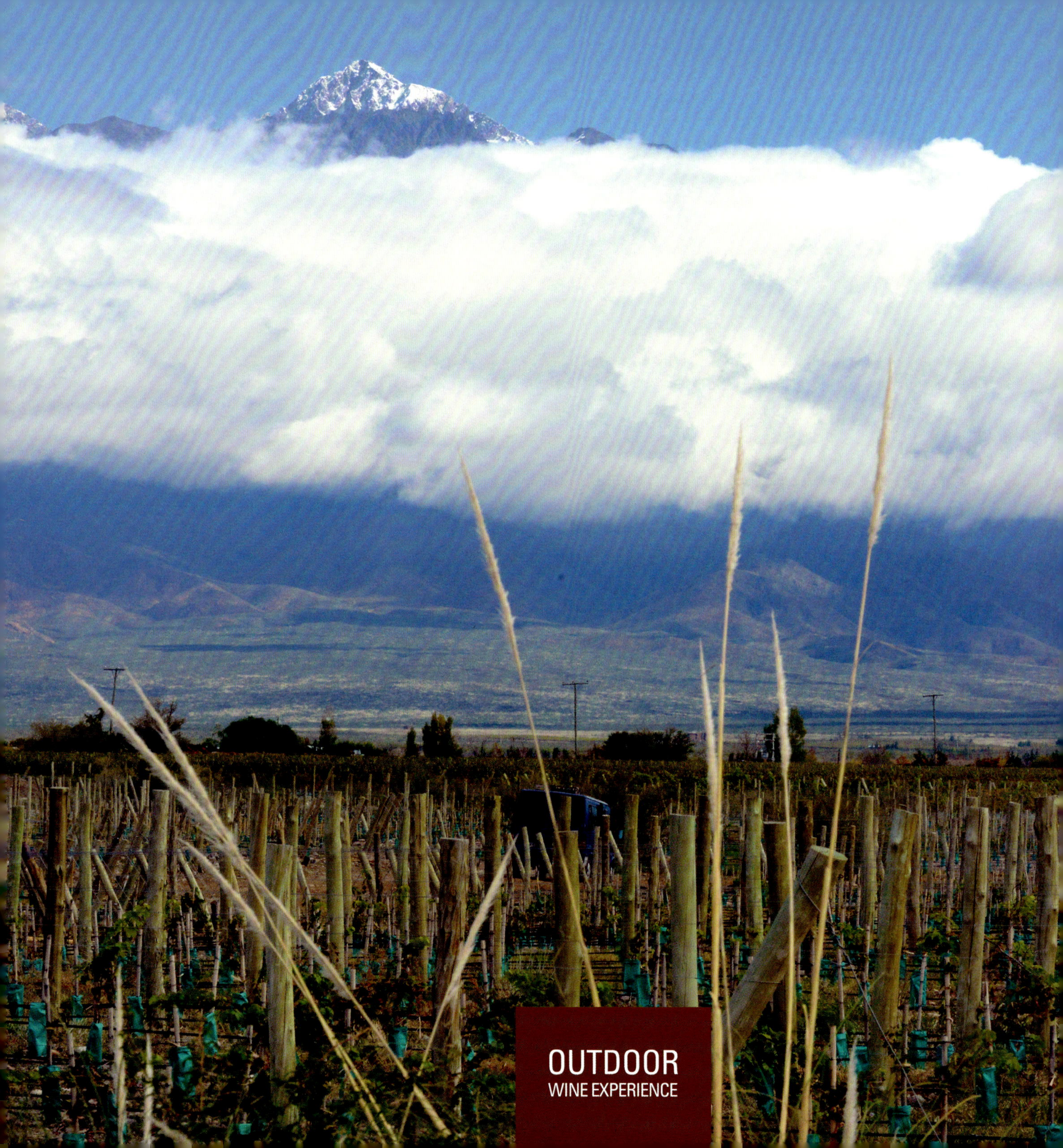
OUTDOOR
WINE EXPERIENCE

FOOD & WINEMAKING PASSION

For four generations, the Giménez and Riili families have shared the love for making wine in Argentina. In 1890 Don Fernando Riili came to Argentina from Sicily and in 1905 Don Pedro Giménez from Spain. This Italian/Spanish love-affair finally consummated in their grandchildren's marriage of 1967 creating the Giménez Riili Winery of family passions for acquiring choice vineyard properties in Mendoza and making their special wines.

Magnificent Vista Flores, Expansive Maipú and a very special 1.5-acre vineyard of 50-year-old Malbec in *Famed Altamira*, has created a delicious lineup of extraordinary wines. Plus, they have recently built a winery in the new *Winemakers Village* in Tunuyán.

Being a huge fan of Altamira Malbecs, this unique property becomes a special single-vineyard bottling as their *Gran Familia Malbec*. 100% Malbec, 100% Altamira, 100% extraordinary. When I was welcomed with open arms by Federico Giménez Riili with an open bottle of Gran Familia Malbec, I knew I had arrived at a very special place.

Second youngest of five great-grandson brothers, Federico is the CEO managing the family's Giménez Riili Winery. Young and fresh with ideas, personable and carrying on the family tradition of friendship and passion for their land, wine and the people who wish to share special moments of life with them.

THE WINEMAKER'S VILLAGE

Giménez Riili is located at the entrance of The Vines, Private Vineyard Estates and Resort & Spa, in a very cool project called *The Winemakers Village*... a boutique collection of 12 small, high-quality wineries that are joined by a walking path along a meandering stream of snowmelt Andes water.

The Village includes some of the best winemakers from Argentina and USA. Federico's older brother Pablo Giménez Riili is a cofounder of The Vines (next page) and as such, Giménez Riili is the first to plant vineyards, build a winery and establish themselves in this unique Winemakers Village.

A UNIQUE FAMILY, WINE & FOOD EXPERIENCE

Enjoy the warmth of this family friendship and spend the afternoon with them. Tour their winery, see the tanks, barrels and vintage gallery. Wander their gardens and learn about the native flora and wildlife of the valley. And, join them for their daily traditional Argentine BBQ under outdoor cabanas overlooking vineyards and the Andes mountains.

An all-you-can-eat five-course menu of fresh-baked empanadas in their clay oven, grilled trout salad with beets and guacamole, chicken stew in an open pot of vegetables, herbs and spices, asado of rib eye and tenderloin, and a dessert of Malbec-infused peaches served with homemade vanilla ice cream... all paired with a different wine.

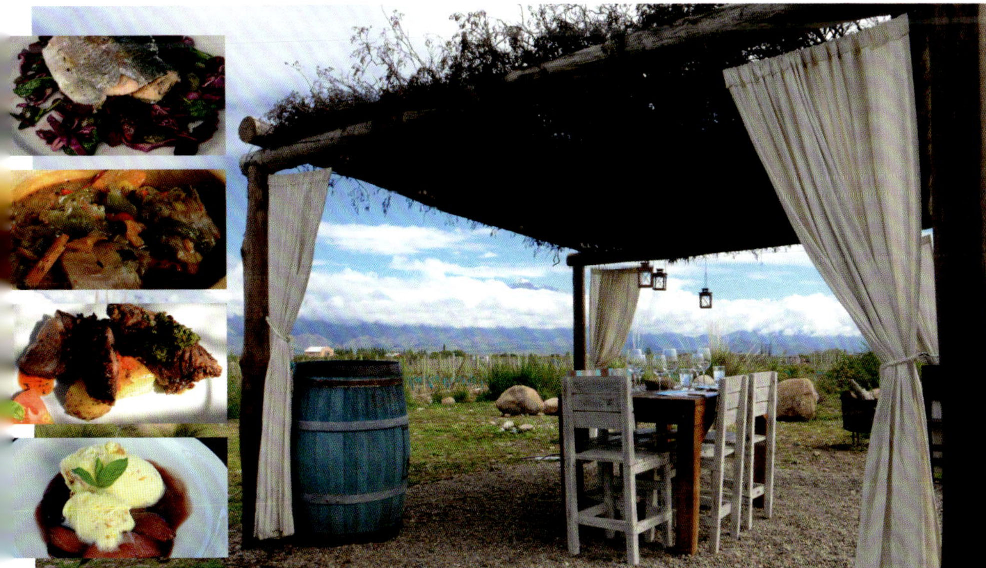

MENDOZA **VALLE DE UCO** TUNUYÁN

Winery (Bodega) • Asado (BBQ)

GIMÉNEZ RIILI

Ruta 94, 8 km from Manzano Histórico
(Los Sauces, **Tunuyán,** Valle de Uco)

011 (+54 261) 498.7863
turismo@GimenezRiili.com

GimenezRiili.com

English & Español
150,000 bottles produced annually

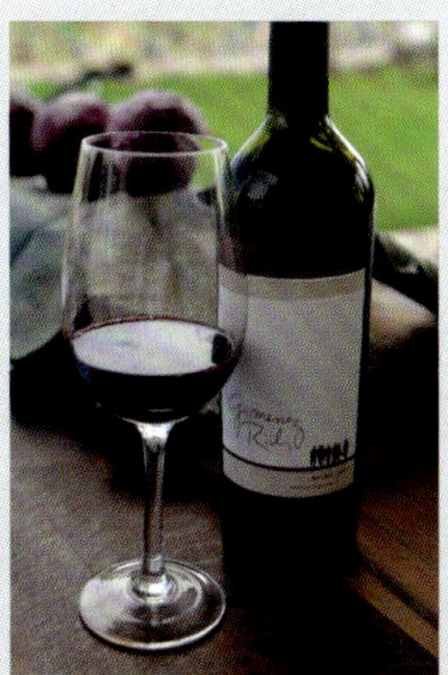

Michael's Favorite Pick
Gran Familia - Malbec (100% Malbec from Altamira)

Total Collection of Wines
Gran Familia - Malbec (from Altamira)
Gran Familia - Syrah (from Vista Flores)

Joyas De Familia - Gran Blend (Altamira & Vista Flores)
(45% Malbec, 25% Syrah, 15% Cab, 10% Cab Franc, 5% Merlot)

Padres Dedicados - Malbec
Padres Dedicados - Cabernet Sauvignon
Padres Dedicados - Cabernet Franc

Buenos Hermanos - Malbec
Buenos Hermanos - Malbec Rose
Buenos Hermanos - Torrontés

To get Giménez Riili wines in the USA
Write to the winery directly and they will ship 12-bottle cases to the USA: info@GimenezRiili.com

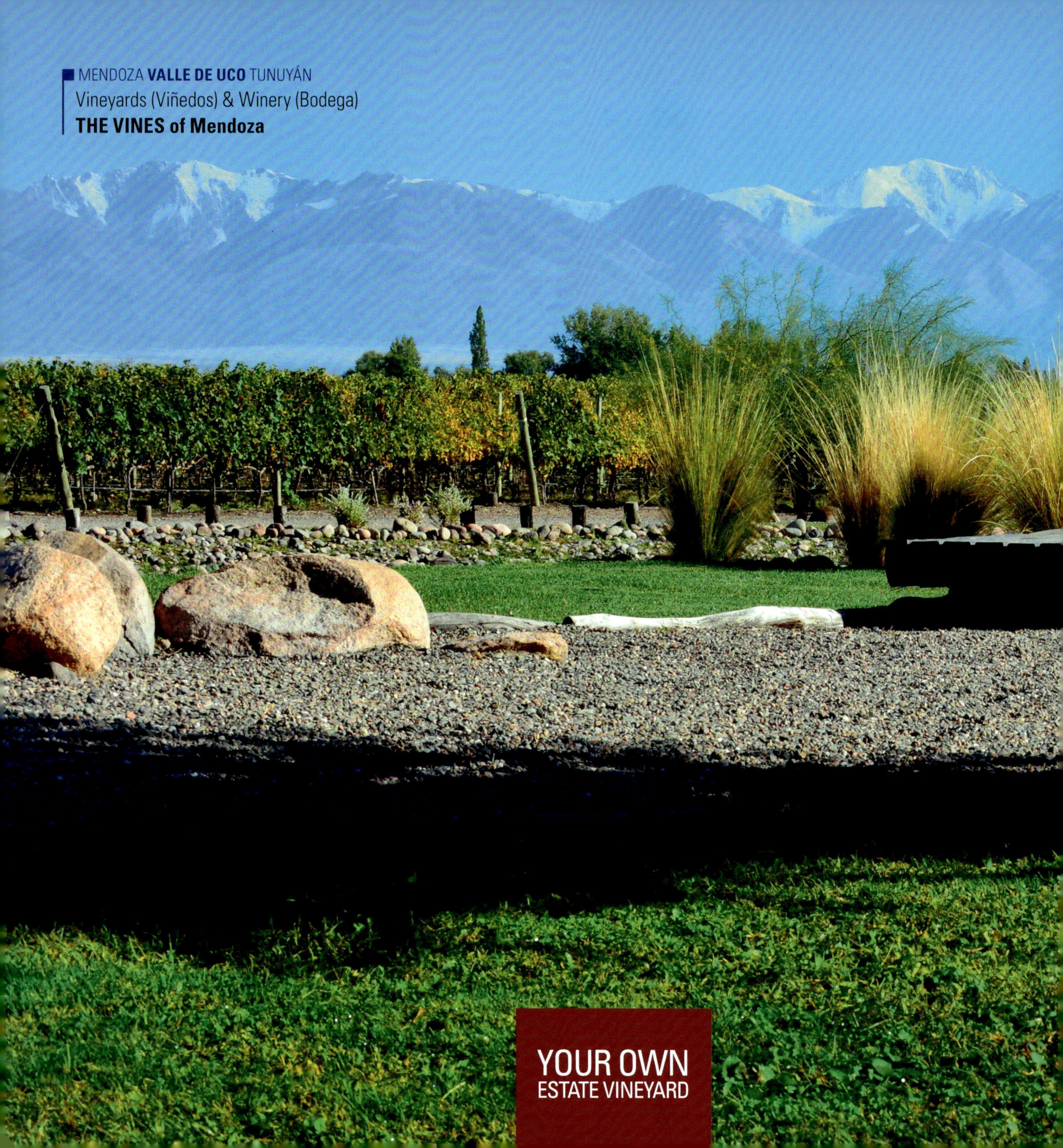

YOUR OWN
ESTATE VINEYARD

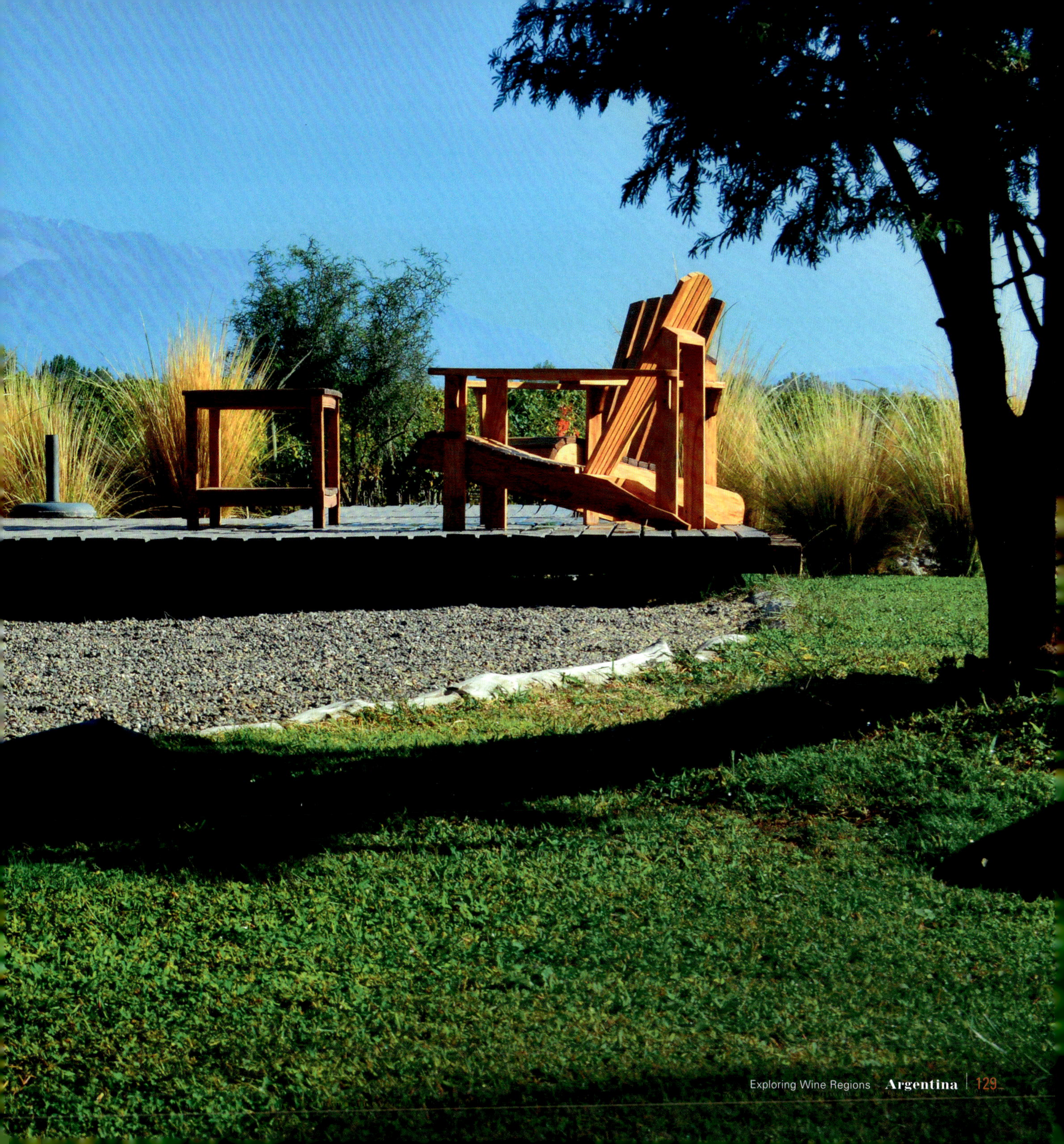

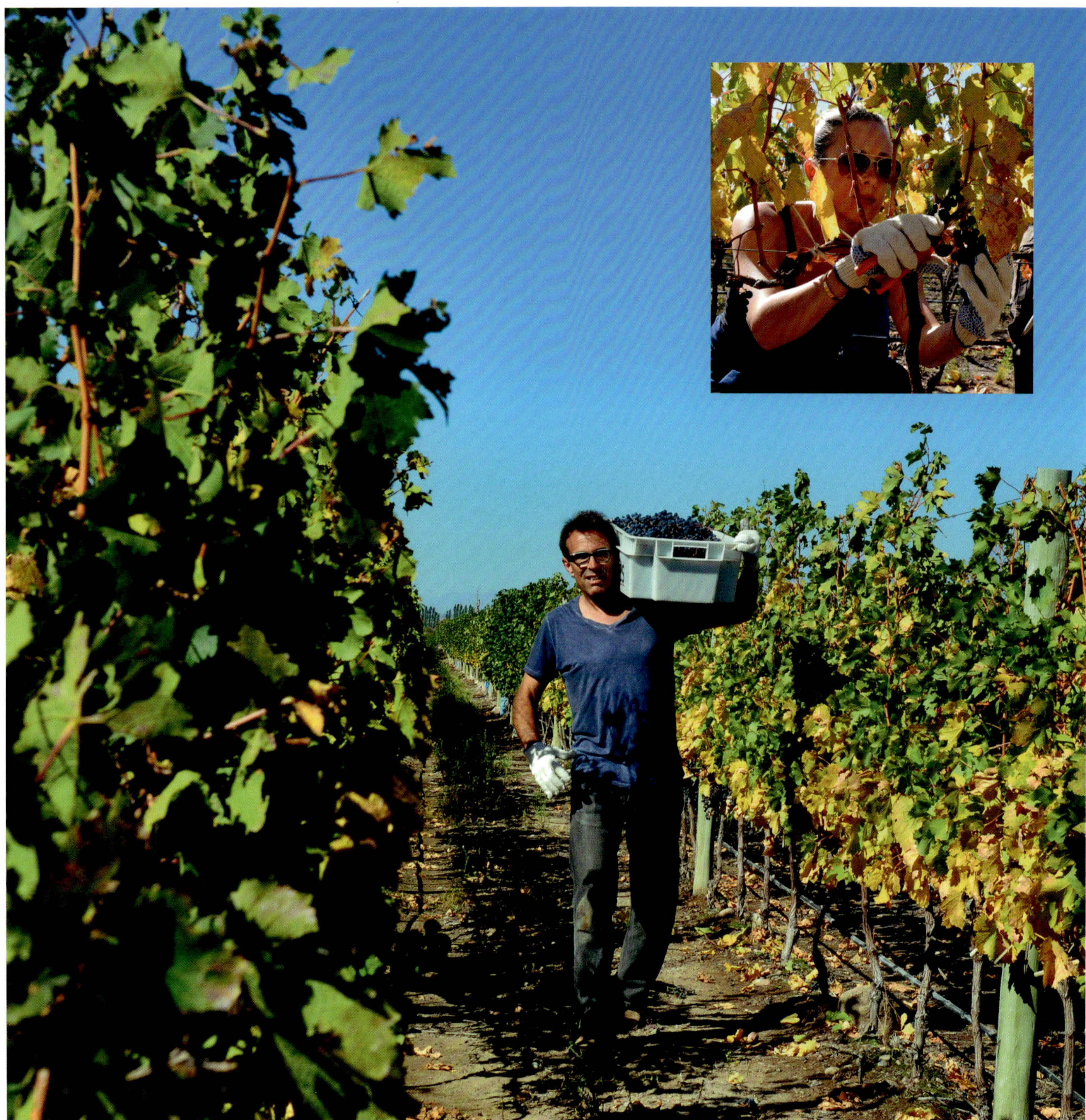

Private Vineyard Estates in Valle de Uco

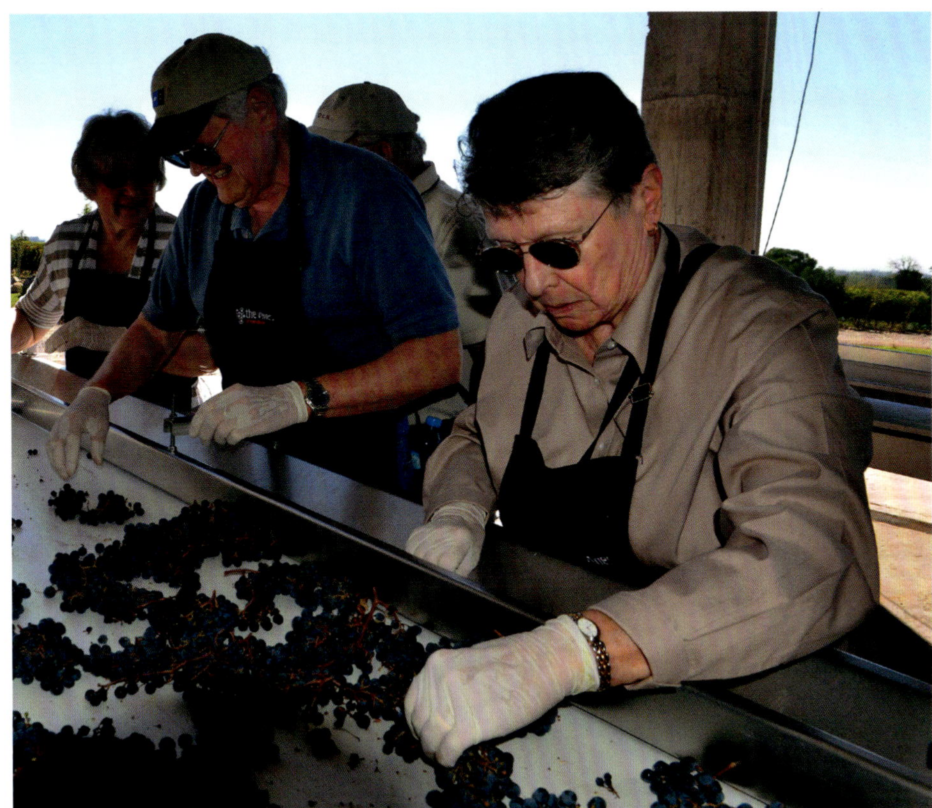

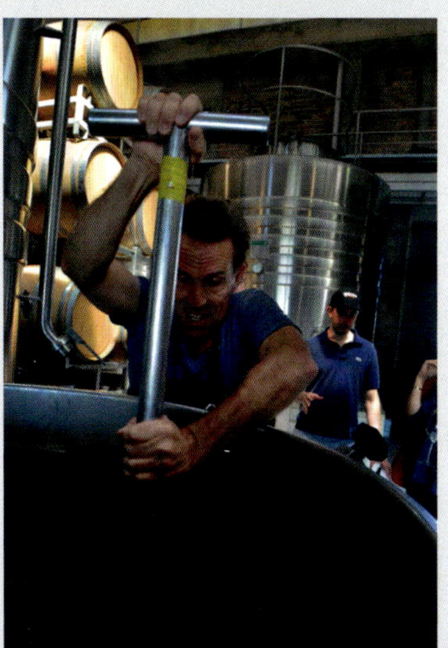

LIVING THE VINTNER LIFE

Here is a unique opportunity to own your own private vineyard within a 1,500-acre acclaimed estate in Valle de Uco, and to become your own vintner with a team of highly accomplished winemakers.

I have been following the development of ***The Vines of Mendoza***, and everything I see is first-class. Their initial vintage received 92 points by Robert Parker. Their consulting winemaker is none other than Santiago Achaval (see Kobe Grape on page 36). They have assembled a top-notch team of vineyard management and wine making professionals... all participating to help you make world-class wines.

The property is grand. Nestled against the Andes at 3,600-foot elevation, fed by fresh snowmelt water, pristine air, and has the special alluvium soil of Valle de Uco. They already have 130 vineyard owners, growing 18 different grape varietals, producing 230 entirely unique wines.

And the investment makes sense. Private Vineyard Estates are available from three to 10 acres in size. Vineyards are US $85k per acre... complete! The complete part is extraordinary... your acres are fully developed, including professional management while you are not there. You choose the grape varietal(s) you want on your property and they do the planting, irrigation system, pruning, harvesting, and vineyard management. Plus, you get use of the winery and the professional winemaking staff (including winemaker Santiago Achaval), the numerous equipment, cellar, bottling, labeling, even shipping... everything you need is included for you to make your dream wine or commercial wine venture.

Do it all yourself or manage the process, or anything in-between... with numerous wine professionals at your disposal.

All this among a five-star, all-villa resort, with spa and extraordinary restaurant.

Private Vineyard Estates

94 Ruta Provincial
(**Tunuyán,** Valle de Uco)

(617) 398-7830 • USA
VinesOfMendoza.com/Private_Vineyard

LEFT PAGE, hand-harvesting your own vineyard is a rewarding experience; getting in touch with nature and your prized grapes.

ABOVE, de-stemming and sorting your own grapes; punching down the skins as your grapes ferment into your dream wine.

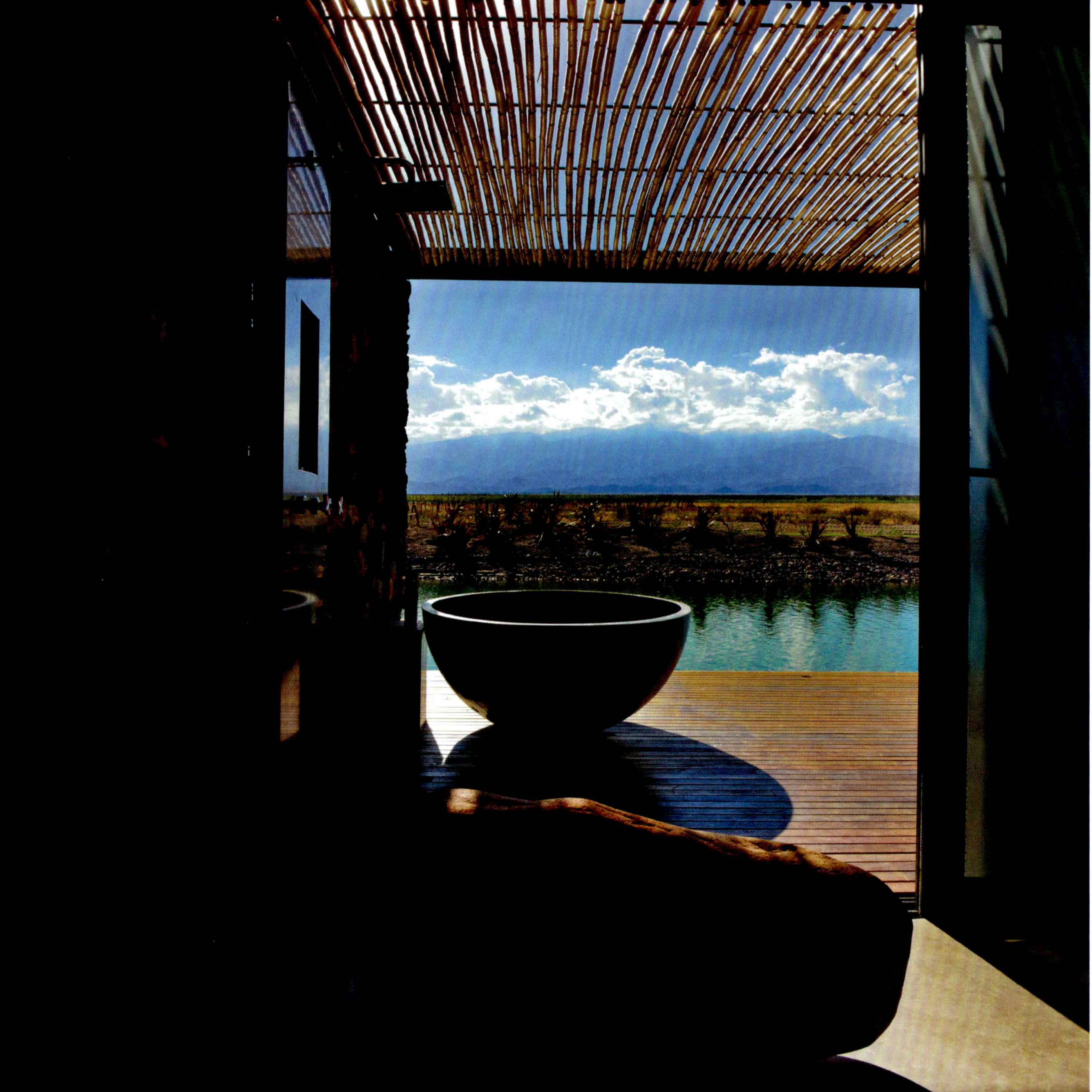

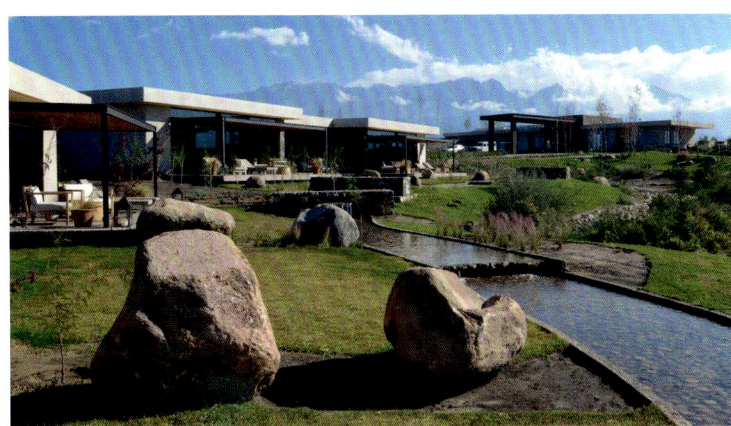

MENDOZA **VALLE DE UCO** TUNUYÁN
Winery Resort & Villas
THE VINES Resort & Spa

94 Ruta Provincial
(**Tunuyán,** Valle de Uco)

(707) 737-0222 • USA
011 (+54 261) 461.3900
info@VinesResortAndSpa.com

VinesResortAndSpa.com

English & Español

MODERN LUXURY VILLAS

Amid the private vineyards, The Vines built a beautiful upscale All-Villa Resort. These villas are far above your typical five-star hotel. Designed by renowned architects Bormida & Yanzon, built with a mix of rustic and modern materials in an ultra-contemporary design, with no stone unturned, literally, the huge stone you see in the indoor/ outdoor shower (photo left page) is conveniently for resting your foot while shaving your legs.

Twenty-two spectacular one- and two-bedroom villas take in the natural light in their open floor to ceiling windows and massive indoor and outdoor living spaces... creating expansive views of the vineyards and Andes Mountains. Beautiful furnishings, full custom kitchens, state-of-the-art technology and meticulous attention to detail.

Outdoor living spaces are just as beautiful and inviting. Expansive natural wood decks, private rooftop terraces, gas fireplaces, outdoor soaking tubs and showers, and plunge pools that double as a hot tub.

The resort villas are available as nightly rentals for vacation getaways. Or, private villas are offered for purchase as exclusive residences, with resort privileges, maintenance-free living, 24-hour security, and may be placed in the resort's rental program with seamless professional management.

VILLA AMENITIES
One and Two Bedrooms
Spacious 1,000 to 2,700 sq'
Indoor and Outdoor Living Space
Floor-to-Ceiling Windows
Spa-Inspired Bathroom
Well-Equipped Modern Kitchen
Flat-Screen Television with DirecTV
Hot Tub and Fireplace

RESORT AMENITIES
Infinity Pool with
Private Cabanas & Hot Tub
Spa, Fitness Center & Bocce Ball Court
Spectacular Restaurant & Wine Bar
Winery & Winemaking Activities
Running Trails & Horseback Riding

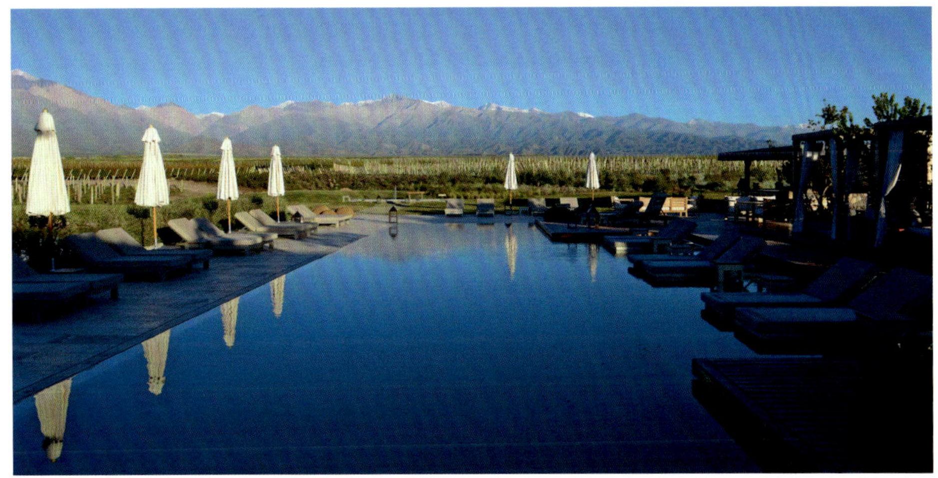

LEFT PAGE, indoor and outdoor, shower and bath, in your private villa overlooking the Andes

ABOVE, front entrance to the resort, with three private villas sprawling to the left

BELOW, spectacular pool, aside the magnificent Andes

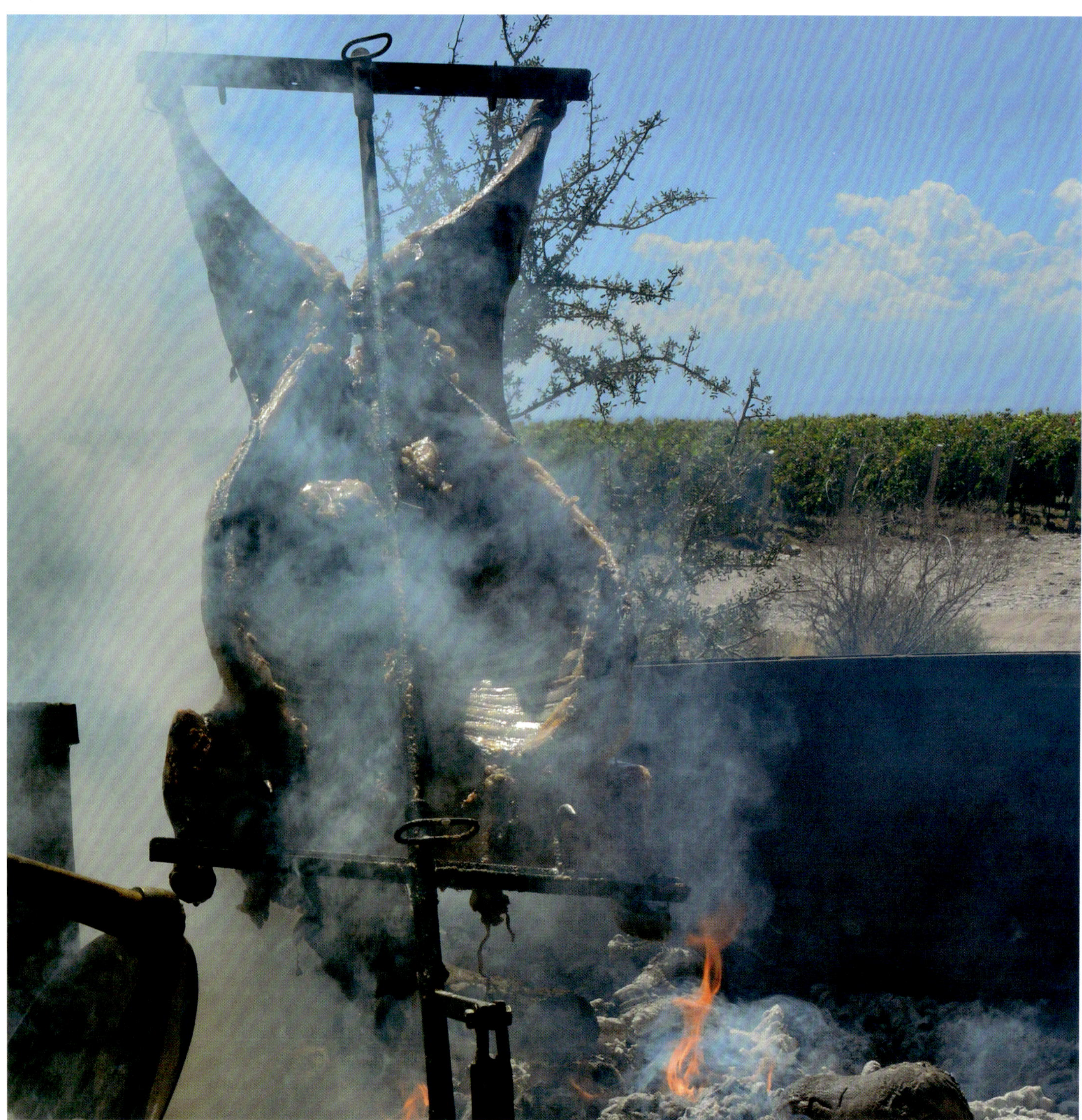

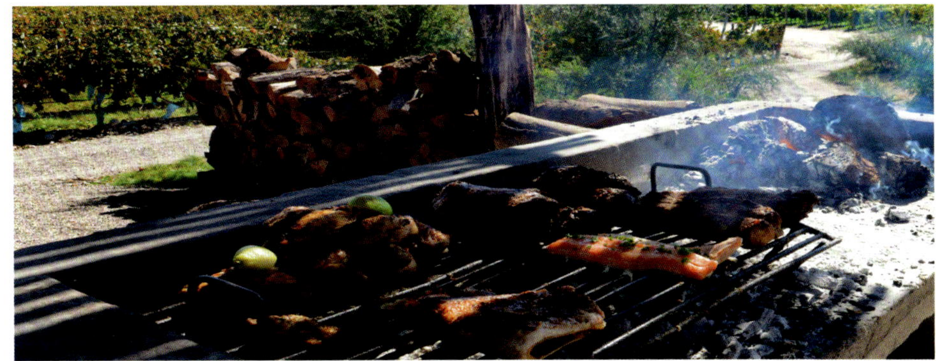

MENDOZA **VALLE DE UCO** TUNUYÁN

Restaurant

THE VINES
SIETE FUEGOS

94 Ruta Provincial
(**Tunuyán,** Valle de Uco)

011 (+54 261) 461.3910
7Fuegos@VinesResortAndSpa.com

VinesResortAndSpa.com

English & Español

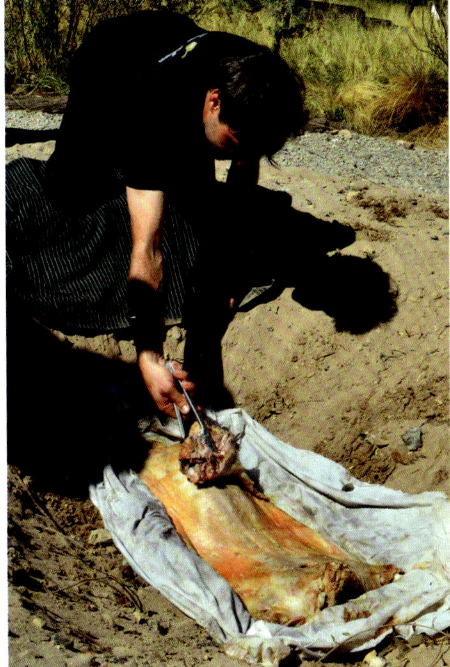

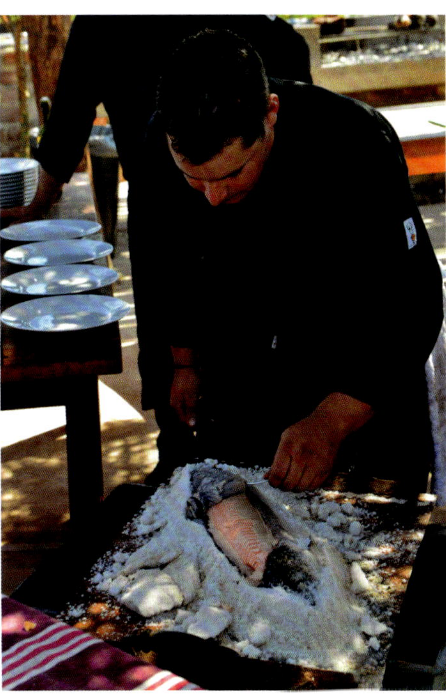

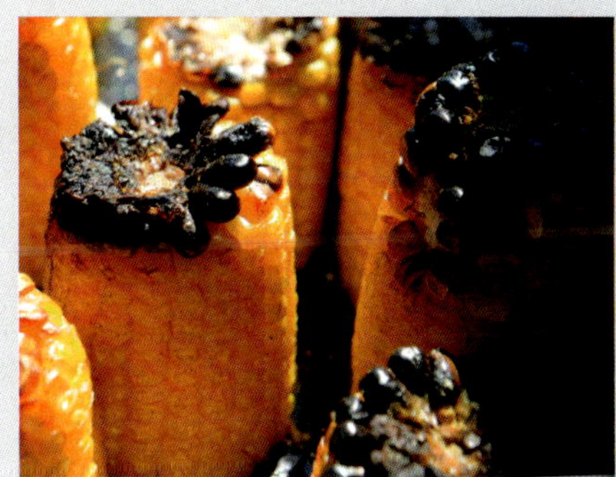

LEFT PAGE,
Butterflied Lamb slowly roasting on an open fire

ABOVE,
Outdoor **Parrilla** preparing for a feast of **Asado**

LEFT,
Goat roasted underground with rosemary leaves and jarilla spice in the coals under the goat.

CENTER,
Peeling the skin off of the **Salt Encrusted Salmon**, cooked above and below a rack of burning embers.

CHEF FRANCIS MALLMANN . . .

Siete Fuegos (translated is Seven Fires) is Francis Mallmann's tradition of the untraditional in open-flame cooking techniques. With fire... over it, under it, in it, and around it... an entertaining experience that can be viewed from your table at Mallmann's new restaurant at The Vines Resort.

Internationally acclaimed culinary author and chef, Francis Mallmann creates inspired dishes of Argentina's famous beef, and other meats and fish. See the photos, open flame cooking in action. Beyond the entertainment, Mallmann's asado

PLAYING WITH FIRE

may just become one of your most memorable barbecue flavor experiences ever.

Eye-opening, mouth-watering and fiery flavors led me to enjoy a nine-hour slow-grilled rib eye with a chimichurri topping to permanently impregnate my senses.

Consider his salt-encrusted salmon, the entire fish thickly encased in salt, baked on cast-iron rack with wood embers burning above and below. After, the skin just rolls back as the beautiful meat is exposed (above).

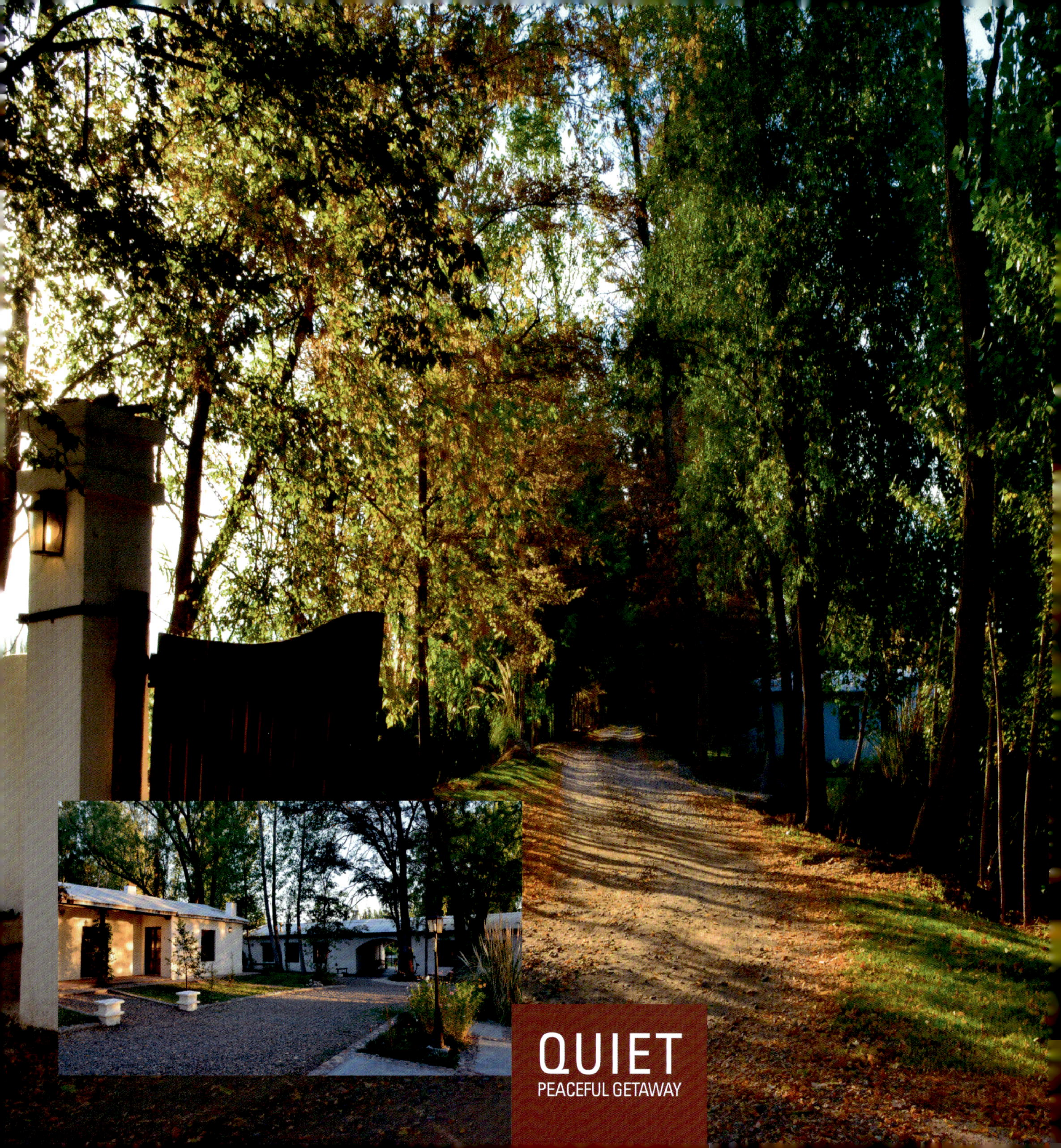
QUIET
PEACEFUL GETAWAY

Boutique Vineyard Hotel

POSTALES HOTELES BOUTIQUE

Tabanera s/n - Colonia Las Rosas
(Colonia Las Rosas, **Tunuyán,** Valle de Uco)

011 (+54 261) (15) 545.7658
Reservas@PostalesArg.com

PostalesArg.com

English, Español & Français

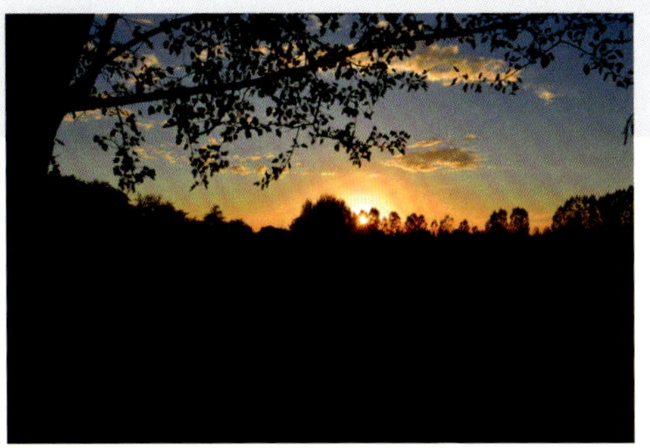

BOUTIQUE TRANQUILITY

Wake up in the morning to a quiet and peaceful serene setting. To crisp clean air. Brilliant sunshine. In the middle of Malbec vineyards. Under enormous weeping willows, pines and alamos trees. Snow-capped Andes for a backdrop. A tranquil getaway from it all, and yet in the center of Valle de Uco convenient to the many wineries and outdoor activities this valley and mountain area offers.

There are only nine quaint rooms in this park-like setting, with swimming pool and benches to gaze out through the vineyards at the majestic Andes mountains. Freely wander through their vineyards, watch the sun rise yellow through the vines, and take in the harmony of nature.

Built of authentic adobe walls and open beam ceilings of logs and bamboo, custom wood doors, and antique furniture. A charming place filled with authenticity and personal service.

Enjoy a complimentary breakfast as you prepare for your day. WiFi included. Staff knows the area and can connect you with what you want to do. Or do nothing within an environment that invites you to relax and stay awhile.

It may be a small place; however, they have a gourmet chef who visits them in the evenings after gathering local ingredients from the valley. Raspberries, eggs, ducks, figs, for example, as he custom-makes the dinner offering.

Postales is at the heart of Valle de Uco, in a tiny town called Colonia Las Rosas, at the intersection of the roads leading to Tunuyán, Tupungato and San Carlos. It's a stroll along a beautiful tree-lined street into this quaint little town of just 2,000 inhabitants.

Three miles away is the town of Vista Flores (pop 4,500). The family who owns Postales also owns Familia Stortini Winery, on the land where their grandfather started farming 100 years ago... exploring the virtues of planting in arid soils, Francisco Stortini became one of the pioneers of Valle de Uco. Today they produce a line of wines called "etc." from Malbec vines that are 30, 50 and 94 years old.

Of course, Postales will arrange for a visit.

Postales. Nice place. Nice price. Nice environment. Nice people. Enjoy.

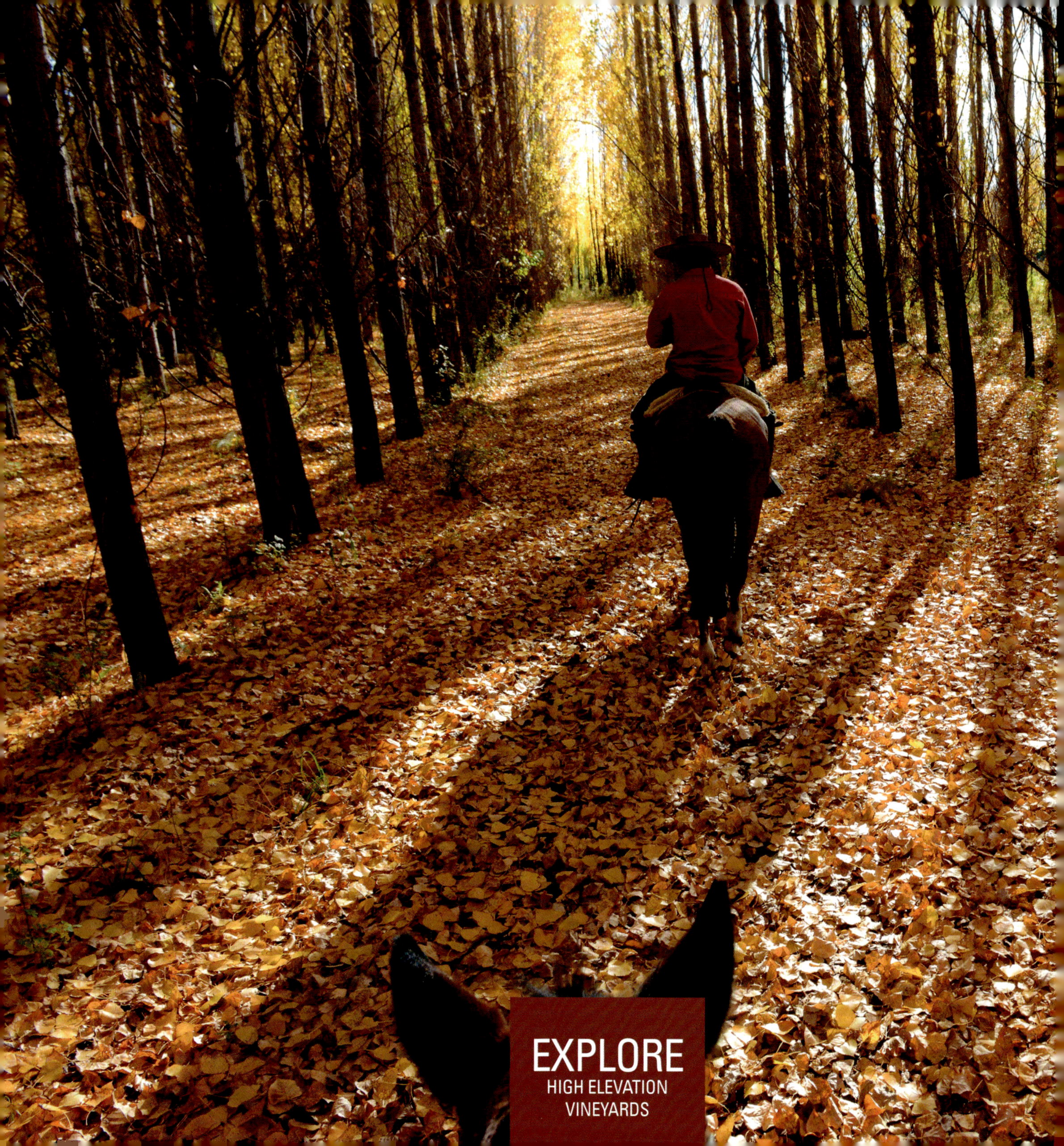
EXPLORE
HIGH ELEVATION
VINEYARDS

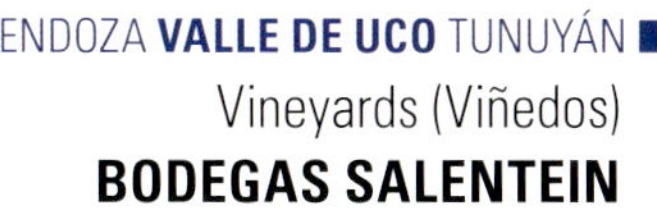

HIGHEST ALTITUDE VINEYARDS IN VALLE DE UCO

Bodegas Salentein is likely the largest winery estate in Valle de Uco with 5,000 acres (2,000 planted with vineyards), stretching 14 linear miles through elevation of 3,400 to 5,600 feet, well into the foothills of the Andes Mountains where the growing cycle is short and the climate cool. As Salentein is discovering, this is ideal terroir for the short-cycle varietals of Chardonnay, Pinot Meunier and Pinot Noir.

Head on up to their horse corral and get yourself a gaucho (cowboy) to take you horseback riding up into the high elevations of their property. Meander through walnut orchards and towering alamos trees (photo left page), while experiencing history as you pass the ruins of Casa Grande, an old farmhouse of indigenous Jesuit missionaries who came to the region in the 17th century. Ultimately arrive at Finca San Pablo, their 5,577′ elevation vineyards (photo below) where grapes are grown at altitudes possibly the highest in all of Valle de Uco, and are irrigated with pure mountain run-off, creating lower pH in the grapes and higher acidity, more color in the wine and greater ageability. The intense sunlight at altitude with much cooler night-time temperatures creates greater thermal amplitude ranges in which the grapes thrive. The result is showing spectacularly...

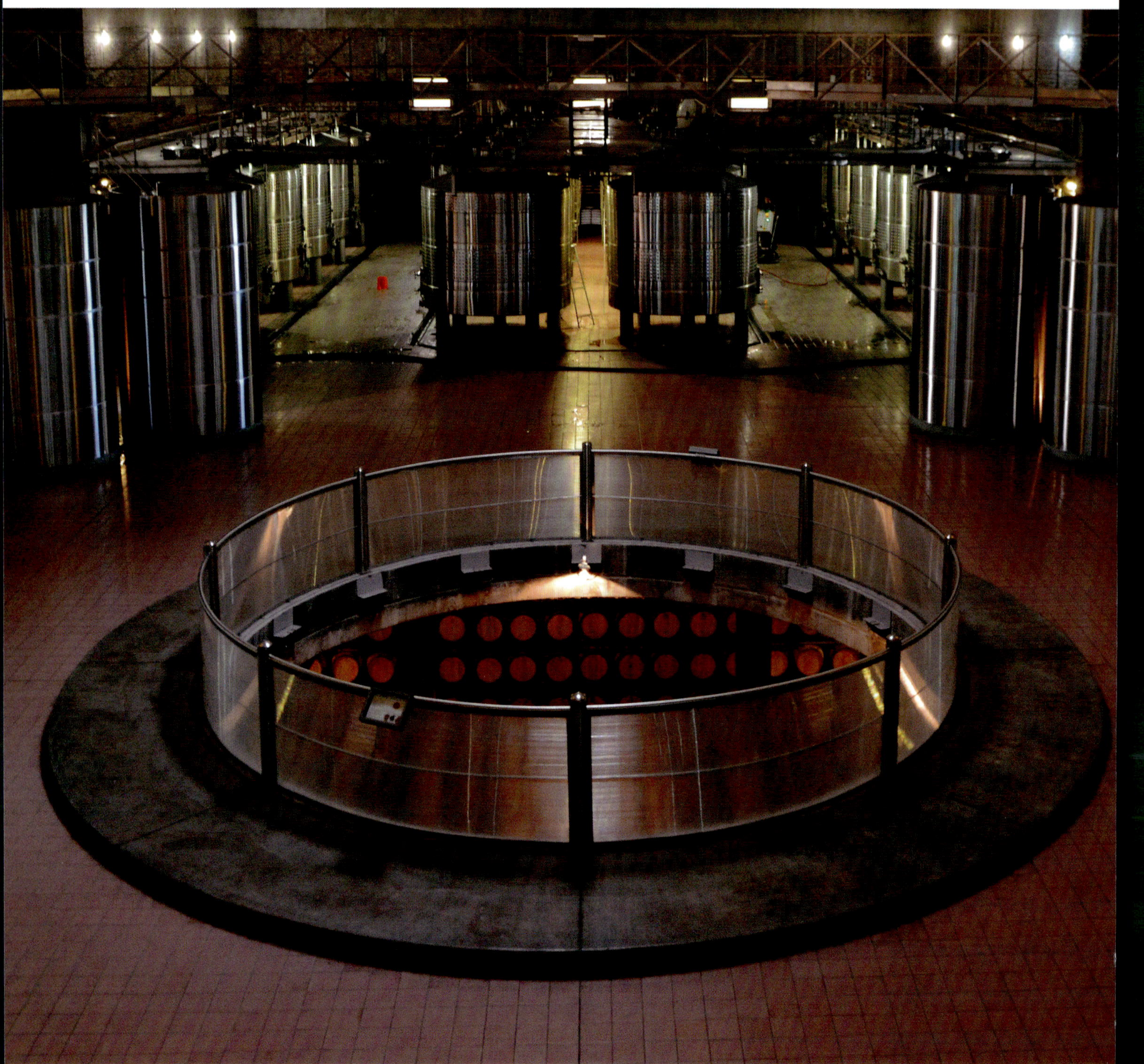

BODEGAS SALENTEIN

Bodegas Salentein has been experimenting with the full range of their estate's diverse terroir and five different micro-climates. Their fincas (vineyards) include many diverse elevations, climates and soils, creating varying conditions for ripening of different varietals. Salentein is primarily a red wine producer and they are making great use of the different conditions to maximize the quality of each wine.

Salentein has three fincas of lower, middle and upper elevations. The vines range from just-planted to over 30 years old. They claim it has taken them 10 years to learn the secrets of their property... to fully understand which varietals render the best results in which locations. Today, they say a new Salentein has been born from this arduous tenure. When you taste their wines, as I did, you will be very impressed with what they have created.

El Oasis is their lower finca, ranging from 3,445' to 3,937' in elevation, planted with all their varietals, and sports the longest full growing season. As their primary and largest finca, it produces much of their volume wines for the Portillo and Killka labels. As seen with other large wineries in the world, Salentein benefits from the profits derived from the volume wines to invest into creating super-premium wines.

La Pampa is their middle finca which lies at 3,937' to 4,265' elevation, and is their primary source of grapes for their premium and reserve wines, single vineyard wines, and their Gran Corte. These vineyards benefit from the varying micro-climates and natural alluvial soil which reaches depths of 12 to 16 inches, containing sand and many stones, causing the roots to grow deep in search of water. In 2006, they stopped turning the soil between the rows and allow natural herbs to grow, beneficial to the health of the vines and fruit.

San Pablo, as discussed earlier, is their upper finca sitting at 5,577' elevation and planted with predominantly Chardonnay, Pinot Noir and Pinot Meunier for their sparkling wines, and extra special luxury vintages. I had the privilege to taste one of their most recent experimentations... a single bottle, single-vineyard, 100% Pinot Noir, all from Finca San Pablo... without label and with full capacity to be a superb and luxurious Pinot Noir.

Mendoza is not exactly the best terroir for Pinot Noir as is found in the Patagonia Wine Region; however, the higher altitude environment has similar characteristics to Patagonia with shorter growing seasons and much cooler daytime temperatures. The results are becoming extraordinary.

The Bodegas Salentein winery was designed in the shape of a cross for both beauty and function. In each of the crosses' four wings is a small winery in-and-of-itself to focus on optimizing quality. Two levels allow a gentle flow of the grapes from tanks to barrels by a traditional gravity transfer system, and reducing the distance wine needs to be moved between winemaking steps.

The ground level houses stainless steel tanks (photo left page) and French wooden vats for fermentation and storage, and the underground for aging wine in oak casks. The four wings converge in a circular central chamber, which resembles an amphitheater and was inspired by ancient classical temples (see photo next page).

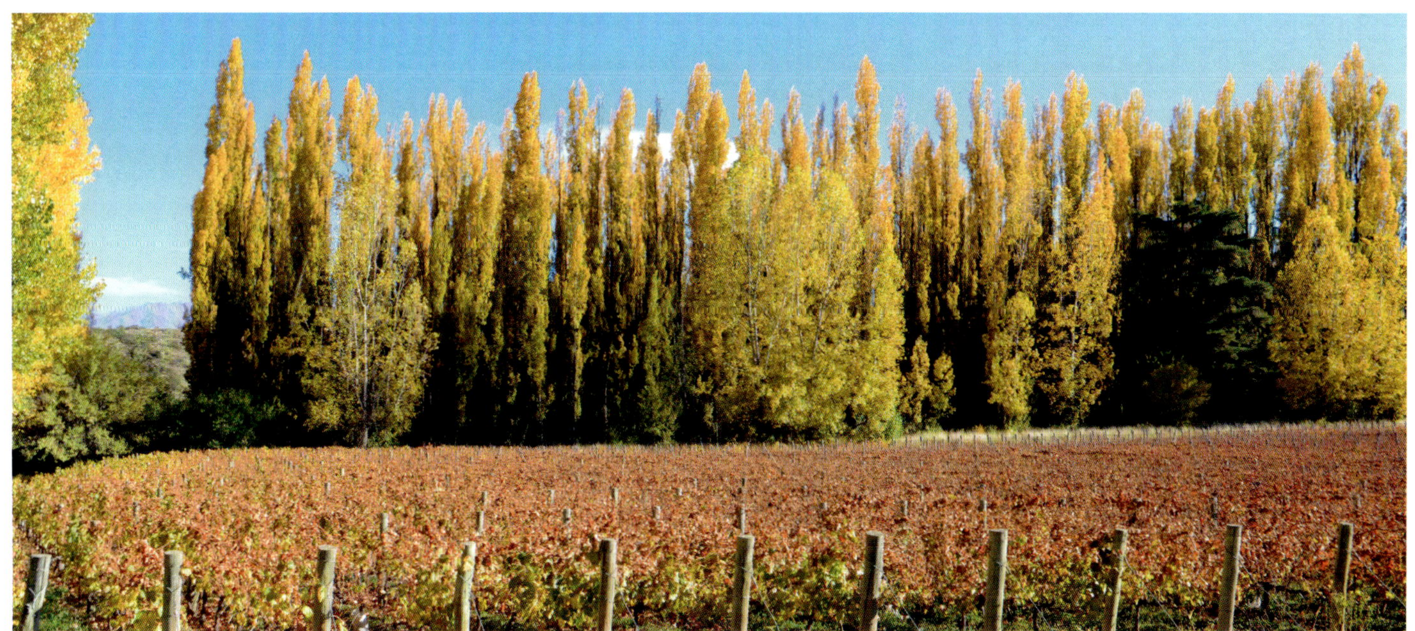

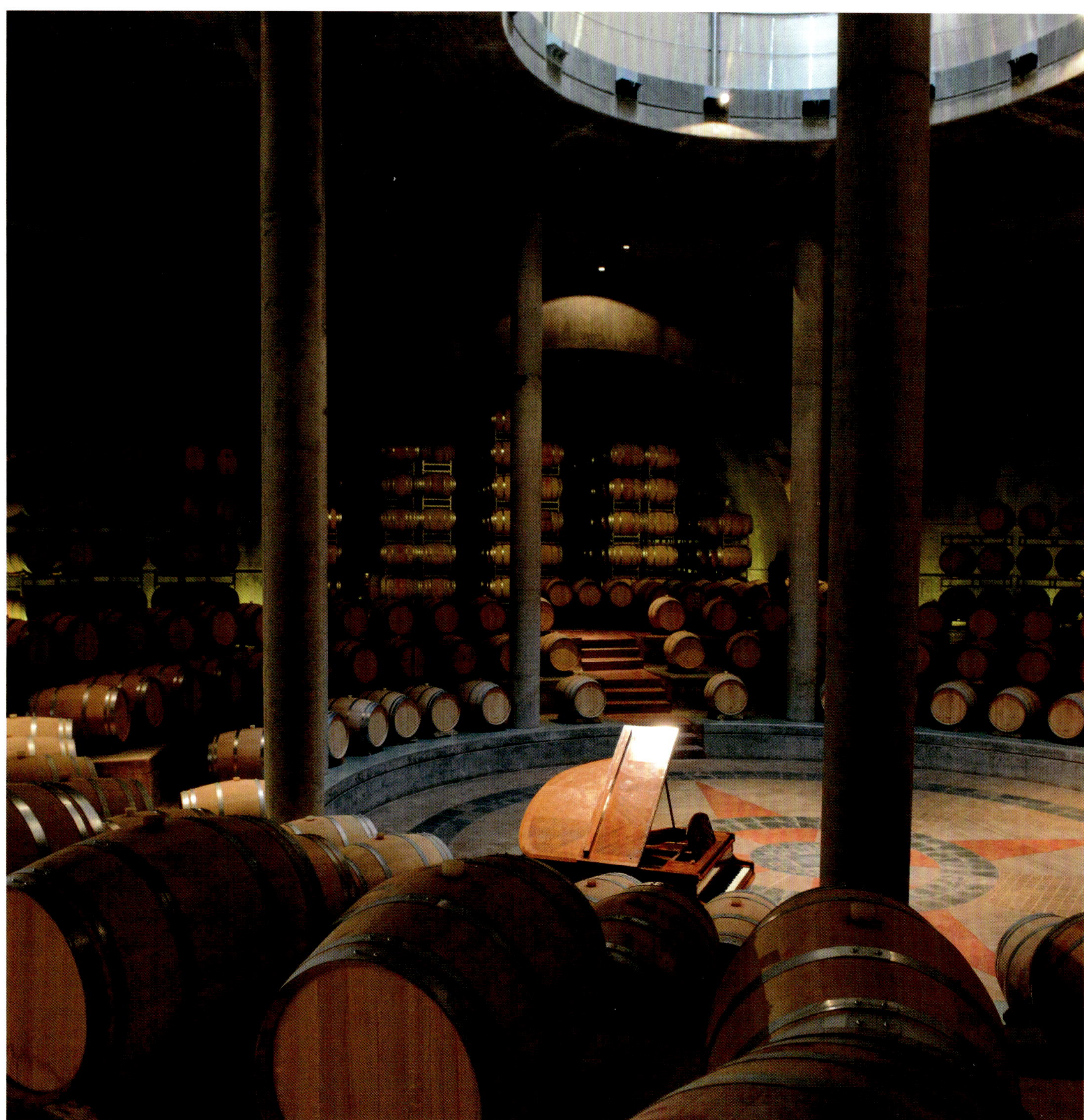

Meet José Antonio Galante (below), an important pioneer of the Argentina Malbec movement in the United States, who is the Chief Winemaker leading the success of Bodegas Salentein. Galante worked 34 years for Catena Zapata, the pre-eminent winery responsible for creating Malbec's iconic status and elevating Argentina as one of the world's most important wine-producing regions.

Today, nearly 50% of the Salentein portfolio is Malbec, and Galante is orchestrating an exciting lineup of different expressions of Malbec...

Single-Vineyard Malbecs which express the specific terroir of its landscape.

Blended Malbecs combining the distinguishing qualities of each micro-vineyard into a complex expression of the entire estate; integrating lower vineyards for fruitiness, middle vineyards for fresher fruit and floral aromas, upper vineyards for minerality, choosing particular grapes to create a great nose and other grapes for the mouth.

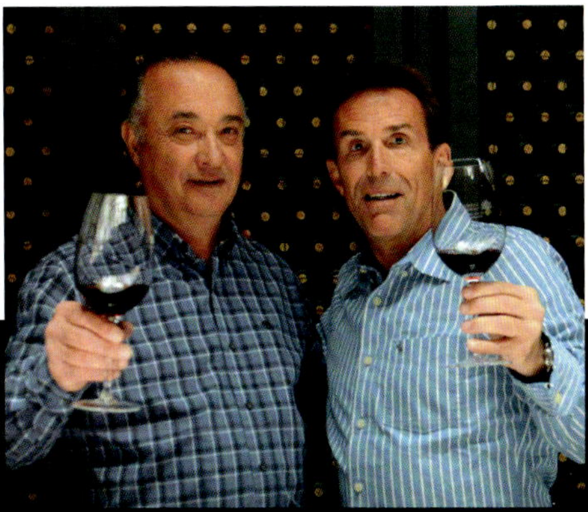

Malbec Blends with other Bordeaux varietals; my personal favorite, the *Salentein Numina Gran Corte*, an Argentine-style Bordeaux blend using all five grapes, with Malbec leading the blend: 64% Malbec, 18% Cabernet Sauvignon, 11% Merlot, 5% Cabernet Franc, and 2% Petit Verdot.

José Galante has made it his mission to understand the micro-climates occurring throughout this massive estate, and with such knowledge of this land, he can deliver wines with strong personalities and varietal expression. In the cellar, he plays music to his wines as they rest, aging (photo left page), Galante is the maestro of his wizardly skills in bringing forth a masterpiece of classical wines.

José and I tasted a lineup of 10 of his wines (photo below). All remarkable! Not possible to have a favorite among so many phenomenal Malbecs, even the stunning *Numina Gran Corte*, or the *Reserve Pinot Noir* next to a new high-altitude experiment of *San Pablo Pinot Noir*.

In the end though, the wine that sang to me most was the *Numina Cabernet Franc*. Bright aromas of blueberry and cloves with rich sweet ripe black fruits in your mouth, and only available at the winery (worth the trip from wherever you live).

All 10 wines showed masterfully just how extraordinary wines become with a property like this, and a maestro orchestrated their perfect harmony.

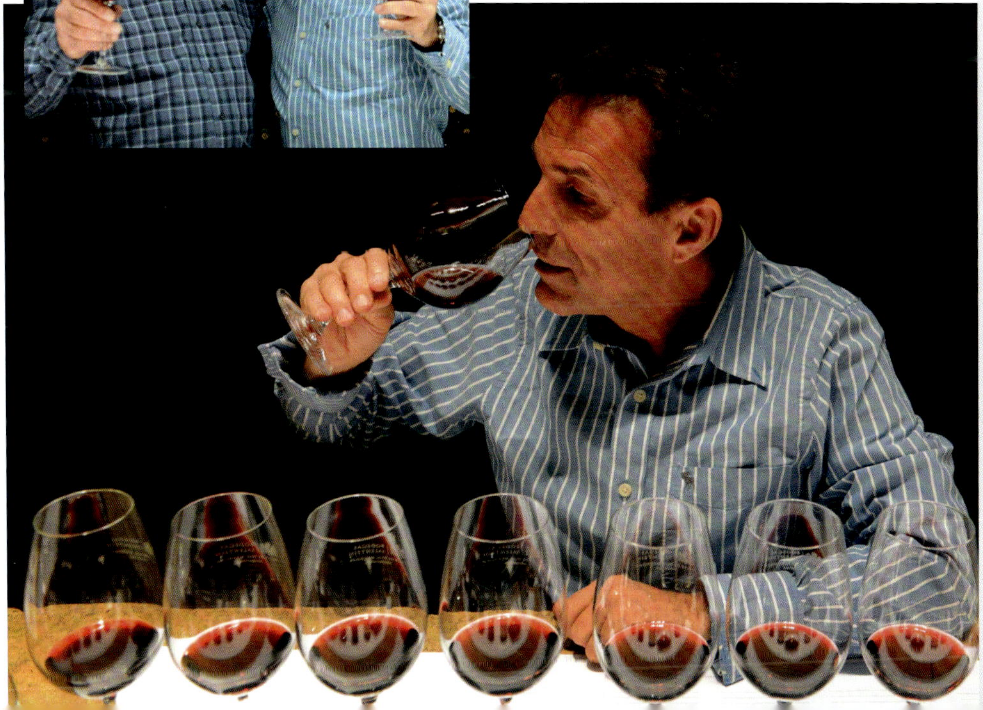

MENDOZA **VALLE DE UCO** TUNUYÁN

Winery (Bodega)

BODEGAS SALENTEIN

Ruta 89 S/N, km 14, Los Árboles
(Los Árboles, **Tunuyán,** Valle de Uco)

011 (+54 262) 242.9500
reservas.killka@BodegasSalentein.com

BodegasSalentein.com

English & Español
12,000,000 bottles produced annually

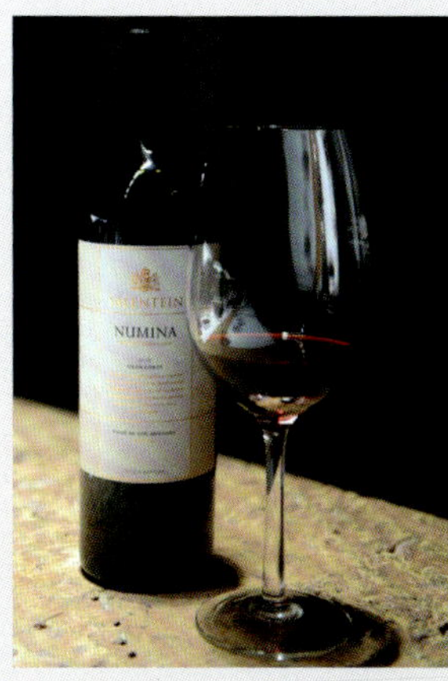

Michael's Favorite Pick
Salentein Numina - Gran Corte
(Malbec, Cab Sauv, Merlot, Cab Franc, Petit Verdot)

Total Collection of Wines

Salentein Numina
Gran Corte • Cab Franc • Syrah • Malbec
Gran VU Blend • Gran Uco Blend

Salentein Primus
Malbec • Merlot • Pinot Noir • Chardonnay

Salentein Single Vineyard
Malbec • Pinot Noir • Chardonnay
• Late Harvest Sauvignon Blanc

Salentein Reserve
Malbec • Merlot • Pinot Noir
Cabernet Sauvignon • Chardonnay
• Sauvignon Blanc

To get Bodegas Salentein wines in the USA
Their Importers have a zip code search at:
PalmBay.com/wine_locator_retail.asp

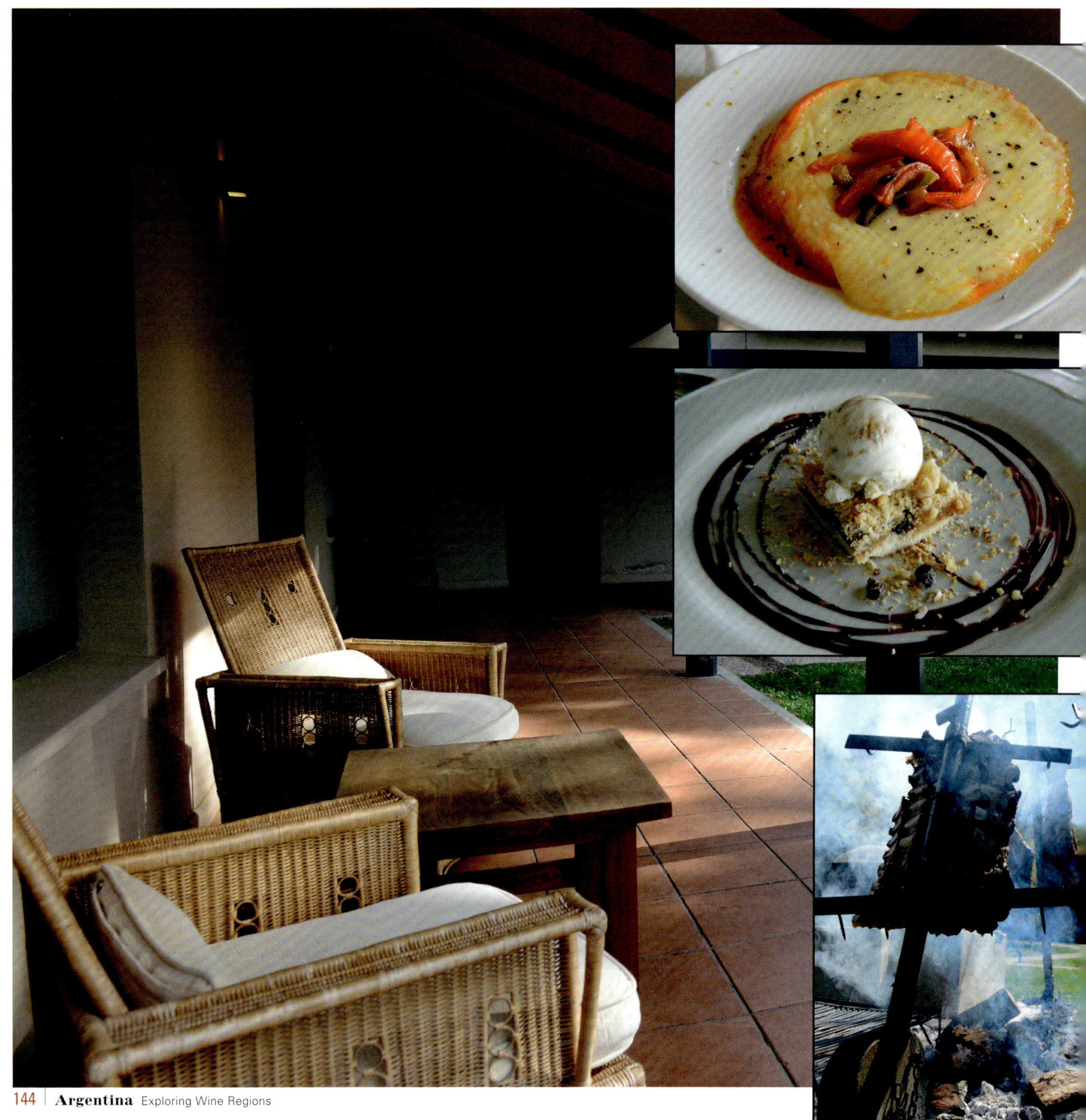

A KILLKA TOURISM DESTINATION

Imagine a place where nature, art, culture, food and great wine all come together for an awe-inspiring experience for the day, or more.

In a breathtaking atmosphere of native plants and natural materials used for construction, comes art... sculptures within the landscape and buildings, modern architecture and design, a museum of 19th- and 20th-century Dutch paintings, an art gallery of local artist expressing thought-provoking Argentine culture, chefs express their art and taste on the plate, and an innovate winery where great wines are created. All under the backdrop of the Andes Mountains surrounded by vineyards in every direction.

The Killka Gallery & Museum bring together the Salentein Dutch ownership displaying European art, emerging with contemporary Argentina artists in quarterly exhibits of highly talented, thought-inspiring work. Guided tours daily. 262-242-9523

The Killka Theatre has ongoing films about viticulture and cultural topics.

The Killka Restaurant is a space of art, food and wine. Gourmet meals are paired with wines. The wine bar has music and sofas, with wines by the glass or bottle. Reservations 262-242-9570, or restaurante.killka@mp-wines.com

The Gift Shop has the full selection of Bodegas Salentein wines, plus interesting wine gadgets and local crafts for sale.

The Chapel of Gratitude is a contemporary take on traditional Andean architecture. Always welcoming, and mass on Saturdays.

Bodegas Salentein is a magnificent winery open for touring and tasting (photo at bottom). Take in the didactic vineyard between the Killka and Bodega, an educational collection of the different Salentein vines growing on the estate. See how the grapes arrive and gently move through the winemaking process. Take in the architectural marvels. End up in the underground amphitheater of ancient classical temples of 5,000 oak barrels aging their precious wine.

Posada Salentein is a 16-room hotel amid their La Pampa Finca, privately tucked away from the tourism area, at 4,200' elevation overlooking their magnificent estate (photos left and below), and with its own private restaurant. Reservation 262-242-9090, or reservas.posada@mp-wines.com

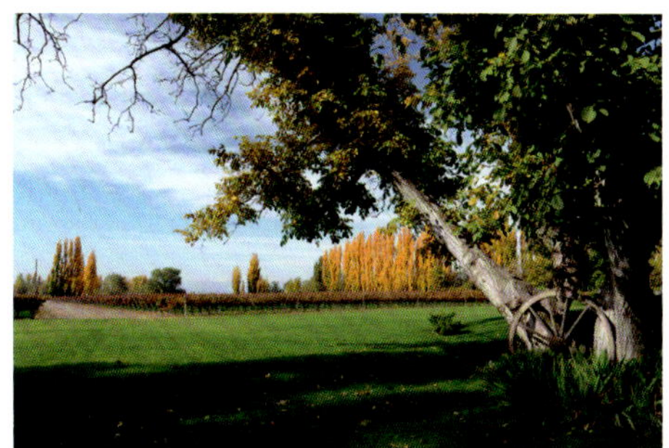

MENDOZA **VALLE DE UCO** TUNUYÁN

Hotel • Gallery • Chapel • Restaurant

BODEGAS SALENTEIN

Ruta 89 S/N, km 14, Los Árboles
(Los Árboles, **Tunuyán,** Valle de Uco)

011 (+54 262) 242.9500
reservas.killka@BodegasSalentein.com

BodegasSalentein.com

English & Español

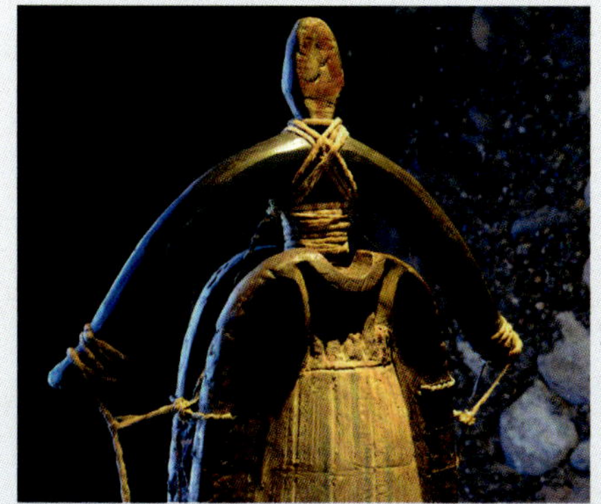

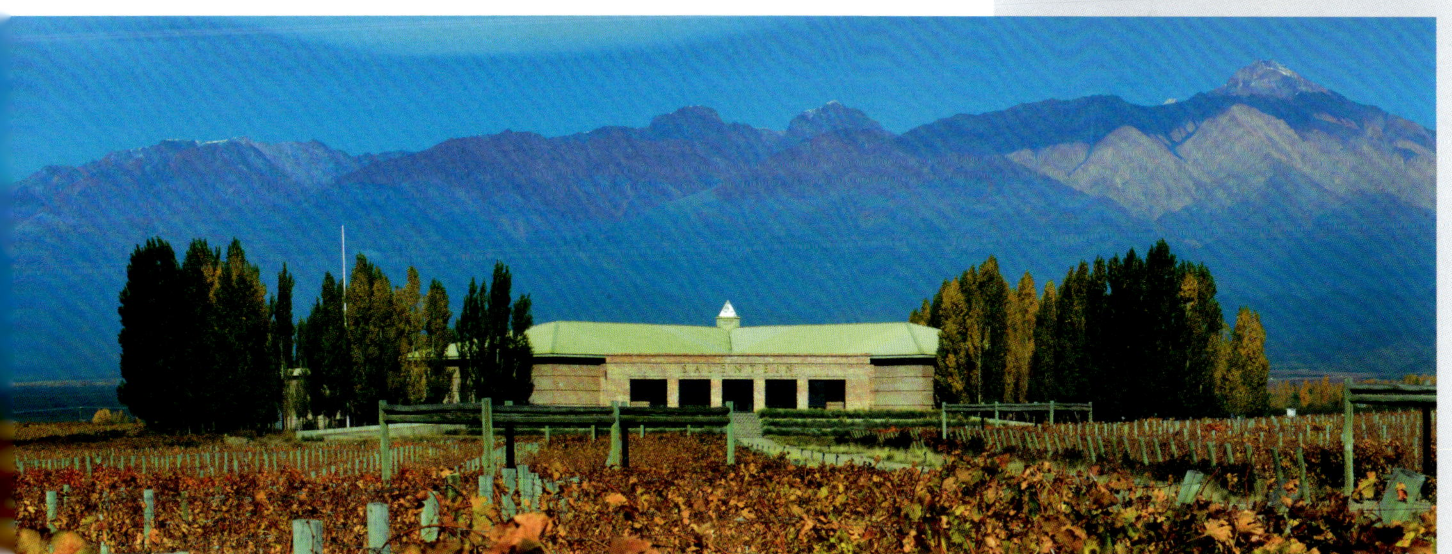

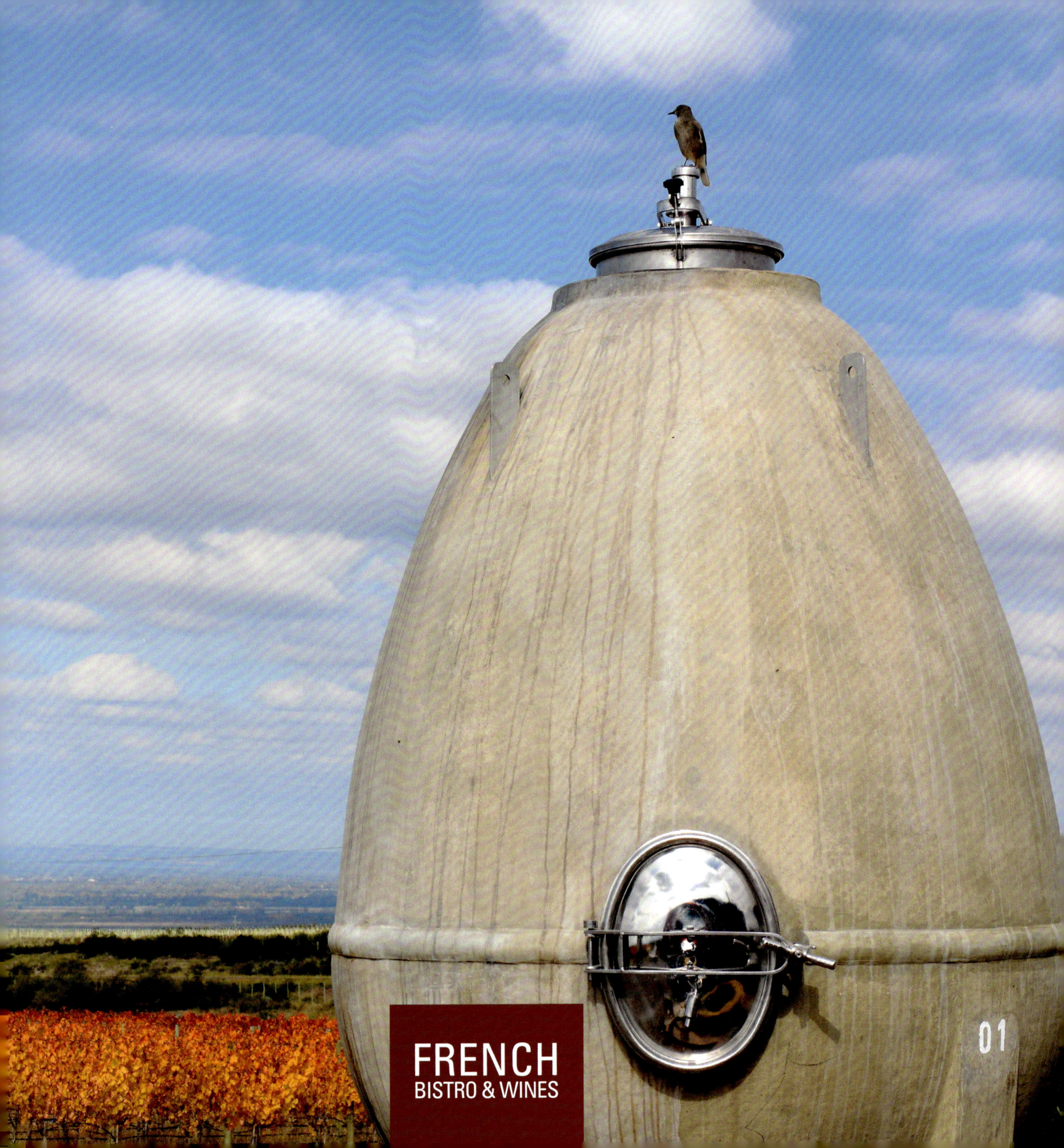
FRENCH
BISTRO & WINES
01

DO LUNCH... AT THE WINE-INDUSTRY'S GATHERING PLACE

You must stop at this roadside bistró, along the highway minutes from Manzano Histórico, and across the road from Casa de Uco and AlPasion. This is not just a gathering of three luxury properties, Finca Blousson is the place where people from all over the world come to talk wine.

While I was there, the owners of a luxury hotel came to have lunch. Also a sommelier from Buenos Aires, and a local winemaker. Everyone mingles, exchanges ideas and stories, eats and drinks special wines... and shares interesting wines.

Patrick Blousson (photo below right with his horse Bones), owner of this small bistró, brought out from his cellar a very rare and unusual wine, a white wine made like a red wine by pressing the skins. This Torrontés, which would normally be a bright fresh yellow color, was orange and rich with flavors. The nose was floral in orange blossoms. We waited an hour, and the second half of the bottle was an entirely different wine, now rich with orange flavors on the mouth. And the group was talking about it. That was a fascinating conversation as you might expect with the type of people present. This is the kind of experience that could only happen at Finca Blousson.

A bistró is, in its original Parisian incarnation, a small restaurant with French home-style cooking, of slow-cooked foods like Finca Blousson's fusion of typical Argentina and French Mediterranean cuisine. This bistró is a French/British fusion dream for couple Patrick and Victoria Blousson, who bought the property in 2008, planted Malbec in 2010 and crafted their first vintage in 2013.

The bistró is small, cozy and warm. This is Patrick and Victoria's home, country-style with a beautiful living room to mingle, eat, and enjoy wine. And a large outside patio overlooking the vineyards, aside the Parrilla (grill) and egg! Yes, a large concrete egg (photo left page) used to ferment their wine.

Outside, this egg sits... exposed to the elements, protecting the precious juice inside. Inside the egg for exactly 30 days from the full-moon harvest of the grapes, after 12 months of full cycles of the moon for growing the grapes. The full moon creates high-tides and raises everything, from the earth to the grapes. Sound superstitious? Maybe. However their winemaker is Michelini, known for his untraditional approach to winemaking, and is very good at it.

Patrick's definition of his bistró is a small place where wine is exchanged, knowledge and experience are shared. Patrick has clearly achieved this, as evidenced by the notable bottles on his mantle (below) signed by their creators who visited his bistró, and by the interesting people I hung out with on my day at the bistró. Now, it is your turn!

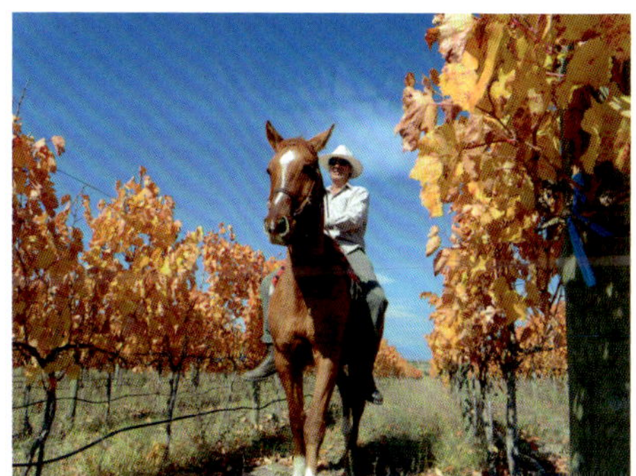

MENDOZA **VALLE DE UCO** TUNUYÁN

French Bistró & Worldly Wines

FINCA BLOUSSON VINS & BISTRÓ

Ruta 94, km 14 (from Vista Flores)
(on the road to Manzano Histórico)
(Los Chacayes, **Tunuyán,** Valle de Uco)

011 (+54 261)(15) 655.3382
reservas@FincaBlousson.com

FincaBlousson.com

English, Español & Français

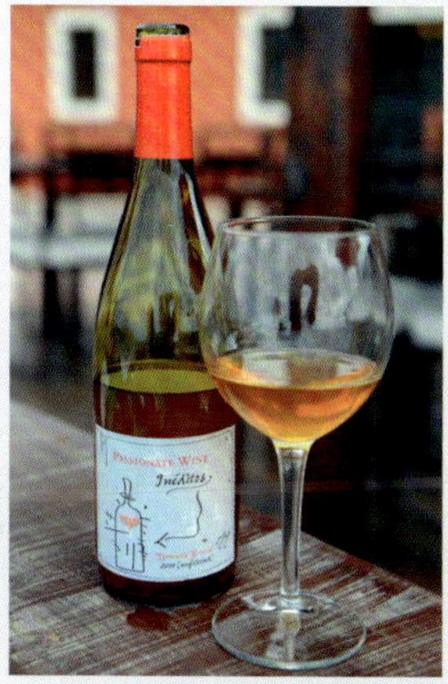

Michael's Favorite Pick
Passionate Winery - Inéditos, Torrontés Brutal

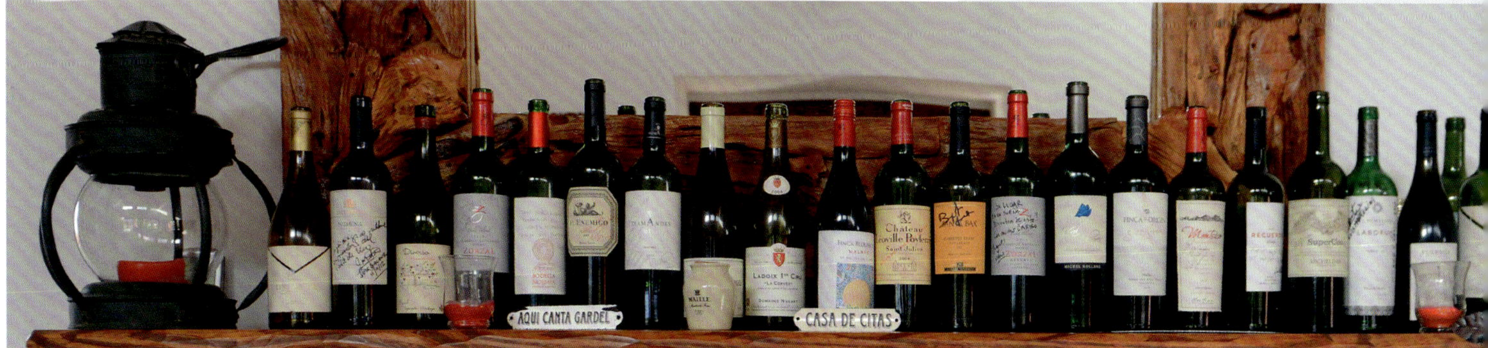

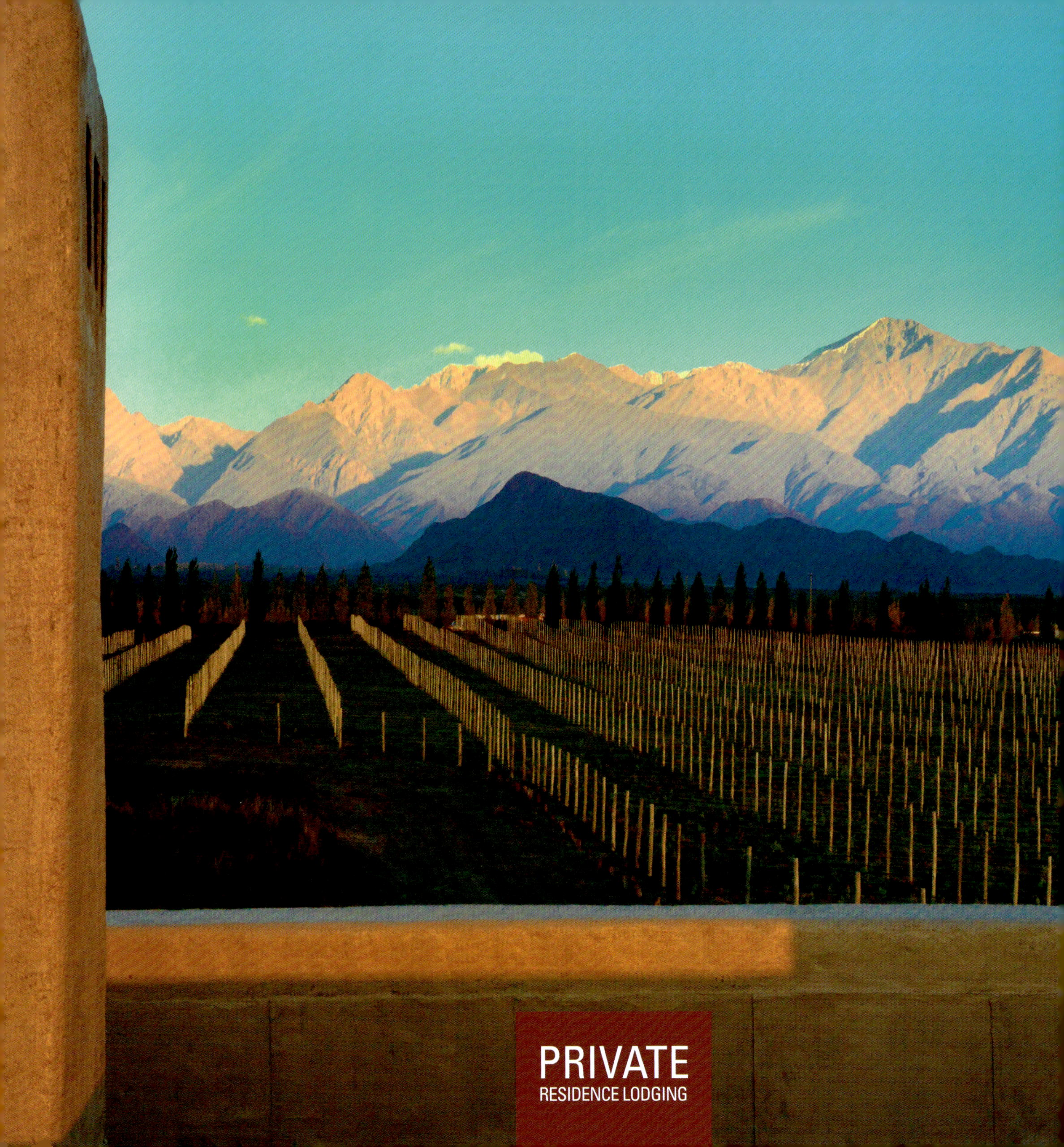
PRIVATE
RESIDENCE LODGING

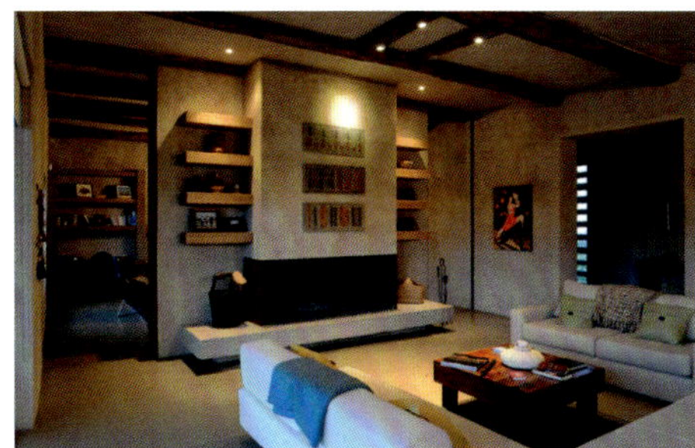
Passion For Living

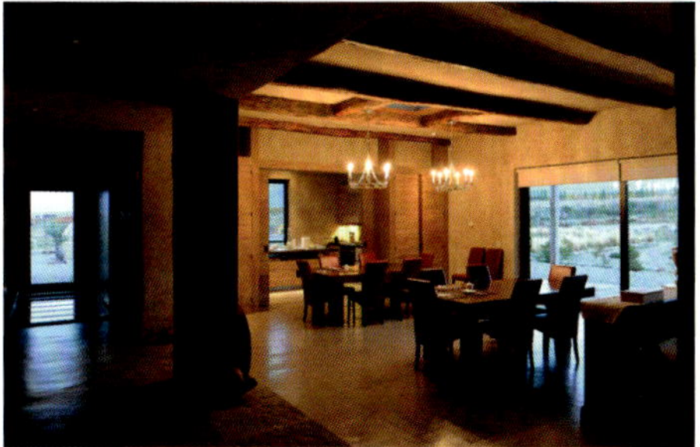
Passionate Dining

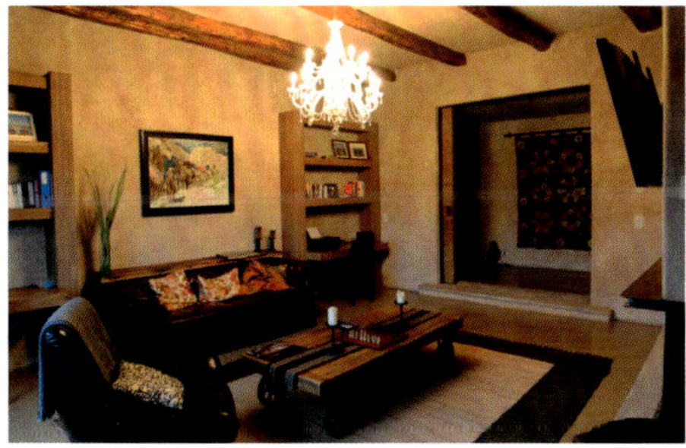
Passion For Relaxing

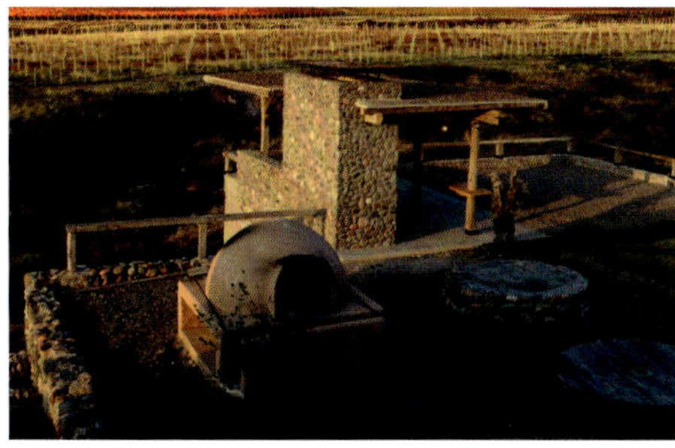
Passionate Entertaining

ALL ABOUT PASSION... ALPASIÓN

Five good friends were sitting around enjoying a few bottles of great wine, becoming inspired by the dream of building a luxury home in Argentina's wine region, and making extraordinary wine to indulge themselves and share their passions with the world.

By December 2012, 28 friends had joined them and they purchased this special property in Valle de Uco and built a beautiful six-bedroom, very spacious and luxurious custom home/lodge. The photos on this page should say it all. The home is staffed, including a gourmet chef for all your meals.

Book a room or the entire home, this is a peaceful wine environment that exudes everything passionate about wine as the owners intended.

148 acres of vines were planted in 2014 (photo left page from rooftop patio with backdrop of the Andes). In the meantime, they have been acquiring premium fruit from neighbors and producing two extraordinary wines: a 100% Malbec and a Malbec blend, my favorite, that will seduce you with its smooth velvety style of merging rich with delicate.

The people behind this project are very passionate wine lovers, adding each of their fingerprints and signatures on every wine label. It is a highly personal, hands-on project, undertaken by a group driven by friendship, passion and quality for all facets of life. And with early success, despite their lack of experience in the business of winemaking... achieving the honor of having their wine chosen to be one of the Top 100 Wines in Argentina on their second vintage.

Join the passion. Stay for a few days, or become part of their future. The passion is all yours.

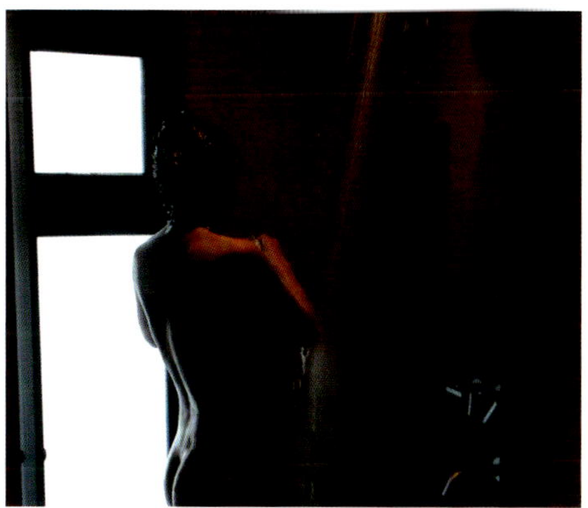
Passionate Bathing

MENDOZA **VALLE DE UCO** TUNUYÁN

Lodge & Winery (Bodega)

ALPASIÓN LODGE

Ruta 94 km 14 (from Vista Flores)
(on the road to Manzano Histórico)
(Los Chacayes, **Tunuyán,** Valle de Uco)

011 (+54 261) 320.2999
reservations@Alpasion.com

Alpasion.com

English & Español
70,000 bottles produced annually

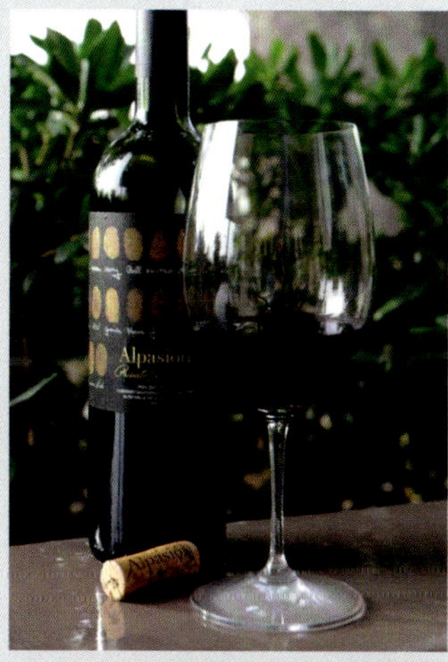

Michael's Favorite Pick
Alpasión - Private Selection

Total Collection of Wines

Alpasión - Private Selection
(50% Malbec, 25% Cabernet Sauvignon, 25% Syrah)

Alpasión - Malbec Crianza
(100% Malbec)

To get Alpasión wines in the USA
Contact them directly at: info@Alpasion.com

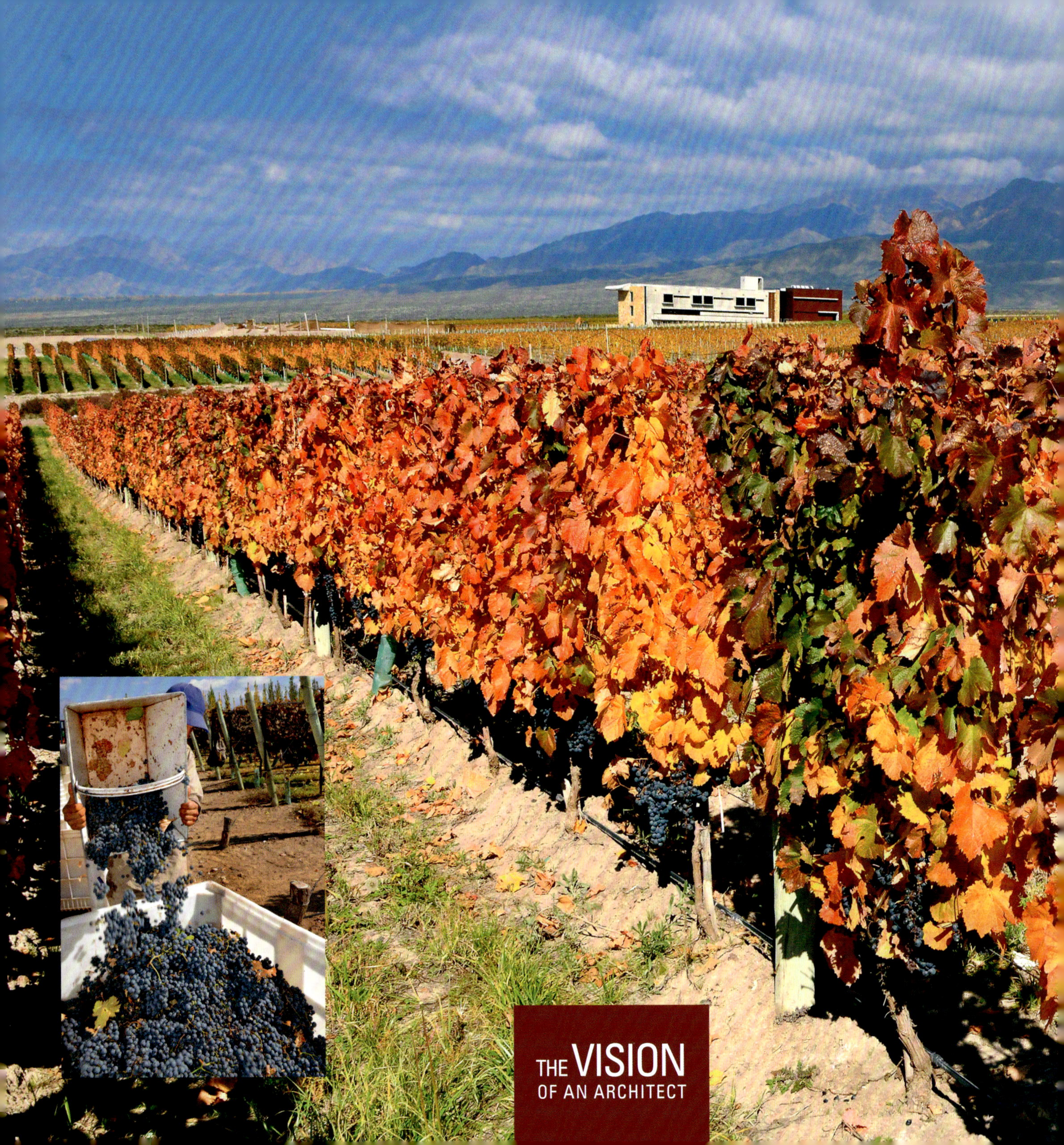
THE VISION
OF AN ARCHITECT

AN ULTRA-MODERN WINE RESORT CONCEPT

Hotel • Spa • Restaurant • Vineyards

CASA DE UCO VINEYARDS & WINE RESORT

It all began with vineyards on this 790-acre estate north of Vista Flores in the Los Chacayes sub-appellation of Tunuyán at 4,100' elevation next to the Andes Mountains. A beautiful backdrop indeed (photos left page and bottom).

In 2007 planting began, primarily Malbec, and by 2012 they harvested and produced 10,000 bottles of wine. From the 2014 harvest they expect to produce 150,000 bottles of wine (photo below left page of 2014 harvest). Also in 2014, the luxury boutique hotel was completed (photo right). Magnificent Bungalows and a state-of-the-art winery are next to be constructed.

Vineyard Opportunities exist if you would like to participate in the growth and development of this property. A minimum of one hectare (2.5 acres) gets you growing and making your own wine, and participating with ownership privileges in the full aspects of the resort. Alberto Antonini is their head winemaker and viticulturist to help you produce quality wine without having to be the expert. Antonio comes with enology and agricultural doctorate degrees from notable universities in Tuscany, Bordeaux and California, and a resulting reputation for creating some of the top wines in the world.

Architect Owner and Visionary of Casa de Uco, Alberto Tonconogy has an illustrious career of designing award-winning buildings... from skyscrapers to luxury homes to bridges. However, when you are the owner/architect (and your partner is your son, Juan Tonconogy, who developed the original vision of this property and the wine expertise connecting all aspects of this resort property together), the design, space and concepts must be brilliant! And they are!

I was there during the final construction stages and had the opportunity to meet Alberto and to see his meticulous attention to all the final details of his masterpiece. When I asked Alberto how he came up with such an unusual structure, he shared with me his challenge of developing a building of modest scale in comparison to the vast desert that it surrounded. It was the stream that zigzagged down from the Andes and onto the property that became the landmark that paved the way for the creation of his master plan and ideas.

This prominent waterway was chosen as the place for the development. By building dams, a number of lagoons were created where the future building would appear. In the absence of any natural element of notable scale, he chose to create by way of tectonic movement. A huge slab was elevated above the lagoons at a height to view the original experience of the landscape. Extending from the development are design elements such as ramps, a floating pool, decks, trees, and paths that branch out like arms settling into the environment.

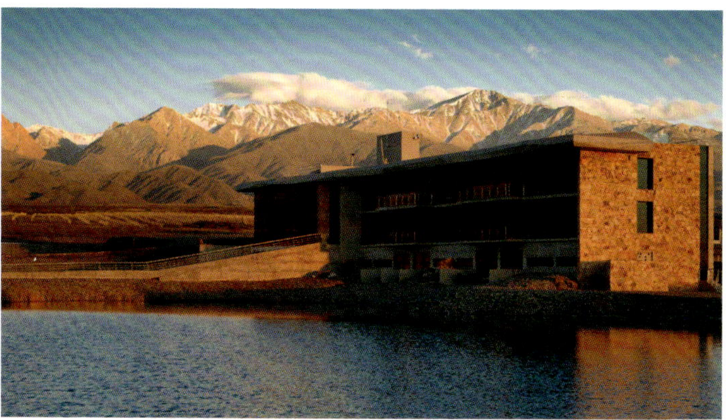

The building itself is presented in different structural parts that are isolated from each other, each one coinciding with a particular internal function.

Inside, the building is separated into two bodies by an asymmetrical space of three floors, where ramps and stairs connect the social area with the rest of its different levels. It is a very interesting design (see photos next page).

Outside, each side is completely distinguishable based on view and sun... a total window treatment faces south (pictured above with the east-facing wooden pattern), electro-hydraulic parasols face west towards the Andes and allows them to gradually adjust for the afternoon sun (and is very cool looking), and an almost solid facade on the north due to the harsh sunshine.

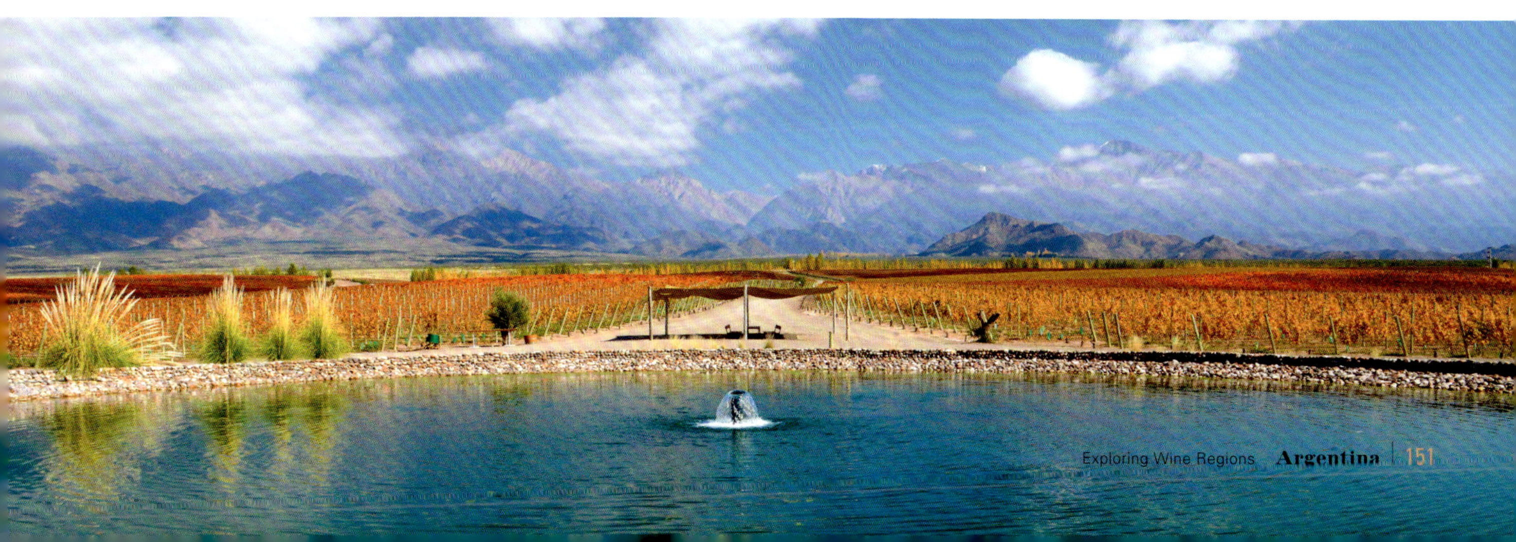

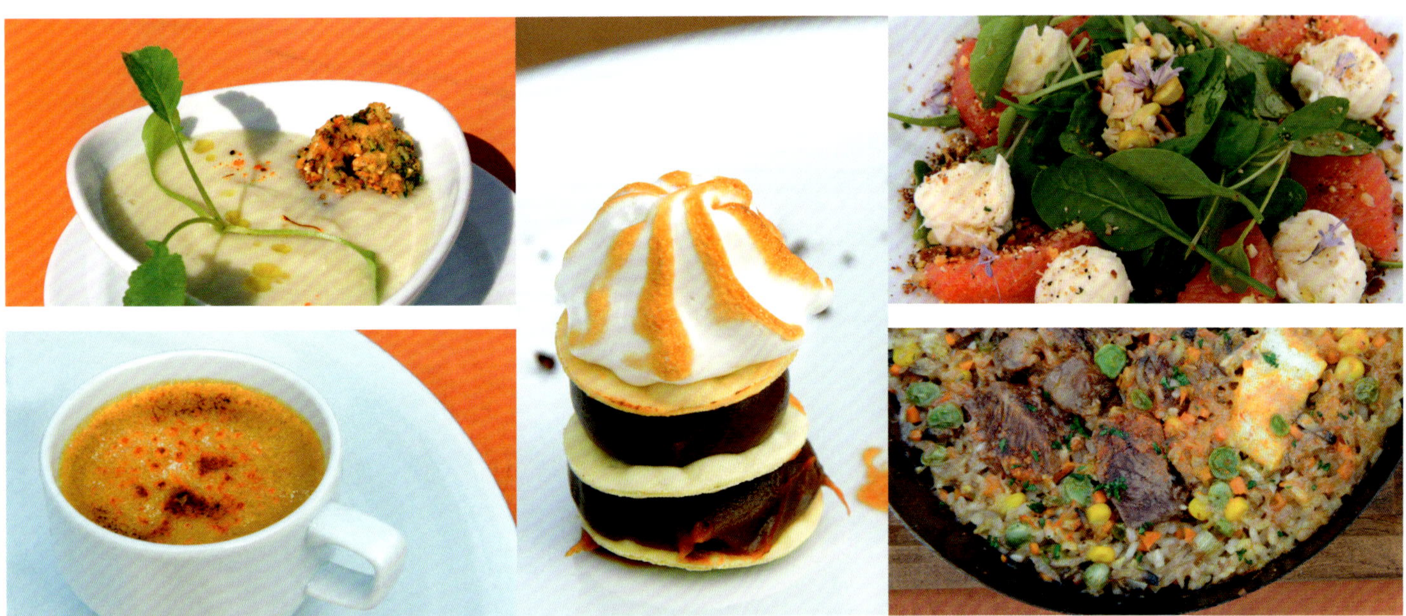

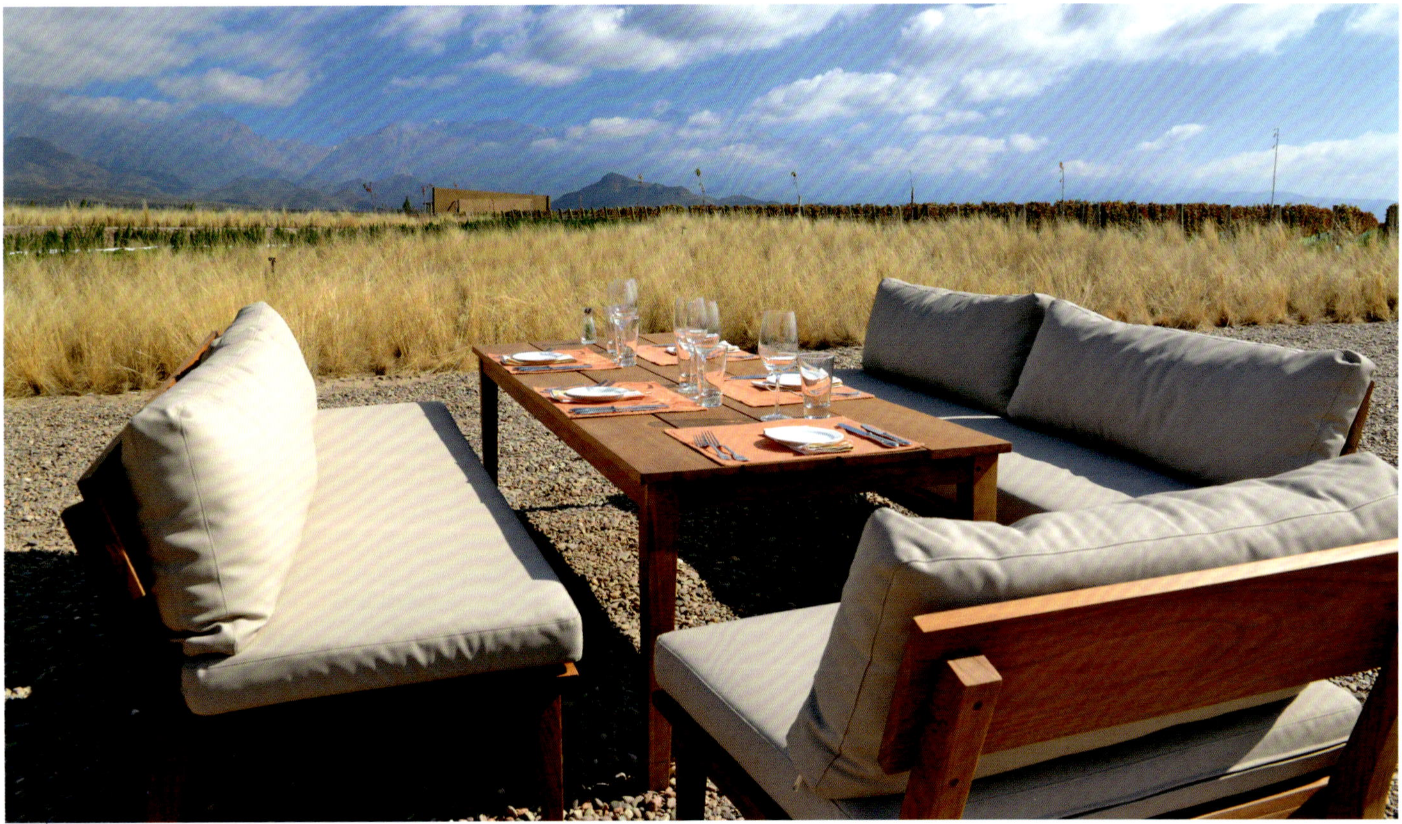

Imagine only 16 rooms in this ultra-luxury hotel... appointed with a gourmet chef, sommelier, underground wine cellar, spa, wine lounge and living room with a grand fireplace, all with extraordinarily attentive service throughout the hotel. You will be received royally, as the service, food, ambiance, and rooms are all top-tier.

As a guest of the hotel, you will be treated to guided tours of the winery and vineyards, including participating in vineyard work if you like, and specially guided wine tastings with their sommelier. Plus access to their spa facilities, use of complimentary mountain bikes, and very cool sulky rides throughout their beautiful property.

The concept with their restaurant is very fresh: they only use local products from the valley and try to manipulate them as least as possible. As such, they regularly create new menus, sometimes daily, especially for their "tapas & wines" menu. Their ultimate is to create five-, six- or seven-course menus, pairing each course with a different wine or cocktail.

The food is gourmet with a celebrated chef on premises; however, the best part is having their sommelier interacting with you throughout your experience. And don't miss the outside Quincho (barbeque), a gathering place for traditional Argentine Asado, amidst lush gardens, lagoons, creeks, and vineyards.

The spa is ultra-modern... with gym, hammam steam room, cedar sauna, relaxation areas and massages with hydrotherapy, body treatments and vine-based therapies.

Casa de Uco can also arrange different adventures and sporting activities... skiing, golf, tennis, cycling, trekking, and horseback riding in the vineyards or the natural reserve (see opportunities next pages).

Enjoy Casa de Uco's tranquil environment... to relax among stunning views of mountains, vineyards and lagoons; to stroll endless paths of the vineyards and gardens; to lounge in the floating pool, hot tub or floating dock; and to enjoy luxurious pampering, wine and culinary experience, and you.

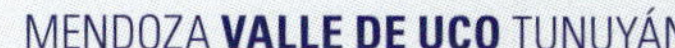

MENDOZA **VALLE DE UCO** TUNUYÁN

Hotel • Spa • Restaurant • Vineyards

CASA DE UCO VINEYARDS & WINE RESORT

Ruta 94, km 14.5 (from Vista Flores)
(on the road to Manzano Histórico)
(Los Chacayes, **Tunuyán,** Valle de Uco)

011 (+54 262) 340.3464
reservas@CasaDeUco.com

CasaDeUco.com

English & Español

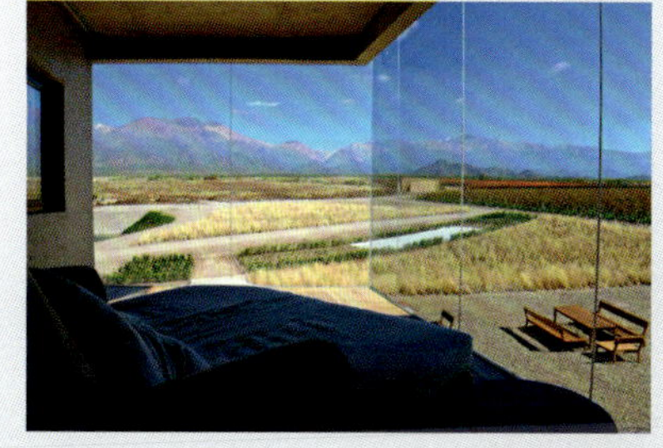

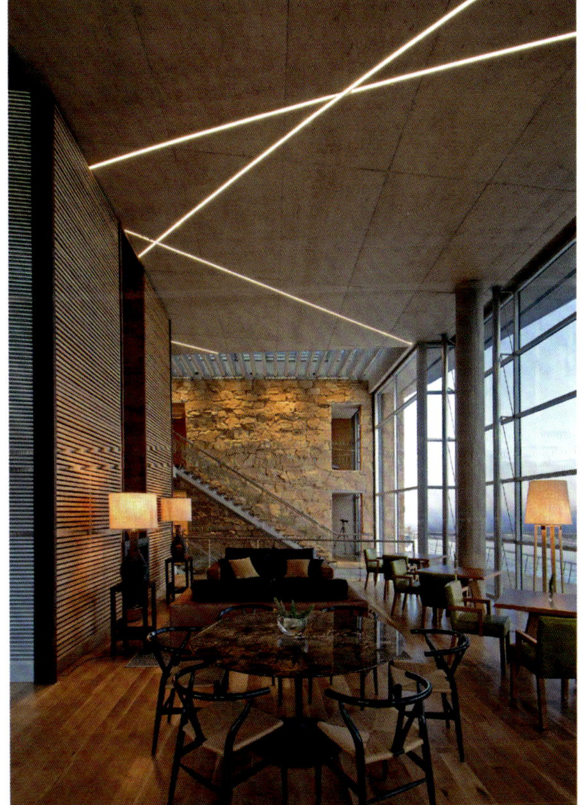

LEFT PAGE, Outdoor dining and mouth-watering cuisine

LEFT, Spectacular hotel dining and lounging with wide open views through the massive windows

BELOW, All bathroom tubs have views

RIGHT, Unique Bay Room, a private area to relax and gaze at the Andes

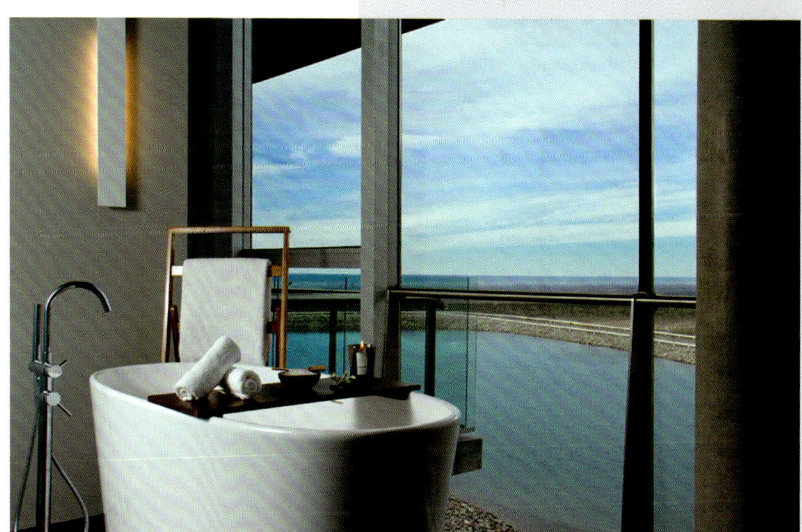

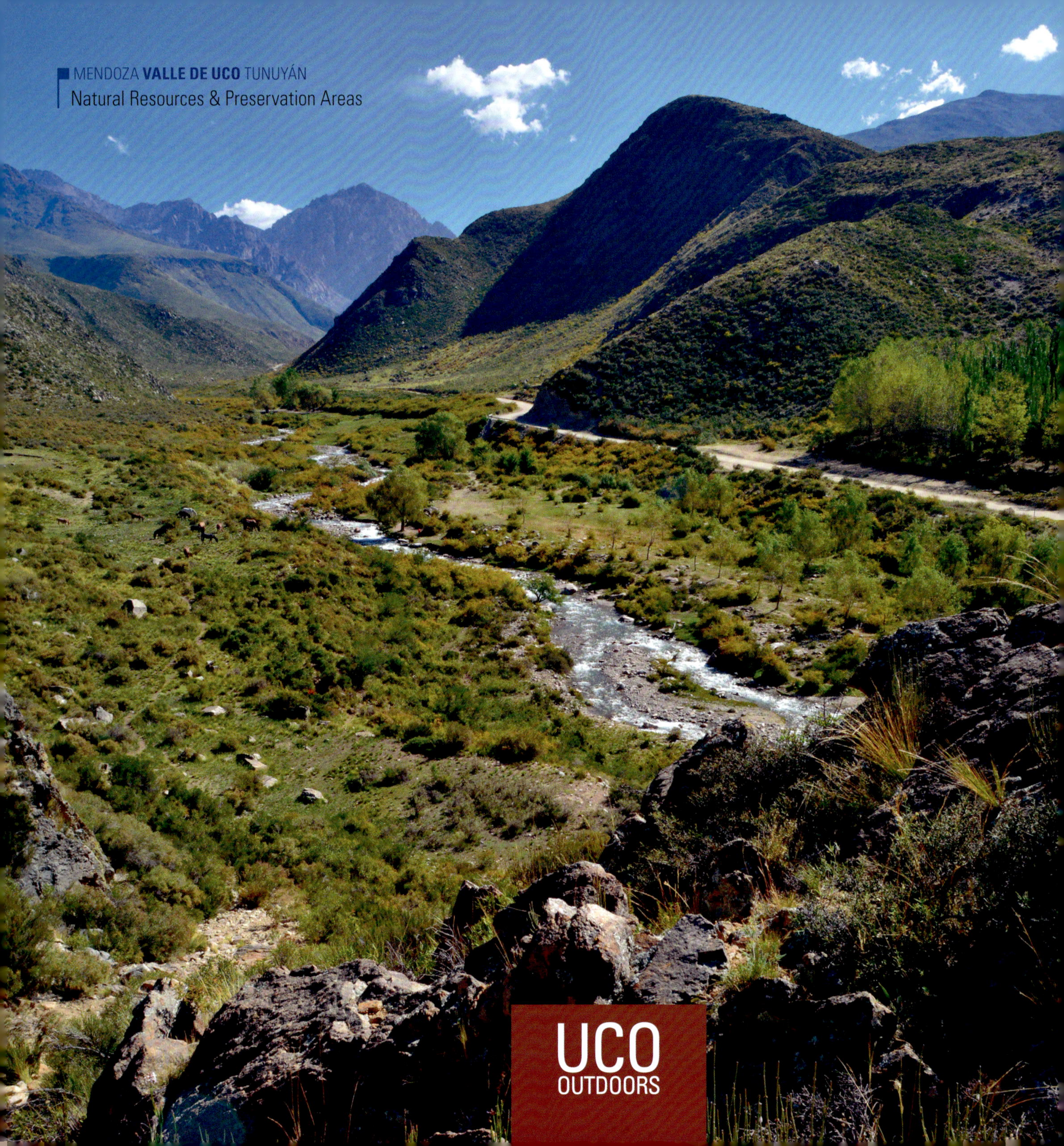
MENDOZA VALLE DE UCO TUNUYÁN
Natural Resources & Preservation Areas
UCO
OUTDOORS

MANZANO HISTÓRICO, GATEWAY TO THE ANDES MOUNTAINS

Manzano Histórico is a large natural and historical reserve, and an important canyon entrance to the Andes Mountains. It is located at the far west edge of Tunuyán where both highways Ruta 94 and Ruta 89 merge and end at the mountains. These highways are where most of the Tunuyán wineries we discussed earlier are located.

Manzano Histórico was made famous by General José de San Martín, who used this canyon as his gateway to the Andes and crossings to Chile where he worked together with his confident Chilean General Bernardo O'Higgins (you just gotta love his name) in fighting for their independence of Argentina and Chile against Spain.

Manzano means apple in Spanish. Collectively, Manzano Histórico is the historical significance of an apple tree that General San Martín made famous as he would sleep here at this spot, in an apple tree. San Martín is highly honored in Argentina as he defeated the Spanish Army, gaining independence for Argentina, Chile and Peru. Sculptures, squares and roads are named after San Martín in most cities throughout the country.

Today there is a monument here with a branch of the old apple tree where San Martín rested, and a huge bronze statue of San Martín and O'Higgins (photo below right).

On a side note, the sub-appellation of La Consulta in San Carlos is only a few miles from Manzano Histórico. San Martín was a very clever warrior, so he "consulted" with the Pehuenche Tribe (the indigenous people who live in the Andes in south central Chile and Argentina) about his plans to defeat Spain. San Martín knew the Pehuenche were beholden to Spain and would tell them of their conversations, so he gave them a fake plan which when conveyed to the Spanish Army led them into his trap. This was a brilliant strategy instrumental in defeating Spain, and now this site of "consultation" has become the town of La Consulta.

Manzano Histórico has a particular micro-climate, unique to other areas of similar elevations, that favors environmental conditions for growth of forest species. This mountainous environment is notable for its landscape beauty and water quality with an ongoing supply of fresh snow-melt water flowing in the rivers and streams from the Andes. This is a great day-visit to enjoy the streams, camping areas and horseback riding. Plus, learn the full lifecycle of salmon by visiting an important fish station which serves to supply the streams and rivers in the province with salmon.

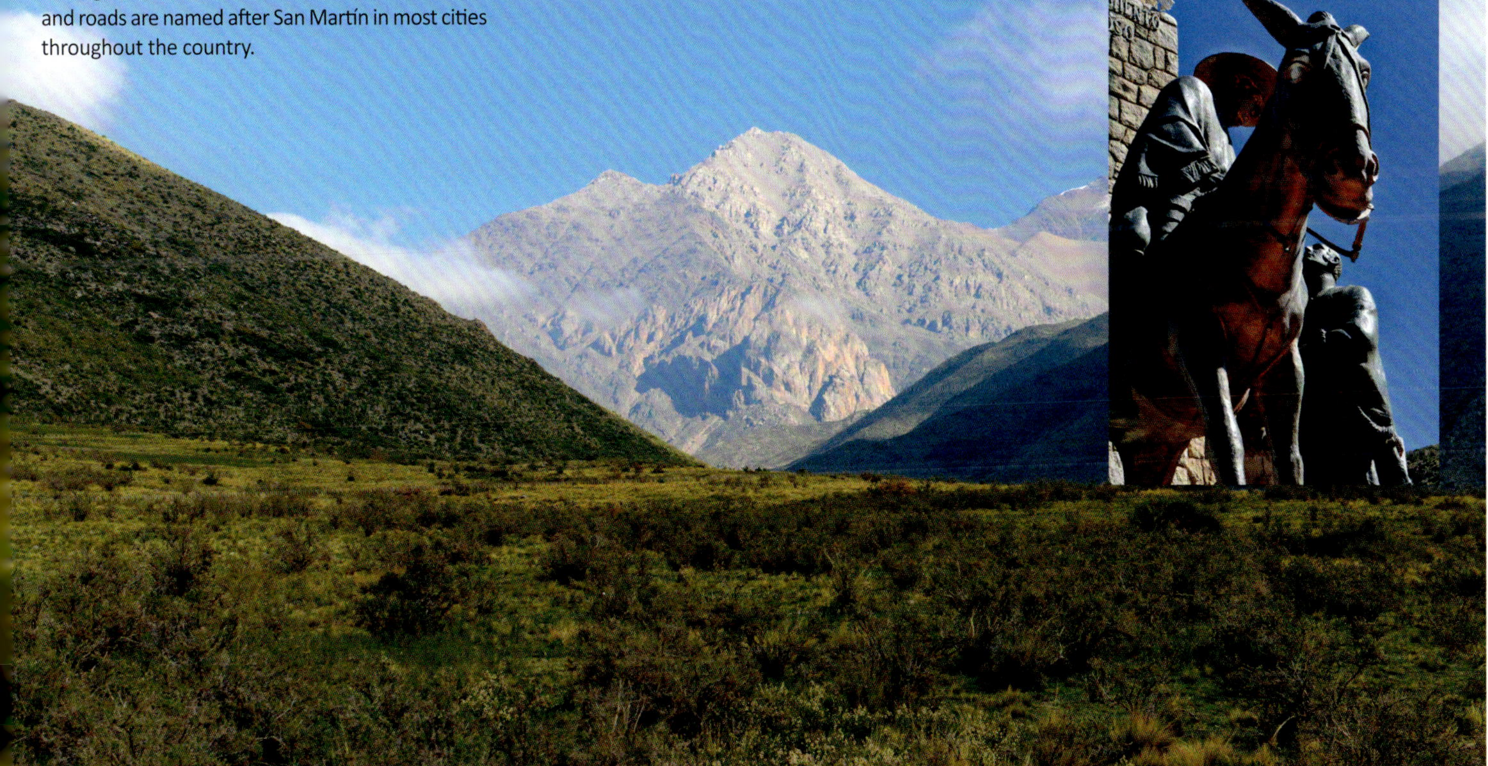

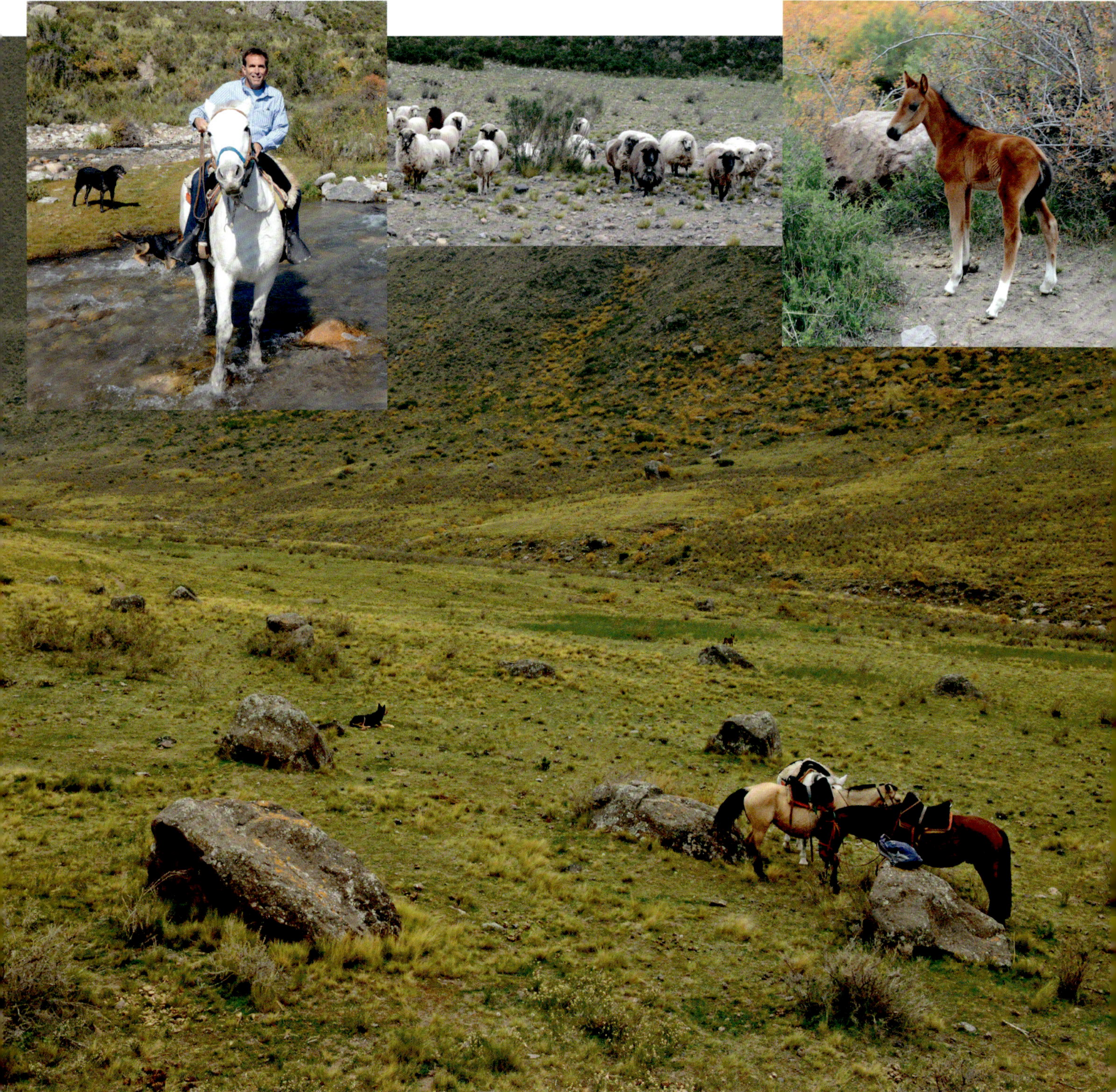

HORSEBACK... RIDE & BARBEQUE

MENDOZA **VALLE DE UCO** TUNUYÁN

Horseback Riding & Whitewater Rafting

LA CIMA TURISMO ADVENTURA

011 (+54 262) (21) 556.0884

LaCimaTurismoAdventura@hotmail.com

Español

Manzano Histórico has remarkable landscapes ranging from 4,000' to peaks of 20,000' of prehistoric aged masses, penetrated by granite and volcanic rocks, with rivers and streams of very high-quality water and fishing.

To truly see this spectacular landscape, you need to venture into the mountains. This is best done on horseback. It is beautiful. Majestic. Meditative. An awe-inspiring experience to explore the wilderness, without trails, just in nature... taking it all in.

After several hours of riding, your gaucho (cowboy) can bring you to a campsite along the river (photo below) where an Asado has been underway for hours. The slow-cooked meats and vegetables are ready for you to enjoy, along with an Argentine Malbec, of course.

Your chef and adventure guide is Roberto Boriero of La Cima Turismo Adventura. I met Roberto when he was cooking for me in the vineyards of the guest house of O.Fournier Winery. His Asado is to die for! Roberto has access to the best horses. You can see it in their physique, eyes and hair as they are well cared for and fed with quality food.

The closest vineyards and hotel to Manzano Histórico is Casa de Uco. They can arrange with Roberto Boriero, or you can contact him directly. Roberto also works at the Casa de Uco resort. Roberto will pick you up and drive you to and from your adventures, and ensure all goes as planned.

Because of the year-round snowmelt, the rivers here are always flowing and make for great whitewater rafting. During the summer months, the rivers flow bigger and offer the most exciting rafting. Roberto will get you hooked up.

It is truly an extravaganza of outdoor activities. It all depends on how deep you want to go?

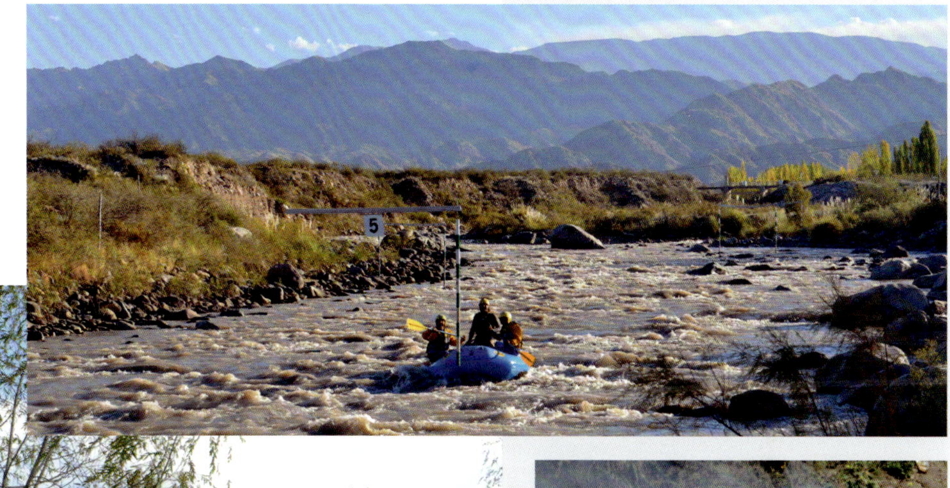

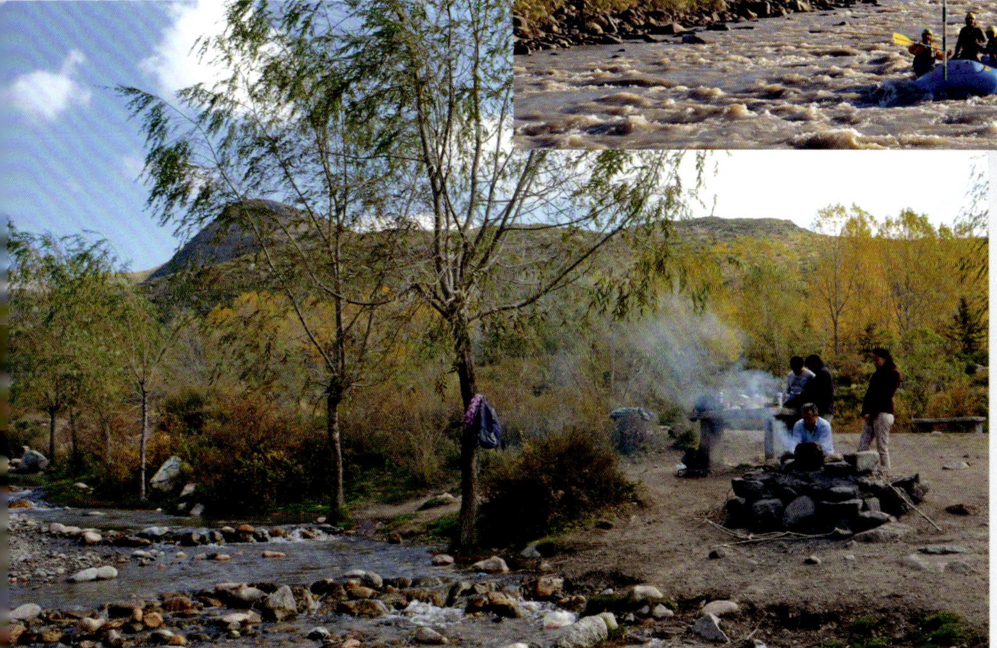

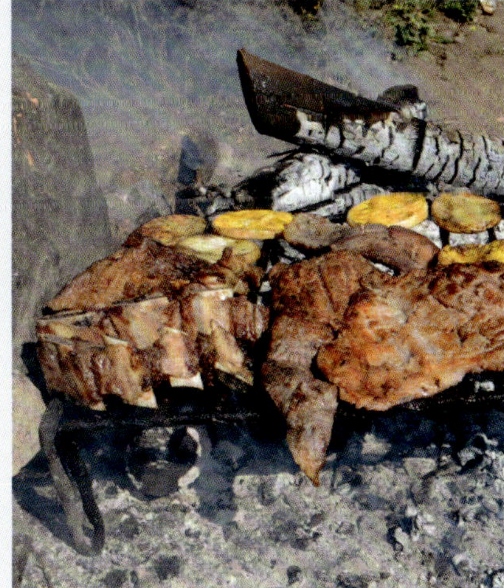

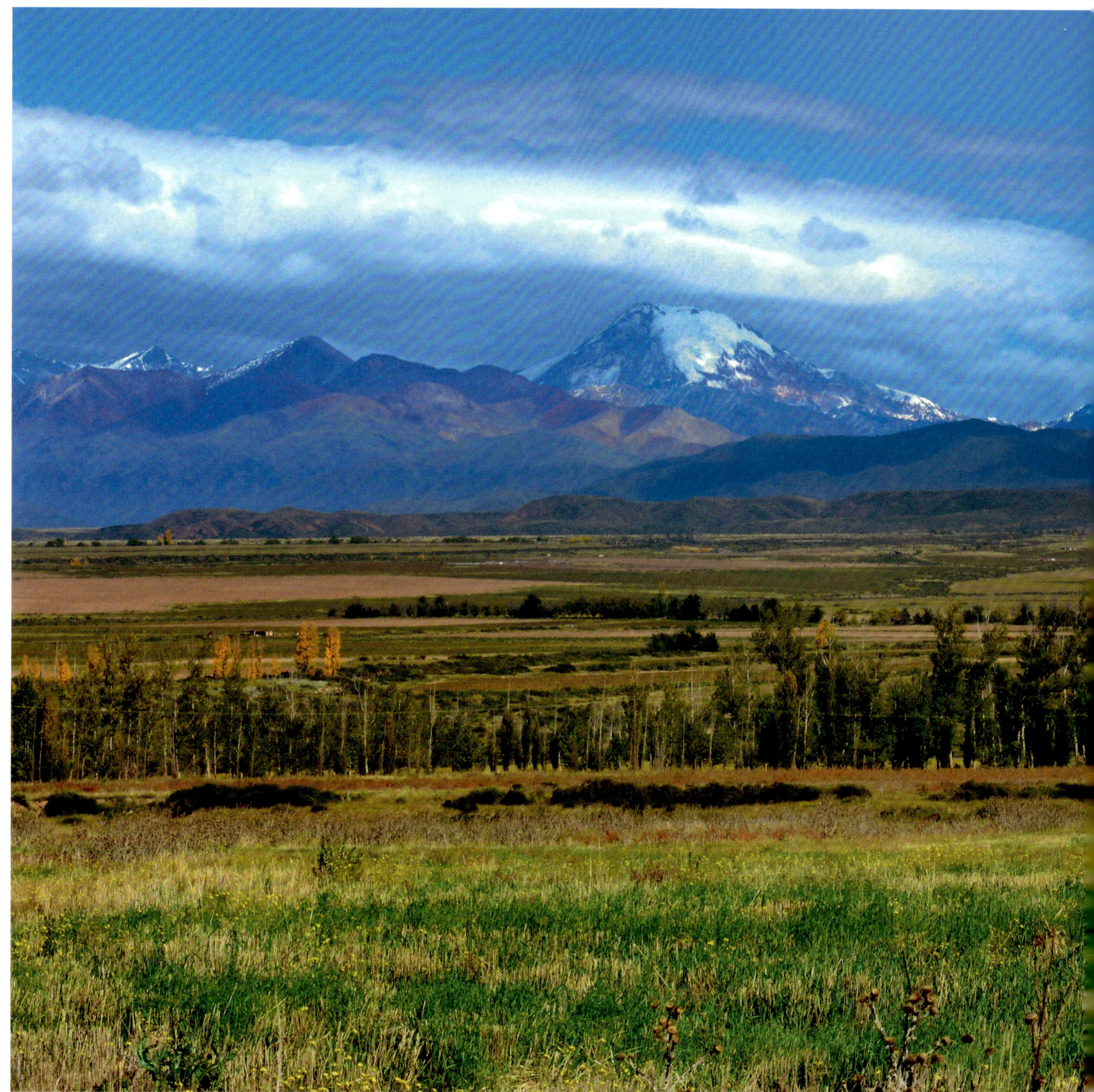

MENDOZA **TUPUNGATO**

*Including the Sub-Appellation of **Gualtallary** in This Sub-Region of **Northern Valle de Uco***

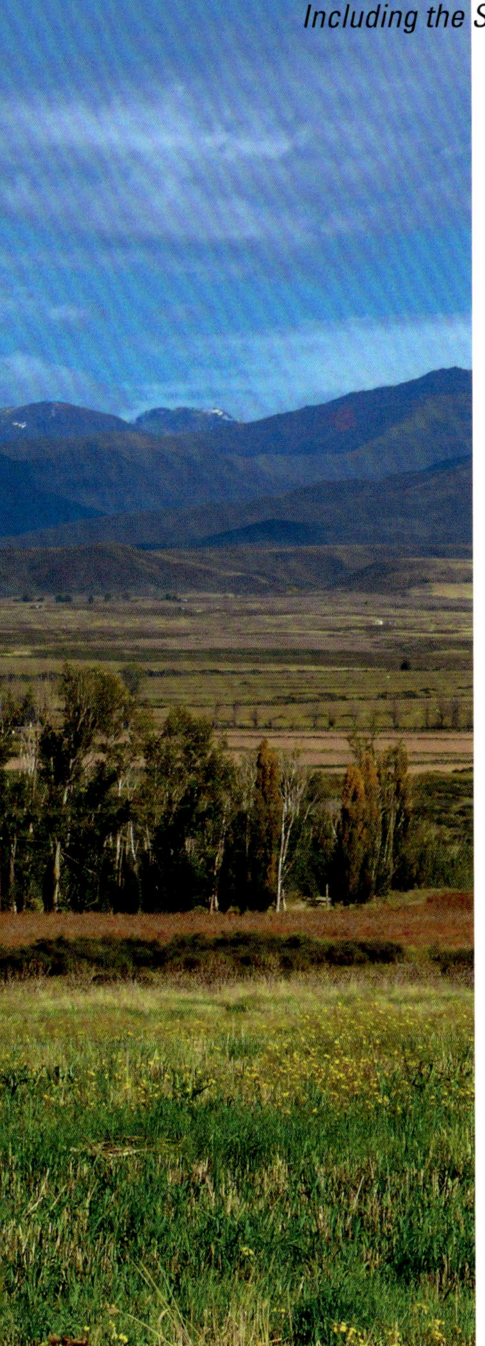

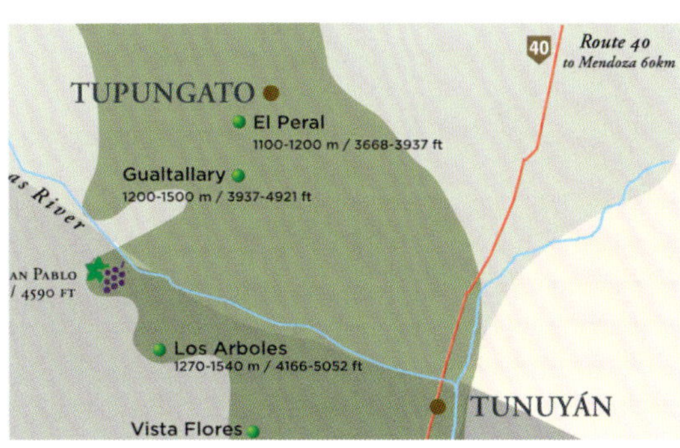

EXPLORING TUPUNGATO

Valle de Uco's northern wine sub-region is Tupungato, identified as being north of the Las Tunas River, with Tupungato (the city) being the largest (pop 43,000) city in the valley. Valle de Uco slopes higher to the north end of the valley, making Tupungato the highest region with elevations from 4,000' to 5,000' and closer to downtown Mendoza, just to the northeast of the valley along Ruta 86.

The Tupungato region is underdeveloped in terms of wineries, and enjoys vast landscapes of untouched beauty. Some of the smart winemakers have invested in properties in Tupungato and planted vineyards to take advantage of its high-altitude terroir, particularly in Gualtallary.

Gualtallary is Tupungato's most famous sub-appellation, and the reason why such highly regarded winemakers as Sebastian Zuccardi and Nicolas Catena have purchased large acreage here, and planted a diversity of grape varietals.

Gualtallary is located on the north bank of the Las Tunas River with soils formed from the sediments of the Las Tunas River basin and other streams in the foothills. The altitude produces high winds carrying sandy topsoil and other sediments. Under, the soils contain hard compacted layers of lime and clay with lime covering small stones, of which Malbec thrives.

The Michelini Brothers have not only planted vineyards in Gualtallary, they built their Zorzal Winery here and are making their highly innovative wines for which they are known.

What is most spectacular about Tupungato is its towering volcano, Mount Tupungato (photo left page). Standing at 21,560' it is one of the highest mountains in the Americas, a massive Andean stratovolcano dating back to the Pleistocene era. Immediately to its southwest is the active Tupungatito volcano, a high-altitude crater (18,909') which last erupted in 1987.

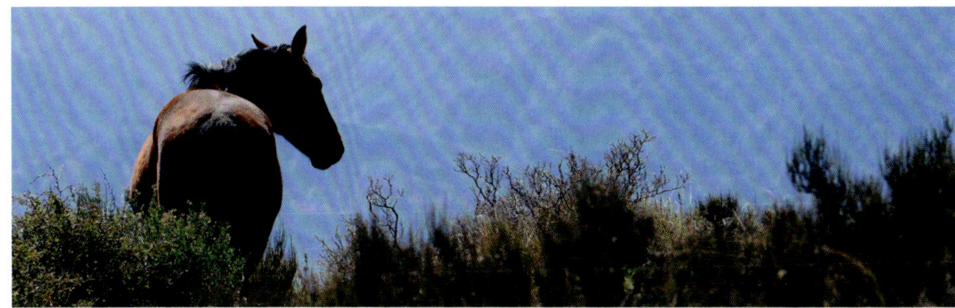

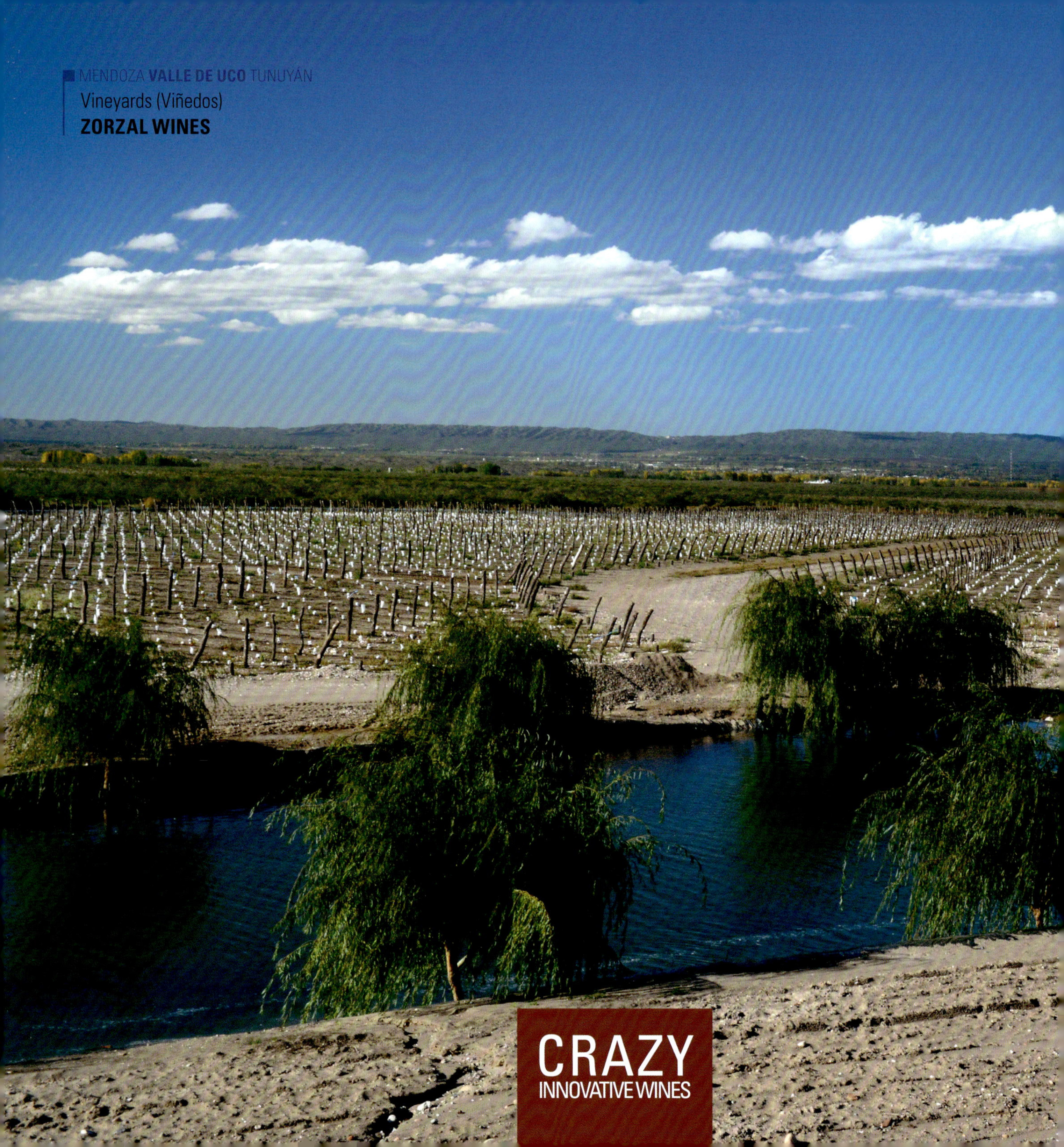

MENDOZA **VALLE DE UCO** TUNUYÁN
Vineyards (Viñedos)
ZORZAL WINES

DEFYING THE MYTHS OF WINEMAKING

The three Michelini Brothers of Zorzal Winery are quite the untraditional winemakers. They desire to explore, invent and experiment, always pushing new ideas and breaking ground where no one has been before. Hits and misses, like brilliant scientists, and now their success are at the forefront of winemaking innovation.

They are innovating new wines... like vinifying grape juice *outside* and in concrete eggs; harvesting Cabernet Sauvignon and Malbec simultaneously and then co-fermenting them together, planting Pinot Noir vines east/west so they have no exposure to the sun; making white wine as you would red wine by pressing the skins and turning Torrontés into an orange wine... and it doesn't stop there...

The Michelinis chose to build their winery away from the crowd, not that this should surprise us, however they chose the notable location of Gualtallary at 4,400' in the highest vine-growing zone in Mendoza at the foot of Tupungato volcano.

As typical brothers, they don't always agree. When Juan Pablo Michelini (photo below in barrel room) made a secret concoction of Pinot Noir, he had to do just that... keep it a secret. When his two brothers told him the wine tasted bad, he took his three barrels of innovation and hid them in the back of the winery, under and behind other barrels. He hid them for two years! Until one day he asked his brothers to try something new, and when the smiles grew on their faces, he unfolded his secret to them.

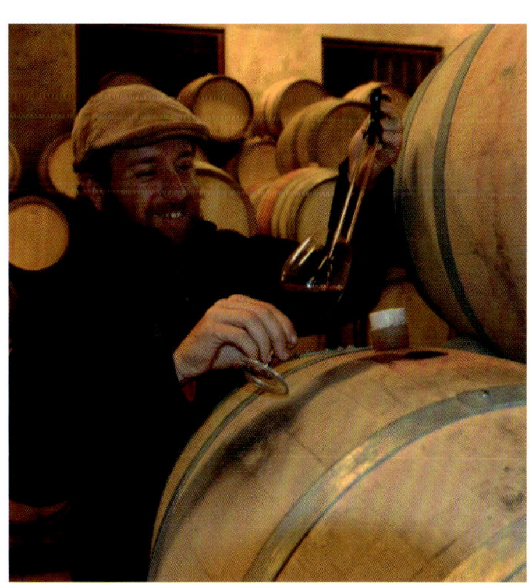

The Michelinis are not just a bunch of mad scientists, their winery is renowned for having state-of-the-art technology in crushing, fermenting and aging. In order to achieve natural wines of the highest quality, the winery was designed on four levels to transport grapes and wines by gravity, without the use of pumps. At the same time, the winery has an automatic temperature control system (designed in New Zealand), which can be operated by Internet from anywhere in the world.

In their search to get the best out of the Gualtallary terroir, the Michelini brothers are constantly innovating processes. This has evolved to bringing in roll fermenters and the egg-shaped vats (photo below), in addition to introducing staggered harvesting and micro-vinifications in casks.

This has all happened since 2008, and they are quickly receiving recognition for their results... **Winery of the Year** awarded by multiple organizations, scoring **94 points with Robert Parker** on their Field Blend; and the **Best Malbec Over US $50** in the Argentina Wines Awards.

For these brothers, who have no limits and share passion for seeking the unthought-of, they do have one official rule... *lose your fear of breaking rules.*

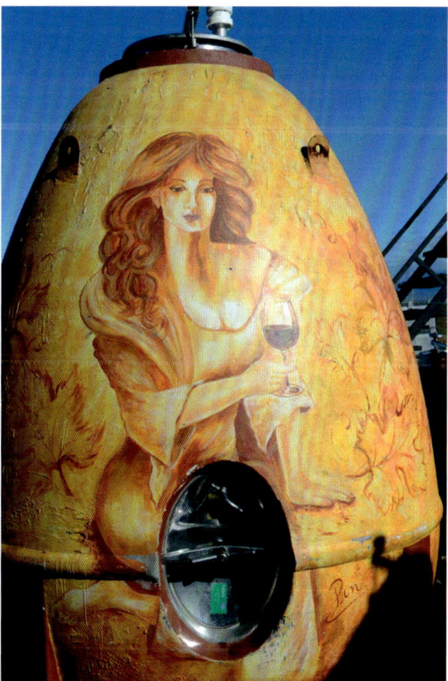

MENDOZA **VALLE DE UCO** TUPUNGATO

Vineyards (Viñedos) • Winery (Bodega)

ZORZAL VINEYARDS & WINERY

Calle Estancia Silva (16 km sw of Tupungato)
(Ruta 89 south to roundabout, then west onto Silva)
(Gualtallary, **Tupungato,** Valle de Uco)

011 (+54 261) 424.5249
reservas@ZorzalWines.com

ZorzalWines.com

English & Español
300,000 bottles produced annually

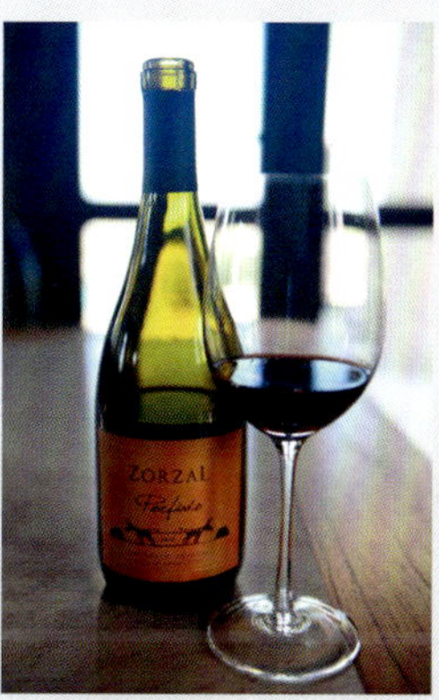

Michael's Favorite Pick
Zorzal - Porfiado Pinot Noir

Total Collection of Wines

Zorzal Especialidades
Porfiado Pinot Noir
Field Blend (45% Cabernet Sauvignon 55% Malbec)
EGGO Tinto de Tiza (92% Malbec, 5% Cab Franc, 3% Cab Sauv)
EGGO Blanc de Cal (100% Sauvignon Blanc)
EGGO Filoso Pinot (100% Pinot Noir)

Zorzal Gran Terroir
Malbec • Pinot Noir • Cabernet Sauvignon

Zorzal Terroir Único
Malbec • Pinot Noir • Cabernet Sauvignon
Malbec Rosé • Torrontés • Chardonnay
Sauvignon Blanc

To get Zorzal wines in the USA
Contact Their Importer: BrazosWineImports.com

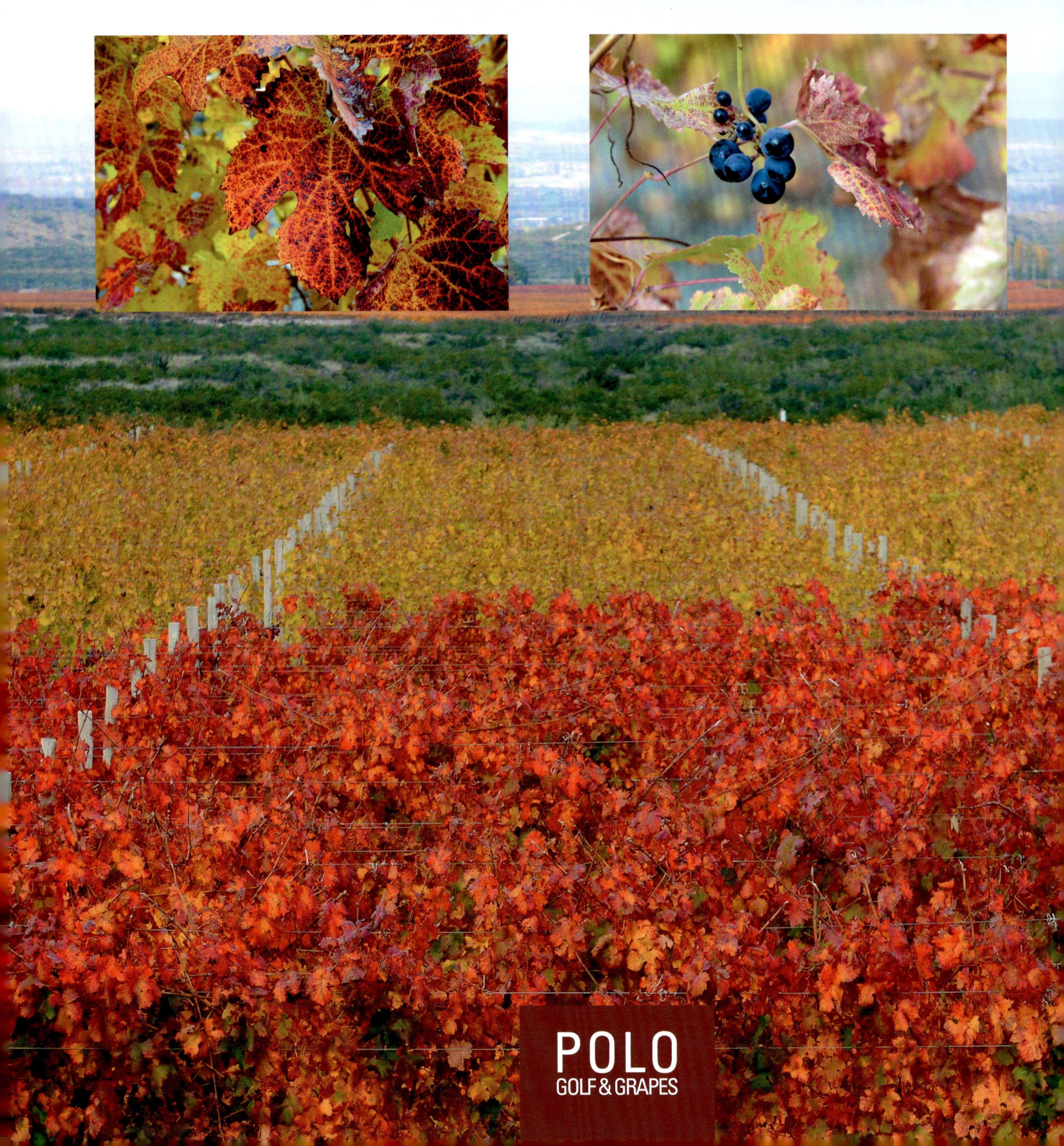
POLO
GOLF & GRAPES

THE FIRST WINE COUNTRY CLUB

Imagine a 2,000-acre estate in Valle de Uco, in none other than the notable Gualtallary sub-appellation, with more than just vineyards... beautifully natural golf course, two professional polo fields, state-of-the-art community-use winery, and gourmet restaurant, lodge and spa... all in a vast open landscape under the majestic Tupungato Mountain, in a private gated community with individual home-sites overlooking these activities. Tupungato Winelands is a place where the wine experience is combined with world-class activities in what they call the *First Wine Country Club in the World*.

Golf. Tupungato Winelands Golf Course is a natural design that preserves and enhances the scenery of the desert, blending green brushstrokes into this magical landscape. This is Argentina's first golf course where only fairways and greens are irrigated, thus preserving native vegetation and making the most out of natural topography while enhancing the landscape and its flora. The course is open for the homeowners, guests and tourists.

Polo. From the moment Argentina was founded, polo has become the quintessential sport among wealthy families. Polo has gained so much importance over the years that it is currently considered a national sport, and the excellence of Argentine players and horses has made them world champions for over 50 years. Tupungato Winelands continues this legacy with regular tournaments on their two professional polo fields.

Grapes. Half of Tupungato Winelands is dedicated to vines, after all, this is Gualtallary. 1,000 acres are devoted to vineyards and the private homes that are within them.

Homes. Enjoy an estate with private vineyards, or a plot of land overlooking the magnificent golf course, or a villa with private terraces at *Villas del Polo,* being built overlooking the polo fields and surrounded by small lakes. Golf lots range from one to 2.5 acres and vineyards from six- to 11-acre fincas, in which you design your own custom home on your own deeded lot.

Wine. Produce your own wine from this superior appellation, under the supervision of highly qualified professionals, including the world-famous winemaker/consultant Michel Rolland. You make your wine while following extremely high-quality standards in this community's boutique winery with the latest technology available for vinifying and aging your own personalized wine.

MENDOZA **VALLE DE UCO** TUPUNGATO

Polo • Golf • Wine • Homes

TUPUNGATO WINELANDS

Ruta 89, La Costa s/n
(Gualtallary, **Tupungato,** Valle de Uco)

011 (+54 261) 645.2434
info@TupungatoWinelands.com

TupungatoWinelands.com

English & Español

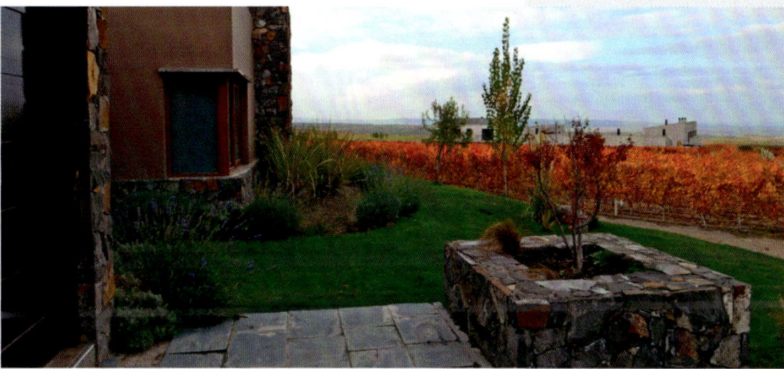

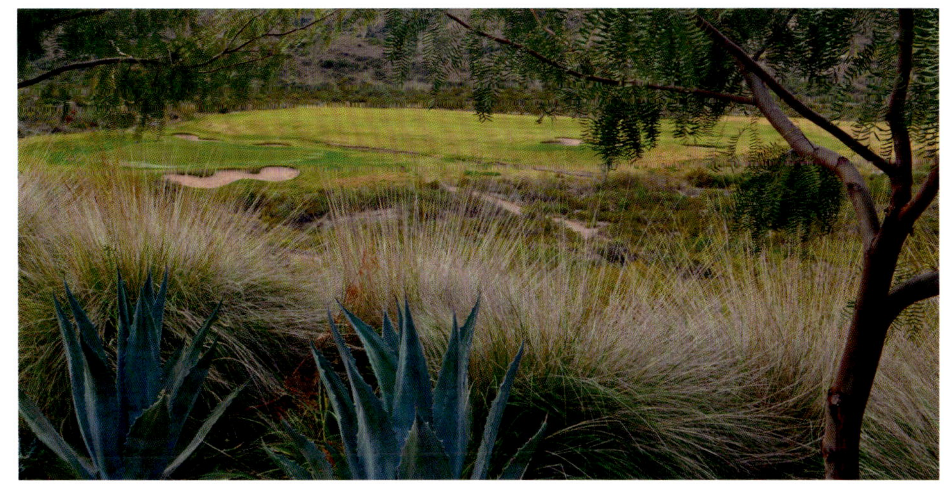

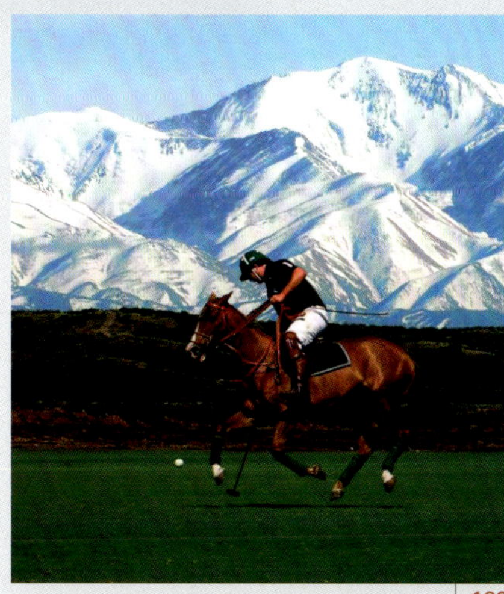

DISCOVER THE ANDES

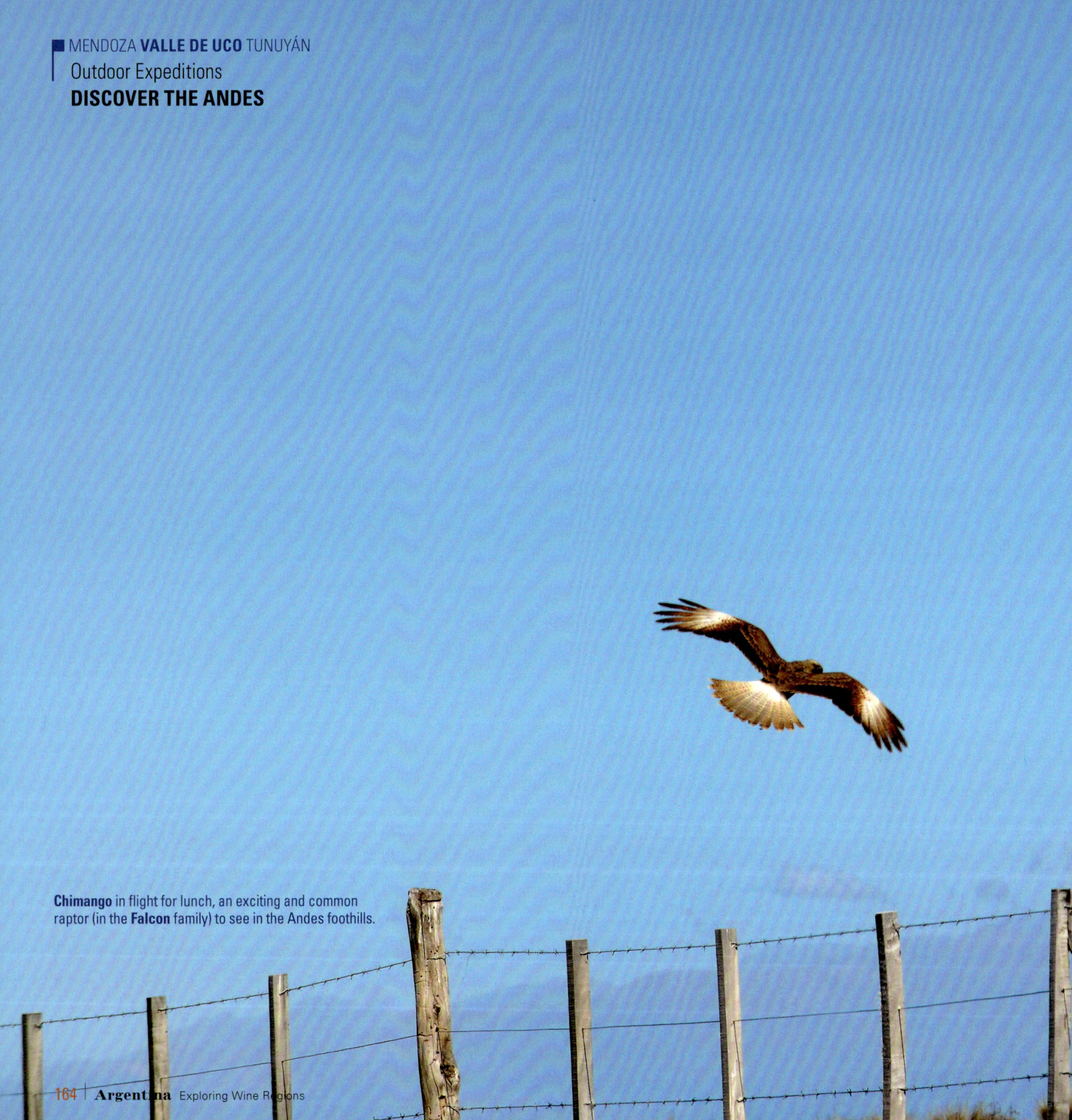

Chimango in flight for lunch, an exciting and common raptor (in the **Falcon** family) to see in the Andes foothills.

EXPLORING... WAY BEYOND THE FENCE

As a pilot, I am always fascinated with our winged friends. Birds figured out the secrets of flight long before us, and they still have it mastered beyond us. With the keen vision and aerodynamic mastery, they have the ultimate access of the Andes Mountains.

Absent eagle characteristics, I suggest you contact *Discover the Andes*... 25-year veterans of expeditions into the Andes. They can take you on serious adventures deep into the Andes, or keep is simple and show you the outdoor magic found in the foothills of this massive mountain range.

Whatever your adventure, bring your binoculars. In this vast land you will find an extensive array of birds. Among our flying friends, the **Andean Condor** is the most popular bird to go spotting. As one of the largest birds in the Western Hemisphere, its wingspan exceeds 12 feet. It is midnight black with tuffs of white feathers around its neck. A sure sight to see! *Discover the Andes* has a special relationship with *Quebrada de los Cóndores* (Ravine of the Condors) a natural reserve, deep into a canyon with steep cliffs, where the condors live protected by an inapproachable terrain. Trek up to the base and see the habits of these majestic birds which will impose their presence from above. Learn interesting characteristics... as in the way they mate for life and, according to tradition, when one of them dies, the other soars and commits suicide by going into a tailspin and crashing into the rocks of the mountain.

The **Chimango** is a beautiful cinnamon-colored bird that is very smart and known as a great survivor in the driest and harshest of landscapes as the Andes.

The **Pirincho**, more commonly known as the **Guira Cuckoo**, is beautifully distinct with its spiky hairdo, pinky orange beak, yellow breast, and brown and white stripes down its back. You will find them in the wide-open and semi-open habitats in the foothills of the Andes.

The **Nandu**, also known as **Rhea**, is a long-legged bird like an ostrich, with a proud plume of feathers on its round body. The male's mating call is quite a show as he lifts up his plumage, makes loud booming noises and runs around the female manically. You will find them walking around, primarily in the flatlands.

And, the vineyards themselves are home to an unusual population: **Owls**. They are small and quiet, and spectacularly beautiful! Their faces are a sight to behold. They can be seen during daylight too.

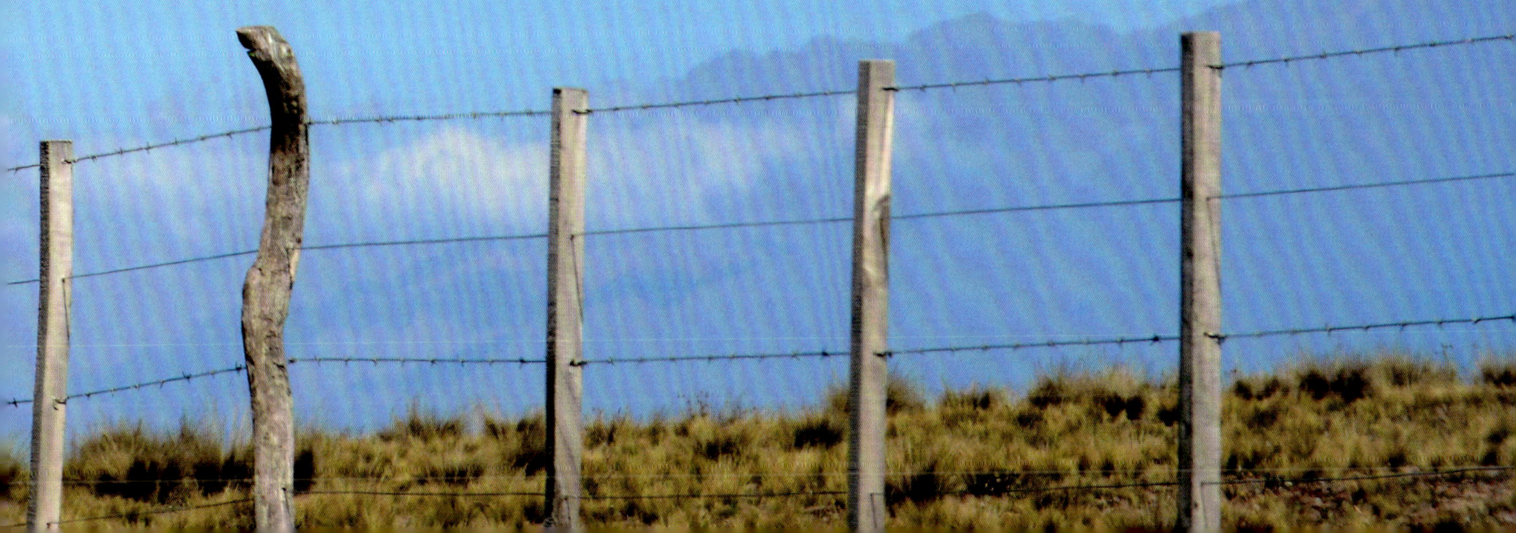

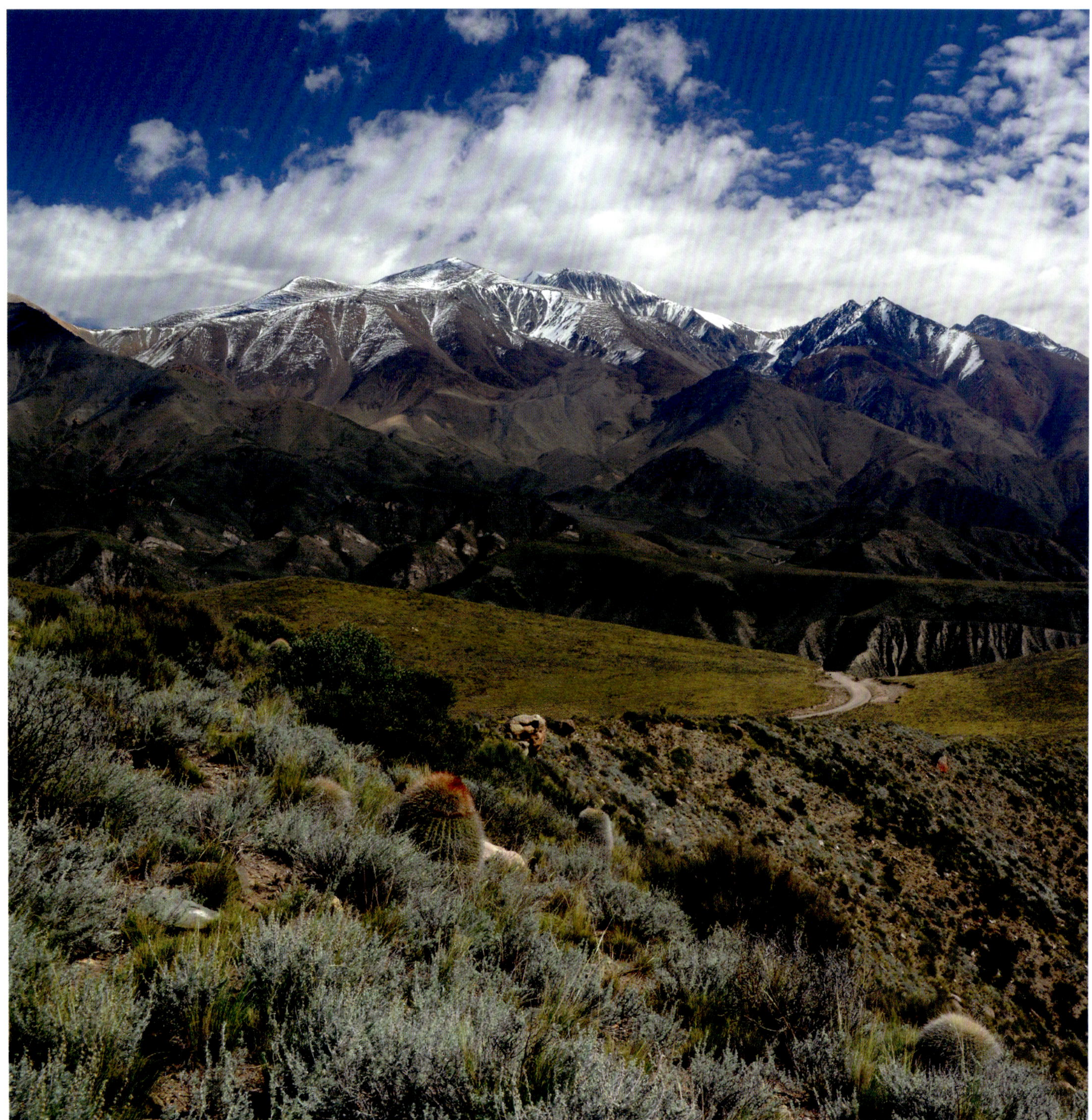

With Valle de Uco nestled into the foothills of the Andes Mountain range, this provides direct access to an abundance of outdoor adventures. The natural areas are extensive in Valle de Uco with many preservation areas. And into the Andes, the wilderness is endless with opportunities.

Discover the Andes is an organization of 12 mountaineers with extensive knowledge of the Andes opportunities, and its terrain, wildlife, flora and fauna. They have been welcoming visitors of all levels of outdoor experience for the past 25 years. Each trip they provide is customized to your exact skills and desires. **Kayaking** and **Whitewater Rafting** in the rivers fed from the mountains. **Horseback Riding** can take you back into the mountains as extensive as you wish to pursue. **Trekking** and **Rappelling** the rocks and canyons, **Snowshoeing** to glaciers, **Hiking** and **Mountain Biking**, all are endless. **Fly Fishing** is great in the many lakes and streams. **Photo Safaris** from four-wheel drive vehicles and year around **Snow Skiing** is possible with the altitude of the Andes.

Checkout these possible trips...

Crossing Over the Andes, Argentina to Chile, a five-day journey following the same crossing as the English biologist Charles Darwin did in 1835 and General San Martin in 1817... through the Manzano Histórico canyon entrance.

Climbing Mt. Aconcagua, the second highest mountain in the world, here in the Mendoza province (see photo and description on page 16). It really needs no introduction... if you want to go, *Discover the Andes* will take you there. Or take you to **Parque Provincial Aconcagua** where you can explore lower elevations of magnificent scenery.

Tupungato Volcano, within the Provincial Park Volcán Tupungato, is a sight to see, comprising of approximately 370,000 acres, protecting an important sector of the central Andes.

Puente del Inca Preservation Area is a place of untold beauty with a natural bridge considered to be a unique geo-shape in the world. Due to its particular characteristics, it will likely be designated a world heritage site soon. It's a natural bridge formed by minerals and microbiological organisms such as algae located over the Cuevas River. It is believed that thousands of years ago a bridge of ice was formed, that with the subsequent avalanches, the hot springs and time solidified its construction along with the bio-mineral components that give the reddish color to the bridge.

With Valle de Uco adjacent the Andes, these foothills offer a huge variety of outdoor activities. *Discover the Andes* believes in mountaineering as an activity to get close contact with the environment and develop moments of deep introspection. It's all part of what they love and want to share. Truly an extravaganza of outdoor adventures and spectacular sights. It all depends on how deep you want to go?

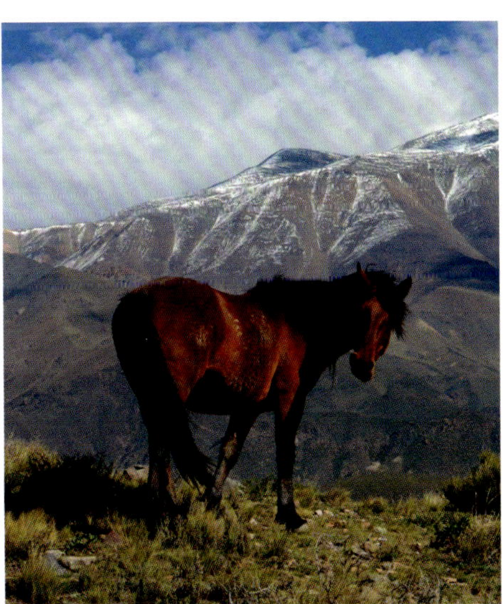

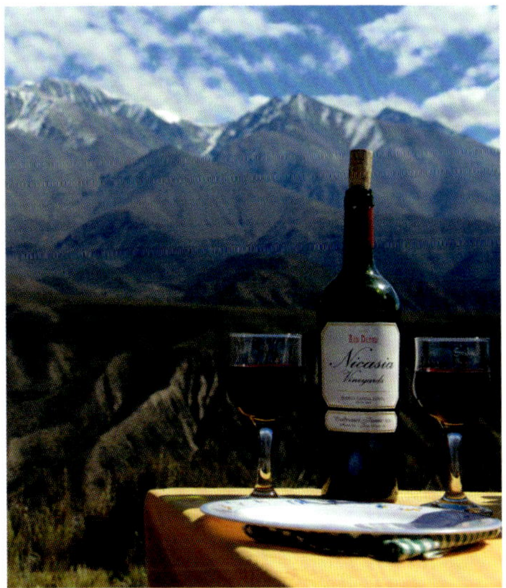

Outdoor Expeditions
DISCOVER THE ANDES

Throughout Valle de Uco
(**Tunuyán**, Valle de Uco)

011 (+54) (9) (261) 639.2757
EduardoSoler@DiscoverTheAndes.com

www.DiscoverTheAndes.com

English, Español and Português

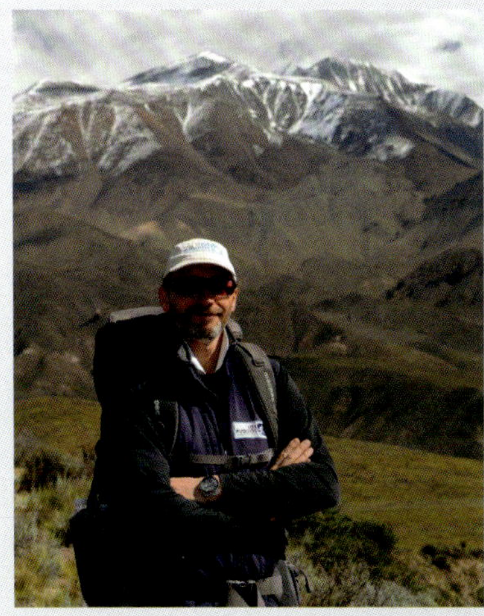

Eduardo Soler
Partner, Discover the Andes, Private Tours
Professional Outdoor Adventure Guide

I had the pleasure to spend the day with Eduardo. He is truly an outdoorsman, a mountaineer who knows his way around the wilderness, knowing geology and geography in a very educational way.

Eduardo is a highly experienced explorer of the Andes... trekking, mountain biking, horseback riding or by 4x4 vehicles... he knows how to get you into (and out of) any place you want to go.

Eduardo is also a sophisticated wine and art aficionado, with numerous connections for insider tours and introductions of special experiences.

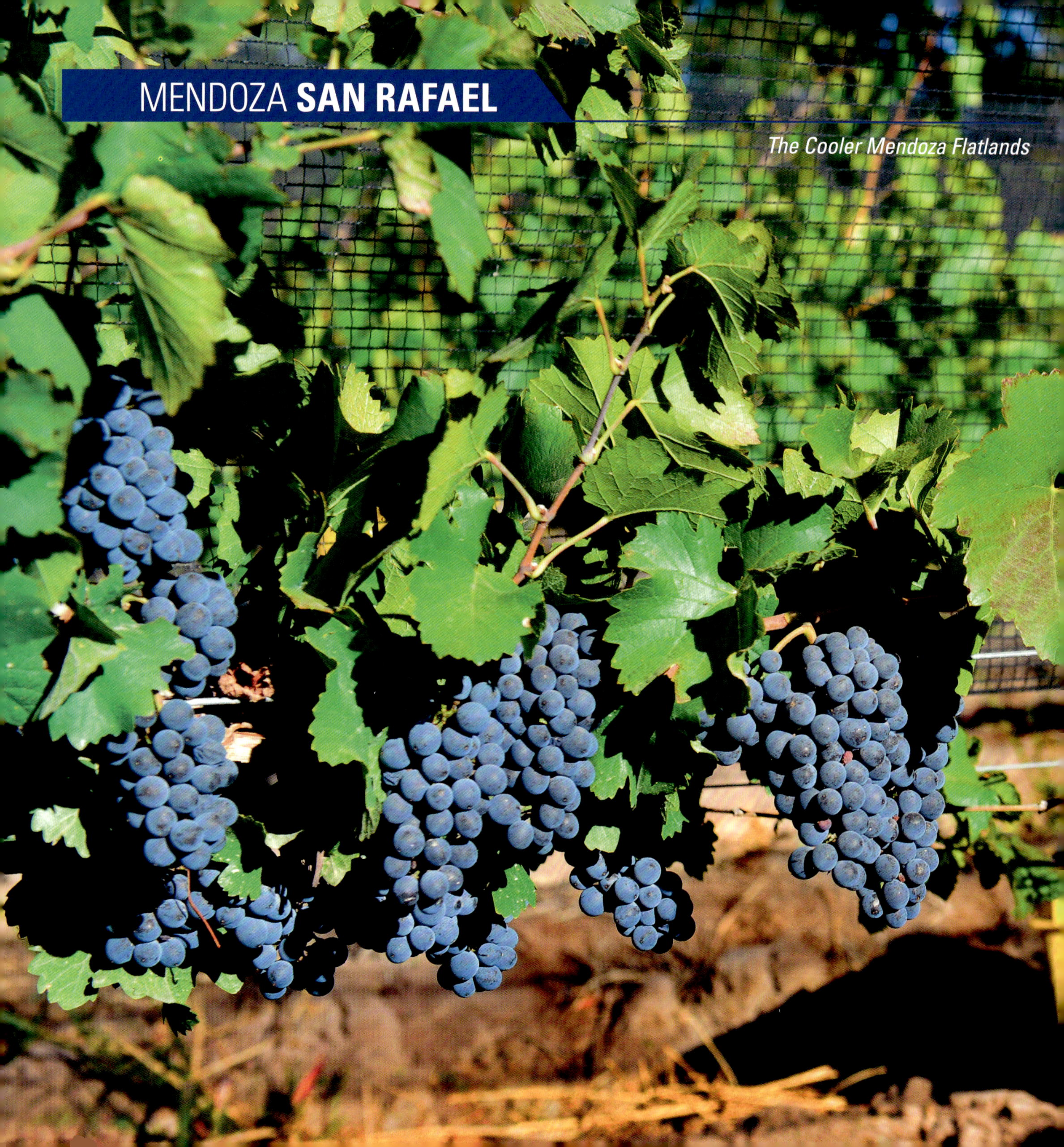

MENDOZA **SAN RAFAEL**

The Cooler Mendoza Flatlands

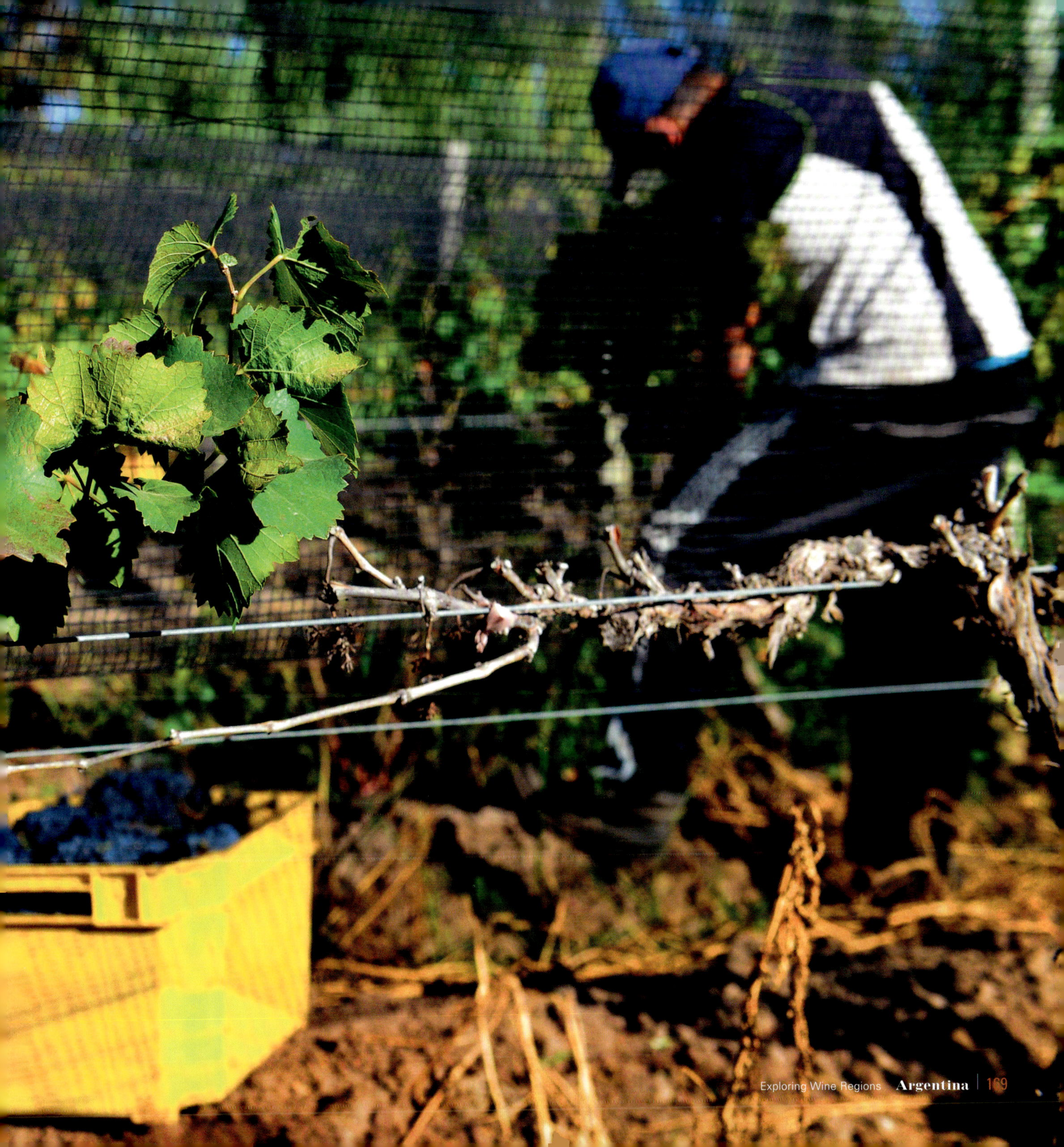

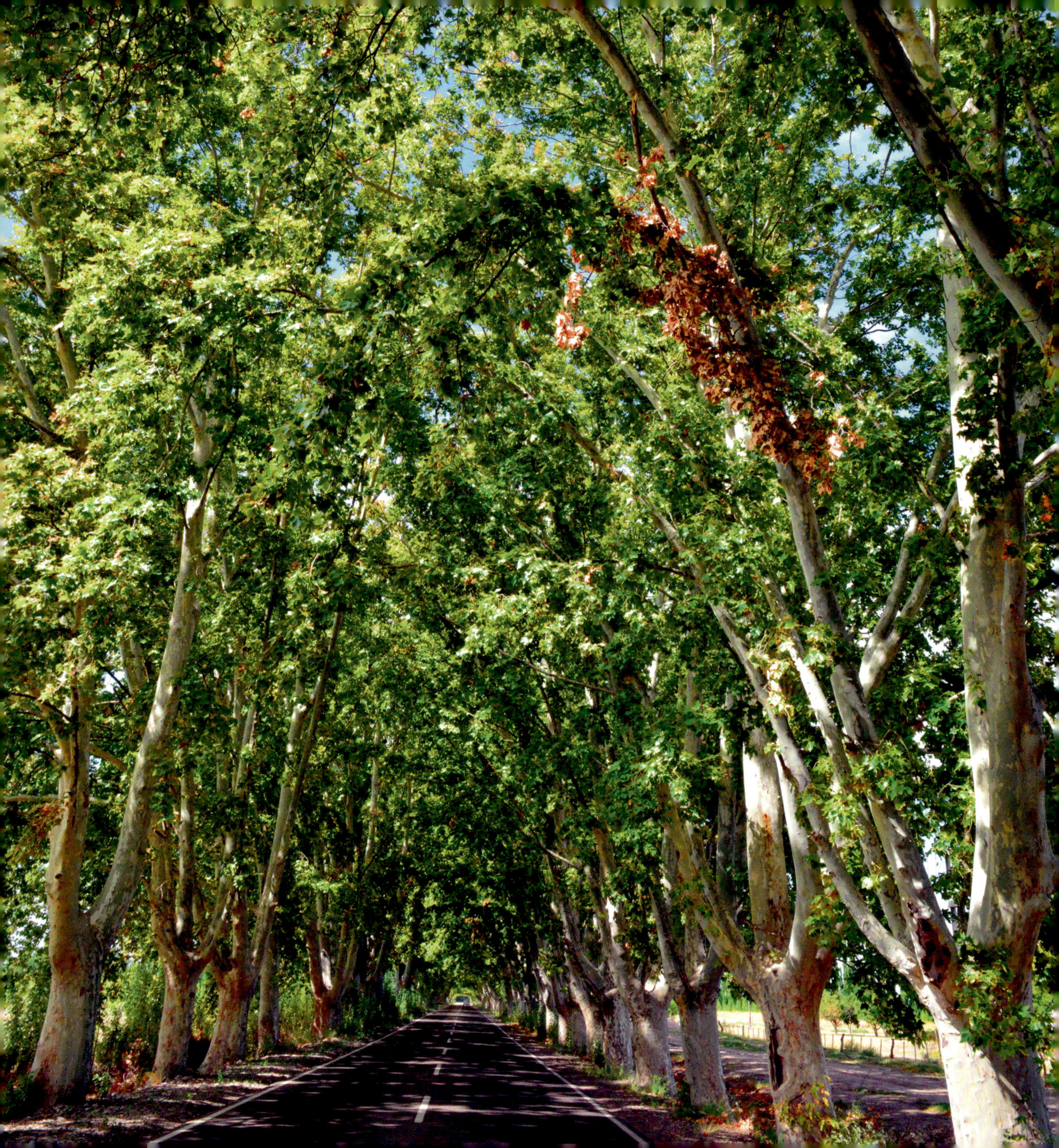

GET OUT OF TOWN, AND

...experience the local community of San Rafael, not a tourist attraction, where you can enjoy real live Argentine culture in a city of 200,000 sanrafaelinos.

San Rafael is a modern city today celebrating its rich history and culture with 15 or more museums and other cultural places to visit. There is a town square, a historic train station, numerous parks, great shopping, and many interesting neighborhood restaurants to taste the local flavor. You can even get a good steak dinner, with a bottle of wine, for only US $15.

The charm of the majestic old sycamore trees and open irrigation channels lining the streets will get you in the San Rafael mood of relaxation. Being in the flatlands away from the Andes, walking and wondering the streets on bicycles (many rentals) are common activities.

There are olive oil factories and a several dozen interesting and different wineries to tour. Three sparkling wine bodegas, including the famed French and California Mumm Champagne, have set roots here. It is a different climate, cooler, so you will experience softer Malbec, Syrah and Bonarda. And with Pinot Noir being used by the sparkling bodegas, Pinot is now being explored by a couple of wineries for single varietal vintages. Algodon Wine Estates might just have created a big winner for their 2012 Pinot!

San Rafael is located in the southern part of the Mendoza region, away from the other wine regions we have been exploring. It is a three-hour drive south of the city of Mendoza. They also have an airport with commercial flights, and a large winery adjacent to the airport – Bodega Valentin Bianchi.

Just south of the city is Valle Grande and Cañón del Atuel, a mini Grand Canyon, with a large majestic reservoir and a year-round flowing river... hosting numerous outdoor sports including boating, sailing, fishing, kayak, canopy, whitewater rafting, hiking, mountain climbing, four-wheeling, horseback riding, and mountain biking.

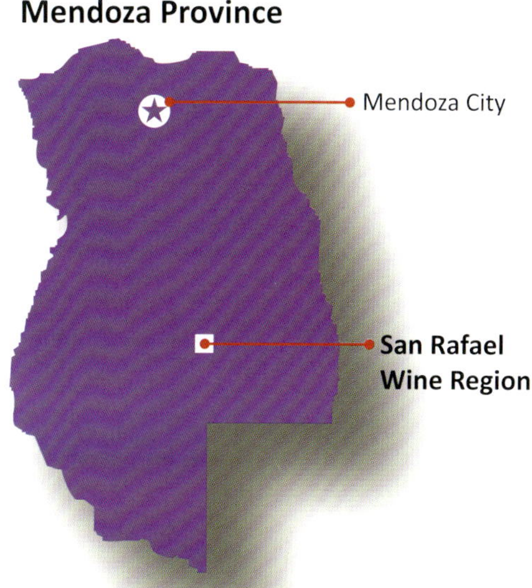

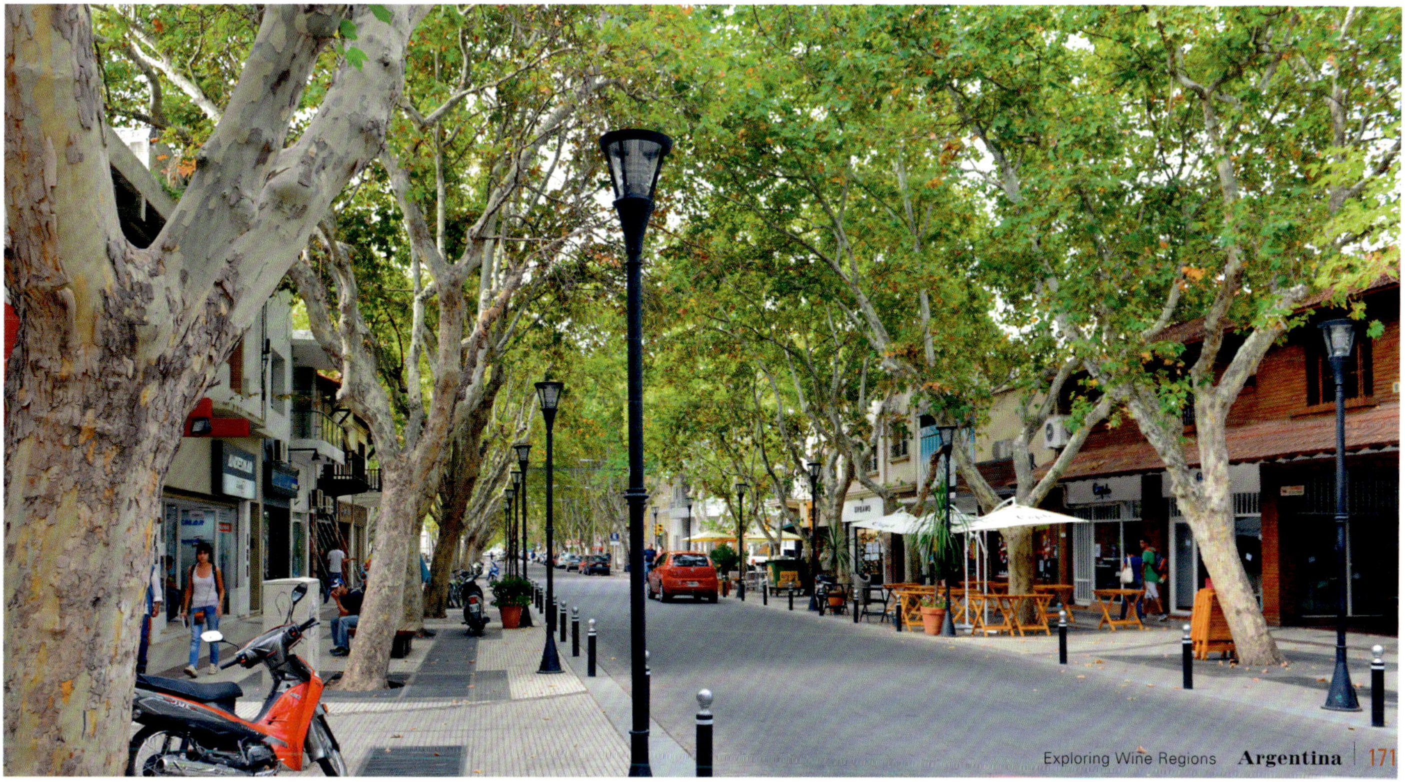

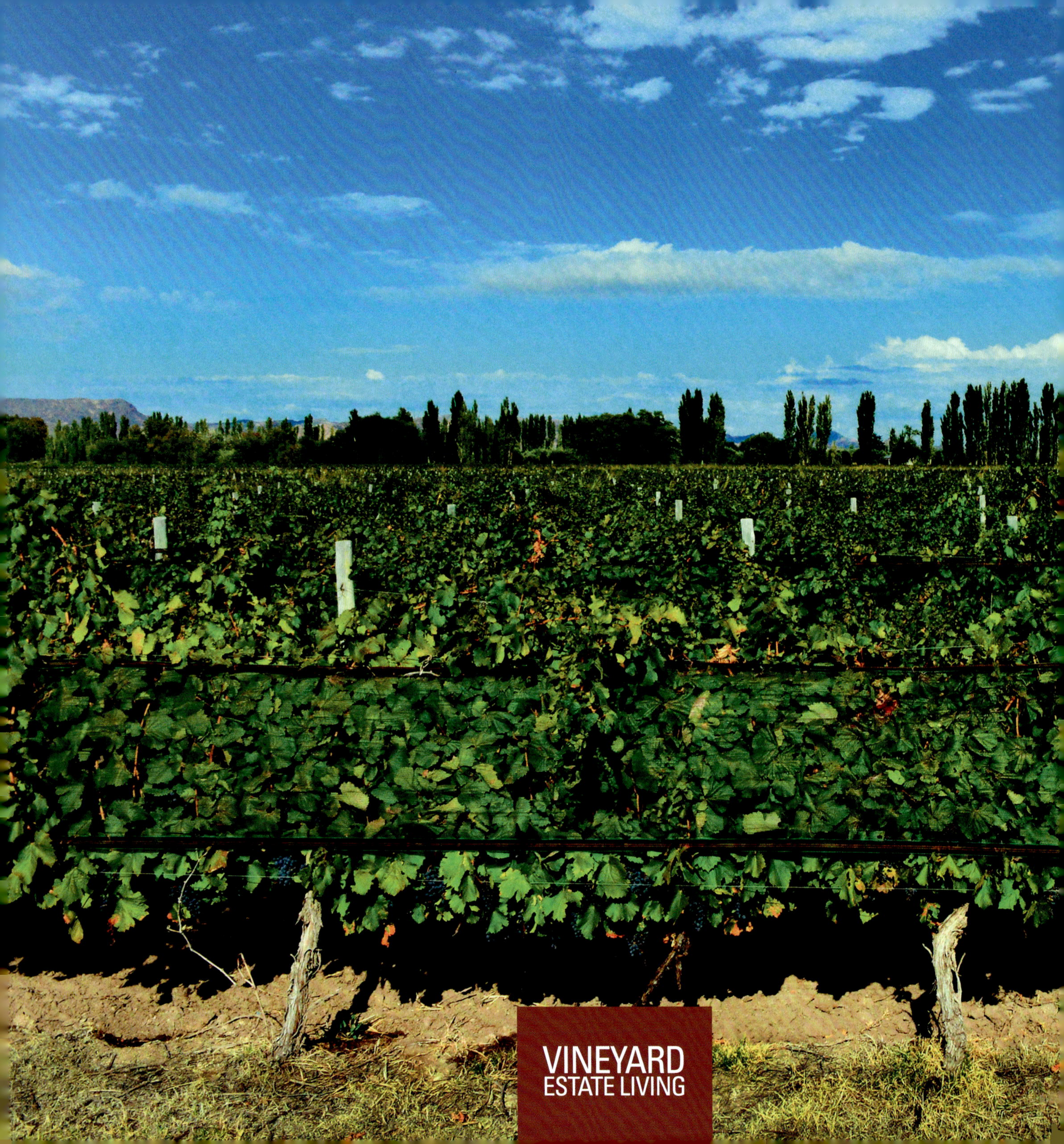
VINEYARD
ESTATE LIVING

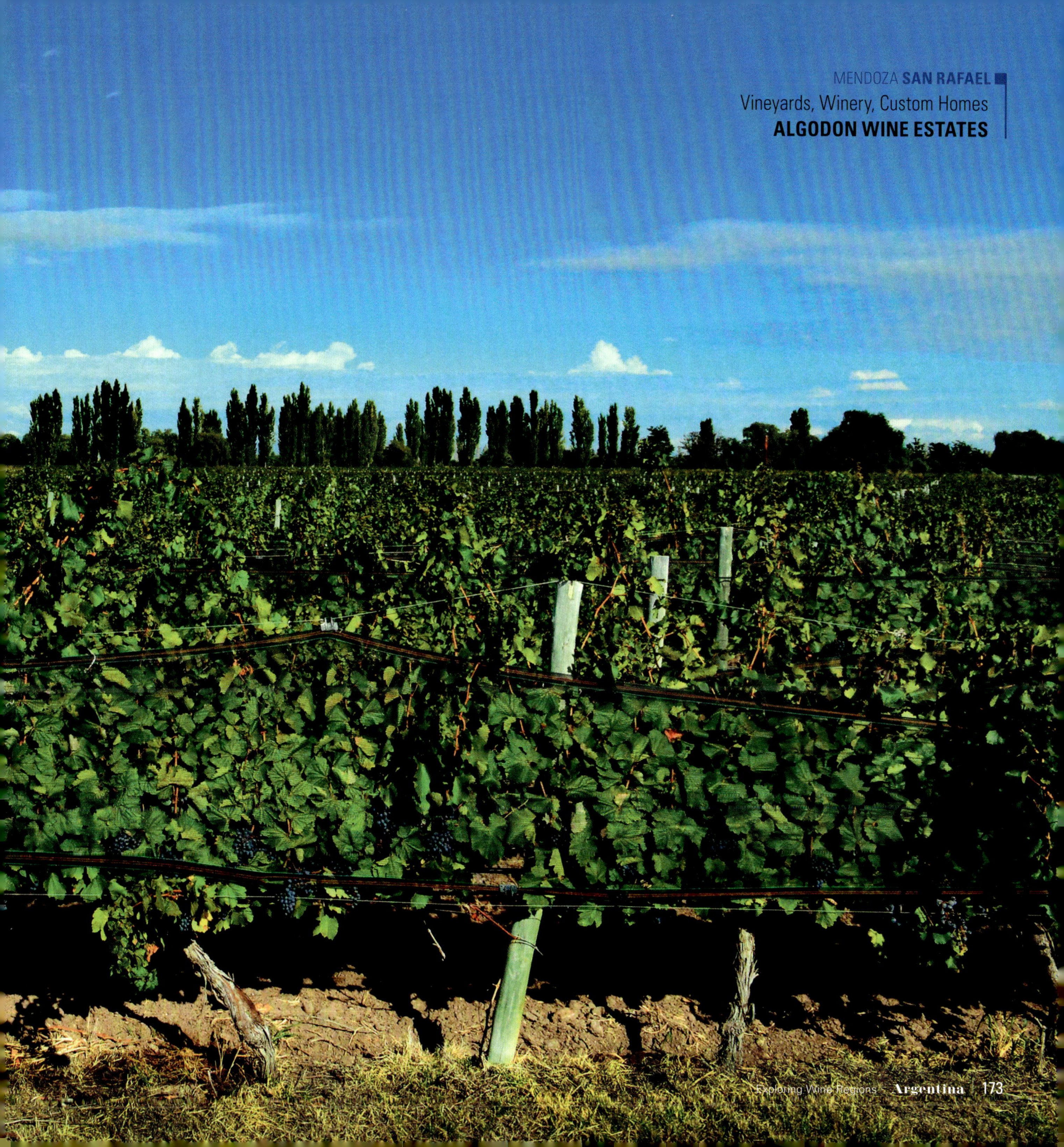

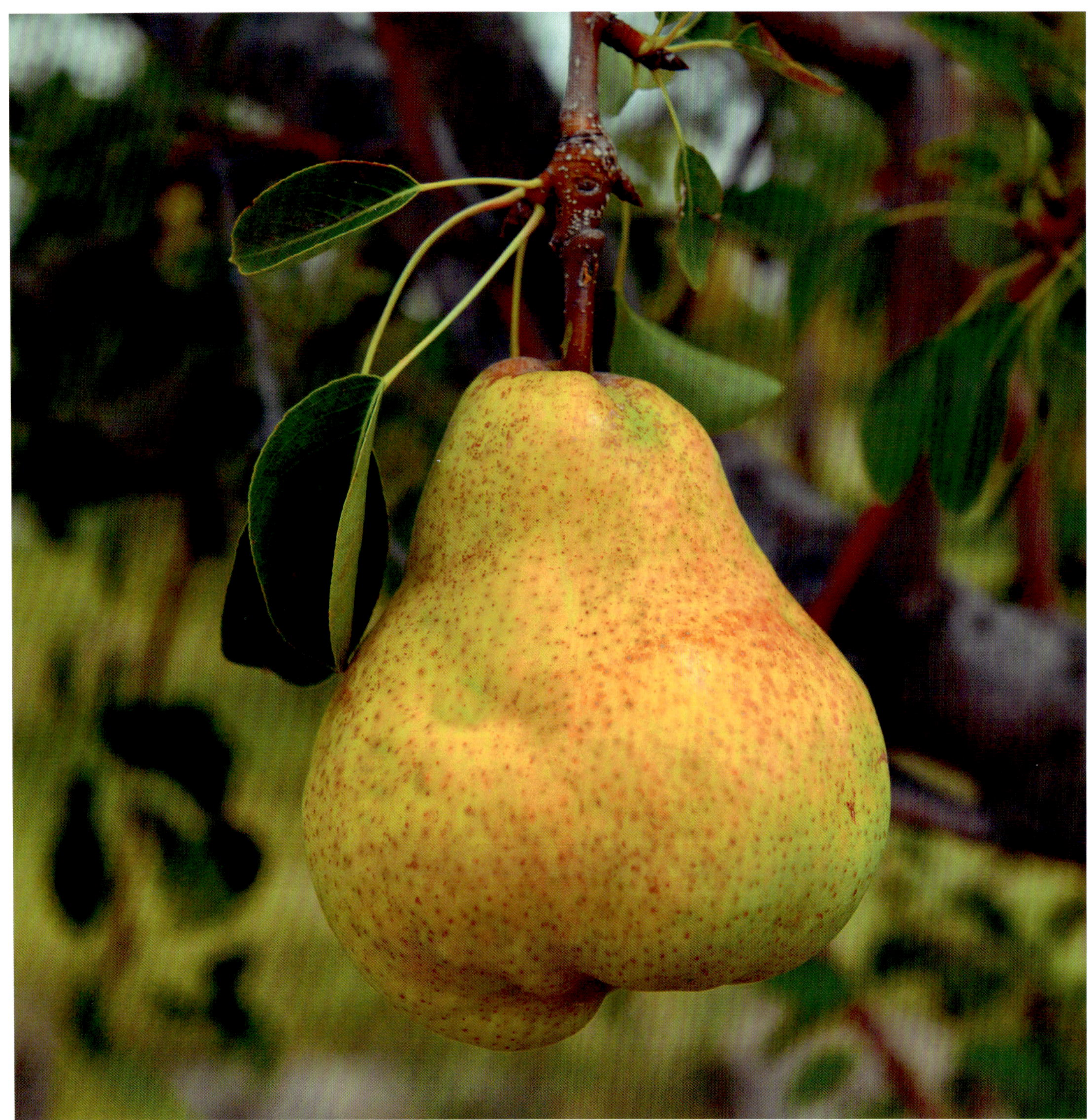

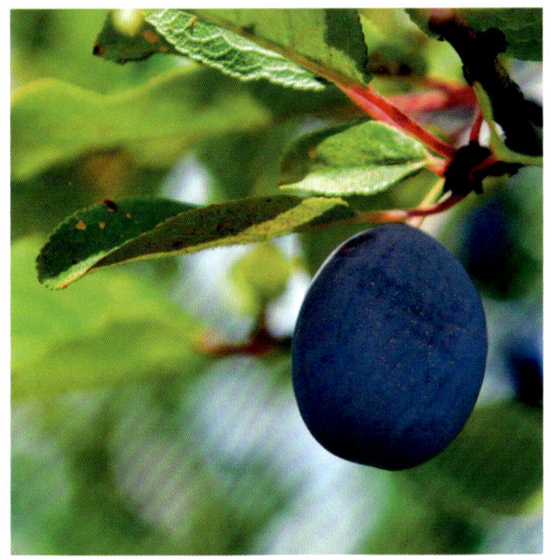

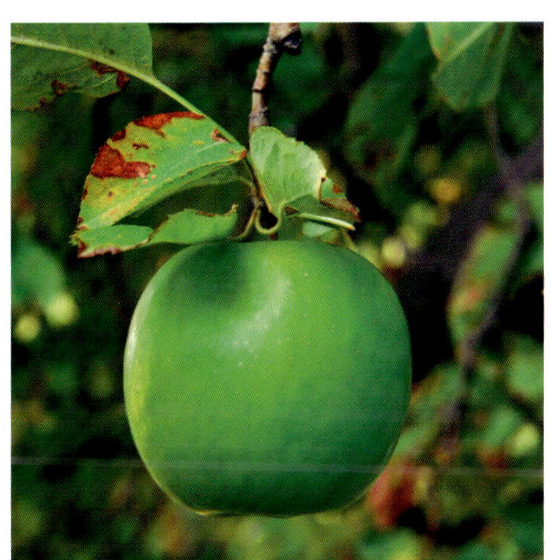

A WINE-INSPIRED LIFESTYLE

Imagine strolling through 2,000 acres of orchards, vineyards, golf, and your own private custom estate home... picking a fresh peach off the tree and pondering life. And just how good it is...

The apple doesn't fall far from the tree, so you can choose to build your own dream home in the center of various fruit orchards, or on your own estate vineyard of your favorite grape varietal, or right alongside one of the beautiful green golf fairways... overlooking it all.

Thirty minutes outside the city of San Rafael, the Algodon Wine Estates is poised to be a luxury community of large estate homes amongst orchards, vineyards, golfing, tennis, hotel, restaurant, and winery. Numerous homes are already under construction or completed, averaging 4,000 square feet.

I had the pleasure to meet the visionary behind Algodon Wine Estates, New York investment banker Scott Mathis, who wants to create a utopia for the oenophile's dream to participate in the vineyard and winemaking process, without any of the headaches. And to get back to nature, living part or full time, within a beautiful countryside estate, away from it all and yet close to everything you need.

Scott grew up on a cotton farm in Mississippi and now lives in the Big Apple. He, like other successful people living in big cities, wants to get back to nature. Algodon, meaning cotton in Spanish, is his vision to do just that.

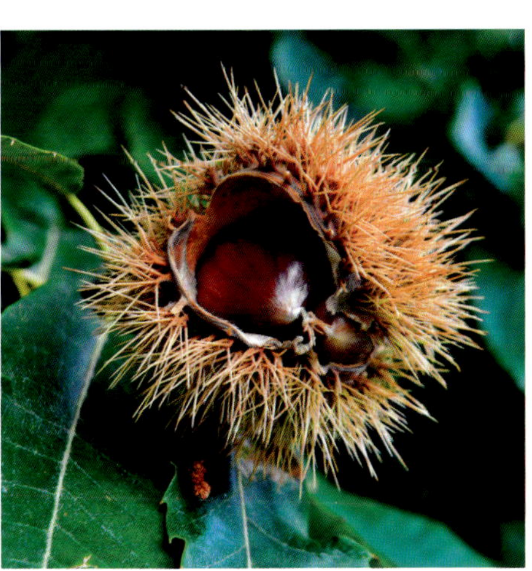

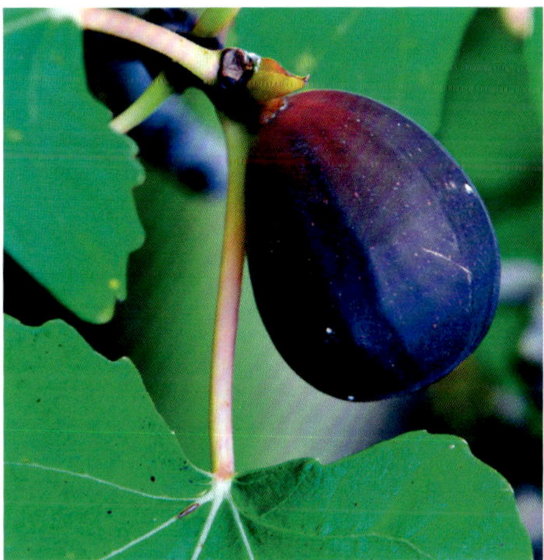

MENDOZA **SAN RAFAEL**

Custom Homes, Golf & Tennis

ALGODON WINE ESTATES

674 Ruta Nacional
(Cuadro Benegas, San Rafael)

011 (+54 262) 742.9020
info@AlgodonWineEstates.com

AlgodonWineEstates.com

English & Español

CNN Money boasts San Rafael as the *Fourth Best Place* in the world to retire

Fruit and nut orchards are abundant on Algodon Estate.

LEFT PAGE, is a delicious ripe pear; ABOVE to BELOW, are the delights of ripening plum, apple, chestnut and fig.

Also on the 2,000-acre estate are peaches, apricots, walnuts, almonds, olives, and 297 acres of vineyards.

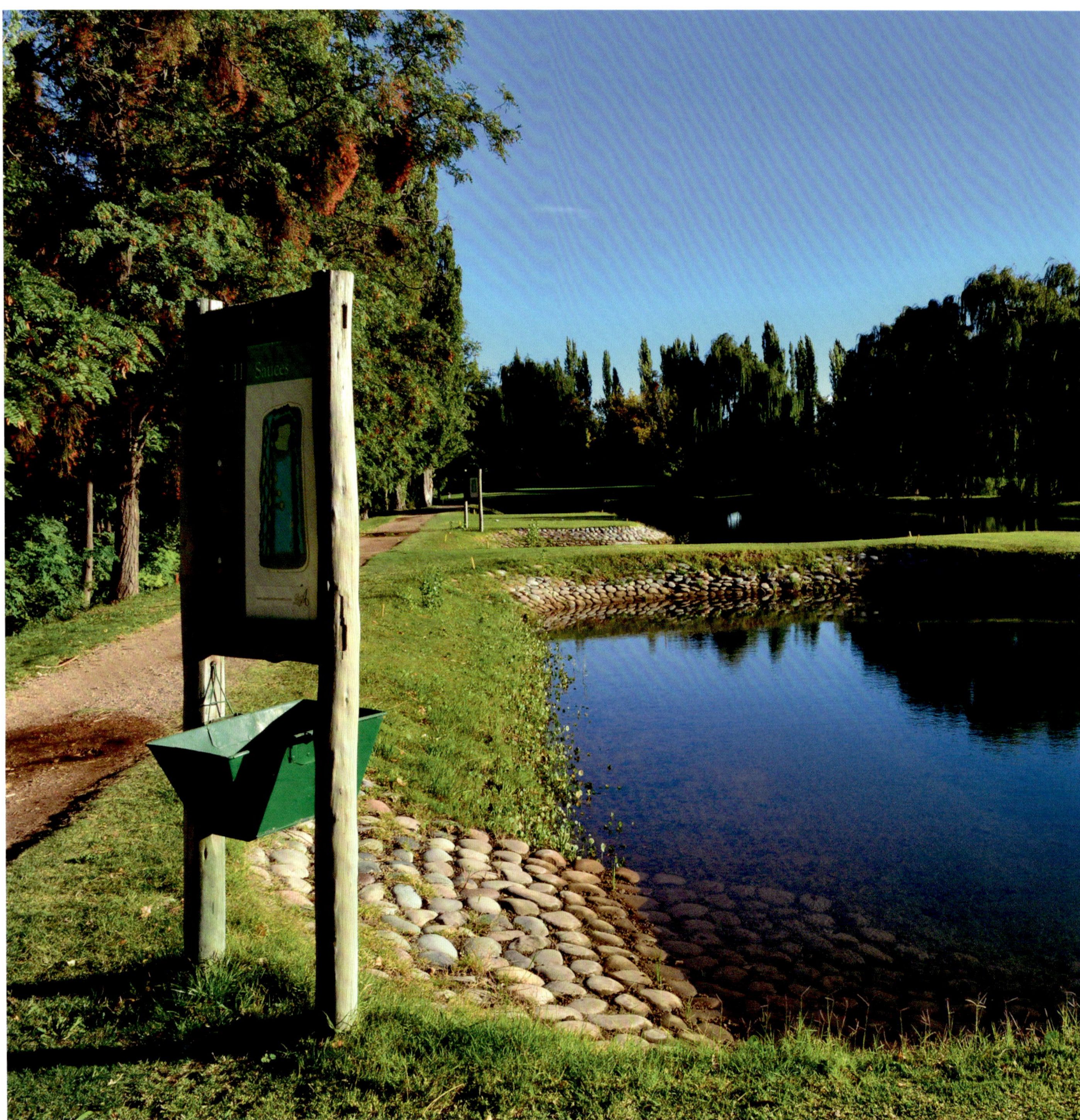

MENDOZA **SAN RAFAEL**

Sports, Restaurant, Hotel

ALGODON WINE ESTATES

674 Ruta Nacional
(Cuadro Benegas, San Rafael)

011 (+54 262) 742.9020
info@AlgodonWineEstates.com

AlgodonWineEstates.com

English & Español

GOLF

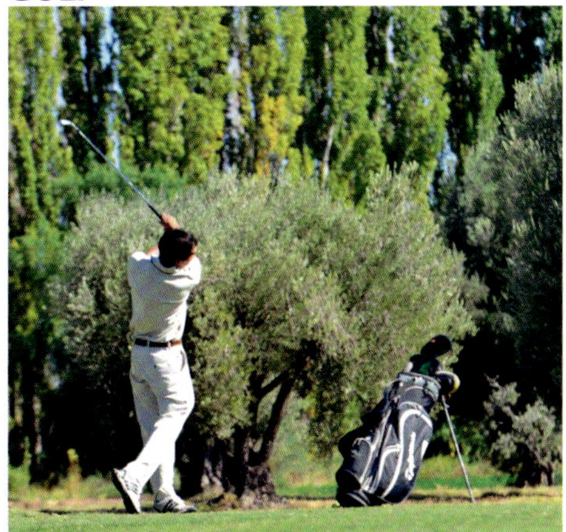

Combining vineyards and golf, Algodon has a unique offering of 18 holes of spectacular golf vistas, meandering through walnut, pear and plum orchards, olive groves, old farmhouses, horse pastures, tree-lined roads, trickling brooks, natural water reservoirs, and numerous vineyards... with history dating back to 1946. Clubs and cart rentals, driving range, clubhouse and restaurant.

TENNIS

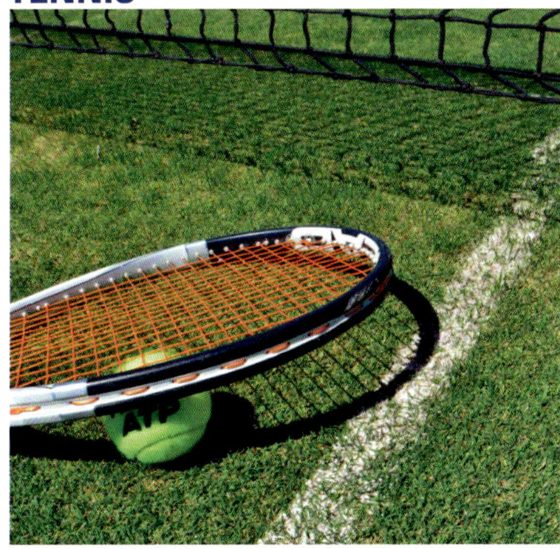

Not just another tennis facility, and way beyond its gorgeous setting amidst half-century old olive groves and vineyards, this is a professional tennis environment. Have you ever played tennis on clay courts, or a grass court? This is a totally unique experience to add challenge and to intrigue you to the game. Seven clay courts, one hard court, and the only two grass courts in all of Mendoza.

HOTEL

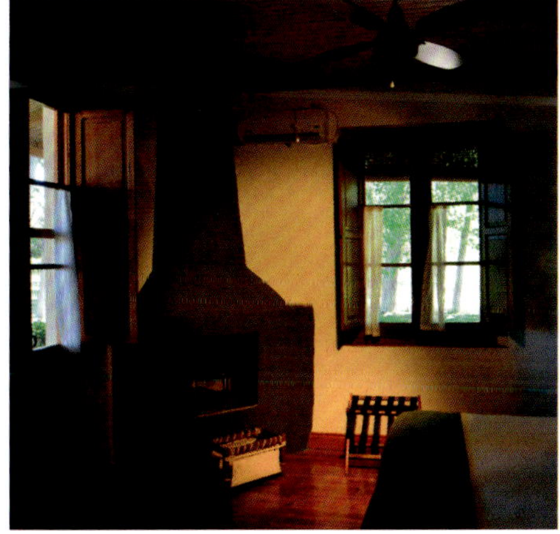

Amid a grass park-like setting, vineyards and fruit trees, is a small lodge on the property converted from a 1921 farmhouse. Charming with basic features in a lodge, private porches, swimming pool and a vine-covered barbecue area. If you can tolerate old infrastructure issues (like no water for hours) and no customer service, this is a nice getaway with comfortable accommodations.

RESTAURANT

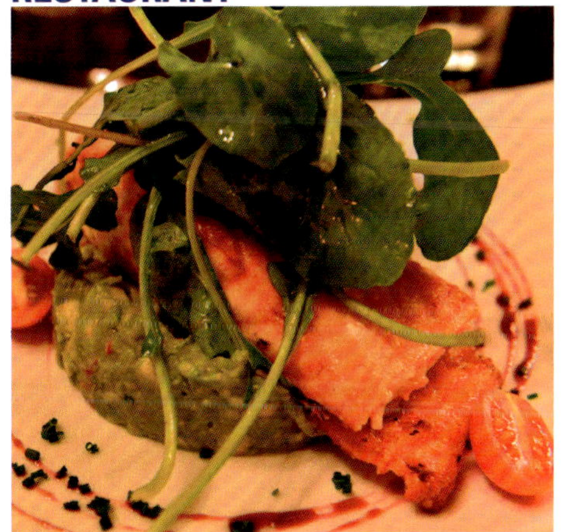

An indoor lodge-type restaurant with fireplace, plus wonderful outdoor dining settings, their restaurant *Chez Gaston* has authentic Argentine cuisine made from the traditional Argentine clay oven and flame broiling pit. Serving breakfast, lunch and dinner, and prepared from local ingredients from their own plantation and those of their neighbors. Cooking classes and seminars are regular year-round.

HORSES

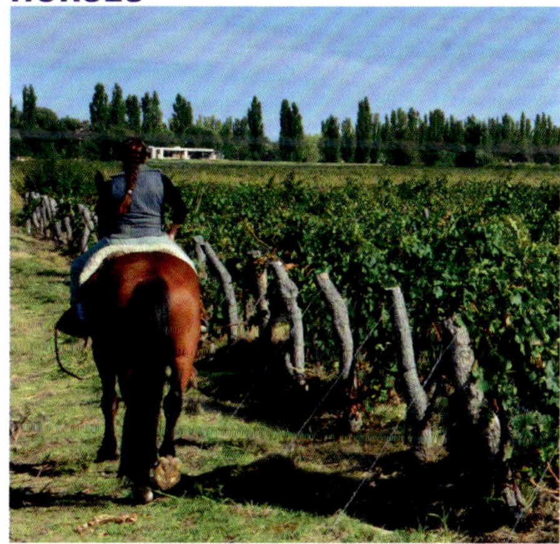

Polo and horseback riding are part of this large estate. A Championship Polo Center is in the master plan to be built. In the mean time, horseback riding is a real treat across these 2,000 acres. Nothing like the altitude of a horse to see across the vineyards to the magnificent landscapes. Stop along the way to eat a fresh plum ripened on the tree, or to take a photo of the many alluring sites.

Vineyards (Viñedos)

ALGODON WINE ESTATES

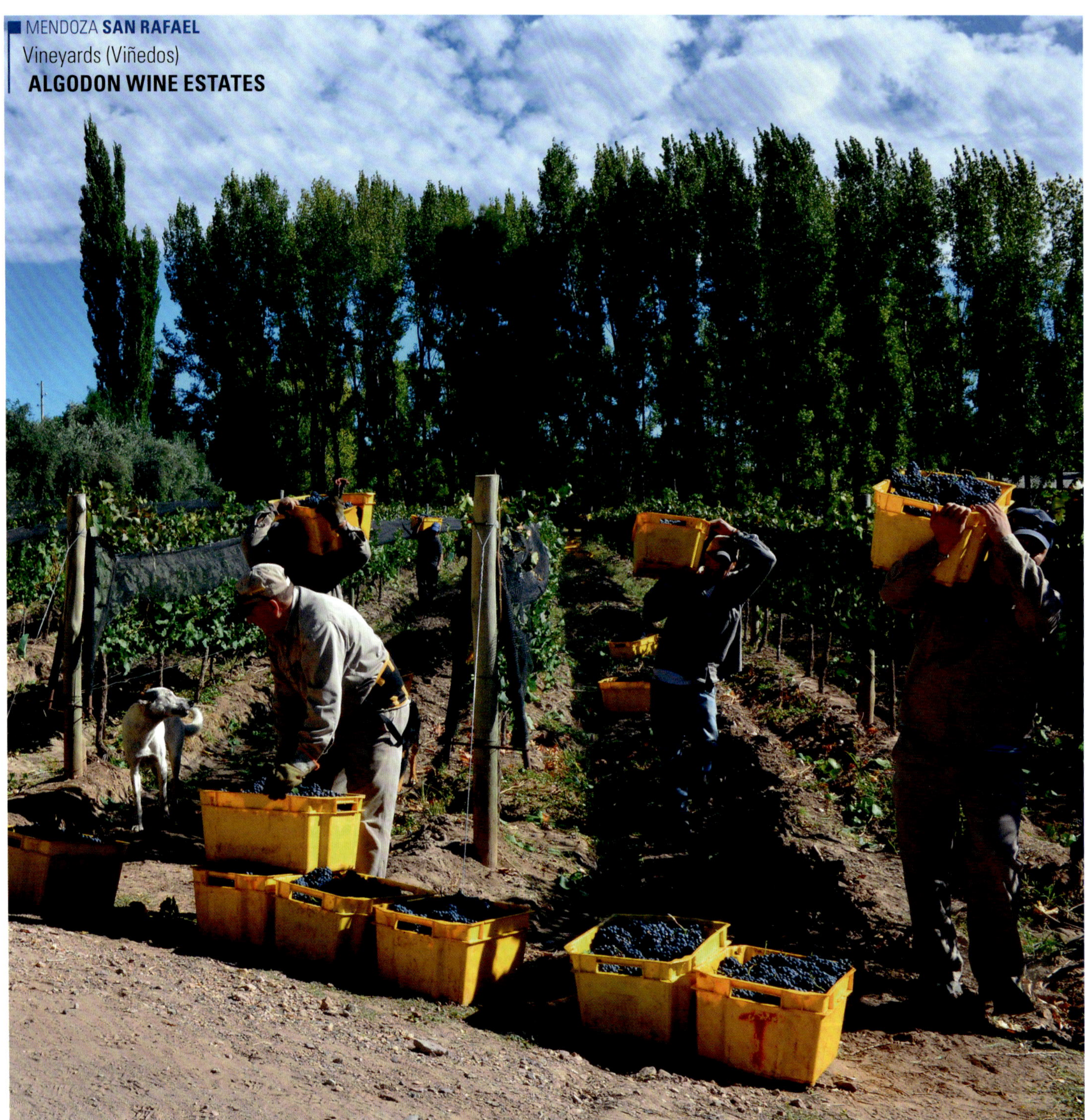

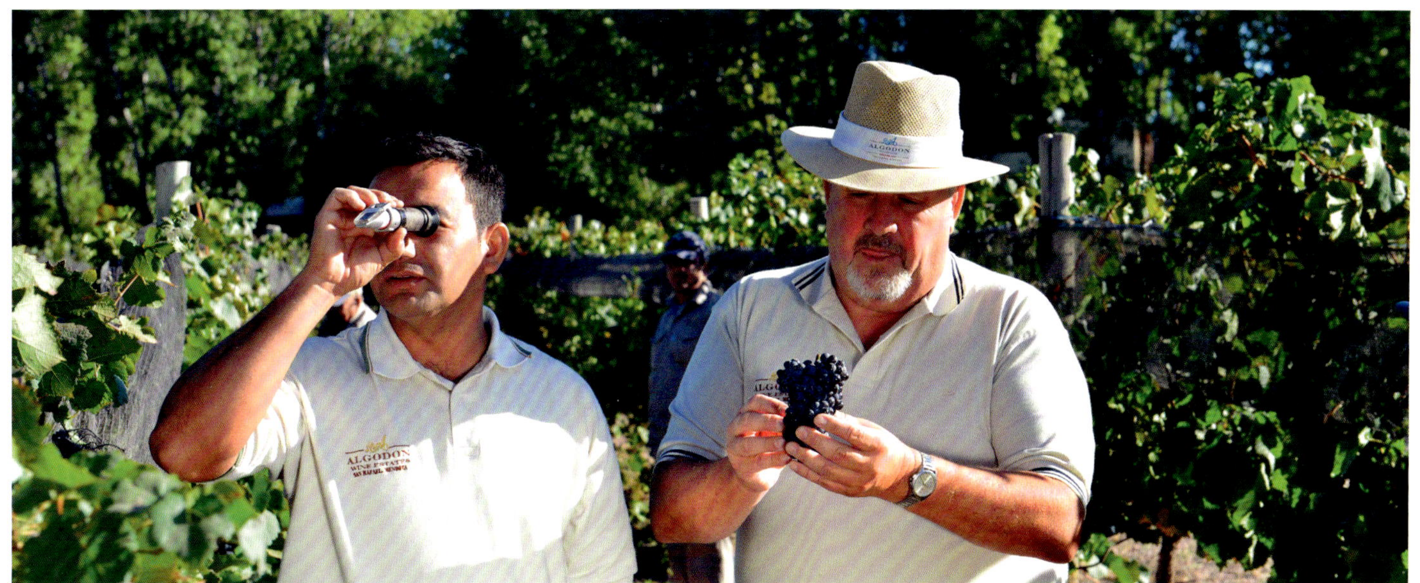

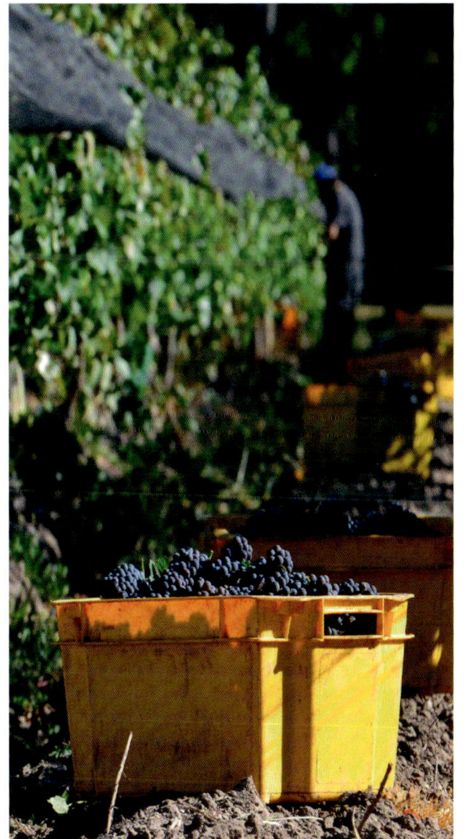

PERFECTION IN THE VINEYARD

It is often said that the wine quality is made in the vineyard. With over 2,000 acres to choose from, and 300 already planted, some vines dating as far back as 1946, Algodon Wine Estates has an ideal environment to grow the very best grapes possible! Most of their 300 acres of grapes are sold to other wineries, so Algodon hand-picks their absolute finest harvest for their own wines. No wonder they are winning awards!

The Algodon property is located in the foothills of the Sierra Pintada Mountains between two rivers fed by the Andes Mountains. For centuries, these rivers have nourished their valley with its fresh water and rich minerals creating distinctive qualities to their vineyards and wines.

One very special and unique vineyard is the one you see harvested in the photographs of these two pages. It's a small four acres of Pinot Noir, not what you would expect in Mendoza. However, San Rafael is a cooler environment for Mendoza, attracting Champagne producers growing Chardonnay and Pinot Noir for their sparkling wines. Algodon is on a unique mission to produce a single vintage, single vineyard, Pinto Noir (not sparkling) of great quality. I tasted the 2012 vintage, only 12 months from harvest, and the possibility, as they expect, are in order to get 95 points for this wine!

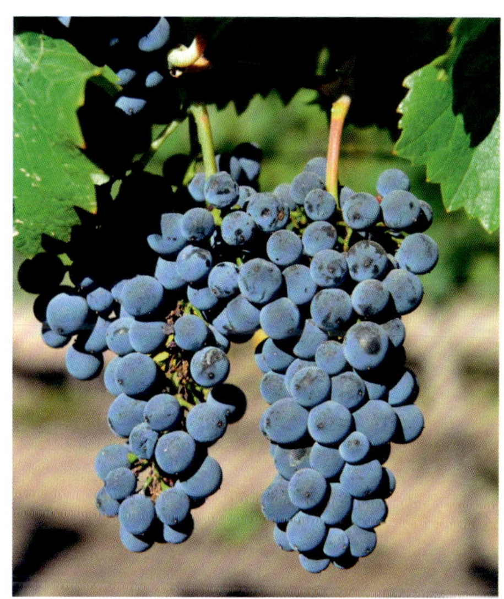

LEFT PAGE, the 2013 Pinot Noir harvest at Algodon;

TOP, Vineyard Technical Manager, Marcelo Hernandez, (reading the Refractometer) and Agronomist, Coco Arenas, are analyzing distinguishing attributes of the Pinot Noir grapes to make important and discerning decisions regarding the day's harvest.

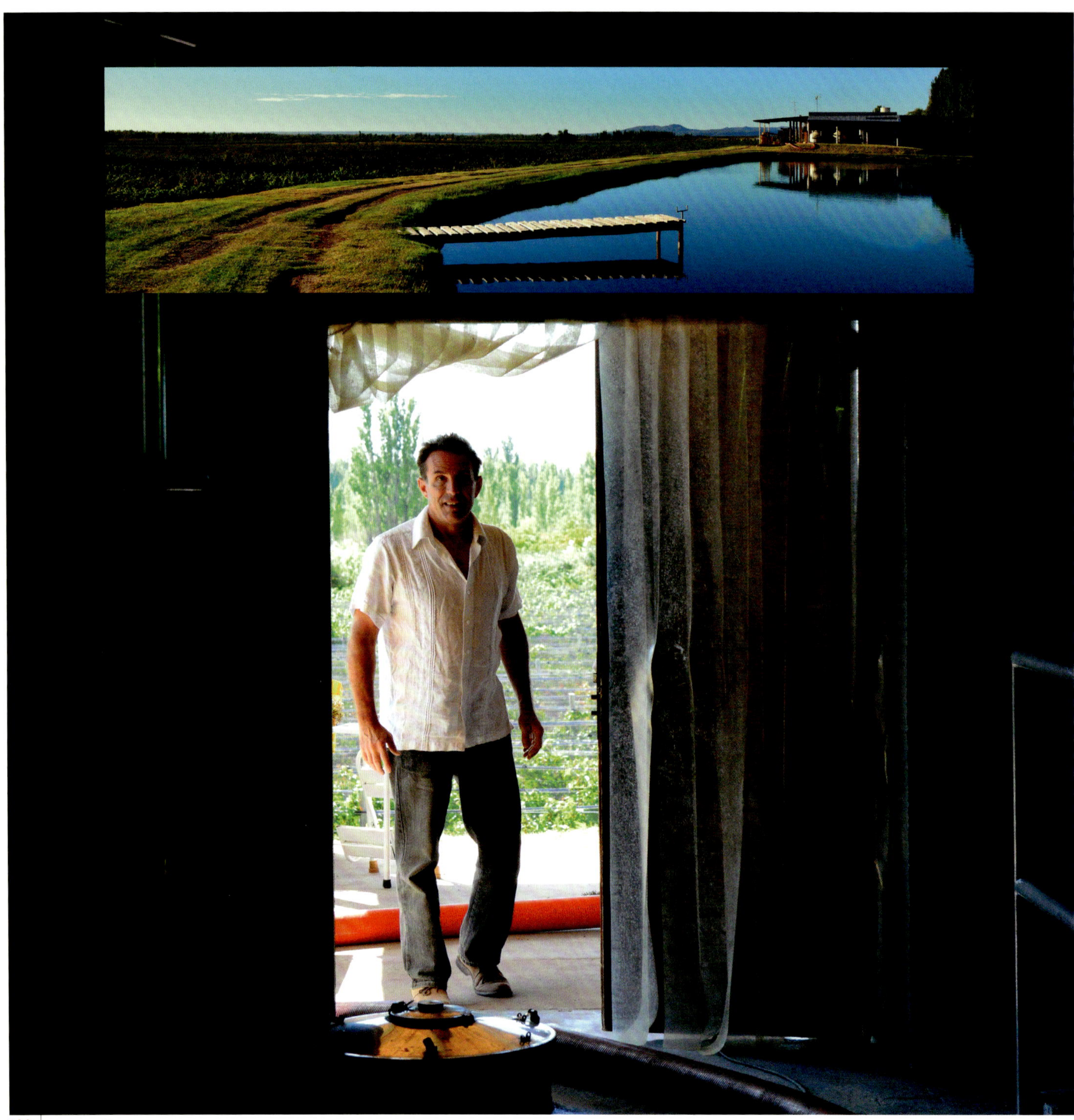

MENDOZA **SAN RAFAEL**

Winery (Bodega)

ALGODON WINE ESTATES

674 Ruta Nacional
(Cuadro Benegas, San Rafael)

011 (+54 262) 742.9020
info@AlgodonWineEstates.com

AlgodonWineEstates.com

English & Español
75,000 bottles annually

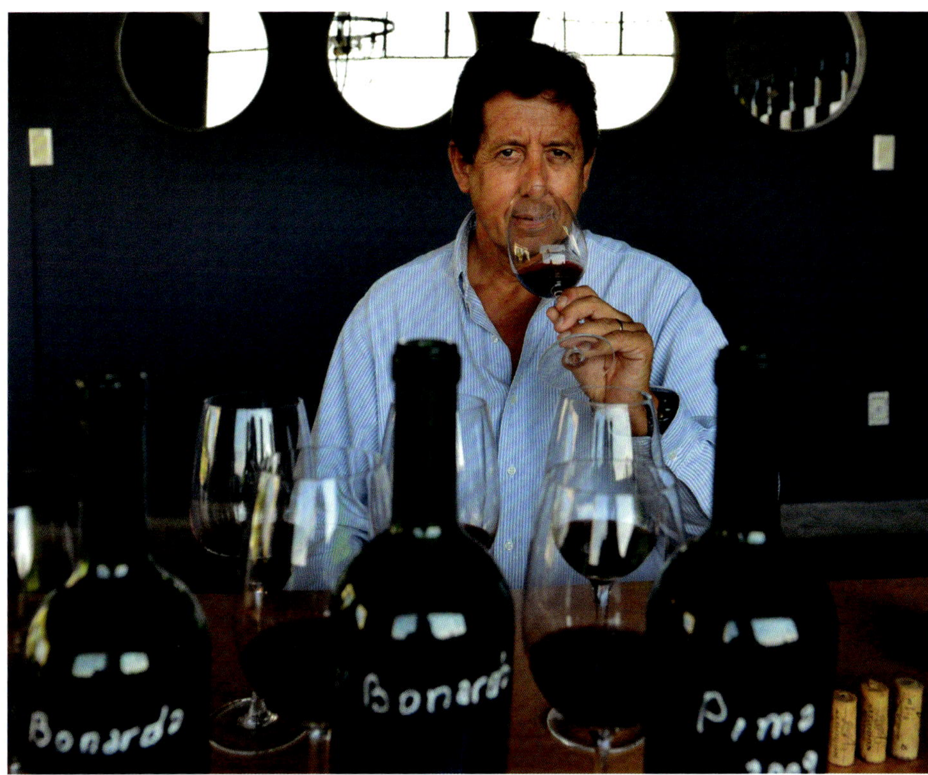

Let's walk inside the Algodon winery now. So, they have started with the best of the best grapes their estate offers, now what? Hire the very best winemaking team. Like Marcello Pellerita who recently received 100 points for his Chateau La Violette he made in Pomeral, France. And, Anthony Foster, who became a Master of Wine after passing the most arduous tasting and theoretical qualification in the industry. Plus, Mauro Nosenzo, who has both winemaking and business degrees, 20 years senior winemaker experience, and judges wine competitions in both Chile and Argentina.

Mauro is Algodon's on-site winemaker and oenologist from the inception, producing the award-winning wines that consistently achieve 90-plus scores. He believes in the exact timing of each varietal's harvest, and manages the vinification process from the moment it is hand-picked to the time it is bottled. Mauro utilizes micro-vinification for producing his premium varietals and blends. Not as a scientific experimentation (as is the common practice), instead as his regular method of maturing the wine completely in one single oak barrel. This is a small-scale production technique to be precise in making super-premium wines.

Winemakers, enologists and sommeliers are available year-round to create a one-of-a-kind viniculture and wine tasting experience at their winery. And they offer group classes in a variety of wine and gourmand related seminars.

Bonarda is another up-and-coming grape in Argentina. Although great on its own, Bonarda works extremely well in blending with Malbec. Very much like what Merlot does when blended with Cabernet. Algodon's Malbec Bonarda is an exciting wine to try. I had the opportunity to taste each of these varietals separately, and then see how they work together. Magic!

LEFT PAGE, Lakeside, overlooking the 1946 Malbec Vineyards, is Algodon Winery; yours truly entering the Winery to discover the makings of their wines;

TOP, Mauro Nosenzo, Algodon Winemaker is sampling the 2012 Pinot Noir, pondering a 95 score for his wine.

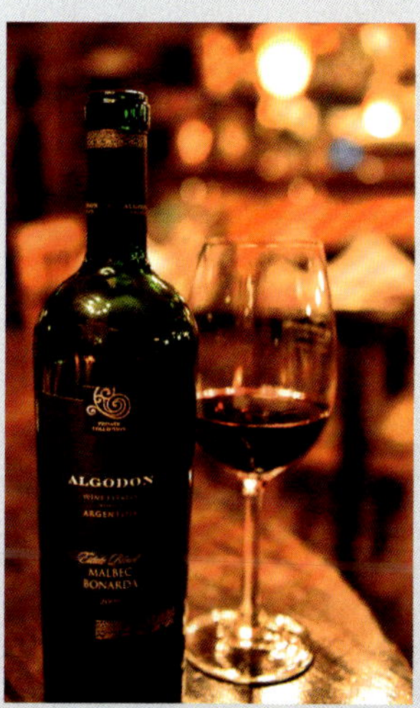

Michael's Favorite Pick
Malbec Bonarda
(70% Malbec, 30% Bonarda)

Total Collection of Wines
Malbec
Bonarda
Malbec Bonarda
Malbec Bonarda Rose
Cabernet Sauvignon
Cabernet Syrah
Pima Blend
Pinot Noir
Chardonnay

To get Algodon wines in the USA
Direct from: OrderWineDirect.com
Use Code: algoinvestors35 for 35% discount

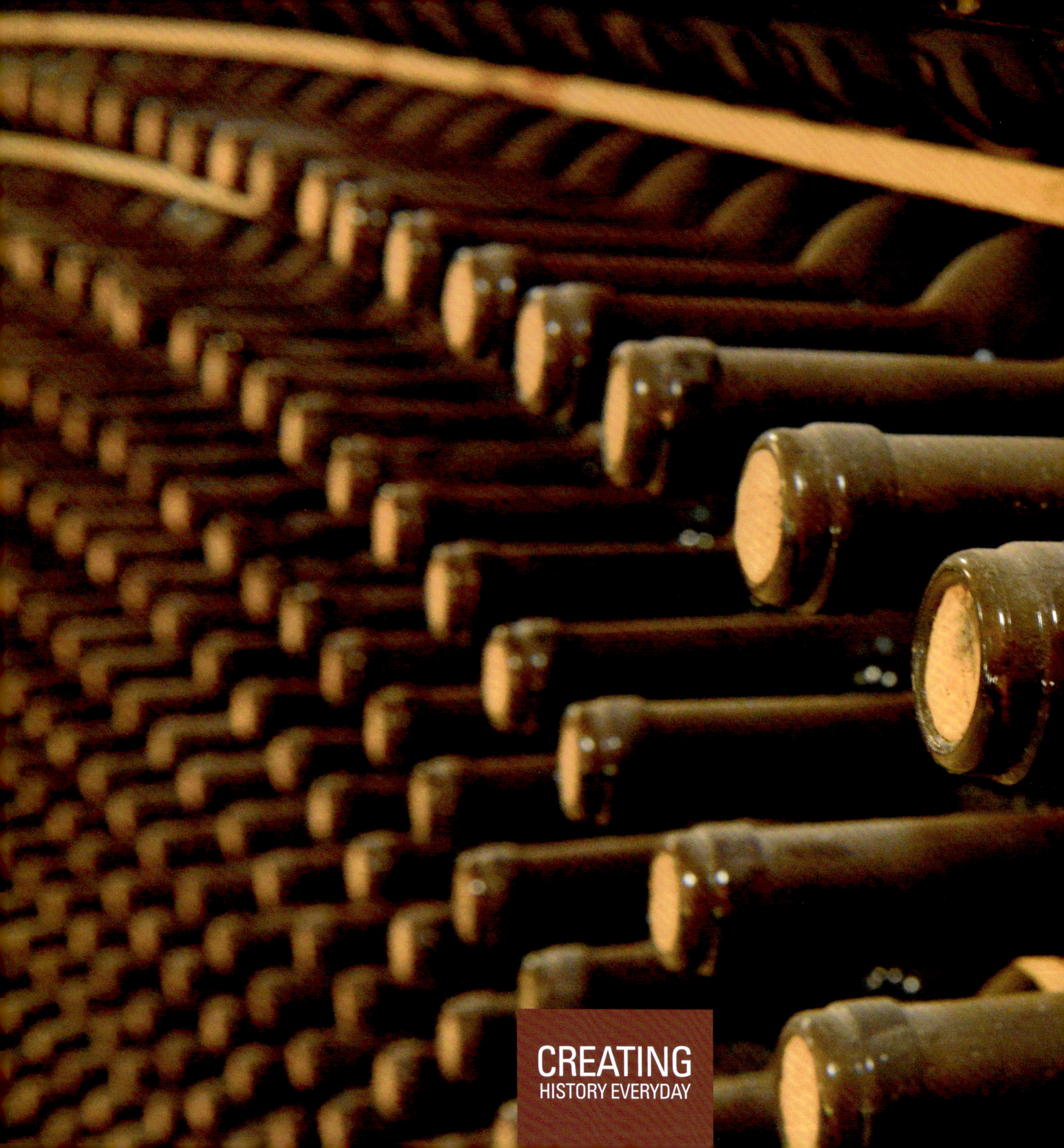
CREATING
HISTORY EVERYDAY

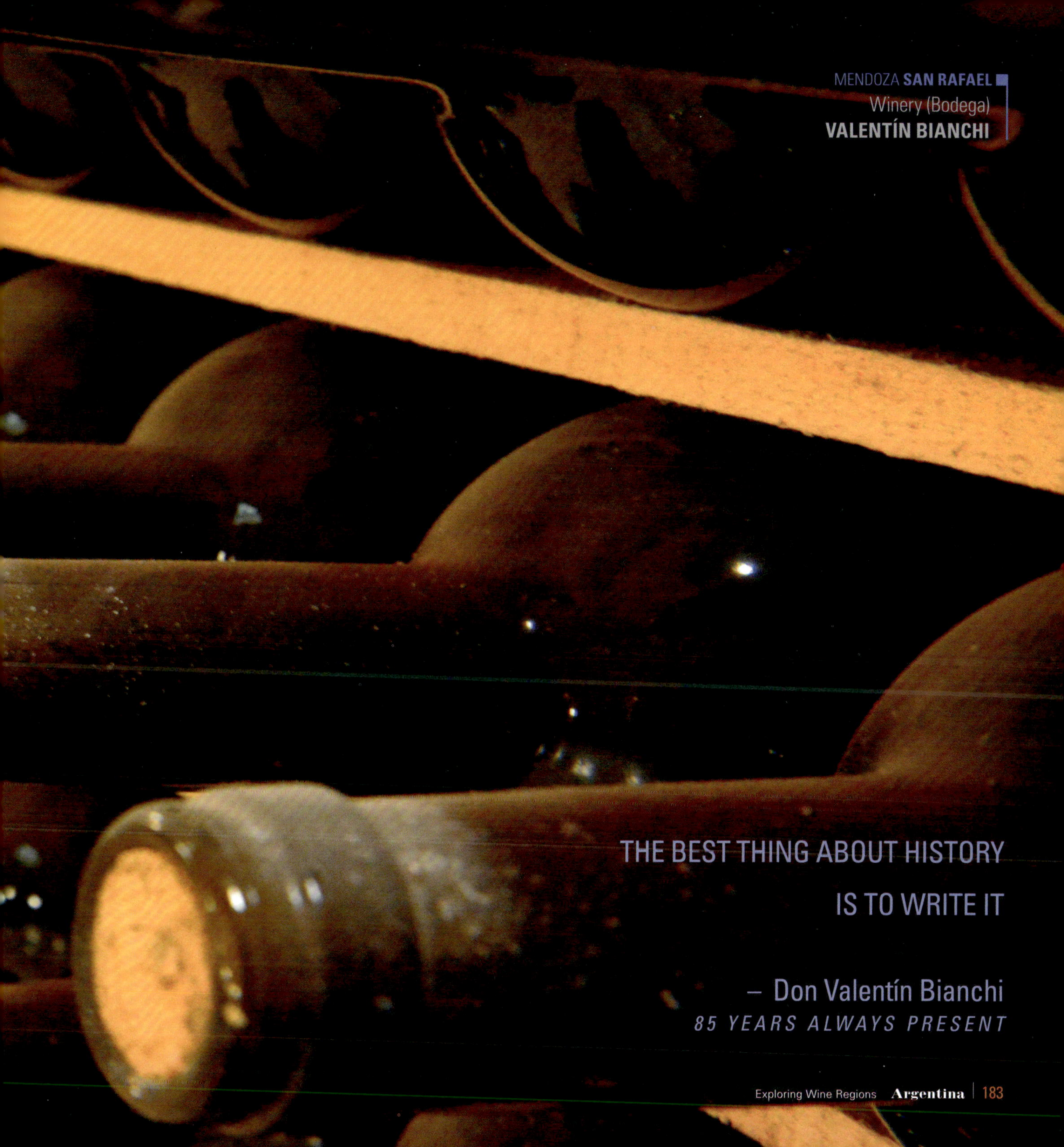

THE BEST THING ABOUT HISTORY IS TO WRITE IT

– Don Valentín Bianchi

85 YEARS ALWAYS PRESENT

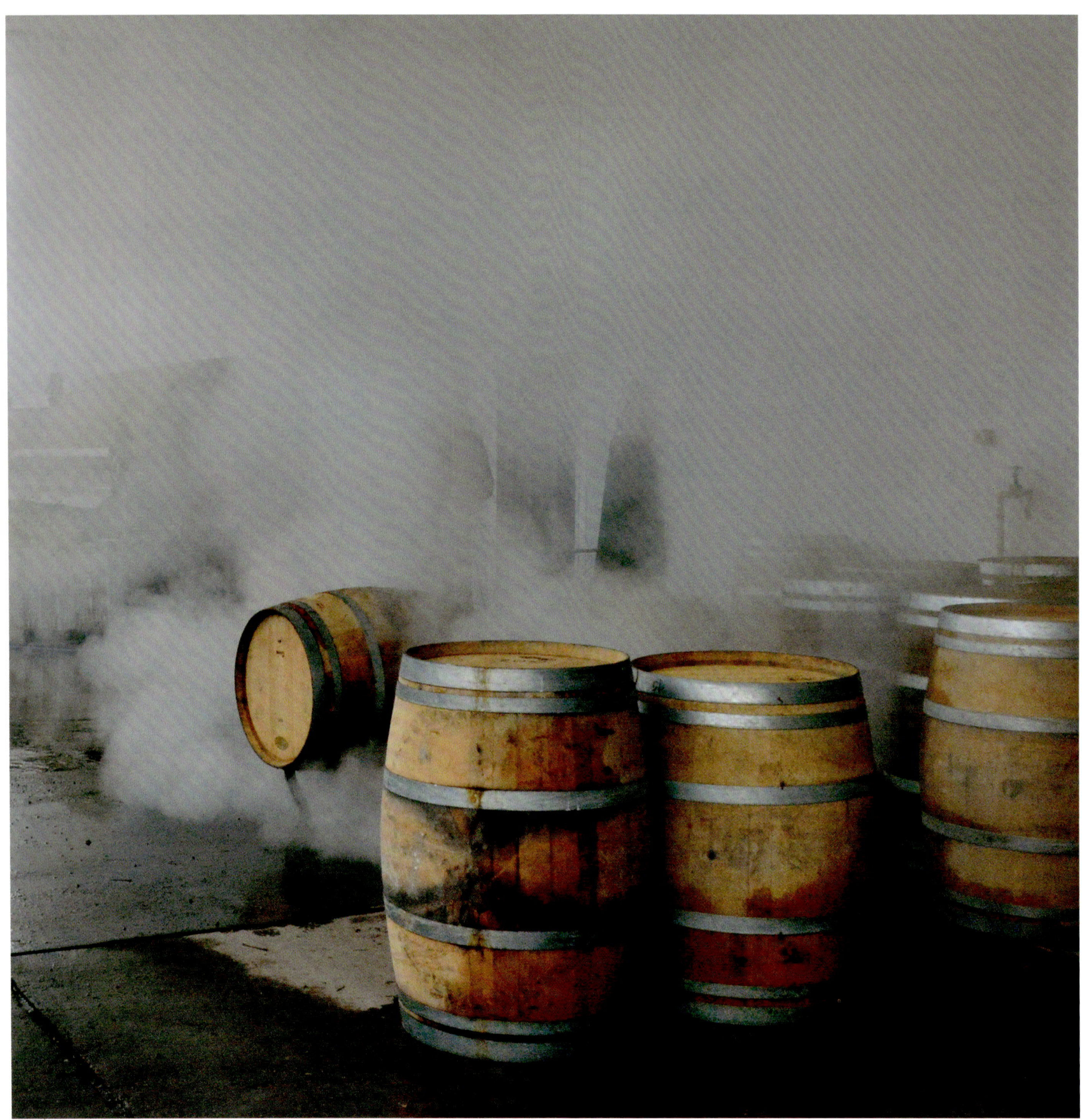

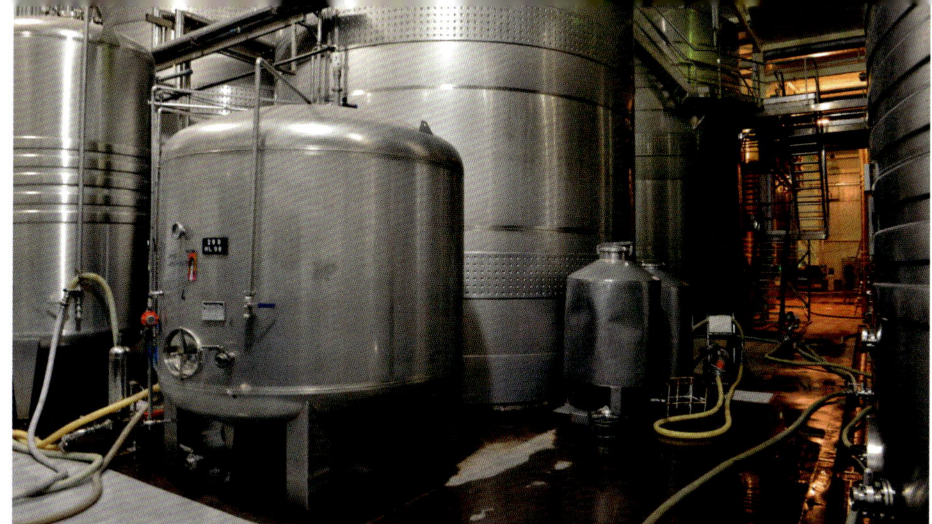

MENDOZA **SAN RAFAEL**

Winery (Bodega)

VALENTÍN BIANCHI

Ruta 143 & Valentín Bianchi St.
(Las Paredes, San Rafael)

011 (+54 260) 444.9600
turismo@CasaBianchi.com.ar

ValentinBianchi.com

English & Español
21,000,000 bottles annually

This is a very large winery operation. Three generations of numerous family members creating the growth of this highly diversified winery business. Bianchi cultivates over 160,000 acres of vineyards and is building a 55,000 sq' facility for US$10 million to develop the ultimate in technology facility for making wine.

It all began in 1910 when Don Valentín Bianchi immigrated from Italy and dabbled in various types of work... the state railway, a French bank, auctioneer, general alvear, master builder, founded a bus company, and councilman for the City of San Rafael. Eighteen years later he discovered his love... growing grapes and making wine, and in 1928 he started his winery.

Today, Valentín Bianchi has created 20 unique wine brands with labels representing 56 different wines. The volume wines are making them huge profits to invest in creating super-premium wines that will get your attention.

For example, *Los Stradivarius de Bianchi - L'Elisir d'Amore* (named after the famed Italian opera and violins). Under certain conditions a fungus (botrytis cinerea) will attack and grow on the grape skins producing large concentrations of sugar. Bianchi produces this dessert wine under the traditional method of making French Sauternes - harvesting Semillón very late in May (southern hemisphere), pressing the grapes and allowing the must to ferment in French oak barrels until the winter cold fermentation stops due to low temperatures. In the spring the fermentation is continued until it finally stops and the resulting wine is with a high concentration of natural grape sugars.

Another example is *Espumante Cabernet Sauvignon*. Made in the classic French champenoise method to make an elegant white Champaign from these rich red cabernet grapes.

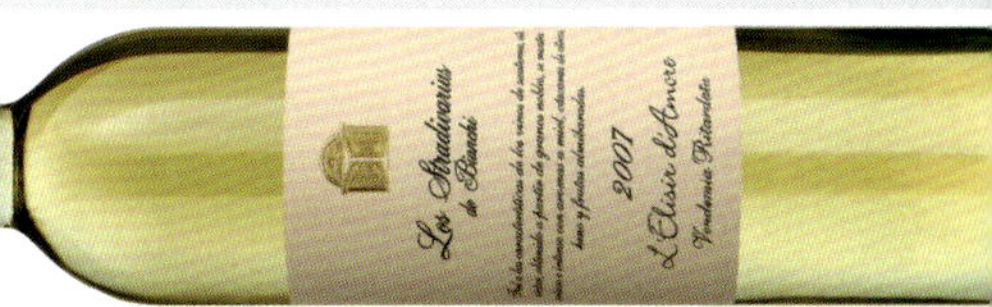

Further, this winery is way ahead of the technology curve. Bianchi employs the technology of infrared photographs, using satellite images and photographs from aircraft, combining the data from GPS, dielectric resonance and automated weather stations... all these to minimize the variance of the crops in their vineyards.

Now, consider just how interesting the tour at this winery will be. The place is huge, so they have a lot to show you. Plus, they have several different types of tastings...

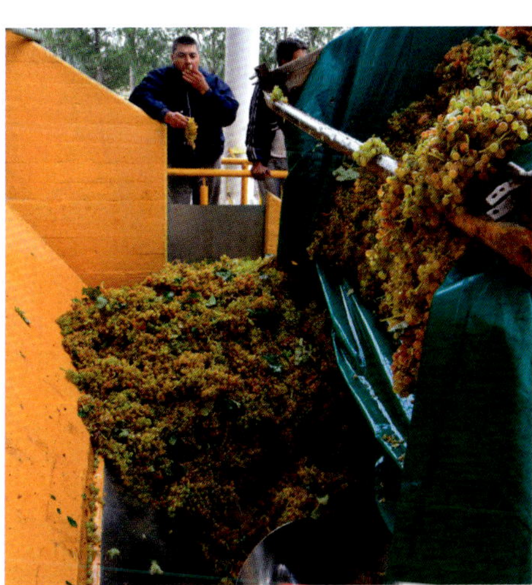

Michael's Favorite Pick
L'Elisir d'Amore
(95% Semillion, 5% Bonarda)

Super-Premium Labels
Enzo Bianchi
Gran Cru
Maria Carmen
Criado En Barricas de Roble, Chardonnay
Los Stradivarius de Bianchi
L'Elisir d'Amore
Espumante Cabernet Sauvignon
Porto de Magoas

Premium Labels
Famiglia Bianchi
Malbec
Cabernet Sauvignon
Chardonnay
Sauvignon Blanc
LEO
Malbec
Malbec Premium
Torrontés
Extra Brut
Bianchi Particular
Malbec
Cabernet Sauvignon
Merlot

To get Bianchi wines in the USA
Importer: QuintessentialWines.com
Call Importer for Retailers: 707.266.5209

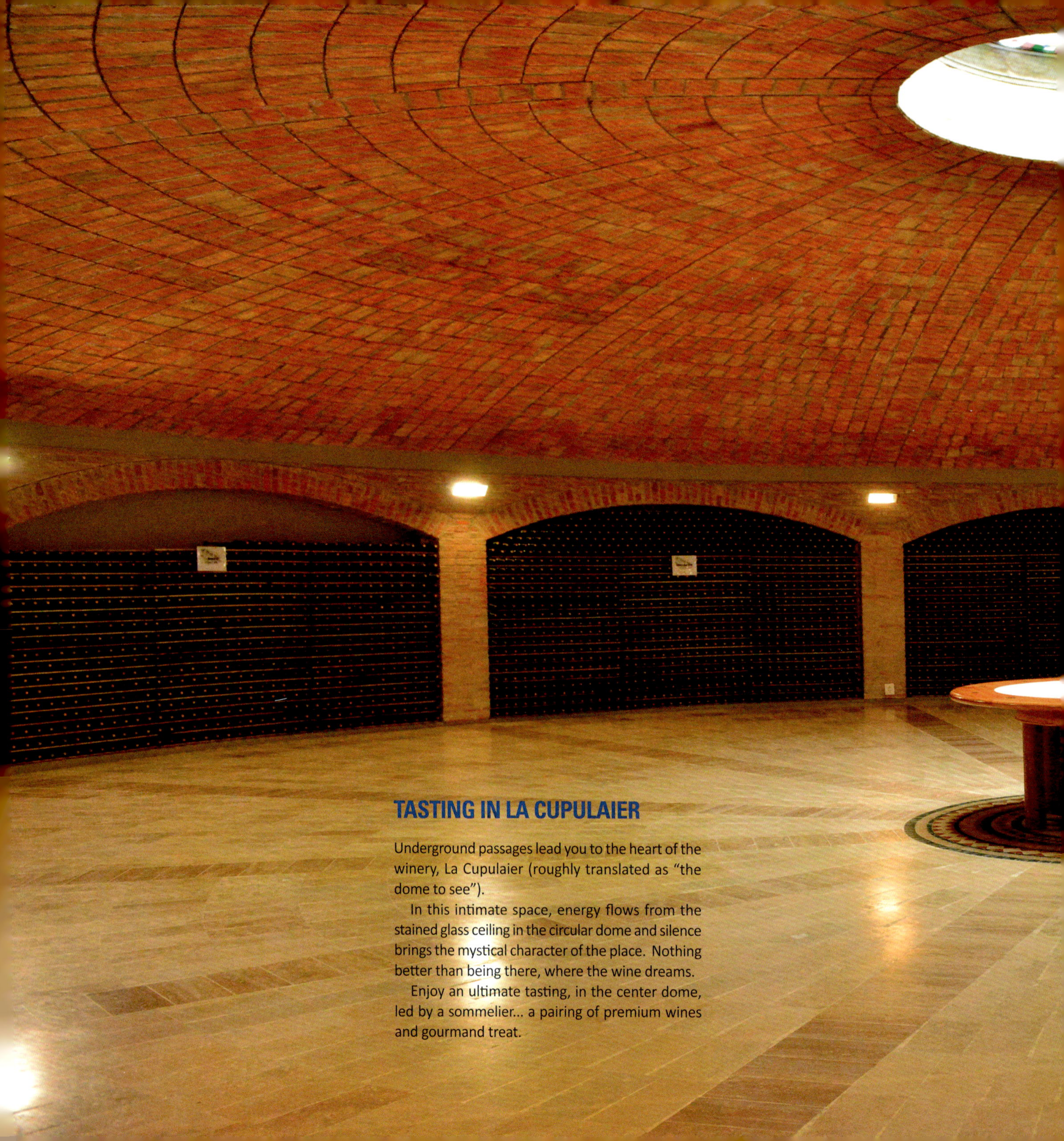

TASTING IN LA CUPULAIER

Underground passages lead you to the heart of the winery, La Cupulaier (roughly translated as "the dome to see").

In this intimate space, energy flows from the stained glass ceiling in the circular dome and silence brings the mystical character of the place. Nothing better than being there, where the wine dreams.

Enjoy an ultimate tasting, in the center dome, led by a sommelier... a pairing of premium wines and gourmand treat.

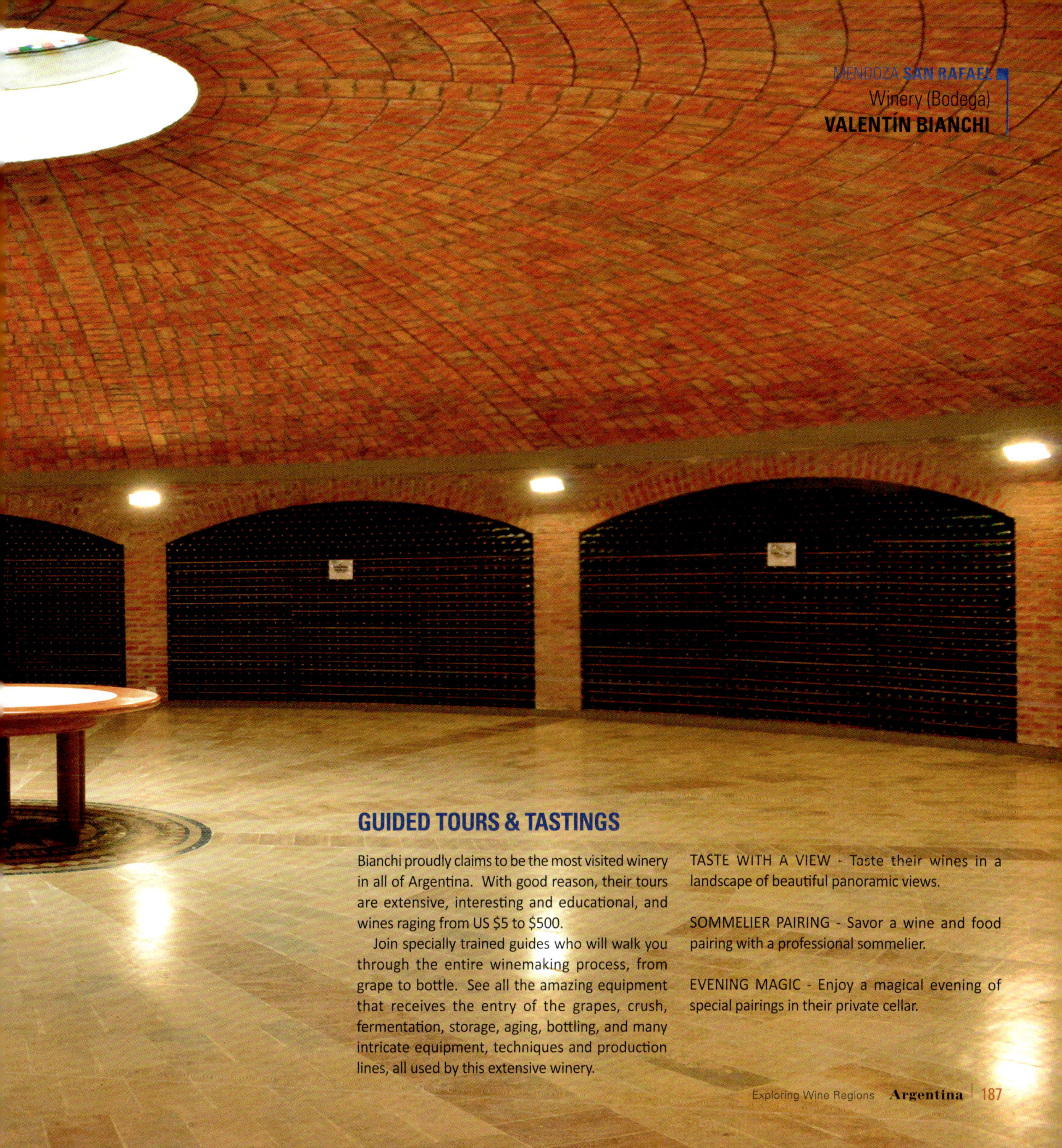

GUIDED TOURS & TASTINGS

Bianchi proudly claims to be the most visited winery in all of Argentina. With good reason, their tours are extensive, interesting and educational, and wines raging from US $5 to $500.

Join specially trained guides who will walk you through the entire winemaking process, from grape to bottle. See all the amazing equipment that receives the entry of the grapes, crush, fermentation, storage, aging, bottling, and many intricate equipment, techniques and production lines, all used by this extensive winery.

TASTE WITH A VIEW - Taste their wines in a landscape of beautiful panoramic views.

SOMMELIER PAIRING - Savor a wine and food pairing with a professional sommelier.

EVENING MAGIC - Enjoy a magical evening of special pairings in their private cellar.

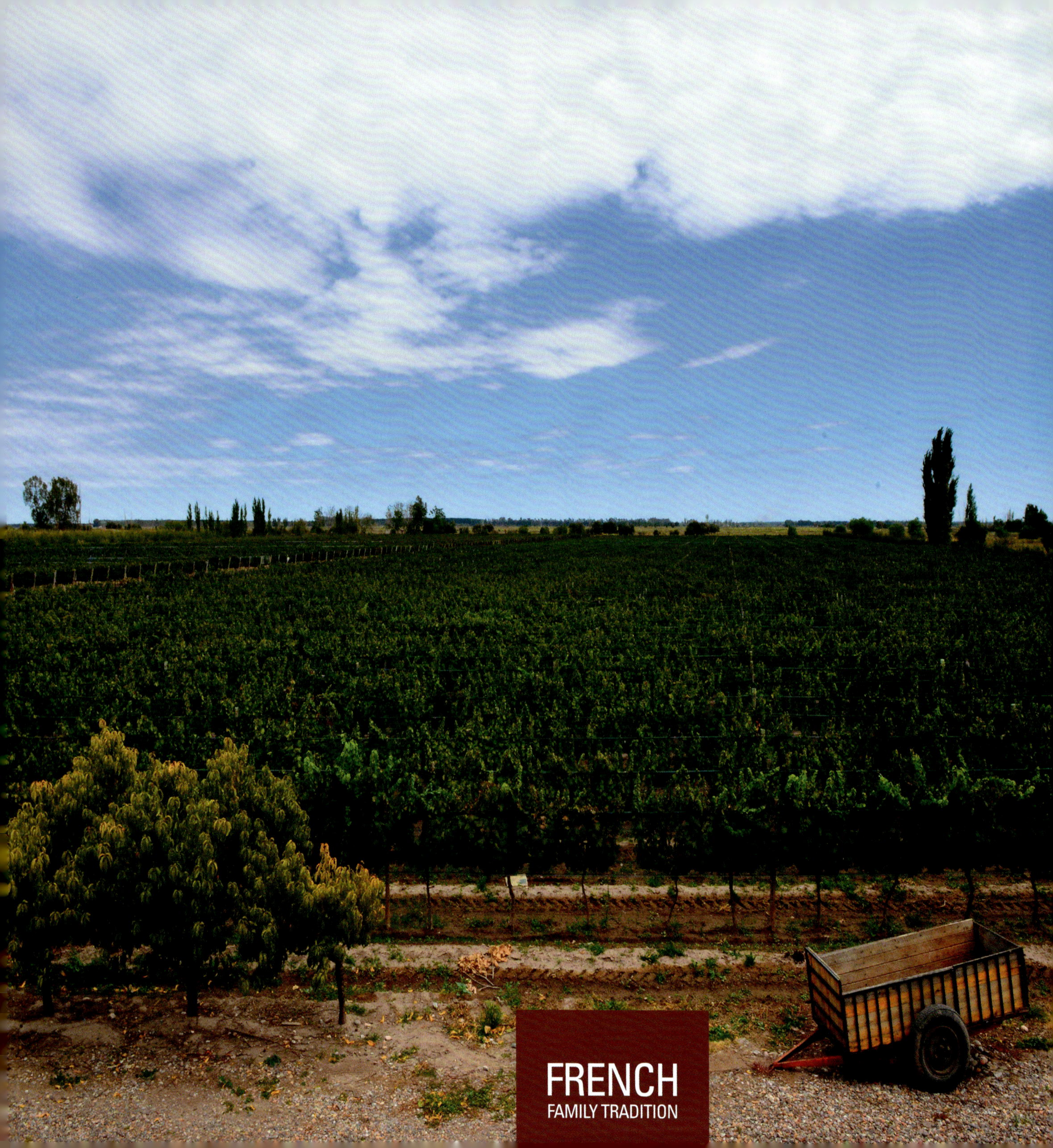

FRENCH
FAMILY TRADITION

THE UNIQUE CORBEAU GRAPE

I really like this winery. The wines are amazing, and the family are the nicest people you will meet.

This is a French family business. Centuries ago, their ancestors started in the wine business in France, then immigrated to Argentina last century. Recently, they bought a small plot of land with established vineyards, and also planted new.

This is a small hand-crafted winery, with extensive attention to the vineyards to maximize the fruit quality. Their aim is a French tradition of the very best wine possible. And they are making some of the very best wines you will taste in Argentina.

Two of their wines were just written up as the **Top 100 Wines of the World** by the *World Association of Wine Writers & Journalists*. They scored 14th and 29th for their Cabernet Sauvignon and Malbec blend, respectively.

Bournett is very precise about their craft. They go so far as to certify their vineyards, and has become the first company to certify *San Rafael Geographic Indication* for their vineyards. By complying with the strict regulation demands for their Malbec, Bonarda, Cabernet Sauvignon, Merlot, and Corbeau vineyards, they have been granted this certification, which is identified as "IG" on their bottles.

Further, Bournett distinguishes their Corbeau from Bonarda. The Bonarda grape varietal has experienced a contested and confused history. It has been classified as Bonarda Piemontese from Italy, and also classified instead, as an ancestor of Corbeau from Savoie, France. Genetic tests have compared the Argentine rootstock to those of Piemontese and Corbeau, and the study found identical molecular markers.

Bournett though says this is a mix-up and not a comparison of different rootstocks. They claim that when phylloxera was destroying the vineyards in France, Corbeau rootstocks were taken to Italy, and became mixed-up with the Bonarda rootstocks when the Italians brought them to Argentina. So today, with the grapes being so similar, someone is not going to distinguish a difference without very close examination and understanding.

Bournett has a very seasoned agronomist working in their vineyards who one day brought to their attention differing leaf and grape clusters, showing them a distinction between what he knew was Corbeau and Bonarda differently. So, Bournett brought this to the Instituto Nacional de Vitivinicultura (Argentina's National Institute of Viticulture) for review and further examination.

Together, with other agronomists, engineers and ampelógrafos, including international experts, it was determined that Bournett's strain of Corbeau is actually distinct from Bonarda, and matched the original molecular structure of the Douce Noir (Corbeau) grape from Savoie, France. This has led to the Institute recognizing Bournett's Corbeau separate from Bonarda, and certifying Bournett as the exclusive winery authorized to put Corbeau on its label.

Regardless of its origin and emigration, Bonarda has adapted extremely well to Argentina and today is considered its own grape identity. In 2011 the name Bonarda Argentina was accepted by the Instituto Nacional de Vitivinicultura recognizing the distinct vitus vinifera varietal grown only in Argentina.

So... the Corbeau or Douce Noir grape from Savoie, France -- is distinct to the Bonarda from Piemontese, Italy -- is distinct to the Bonarda Argentina -- and to add further complication, this same grape vinified in California is called Charbono.

Now... Bodega Bournett is the only place where you can taste these distinctions, see their unique 10 acres of 18-year-old Corbeau, and buy this proprietary estate exclusive of Corbeau.

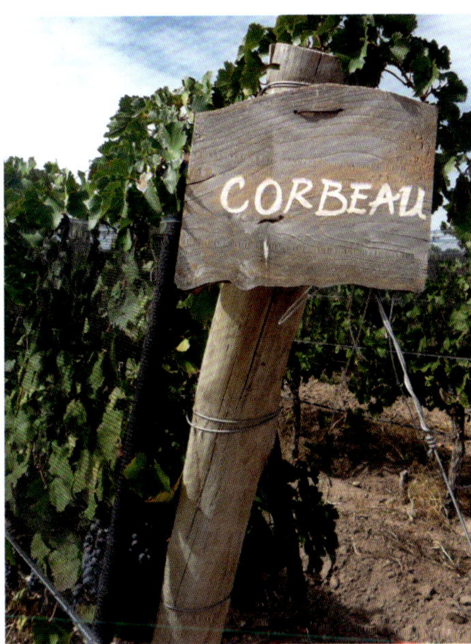

MENDOZA **SAN RAFAEL**

Winery (Bodega)

BODEGA BOURNETT

154 Ruta Sarmiento Street
(Cuadro Nacional, San Rafael)

011 (+54 260) 444.2021
info@Bournett.com.ar

Bournett.com.ar

English & Español
100,000 bottles annually

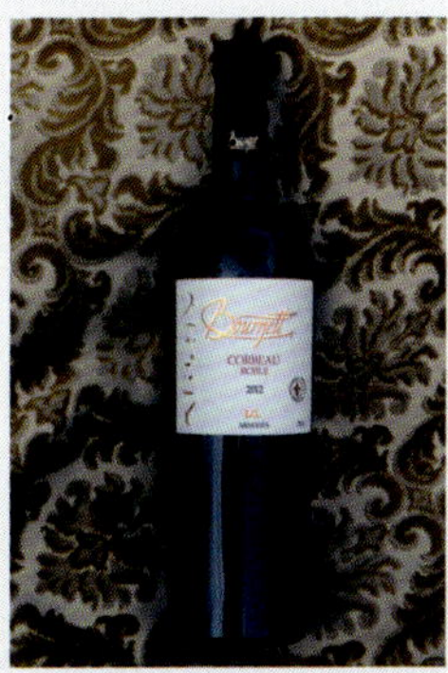

Michael's Favorite Pick
Corbeau Roble I.G.
(100% Corbeau, Proprietary Estate Exclusive)

The IG Line
(Geographic Indication)
Corbeau Roble I.G.
Malbec Roble I.G.
Merlot Roble I.G.
Cabernet Sauvignon Roble I.G.
Malbec Rosé I.G.

Numbered Malbec

Oak Prestige (Merlot/Malbec)
Prestige Chardonnay

Champagne
Extra Brut (Champenoise Method)
Extra Brut (Charmat Method)

To get Bournett wines in the USA
Travel to San Rafael, Argentina
and bring back a case or two

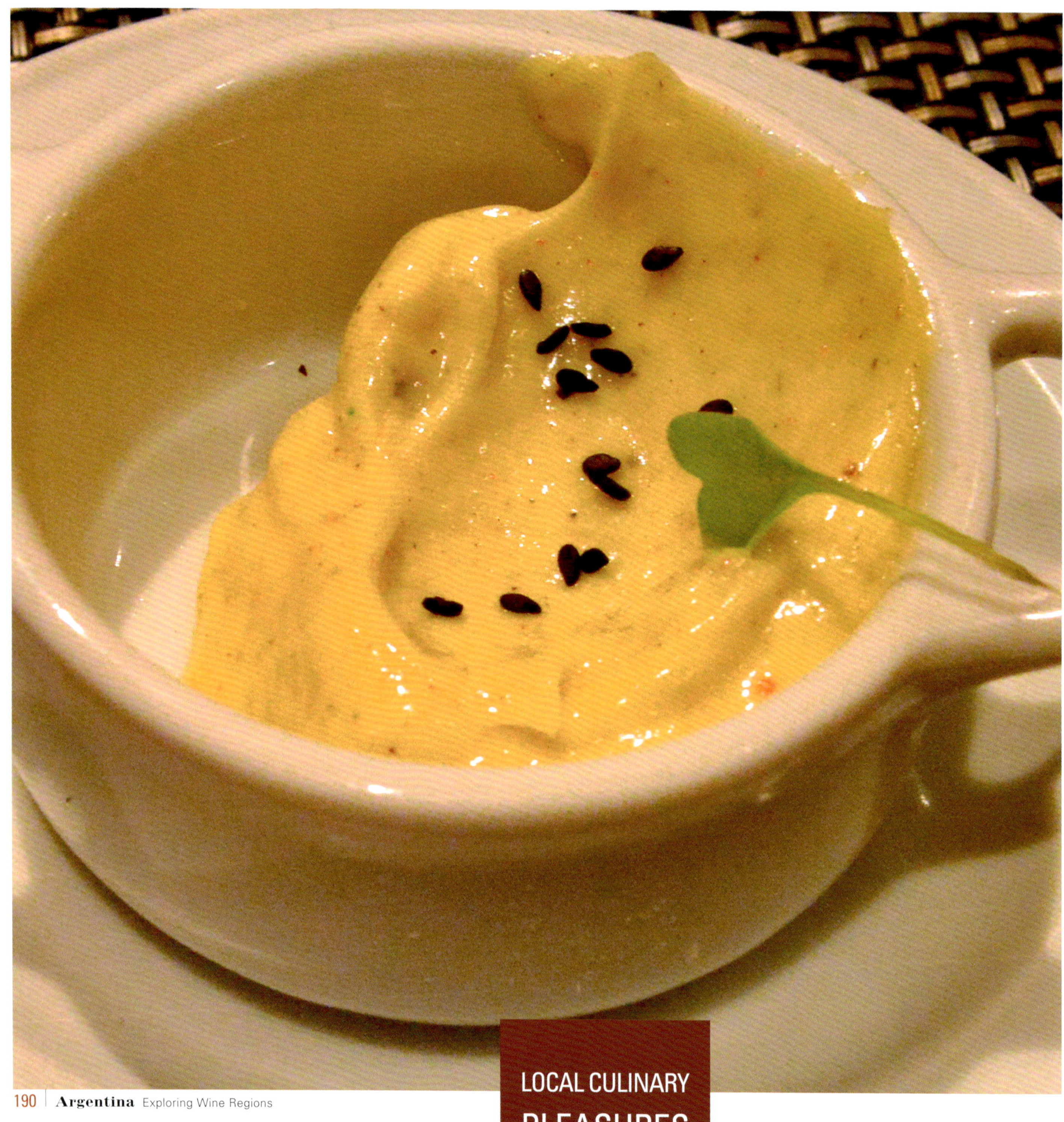

LOCAL CULINARY PLEASURES

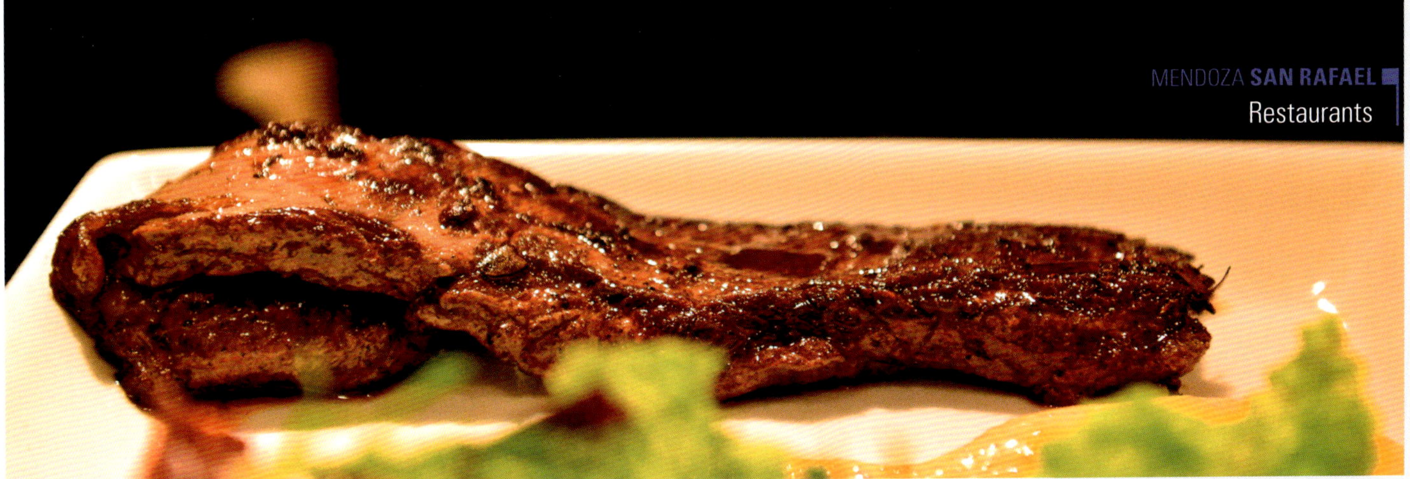

FRANCCESCO RISTO

This might just be the best restaurant in San Rafael. Fancy and creative ideas. Even the butter is gourmet! Fresh churned, with herbs of basil, parsley, dill, thyme, and oregano (photo left page). This compels me to consume bread!

The menu is exquisite, innovative and full of flavors. Many fish choices. The steaks are also incredible; the best I tasted in San Rafael (photo above). And a great wine list of many special wines of this region.

The service is very attentive, knowledgable and friendly. And a beautiful atmosphere with a modern decor and mood lighting.

The guests next to me, sanrafaelinos, make Franccesco's a frequent dining date, claiming: *it always is a great experience*. Looking at the steak above, is reminding me why I will be back for more.

Reservation is a must
31 Champagnal, San Rafael
011 (+54 260) 443.7024

THE JOCKEY CLUB

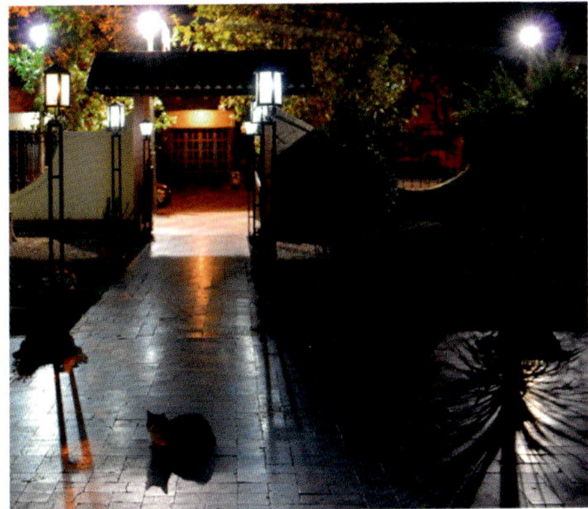

Tucked away, off the street. Downtown. Originally the home of Poet Alfredo Bufano, later expanded into The Jockey Club where large and small groups could meet and dine. Open to the public. Authentic Italian cuisine. Extensive menu. Huge portions. Many private spaces for a quiet business meeting, or a romantic dinner, or room to party.

330 Belgrano, San Rafael
011 (+54 262) 743.0237

LA TRANQUERA CENTRAL

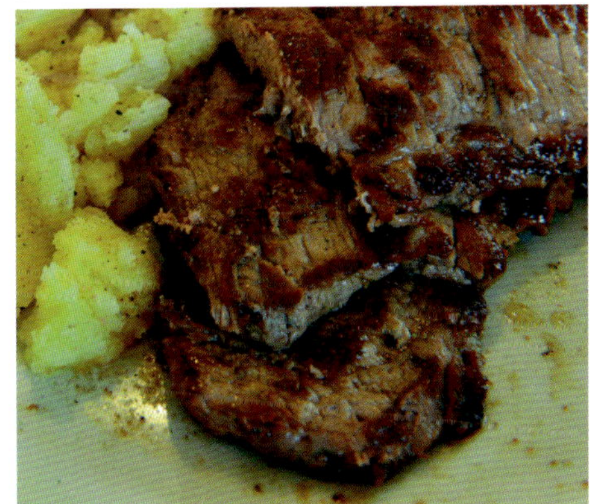

And along came Nery. I was desperate. Starving. 8:00 pm, and early for dinner. Nery saw me wandering the street, and helped... he talked to the owner of La Tranquera to open his kitchen and cook me dinner. I ordered a bottle of wine, Nery had a couple of beers, and we created a wonderful friendship. Good food, nothing fancy. And open.

538 Hipólito Yrigoyen, San Rafael
011 (+54 260) 442.9726

YANCANELO OLIVE OIL

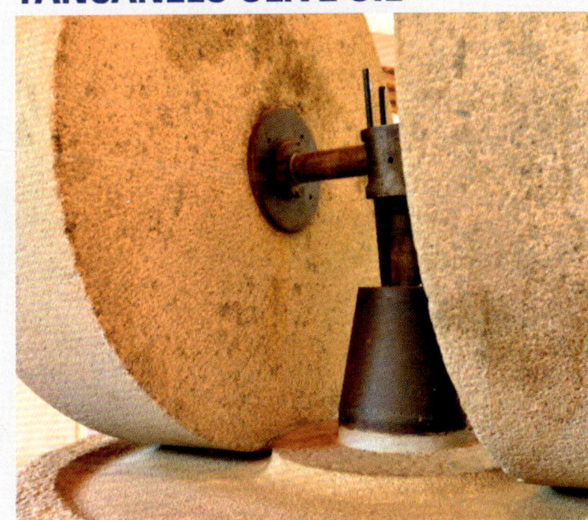

See the staple of Italian cooking, olive oil, from harvest (May and June) through processing. The machinery and tools used have changed dramatically through the years, and the Yancanelo Factory, established in 1942, will show you both, with an extensive history museum and a tour of the interesting modern processes of today.

4030 Hipólito Yrigoyen, San Rafael
011 (+54 260) 442.3879

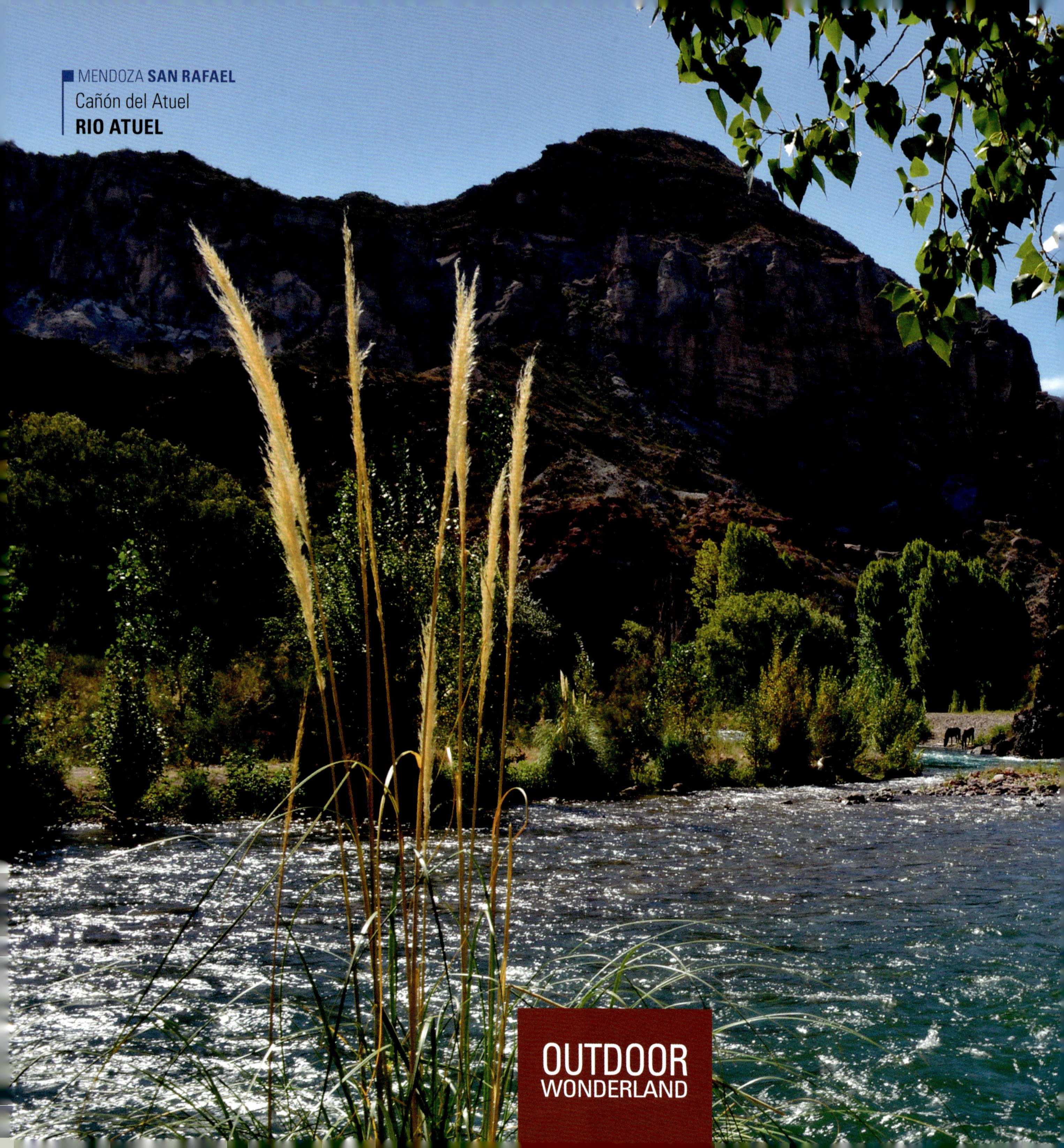
MENDOZA SAN RAFAEL
Cañón del Atuel
RIO ATUEL
OUTDOOR
WONDERLAND

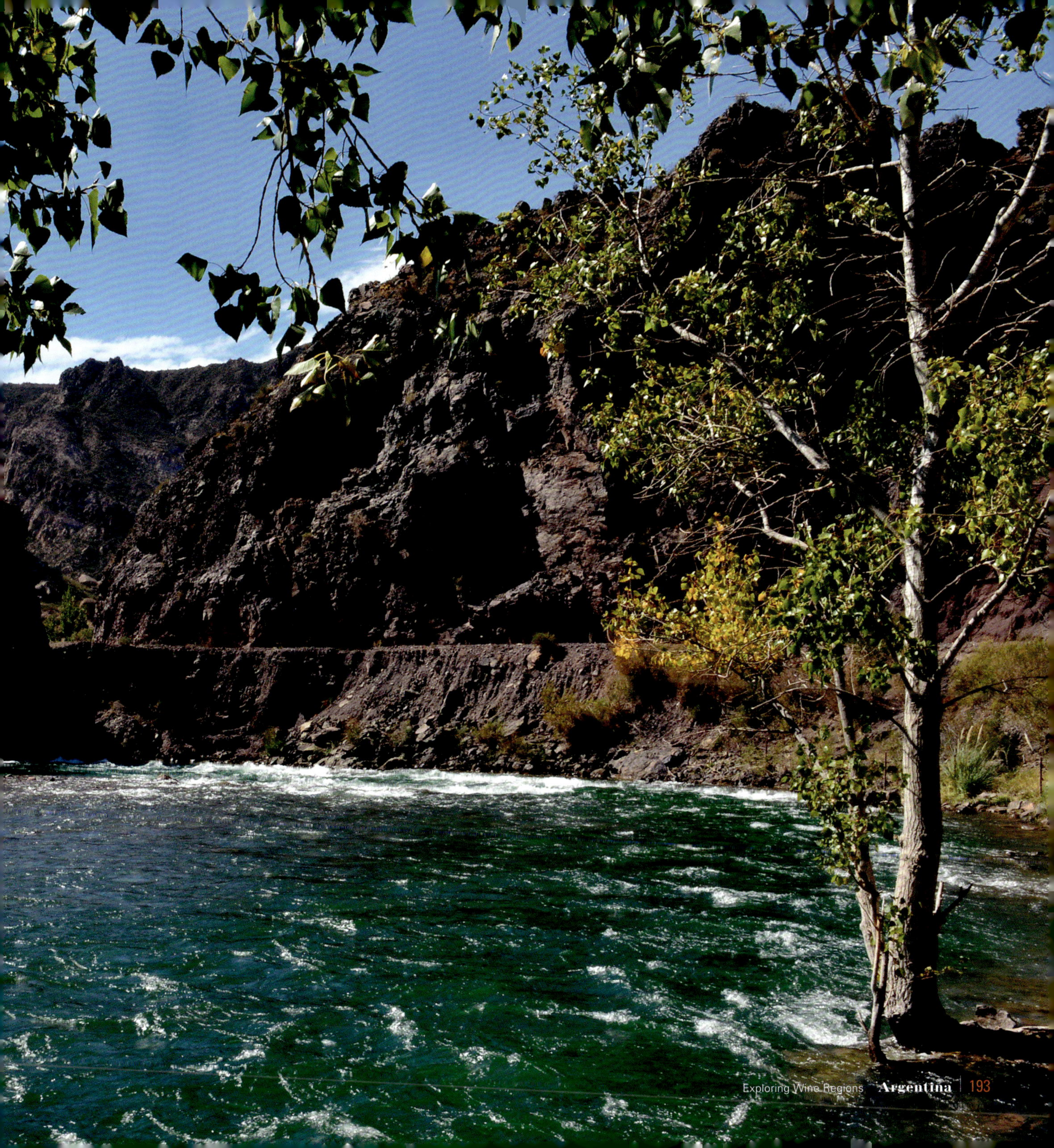

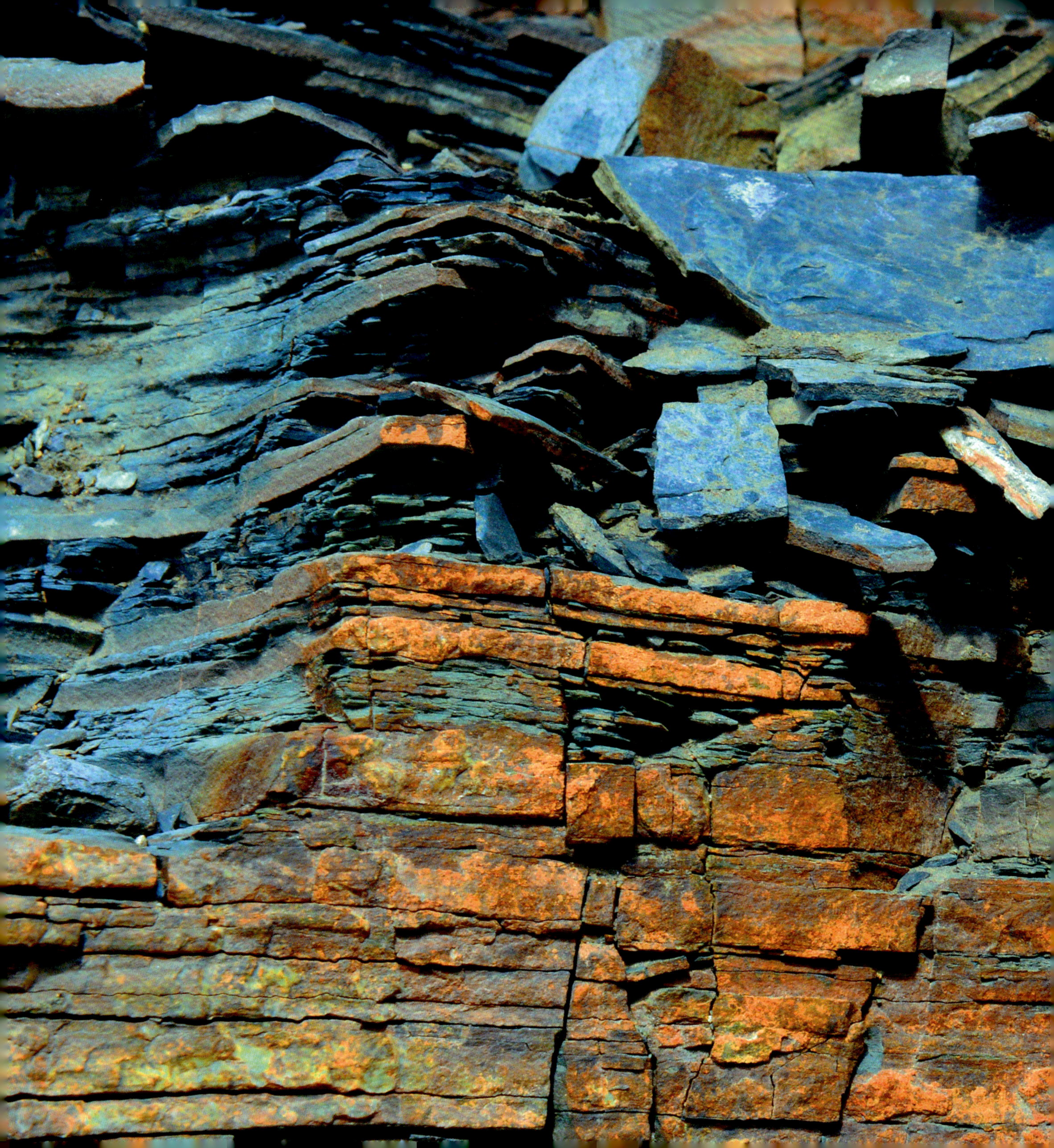

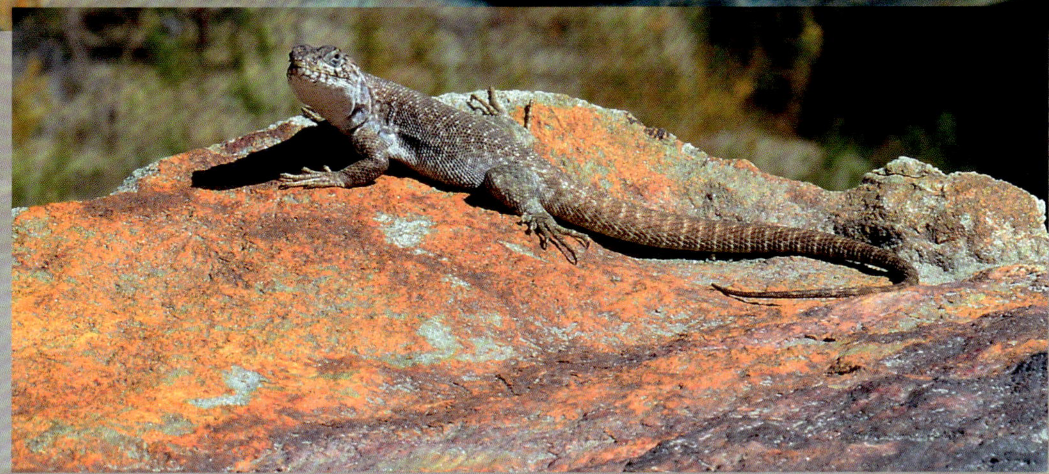

MINI GRAND CANYON

Cañón del Atuel is a mini grand canyon just south of San Rafael. With Atuel though, you get to drive the bottom of the canyon, meandering the river and seeing the inside geography up close and personal. Rio Atuel is the longest river in Mendoza, born in the Andes, at 10,000-foot elevation, from the glacial Atuel Lake.

A great trip starts with a beautiful drive from San Rafael south through the desert for about one hour to arrive at El Nihuil, a large lake on the Atual River flourishing with aquatic wildlife, attracting fisherman and water sport enthusiasts.

From there, you can enter the canyon on a very well-maintained dirt road. Rio Atual flows south to north, from El Nihuil Lake through the canyon, flowing into Valle Grande (lake). Past Valle Grande, Rio Atual continues with roaring rapids for exciting whitewater rafting.

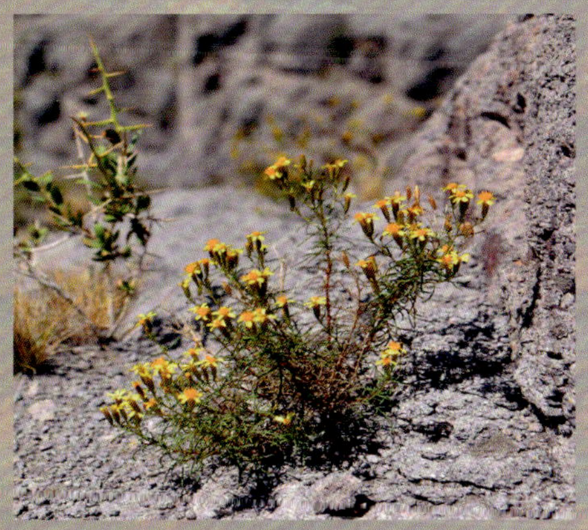

This is a great day-trip exploring Cañón del Atuel. The road follows the river as you journey the canyon. The origins of the Earth are visible here. It is a mineral and geological discovery. See how the river, the winds and the rain have chiseled away at this canyon for millions of years. Take your time. Explore. Penetrate the origins of the world here. Discover interesting geographic sculptures, some of which are named: Armchair Rivadavia, the Lizard, the Old, the Monster, the Enchanted City, the Beggar, the Hanging Gardens, the Monks, etc.

When you reach the end of Cañón del Atuel, you will drive up onto a mesa and when you turn the bend, you will be confronted with one of the most amazing sights.. overlooking the spectacular Valle Grande. Valle Grande translated into English means "large valley" as it once was prior to the Valle Grande Dam, which now holds back a massive lake reservoir with a beauty that will captivate you for hours. Returning late in the day from your Cañón del Atuel adventure, will position you to watch a beautiful sunset over the lake.

In Valle Grande, the lake and river offer numerous aquatic sports, including extreme sports. Sailing, windsurfing, kayaking, canoeing, swimming, diving, skiing, rowing, parasailing, catamaran ride on the lake, windsurfing, jet skiing, quads, Class II, III and IV whitewater rafting, mountain biking, zip-line canopy, trekking, horseback riding, rappelling, rock climbing, and hiking.

LEFT PAGE, the minerals found in the rocks of the canyon are rich and magnificent;

ABOVE, lizards of the Atuel enjoy sunning themselves in the warmth of the day;

BELOW, wildflowers add color to the vast desert landscape.

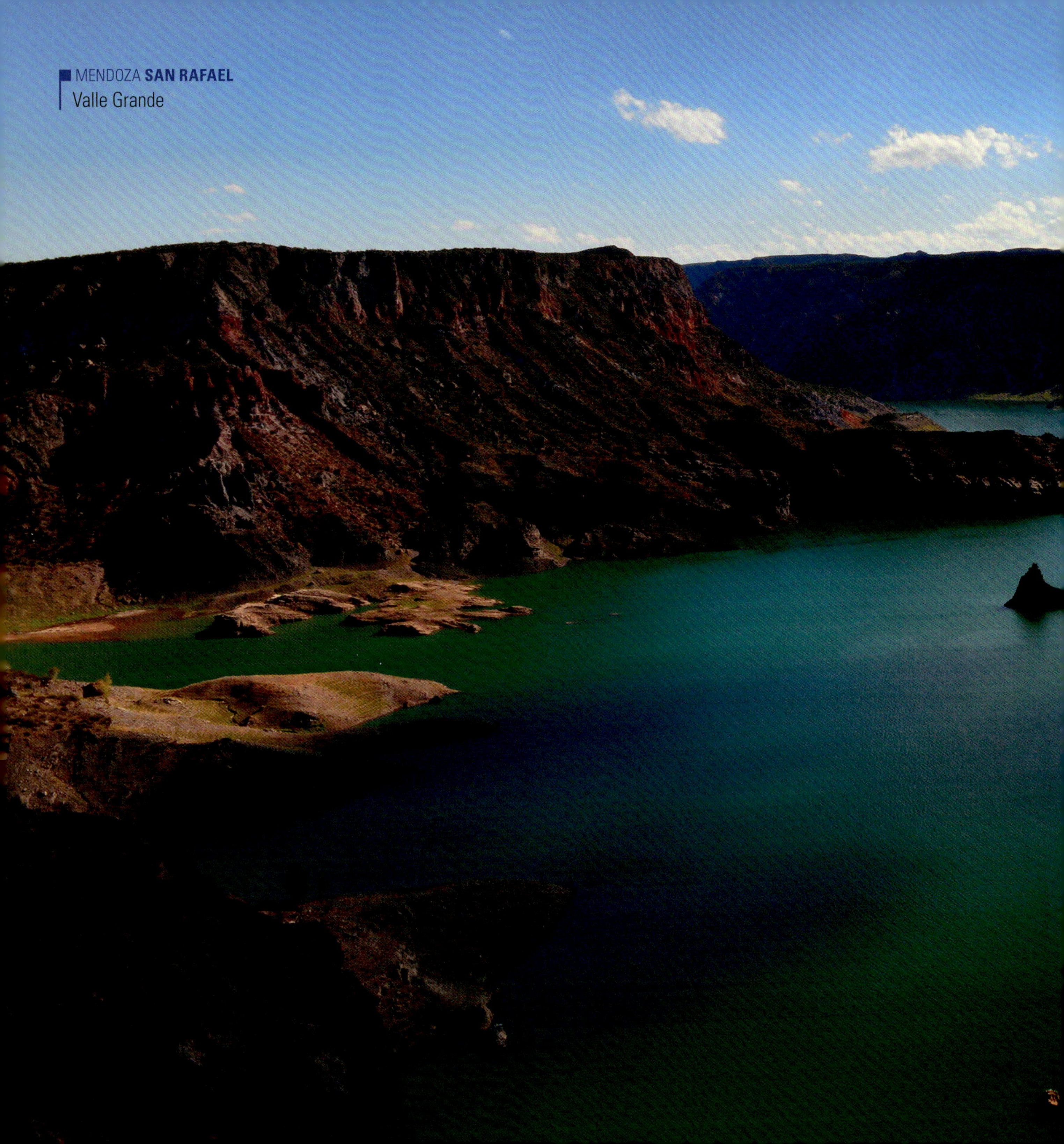
MENDOZA **SAN RAFAEL**
Valle Grande

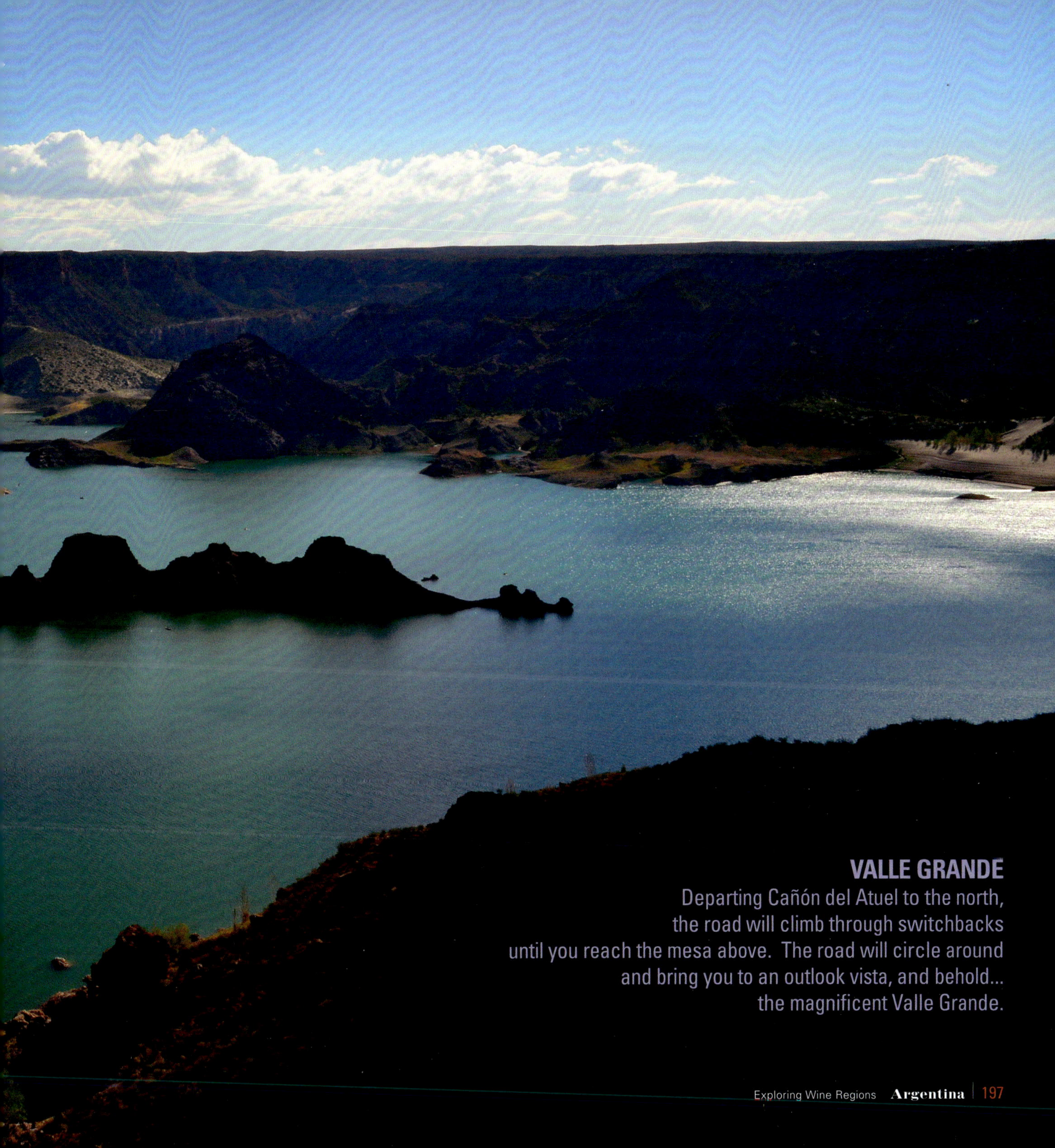

VALLE GRANDE

Departing Cañón del Atuel to the north, the road will climb through switchbacks until you reach the mesa above. The road will circle around and bring you to an outlook vista, and behold... the magnificent Valle Grande.

Valle Grande

RAFFEISH ADVENTURES

Ruta 173 (Below the Dam)
(Valle Grande, San Rafael)

011 (+54 260) 443.6996
info@Raffeish.com.ar

Raffeish.com.ar

English & Español

Directions:
from Ruta 173 (Route 173)
at the Valle Grande Lake,
drive past the Valle Grande Dam
three miles north of the dam, down river

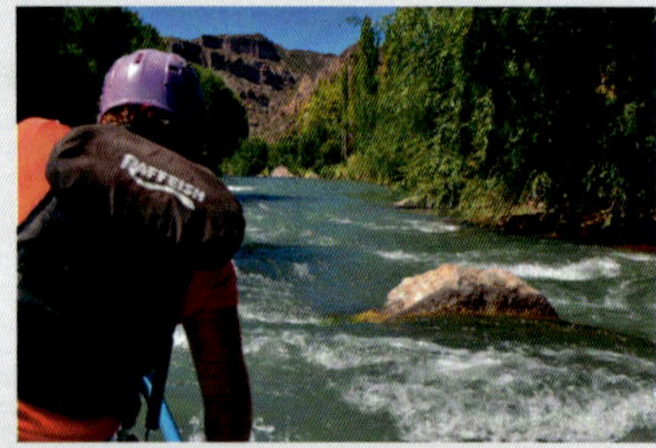

Numerous Water Sports
Just Below the Lake On the River

A very experienced company
Highly-knowledgable expert guides
Safety and first-aid oriented
Utilizing latest equipment

White Water Rafting
Catamaran
Col River
Doky
Canoeing
Kayaking
Trekking

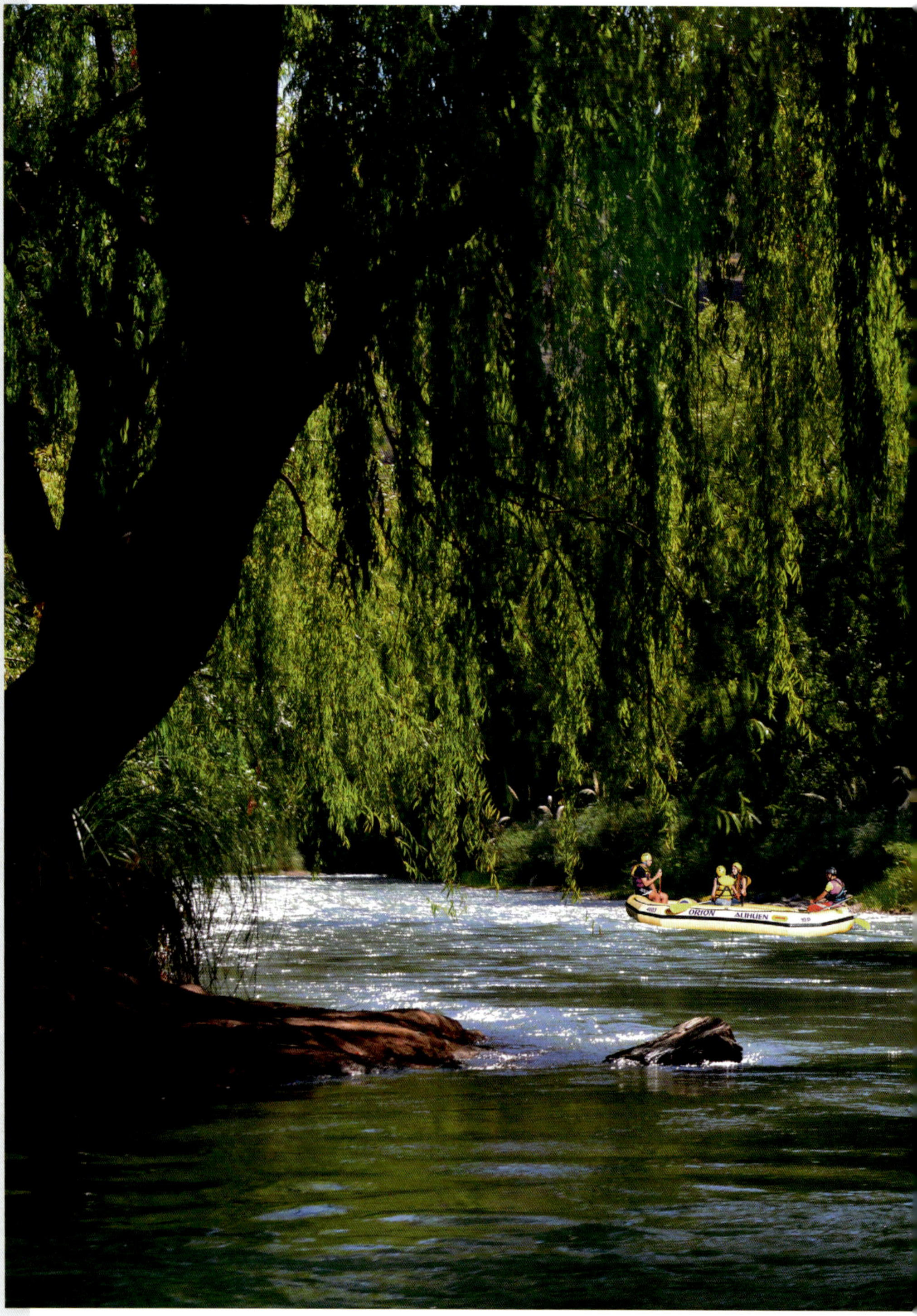

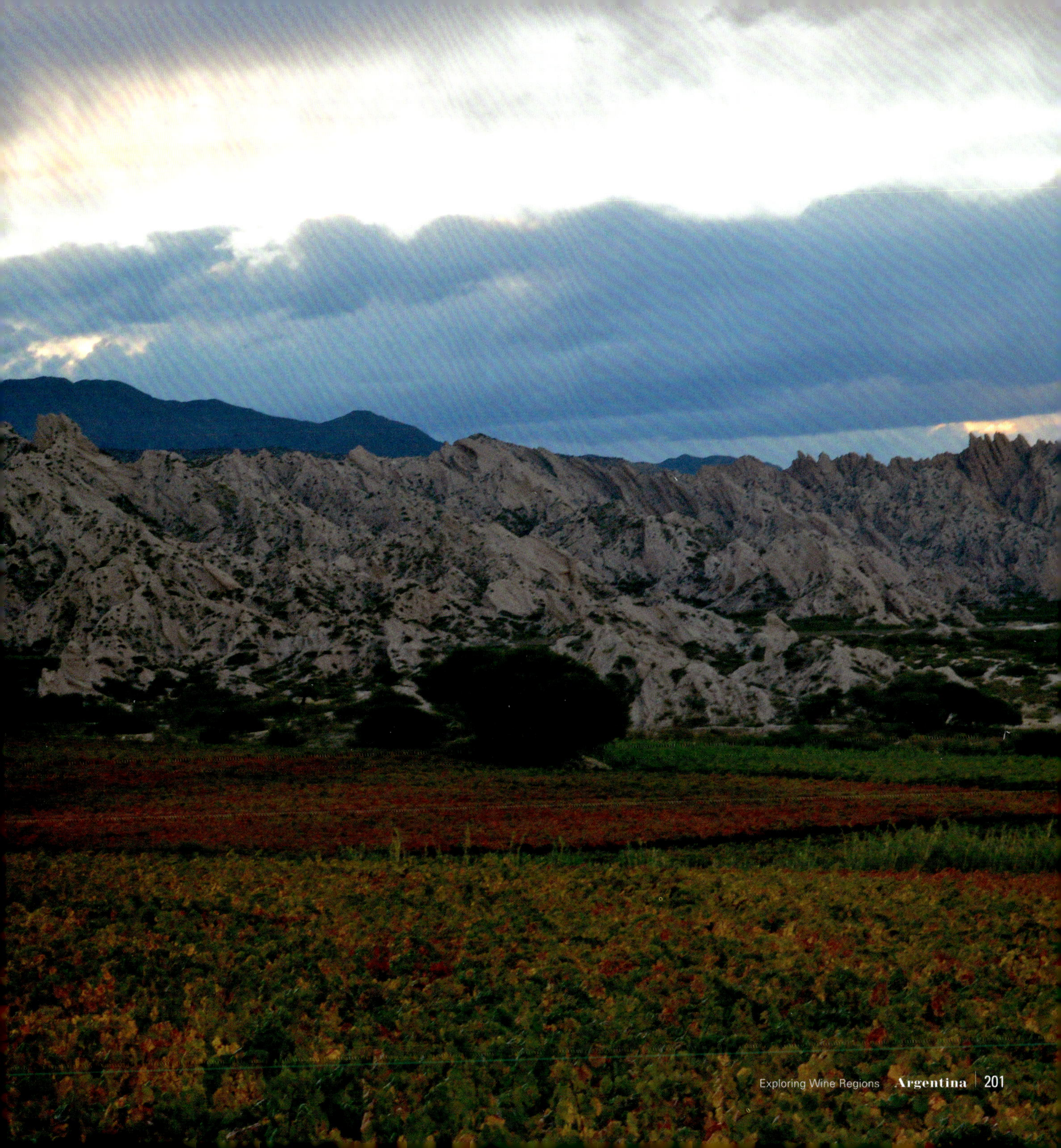

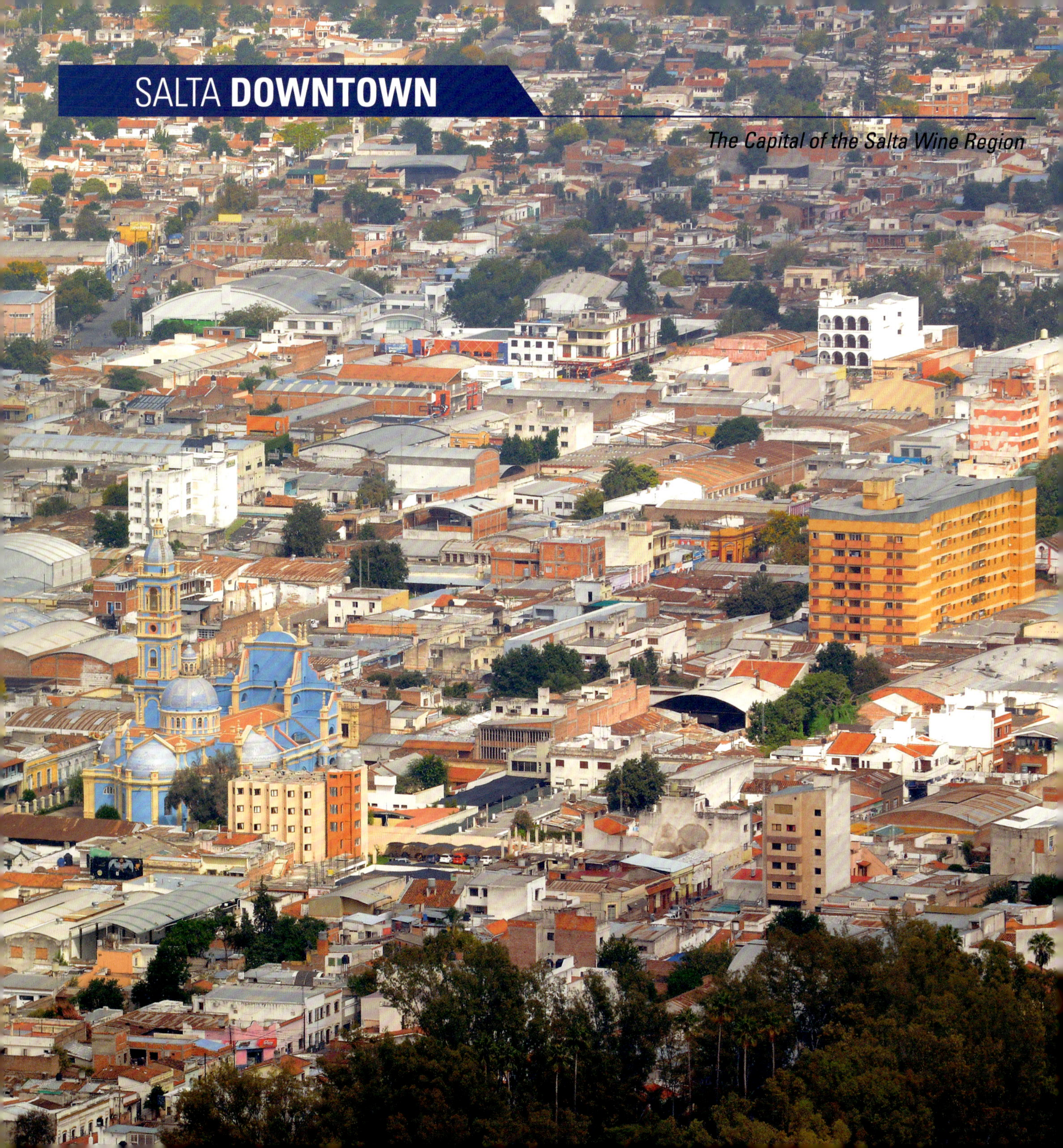

SALTA **DOWNTOWN**

The Capital of the Salta Wine Region

COLONIAL COLORS

Salta is a state, and the capital city of the province, located in the far northwest of the country at high elevations in the foothills of the Andes Mountains 600 miles north of Mendoza and bordering Bolivia, Paraguay and Chile.

This is Argentina's second largest wine region becoming famous for its unique grape... Torrontés. Another unusual grape grown here is Tannat. Plus they grow Argentina's notable Malbec, in addition to Merlot and Cabernet Sauvignon.

In all of Argentina, Salta is considered the city which has preserved its colonial architecture the best. Nicknamed Salta La Linda (Salta the beautiful), it has become a major tourist destination due to this old and restored colonial architecture.

Salta is the city you must fly into in order to venture out to the wine regions. It has a population of 600,000 and an elevation of 3,780' with many exciting tourism opportunities. Since the wine regions are at least two hours away, you might as well explore Salta for a day or two on your way.

Besides the architecture, Salta has naturally beautiful scenery created by its subtropical highland climate, different from the desert climate of its wine regions. Salta's architecture is beautifully colorful as seen in the photo (left page) taken from atop **San Bernardo Hill**, 968' above the city and accessible by aerial tram (photo below).

The tallest bell tower in South America is located in Salta. **Iglesia San Francisco's** tower stands 177' high and has history dating back to 1625. It has been rebuilt several times to retain its impressive aesthetic form and bold contrasting colors of Italian-influenced architecture.

The perfect starting point for numerous attractions is the palm tree laden **Plaza 9 de Julio** at the heart of downtown, surrounded by buildings of religious, cultural and historical significance. See their crown jewel of colonial architecture **El Cabildo**, the **Historical Museum of the North**, the renowned **Museum of High Altitude Archeology** that holds three frozen Inca mummies found at the Llullaillaco volcano at 22,000 feet elevation, and the massive **Cathedral of Salta** (photo below).

Within a few blocks of the plaza is **Pasea Balcarce** (photo below right), an eight-block stretch of 100-year-old buildings restored into the cultural centre of the city. It is the new hip nightspot with loads of chic and character-laden venues of snazzy cafes, innovative restaurants like **José Balcarce** (next page), cool clubs and unique luxury hotels like **Delvino Boutique Hotel** (following page).

SALTA **DOWNTOWN**

Restored Colonial Architecture

Salta Wine Region

Salta Province

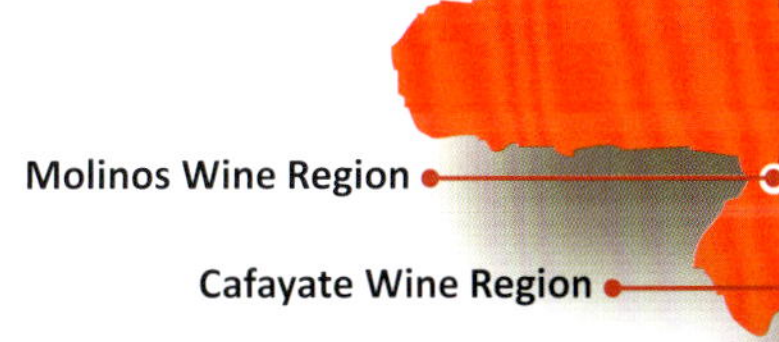

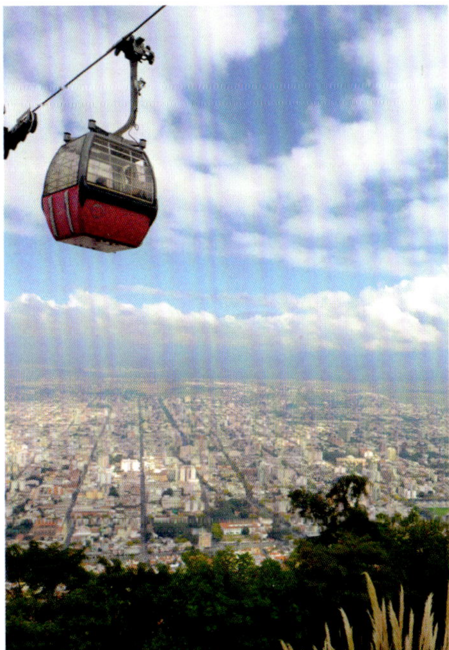

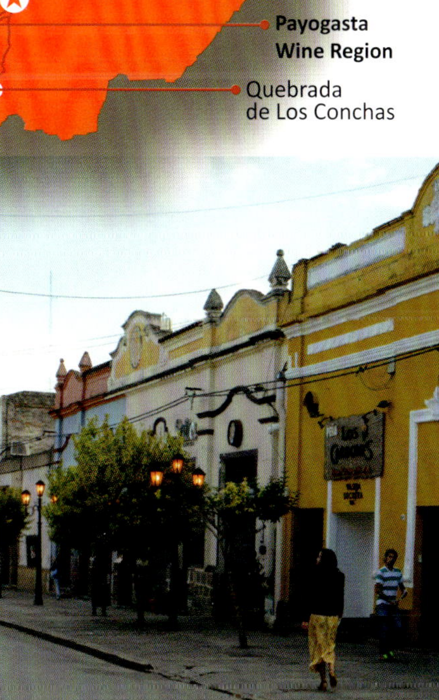

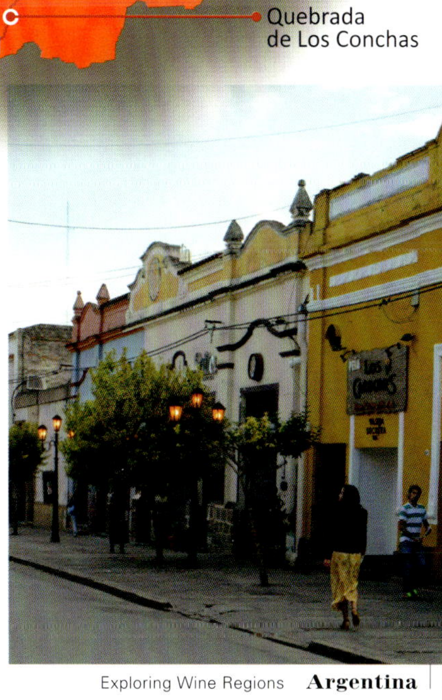

SALTA **DOWNTOWN**

Authentic Northern Argentina Cuisine

JOSÉ BALCARCE

594 Necochea
(downtown in Paseo Balcarce district)

011 (+54 387) 421.1628
JoseBalcarceSalta@hotmail.com

Dinner: Seven Nights (8:00 pm - 1:00 am)

JoseBalcarce.com.ar

English & Spanish

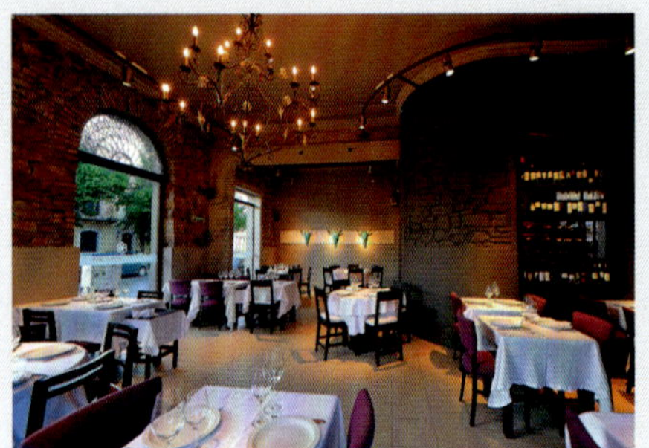

TRADITIONAL ANDEAN RECIPES

The cuisine in high-country northwest mountain region of Argentina is different from the rest of the country. And José Balcarce focuses on this local flavor... even rescuing pre-conquest and pre-Colombian Andean recipes, with interesting ingredients and nutrients, like amaranth, quinoa, llama and api (purple wheat).

Located in the trendy Paseo Balcarce district downtown, and in a beautifully restored 120-year-old house, José Balcarce has a stylish atmosphere that contrasts rustic stone walls with white tablecloth linens in an intimate setting.

I call their cuisine comfort food, and realized that the mountainous environment has evolved heartier foods of sustenance. I was treated to the top-five typical Salta dishes (below left, counterclockwise)...

Locro – hearty thick soup of corn, alubia (white beans), filet mignon, sausage slices, bacon, red peppers, and green onions.

Empanadas – baked pastry turnover filled with finely chopped beef, green onions and potatoes. Onion, tomato and chile pepper sauce.

Humita – slowly steamed hominy, grated corn, onions, red peppers, oil, mozzarella cheese, and basil in a clay pot with corn husks.

Cheesecake – Dulce de leche, atop a base of chocolate and topped with praline nuts.

Quesillos – dessert of thinly-sliced cheese layers filled with fig and peach jam (cooked for two hours), topped with walnuts.

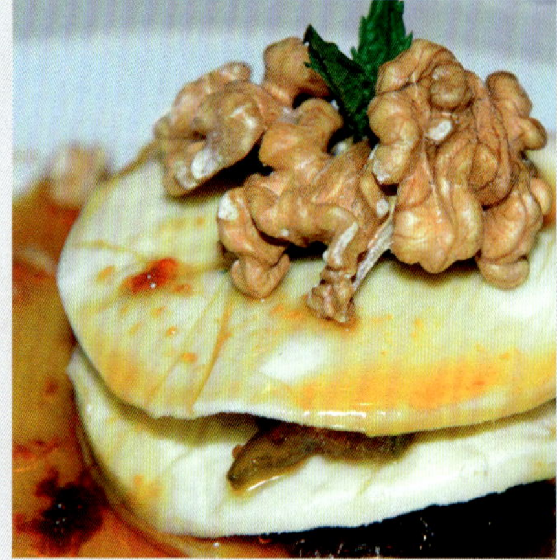

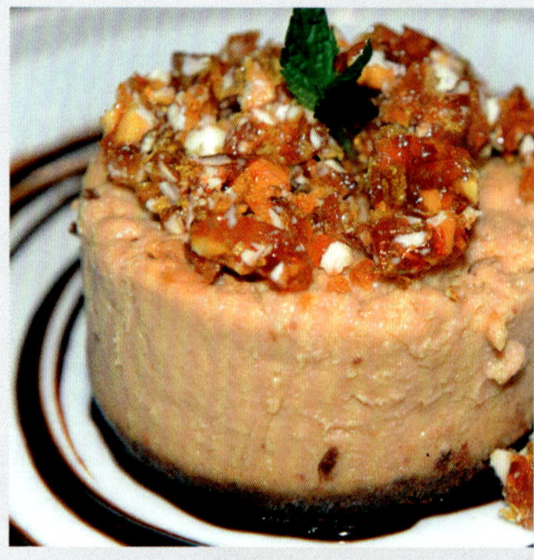

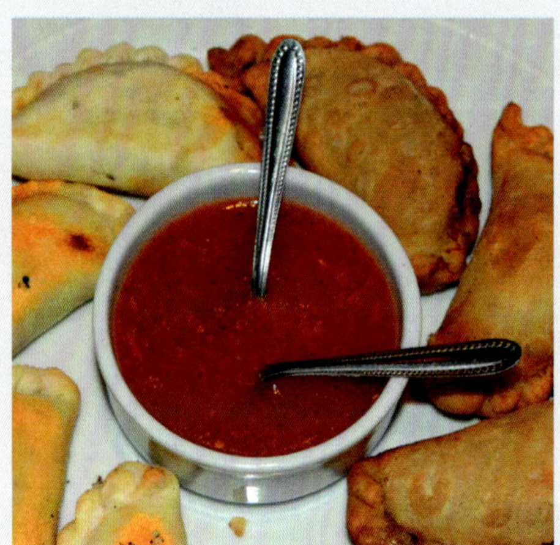

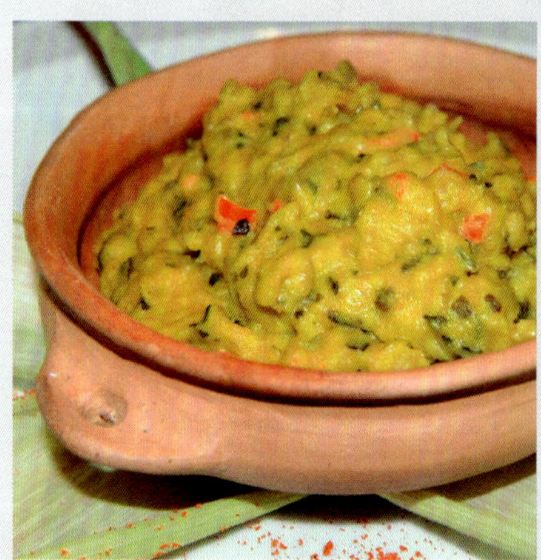

WINE HOTEL IN SALTA

The Delvino Boutique Hotel is the perfect hotel when on a wine region adventure to Salta. Delvina will get you in the wine mood. The entire hotel is themed and focused on wine.

When you arrive, you will be greeted with a glass of local Salta wine and personally escorted to your wine-themed room. Each room is named after a wine grape and decorated with the varietal's theme. The *Malbec Room* has red Malbec walls, paintings and other art, all in the theme of Malbec.

My favorite is the *Torrontés Room*, the grape famous for Salta and the hotel's premium suite. It has crisp green walls just like the Torrontés grape and wine region paintings of the vineyards and wineries of Salta. It is spacious with a large living room and in-room hot tub (photo below) overlooking the hills of the city.

Delvino is an old home restored into a hotel, with a central courtyard and casual homestyle ambiance. It is perfectly located in downtown Salta, just two blocks from the new hip *Paseo Balcarce* district of cool restaurants, clubs and shops, and a scenic five-minute walk to *Plaza 9 de Julio* central square, with many things to see and do.

The Delvino Vinoteca is a cozy little wine bar in the front of the hotel. They carry a huge variety of the Salta region wines, and do tastings, blind tastings, food and wine pairings, and invite winemakers from the region to talk and taste their wines. The staff is very knowledgable about the local wines, and they can serve you in the Vinoteca, their lounge, by the hotel pool, in your room, or sell you bottles to take with you.

I found it valuable to stay in the Delvino on my way to the wine regions to get an advanced view of the coming attractions, and then after exploring the wine regions to recap the experience and purchase wines I remember I wanted.

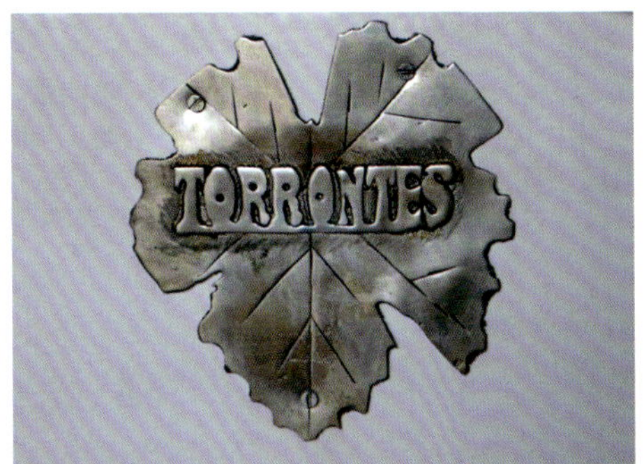

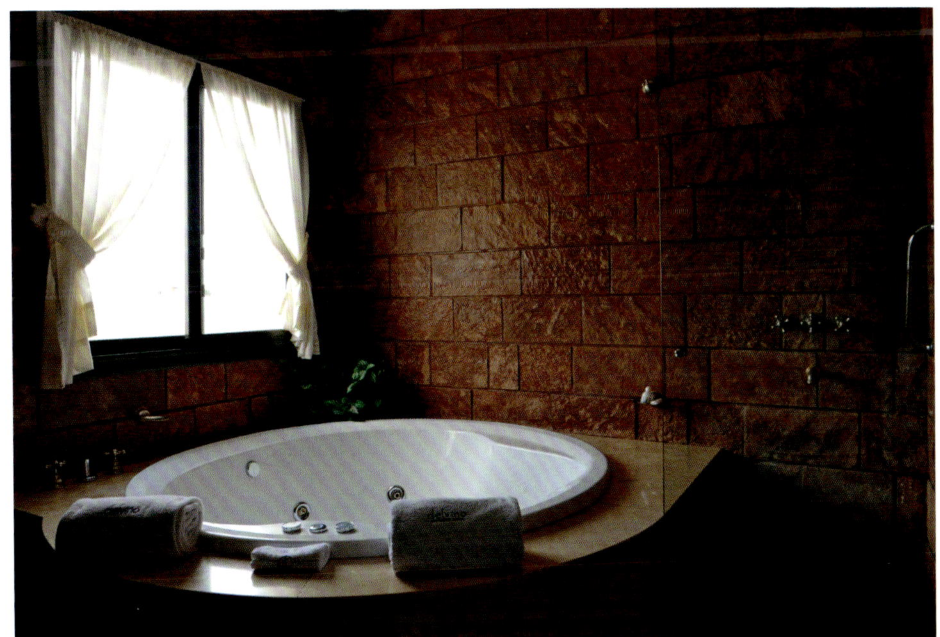

SALTA **DOWNTOWN**

Hotel • Vinoteca

DELVINO BOUTIQUE HOTEL

555 Ameghino

(Paseo Balcarce, **Downtown,** Salta)

011 (+54 387) 432.0092

hotel@DelvinoSalta.com.ar

DelvinoSalta.com.ar

English & Español

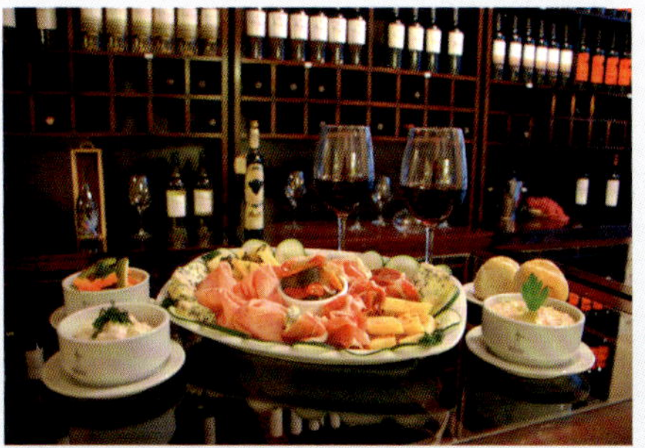

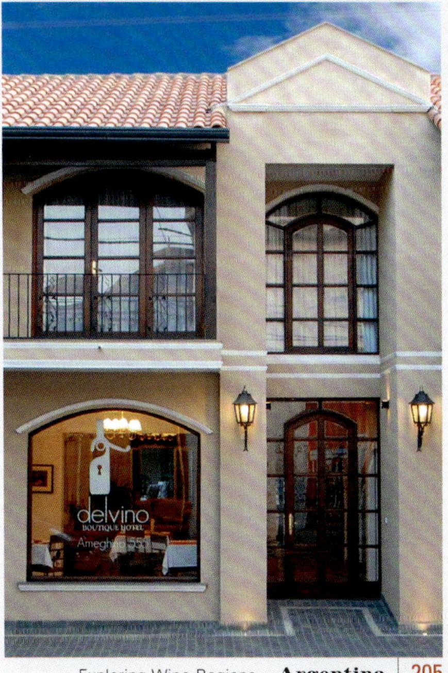

SALTA **CAFAYATE MAP** DOWNTOWN & BEYOND

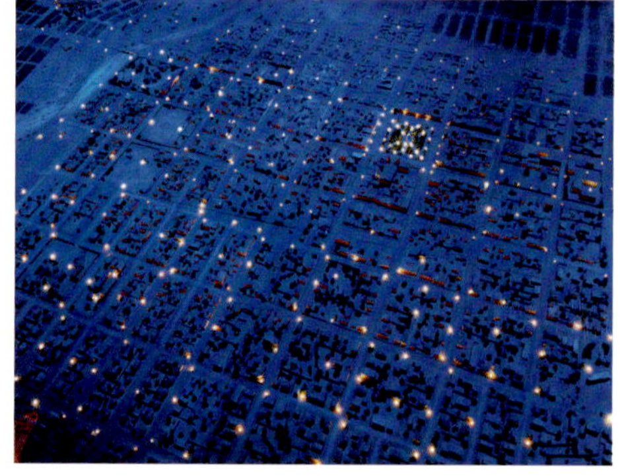

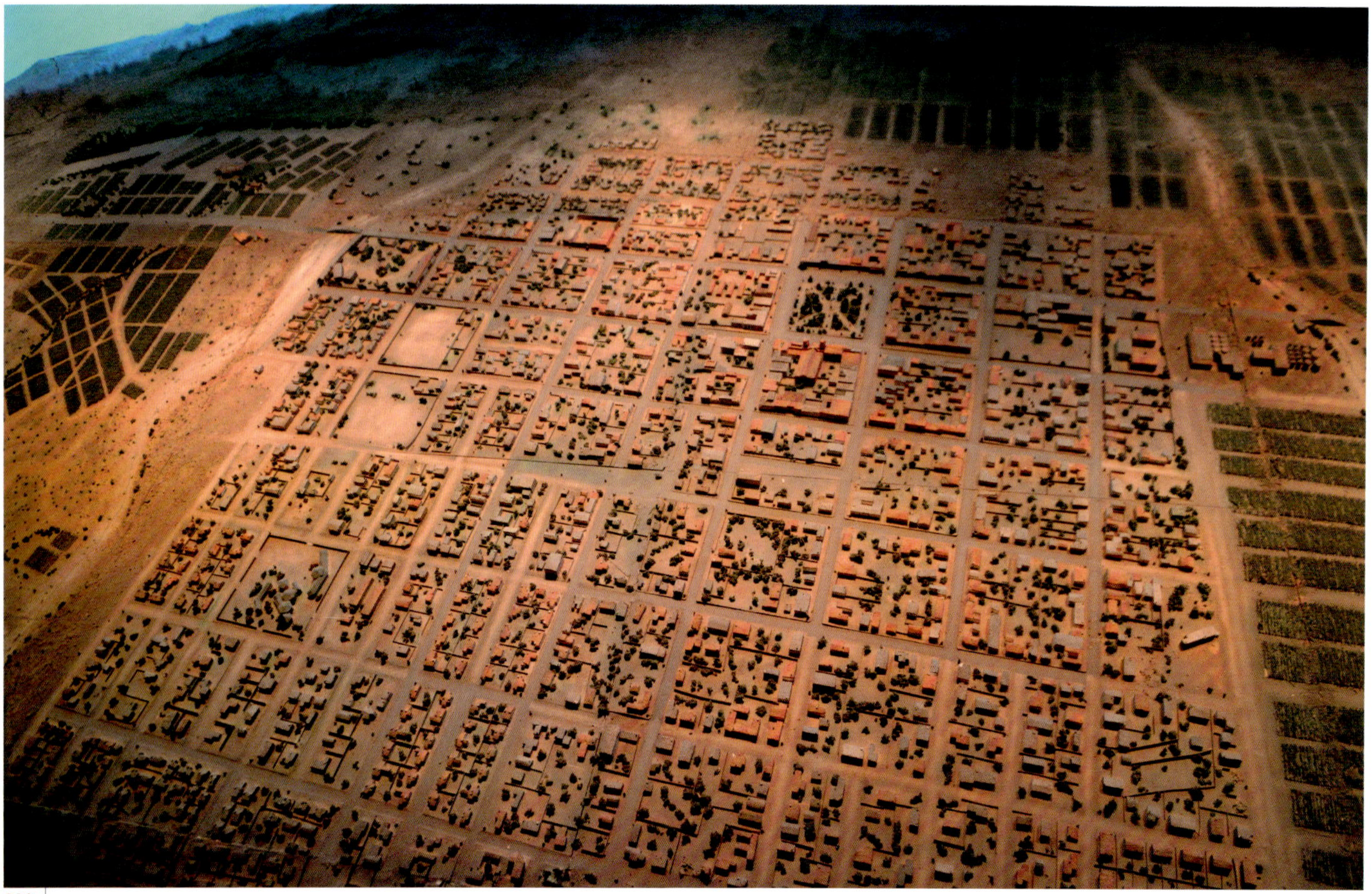

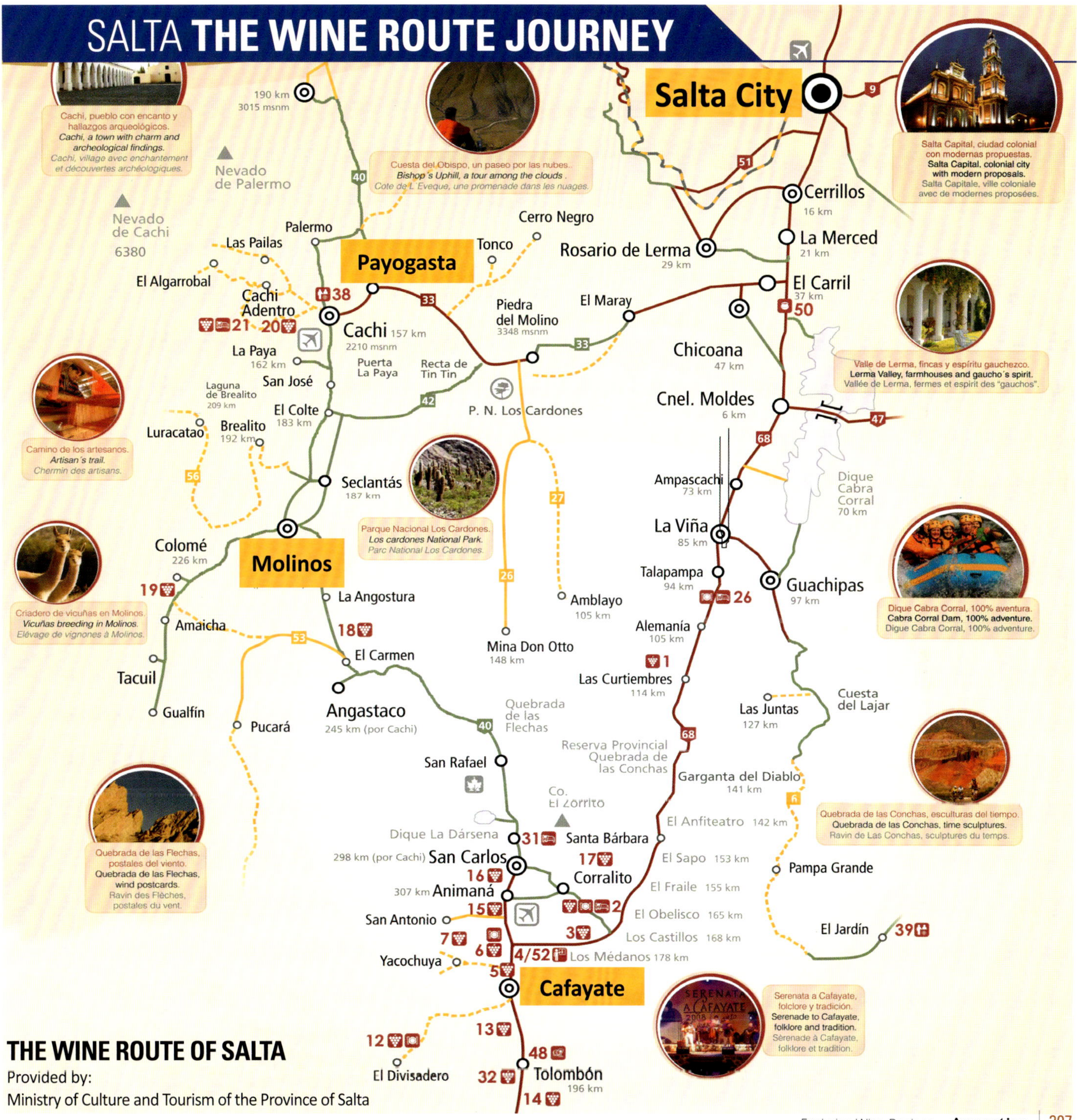
SALTA THE WINE ROUTE JOURNEY
Salta City
Cachi, pueblo con encanto y hallazgos arqueológicos.
Cachi, a town with charm and archeological findings.
Cachi, village avec enchantement et découvertes archéologiques.
190 km
3015 msnm
Nevado de Palermo
Nevado de Cachi
6380
Cuesta del Obispo, un paseo por las nubes.
Bishop's Uphill, a tour among the clouds.
Cote de L'Eveque, une promenade dans les nuages.
Salta Capital, ciudad colonial con modernas propuestas.
Salta Capital, colonial city with modern proposals.
Salta Capitale, ville coloniale avec de modernes proposées.
Cerrillos
16 km
La Merced
21 km
Rosario de Lerma
29 km
Cerro Negro
Tonco
Palermo
Las Pailas
El Algarrobal
Payogasta
38
33
Cachi Adentro
21
20
Cachi
157 km
2210 msnm
Piedra del Molino
3348 msnm
El Maray
El Carril
37 km
50
Chicoana
47 km
La Paya
162 km
San José
Laguna de Brealito
209 km
Puerta La Paya
Recta de Tin Tin
P. N. Los Cardones
Valle de Lerma, fincas y espíritu gauchezco.
Lerma Valley, farmhouses and gaucho's spirit.
Vallée de Lerma, fermes et espirit des "gauchos".
Cnel. Moldes
6 km
47
68
Camino de los artesanos.
Artisan's trail.
Chermin des artisans.
Luracatao
Brealito
192 km
El Colte
183 km
42
56
Seclantás
187 km
27
Ampascachi
73 km
Dique Cabra Corral
70 km
Parque Nacional Los Cardones.
Los cardones National Park.
Parc National Los Cardones.
La Viña
85 km
Colomé
226 km
Molinos
19
26
Amblayo
105 km
Talapampa
94 km
26
Guachipas
97 km
Dique Cabra Corral, 100% aventura.
Cabra Corral Dam, 100% adventure.
Digue Cabra Corral, 100% adventure.
Criadero de vicuñas en Molinos.
Vicuñas breeding in Molinos.
Elévage de vignones à Molinos.
La Angostura
Amaicha
18
53
El Carmen
Mina Don Otto
148 km
Alemanía
105 km
1
Las Curtiembres
114 km
Tacuil
Gualfín
Pucará
Angastaco
245 km (por Cachi)
40
Quebrada de las Flechas
Las Juntas
127 km
Cuesta del Lajar
Reserva Provincial Quebrada de las Conchas
68
San Rafael
Garganta del Diablo
141 km
Co. El Zorrito
El Anfiteatro 142 km
6
Quebrada de las Conchas, esculturas del tiempo.
Quebrada de las Conchas, time sculptures.
Ravin de Las Conchas, sculptures du temps.
Dique La Dársena
31
Santa Bárbara
17
El Sapo 153 km
298 km (por Cachi) San Carlos
16
Corralito
Pampa Grande
Quebrada de las Flechas, postales del viento.
Quebrada de las Flechas, wind postcards.
Ravin des Flèches, postales du vent.
307 km Animaná
El Fraile 155 km
15
2
El Obelisco 165 km
San Antonio
3
Los Castillos 168 km
El Jardín
39
7
6
4/52
Los Médanos 178 km
Yacochuya
5
Cafayate
Serenata a Cafayate, folclore y tradición.
Serenade to Cafayate, folklore and tradition.
Sérenade à Cafayate, folklore et tradition.
13
12
48
El Divisadero
32
Tolombón
196 km
14
THE WINE ROUTE OF SALTA
Provided by:
Ministry of Culture and Tourism of the Province of Salta

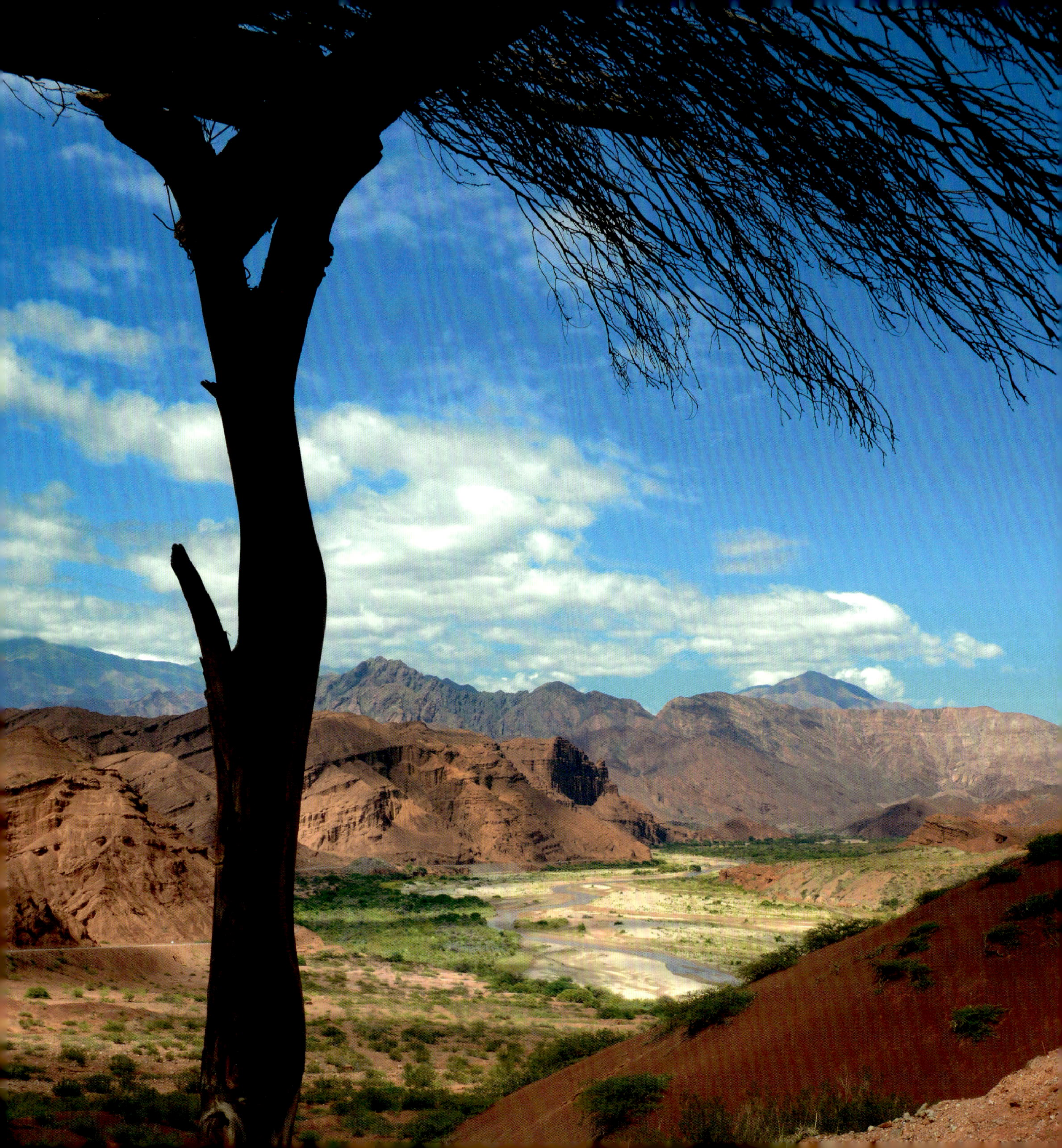

SALTA **QUEBRADA DE LAS CONCHAS**

*A Spectacular Drive Through the Hills between the Towns of **Salta** and **Cafayate***

To get from the city of Salta to the town of Cafayate (the primary wine region of Salta) you drive about 120 miles southwest on Route 68 through some very picturesque landscapes. The road is mostly paved and well maintained when hard-packed dirt.

Both Salta and Cafayate are in valleys, Lerma and Calchaquí respectively, divided by a mountainous region known as Quebrada de las Conchas. It is a scenic drive leaving Salta through the valley of Lerma, a green subtropical highland climate, traversing through the dramatic scenery of Quebrada de las Conchas, and then into the Cafayate valley of Calchaquí, a dry desert climate.

Quebradas de las Conchas translated as *Ravine of the Shells* and is a nature reserve with much prehistoric oceanic sediments of inland marine limestones rich in fossils and even dinosaur footprints. The landscape has magnificent geological rock formations of red and lavender colors within sharp cliffs and gorges along a ravine in which you drive. Plenty of stopping points to take it all in, and capture beautiful photography.

You won't miss **La Garganta del Diablo** as it appears when the gorge narrows and its walls are higher. This interesting formation of textured and oblique shapes resembles a human trachea, translated is *The Throat of the Devil.* It consists of a sequence of sedimentary rock composed of materials that accumulated about 90 million years ago. The shape is due to water penetrating the pores and crevices of rocks, wearing away and molding them. The floor is preserved despite the passage of time since it consists of harder rocks originating from 500 million years ago.

Other interesting must-see formations are... **The Amphitheater,** an open-topped cavern of reddish sedimentary rocks; **Mirador Tres Cruces**, a hillside series of three crosses along the valley gorge; and **The Dunes** of fine sand glittering with mica. Throughout the ravine, you will find palettes of brick red, pale orange, yellow, white, green, slate blue, and rich purple as big as hillsides and as small as a few feet.

Enjoy the drive, make this a day trip!

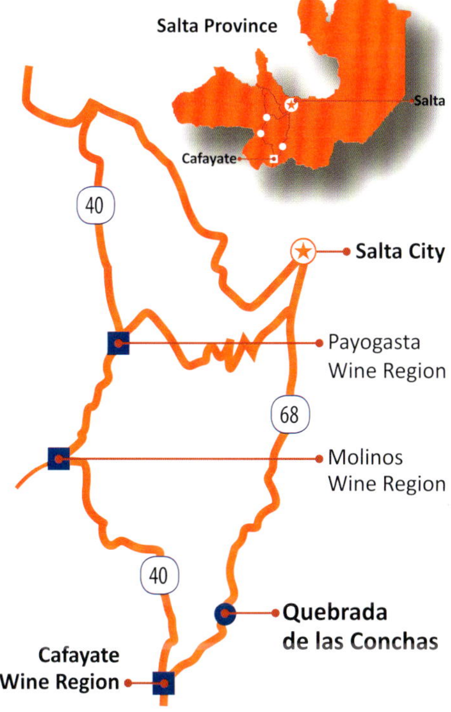

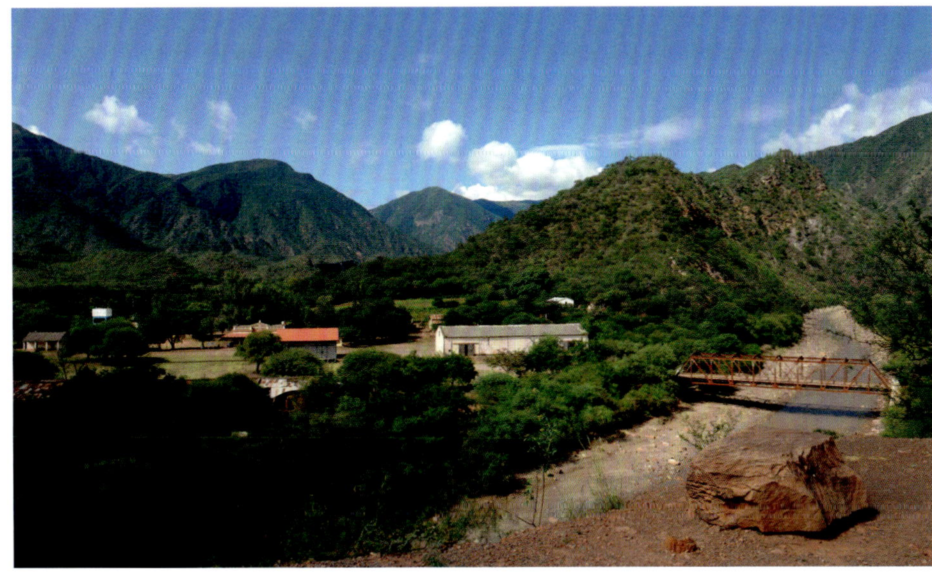

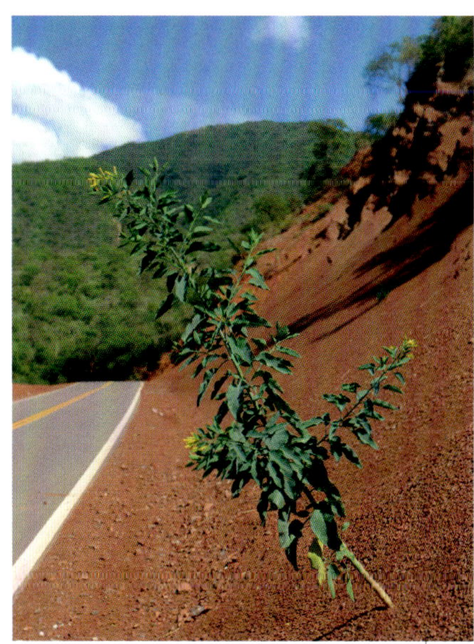

SALTA **CAFAYATE**

*Central to the **Valle de Calchaquí** Wine Region*

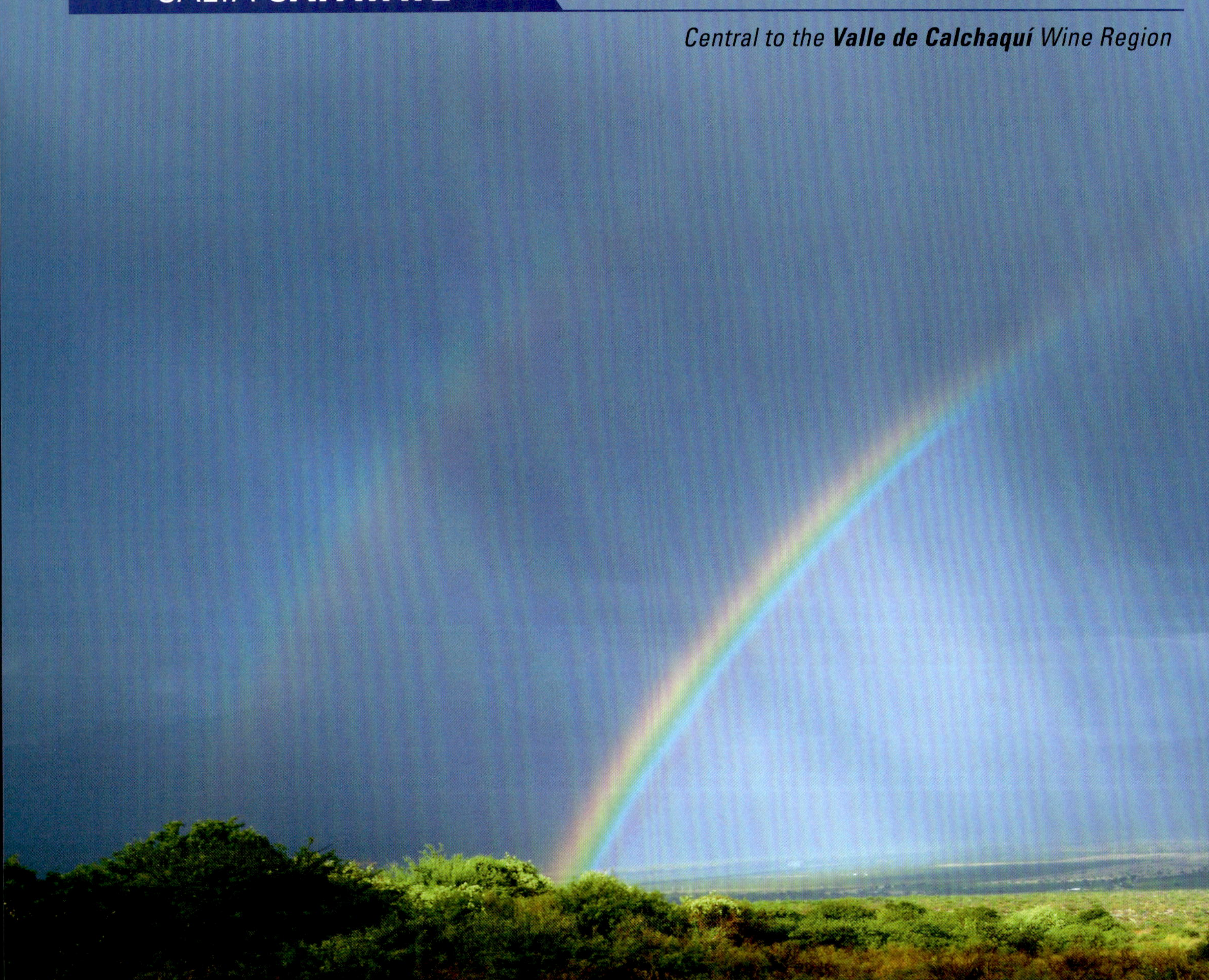

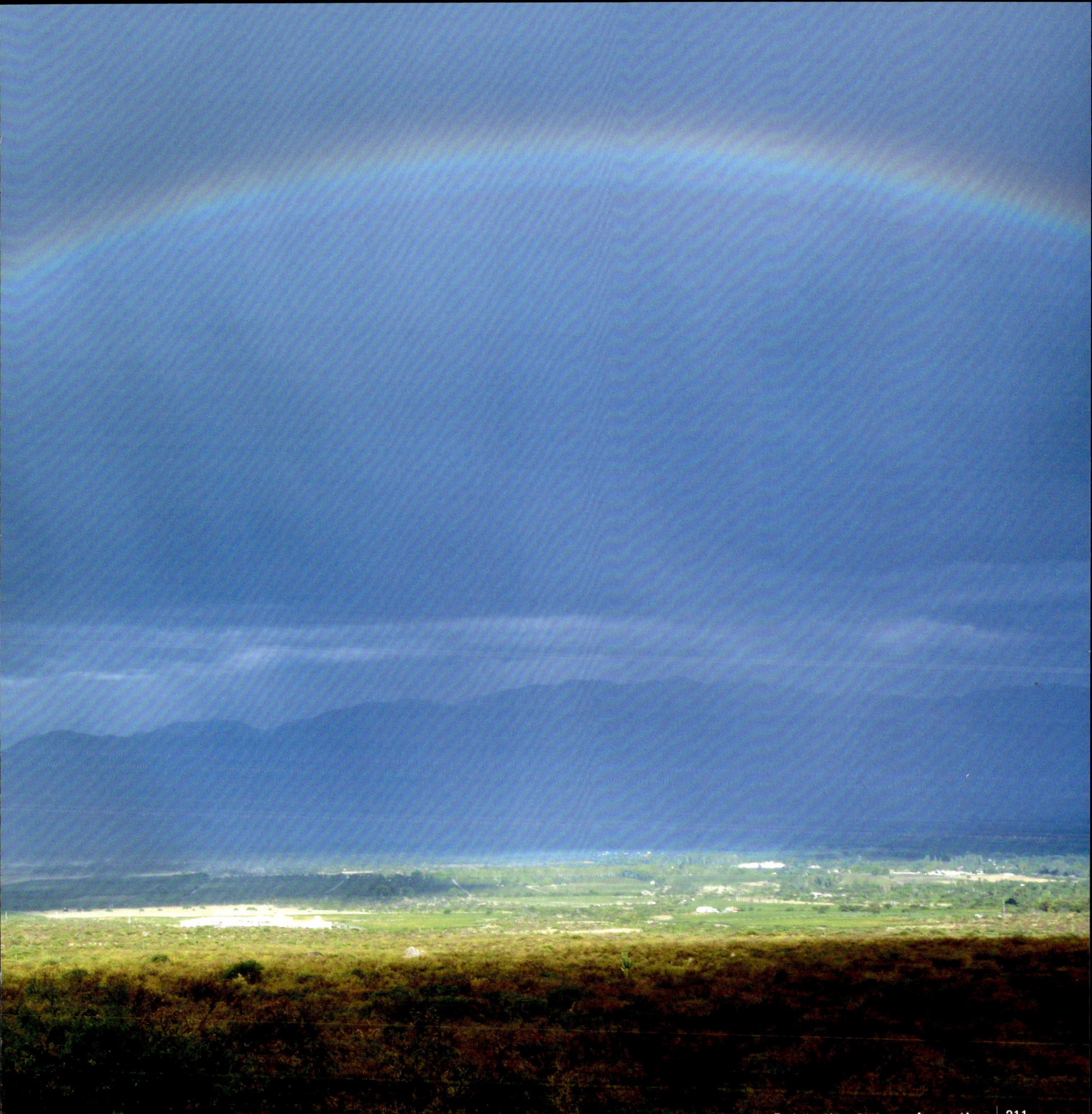

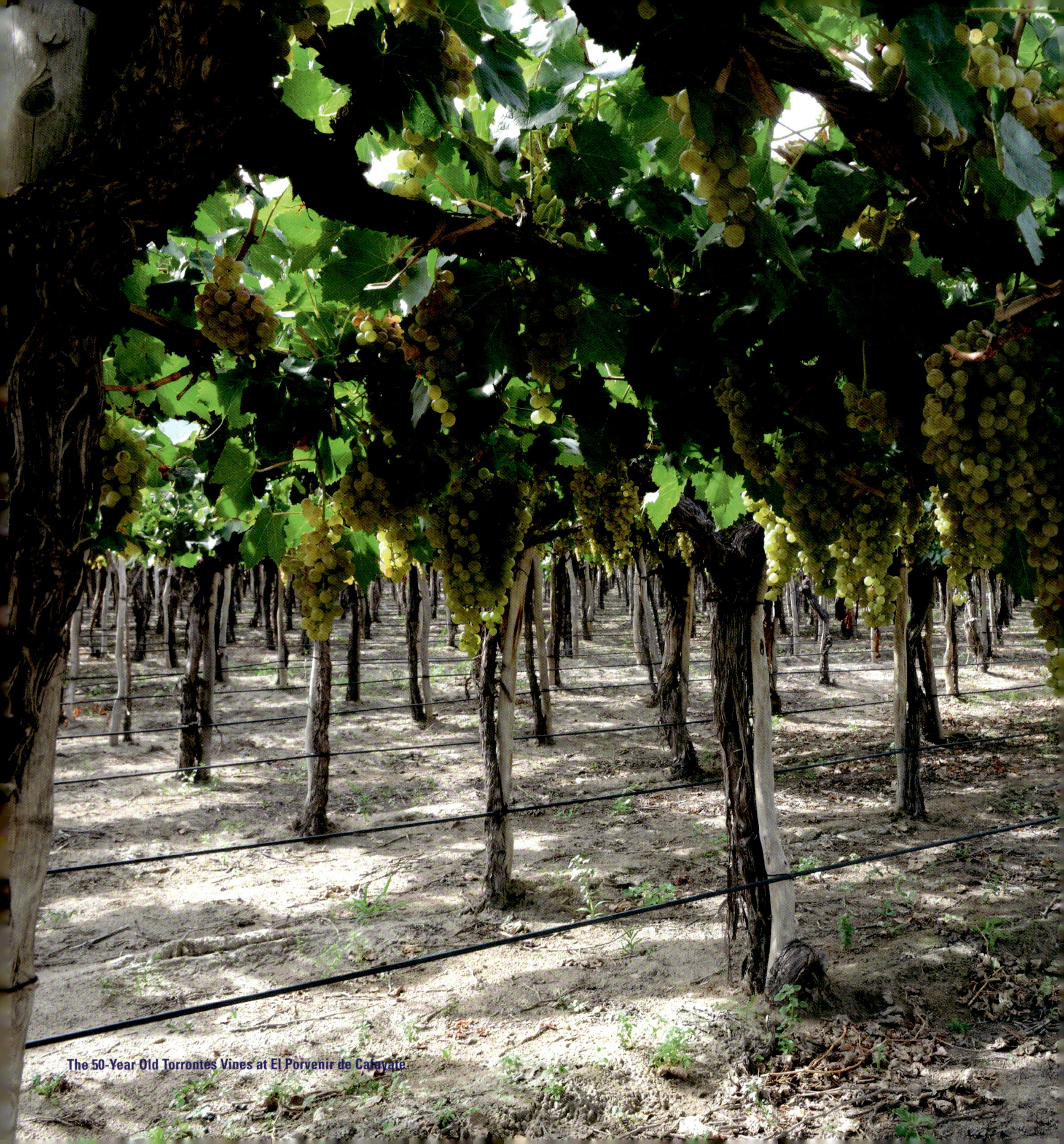

The 50-Year Old Torrontes Vines at El Porvenir de Cafayate

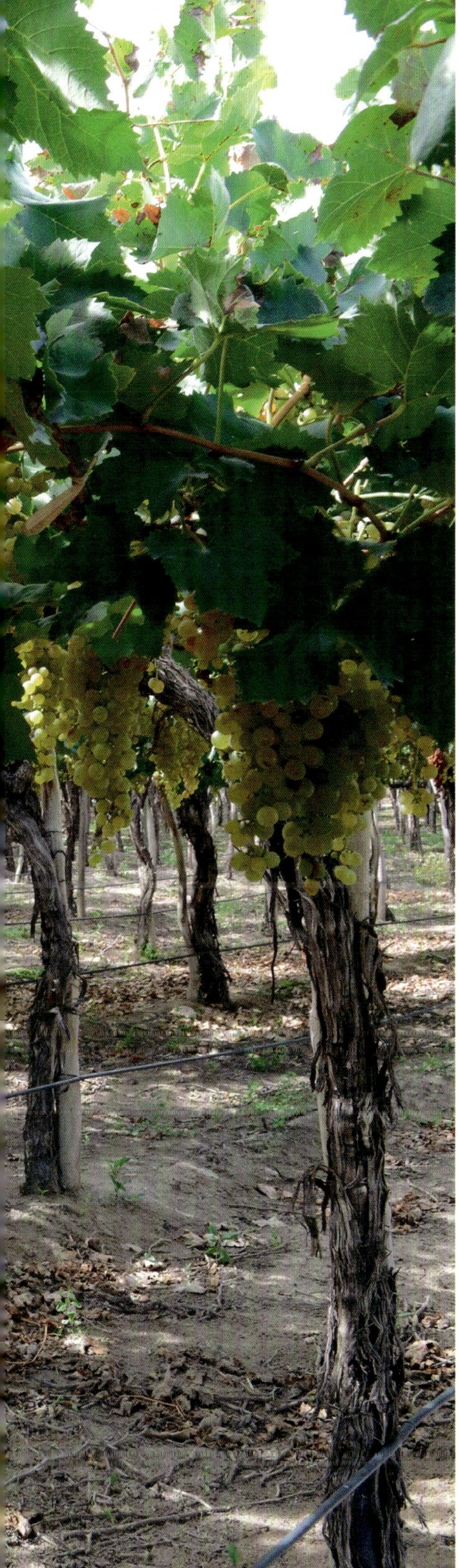

SALTA **CAFAYATE**

The Land of High-Altitude Growing of Argentina's Unique Grape - Torrontés

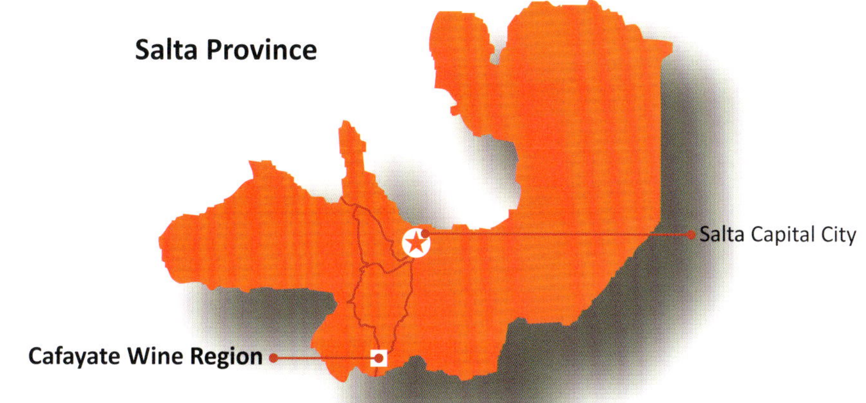

EXPLORING CAFAYATE

With so much attention on Mendoza and Malbec, how can Salta and Cafayate get any attention? From Torrontés... it's the quintessential grape of Salta, and it thrives at the high altitudes of Cafayate. The town of Cafayate is at 5,500' elevation with vineyards extending up the sides of the valley floor into the foothills with elevations exceeding 6,500'. Salta is the highest wine growing region in the world with vineyards as high as 10,000' elevation.

Torrontés is a white grape varietal exclusive to Argentina and with a very strong personality. It is affectionately nicknamed **The Liar,** because of its sweet floral and fruity nose of ripe peaches, followed by a surprise of dry crisp finish of grapefruit on the mouth. Torrontés is typically grown in a canopy-style (photo left page) to protect the grapes from the high-altitude sun exposure here.

Cafayate is located in the southern most part of the Salta Region in the Calchaquíes Valley. Further north up the valley are the 10,000' vineyards, which we will explore after Cafayate. Cafayate is the primary wine growing region in Salta with roughly 35 wineries, most are small family operations. Cafayate is a quaint little colonial town with a population of only 12,000 people. It has a lively square in the center of town, nice restaurants and a very interesting museum about this wine region. Being only eight square blocks, you can easily stroll around and visit the shops, restaurants, church, and the 10 or so wineries located in the town.

This is Argentina's most radical wine region... The vineyards sit more than a mile above sea level, planted within mountainous jagged red-rock formations, growing unusual varietals as Torrontés and Tannat, and the winemakers are constantly reinventing how they produce and market their wines as a very progressive endeavor.

The wines from Cafayate are strong and flavorful, and with intense color, because of the high altitude. This intense exposure to the sun, the hot days with cold nights, temperature differences exceeding 35 degrees, and a tropical humidity that drifts south from the Amazon, all have created a micro-climate perfect for naturally balanced acidity, luminosity and richness in the wines produced here.

Cafayate is also ideal for warm weather varieties, including Malbec, plus Tannat, Cabernet Sauvignon and Merlot. The climate brings out their full-bodied big redness easily, so winemakers have learned to tame the inherent wild spirit of these vines by picking earlier and managing sun exposure to make great wines.

This is a land of extremes... extreme altitude, extreme sunlight and extreme beauty.... ultimately, this is one spectacular place to explore. It really is in the middle of nowhere, and you will love it!

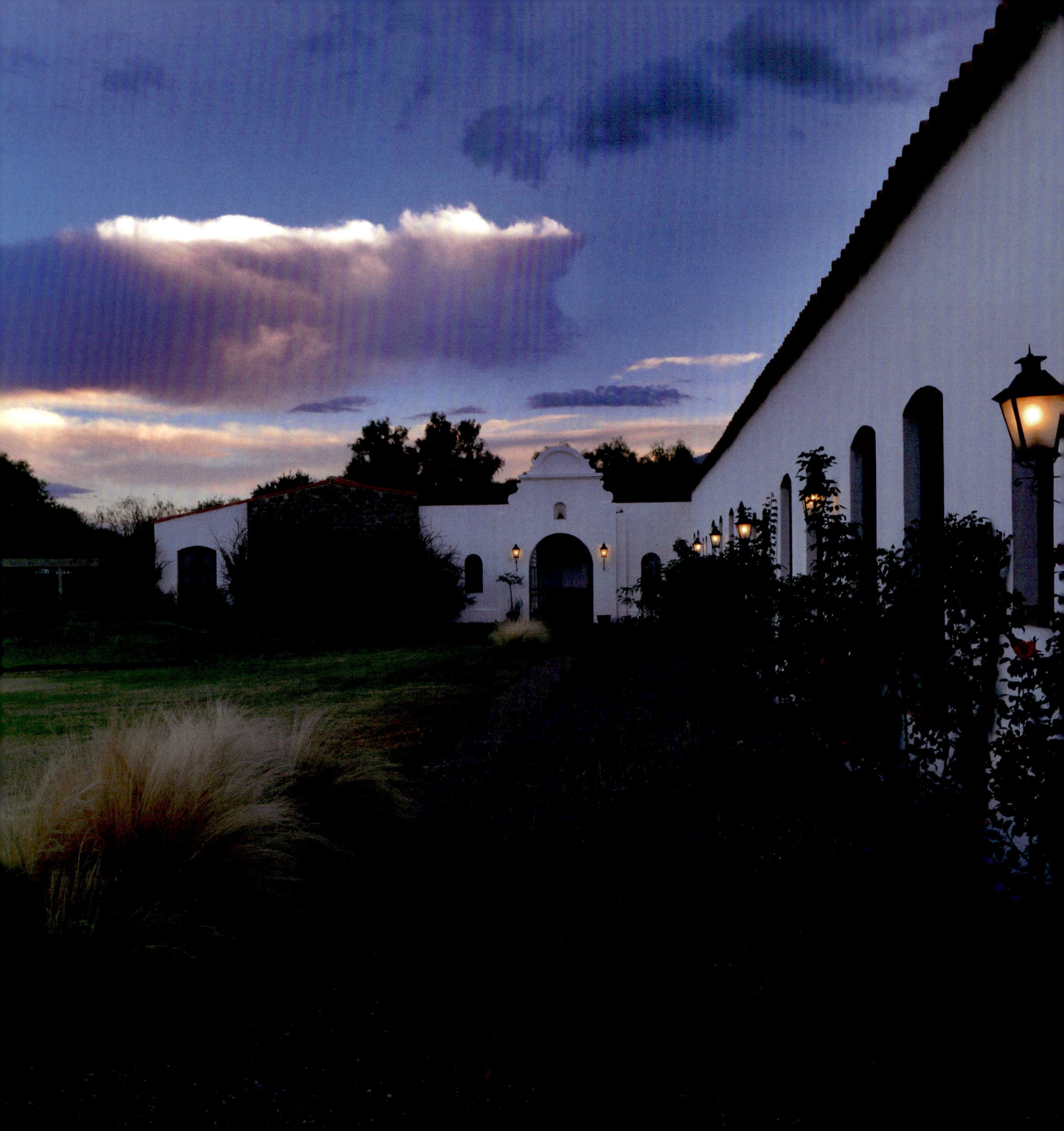

THE HOTEL AT EL ESTECO WINERY

Actually, Patios de Cafayate is a beautiful Spanish-style hacienda, the former home of the Michel Torina family, founders of El Esteco Winery in 1892. Thirty-two bedrooms with private baths surround courtyards and elegant gardens of colonial beauty in what today is a luxury boutique hotel.

Enjoy the peaceful serene environment of this hotel and winery set amidst 1,000 acres of vineyards, and well off the road down a long driveway after a guarded entrance into the grounds and then through a majestic iron gate into a private world of the hacienda. It is quiet. Romantic. A grandeur of luxury of a era past.

Sit pool-side on their patio with a special glass of one of El Esteco's wines and enjoy the uniqueness of an east-facing sunset. The hills light-up with magnificent colors from the desert-sun setting behind the hotel and onto the palate of your view.

Dining at Patios de Cafayate will feel like you are in your own home, with your private chef and high-class staff. They serve authentic Andean cuisine made with local ingredients from recipes passed down through generations. And the winery is only on the other side of the wall, so a fabulous bottle of wine is at your fingertips.

The hotel will arrange special tours of the vineyards and the winery, and for specific tastings of their wines. I recommend a food & wine paring at the hotel restaurant and winery are adjacent buildings. A great combination is offered here.

The rooms are authentic, outfitted with antique furniture, handmade carpets, ceramic and wood floors. The rooms reflect the local culture, with tapestries designed by renowned Calchaquí artist Héctor Cruz and original features still in tact such as loom woven carpets and oven-baked clay tiles.

And more... a wine spa of local ingredients and culture, a magnificent outdoor swimming pool, extensive grounds to meander, llamas friendly enough to pet, and an original chapel of the hacienda, which is adorned with hand-painted images, the Cross and the Via Crucis which was made in Cusco.

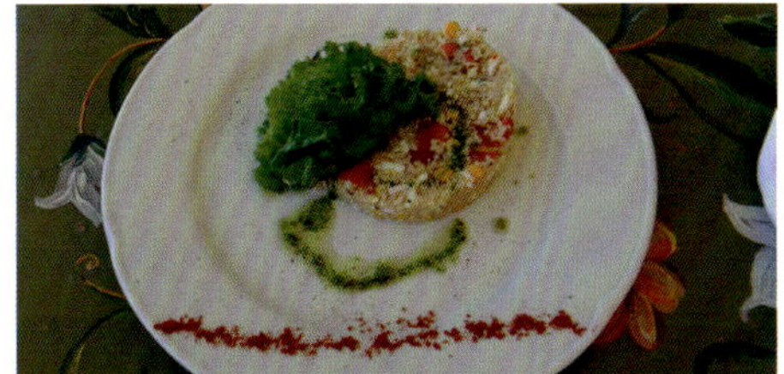

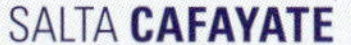

Hotel • Wine Spa • Restaurant

PATIOS DE CAFAYATE

On Ruta 40, at Ruta 68 Intersection
(North Edge of Downtown **Cafayate,** Salta)

011 (+54 386) 842.2229
reservas@PatiosDeCafayate.com

PatiosDeCafayate.com

English & Español

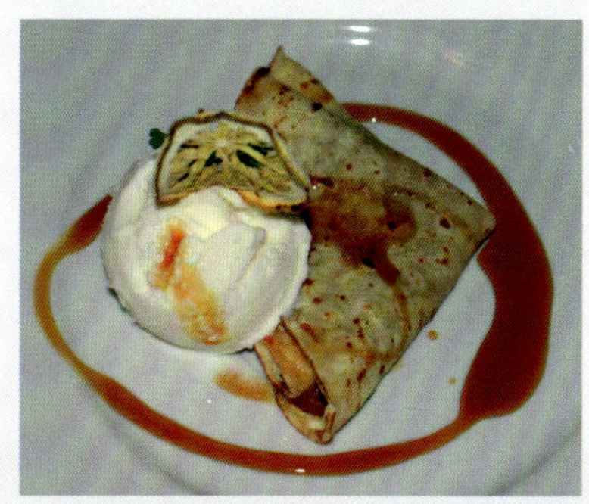

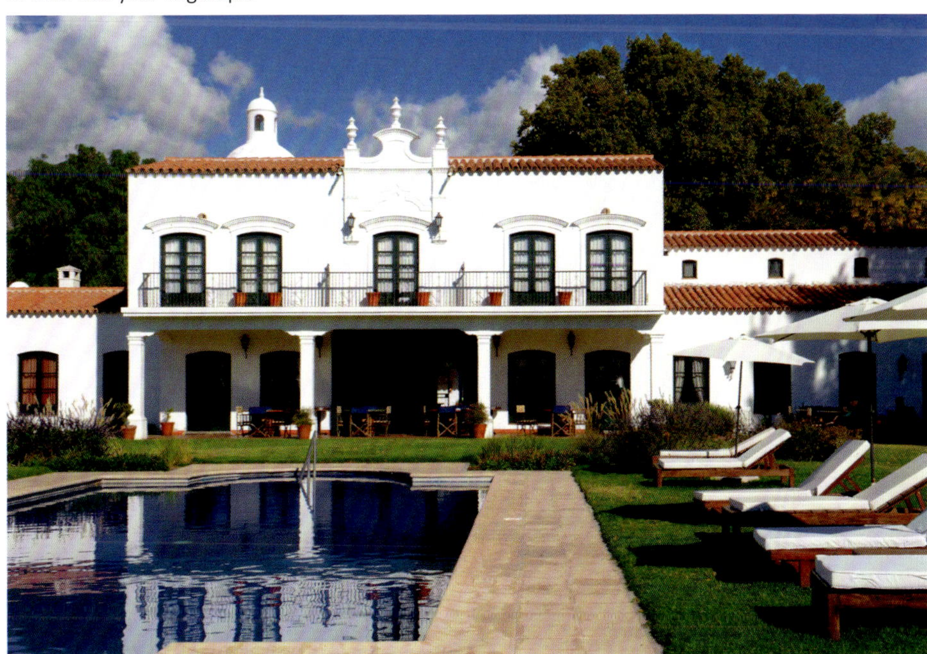

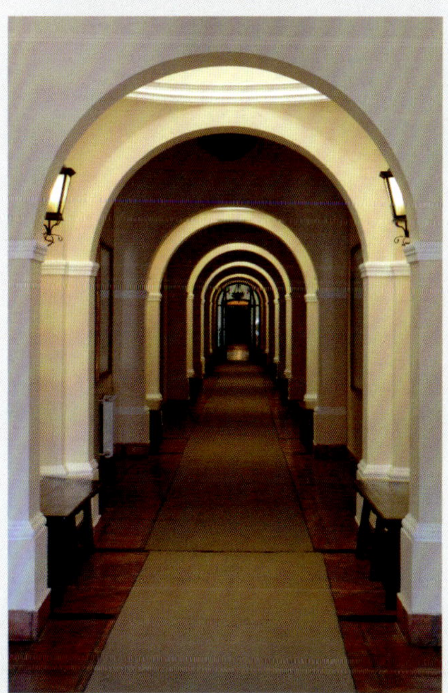

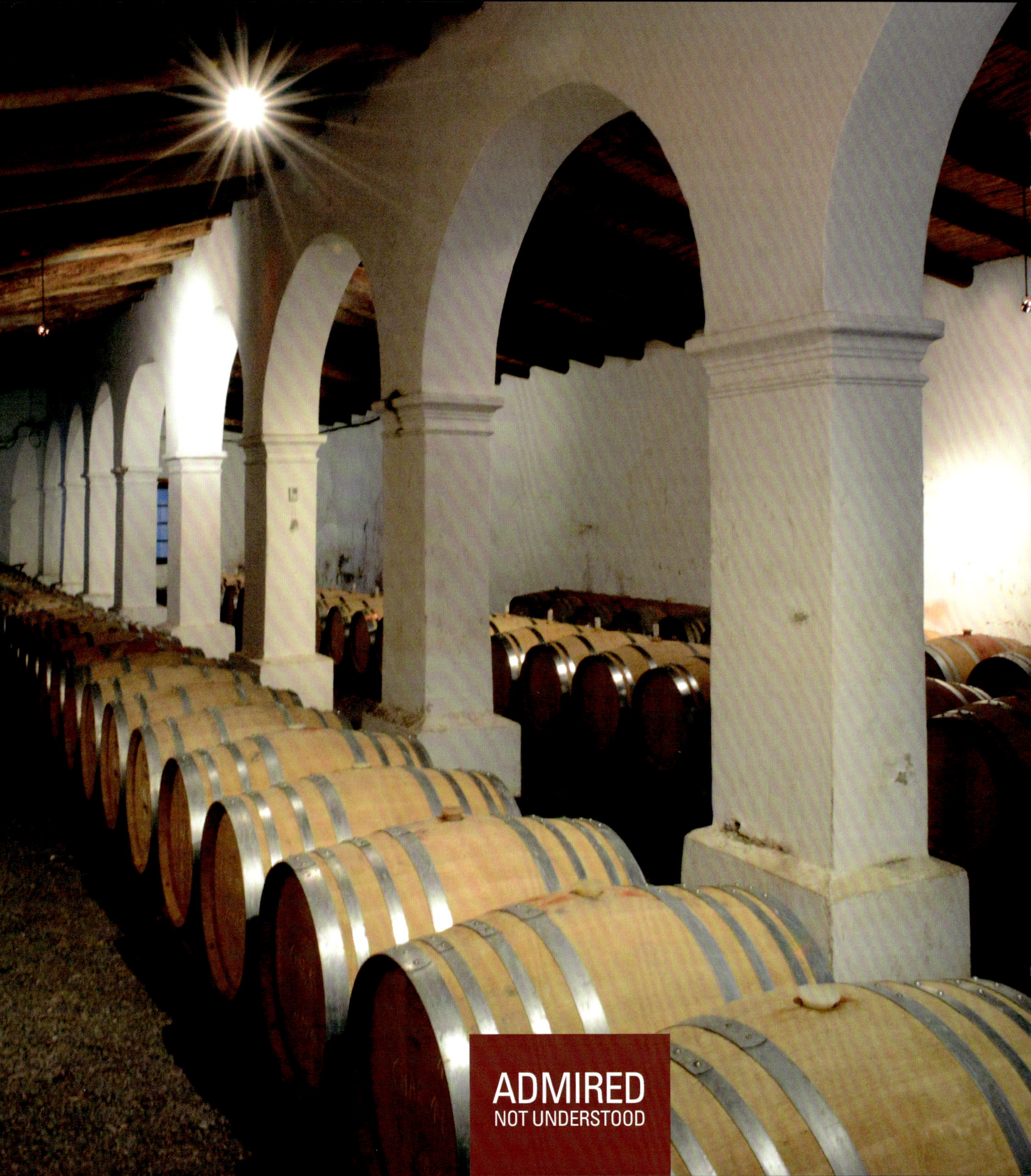
ADMIRED
NOT UNDERSTOOD

A LARGE COLLECTION OF ALL PREMIUM WINES

At Bodego El Esteco, they view their region, the Calchaquí Valley, as a magical place to be admired, not understood. Of course it does not make sense... this is like no other wine region in the world. Very high altitude. Extremely poor soil. Extreme temperatures. It resembles Mars, or some other odd-looking planet. It does not make sense that extraordinary wines can be produced in this harsh environment.

Further incomprehensible is that El Esteco produces eight different labels with 50 different wines in 13 million bottles annually, and yet they are all premium wines. I tasted across their various labels, at least a dozen different wines, and I can tell you the results are admirable, quite admirable!

Each label has a concept, and in that concept, the wine has a purpose exploiting a specific style or characteristic of wine. Their wines are interesting, with very attractive flavor profiles, some are very high-end premium results, with numerous awards to show. The wines are magnificent.

The two men behind these successful wines are winemaker Alejandro Pepa and agronomist Francisco Xavier Tellechea (pictured below, left and right, respectively).

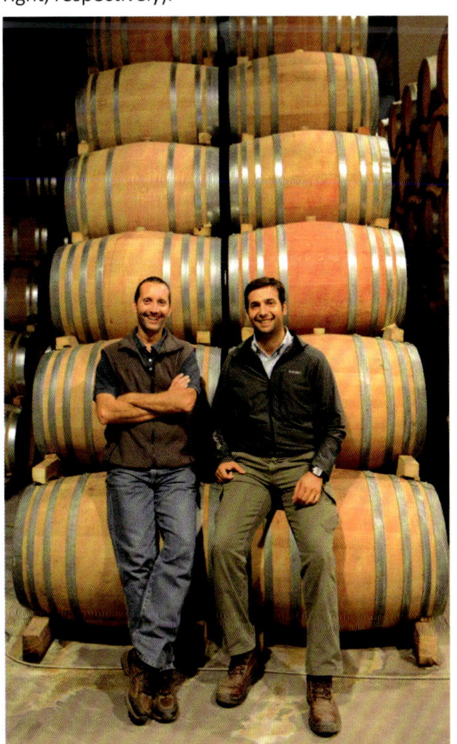

SERIE FINCAS NOTABLES

This is El Esteco's top-of-the-line, single vineyard, wine. As the name translates, it is a *series* of wine from their most *outstanding properties*. As an agronomist, this is Francisco's dream wine because it is the epitome of creating the wine in the vineyard, the perfect fusion between having the wisdom of nature and applying your best skills.

This single vineyard series was born out of keeping small amounts of juice being used for their Altimus wine when showing amazing character in 2011. Each year thereafter they honor the very best vineyard harvest into this ultra-special wine.

ALTIMUS

This is El Esteco's top-of-the-line wine resulting from the *winemaker's* meticulous attention to creating the ultimate wine possible. Latin for *the highest*, Altimus is Alejandro Pepa's highest choice of grapes, which he ages separately for 12 months in new French oak barrels, then blends and ages for an additional six more months.

EL ESTECO CHAÑAR PUNCO

This label is also unique as it is made from grapes, regardless their variety, grown from vineyards on their most unusual terroir... above 7,800' elevation.

DON DAVID RESERVE

This wine is in honor of the winery's founder, Don David Michel, whose name it takes, and was inspired by his distinction and elegance.

AMARU

This wine is named after the deity of the economics of water to irrigate farmland and symbolizing the vitality of water that allows the existence of Aymara people. Like its name, this wine encompasses the mystic spirit of the Calchaquí Valley and its strong character of the desert... intense and distinct aromas, concentrated textures and the vibrant vitality of the soil and water of the desert.

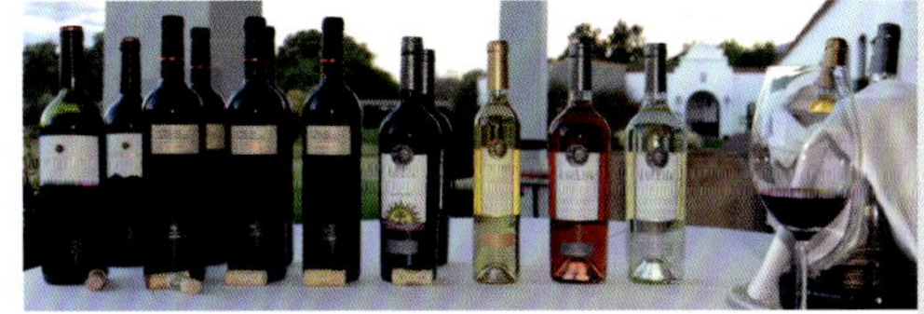

Vineyards (Viñedos) • Winery (Bodega)

BODEGA EL ESTECO de Cafayate

On Ruta 40, at Ruta 68 Intersection
(North Edge of Downtown **Cafayate,** Salta)

011 (+54 115) 198.8000
reservas@ElEsteco.com

ElEsteco.com

English & Español
13,000,000 bottles produced annually

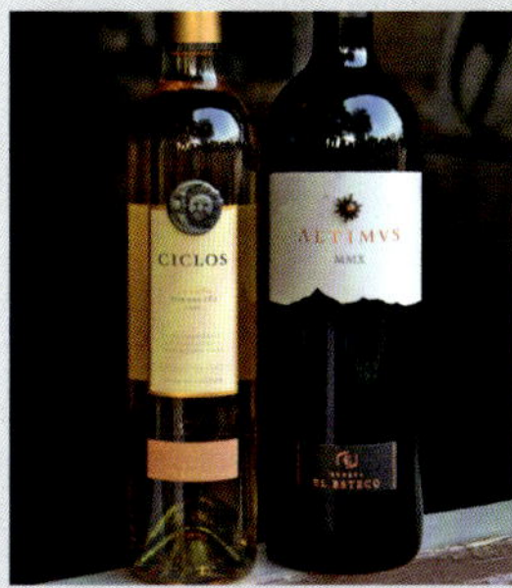

Michael's Favorite Pick
Tardío Torrontés (late harvest) & Altimus XXM

Total Collection of Wines

Serie Fincas Notables
Malbec • Cabernet Sauvignon • Tannat
(very limited production, only available at the winery)

Altimus MMX (2010)
54% Malbec, 25% Cab Sauv, 11% Cabernet Franc, 10% Tannat

El Esteco Chañar Punco
Grapes Grown Exclusively Above 7,800' Elevation

El Esteco
Malbec • Cabernet Sauvignon

Ciclos & Ciclos Sparklings
Icono • Malbec • Cabernet Sauvignon • Torrontés
Tardío Torrontés • Cabernet Sauvignon Blanc • Malbec Rosé
Sparklings: Torrontés Semi Seco • Rosé • Extra Brut

Don David Reserve
Malbec • Cabernet Sauvignon • Tannat
Syrah • Bonarda • Torrontés • Chardonnay

Amaru
Malbec • Cabernet Sauvignon
Torrontés • Torrontés Rosé

To get El Esteco wines in the USA
Contact their Importers at FrederickWildman.com

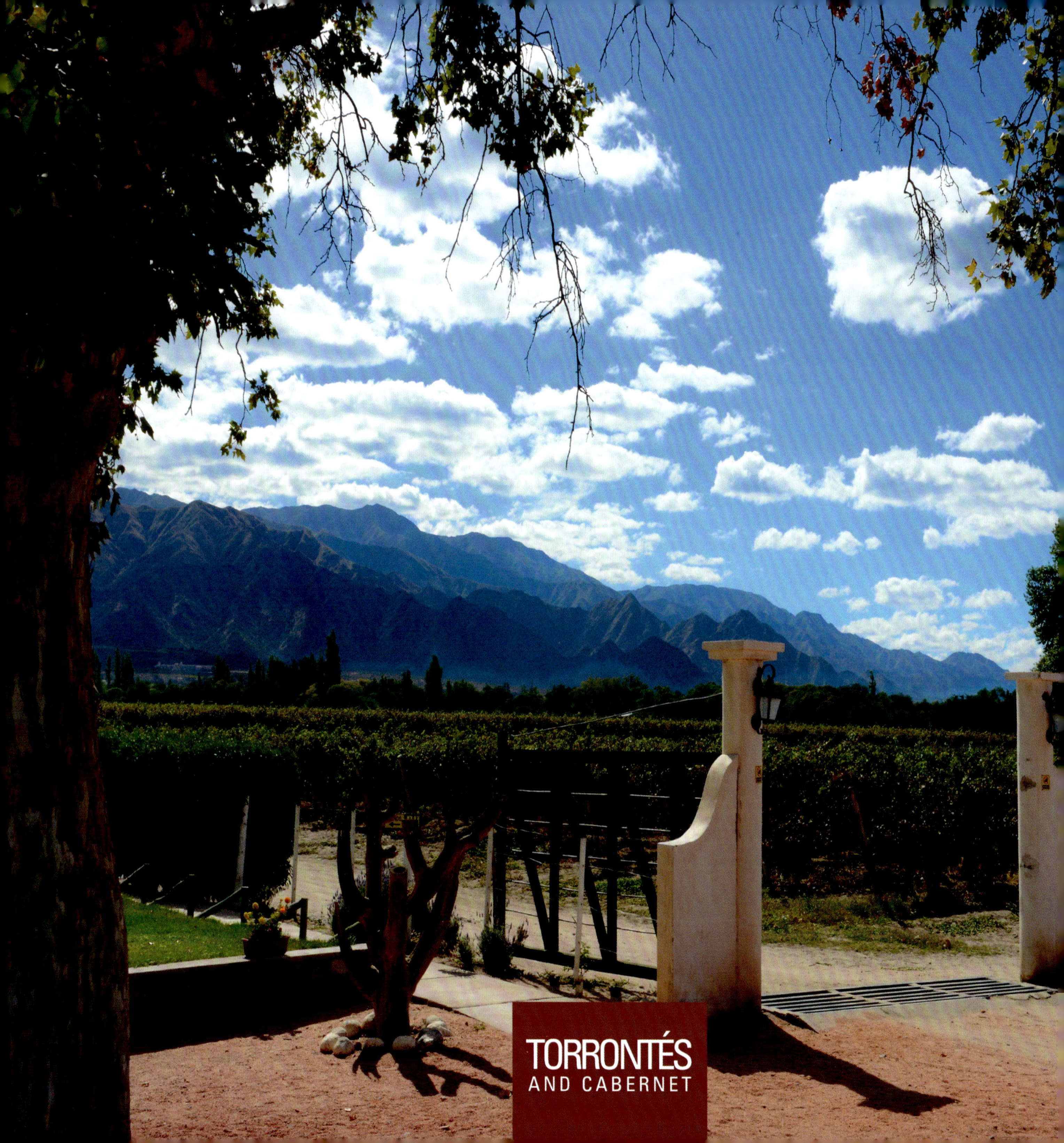

TORRONTÉS AND CABERNET

THE ORIGINS OF CAFAYATE WINE

Vasija Secreta Winery is right across the street (Ruta 40) from El Esteco Winery at the entrance to the town of Cafayate. They claim to be the oldest winery in the Calchaquí Valley, dating back to 1857. In these early days, wine was stored and sold in big clay mud vase-like jars, hence the name Vasija Secreta translated is *Secret Vase*.

Their vineyards here have an extra special terroir to grow the grapes... as their vines were planted between the Esteco Stream and Chusha River. Mesopotamia is a Greek concept of planting on land between rivers, and here Vasija Secreta benefits from both the dry sunny desert environment blended with underground humidity greater than the rest of the valley, giving them different soil and vine behavior to their advantage.

Their Torrontés vines have a higher solar exposure from their location on high slopes, whereas their Cabernet Sauvignon vineyards flow along sediment-rich lowlands with mean temperatures.

With such origins dating back to the last mid-century, Vasija Secreta has been the tradition of Salta inhabitants. Initially they focused on Torrontés and Cabernet Sauvignon, and have since expanded to include other varietals.

THE PETIT WINE MUSEUM

The current owners of the winery, the Córdova-Murga family, are very proud of the history of their wines and property. They have restored the old adobe-walled and mud-cake-roofed buildings, and saved numerous original winemaking equipment which gave birth to the winemaking industry in Salta.

With more than 300 historical pieces, Vasija Secreta opened the Petit Wine Museum as an educational and cultural place at the winery. See agricultural and industrial machinery equipment with some craft elements, restored oak and carob barrels in complete cooperages, plus personal belongings and information from the old owners who did so much to contribute to the social and cultural work of the region... elements of history of those who fought under most adverse conditions, their sacrifice could not be ignored.

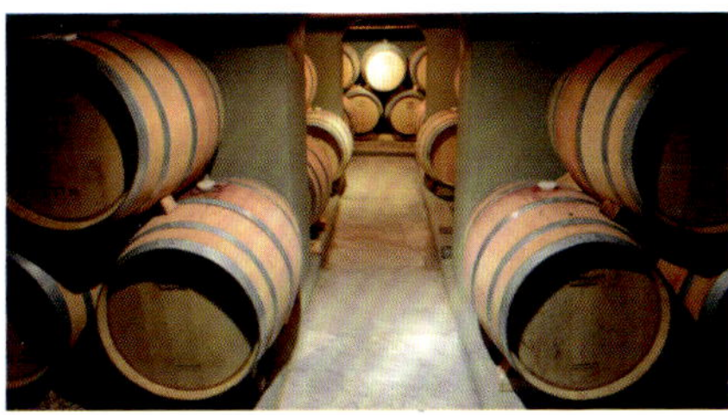

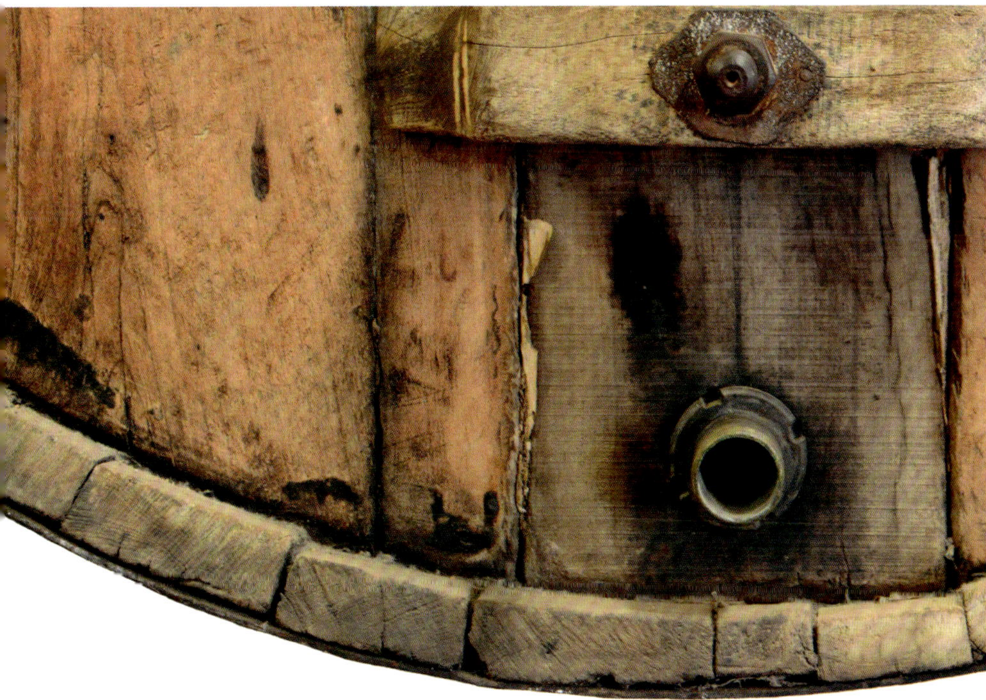

SALTA **CAFAYATE**

Winery (Bodega)

VASIJA SECRETA

On Ruta 40, at Ruta 68 Intersection
(North Edge of Downtown **Cafayate,** Salta)

011 (+54 386) 842.1850
turismo@VasijaSecreta.com

VasijaSecreta.com

English & Español
800,000 bottles produced annually

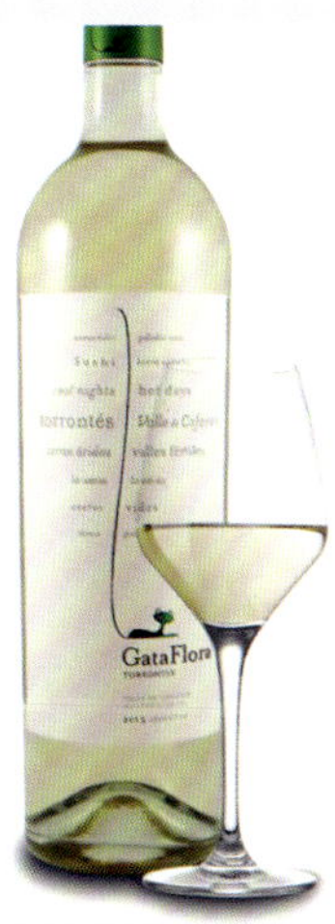

Michael's Favorite Pick
Gata Flora Torrontés

Total Collection of Wines

Vasija Secreta
Torrontés • Cabernet Sauvignon

Lacrados
Torrontés • Malbec • Cabernet Sauvignon

Gata Flora
Torrontés • Malbec
Cabernet Sauvignon • Pink (Rosé) • Tannat

VAS Reserva
Torrontés • Malbec • Cabernet Sauvignon

To get Vasija Secreta wines in the USA
Contact Importer: PedrosWineCollection.com

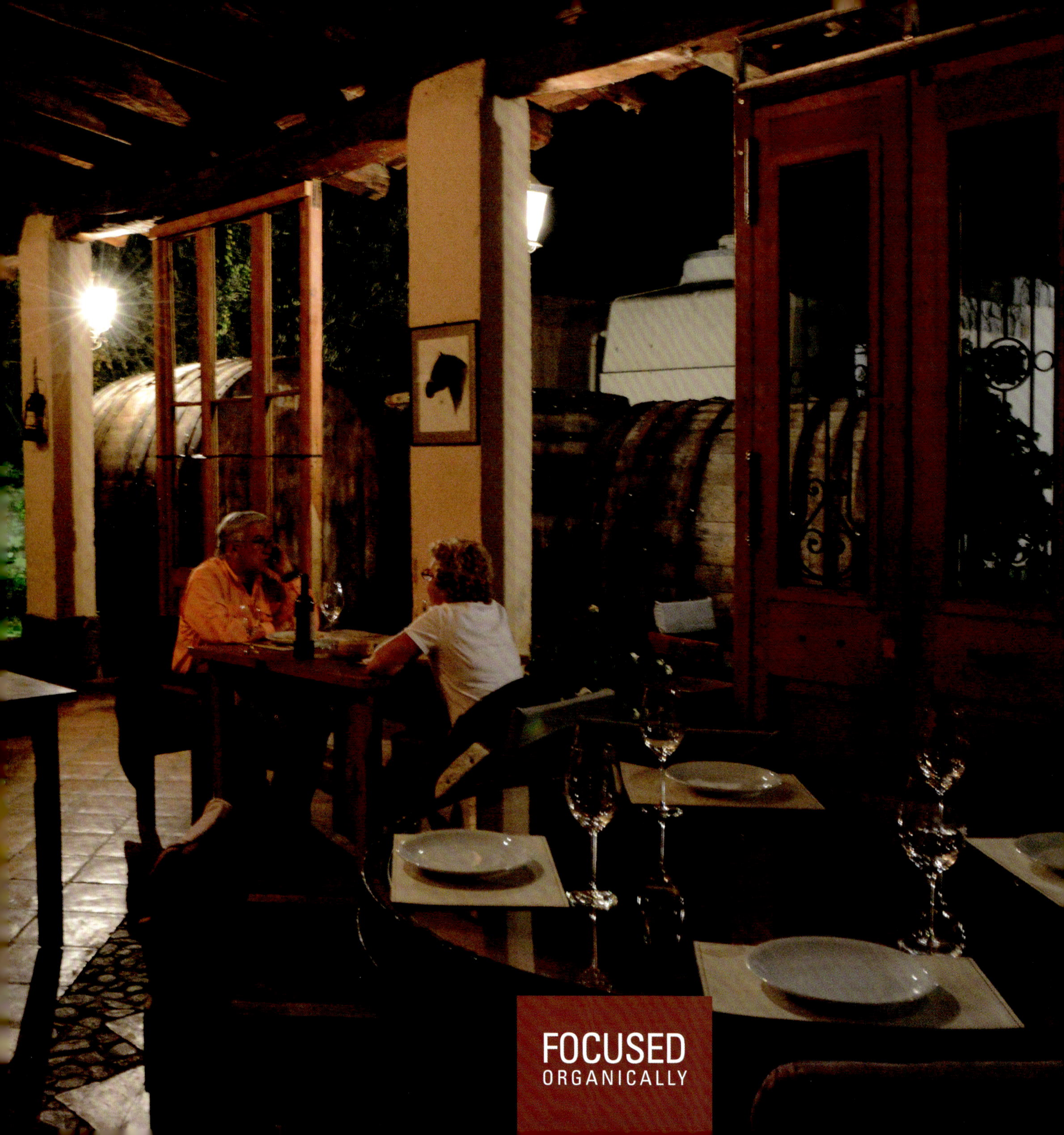

FOCUSED
ORGANICALLY

GOURMET FOOD & WINE PAIRING

Bodega Nanni is a special experience in food and wine culture. Just a block and a half off the central square, Nanni opens into a central courtyard park setting with a unique gourmet restaurant.

Three great-grandchildren run this fourth generation business, and while one brother José Eduardo went to college to study enology and business management, the other brother Juan Pablo only pretended to study winemaking to make his father happy. In truth, he was secretly in culinary school. After graduating as a chef, he advised his father that he was now ready to open the winery's gourmet restaurant. Add to this, their sister Jimena created Nanni as a tourism destination incorporating both her brother's talents.

This is where you want to be for lunch or dinner. Truly gourmet, and the wines are excellently paired. The wines are also used in his cuisine... Malbec reduction sauce over the grilled steak, and Torrontés flan with Torrontés grapes (photos below).

Their wines are fresh and fruit-forward in their taste, no oak. A tradition passed down from their father, who says: "*If I wanted to taste wood, I would chew on a tree*." And their fruit is very fresh and healthy, organic from the beginning in 1897, and now **Certified Fully Organic**. They have always been convinced that taking care of the environment and using the most natural methods provides them with healthier top-quality grapes.

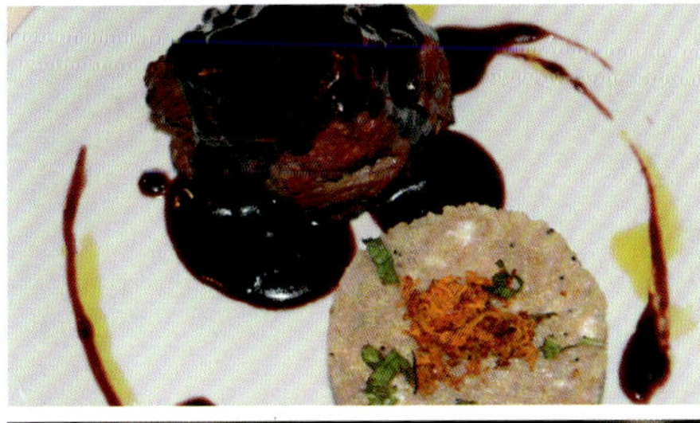

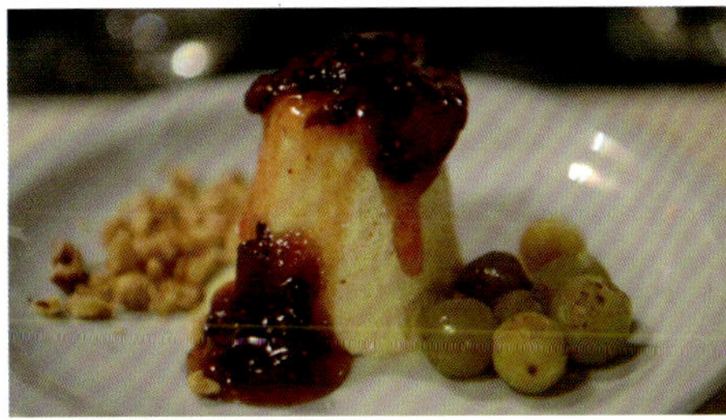

Their farm is outside the city and across the valley in an isolated area of high winds and extreme temperatures (105°F day, 40°F night). This is a fully biodynamic environment derived from their ecological management system that fosters and heightens the ecosystem health and soil fertility, allowing the powerful laws of nature to increase the yield and resistance of crops. The result is rich healthy fruit flavors in their wines that are also unmasked by oak or other external elements.

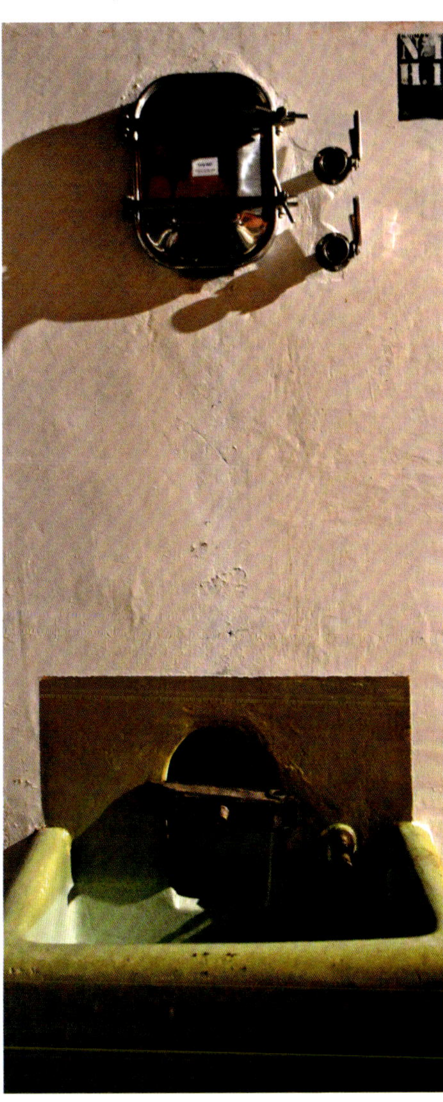

Winery (Bodega) • Restaurant

BODEGA NANNI

151 Silverio Chavarría (one block east of square)
(Center of Downtown **Cafayate,** Salta)

011 (+54 386) 842.1527
info@BodegaNanni.com.ar

BodegaNanni.com

English & Español
35,000 bottles produced annually

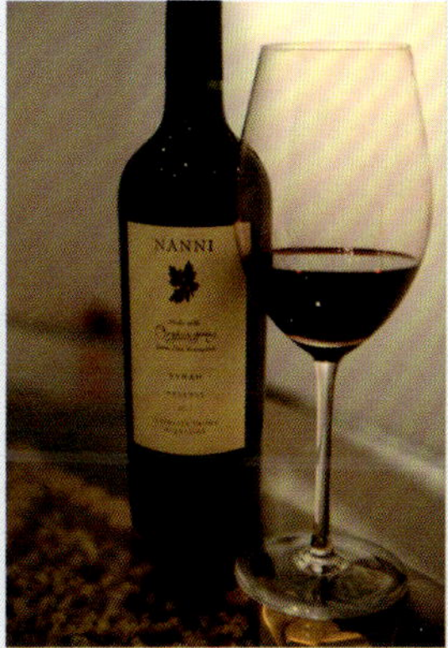

Michael's Favorite Pick
Nanni Syrah Reserve
(limited production, available only at the winery)

Total Collection of Wines

Linea Gran Reserva
Arcanus (secret blend of Tannat and Malbec)

Linea Reserva (ages in oak)
Malbec • Tannat • Syrah
Cabernet Malbec • Bonarda

Linea Joven (young, no oak)
Malbec • Cabernet Sauvignon • Tannat
Torrontés • Rosado (Cabernet Sauvignon Rosé)
Torrontés Tardío (late harvest)

To get Nanni wines in the USA
Contact their Importer: VinosArgentinos.us

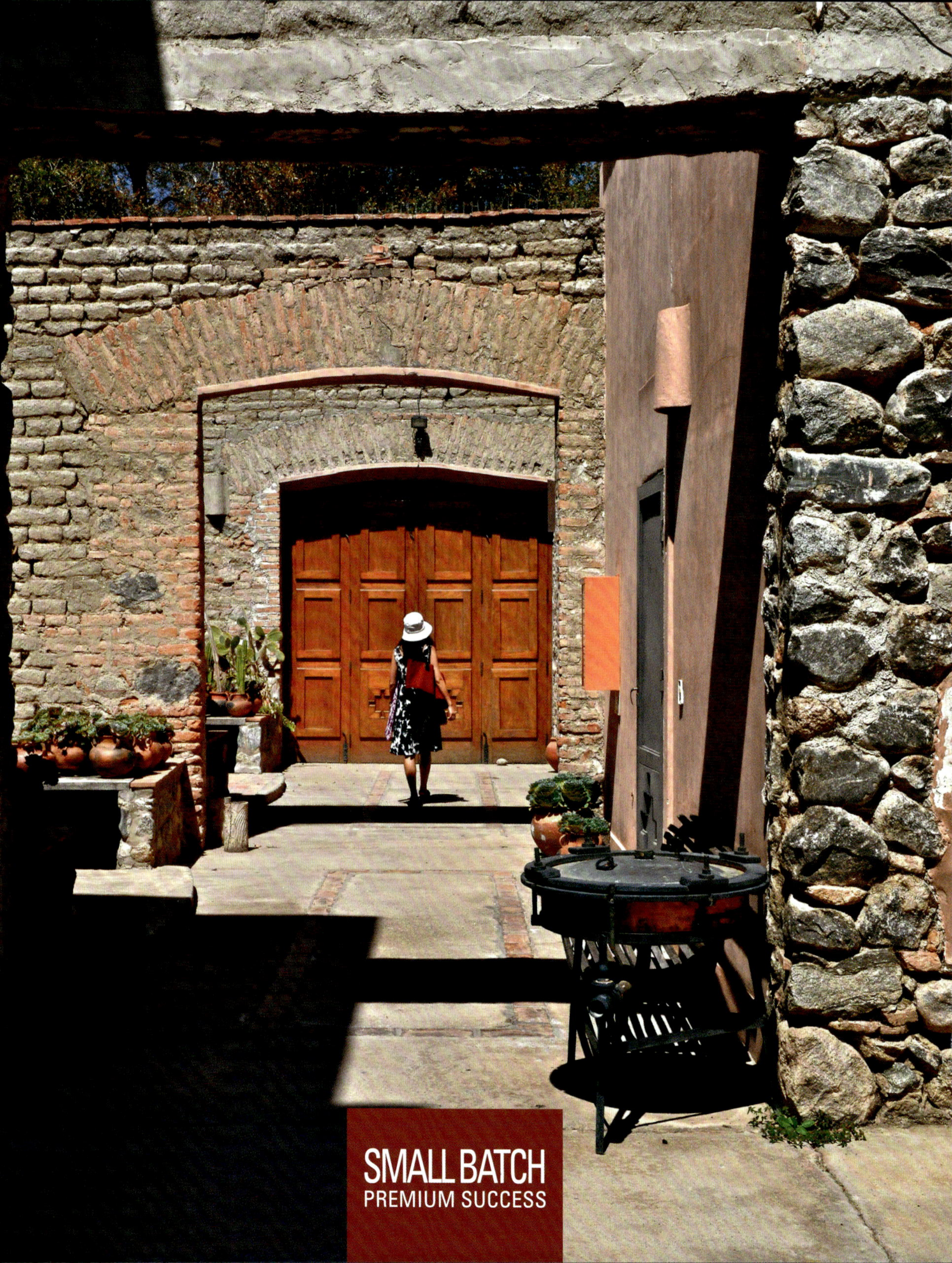
SMALL BATCH
PREMIUM SUCCESS

INGENUITY OF A NEW OLD WINERY

This is a special winery to explore. It is now run by grandaughter Lucía Romero who has a new direction for the family business. After growing up in this wine family, playing in the vineyards as a child and studying at the Bordeaux Business School for her Wine MBA... Lucía has designed a new premium winery for small batch wines of very high quality. Not surprising the new name of the winery would be El Porvenir, meaning *the future*.

With this premium wine objective, she acquired an old winery in downtown Cafayate (two blocks from the square) and, while she brought it up to date with the latest of technology (photo below), she also restored the beauty of the architecture and artifacts of the era past (photo left page).

At the same time, she successfully restored the family's 60-year-old vineyards of Torrontés (photo right) and Tannat. In 2010, Lucía engaged the expertise of **Paul Hobbs**, the notable authority of how to achieve super-premium wines in Argentina.

In love with this terroir, Lucia added Malbec, Cabernet Sauvignon, Merlot, Petit Verdot, Syrah, and Chardonnay to her new vineyards.

As the future would hold, I had the opportunity to be one of the first to taste the next bottling of El Porvenir, their top-of-the-line blend of at least four varietals from the best of their vineyards. Unlabeled (photo far right), and rich with black fruits on the nose followed by big intense flavors, sweet tannins and a very long desirable finish.

Also, you must experience their Torrontés fermented in oak barrels. An exciting twist in a land of extraordinary Torrontés. Fermented with selected yeast for 25 days in new oak French barrels, plus eight more months aging in new French oak.

The ingenuity continues with their harvesting of the Torrontés. First harvest is for the nose to gain floral, citrus and freshness. Then a second harvest for the mouth to obtain tropical and honey flavors.

All wonderful palette surprises worth exploring.

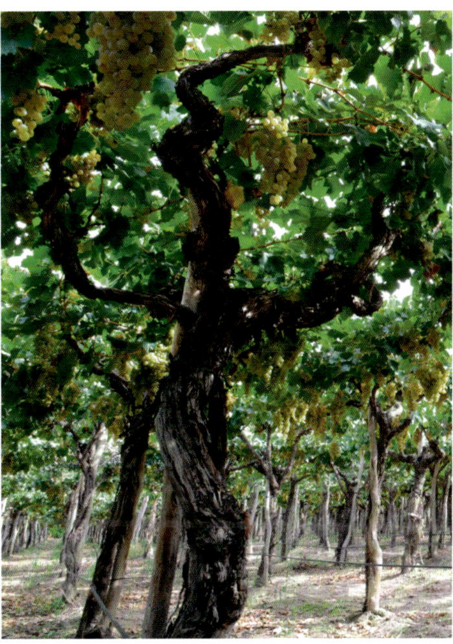

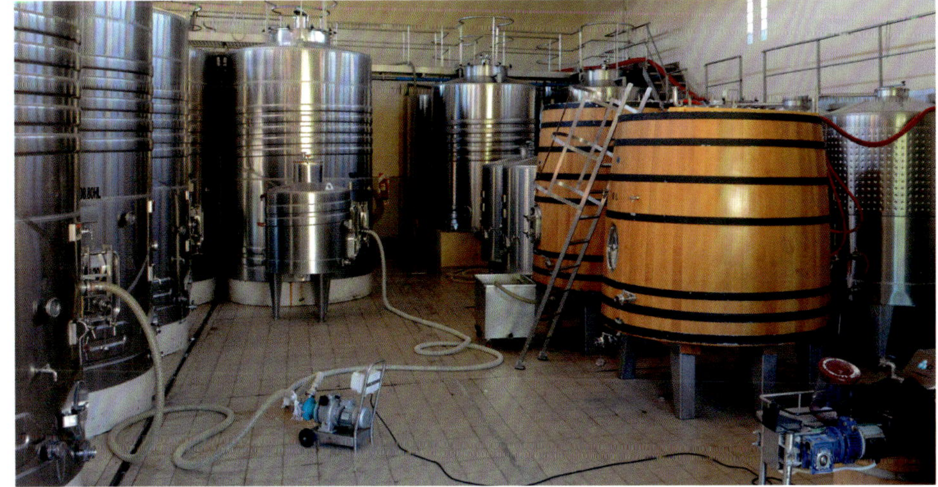

SALTA **CAFAYATE**

Winery (Bodega)

EL PORVENIR DE CAFAYATE

32 Córdoba (two blocks north of the square)
(Center of Downtown **Cafayate,** Salta)

011 (+54 386) 842.2007
Adriana@ElPorvenirDeCafayate.com

ElPorvenirDeCafayate.com

English & Español
250,000 bottles produced annually

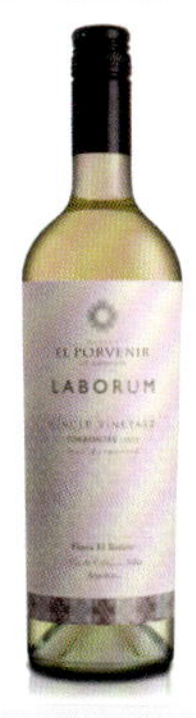

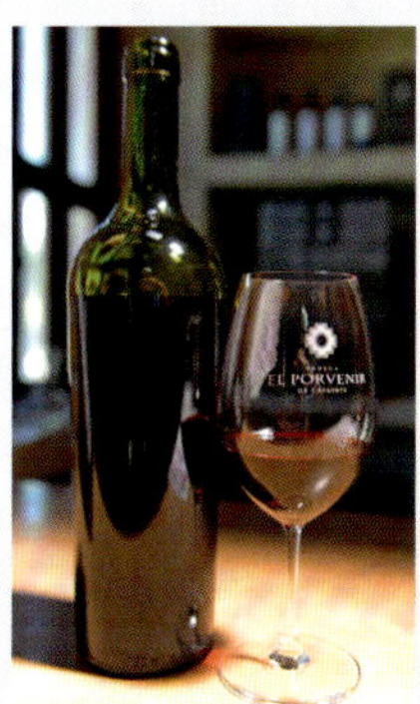

Michael's Favorite Pick
Laborum Torrontés Oak Fermented

Total Collection of Wines

El Porvenir (aged luxury)
(Malbec, Cabernet Sauvignon, Tannat, Syrah, Petit Verdot)

Laborum (single vineyard)
Torrontés • Torrontés de Otoño
Torrontés Oak Fermented • Chardonnay
Malbec • Malbec Tardío • Rosado de Malbec
Cabernet Sauvignon • Tannat • Syrah

Amauta Corte (blends)
Corte I - Inspiration (Malbec, Cabernet Sauvignon Syrah)
Corte II - Respect (Cabernet Sauvignon, Merlot)
Corte III - Reflection (Malbec, Cabernet Sauvignon)
Corte IV - Innovation (Malbec, Tannat, Petit Verdot)

Amauta Absoluto (varietal)
Malbec • Tannat • Torrontés

To get El Porvenir wines in the USA
Contact their Importers at PaulHobbsImports.com

SALTA **CAFAYATE**

Museum of Vine and Wine

MUSEO DE LA VID Y EL VINO

201 Güemes Ave Sur (Ruta 40)
(two blocks south of the square)
(Center of Downtown **Cafayate,** Salta)

011 (+54 386) 842.2322
info@MuseoDeLaVidYElVino.gov.ar

MuseoDeLaVidYElVino.gov.ar

English, Español, Français & Português

The Museum of Vine and Wine
An Interactive Education

This is a museum like no other...
It is not a museum of artifacts
(although they do have many historical pieces).
This is a museum that uses modern technology to present the past and present of grape growing and winemaking.

Displays are interactive.
Evolutionary and time progressive.
Transcending seasons.
Landscapes go from day to night in minutes.

Sun, Water, Earth, Men
Day & Night
High Elevations

A Virtual Guide (10 inches tall)
follows you through the museum.
Magically appearing at strategic points
and guides you through the journey.

Wine Itself Tells The Story
An interesting film ends the museum journey...
Where wine itself tell its own
story about its life on earth.

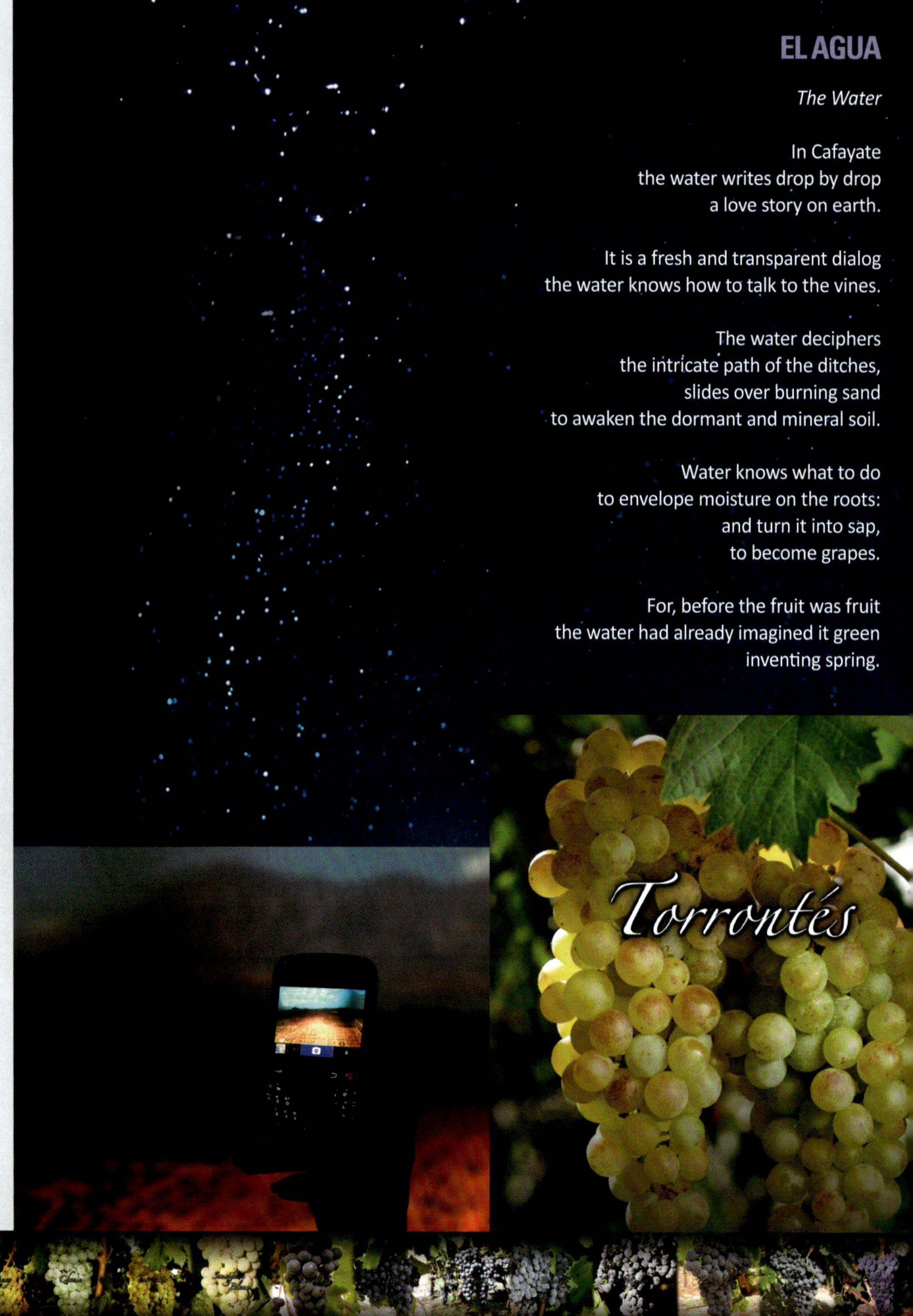

Restaurant

TERRUÑO GASTRONOMÍA GOURMET

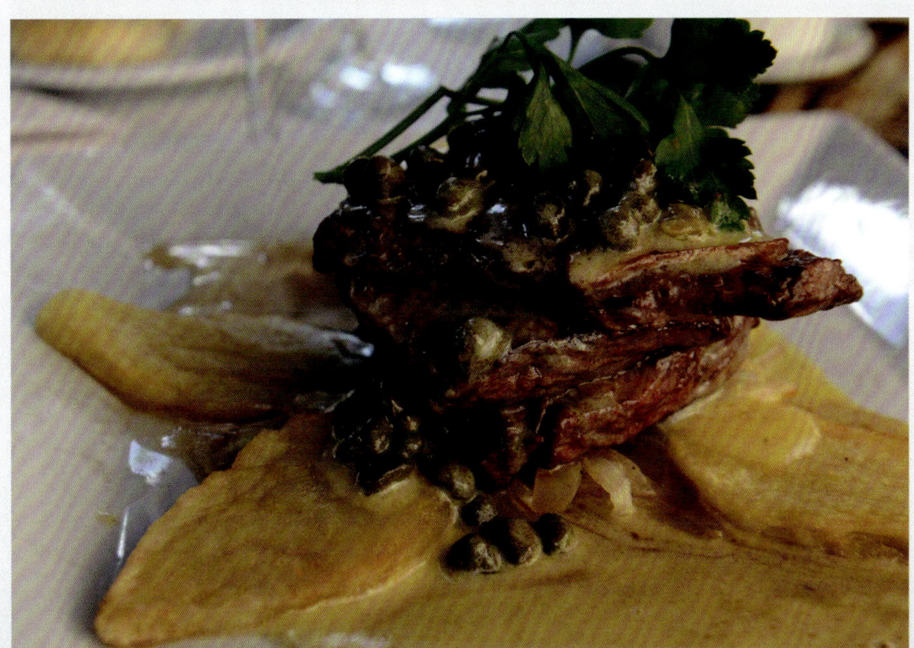

28 So Guemes Ave (Ruta 40) (on the Square)
(Center of Downtown **Cafayate,** Salta)

011 (+54 386) 842.2460

Terruno.TodoWebSalta.com.ar

English, Español & Português

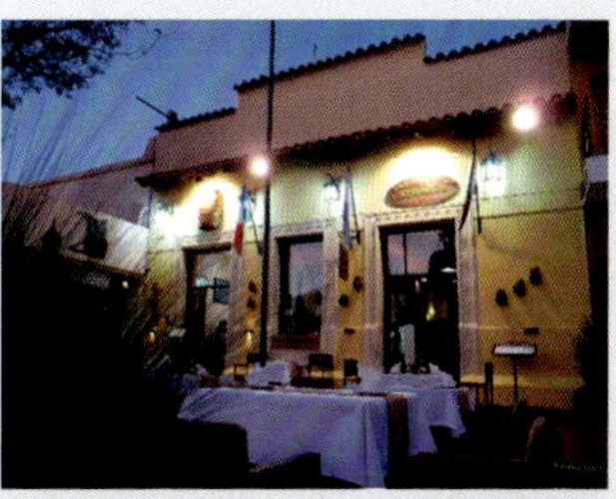

Hard to imagine you would find a gourmet restaurant in the middle of this small village of Cafayate.

Enjoy a truly gourmet treat by Chef Carlos Manuel Amante in a very special location... right on the central square overlooking the park of Cafayate.

Outdoor dining in a beautiful atmosphere of live plants and flowers and restored architecture.

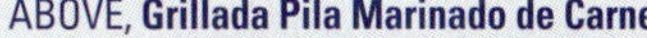

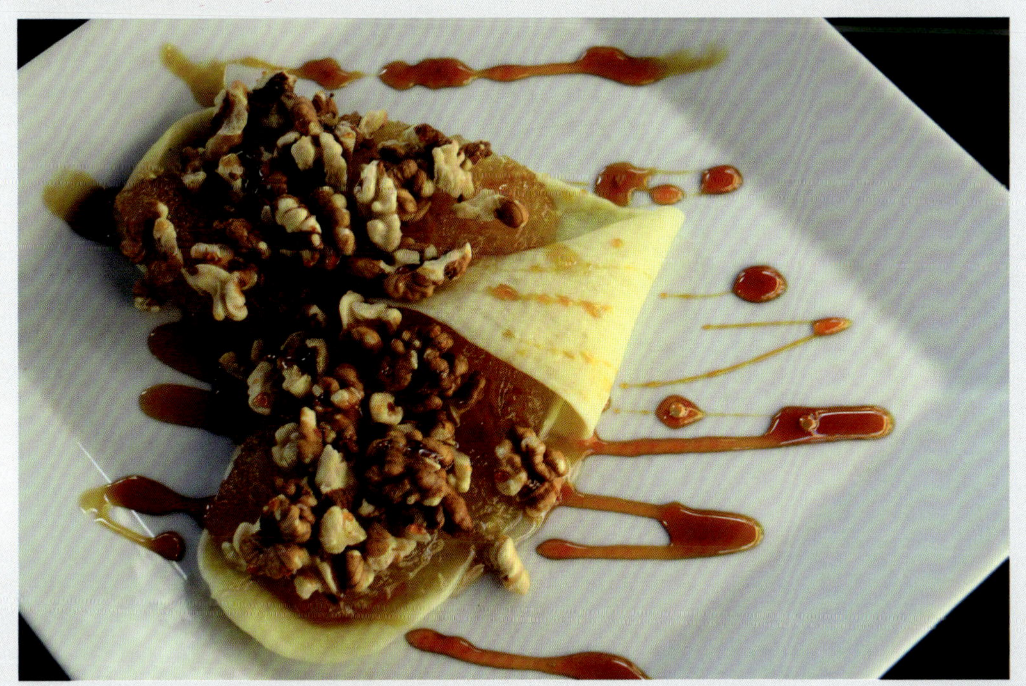

ABOVE, **Grillada Pila Marinado de Carne**
Grilled sirloin marinated in Torrontés wine and honey gravy, served with grilled potatoes and onions, topped with peas sauteed with vinegar.

BELOW, **Milhojas de Quesillo**
Cheese strudel confection of thin pastry, covered with puree of mango sauce, topped with diced pineapples and walnuts, rolled into a special dessert of love (heart).

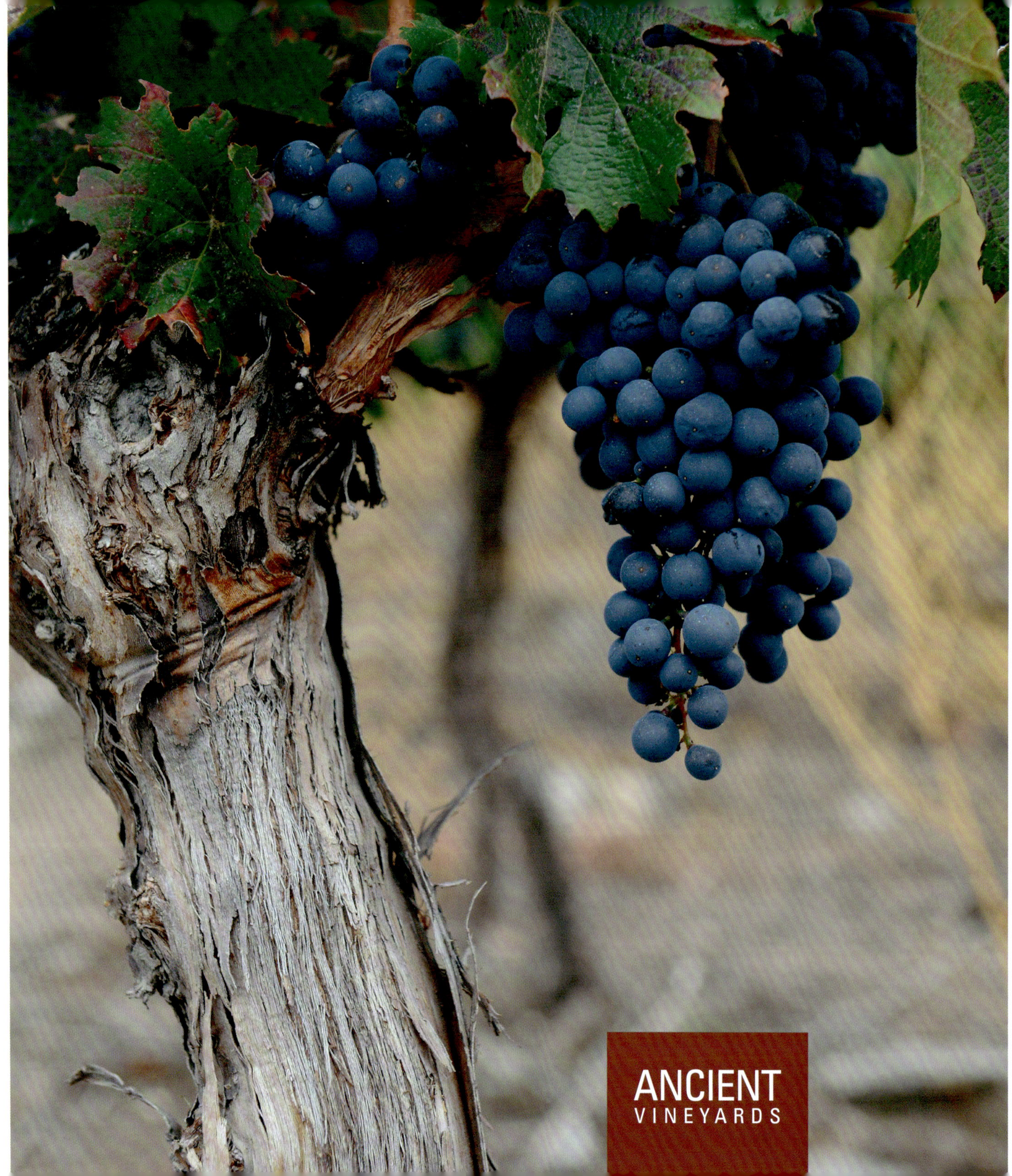
ANCIENT
VINEYARDS

BIG, FULL-BODY TORRONTÉS

With 60-year-old vines, the Yacochuya wines are of a unique flavor worth your attention. A lot less liar I would say about the Torrontés, not faking you out on the sweet floral fruit nose upfront. On the mouth, it is bigger, very full-bodied... a red wine drinker's white wine!

San Pedro de Yacochuya is quite focused in their winemaking. Only three wines, and very distinct. A Torrontés, a Malbec and a Blend (Malbec and Cabernet Sauvignon). All from ancient vines in this mountainside terroir of 6,700' elevations on the westward slopes of the Calchaquí Valley northwest of the town of Cafayate. Some vineyards exceed 100 years old, as you can see behind Yacochuya owner Marcos Etchart standing in front of his treasured vineyard in the photo below.

Etchart is very careful not to let his ancient vines become extinct. If a vine is ready to retire its livelihood, a new trunk is formed and the old vine cut, saving the history of the root structure which continues to feed the depths of its history to the new berries (see photo top right).

In 1988 the Etcharts coerced the notable French master-winemaker **Michel Rolland** to come to Argentina to make magic from these ancient vines. Just two years later, Etchart and Rolland released one of the very first premium wines of Argentina, *Etchart Cosecha*, with Rolland himself featured on the cover of Wine Spectator magazine.

Not exactly easy to find; however, worth the adventure of the four-mile drive, on a windy dirt road, up from the valley. On Ruta 40, make your first left turn (onto a dirt road) after the Ruta 68 intersection, one mile north of Cafayate.

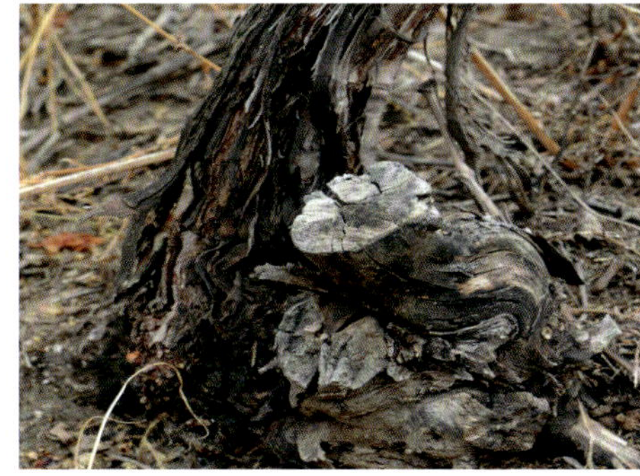

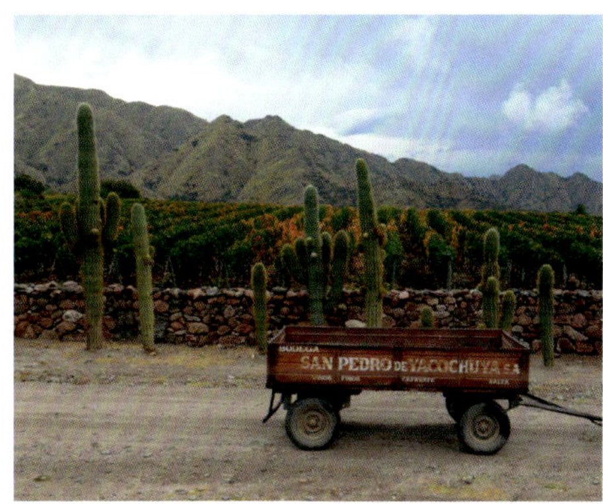

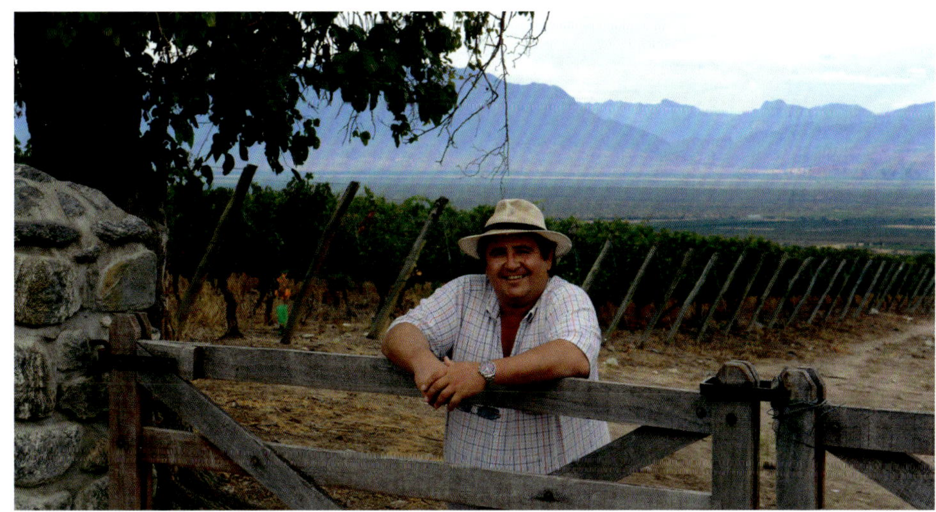

SALTA **CAFAYATE** YACOCHUYA

Winery (Bodega)

SAN PEDRO DE YACOCHUYA

Ruta 2, km 6 (6 km on Ruta 2 from Ruta 40)
(8 km North of **Cafayate,** Salta)

011 (+54 387) 431.9439
info@SanPedroDeYacochuya.com.ar

SanPedroDeYacochuya.com.ar

English & Español
200,000 bottles produced annually

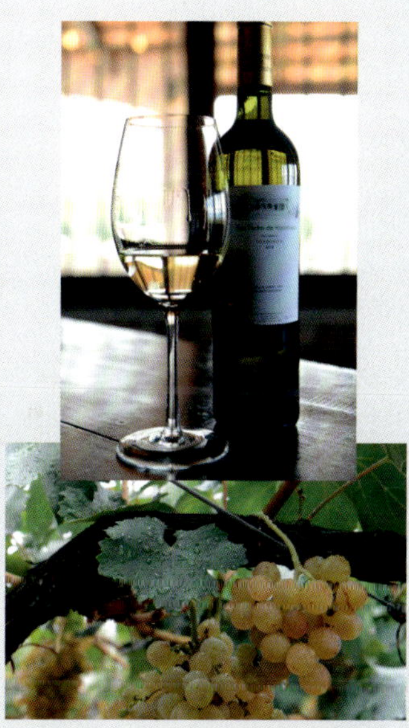

Michael's Favorite Pick
Yacochuya Torrontés

Total Collection of Wines

Yacochuya Red Wine
(85% Malbec • 15% Cabernet Sauvignon)

Yacochuya Malbec

Yacochuya Torrontés

To get Yacochuya wines in the USA
Contact their Importers at VineConnections.com

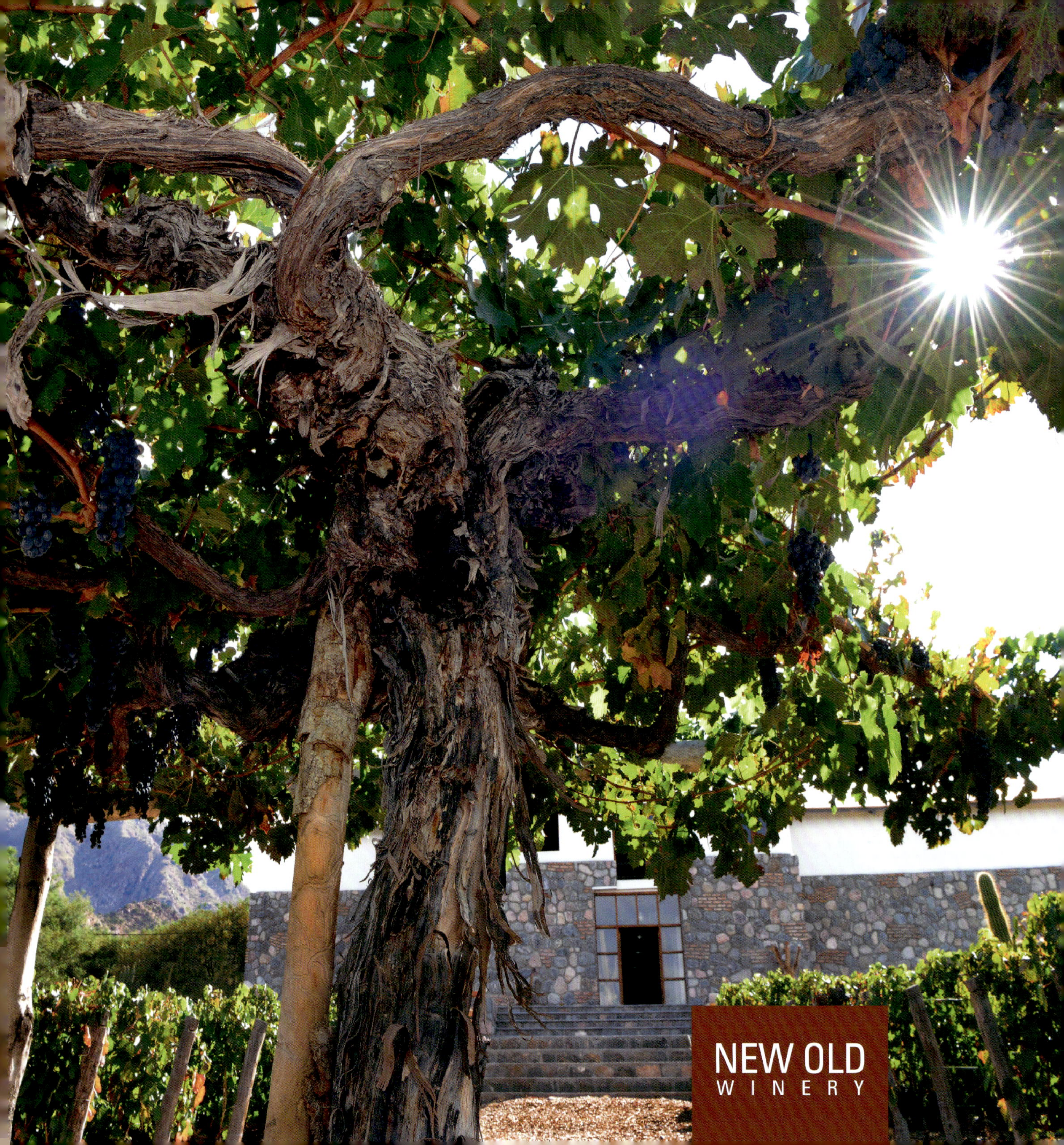
NEW OLD
WINERY

WHY NOT TANNAT ?

When you begin exploring Cafayate, you will come across Tannat, a rare French varietal now growing in South America, and unique to the Calchaquí Valley in Argentina. Originally from the Basque Region (a region that straddles parts of north-central Spain and southwestern France), Tannat was initially brought to Uruguay and is now considered their national grape.

Tannat is a full-bodied red wine grape. My first reaction to tastings of Tannat was, so what. It had no special characteristics, just big, bold and red. If I want big red wine, I would choose Malbec or Cabernet Sauvignon, because these two wines have unique and delicious flavors.

When Domingo Molina winemaker Rafael Domingo heard of my sour opinion of Tannat, he became eager for me to try his Tannat and change my perception forever. And so he did! The 2013 Domingo Molina Tannat is extraordinary. It had fruit of ripe blackberries, softer tannins, and less bitterness. Still big, yet velvety. Now I was tasting a flavor profile I could desire, again and again.

The Domingo Molina Tannat is grown in a very special terrior at 7,400' elevation 30 miles north of Cafayate and 10 miles west of the tiny village of San Carlos, in Rupestre Valley. In the middle of nowhere, this property looks like another planet (see photo next page) and it might as well be with its clay and rock soils, and rock formations of something similar to the Planet of the Apes.

Rafael's brother Osvaldo Domingo is the agronomist who cares for their vineyards. Finca Cafayate for Torrontés, Finca Yacochuya for Malbec and Cabernet Sauvignon, and Finca Rupestre for Malbec, Cabernet Sauvignon and Tannat.

This is the second generation of the Domingo family winemaking business. Rafael and Osvaldo's father Palo Domingo started Domingo Hermanos winery in downtown Cafayate in 1977 to produce volume wines, in three- and five-liter bottles. Palo had a vision though, for the future of high-quality wines. This is why the Finca Rupestre property was purchased and with Palo's crazy and stubborn conviction, vines were planted and nurtured into a whole new profile of grapes.

In 2000, the Domingo Molina winery was built on their Yacochuya property with the latest of winemaking technology to produce super-premium wines (photos below and left page).

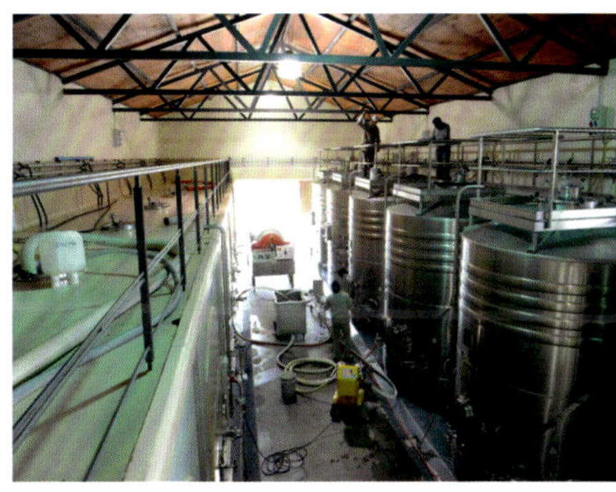

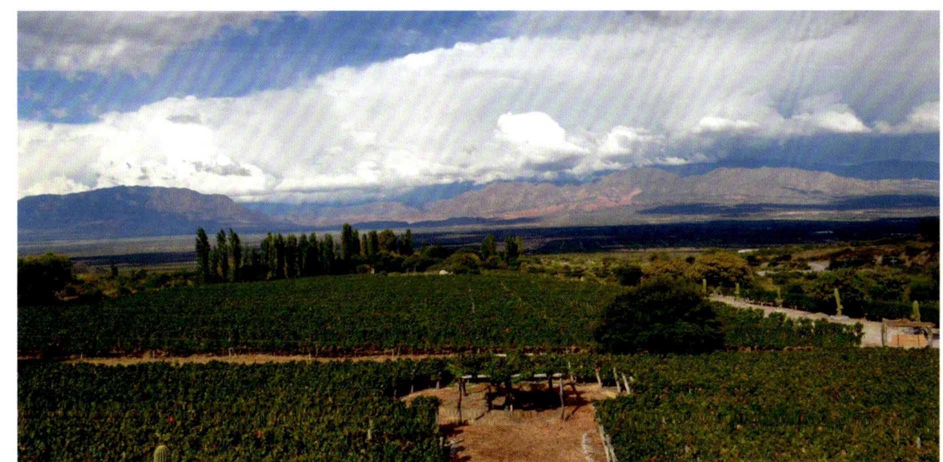

SALTA **CAFAYATE** YACOCHUYA

Winery (Bodega)

DOMINGO MOLINO

Ruta 2, km 6 (6 km on Ruta 2 from Ruta 40)
(8 km North of **Cafayate,** Salta)

011 (+54 9 386) 845.2887
info@DomingoMolina.com.ar

DomingoMolina.com.ar

English & Español
200,000 bottles produced annually

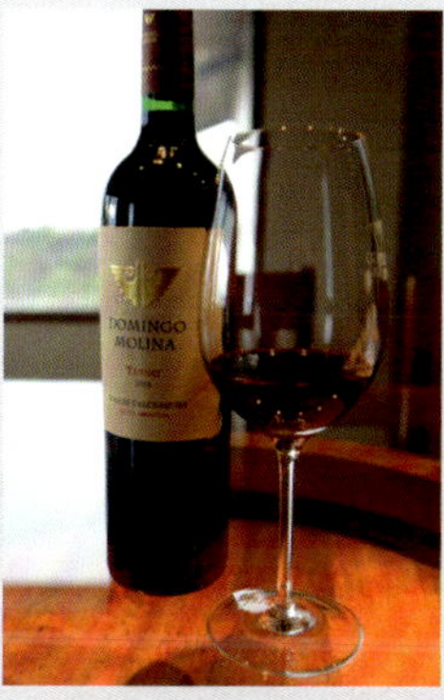

Michael's Favorite Pick
Domingo Molina Tannat

Total Collection of Wines

Palo Domingo Vino Tinto
(80% Malbec • 20% Cabernet Sauvignon)

Rupestre Blend
(80% Malbec • 10% Merlot • 10% Tannat)

Domingo Molina (their big wines)
Tannat
Malbec
Torrontés
Cabernet Sauvignon

Finca Domingo (young wines)
Malbec
Cabernet Sauvignon
Torrontés
Torrontés Dulce Natural

To get Domingo Molino wines in the USA
Contact their Importers at VineConnections.com

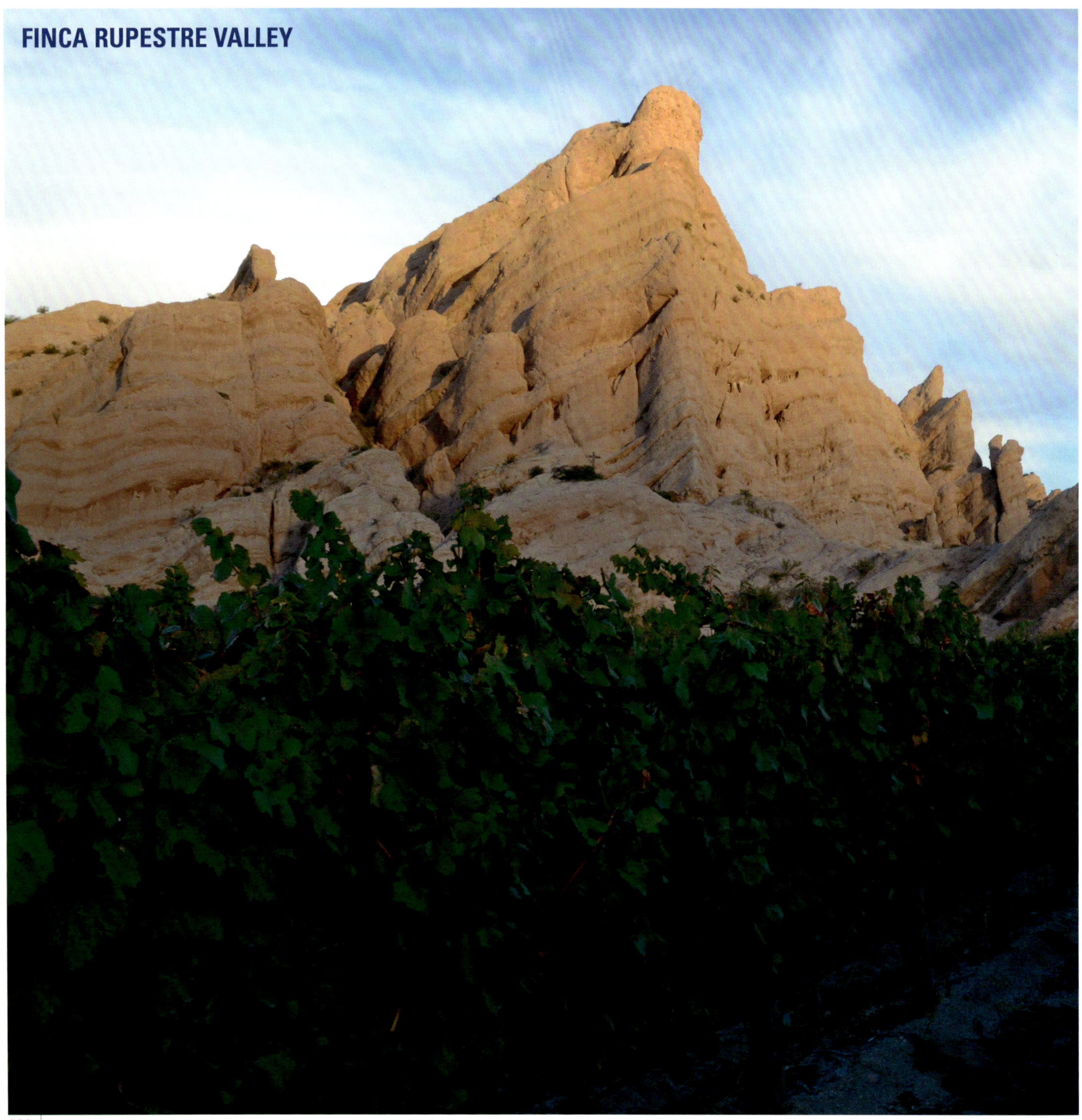
FINCA RUPESTRE VALLEY

Finca Rupestre is a magical place. Its barren silence is stunning in its peaceful senses. Arid, for the water harvested from the mountains. Green vineyards contrast against a backdrop of soft hues and gentle sounds of the whispering winds. The environment of this 7,400′ mountainous desert is an oasis for the taste of sensational fruit cultivated from this terroir.

Finca Rupestre is not just for the spectacular Tannat, in which I was transformed earlier, Domingo Molina produces a Malbec from this estate, **Finca Domingo Malbec**, which is also notable.

Creativity is very much a part of this new winery's premium packaging. The **Palo Domingo Vino Tinto** has a thick leather-branded label and is packaged in a hand-made burlap satchel (photo bottom right).

Among their three properties, the new winery of Domingo Molina in Yacochuya Norte is where they receive visitors, have tours of the winery and vineyards, and tastings of their various wines.

Not exactly easy to find; however, worth the adventure of the four-mile drive, on a windy dirt road, up from the valley. One mile north of Cafayate on Ruta 40, make your first left turn after the Ruta 68 intersection (onto Ruta 2, a dirt road). Proceed four miles on Ruta 2 to the winery.

SALTA **CAFAYATE** YACOCHUYA

Vineyards (Viñedos)

DOMINGO MOLINO

Ruta 2, km 6 (6 km on Ruta 2 from Ruta 40)
(8 km North of **Cafayate,** Salta)

011 (+54 386) 842.1225
info@DomingoMolina.com.ar

DomingoMolina.com.ar

English & Español
200,000 bottles produced annually

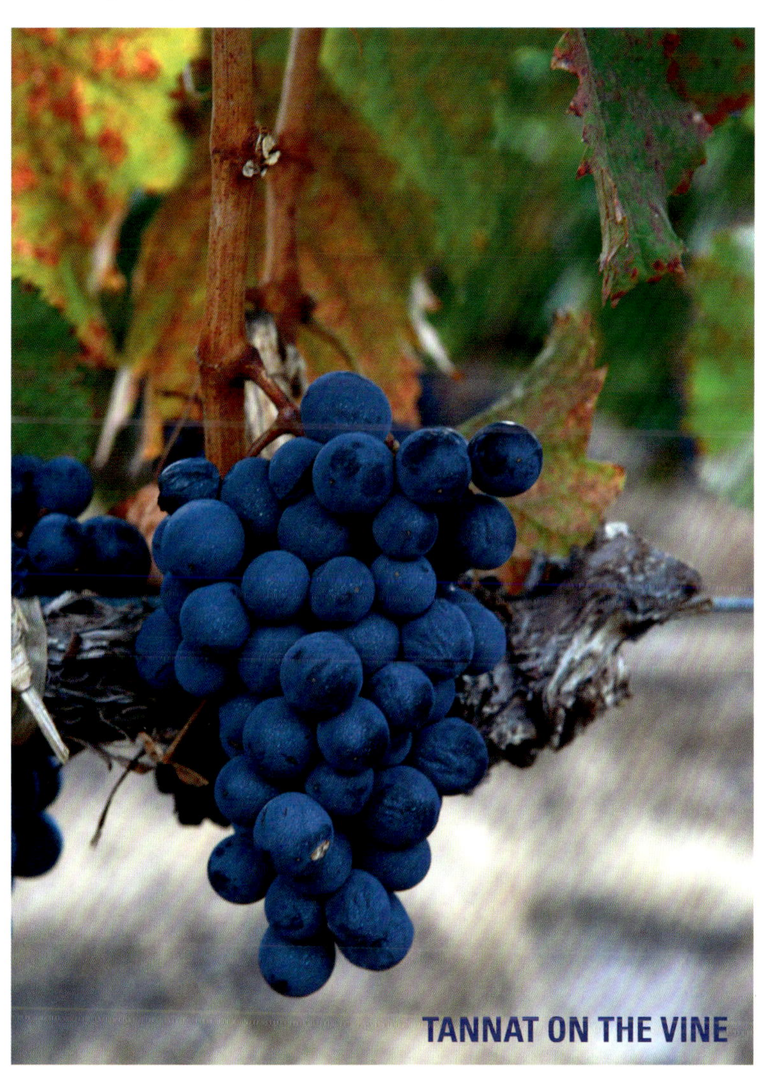

TANNAT ON THE VINE

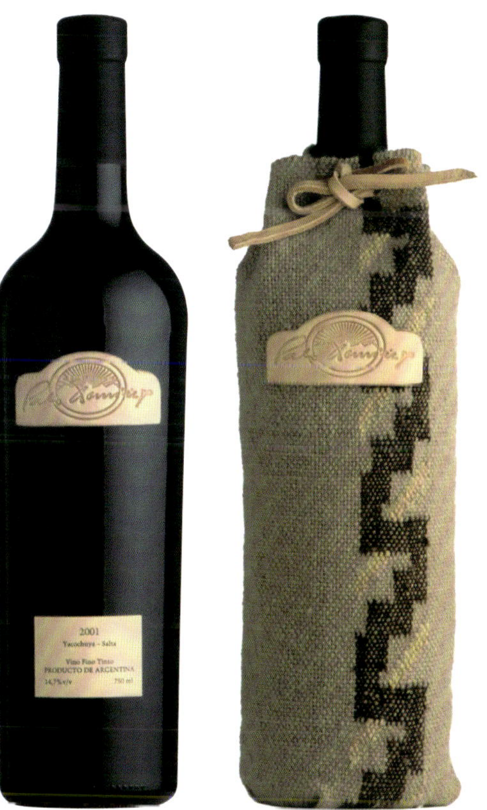

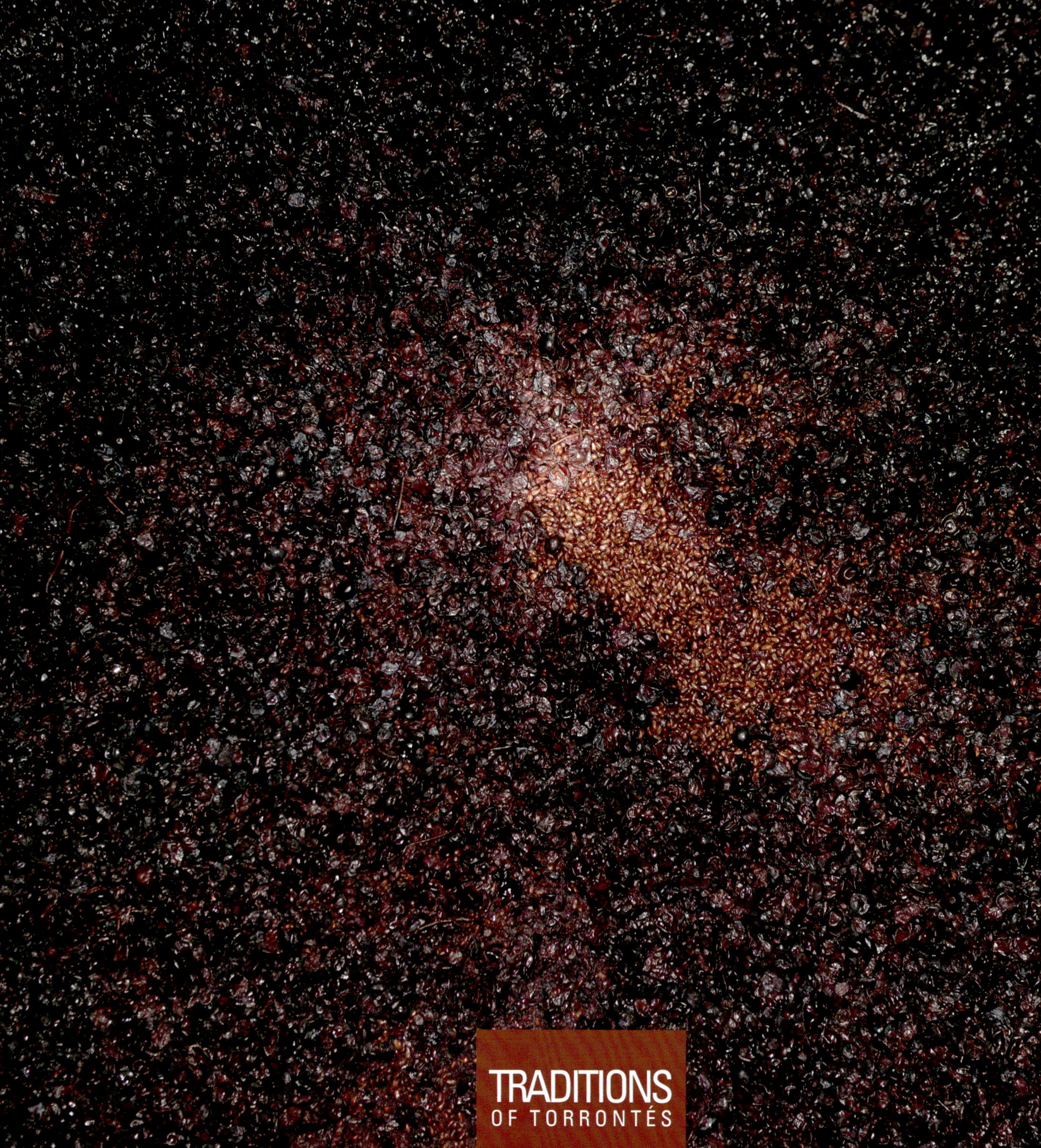
TRADITIONS
OF TORRONTÉS

THE KINGDOM OF TUKMA

As it all began, nearly 2,000 years ago, with the *Diaguita Tribes* inhabiting this land and mastered very sophisticated farming techniques which started the cultivation of this area. Later, the *Inca Empire* invaded and took over this farming community, improving upon its agricultural opportunities. When the *Spaniards* showed up in the 16th century with grape vines, they adopted the ancient agricultural traditions to care for the vineyards.

This region was known as *Tukmanao* in the native language, and their ruler was *Chief Tukma*. It is unknown when the village of Tolombón was founded, however, the Incas conquered it in 1480 and the Conquistadors invaded again in 1535. Today, Tolombón feels authentic of a place that has not changed with the passing of time. Currently 255 people live in this little village of Tolombón.

Tukma Winery adopted the chief's name in honor of the land and the artisanal manner in which they craft their super-premium wines. Tukma Winery also embraces Argentina's native varietal Torrontés, by hiring winemaker José Luis Mounier, the expert in this varietal and known as *Mr. Torrontés* by his colleagues.

Born in Argentina, José is a fourth generation winemaker. His great-grandfather was a noted winemaker in Cognac, France. His degree is in enology from Mendoza, and his experience includes Bodegas Etchart (San Pedro de Yacochuya) where he worked with Michel Rolland, including studying vinification with Michel in Pomeral, France.

Tours of the winery can be arranged though Tukma's *Casa de Vinos Boutique Hotel* (next page) where they can also set up tastings at the hotel with delicious pairings. The winery is just two miles south of the hotel and shares the same ownership.

This is a great place to explore Torrontés as they make three different styles of Torrontés... Gran Torrontés, Torrontés Reserva and Torrontés Tardío (late harvest). Plus, the gourmet foods at Casa de Vinos can be perfectly paired as you will discover on the next page. The Torrontés Reserva got my attention, wow! It also has the attention of numerous critics, including Robert Parker, as it is winning numerous awards and accolades from this wine.

LEFT PAGE, grapes in vintification, skins floating to the surface and the seeds collecting in the center. LEFT, Jose Luis Mounier inspecting his wine. RIGHT, punching down the skins during barrel fermentation.

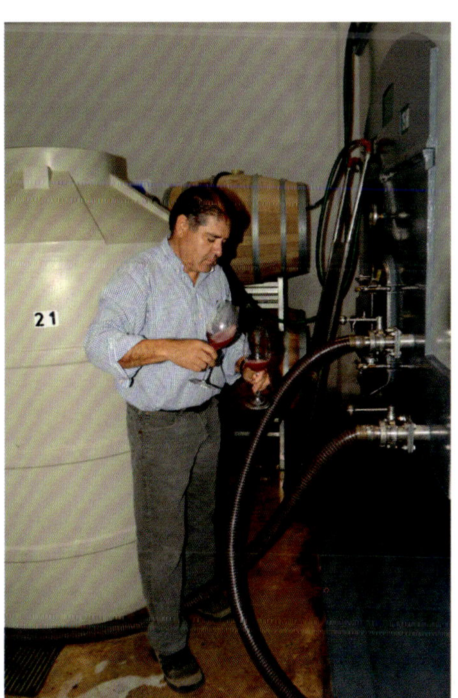

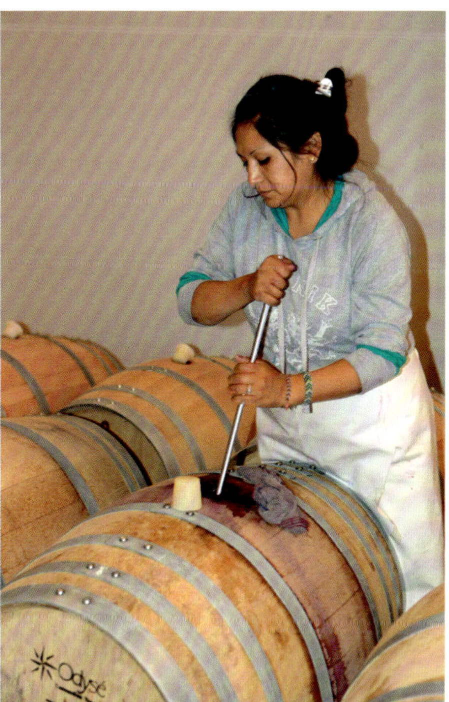

SALTA **CAFAYATE** TOLOMBÓN

Winery (Bodega)

BODEGA TUKMA

Ruta 40 km 4324 (4324 mile-marker on Ruta 40)
(**Tolombón** [11 miles South of Cafayate], Salta)

011 (+54 387) 461.0283
info@Tukma.com

Tukma.com

English & Español
100,000 bottles produced annually

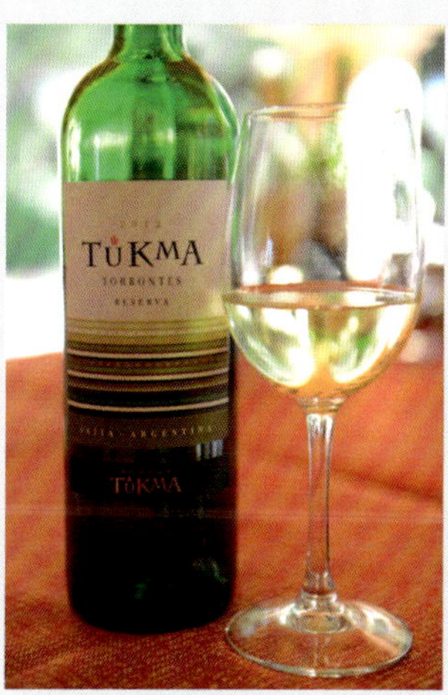

Michael's Favorite Pick
Tukma Torrontés Reserva

Total Collection of Wines

Tukma Wines

Gran Corte (Malbec, Tannat, Cabernet Sauvignon)
Gran Torrontés • Torrontés Reserva • Torrontés Tardío
Altura 2670 (Sauvignon, Blanc at 2670 meters)
Malbec Reserva • Cabernet Sauvignon Reserva
Rosé (Malbec, Cabernet Sauvignon)

Finca Las Nubes (Mounier's vineyards)

Blend (Cabernet Sauvignon, Malbec)
Malbec • Torrontés • Rosé (Malbec)

To get Tukma wines in the USA
Direct from the Importer: CopaFina.com
at CopaFina.com/**tukma**buywine.html

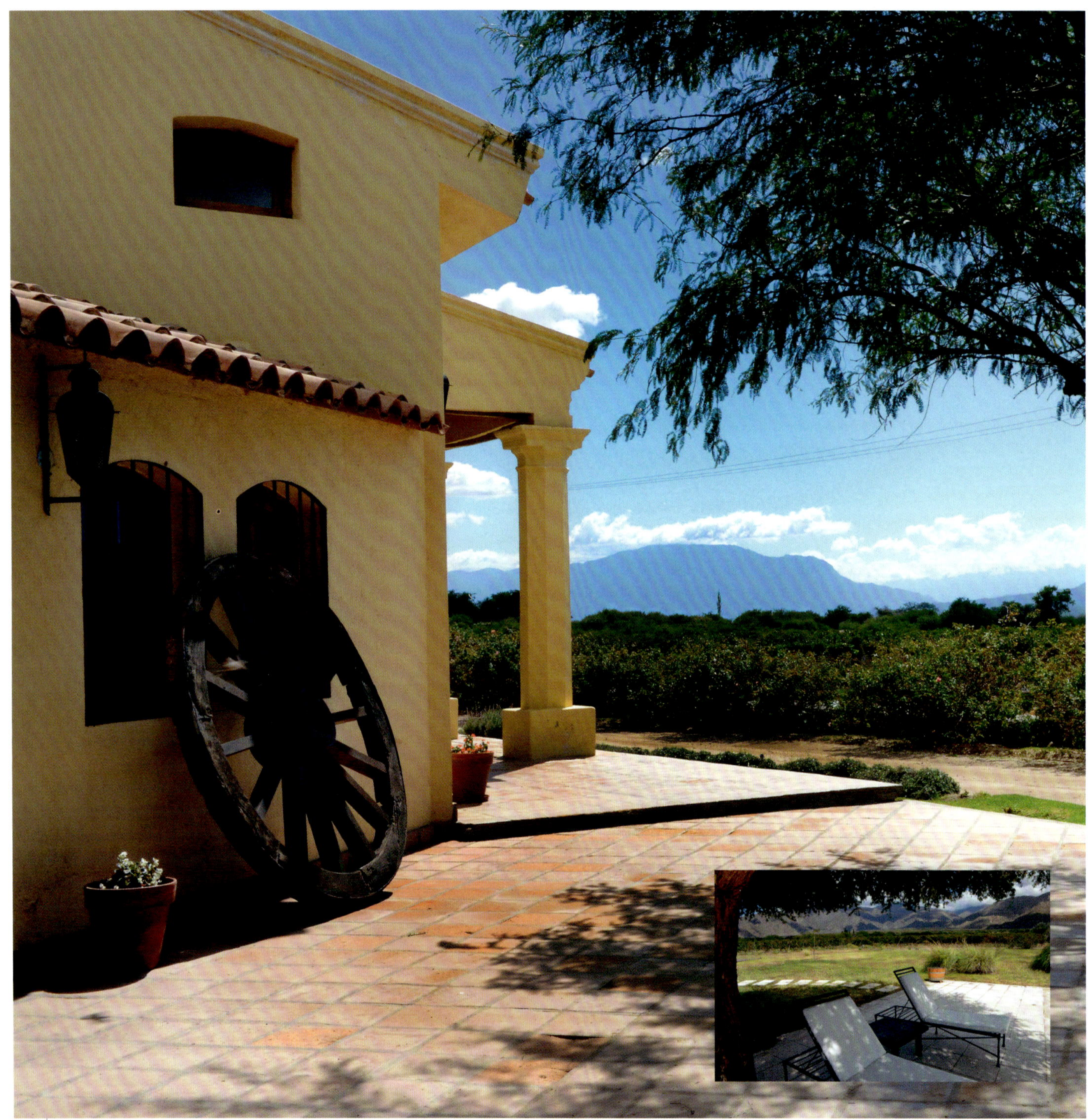

Here you are, in this quaint little village of Tolombón, nine miles south of Cafayate, where is appears that time has stood still for hundreds of years. Now, this is a place to relax. You are literally away from everything. Quiet. Peaceful. Picturesque. Pure clean air. Cloudless skies. And a sky that decorates the night with stars galore!

And, in this oasis is a charming historical manor, *Tukma Casa de Vinos Boutique Hotel & Spa*, built in 1892 and restored to a beautiful relaxing getaway.

Relax pool-side (inset photo left page) gazing at the surrounding vineyards and mountains in the distance. Bar and restaurant service is available. You can borrow their bicycles to explore the area and town, or arrange a tour of their winery *Bodega Tukma* just two miles south of the hotel.

The rooms are large and spacious, with all the amenities of resort hotel.

The property is filed with many large trees for a park-like setting to doze off in the shade, or have a picnic of authentic country-style foods prepared in their kitchen. Of course a bottle of *Tukma Torrontés Reserva* is the best way to spend the afternoon.

A gourmet chef is on premises to offer you an incredible gastronomic journey, offering a menu of authentic local foods designed in a gourmet menu. An organic garden on premises supplies the kitchen with seasonal vegetables. The chef can specifically prepare foods for a wine tasting to bring out the best in pairings with Tukma wines.

The Casa de Vinos Spa is a separate building isolated at the back of the property to relax, unwind and enjoy the unobstructed views across vineyards into the surrounding hills.

They have wet and dry saunas, Scottish showers (photo below), relaxation room, massage rooms and gym. Indulge in a great massage at an even greater price. The spa offers a wide variety of natural juices and salads.

SALTA **VALLE CALCHAQUÍ** TOLOMBÓN

Hotel • Restaurant • Spa

CASA DE VINOS BOUTIQUE HOTEL

Ruta 40 km 4327 (4327 mile-marker on Ruta 40)
(**Tolombón** [9-miles South of Cafayate], Salta)

011 (+54 387) 461.0283
info@Tukma.com

Tukma.com/hotel

English & Español

BELOW LEFT TO RIGHT,

Empanadas Traditcionales Salteñas
Beef and cheese empanadas, a classic stuffed pastry of Salta, served with fresh with salsa criolla.

Sorrentinos de Cabrito, Ricotta y Verduras
A special Argentine style of ravioli filled with roasted baby goat, ricotta cheese and vegetables in creamy bolognese sauce, topped with fresh herbs. Sorrentinos are a unique round sombrero-like shape of ravioli pasta of this classic Argentinian dish.

Locro Altalaluna
A hearty thick stew made of Locro (a specific kind of potato called *papa chola*), and pumpkin, beans, corn, cucurbita (squash), meat, and sausage. A traditional dish of the Andes Mountain region, and one of the national dishes of Argentina, a unique taste difficult to find outside this area.

...all dishes perfectly pair with a Tukma Torrontés.

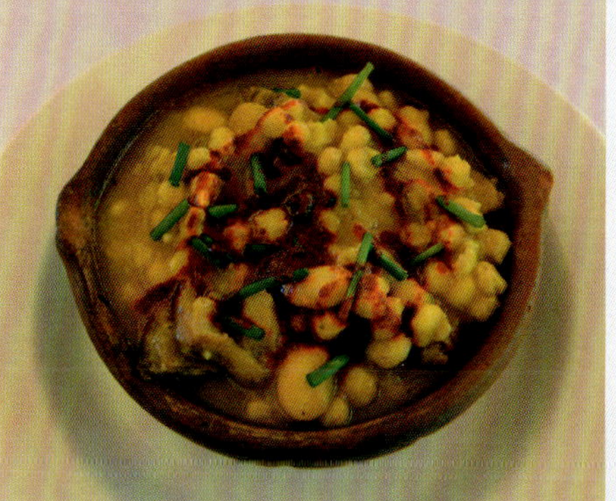

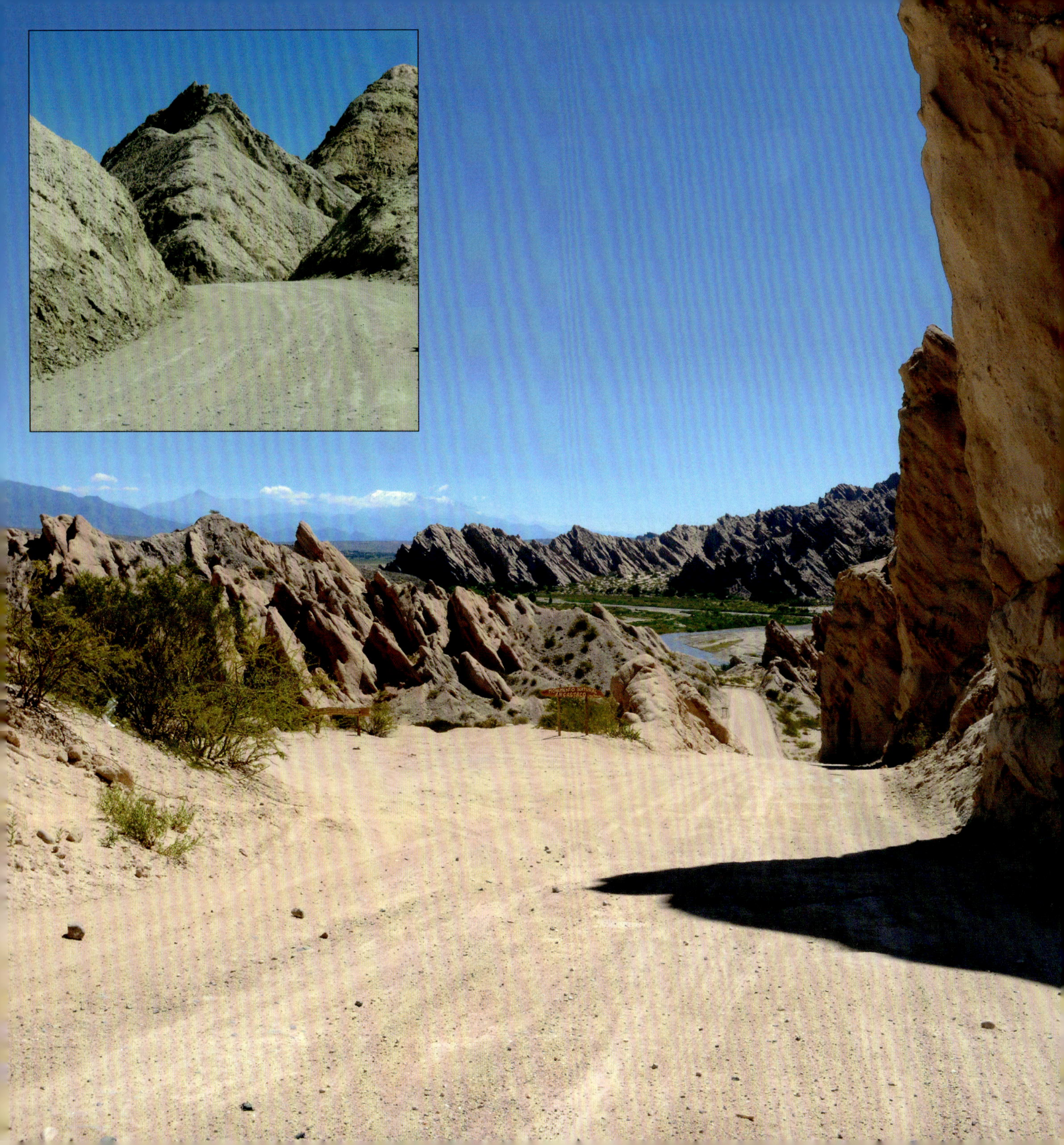
NATURAL
ANGASTACO

SALTA **RUTA 40 - THE ADVENTURE**

*A Wild Adventure Driving Through the Hills between the Towns of **Cafayate** to **Molinos** to **Payogasta***

Departing Cafayate to the north is a wild adventure on **Ruta 40 (RN 40)** as you venture through the Calchaquí Valley to the little village of **Molinos**, the next wine region we will explore. This highway is primarily dirt, sometimes as narrow as the car itself (photo left page) and reaches 16,404' elevation in the very north of the Salta Provence, making Ruta 40 the highest highway in the Americas.

Ruta 40 is also one of the longest highways in the world, and Argentina's main north/south artery stretching 3,107 miles longitudinally along the Andes Mountain Range. It starts at sea level from the very south of Patagonia through small villages, large cities, crossing 20 national parks, 18 major rivers, 27 passes on the Andes, connecting 11 provinces, and goes directly through the wine regions of Patagonia, Mendoza, Salta, and beyond.

Through the Calchaquí Valley, traversing this terrain would best be done in a SUV; however, I did it in a regular economy car. In this northern region, the road winds up the valley along the Calchaquí River (photo below) presenting breathtaking views of the hills and mountains, over plateaus offering spectacular views of the landscape showing the mountains in a multitude of colors with lush green agriculture in the valley floor. The unique scenery will make you feel at times you are on another planet. In this northwest, the beauty of nature equals the cultural richness, since Inca and Kolla traditions are well intact, alive and everlasting in each town and every inhabitant of these highlands.

Mile-markers make navigation easier, as you see in the photo below right, where this one identifies 4,389 kilometers distance from the Patagonia beginning. In the little villages, the roads are paved, and you will enjoy exploring them as a labyrinth to find your way out to the exiting dirt highway.

When you reach **Molinos**, **Ruta 53** will take you on a more adventuresome road down the **Tacuil Valley** to three very unique wineries.

Enjoy the drive, make this a day trip!

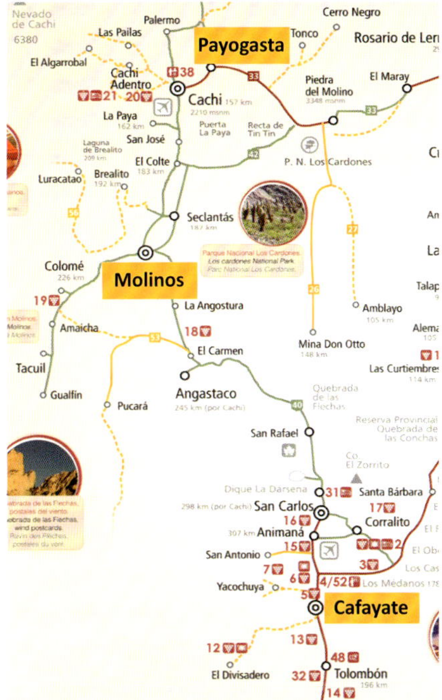

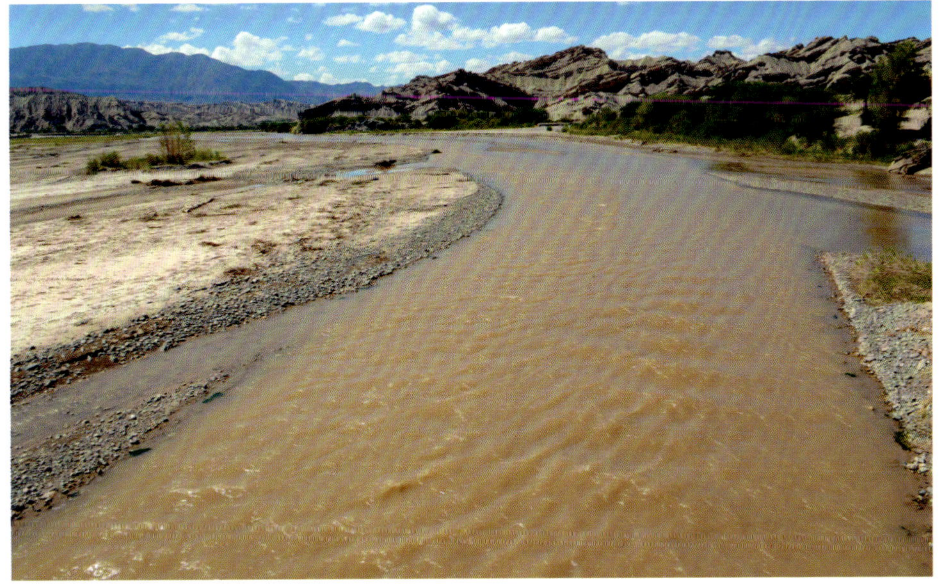

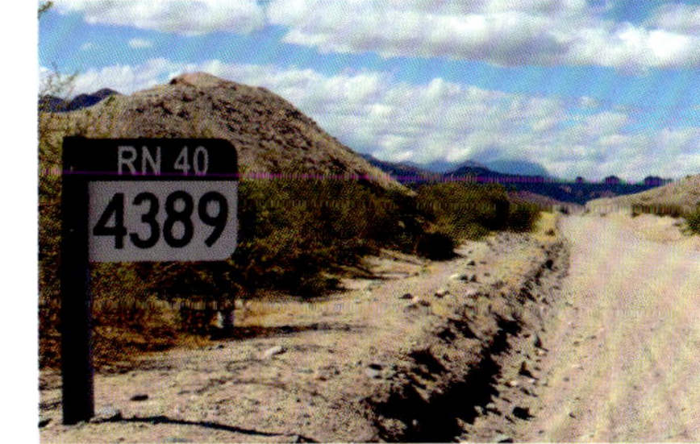

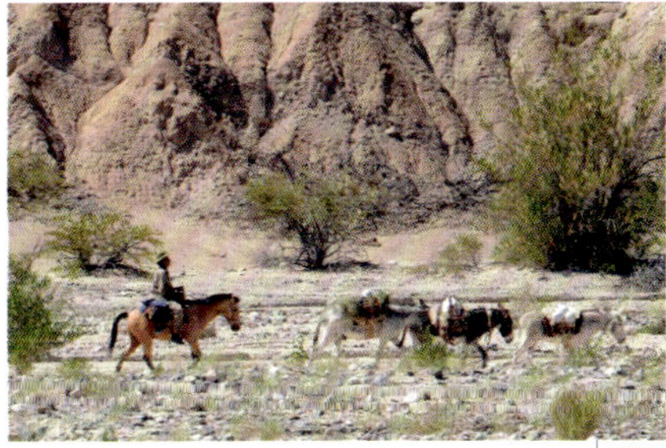

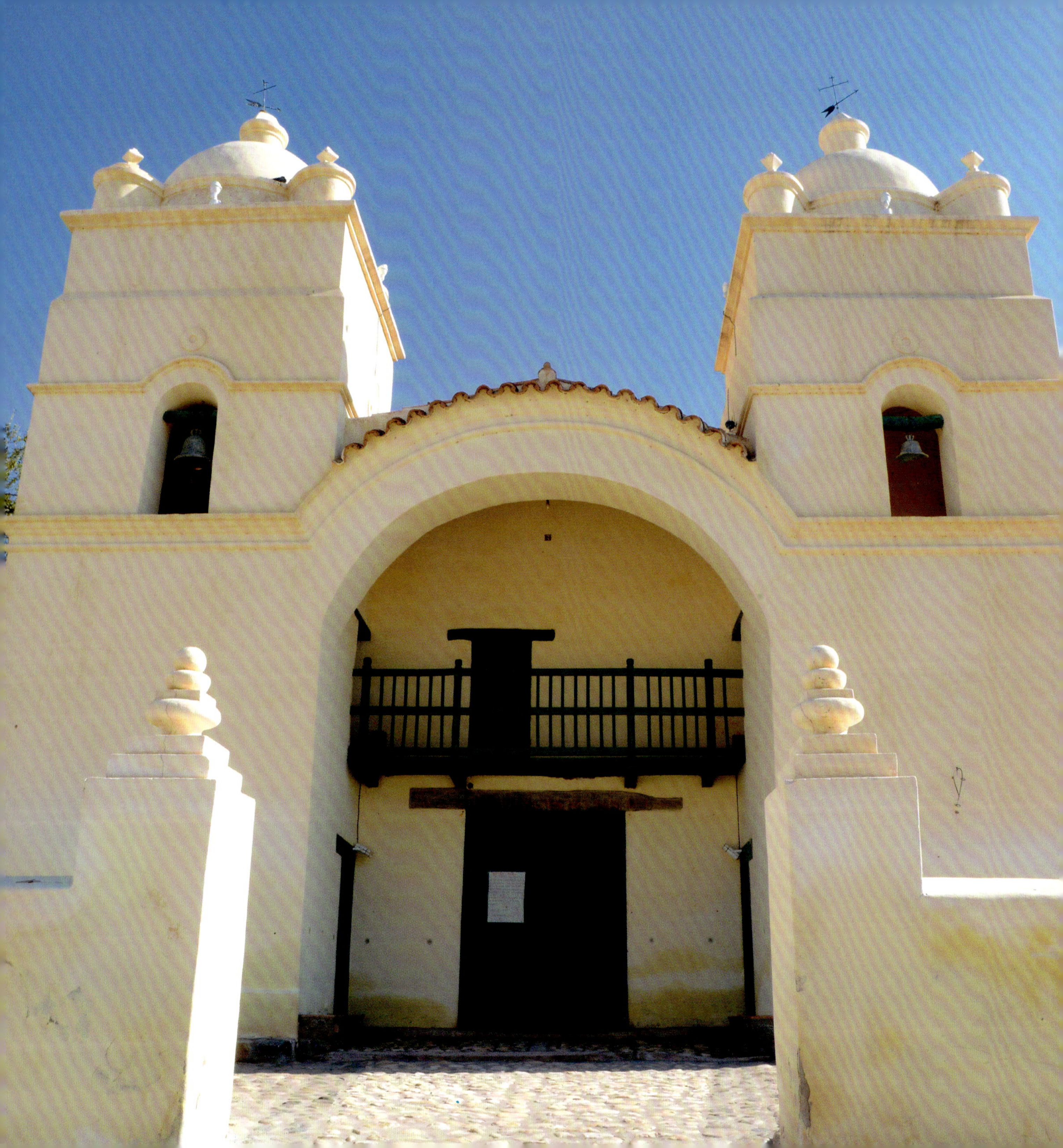

SALTA **MOLINOS**

An Authentic Village of Historical Significance

This little **Molinos Village** is a preservation of history, authentic of 17th-century native culture. The Molinos Valley is one of the pre-Hispanic places which still reflects the history of Argentina and the origins of the Spanish conquest and colonization in the Argentine territory.

These lands were originally inhabited by the people of Tiahuanaco who developed irrigation systems, and the Incas who struck a deal of sovereignty with them. Today, you can see this culture alive and well in Molinos and its valley.

Typical towns in Argentina have religious origins and were built around the parochial church in the center of town next to a central park. Molinos is different, as the village was created and developed around the **Hacienda of San Pedro Nolasco de los Molinos** (photo below), the home of General Diego Diez Gómez who protected the land, which the native inhabitants came to depend upon.

In Molinos, the church was built across from the hacienda, making the town's layout significantly different from the typical colonial layout where the church is situated opposite the main park with traditional squares and narrow streets.

Today, the church, **Iglesia San Pedro Nolasco de los Molinos** (photos left page, and right), is a National Historical Monument and the hacienda is a beautifully restored hotel **Hacienda de Molinos**, both right opposite each other.

Hacienda de Molinos was built by General Diego Diez Gómez in the second half of the 17th century on the Tacuil Region gifted to him in return for the services he rendered to Spain. Later, it became his daughter (Magdalena Diez Gómez) and his son-in-law's (General Domingo de Isasi Isasmendi) residence. When Isasi Isasmendi died in 1767, the hacienda was inherited by his eldest son Nicolás Severo de Isasmendi who was the last governor of Salta who was appointed by the King of Spain.

Hacienda de Molinos is a very traditional hacienda that has been refurbished to provide all the comforts expected in a 21st-century hotel, while preserving the essence and typical features of these colonial times. The hacienda has typical thick and tall adobe walls surrounding a central patio, which is shaded with a huge pepper tree. The rooms are authentic with antiques, iron window bars and ceilings made of carob trees and reeds.

Molinos has a population of 900 people, an elevation of 7,300' and the village is roughly four blocks wide by seven blocks long. The streets are romantically lit by lanterns at night to silently express part of their history and culture.

Ruta 53 runs through the center of town and upon departure, you cross a wide riverbed and head into the valley of vineyards and wine.

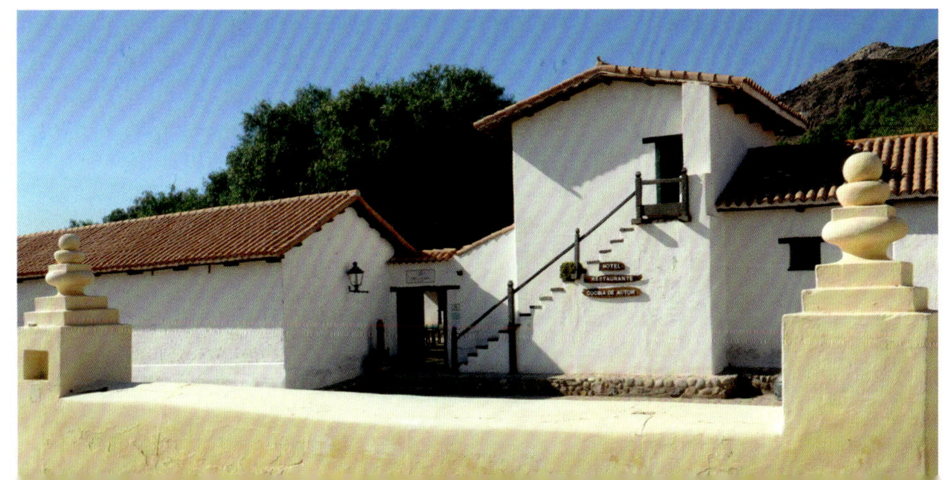

Hotel • Restaurant

HACIENDA DE MOLINOS HOTEL

Abraham Cornejo s/n
(1/4 mile west on Ruta 53 from Ruta 40)

011 (+54 386) 849.4094
Reservations 011 (+54 114) 963.1110
info@HaciendaDeMolinos.com.ar

HaciendaDeMolinos.com.ar

Español

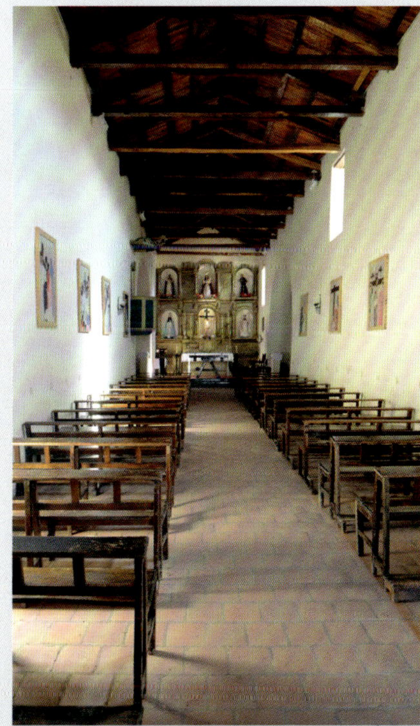

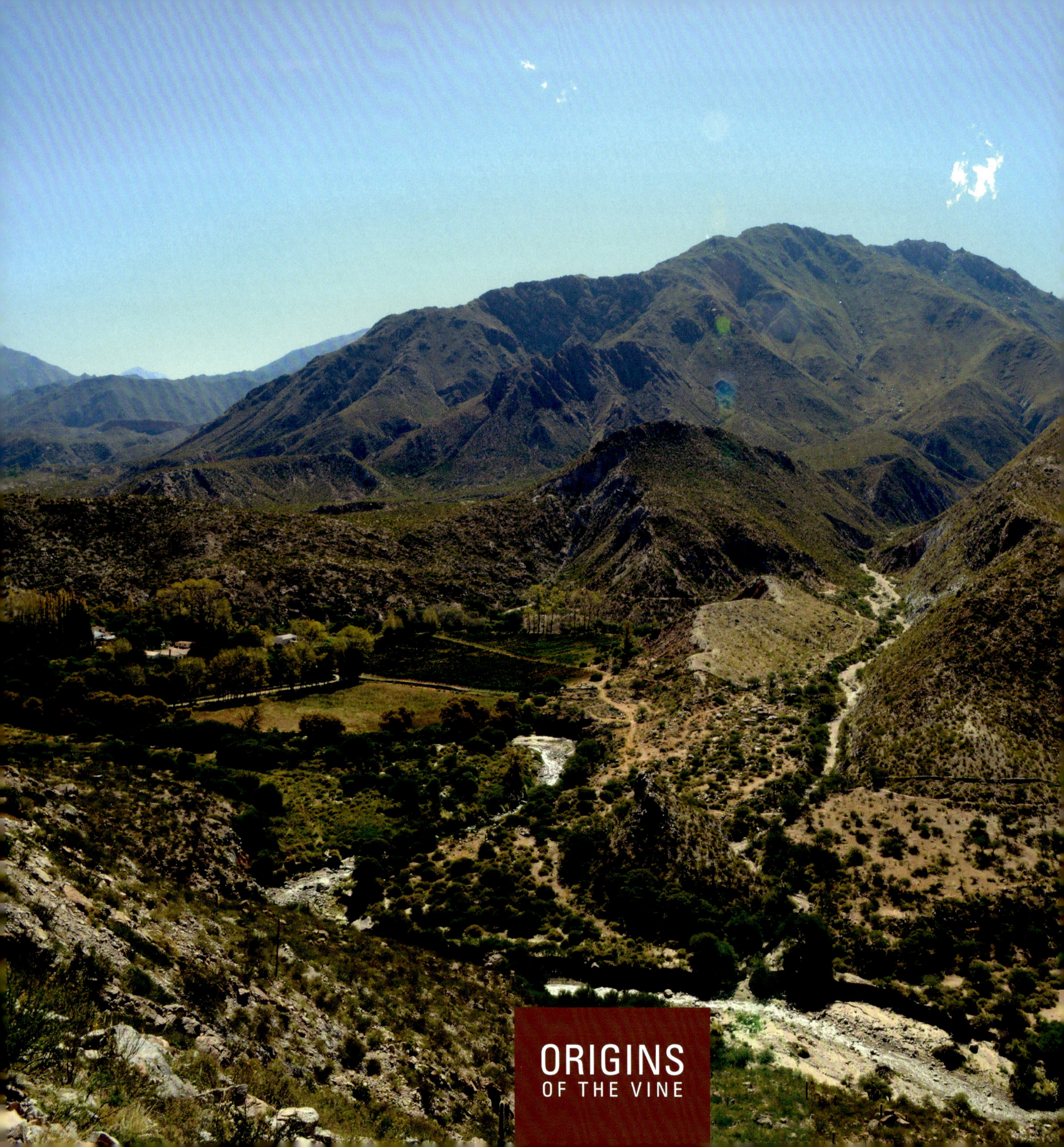
ORIGINS
OF THE VINE

THE FIRST RECORDED WINERY IN ARGENTINA

As it all began in the 17th century when **General Diego Diez Gómez** defeated the invaders from the north (Bolivia and Paraguay) and the King of Spain told him to go to the top of the hill and look out as far as he could see, and that was his property in recognition of his service to his country. What he saw was an endless valley which became his enormous estate known as Tacuil.

The legacy continued with his son-in-law **General Domingo de Isasi Isasmendi** who willed the territory to eldest son **Nicolás Severo de Isasmendi** who became the last Governor of Salta appointed by the King of Spain. His daughter **Doña Ascención Isasmendi de Dávalos** (whose husband Dr. José Benjamín Dávalos also became Governor of Salta) took over the estate and started the **Colomé Tacuil** vineyards by acquiring high-quality strains of vines from France, beginning the industrialization of wine in the Calchaquíes Valleys in 1831.

Doña Ascención's grandson, a retired Capitán de Fragata (warship captain), **Raúl Dávalos Rubio** took over the family business and restored their ancient vines and their production of high-quality wines known as **Bodega Colomé** (next page) and ultimately sold the winery to Donald Hess's American Hess Collection (Napa Valley) in 2001.

Raúl Dávalos Rubio kept his **Tacuil Fincas** (farms), a very special property of 80 square miles with vines growing at altitudes of 8,600' and topsoil of a meter of sand with depths of clay and no salt. This terroir provides him with wines of great minerality and beautiful aromas, and with *no oak barrels used*, fully expressing the fruit and flavors of his land.

Dávalos has developed a commune of 50 families on the Tacuil Fincas who live off the land and care for the crops of peppers, paprika, cumin, quinoa, pallar, quince, walnuts, and grapes of Cabernet Sauvignon, Malbec, Torrontés and Sauvignon Blanc.

To get there, drive 35 kilometers to the very end of Ruta 53, and when you think you are at the end of the valley, you climb over another hill and down the side of a cliff (Raúl had to dynamite) into the beautiful valley of Tacuil Fincas (photo left page).

The Bodega Tacuil wines celebrate their heritage. While we can be enchanted with this illustrious family of generals, captains and governors, they also have the *Crazy Uncle* who is represented on their bottle of *33 de Dávalos*. From rocky soil as harsh as this brazen uncle who was famous for breeding Peruvian and Arabian horses, and branded with the crazy-man number of 33!

33 de Dávalos is my favorite, as the boldest, spiciest and most minerally of their wines. 80% Malbec, 20% Cabernet Sauvignon.

Doña Ascención, also 80% Malbec, 20% Cabernet Sauvignon, celebrates Doña as the woman of the family who provided the vision and fortitude.

RD is **R**aúl **D**ávalos's pride as winemaker of a completely organic, bottled by hand wine, without any purification or filtering.

Viñas de Davalos are their main wines expressing the terroir of the uniqueness of their property.

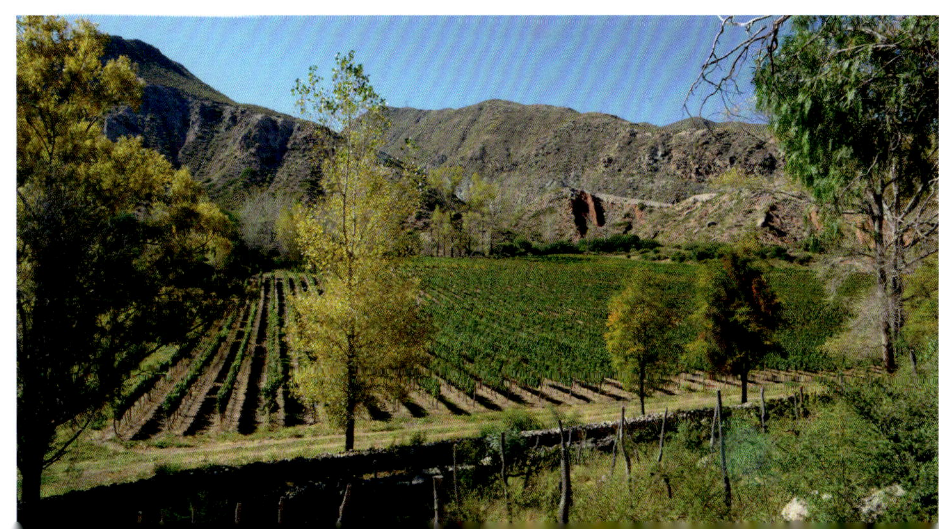

SALTA **VALLE CALCHAQUÍ** MOLINOS

Winery (Bodega)

BODEGA TACUIL

Ruta 53, 36 km

(36 kilometers from Molinos on Ruta 53)

011 (+54 386) 849.1072

VinosDeAltura@Tacuil.com.ar

Tacuil.com.ar

English & Español

35,000 bottles produced annually

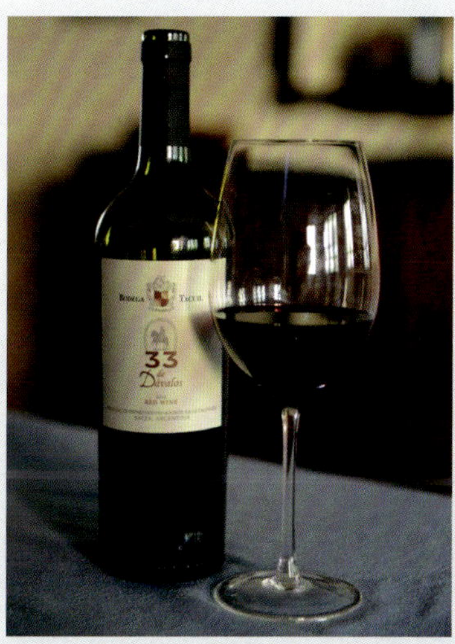

Michael's Favorite Pick

Bodega Tacuil 33 de Dávalos

Total Collection of Wines

Viña de Dávalos Tinto (red)
(50% Malbec, 50% Cabernet Sauvignon)

Viña de Dávalos Blanco (white)
(Torrontés and Sauvignon Blanc)

33 de Dávalos
(80% Malbec, 20% Cabernet Sauvignon)

RD (Raúl Dávalos)
(80% Malbec, 20% Cabernet Sauvignon)

Doña Ascención (their only wine with oak)
(80% Malbec, 20% Cabernet Sauvignon)

To get Tacuil wines in the USA

Direct from the Importer: VineConnections.com

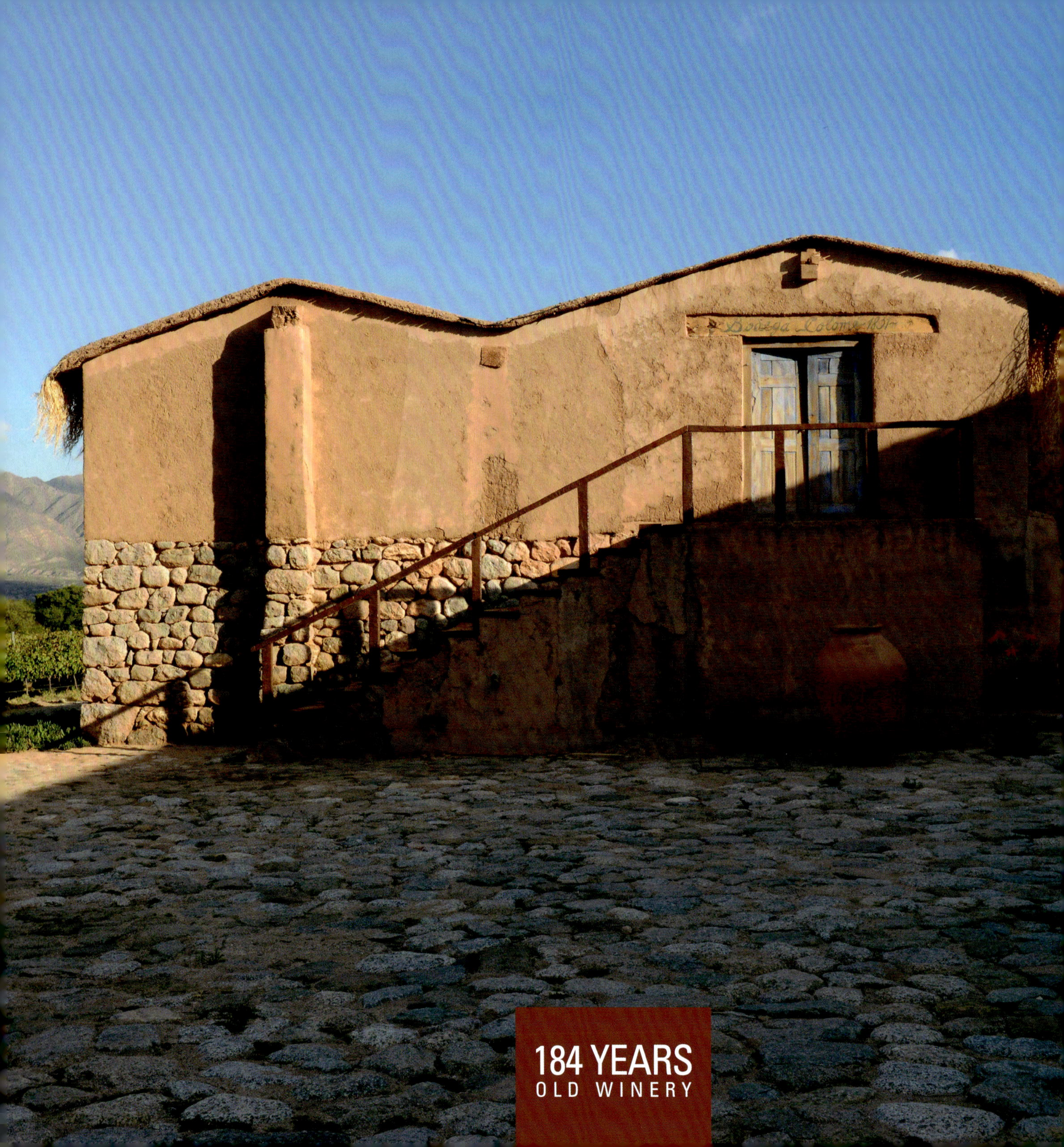
184 YEARS
OLD WINERY

HIGH-ALTITUDE WINES OF GREAT CONCENTRATION AND BALANCE

OK, so Donald Hess went to visit Argentina, had a great time, enjoyed several wine regions, and of course, he is a wine lover (and owns vineyards in Napa Valley). And then there was Tacuil, and Colomé. Donald was awakened by a new style of wine, super-high-altitude wine... and he loved it!

A bottle simply would not do it, nor would a case. He had to have it all... the entire winery sitting on 150,000 acres across the valley, with 650 acres already planted with vines to expand this amazing Colomé Winery, and bring modern technology and marketing to this business.

Beyond the bottle, Donald and his wife Ursula fell in love with this land... the grandeur and natural beauty of Colomé inspired and rejuvenated them to create a home a way from home. This upper part of the Calchaquí Valley is more mountainous and forested, with richer soils than in Cafayate. At nearly 10,000' elevation, Hess built their home overlooking the expansiveness of this Calchaquí Valley.

Bodega Colomé was founded in 1831 and purchased from the Isasmendi-Dávalos family in 2001 (see history in the preceding pages). Completely renovated and revitalized by Donald Hess, Bodega Colomé has **new winery** facilities with the latest technology and equipment, a beautiful **visitors center** with **gourmet restaurant**, a 4,000 sq' **modern art museum**, a **boutique hotel**, and has developed a community of 500 people complete with a school, church, community center, and medical facility, representing five extended families who live on the property and are employed by Colomé.

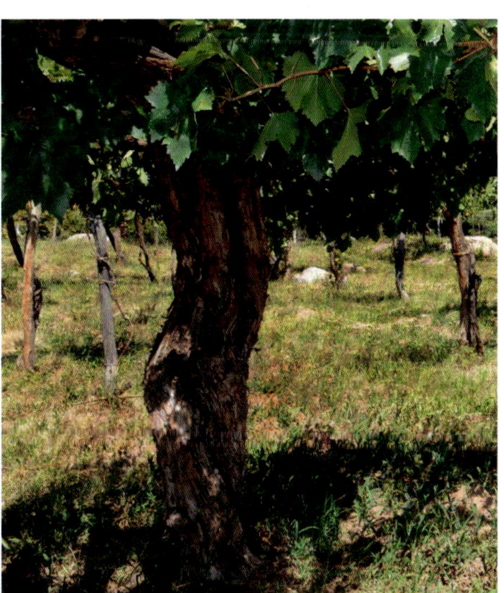

Bodega Colomé focuses on extreme high-altitude farming of the two traditional Argentine varietals of Malbec and Torrontés. Bodega Colomé vineyards are the highest in the world, ranging from 7,500' to 10,206' elevations. This altitude has a significant impact on the quality of the grapes. The higher the altitude, the greater exposure of the fruit to the sun's ultraviolet rays. Grapes develop thicker darker skins to protect themselves from the sun's rays, which later accounts for more intense wines in color, aromas and flavors. The result is receiving high awards and will capture your palate's attention.

Further, the land is farmed using agroecological and biodynamic principles, which consist of fertilization through organic compost and manure produced on their farm and vegetable gardens, the use of biodynamic preparations made up of organic matter and energies that stimulate living processes in the soil and the vines. This energy is also transmitted to the environment and builds up the mystical aura that characterizes Colomé.

Colomé also maintains their ancestral approach to agricultural management, allowing for tasks to be planned in agreement with the sun, moon and planets' rhythms, having a direct influence on the plant's fluids contributing to a more harmonious growing of the vines. The goal is to keep balanced vines throughout the years and to grow healthy nutritious grapes with concentrated aromas, polyphenols and flavors, which will later produce intense, complex and balanced wines.

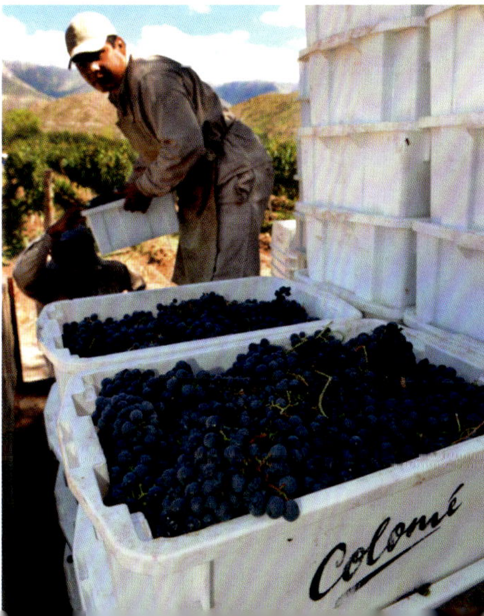

SALTA **VALLE CALCHAQUÍ** MOLINOS

Winery (Bodega)

BODEGA COLOMÉ

Ruta 53, 20 km

(20 kilometers from Molinos on Ruta 53)

011 (+54 386) 849.4200

reservas@BodegaColome.com

BodegaColome.com

English, Español & Portugués

900,000 bottles produced annually

Four wines, from two grapes, at four different elevations, producing over half a million liters of wine, exported to over 25 countries around the world. This is truly a result of Donald Hess's mantra that great wines come from vineyards of distinction.

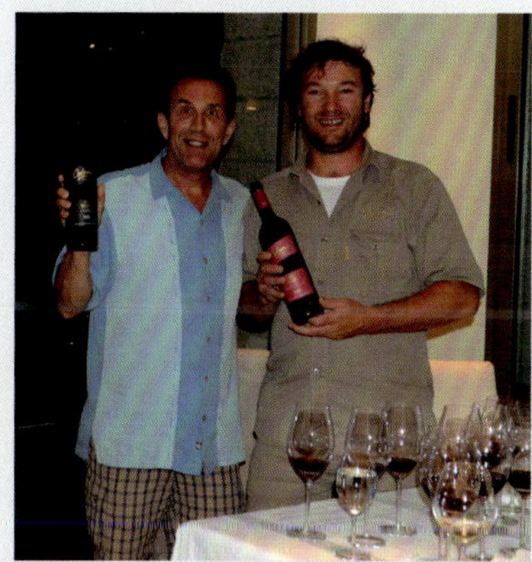

Michael's Favorite Pick

Colomé Reserva Malbec

Total Collection of Wines

Colomé Torrontés

(Torrontés of delicate elegant)

Colomé Auténtico Malbec

(using ancient techniques and no oak)

Colomé Reserva Malbec

(from their oldest vines of 60 to 160 years)

Colomé Estate Malbec

(from their highest vineyards of 8,900')

To get Colomé wines in the USA

Email the Importer: info@HessCollection.com

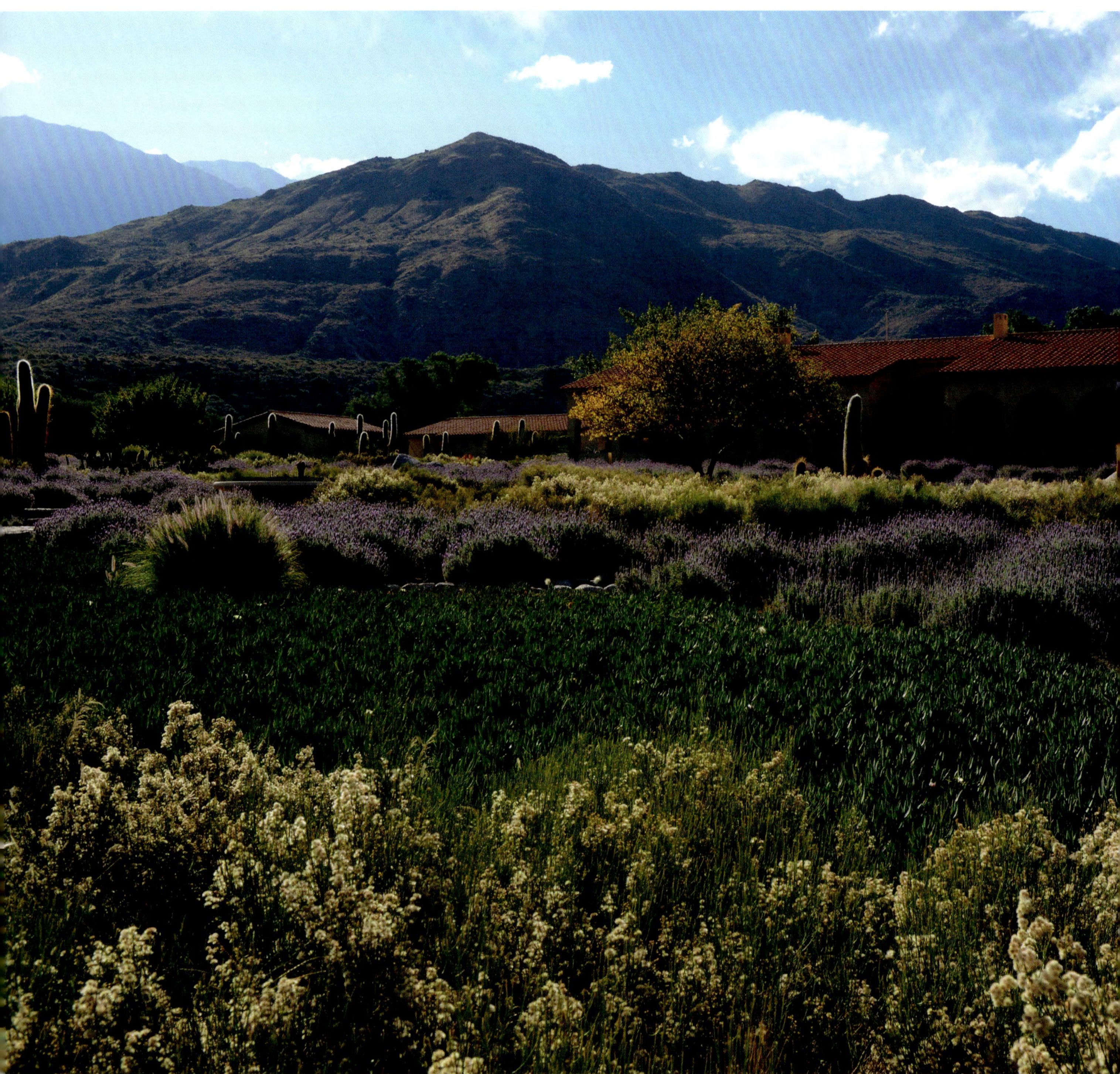

ESTANCIA DE COLOMÉ

Estancia Colomé is a private hacienda where Donald Hess and Bodega Colomé invite special guests in grand style. It has a hacienda-style layout with central courtyard and nine very luxurious rooms surrounding an authentic Spanish courtyard complete with antiques and central fountain to set the mood for kicking your feet up.

If five rooms are being occupied, then Estancia Colomé will open for public reservations, or you can bring four other friends and make it happen. Call or email Connie Bearzi, their travel coordinator.

While Bodega Colomé has a gourmet restaurant, wine bar and tasting room open to the public, Estancia Colomé has private dining of haute-cuisine, private gardens and reading rooms. Each guest room has its own private terrace for gazing outside the hacienda across the beautiful landscape, vineyards and mountains... ideal to enjoy a glass of Colomé wine in the evening while star-gazing at the massively lit-up southern sky!

There are numerous activities that the visitors center can arrange... vineyard, winery and museum tours, plus hiking, horseback riding and trekking in these unique natural surroundings.

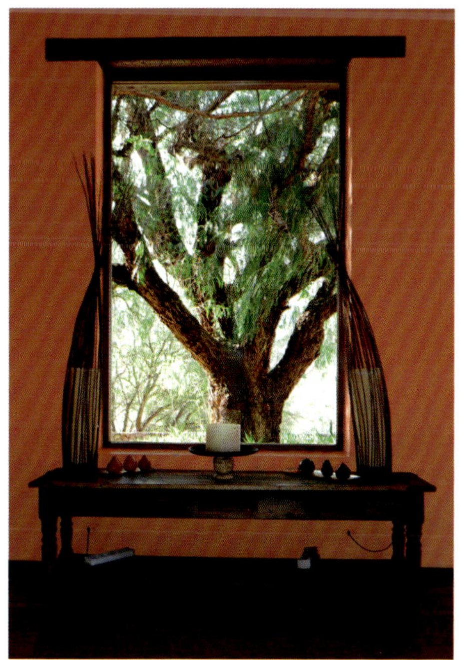

THE JAMES TURREL MUSEUM

This is one of the most unique works of modern art you will ever experience. And it is *an experience!* Interactive, and exclusively with light, you will be in awe with how the light will play tricks on your eyes, mesmerizes and delights your senses.

James Turrell (1943) is one of the world's most renowned contemporary artists, whose work plays with the perception and effects of light within a created space. His work can be found in collections worldwide, including the Guggenheim Museum.

At first, Turrell thought this was a crazy idea, a museum at Colomé, in the middle of nowhere... you must fly to Buenos Aires, then fly to Salta, then drive over poorly maintained dirt roads for many hours... and yet people come from all over the world just to see this exhibit, and a little wine thrown in for some culture.

His palette is exclusively light. Your visit will be guided, going through a process of discovering the images, discovering how they change, and realizing that what you see is not actually what is real. The interactive aspect is magical in its experience.

5,600 square feet of nine exhibits spanning five decades of the artist's career, including *Unseen Blue*, the largest sky-space exhibit in the world... an open view of the sky with the sun creating and changing the art, reaching its maximum intensity at sunrise and sunset.

The environment is sterile, no cameras, no shoes, no pens, and no touching of walls. And then, you will be asked to touch a wall... just to find out that the wall does not exist... except in your mind.

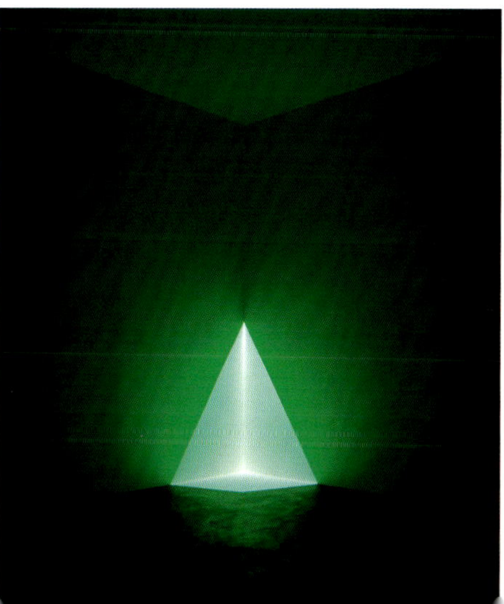

SALTA **VALLE CALCHAQUÍ** MOLINOS

Hotel • Restaurant • Museum

ESTANCIA COLOMÉ

Visitors Center Reservations
(Restaurant, Museum, Winery, Tours)
011 (+54 386) 849.4200
reservas@BodegaColome.com

Travel Agent Estancia
011 (+54 387)(15) 409.0442
Connie.Bearzi@Hess-Family.com.ar

BodegaColome.com

English, Español & Portugués

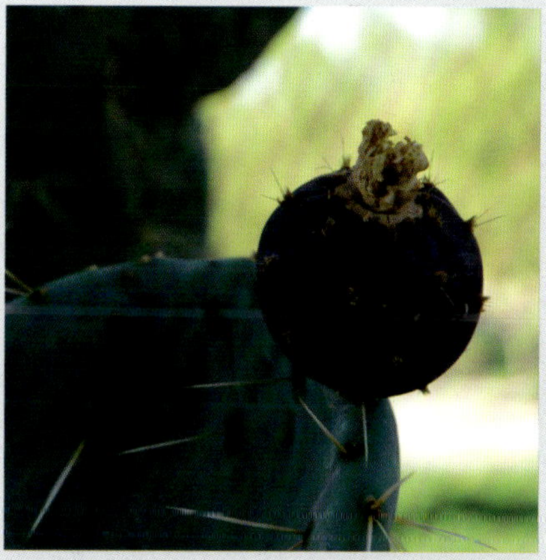

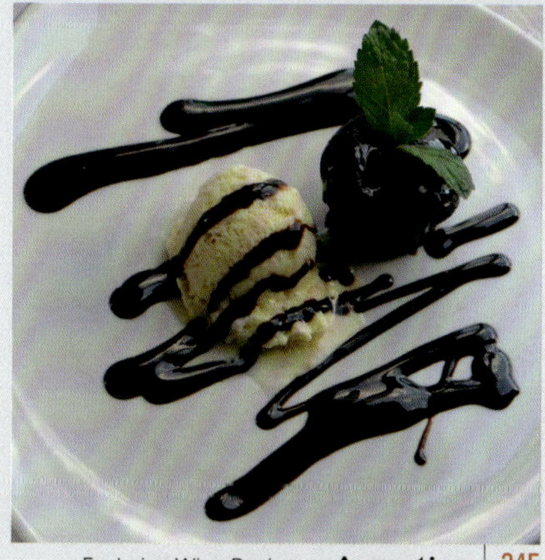

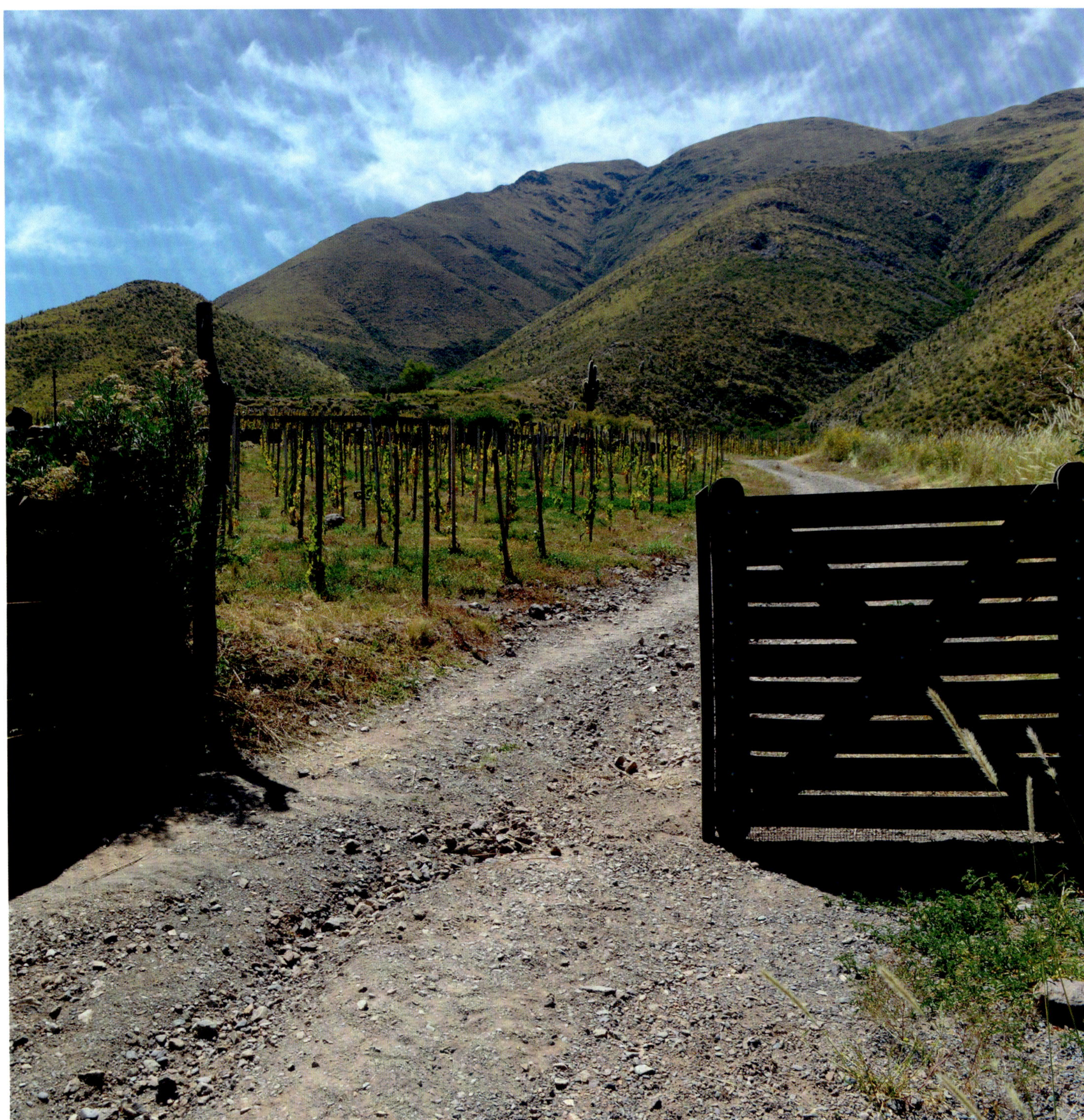

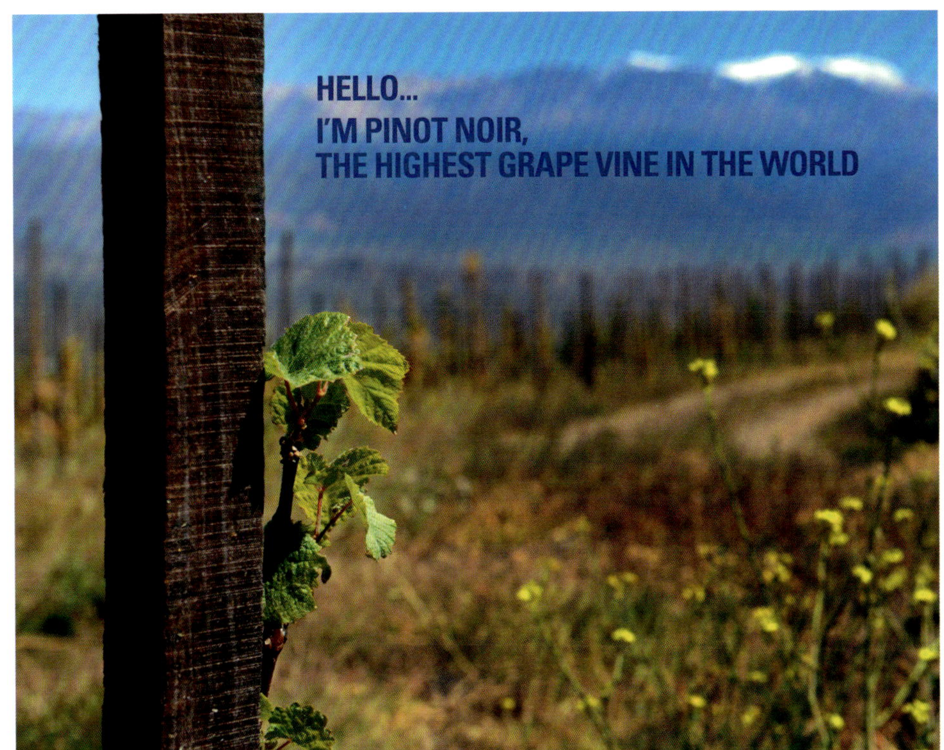

Vineyards (Viñedos)

ALTURA MÁXIMA (Colomé)

Ruta 40, Payogasta

Located at the intersection of Ruta 40 and Ruta 33
59 km north of Molinos
just outside the tiny village of Payogasta

BodegaColome.com

Imagine this little plant, just beginning her life, only her second growing season, struggling to survive at 10,206 feet above sea level. She is a Pinot Noir (photo above) and she is the single tallest grape vine in the entire world. How proud she must be.

This is yet another experiment from Donald Hess in his ultra high-altitude farming in the Calchaquí Valley. Now he is pushing the limits with two farms several hours drive north of Bodega Colomé in the upper region of the Calchaquí Valley.

Finca El Arenal is at 8,858 feet elevation, and **Finca Altura Máxima** is at 10,206' elevation.

There is nothing like this anywhere in the world. At El Arenal the experiment is paying off... 111 acres of Malbec was exclusively planted on this farm and it has now become their *Colomé Estate Malbec* (their highest altitude Malbec), which their French winemaker **Thibaut Delmotte** loves the best.

At Altura Máxima (translated as *maximum height*), Colomé is experimenting with numerous varietals to figure out what will work best at this extreme altitude. Planted already are 86 acres of Malbec, Pinot Noir, Merlot, Syrah; Torrontés, Sauvignon Blanc and Chardonnay.

To engineer this high-altitude experiment, Colomé hired **Ing. Arg. Rafael Racedo Aragón** to take on the challenge. Rafael lives on the 68,000-acre property, in the middle of the Altura Máxima finca, and has established a biodynamic farming environment that he believes will influence the crop's ability to establish themselves best in this harsh environment. He also believes it sets a respectful tone and harmonious ambiance between all aspects of the farm and its workers.

The soil here is poor, sandy with a high percentage of gravel... except, different from the other vineyards in the Calchaquí Valley, it has high concentrations of phosphorus due to the presence of volcanic rock... plus substantial exposure to the sun's rays. The expected outcome is even greater concentrated aromas, polyphenols and flavors of intense, complex and balanced wines.

The very first bottling of **Altura Máxima Malbec** was from the 2011 harvest (photo right), which I had the *máxima* pleasure to sample, paired with roasted goat, at the local eatery in the tiny village of Payogasta, which makes a great lunch stop on this journey.

BELOW, is a rustic outdoor restaurant at Sala de Payogasta in the little village of Payogasta where you can enjoy roasted goat (pictured) and other authentic local Andean cuisine, along with a bottle of Colomé wine.

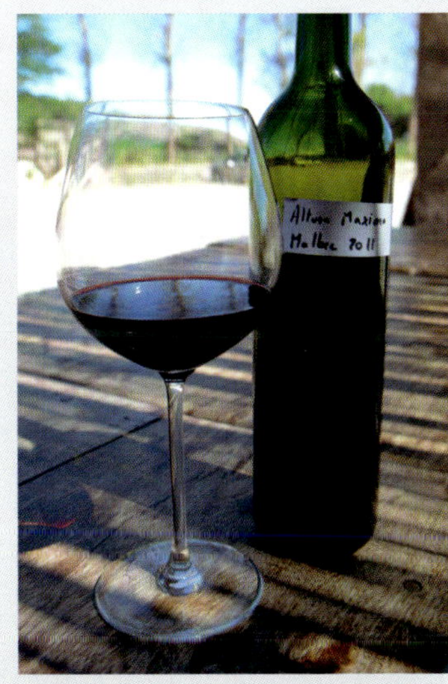

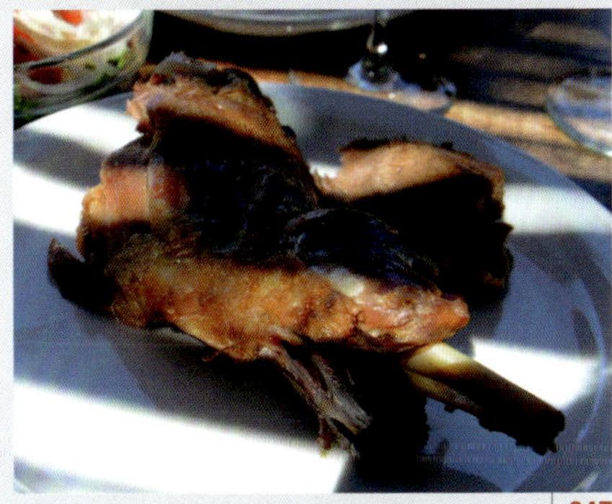

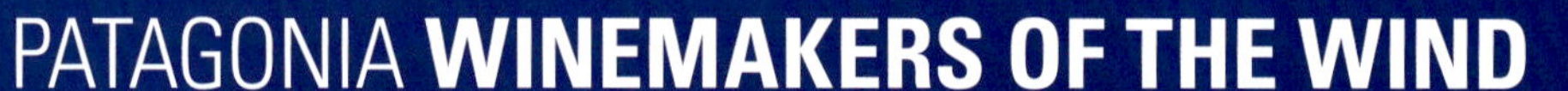

Remarkable Terroir for Pinot Noir, Chardonnay, Merlot, and Cabernet Franc

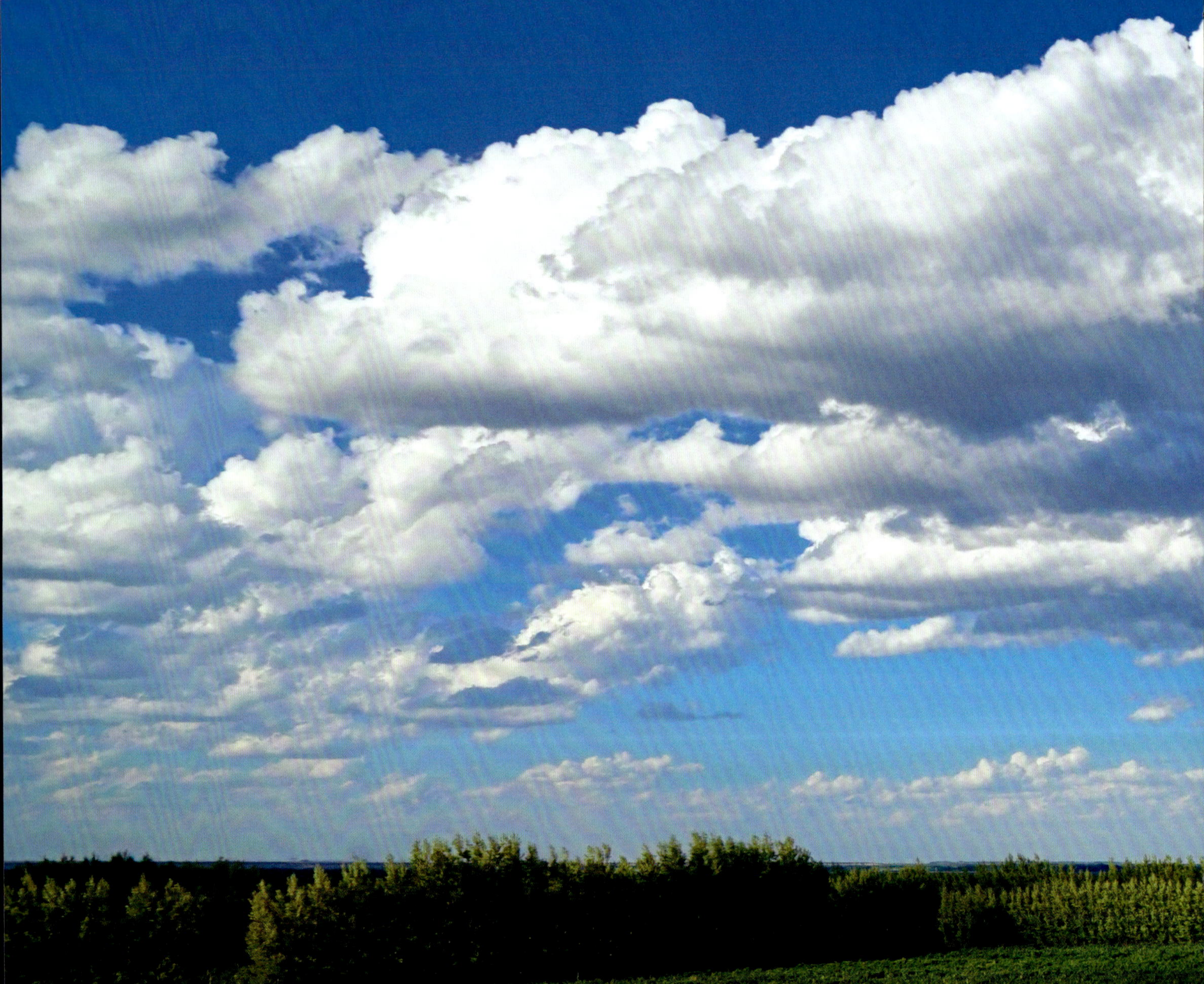

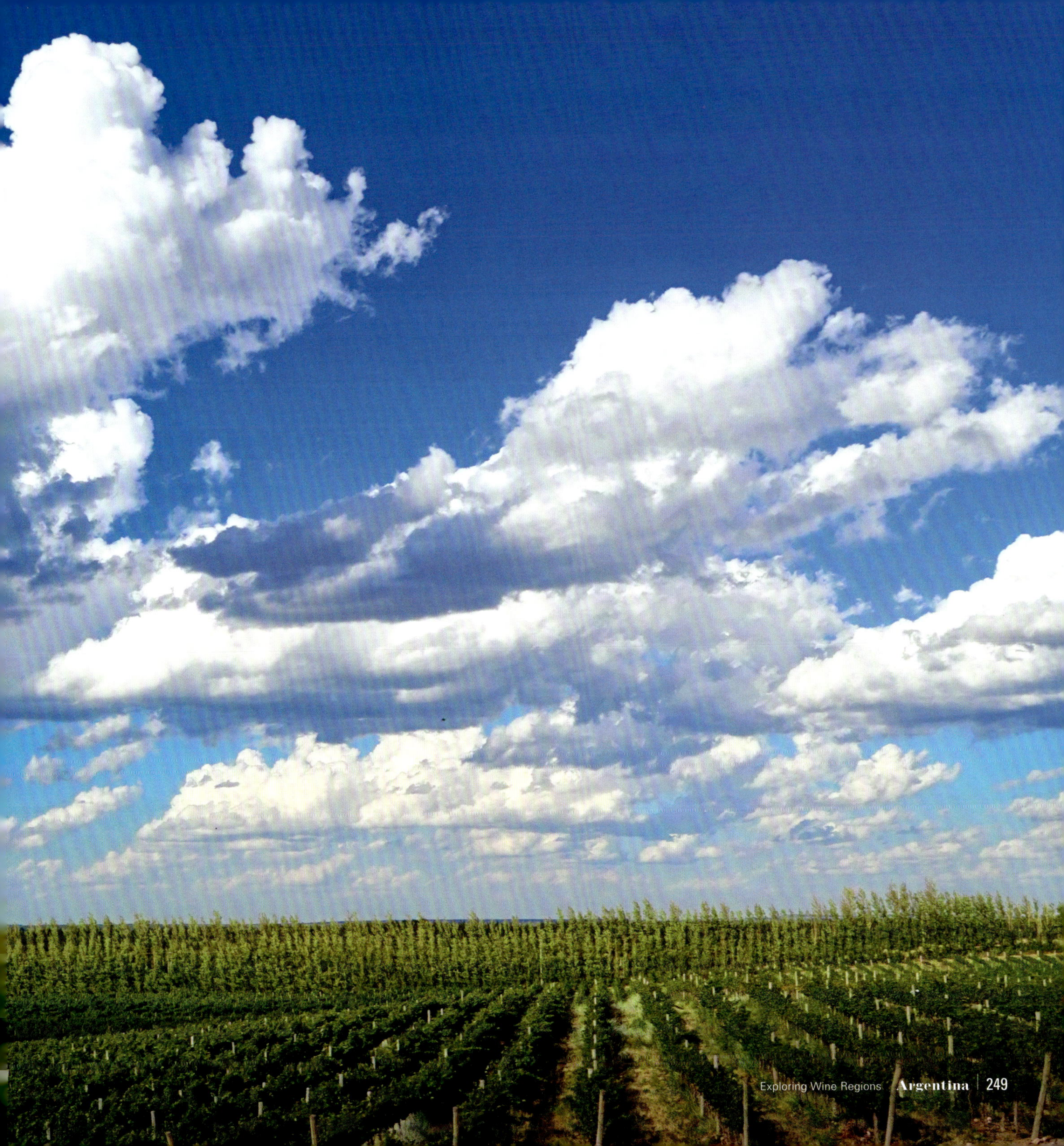

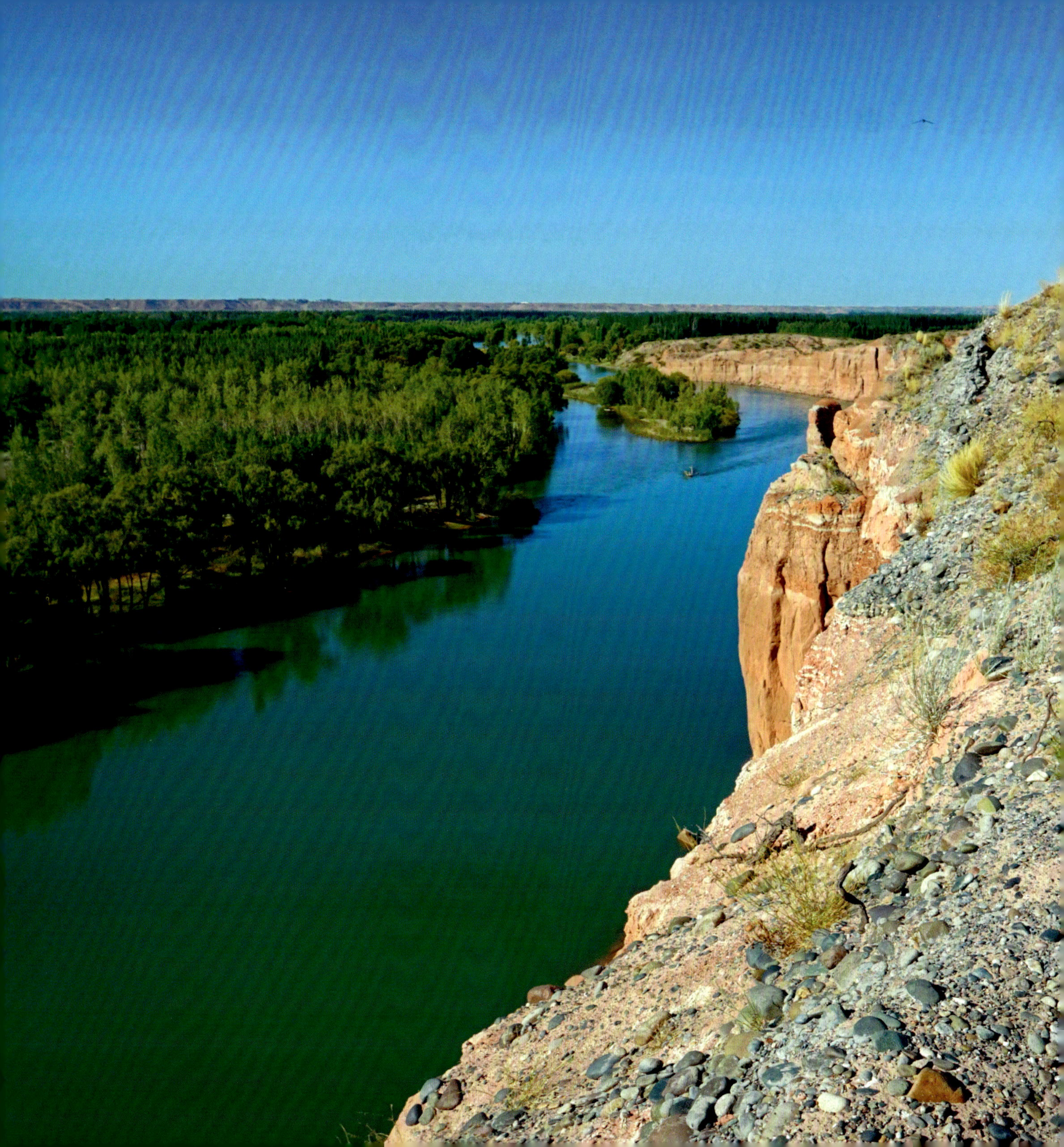

PATAGONIA **WINEMAKERS OF THE WIND**

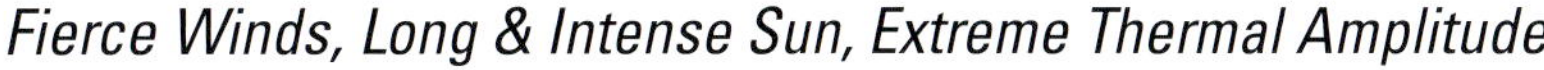

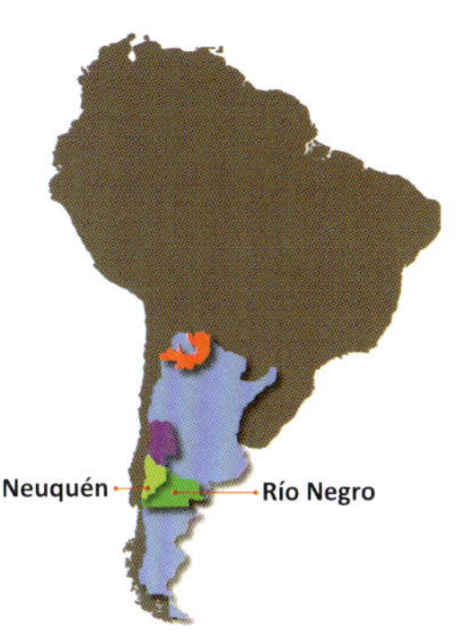

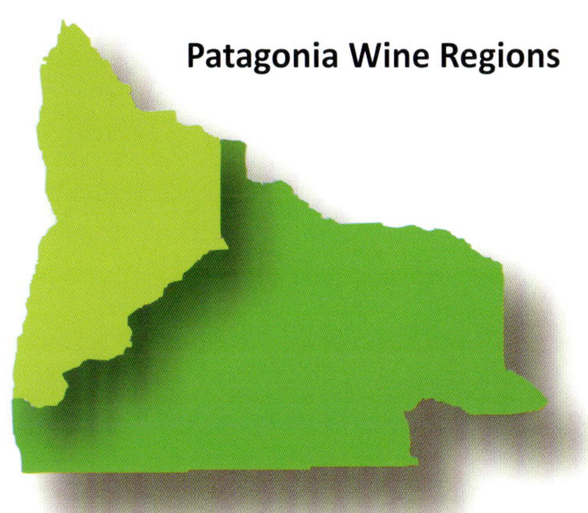

EXPLORING PATAGONIA

Patagonia encompasses the extreme south of the American continent, mostly in Argentina, and represents more than a third of the land mass of Argentina. Argentine Patagonia consists of many provinces (states) of which **Neuquén** and **Río Negro** are located at the northern edge of Patagonia.

Neuquén borders the province of Mendoza (Argentina's primary wine region) directly to the south along the Andes Mountain Range. **Río Negro** is to the east and south of Neuquén extending all the way to the Atlantic Ocean.

The wine regions of Patagonia are located in **Neuquén** and **Río Negro**, and La Pampa. The vineyards are clustered primarily in the areas where the two provinces come together in their north, far from the Andes Mountains, and where the two rivers of Limay and Neuquén merge to become the Río Negro.

What makes this agricultural region possible is these two very big rivers, the **Río Neuquén** and **Río Limay** (photo left page), bringing fresh water from the Andes to irrigate the vineyards, as well as the orchards of pears, apples and cherries.

Neuquén the city (capital of Neuquén Province) is located where these two rivers meet. It is the largest city in Patagonia with a population of 400,000 and growing rapidly as a result of huge oil reserves being discovered in the province. Neuquén city is where the **Neuquén Airport (NQN)** is located that you will fly into to access the Patagonia Wine Regions.

As the southernmost wine region, Patagonia offers a cooler environment for the grapes that thrive in cooler terroir. As such, Patagonia is magic for **Pinot Noir** and **Chardonnay** as we know from other parts of the world. Further, with the softness of **Merlot**, this environment works wonderfully in bringing out its delicate nature. And for a surprise, **Cabernet Franc** is thriving here, and will capture your taste buds in a way you will not forget.

Being farther south causes cooler nights, and it also means longer sunlight days in the summer, plus with a thinner ozone layer, the sun gets very intense. All of these create the greater thermal amplitude range (as much as a 65°F day/night difference) in which wine grapes thrive and produce higher concentrations of fruit, color and balance.

This intense sun also causes the grapes to grow thicker skins to protect themselves – from the sun itself, and of even greater importance, the high winds. During springtime when the grapes are forming, the winds here are regularly blowing at 50 mph, reaching upwards of 100 mph in some places at certain times. Just picture how much the grapes need to protect themselves, and to do so, they grow very thick skins.

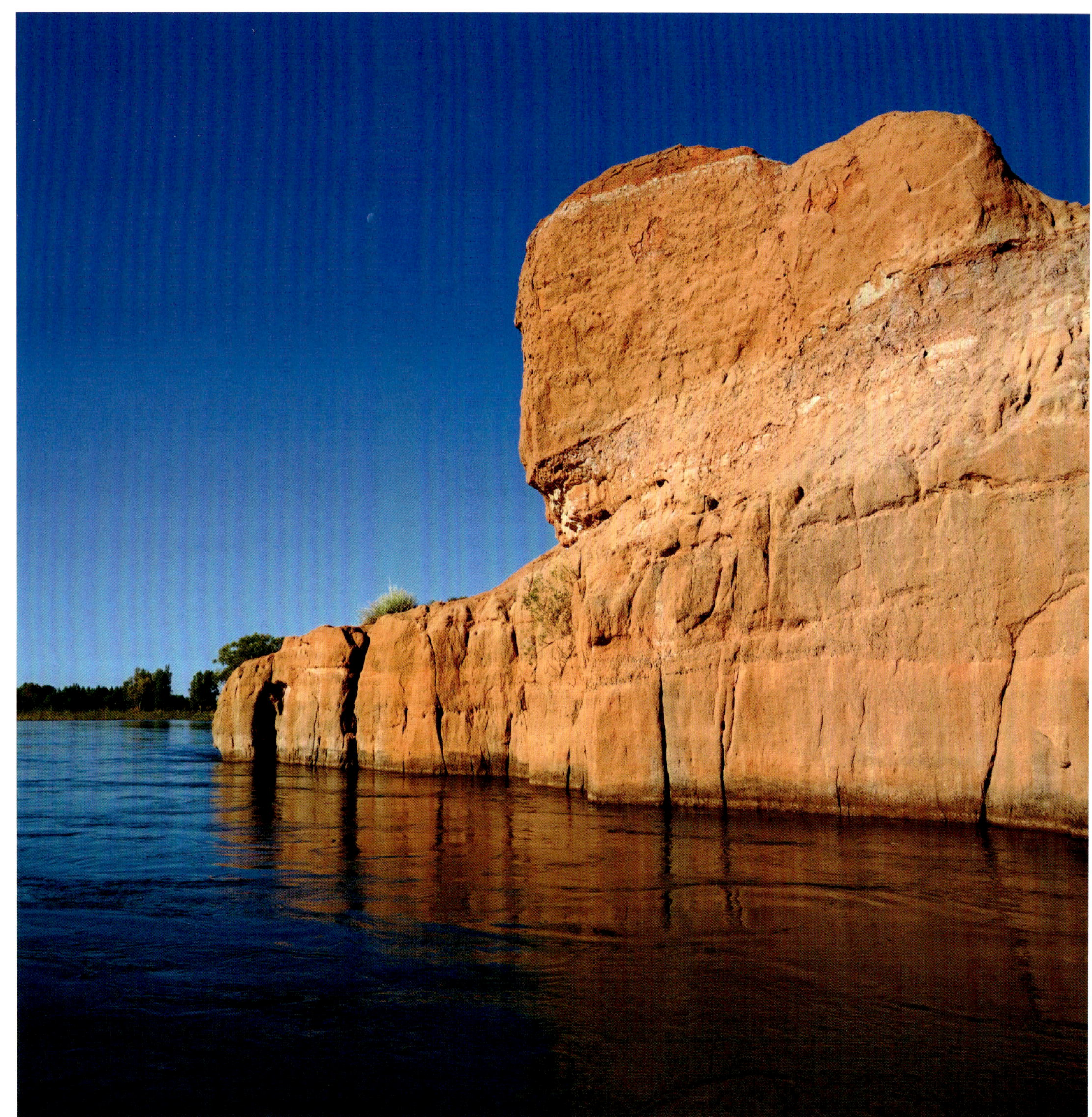

RÍO NEUQUÉN **RÍO LIMAY**

The Two Grand Rivers That Merge Into the Río Negro

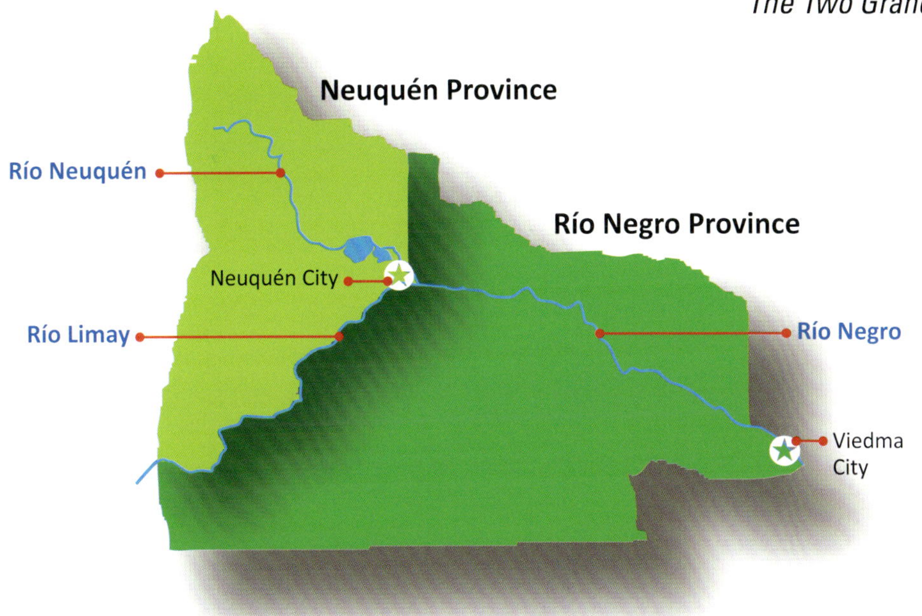

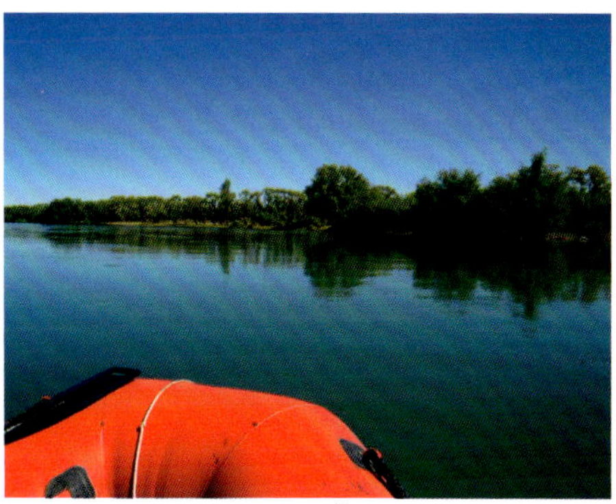

RAFTING IN THE RÍO LIMAY

I had just finished an exciting week in the busy city of Buenos Aires... a fast-paced week of amazing food and wine pairings, nightlife and Tango! It was time to relax and unwind in Patagonia.

Floating down the **Río Limay** (photo left page) was the way to unwind. Relaxation. Tranquility. Beauty. A peaceful drift in a floating raft. No rapids.

This was the way to spend the afternoon. So many species of birds enjoying the river with you. The terrain is diverse and interesting. And numerous photo moments.

I went with the Bakali Viajes & Turismo. They provide all the equipment and experienced boatman. And they will also cook you a BBQ Asado along the river if you desire.

BAKALI VIAJES & TURISMO

(they provide transportation to and from the river)

011 (+54 299) 443.6643
ventas@BakaliTurismo.tur.ar

BakaliTurismo.tur.ar

English & Español

The skins are where wine gets its color. Thicker skins mean more intense colors in the wine, resulting in wines that are highly concentrated in color, aromas and flavors, and also giving greater balance to the acidity and tannins.

Different from the Mendoza and Salta Wine Regions, the Patagonia Wine Region is far away from the Andes Mountains at a much lower elevation of 850'. Being far away from the Andes, this region does not get snow, nor the devastating effects of summer hail. When you see leaf damage in the vineyard, this is from the intense winds.

The wind is a unique and intense aspect to winemaking in Patagonia. These ***Winemakers of the Wind*** are fond of the difficulty the winds bring them, as the results in their wines are magnificent.

Tight rows of Alamos trees are planted in a line along the water canals surrounding the vineyards. This is the common infrastructure agronomists use to protect their vineyards from the winds. Alamos trees grow fast and tall, ideal for blocking the winds and tempering the environment from the intensity that can destroy the vineyards.

Similar to the Mendoza and Salta Wine Regions, Neuquén and Río Negro are deserts with very little rainfall. As such, they also share this same disease absent terroir, poor soil quality, and the ability to control the quantity and timing of water irrigating the vines.

To access the water from the three large rivers in this wine region, the vineyards are planted along the north sides of these rivers, where canals have been created to bring the fresh water directly to the vineyards.

Take a look at the map above...

In Neuquén, the wine region is very small and located in an area north of the city along the Río Neuquén. Neuquén also has one new winery that has begun along the Río Limay, southeast of the city.

In the Río Negro province, the wine region extends the full distance of the Río Negro (river) from Neuquén to the Atlantic Ocean. The primary concentration of wineries; however, is located in the upper valley of Río Negro next to Neuquén.

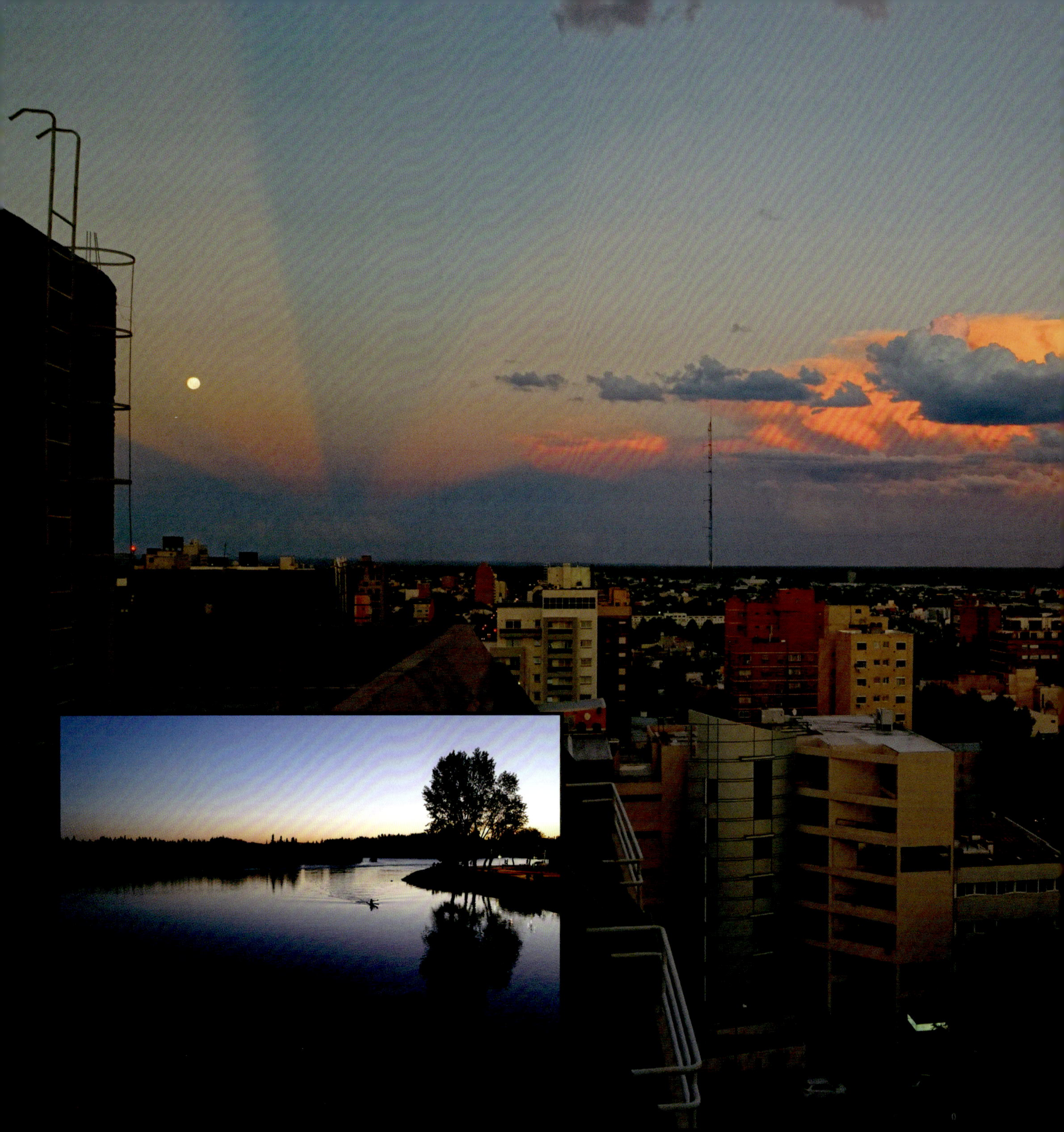

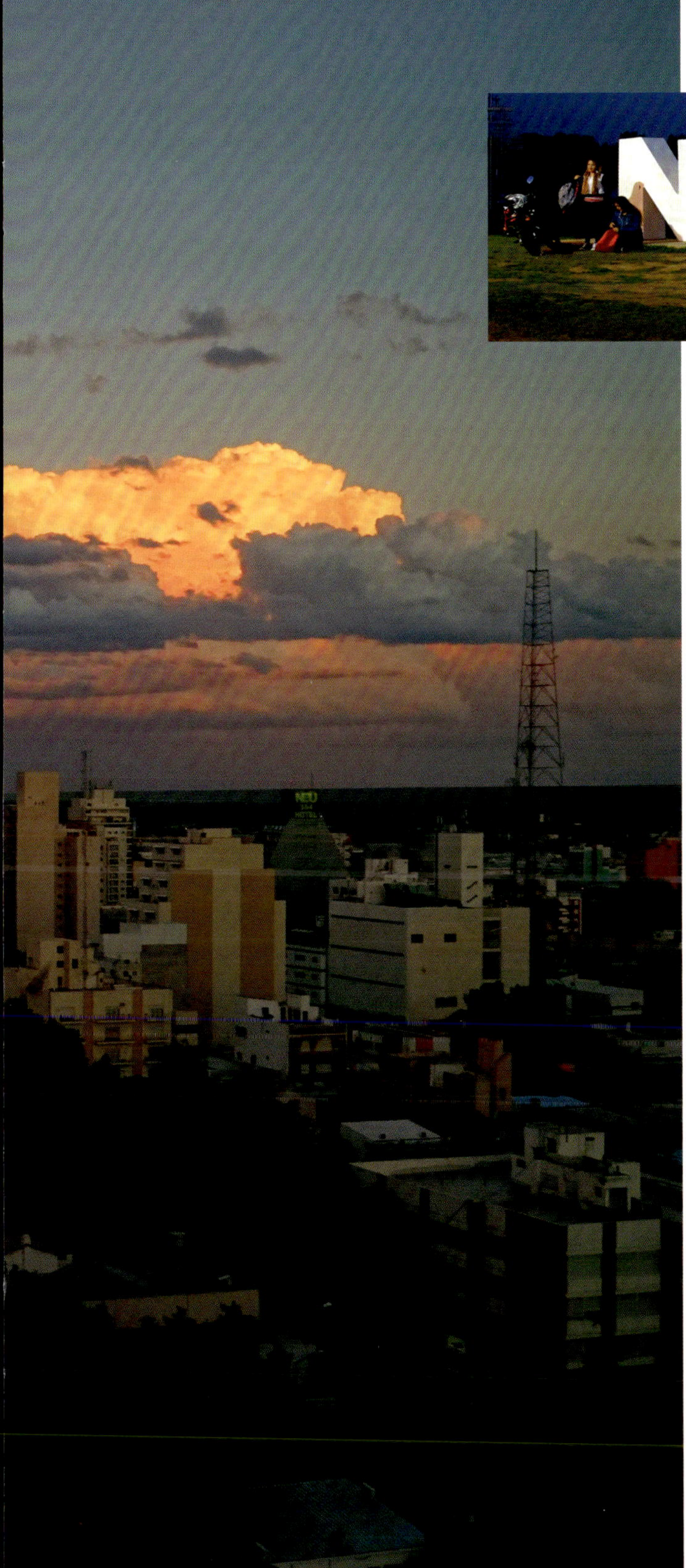

WELCOME

Neuquén, the capital city of the Neuquén province, is central to the Patagonia Wine Region, and also the largest city in both provinces of Neuquén and Río Negro. With its size and fast growth, comes many things to do and see in and around the downtown area. There are some fantastic restaurants too, as you will find on the next few pages.

Downtown Neuquén is a beautiful walking community. Tree-lined streets with extra large walking areas, parks, shops, restaurants, art galleries, museums, and an active night life.

There are actually quite a few **Art Galleries** and **Museums** in Neuquén. They are all located in the **Central Park** area of the city with free admission. What's interesting is the **Sala de Arte Emilio Saraco**, a small funky art gallery located in the old restored train station (8300 Avenida Olascoaga). They present local artists of very creative ideas and expressions. Also... **Museo Paraje Confluencia** and **Museo Gregorio Álvarez**.

Neuquén also has the national art museum: **Museo Nacional de Bellas Artes** (National Museum of Fine Art) of extraordinary artistic heritage. It houses the largest public collection in Latin America with more than 12,000 pieces. Their collection of 19th-century European art is considered the most important in the region. They also consider their collection of Argentine art as the most valuable collection of its kind in the world.

The nicest hotel in downtown Neuquén is the **Neuquén Tower Hotel** at 174 Belgrano (299.447.6551, NeuquenTowerHotel.com.ar). Near the airport is the **Casino Magic Hotel** at 4005 Teodoro Planas (299.445.2600, CasinoMagic.com.ar). Both are very modern and upscale. There are many other hotels in Neuquén, some "claiming" to be nice, so these two you can count on for top level quality and service.

At the very south end of the town, the city borders the Río Limay (photo inset left page) where it has redeveloped the entire area into a very nice park. **Parque Democracia** has numerous benches along a new walkway, grass and trees, all overlooking the majestic river. There are several private clubs adjacent to the park as well. The **Cervecería Owe**, restaurant and brewery (page 258), is just a block up from the park.

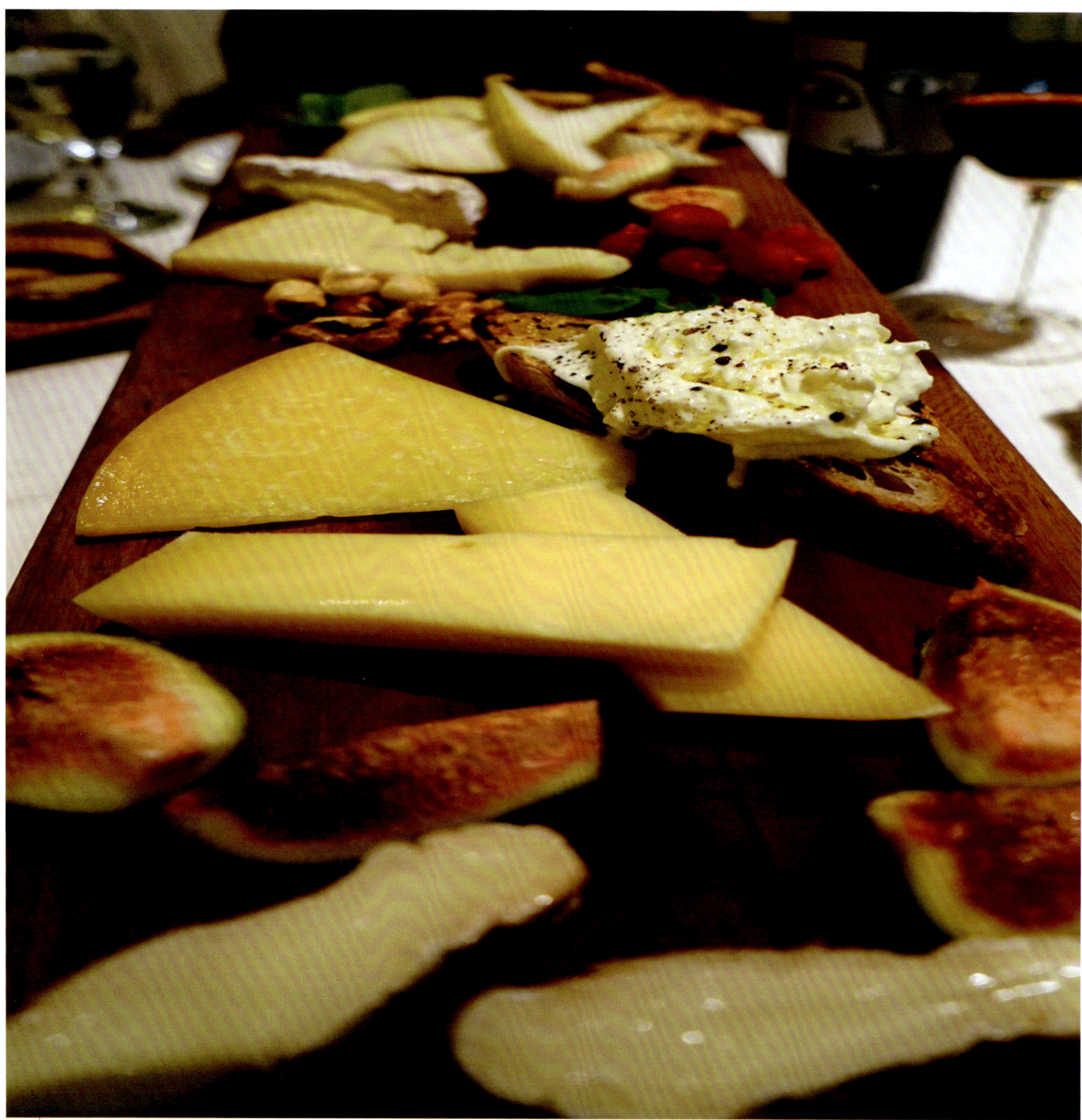

GOAT CHEESE AND FIGS... MI ENCANTA!

It was a very special evening with Chef Mauricio Couly... starting with the most spectacular cheese experience you will ever encounter... Mauricio begins with traditional recipes and adds his creative twist to produce cheeses of uncommon culinary art. It all starts on his farm, where he raises, nurtures and even grooms his special milk-producing friends... goats, sheep and special cows, all with endearing names. These are cheeses made with lots of love.

Presentation is on a large wooden slab (photo left page). It is the cheese platter of all cheese platters. An evening in this restaurant for just the cheese board and a bottle of wine (the Miras Cabernet Franc is a perfect pairing) would be an extraordinary evening.

Fresh goat cheese and tree-ripened figs are only the beginning. His cheddar is made with all three animals and aged for a full year, making it very sharp and flavor-rich. He also has a beautiful fresh sheep's milk cheese, with crunchy crystals inside. His brie, well, I would call it an "Italian Religion" in this restaurant. Simply delectable!

The atmosphere is fantastic. A large open space, open to the kitchen and to a wine cellar (photo right) to pick out your wine of the evening. This Tuscany-style cuisine is achieved by cooking in a massive clay igloo-style oven using apple and pear hardwoods for heat. I feasted on a Patagonia lamb shoulder (photo below) slow-roasted in this oven for seven hours with rosemary, garlic, parsley, and wine. It was fall-off-the-bone tender and juicy... simply delectable!

Chef Mauricio Couly learned his talents at an early age by working with world-renowned chef, Francis Mallman, who took him to his kitchens in Argentina, Uruguay and Brazil, and taught him interesting cooking techniques. Then Couly continued on with learning from other chefs of restaurants in Italy, Spain and England. Now, with his two brothers Darjuanío and Edgard, they opened La Toscana in 2004.

Don't forget to indulge in one of their desserts, they are unique as well. A dulce-de-leche made with sheep's milk, or exotic figs with homemade ice cream of lavender and pistachio with red and yellow raspberries (photo bottom right).

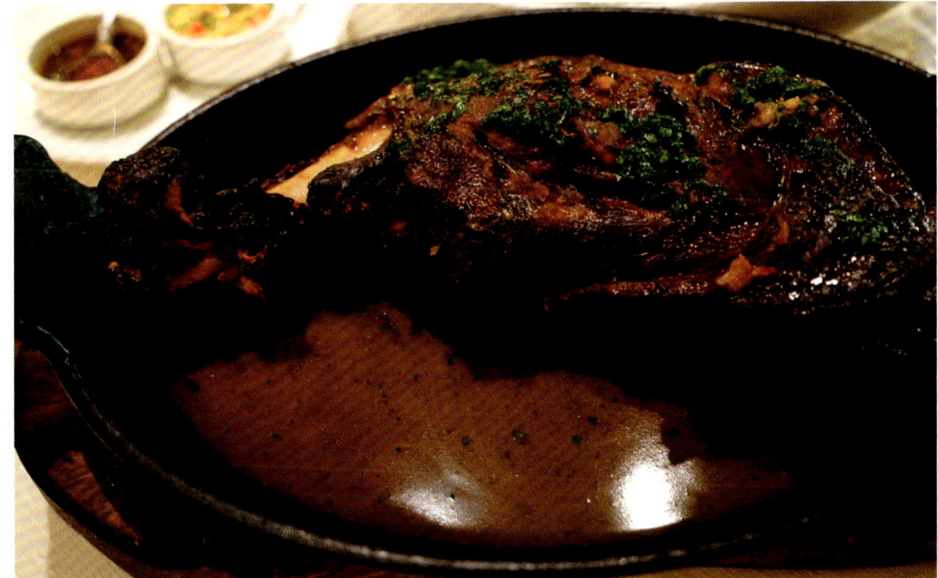

Restaurant
La Toscana

176 Juan Julián Lastra
(Downtown Neuquén, side road along Ruta 22)

011 (+54 299) 447.3322
reservas@LaToscanaRestaurante.com

LaToscanaRestaurante.com

English & Español

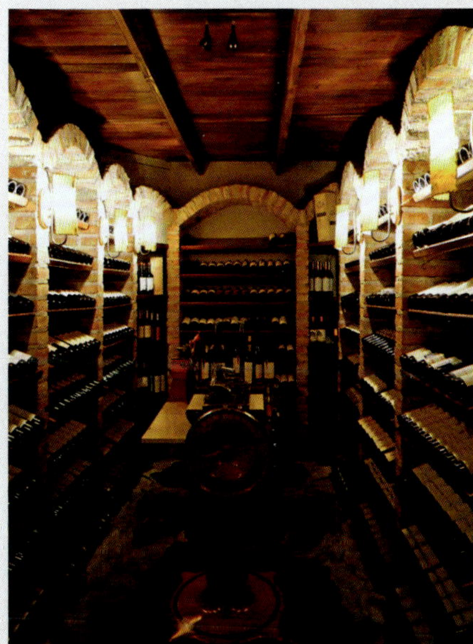

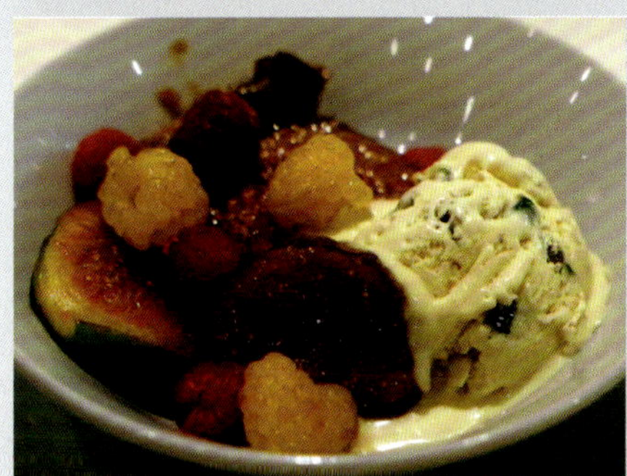

PATAGONIA **NEUQUÉN** NEUQUÉN

Brewery & Restaurant

CERVECERÍA OWE BREWHOUSE

2150 Av Coronel Olascoaga
(Large Restaurant & Brewery, south of downtown)
133 Buenos Aires
(Small Restaurant with Beer, Downtown)

011 (+54 299) 443.7501
info@CerveceriaOwe.com.ar

CerveceriaOwe.com.ar

Español (just say: cerveza por favor)

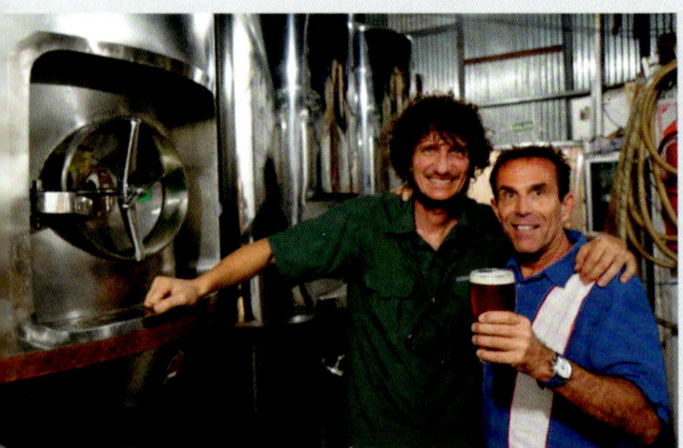

In the land of extraordinary wines, Neuquén also has a local craft brewery... Cervecería Owe.

These are some of the best beers you will drink anywhere, so why not Neuquén. It is said: it takes a lot of beer to make wine, it is the secret ingredient of every harvest. Hot harvest days need cold refreshing beers! So... why not a few remarkable craft beers to get you ready for some exceptional wine tastings. This was my approach (photo above) however... I had to come back for more after the wine tasting.

With all fresh ingredients, creative styles and delicious flavors, all beers are brewed on the premise by Master Brewmeister Marcelo Neme, caught here tasting one of his newest special brews (photo right), an unfiltered Belgian-style beer, only 17 days in the making.

The food is great too... try the pork elbow. It is so tender, it falls off the bone!

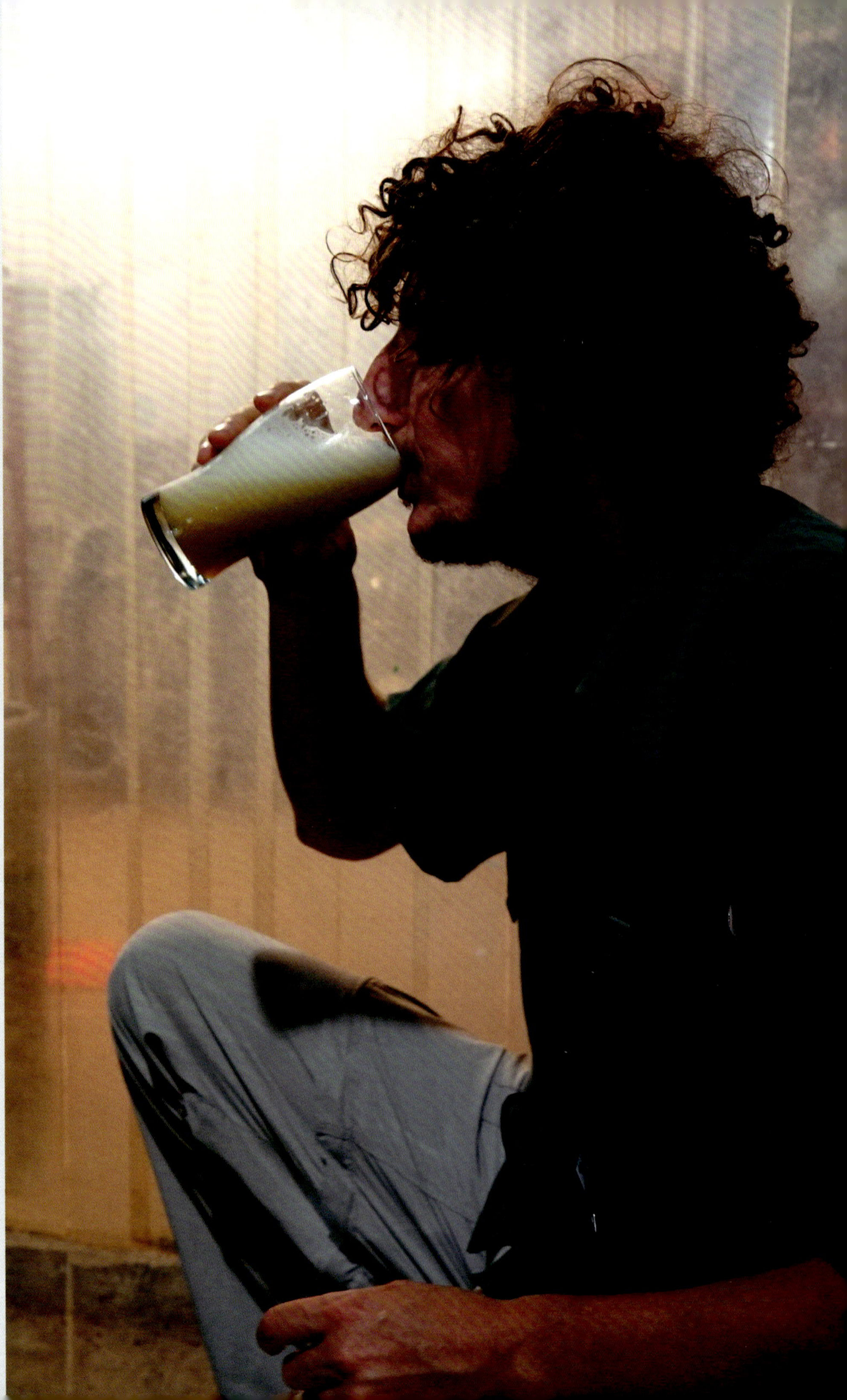

Restaurant
CASA TINTA

166 Fotheringham (Downtown Neuquén)

011 (+54 299) 442.1906
CasaTintaRestaurante@gmail.com

facebook: Casa Tinta Restaurante

English & Español

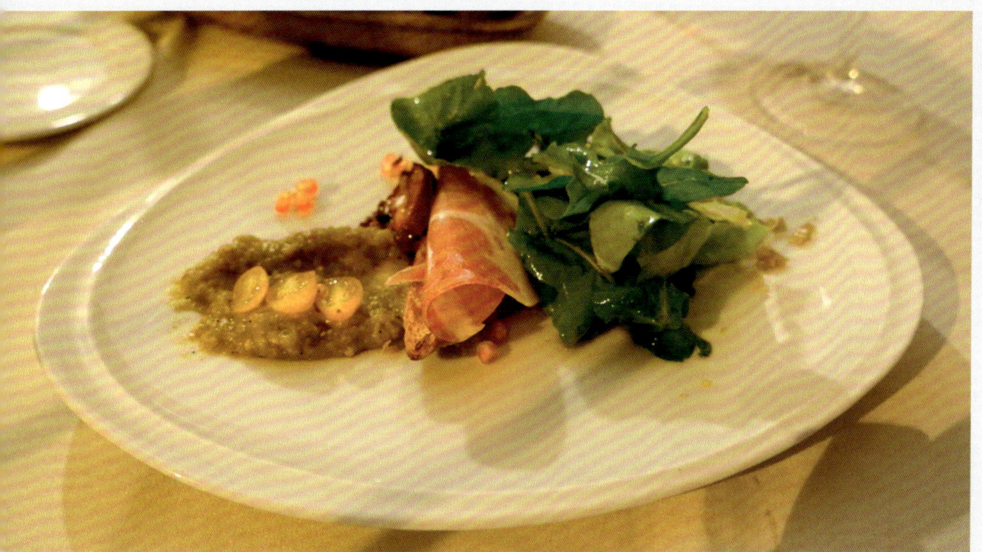

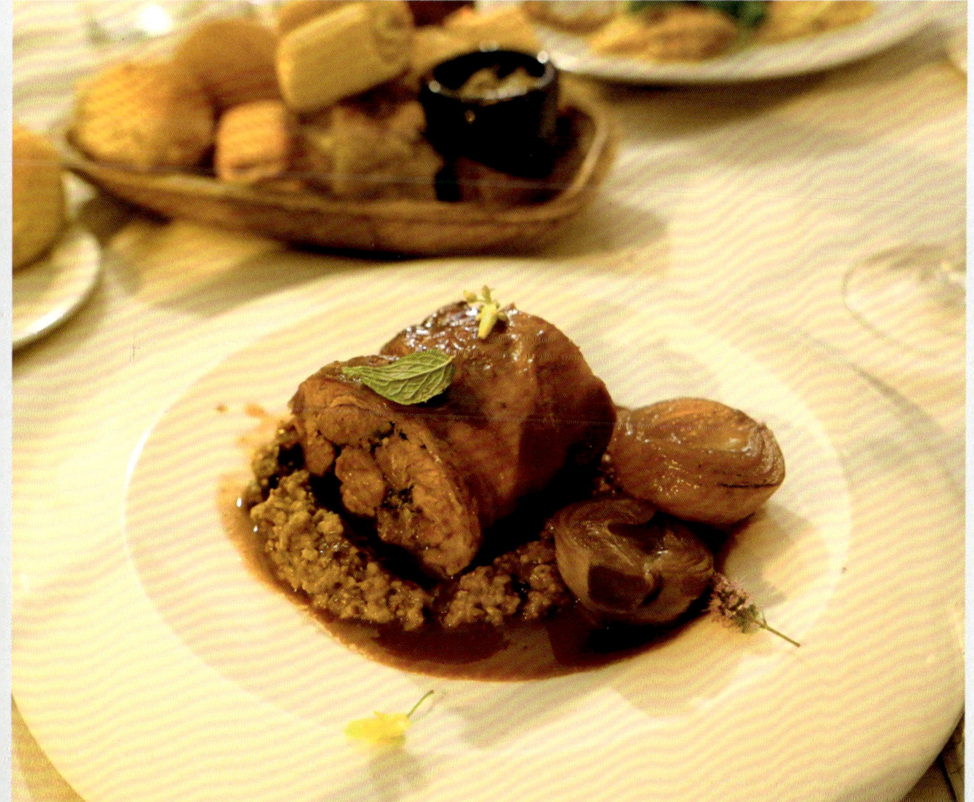

They call their food: **New American Cuisine**. The more I thought about it, the more I realized this was the gourmet plates I would find in New York or San Francisco. It was refreshing to indulge in an American-style fresh salad (photo top left).

I was thinking Patagonia though... because of the lamb. Check out the **Patagonia Lamb Roll** (photo bottom left) with grilled onions and creamy lentils, with ginger and lemon zest. Succulent! Patagonia is known for their superior lamb, and Casa Tinta does it very well. They use a clay oven with natural woods. The lamb was slow-cooked in this oven for four hours.

This is a cozy little place, run by the owners/chef. The menu is created monthly for seasonal offerings. Open since 2013, and they are already winning awards for their cuisine... best menu!

Local wine list of Neuquén wines, as in the 2013 Saurus Select Pinot Noir, from Familia Schroeder.

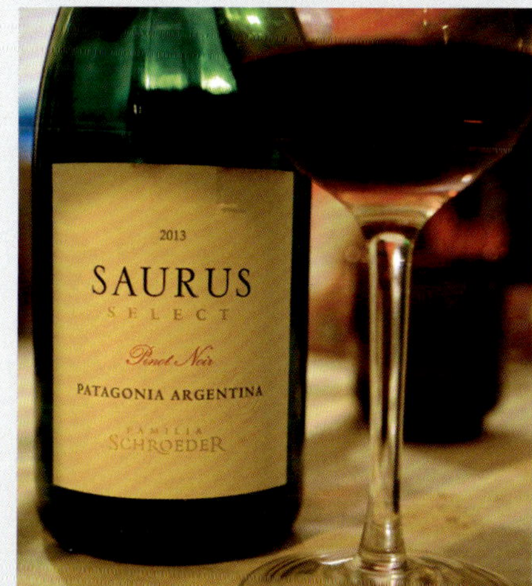

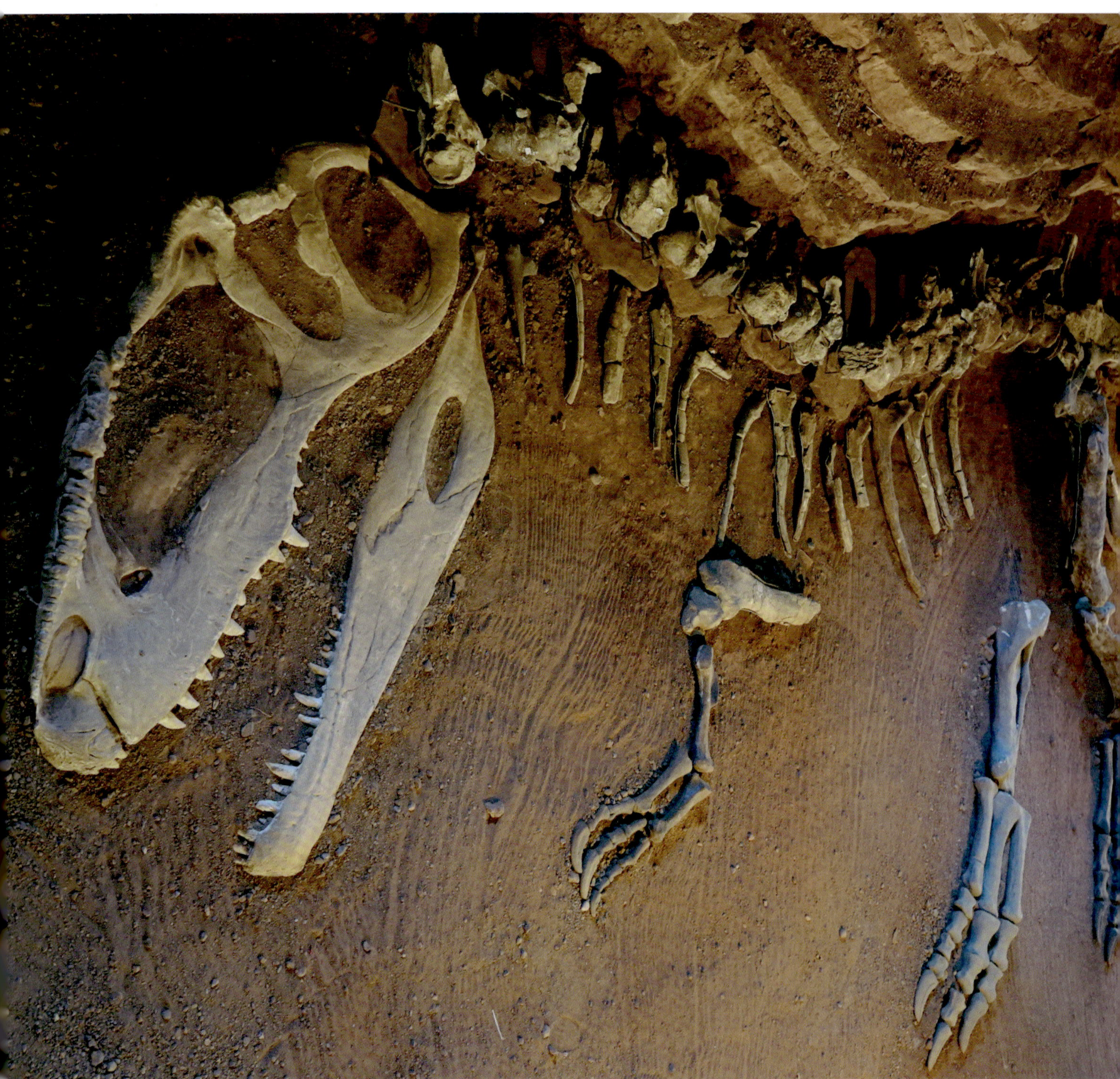

THE LARGEST CARNIVORE WAS RECENTLY DISCOVERED HERE

The oil industry is booming in the Neuquén province as the world's third largest oil reserves are being discovered here. Just five years ago the city of Neuquén had 200,000 population, now it is near 300,000! It is expected to reach a million people in the next 10 years. And we all know who was in the oil business first... ***Dinosaurs!***

Dinosaurs are all over the place in Neuquén. There are numerous museums and Paleontology Centers studying this gigantic group of reptiles that dominated Earth for 165 million years (during the Mesozoic Era 65 million to 230 million years ago).

The largest carnivore of all time, Dinosaur Carcharodontosauridea (meaning, the tooth of the shark), was recently discovered here near Neuquén and is displayed at **Villa El Chocón** (photo left page). This dinosaur was 46 feet long, surpassing the previous record of 42 feet long, and much bigger than the better-known Tyrannosaurus Rex.

There are interesting theories surrounding the dinosaur. It makes the study fascinating. One theory suggests that the Earth went through a dramatic change causing the food sources to be destroyed. The herbivores literally starved to death. And the carnivores followed.

The flying dinosaurs were better survivalists. They could travel larger distances to find food. And from their aerial perspective, they could see food sources with greater advantage to their earthbound counterparts.

I speculate while the flying dinosaurs could still find food, the quantity became less and less for their massive bodies. Over time, the generations became smaller and smaller to adapt to a smaller food supply. Take this over millions of years and I ask you... are these our birds of today?

Paleontologists are now studying the hip structure of the various dinosaurs and how they relate to other reptiles. Most interesting though, is that they have found the flying dinosaur hips to be dramatically different from the other dinosaurs, and having the same characteristics of the flying birds of today. Hmmm...

I can easily imagine the continued survival of these flying dinosaurs/birds through such progressing Earth disasters, such as the Ice Age (2.6 million years ago). Wings sure do have their advantage. Must be another reason why I love being a pilot!

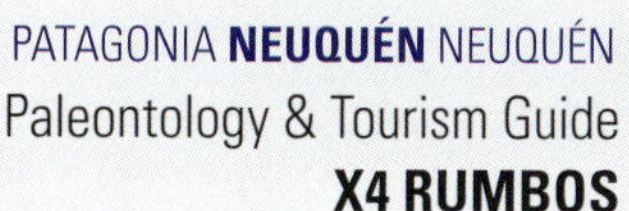

011 (+54 299) 448.8977
info@x4rumbos.com.ar

x4rumbos.com.ar

English & Español

There are many places in Neuquén to see dinosaurs and understand their history. I recommend calling María Huk and spend the day with her. Her business is x4 Rumbos and she is extremely knowledgable about dinosaurs. She can take you to interesting places to hike, where the dinosaurs hiked. And she knows the right Paleontology Centers to visit. Most valuable is that María is an educational experience. She speaks both English and Spanish fluently, and you will end your day fascinated by what you learned from her.

María Huk is a Professional Tourism Guide, and is well versed in wine too. She can take you to the wineries, both in Neuquén and Río Negro. She also offers bird-watching excursions as well as other historical and cultural experiences in the area.

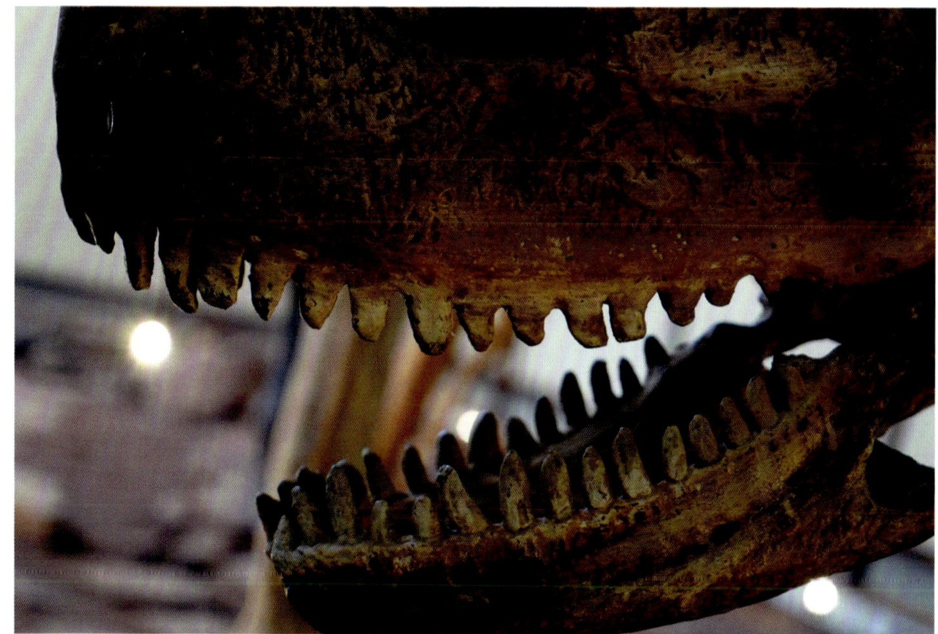

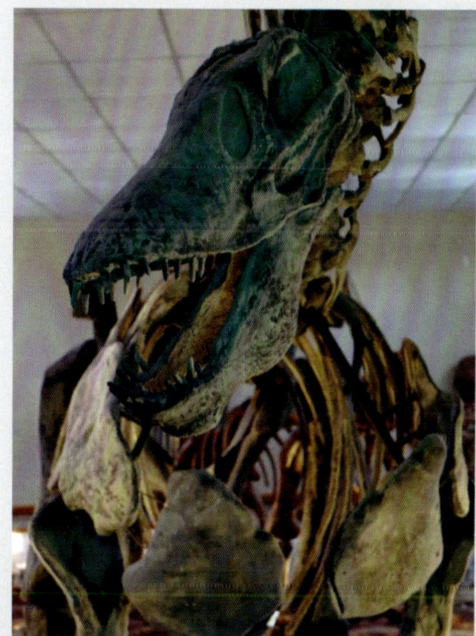

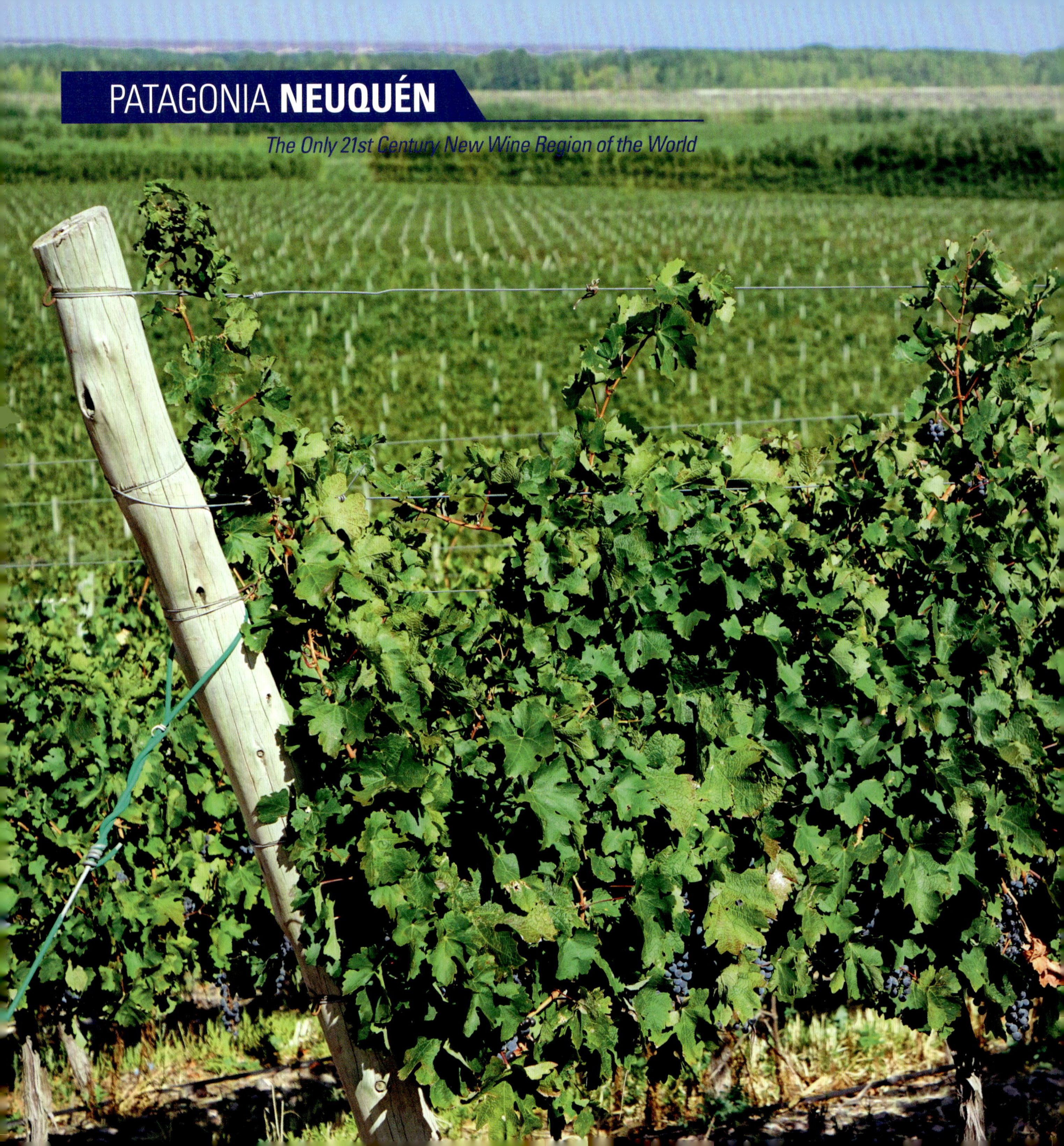
PATAGONIA NEUQUÉN
The Only 21st Century New Wine Region of the World

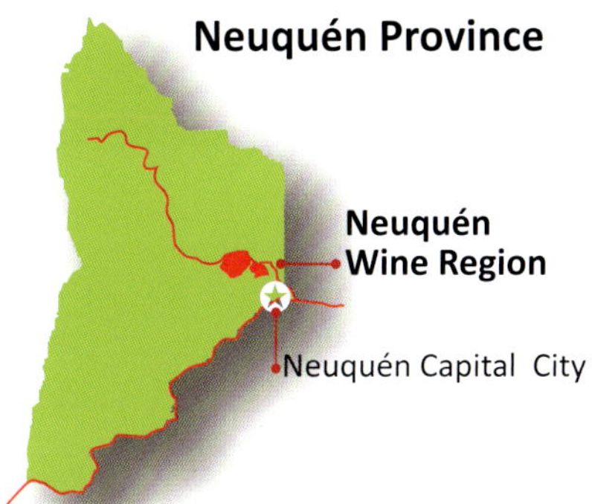

EXPLORING NEUQUÉN

The world's newest wine region has recently been born in Neuquén! Not that long ago, at the turn of the century, the concept of a brand-new wine region was realized by planting 5,000 acres of Patagonia desert with grapevines into a terroir that would produce exclusively top-quality, premium wines. Today, there are five wineries producing more wine than the rest of Patagonia combined.

All five wineries are located on the north side of Rio Neuquén, 37 miles northwest of the city of Neuquén, next to the small village of San Patricio del Chañar, on Ruta 7. The wineries are all practically next to each other, making them easy to visit.

What makes this all possible is canals that were developed a hundred years ago to bring the water from Neuquén River to irrigate pear, apple and cherry orchards. Now they are channelled to the vineyards with an endless supply of fresh water. Since all of the wineries are brand new, they are built using the latest of technology in winemaking.

The soil texture here is ideal for viticulture, with three distinct soil types for the agronomists to work with in maximizing the grape quality and characteristics. The hillside top is rock and sand, while the hillside itself is clay and sand, and the valley floor is just sand. Elevation ranges from 1,000 to 1,300 feet. This is a much lower elevation from Mendoza, and especially Salta, as Neuquén is several hundred miles away from the Andes.

The bone-dry, wind-swept landscape here has been untouched since the dinosaurs. It is the extreme dryness plus wind that prevents vineyard diseases naturally. Longer days and greater thermal amplitude allow slow ripening of the grapes, promoting greater accumulation of sugars, acidity levels, aromas and flavors... giving these wines unique characteristics of the terroir.

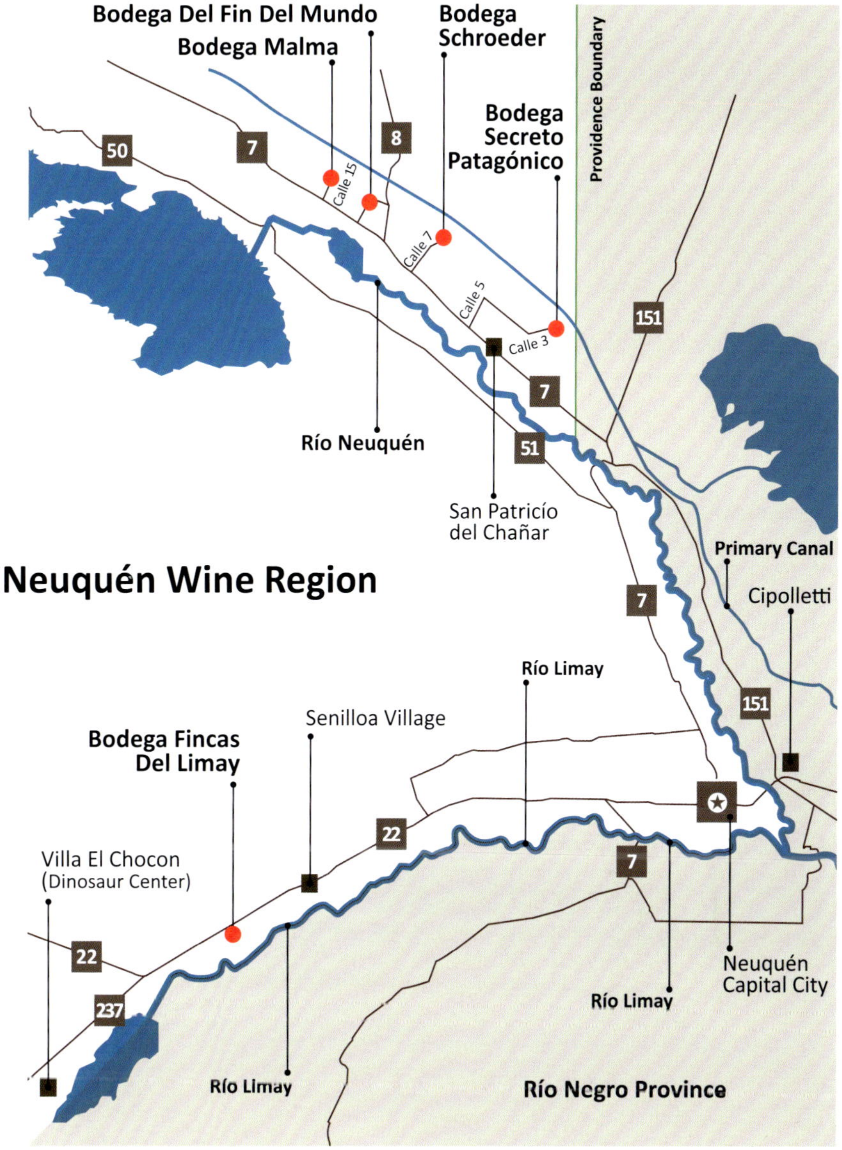

Neuquén Wine Region
Bodega Del Fin Del Mundo
Bodega Malma
Bodega Schroeder
Bodega Secreto Patagónico
Providence Boundary
Calle 15
Calle 7
Calle 5
Calle 3
Río Neuquén
San Patricío del Chañar
Primary Canal
Cipolletti
Río Limay
Senilloa Village
Bodega Fincas Del Limay
Villa El Chocon (Dinosaur Center)
Neuquén Capital City
Río Limay
Río Limay
Río Negro Province
50 7 8 151 7 51 7 151 22 7 22 237

Neuquén wines have great color concentration, intense fruity aromas and great body structure. The cooler climate allows for more elegance in the red wines, especially for Pinot Noir and Merlot, and a Malbec of a different style to Mendoza. Also grown here are Chardonnay, Cabernet Sauvignon, Cabernet Franc and Sauvignon Blanc. The wines express more minerality here, and have deeper more concentrated characteristics.

The next possible wine region on the planet just began in 2005 as yet another Neuquén wine region. This time along the north side of the Limay River, 34 miles southwest of the city of Neuquén, just west of the small village of Senillosa, on Ruta 22. The grapes were planted in 2005 and the first winery is scheduled to be completed in 2015.

Most significant about this area is the presence of sand and gravel from ancient paleobanks of the Limay River. The mineral components of this deep and well-drained soil fill the wines with aromas which make them unique, and with intense colors.

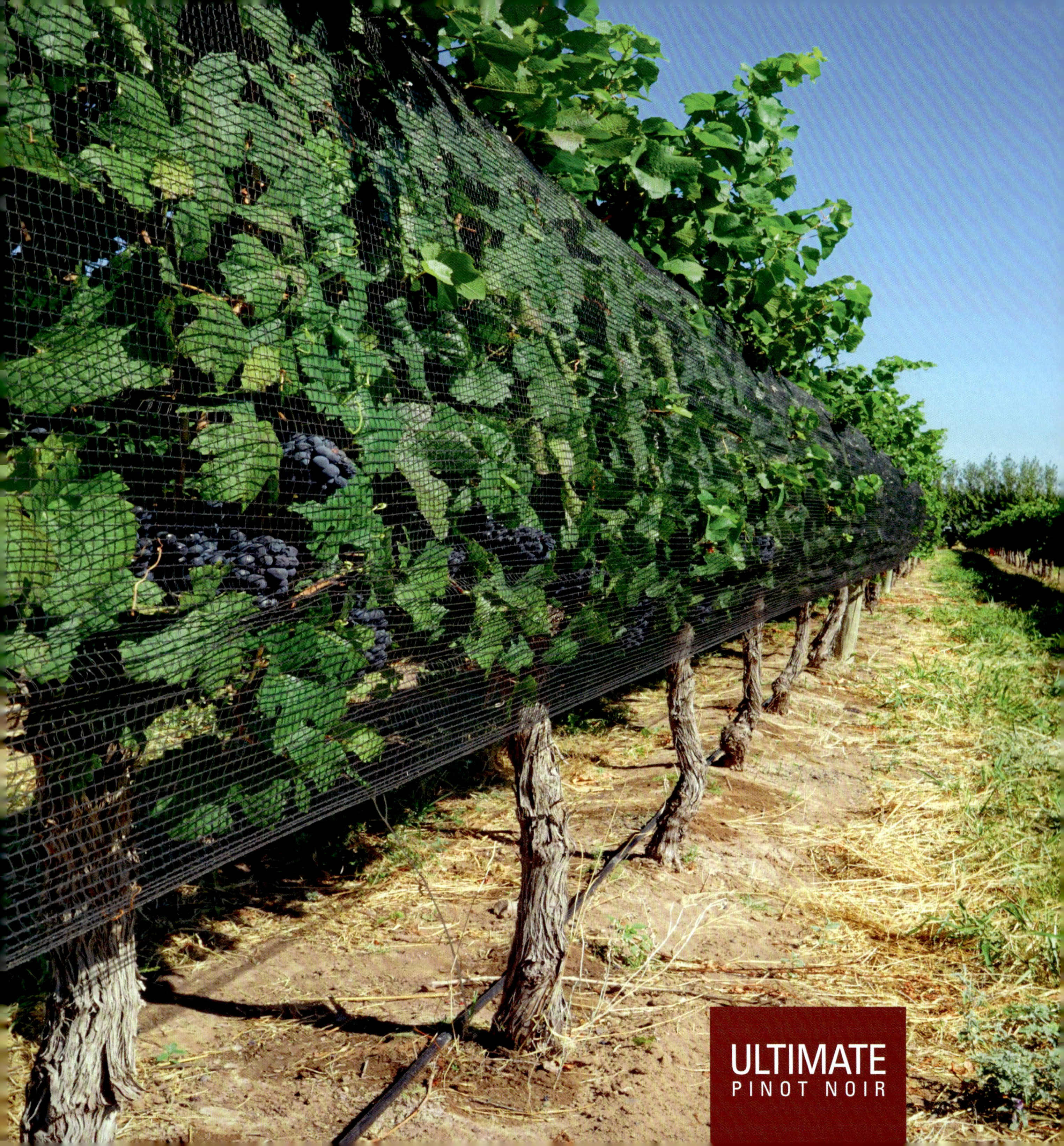
ULTIMATE
PINOT NOIR

Winery (Bodega)

DEL FIN DEL MUNDO

AT THE END OF THE WORLD

It would take quite the visionary to successfully pull off creating a brand new wine region, especially out of the extreme desert of Patagonia. Such visionary is **Julio Viola**, a lover of the land here, who conducted significant research on the soil, climate and other conditions, finding out that the Neuquén terroir surrounding San Patricio del Chañar had ideal conditions for *vitis vinifera*, the wine grape species of the vine. And especially Pinot Noir.

It made sense... being farther south would be cooler than Mendoza, the thermal amplitude range greater, the days longer, the soil as poor, and the water plentiful. And made further sense... that Viola would name his winery **Del Fin Del Mundo** as its literal translation is: **The End of the World**.

Many people compare the Patagonia style of Pinot Noir to French style, not California. The wines are definitely softer like Burgundy; also like the Willamette Valley in Oregon, USA. I feel the wines here include all these qualities, including California. Why? The wind and intense sun! The wind I explained earlier is extreme and so the grapes build up thicker skins to protect themselves. The ozone is thinner in Patagonia, giving greater intensity of sun to the grapes, causing them to further develop thicker skins. Thicker skins bring immense colors to the wines and more concentrated juice that I feel resemble the bigger Pinot Noir style of California and still retain the softness of Willamette and Burgundy.

Plus, there is a unique minerality derived from the soil here that adds further complexity and flavor to the wines that are a magnificent experience in the mouth. When you have this experience, I assure you, you will be back for more.

Vineyard Netting? If the photo (left page) was in California you would think this was *bird-netting* to keep the fruit-thirsty birds away from the precious grapes. If this photo was in Mendoza, it would be *hail-netting* to protect against the drastic summer storms coming from the Andes, throwing large hail stones at the grapes and destroying entire vineyards. Far from the Andes and with vineyard friendly birds in Neuquén, what you see in this photo is *sun-netting*, and the beautiful Pinot Noir grapes (also photo below).

Del Fin Del Mundo nets their most prized vineyards to protect the grapes from the sun's intensity in order to produce even greater softness in their ultimate wines. Del Fin Del Mundo makes a very large number of different wines (next page), which I have tasted through the profile, and I must tell you this Pinot Noir, from this vineyard, stands on top above all their other wines, even the other varietals. Specifically, this is the **FIN Del Mundo, Single Vineyard, Pinot Noir** (bottle photo right and grapes photo below).

This exclusive line of **FIN Single Vineyard** varietals is produced using unique grapes in pursuit of the maximum typicity of the varietal and of which the Neuquén terroir can produce. Singularity in the exact vines is what makes it different from others and demonstrates signature characteristics to the wines. I am a real fan of this line of their wines.

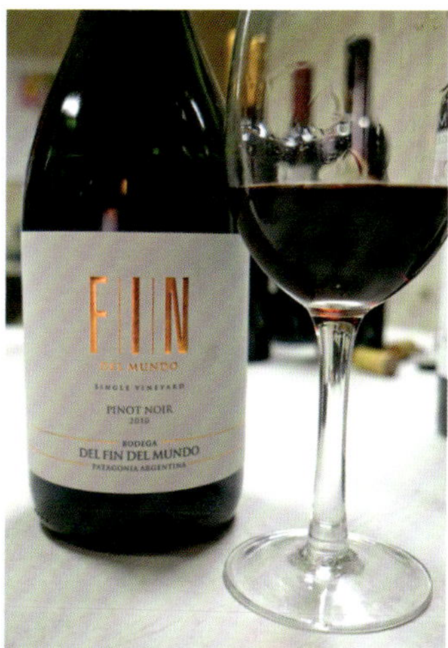

Michael's Favorite Pick
FIN Del Mundo - Single Vineyard - Pinot Noir

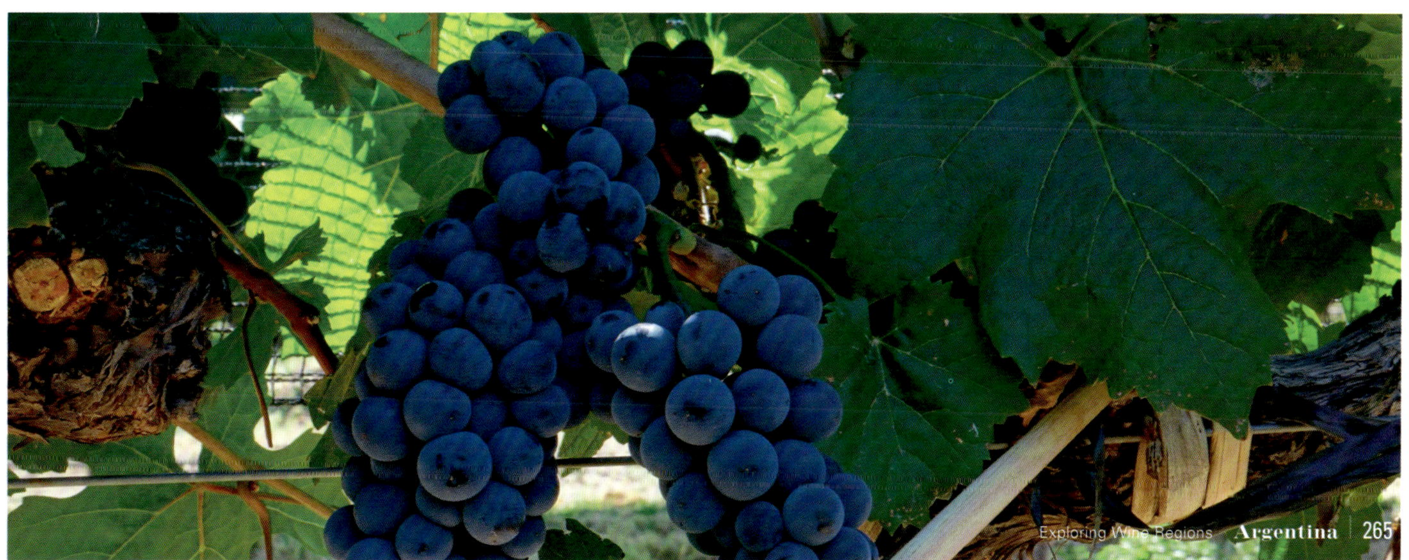

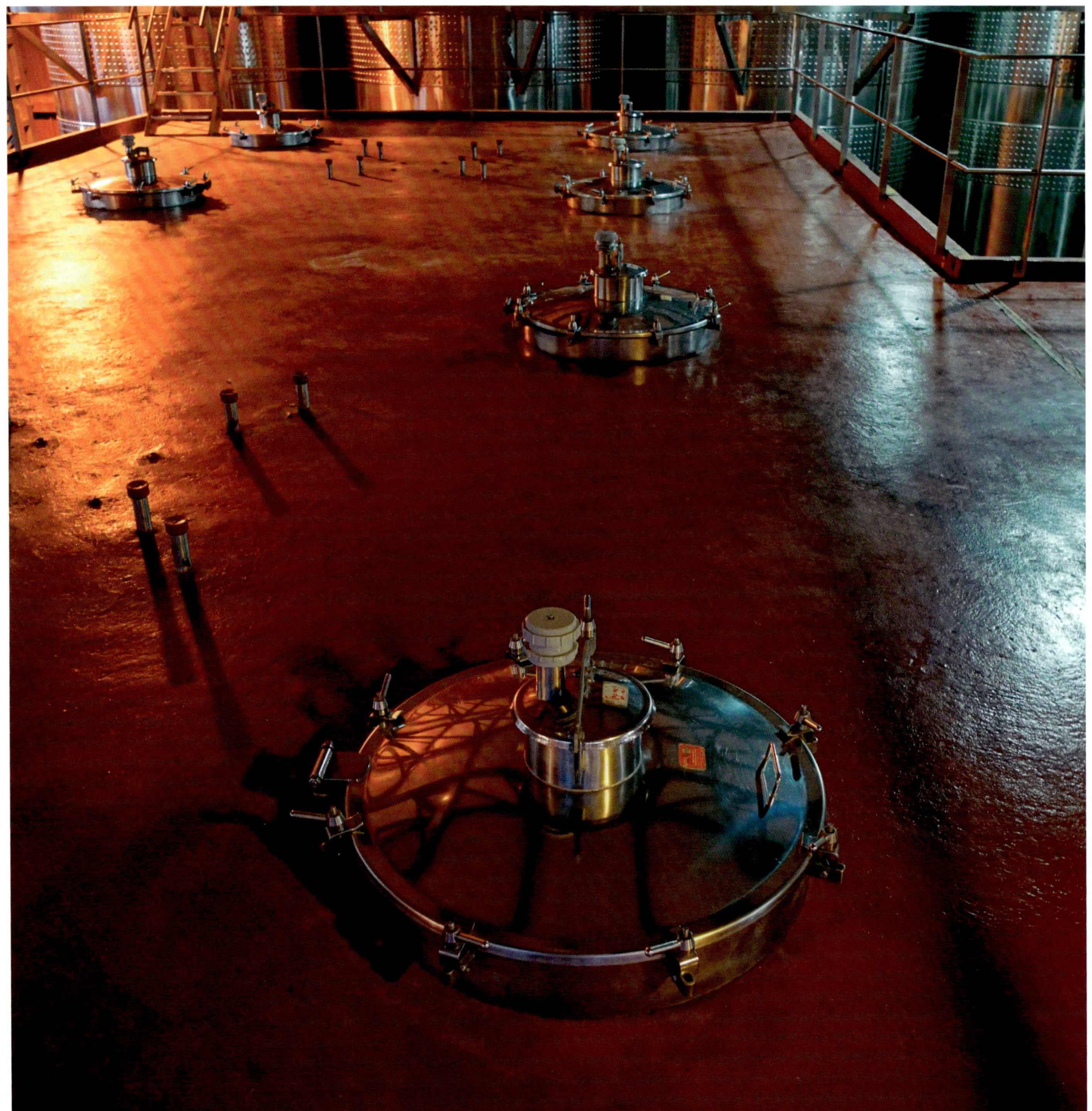

Del Fin Del Mundo was not just first in developing this new wine region in Neuquén, it has become the largest winery in Patagonia, including the wineries of Rio Negro. In fact it is larger than all the other wineries in Patagonia, combined.

Del Fin Del Mundo produces 10 million bottles of wine annually, plus they own the winery next door Bodega Malma (formerly NQN) producing another million bottles, for a total of 11 million of the 20 million total bottles produced in all of Patagonia.

You can begin to see the massive scale of this winery in these photographs (left page and below) of the concrete wine pools and stainless steel tanks, respectively. This winery alone has 104 concrete wine pools, 200 stainless steel tanks, 2,200 oak aging barrels, and four French oak casks of 6,000 liters each... producing wines from their expansive 2,150 acres of estate vineyards.

This winery makes for a fantastic tour as they have built a skywalk which crosses through the winery at elevation, so you can oversee the production of their many winemaking activities. The guided tour begins with a glass of sparkling wine as you are educated about the different aspects of the winery and the winemaking process step by step. You will get to taste wines directly from the stainless steel tanks and from the oak barrels to learn about the differences among the different stages of the winemaking process.

During harvest, February, March and April, you can also tour the vineyards in an educational experience of grape growing, which includes harvesting your own grapes.

In July and August, you can participate in their vine-pruning activities. This is actually a critical activity in preparing the vines for the coming year's harvest. They will explain the unique Patagonian vineyard systems, irrigation, pruning techniques and their benefits as you tour the vineyards.

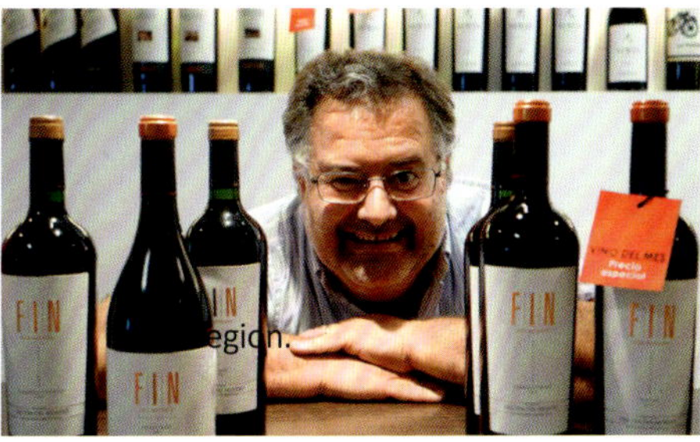

Master Oenoligist - Marcelo Miras

Marcelo Miras is the Chief Winemaker at Del Fin Del Mundo. He came to Patagonia in 1991 from Mendoza, since then has contributed to the success of most of the 20+ wineries in Neuquén and Río Negro.

Miras began his career being mentored by Argentina's most notable viticultural visionary **Don Raúl de la Mota,** who was bestowed the *Best Winemaker of the 20th Century Argentina*. Today, Miras consults with the renowned French winemaker/consultant **Michel Rolland**.

Marcelo comes with a great personality, perfect for inspiring his winemaking team, and experience probably greater than anyone else in Patagonia, plus expertise that creates magic in the winemaking process. When you taste his wines, you will enjoy their amazing qualities!

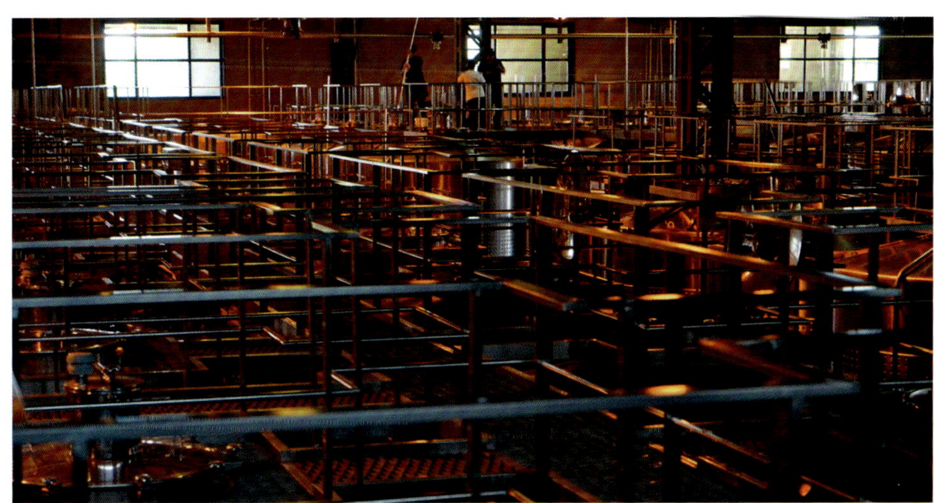

PATAGONIA **NEUQUÉN** SAN PATRICIO

Winery (Bodega)

DEL FIN DEL MUNDO

Ruta 7 at Ruta 8 (9 km N of San Patricio on Ruta 7)
(**San Patricio Del Chañar,** Neuquén)

011 (+54 299) 580.0414
info@bdfm.com.ar

BodegaDelFinDelMundo.com

English, Español & Português
11,000,000 bottles produced annually

Total Collection of Wines

Bodega Del Fin Del Mundo - Special Blend
(Malbec, Cabernet Sauvignon, Merlot)

Del Fin Del Mundo - Gran Reserva
(Malbec, Cabernet Sauvignon, Merlot, Cab Franc)

Del Fin Del Mundo - Reserva
Pinot Noir • Malbec • Cabernet Sauvignon
Merlot • Chardonnay/Viognier

FIN Del Mundo - Single Vineyard
Pinot Noir • Malbec • Cabernet Sauvignon
Cabernet Franc • Merlot • Tannat

La Ponderosa
Viognier • Cabernet Franc & Merlot Blend

Newen - Reserved
Pinot Noir • Malbec • Cabernet Sauvignon
Merlot • Syrah • Sauvignon Blanc • Torrontés

Del Fin Del Mundo - Postales
Roble (Cab Sauvignon, Malbec, Chardonnay)
Malbec • Merlot • Cabernet Sauvignon • Chardonnay
Malbec/Syrah • Cabernet Sauvignon/Malbec
Sauvignon Blanc/Semillón

Ventus
Roble (Malbec/Cabernet Sauvignon/Chardonnay)
Malbec • Cab Sauvignon • Chardonnay/Sauv Blanc
Malbec/Cabernet Sauvignon/Merlot

Cosecha De Mayo - Semillón Tardío (late harvest)

Del Fin Del Mundo - Extra Brut (sparkling)
80% Pinot Noir & 20% Chardonnay

To get Del Fin Del Mundo wines in the USA
Contact their Importer at TestaWines.com
In Florida, Importer at GlobalWinesLLC.com

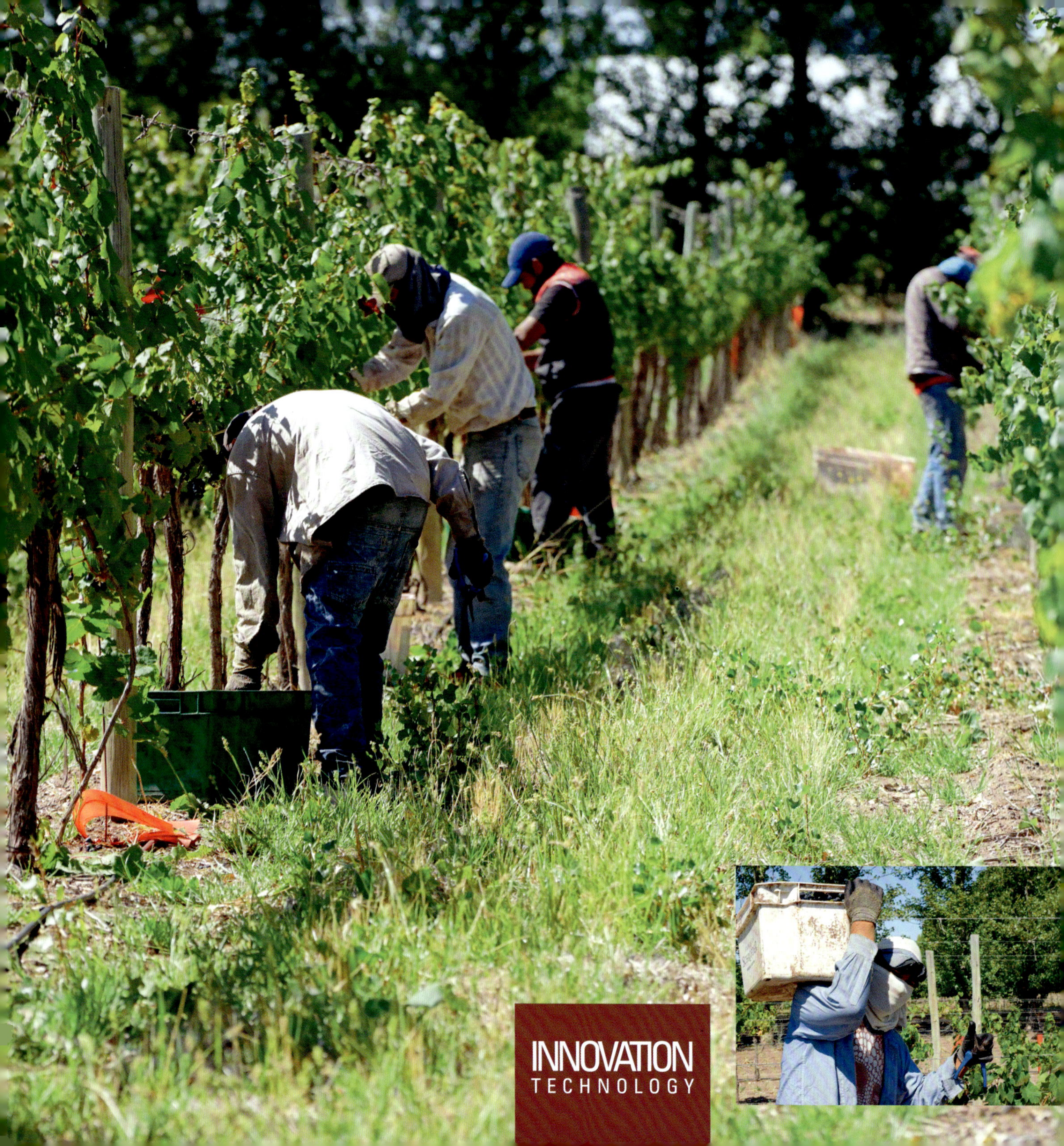
INNOVATION
TECHNOLOGY

HIGHLY ADVANCED WINERY

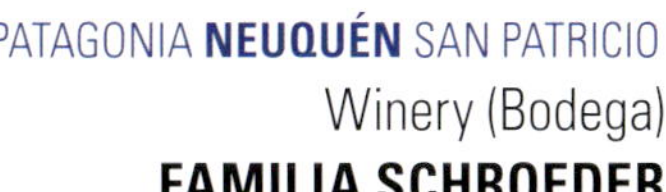

The Schroeder family were also pioneers of this new wine region of Neuquén, planting their first vineyards in 2001 (photo left page of a Pinot Noir harvest) and building their winery in 2003. Today they have 350 acres of vineyards, produce 1.5 million bottles of wine, and have become the largest exporter of Patagonia wine to the USA. They are also the largest producers of sparkling wines in Patagonia with 500,000 bottles annually.

Their success comes from producing extremely high-quality wines, many of which are unique and innovative, setting them apart from their competition. Considering the vines were 10 years old in 2011, releasing many of their red wines in 2014, Familia Schroeder is now at the pinnacle of showing off their creations. Very impressive!

At the helm is oenologist Leonardo Puppato (photo below overseeing a detailed sorting process) who was there from the beginning and designed the most technologically advanced winery you can possibly imagine! This includes the technical aspects of the building design itself, as well as incorporating innovative equipment and processes inside the winery (photo below right).

From the moment the grapes enter the winery, they are received in a spacious cold room to bring their temperature down prior to hand-sorting. As the grapes move through the winery, there is almost no pumping whatsoever to maintain the highly delicate handling of their precious fruit. To achieve this, the winery was built on the side of a slope to take advantage of gravity moving the wine through each step in the winemaking process.

Puppato created a special design for "hanging" his fermentation tanks (versus sitting on the floor) allowing him to drop the fruit from above into the fermentation tanks and then release them at the bottom as they continue to move though the winery without pumping. This also allows for better control of the solids and cleaning.

The temperature of all of the tanks (both storage and fermentation) is controlled from a centralized master panel, along with controlled humidity and temperature in the aging cellars. This is a total integral designed to allow the production of controlled quality with the highest standards.

Leonardo Puppato also consults with **Renowned Oenologist Paul Hobbs**, from whom he finds himself constantly learning and being challenged by his obsession with achieving the highest quality possible. Hobbs also brings a very clear view on the trends of the consumers palate in the quality arena they target for their wines.

As the wine flows to the lowest level of the winery for aging in the cellars, it passes through an exhibit of the remains of a dinosaur discovered during the construction. When they conducted excavations for the cellar, they found fossilized remains of a titanosaurid, one of the largest dinosaurs found wandering this land millions of years ago. Today you can see the remains of **Panamericansaurus Schroederi** in a space specially fitted inside the cellar in the exact place it was found (photo right).

Saurus is now the label for many of the Familia Schroeder wines in honor of its ancestors of this land once lived.

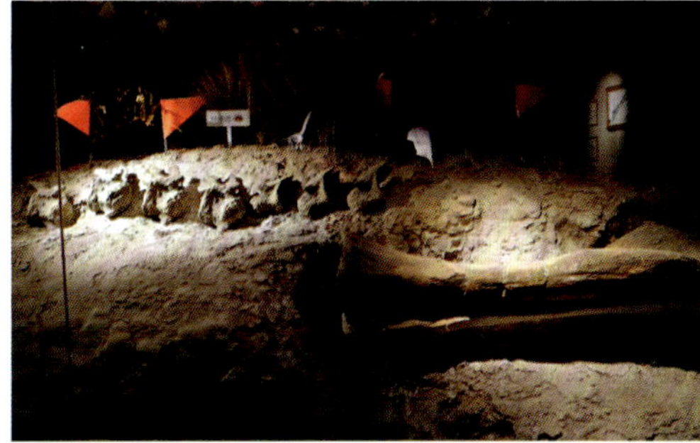

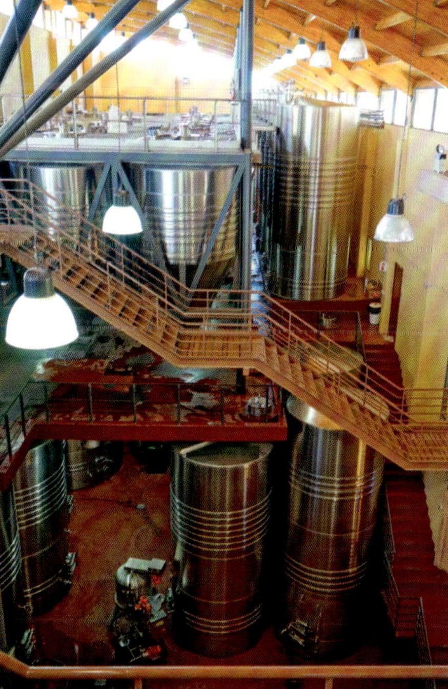

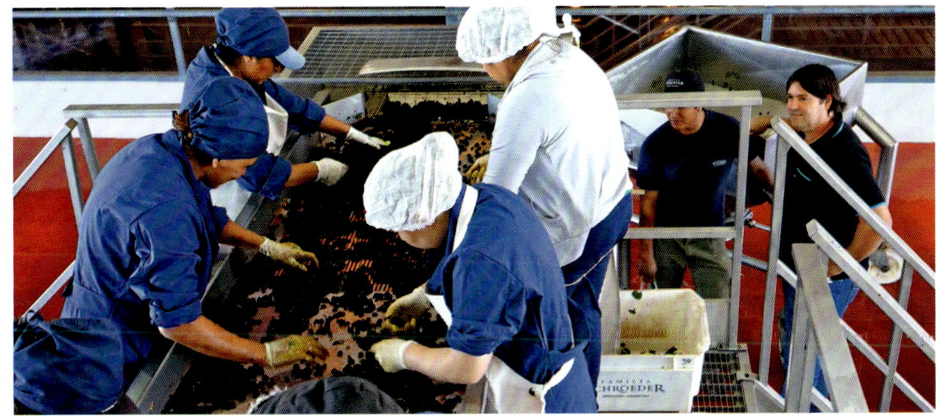

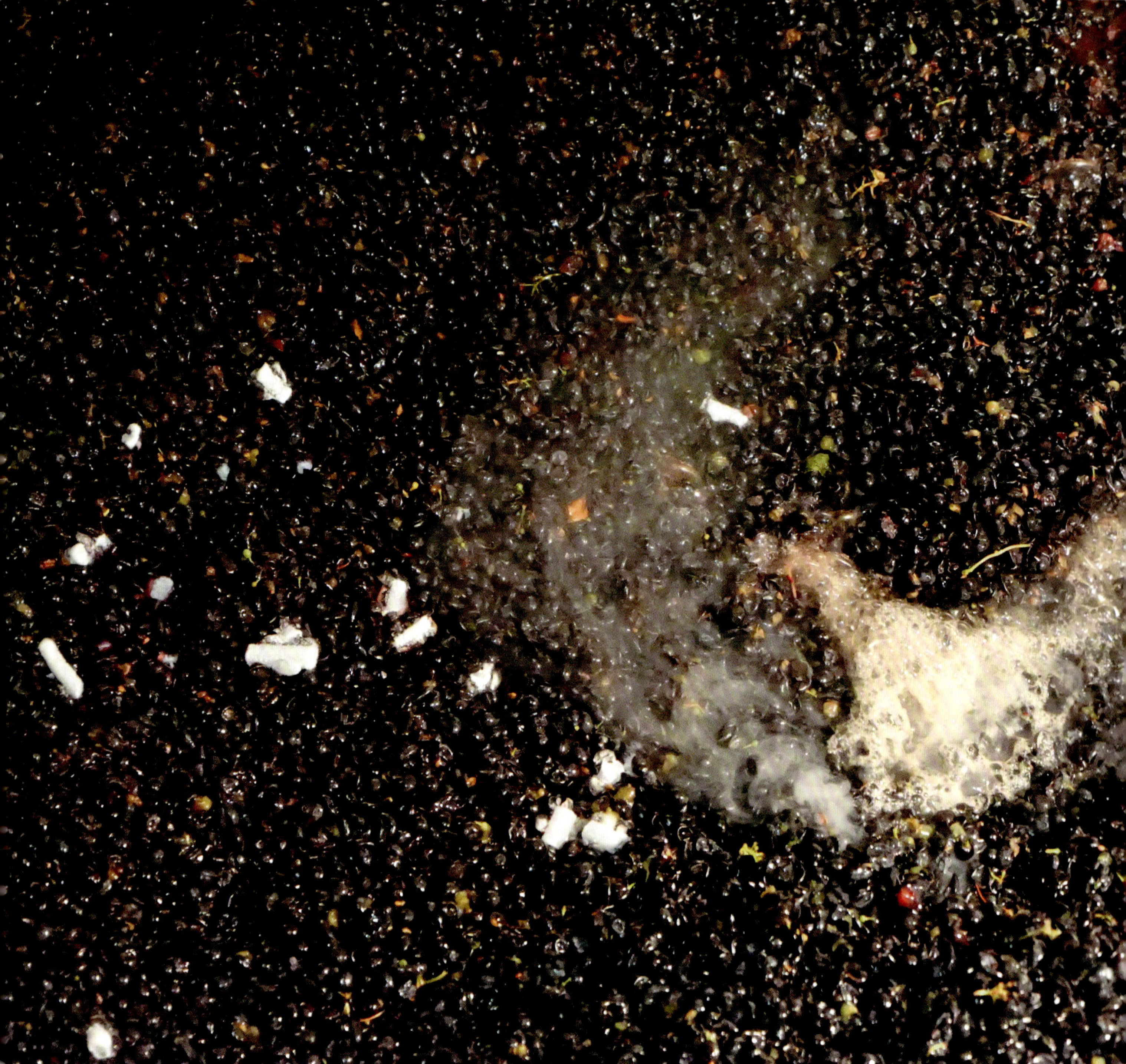

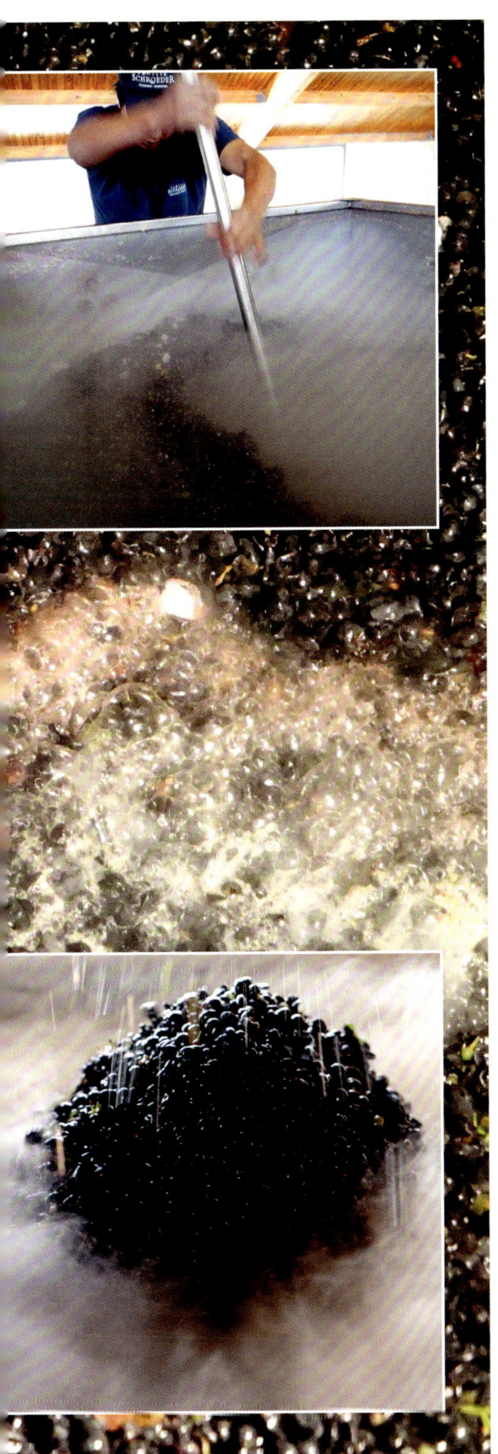

INNOVATIVE WINEMAKING

Dry Ice Winemaking is a unique technique used at Familia Schroeder to create extremely smooth wines. After de-stemming and meticulous sorting, the berries fall into bins of dry ice (photo below left). Then the berries are gently mixed by hand (photo left) so the dry ice mixes throughout the fruit to quickly bring the temperature below 43°F. In the large picture (left page) you can see the pieces of dry ices in and around the grapes, and the cold fog rising from the surface.

Temperature and oxygen are necessary for fermentation to occur. This dry ice is very cold and thwarts off fermentation and absorbs oxygen to maintain a carbonic atmosphere, so they can extend the cold prior to fermentations.

This process is applied to all wines from Select level upwards and is meant to obtain the lightest flavors prior to the fermentation process. The intention is to get the smoothest possible wines while retaining a reasonable amount of tannins for achieving a well-balanced structure, long finish, and keeping a bright fruit profile and fresh juicy mouth feel.

Dead Yeast Winemaking is a special technique used at Familia Schroeder to produce delicate flavors in their sparkling wines.

Lees is the sediment of wine in the barrel, considered worthless with dead yeast and other particles, and is subsequently discarded after fermentation. This dead yeast is the secret, however, to the delicate flavors and elegance of the Schroeder sparkling wines.

Schroeder starts with very high-quality wines and then allows the wines much longer contact with the dead yeast particles. Contact with the lees requires the sparkling wine to sit on the tank at controlled low temperatures for longer periods of time after the fermentation has finished. This means extra costs because of energy to keep the temperature down and investment in tanks to hold the inventory; however, the result is a special elegance and delicateness to the flavors.

Saurus Extra Brut has three to four months of dead yeast, **Rosa de los Vientos** has six months, and the **Brut Nature** has 12 to 14 months of added contact with the dead yeast particles.

Winery (Bodega)

FAMILIA SCHROEDER

Calle 7 Norte (7 km N of San Patricio on Ruta 7)
(**San Patricio Del Chañar,** Neuquén)

011 (+54 299) 489.9600
marketing@FamiliaSchroeder.com.ar

FamiliaSchroeder.com

English and Español
1,500,000 total bottles produced annually
500,000 bottles of sparkling produced annually

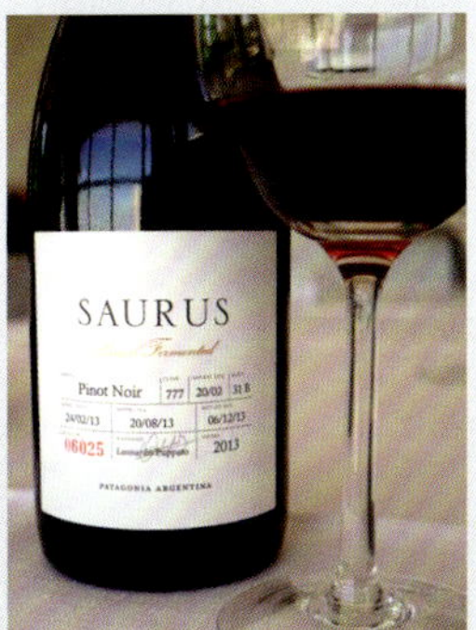

Michael's Favorite Pick
Saurus - Barrel Fermented - Pinot Noir

Total Collection of Wines

Familia Schroeder
Pinot Noir • Malbec • Pinot Noir/Malbec

Saurus Barrel Fermented
Pinot Noir • Malbec

Saurus Select • Alpataco Select • Puestero Select
Pinot Noir • Malbec • Cabernet Sauvignon
Merlot • Chardonnay • Sauvignon Blanc

Saurus • Alpataco • Puestero
Pinot Noir • Malbec • Cabernet Sauvignon
Merlot • Chardonnay • Sauvignon Blanc
Malbec Rose

Espumantes (sparkling wines)
Deseado (Torrontés) • Rosa De La Vientos (Pinot Noir)
Saurus Extra Brut (40% Pinot Noir/60% Chardonnay)
Brut Nature (60% Pinot Noir/40% Chardonnay)
Deseado Rosé (Torrontés/Pinot Noir)

To get Familia Schroeder wines in the USA
Contact their Importer at EcoValleyImports.com

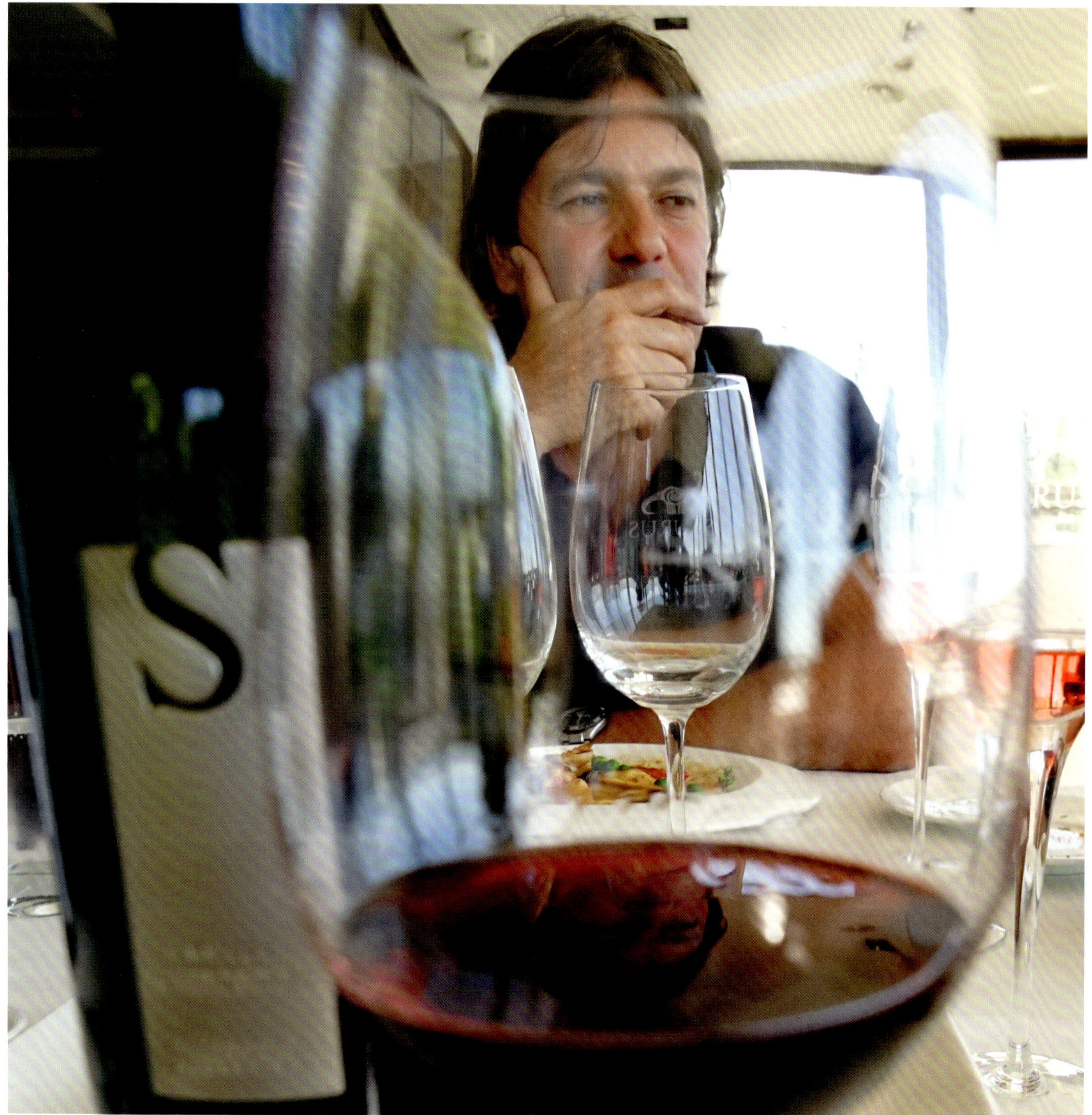

Familia Schroeder's oenologist, Leonardo Puppato, contemplating innovation

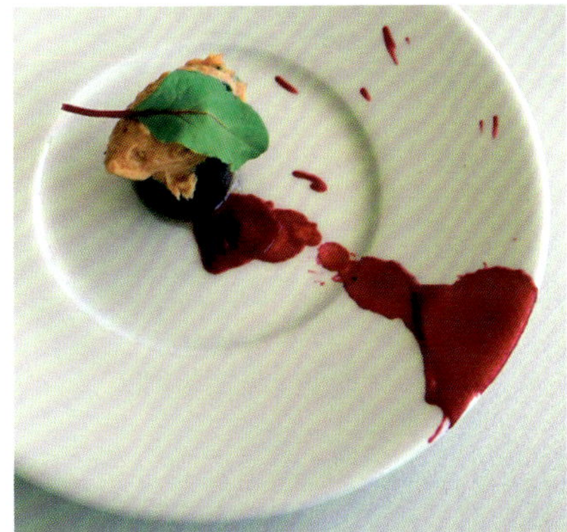

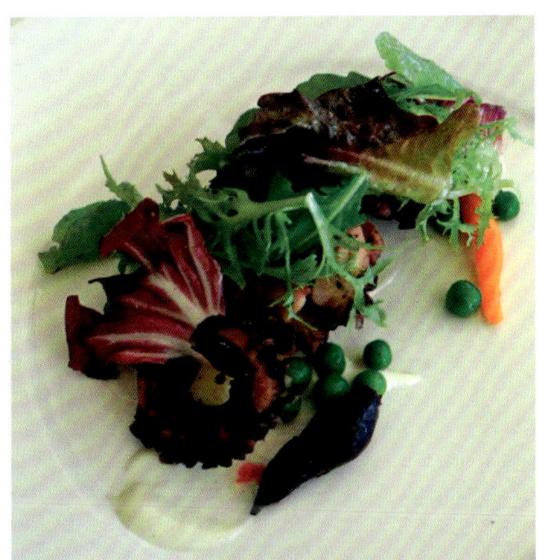

Innovative Blends are also part of Puppato's creative style. Oenologist Leonardo Puppato (photo left page) contemplates his next innovation at the Schroeder Winery after tasting his **2010 Pinot Noir/ Malbec Blend** (55%, 45% respectively) contrasting a big Pinot Noir with a soft Malbec (possibly the only Pinot/Malbec blend in the world) for a sophisticated wine characterizing ripe red fruits.

My *Favorite Pick* is the **Saurus Barrel Fermented Pinot Noir**. These grapes attend a complex process of mixing crushed and full berries with dry ice in oak for five days, followed by removing all solids (including the grapes) and fermenting in oak for an additional 20 days, then aging in oak for six months. This is an extremely delicate and elegant wine expressing the subtleties of the Pinot Noir.

Don't you just love innovative people?

Familia Schroeder has a **Gourmet Restaurant** in the Neuquén wine region, which is open seven days for lunch. They built their winery on a hillside and positioned their ***Saurus Restaurant*** with a view of their vineyards, looking out across the valley.

The Saurus Restaurant employs top chefs who come from luxury restaurants in New York and Paris, and have been trained at the Culinary Institute of America. *Schroeder Winery* and *Saurus Restaurant* are the perfect pairing experience of gourmet European cuisine with top-level wines.

PATAGONIA **NEUQUÉN** SAN PATRICIO

Saurus Winery Restaurant

FAMILIA SCHROEDER

Calle 7 Norte (7 km N of San Patricio on Ruta 7)
(**San Patricio Del Chañar,** Neuquén)

Reservations: 011 (+54 9 299) 409.1754
restautantenbodega@FamiliaSchroeder.com.ar

FamiliaSchroeder.com

English and Español

TOP LEFT, **Amuse-Bouche**
A Nut Bread Bruschetta with Trout Mousse and Beetroot Carpaccio.

MIDDLE LEFT, **Laminas de Pulpo Marnidas**
Clay Oven Baked Octopus, sautéed potato tubes, white garlic aioli, fresh peas, baby carrots and beetroots, plus green leaves seasoned with citrus and olive oil.

BOTTOM, **Dúo de Cabrito Patagonico**
Two versions of the Patagonia Goat... Goat Shoulder braised in clay oven for four hours, then crumbled, seasoned and pressed. Goat Loin which remains juicy, is seasoned with thyme, rosemary, salt and pepper. Served with creamy green risotto, green asparagus and peas, and Pinot Noir Reduction.

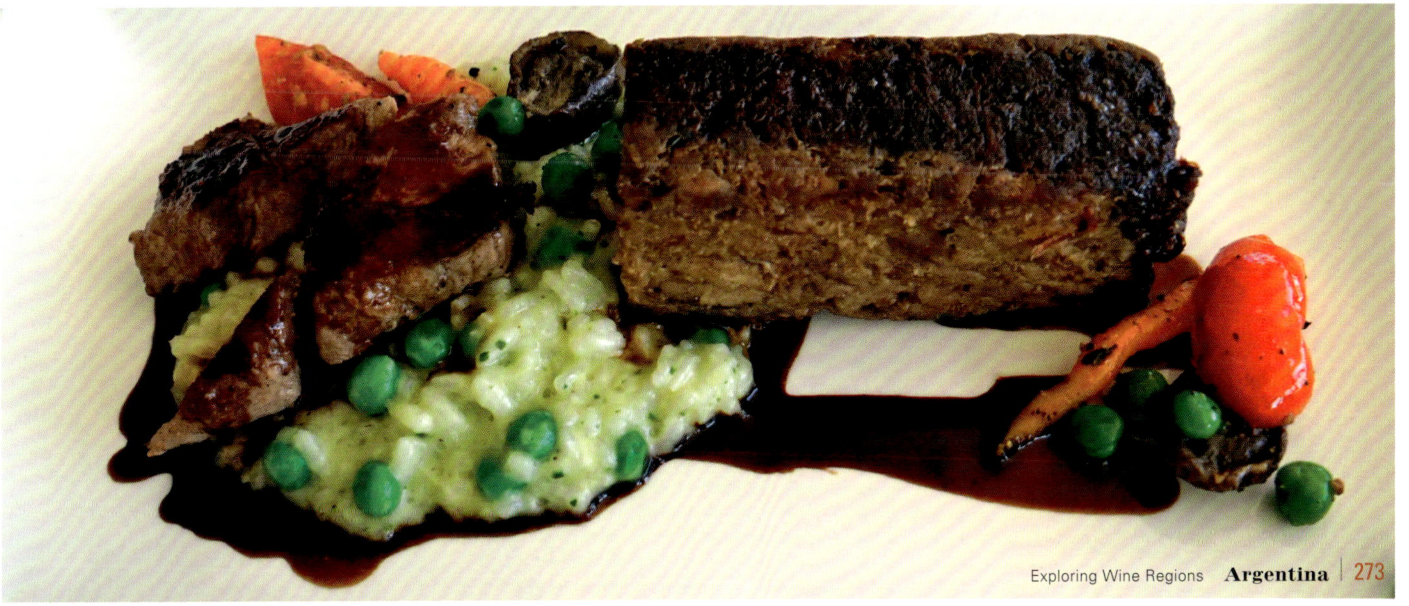

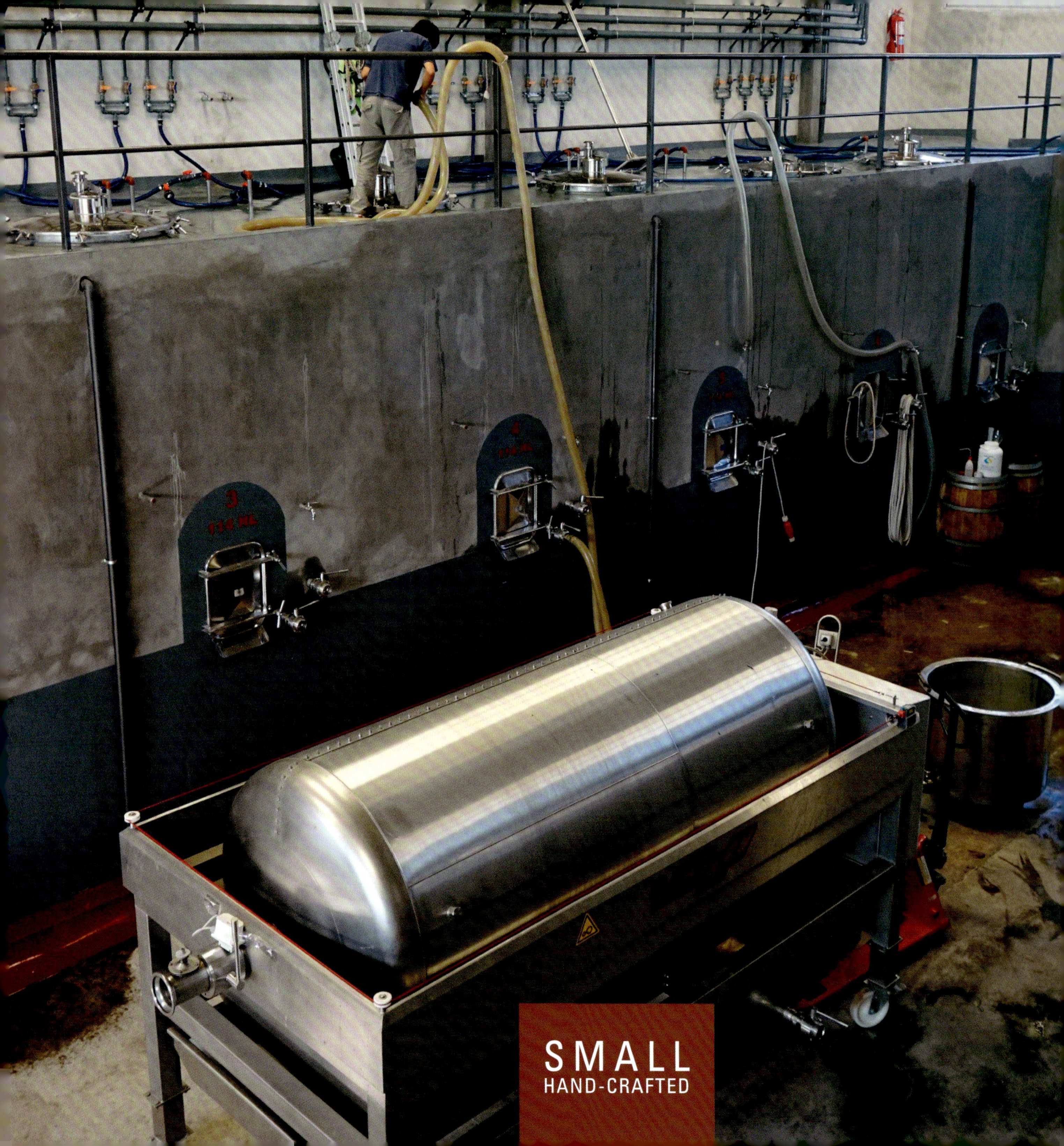

SMALL
HAND-CRAFTED

SMALL BATCH PINOT NOIR

Now for a small winery in the grand scheme of Neuquén... a family-run project of hand-crafted wines. Also pioneers of the region, the Groppo family started planting their vineyards in 2003. This is a real family affair, brother, sister, father, mother, and a very talented winemaker Santiago del Pin. And not to forget, Malbec and Pinot, their two Swiss shepherds who live on the property full time.

Secreto Patagónico is located on one of the highest sites in the Neuquén wine region... on top of the shelf that overlooks the valley. Up here, the rocks are plentiful in the soil offering their wines a unique profile from the other wineries. Plus, this elevation makes for breathtaking views of the valley that you can see in the photo that opens this Patagonia section (pages 248-249).

There are no stainless steel tanks in this winery. They are all 100% concrete wine pools (photos left page and below), and all of small batch sizes for focused vintification of single vineyards to maximize their distinctions of the terroir and typicity. Further, they only harvest in the early mornings when it is cool and only by hand to preserve the integrity of the grapes. The grapes are immediately put into a cold cellar to preserve them until processing begins.

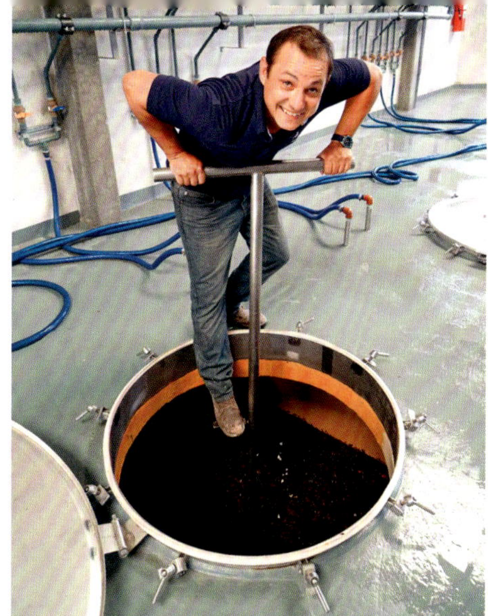

Santiago del Pin (photo above) is the ideal oenologist for the Groppo family as he is an expert with Pinot Noir and his expertise is small-batch, high-quality winemaking. Santiago's philosophy in the winery is minimum intervention in order to create wines that best reflect the terroir. He does this with specified harvests elaborating the signature characteristics of a single plot of land or rows in the vineyard into a limited edition wine. This is the Secreto Patagónico style!

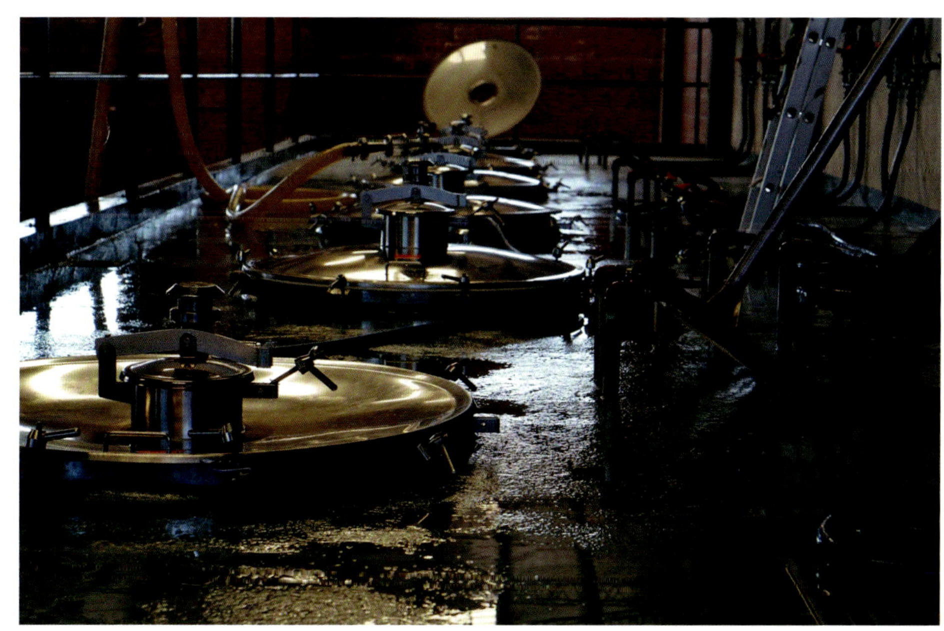

PATAGONIA **NEUQUÉN** SAN PATRICIO
Winery (Bodega)
SECRETO PATAGÓNICO

Calle 3 Norte (5 km N of San Patricio on Ruta 7)
(**San Patricio Del Chañar,** Neuquén)

011 (+54 9 116) 218.9096
turismo@SecretoPatagonico.com

SecretoPatagonico.com

English and Español
50,000 bottles produced annually

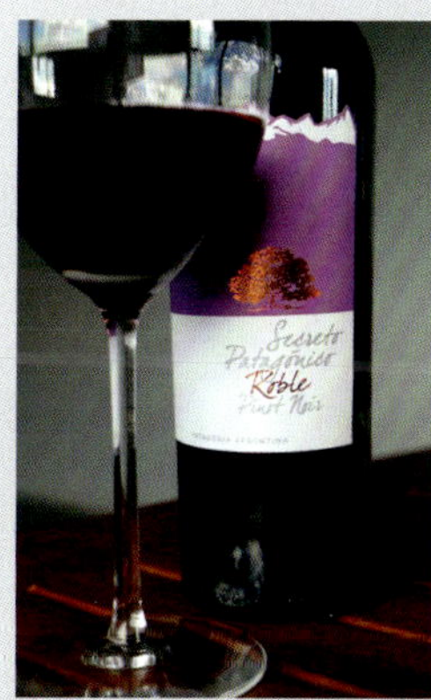

Michael's Favorite Pick
Secreto Patagónico Reserve - Pinot Noir

Total Collection of Wines

Secreto Patagónico Reserve
Pinot Noir • Malbec • Cabernet Sauvignon

Secreto Patagónico
Pinot Noir • Malbec • Cabernet Sauvignon
Merlot • Chardonnay

Secreto Patagónico (sparkling wines)
Extra Brut (Pinot Noir/Chardonnay)
Extra Brut Rosé (Torrontés/Pinot Noir)

To get Secreto Patagónico wines in the USA
Contact Their Importer: GoodyGoody.com

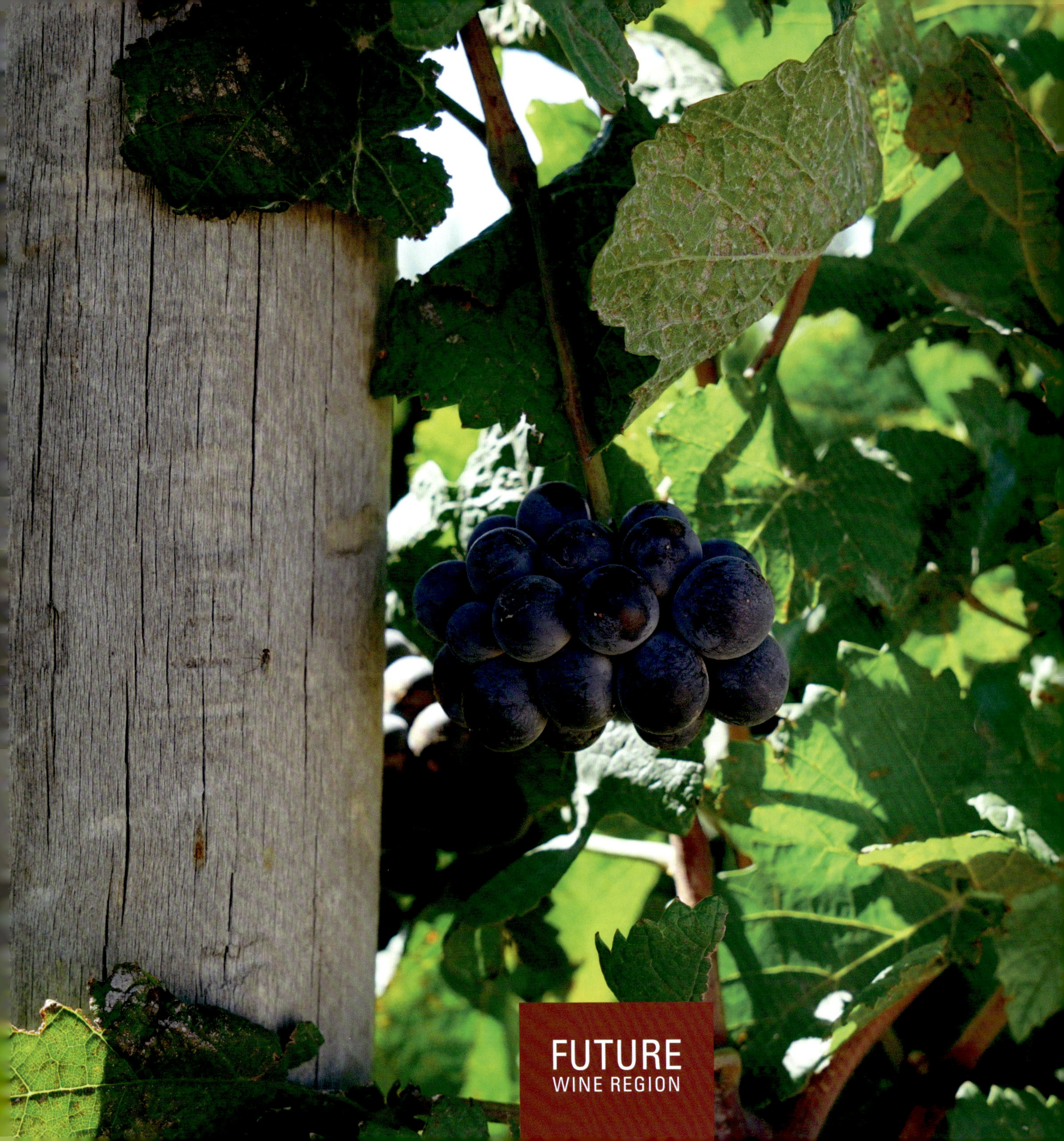
FUTURE
WINE REGION

PROMISED LAND

All the while, the Neuquén Wine Region is blossoming with extraordinary vintages from vineyards growing along the Neuquén River... vineyards are being planted along the Limay River, approximately the same distance from the city of Neuquén in hopes of another phenomenal viticulture success of Neuquén's other major river.

In 2005, the first vineyards were planted, Pinot Noir and Malbec. The first winery is under construction to be completed in 2015 as Fincas del Limay. Concurrently, they are building a restaurant adjacent to the winery to enjoy their wines paired with delicious foods. As the dream continues, they plan to build a luxury hotel, spa and villas overlooking a natural lagoon on their property (photo right).

The terroir here makes sense with the extreme conditions going beyond that found in San Patricio del Chañar... Temperatures can exceed 100°F during the day and can fall to 40°F that night. Winds can reach 90 to 100 miles per hour during spring (August to November). Most significant about this area is the presence of sand and gravel from ancient paleobanks of the Limay River. The mineral components of this deep and well-drained soil fill the wines with aromas which make them unique, and with intense colors.

Wines are already being produced from these vineyards. I tasted the **2012 Huellas Del Limay, Malbec Reserva**, from Fincas del Limay's premium line. They also make a young line of wines called **Zorro y Arena**, named after the Patagonia fox that live on and around their property. The fox are very efficient at protecting the delicate newly planted vines from the insatiable appetite of hares. This young wine line honors these shrewd predators for their preservation of the vines.

As beautiful new grapes are maturing on the vines (photo left page) and a technologically advanced winery is being constructed (photo below of the new Fincas del Limay winery), this new terroir is becoming the place to find great happiness and promise for another new wine region to emerge.

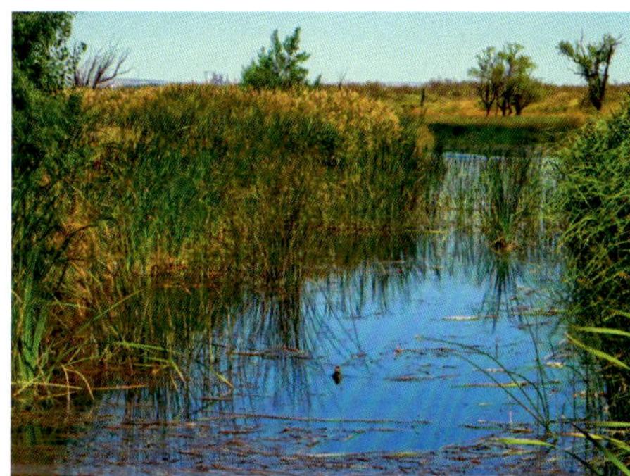

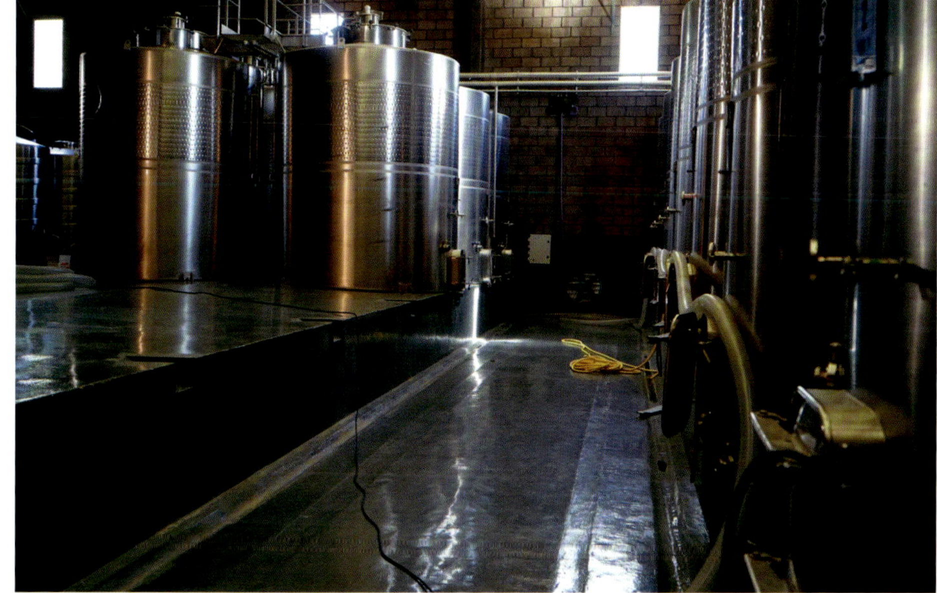

PATAGONIA **NEUQUÉN** SENILLOSA

Winery (Bodega)

FINCAS DEL LIMAY

Ruta 22 km 1262

(34 miles SW of Neuquén, 5 km W of Senillosa on Ruta 22)

(**Senillosa,** Neuquén)

011 (+54 299 15) 531.0674

info@FincasDelLimay.com.ar

FincasDelLimay.com.ar

English and Español

60,000 bottles produced annually

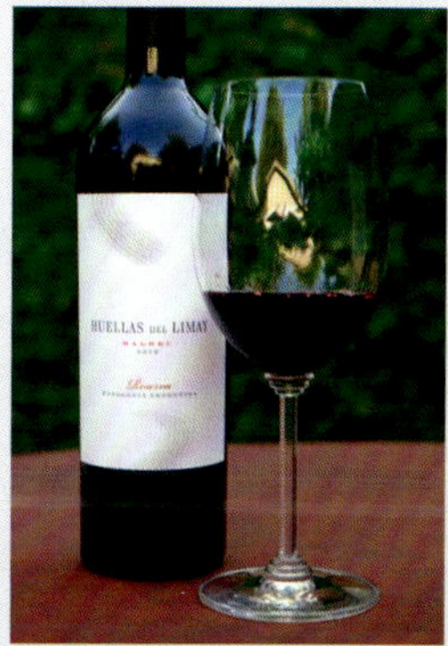

Michael's Favorite Pick

Huellas del Limay - Malbec Reserva

Total Collection of Wines

Fincas del Limay - Premium Wines

Huellas del Limay - Malbec Reserva

Huellas del Limay - Pinot Noir Reserva

Huellas del Limay - Blend Reserva

(Malbec/Merlot/Cabernet Franc)

Fincas del Limay - Young Wines

Zorro y Arena - Pinot Noir

Zorro y Arena - Malbec

Zorro y Arena - Blend Tinto (red)

(Malbec/Merlot/Cabernet Franc)

Zorro y Arena - Blend Noir (white)

(Chardonnay/Sauvignon Blanc)

To get Fincas del Limay wines in the USA

No distribution yet, since they have just begun, travel to Neuquen and bring back a few bottles

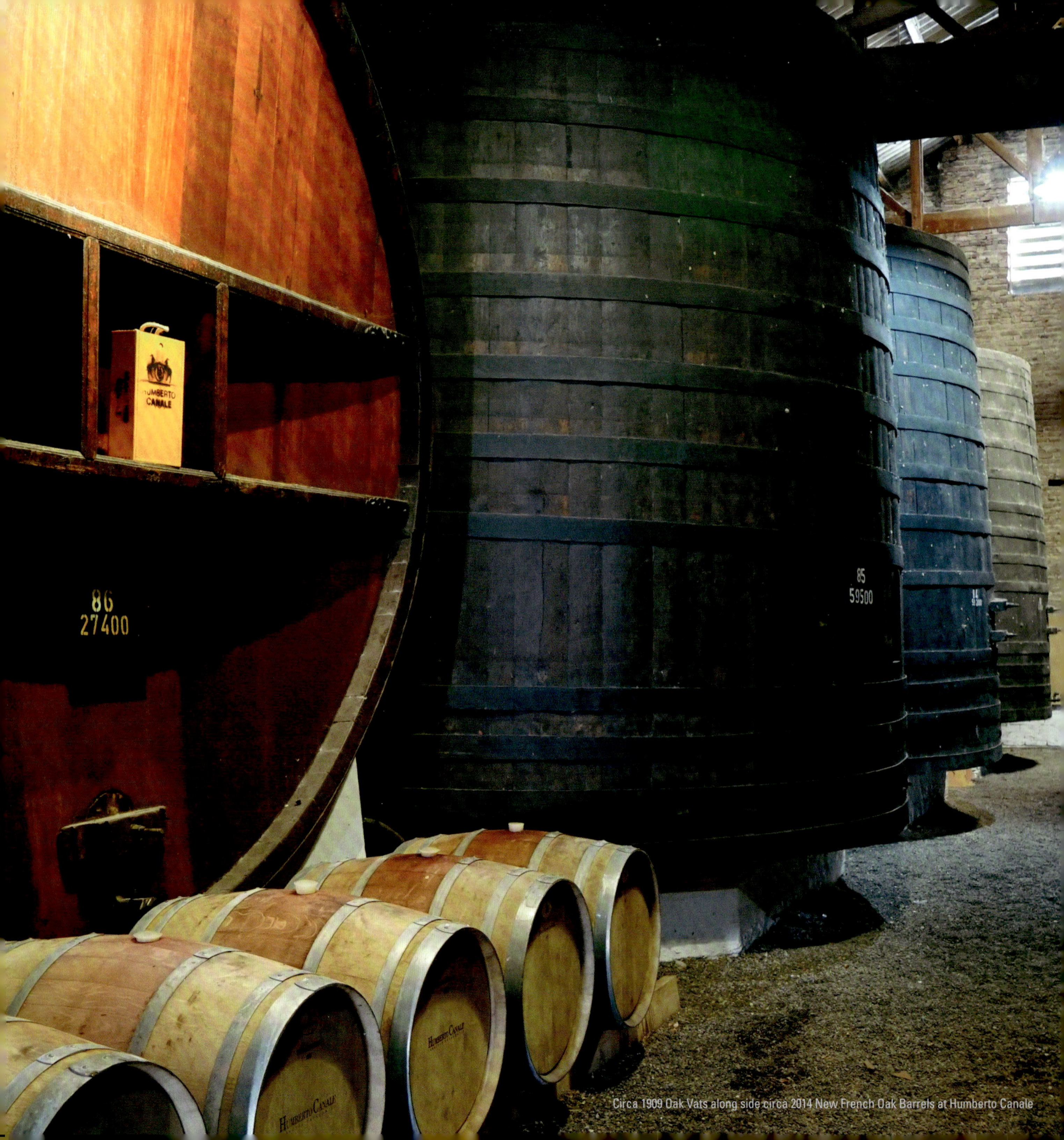

Circa 1909 Oak Vats along side circa 2014 New French Oak Barrels at Humberto Canale

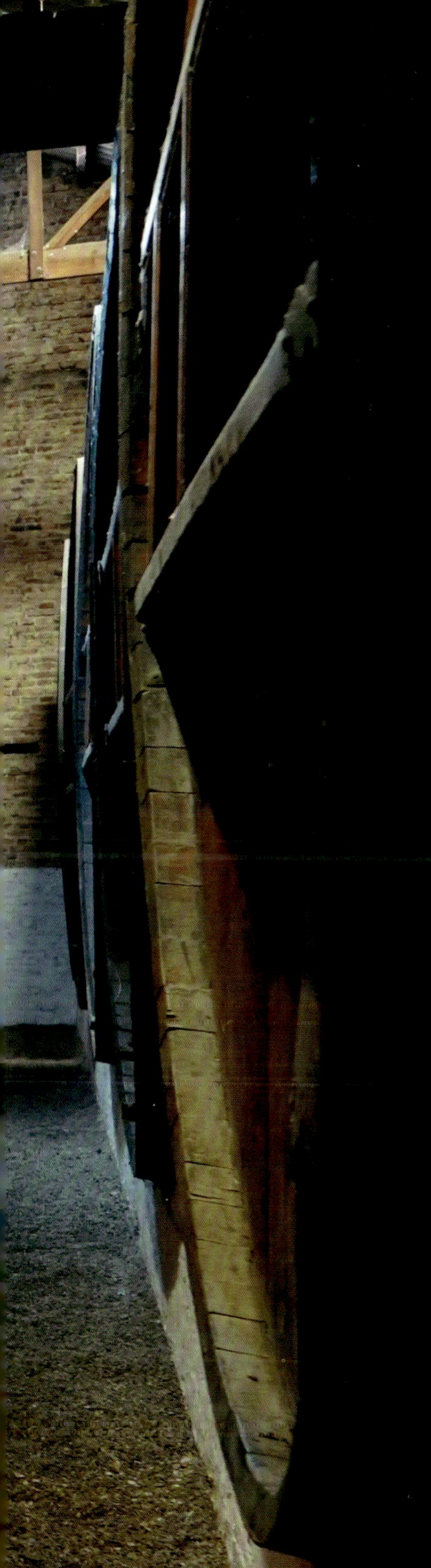

PATAGONIA **RÍO NEGRO**

100 Years of Tradition and Culture in Winemaking

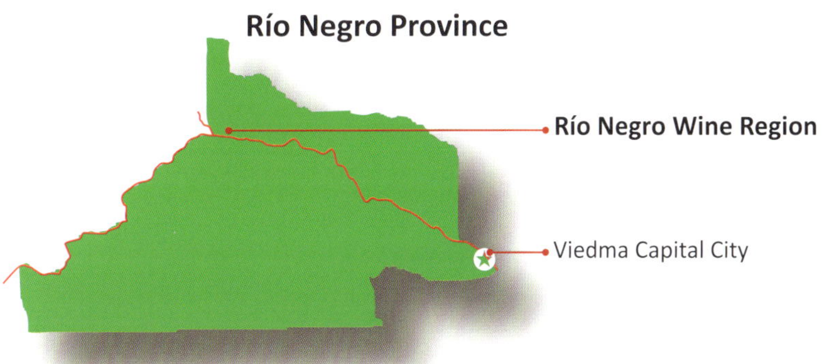

EXPLORING RÍO NEGRO

Río Negro is the world's southernmost wine region. Río Negro is both a province (to the east and south of Neuquén) and a grand river which flows from Neuquén 310 miles to the Atlantic Ocean, creating three agricultural regions in its route.

The Río Negro river is formed at the convergence of the Río Neuquén and Río Limay (at Neuquén city near the Neuquén wine region), and is divided into *Alto Valle* (high valley) at the beginning of the river, *Valle Medio* (middle valley) near Choele Choel, and *Valle Inferior* (lower valley) at the end of the river where it flows into the Atlantic Ocean.

Alto Valle is the most prosperous part of the province with the predominance of the pear and apple plantations, plus most of the wineries and vineyards are here as the **General Roca Appellation** of Río Negro. Ruta 22 runs though the middle of this valley, giving easy access to all the wineries. Here we explore these Alta Valle wineries.

Valle Medio is known as the National Capital of the Tomatoes, and has a couple of wineries. *Valle Inferior* cultivates onions, alfalfa and corn, and also has a couple of wineries.

Being the cooler Patagonia climate, elegant styles of Pinot Noir, Sauvignon Blanc, Merlot, and Malbec are the primary wines produced here.

Unlike other wine regions, the mountains and ocean have very little influence on the vineyards here. It is the river that contributes most to the region's terroir, along with the high winds, thin ozone, longer summer days, and the extreme diurnal temperature variation.

Winemaking in Río Negro has a deep history dating back more than 100 years. Winemaking, and agriculture in general, became possible here in the late 19th century after the **Campaña al Desierto de 1879** (Conquest of the Desert), an Argentina military conquest of Patagonia. This allowed the early settlers from Spain and Italy to bring the wine culture to the area, and the British to develop railways and introduce pears and apples as crops of high economic impact for the region.

The British colonists also dug irrigation channels into this arid desert from Río Negro and Río Neuquén, forming a green belt along the river throughout the valley conducive for agriculture. While viticulture (vineyards) is a significant part of this growth, Río Negro became most famous for its apple and pear orchards.

General Julio A. Roca was the architect of the Campaña al Desierto (and twice President of the Argentina). His name is forever remembered in the legacy endowed as the **General Roca Wine Region** and as its central and primary town **General Roca**.

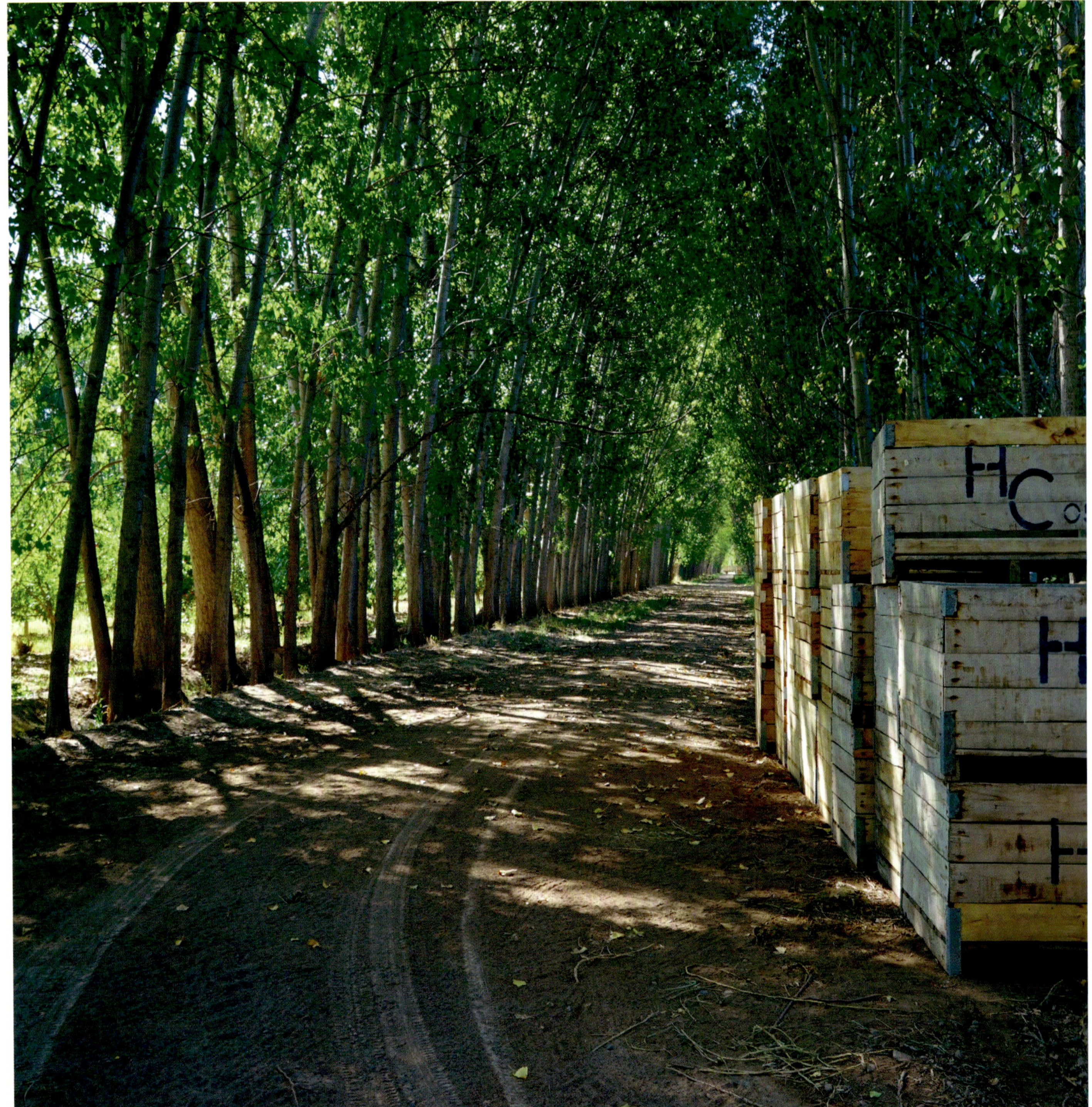

ABOVE, Humberto Canale fruit orchard crates; RIGHT PAGE, harvesting the PAI Brand pears Canale sells worldwide

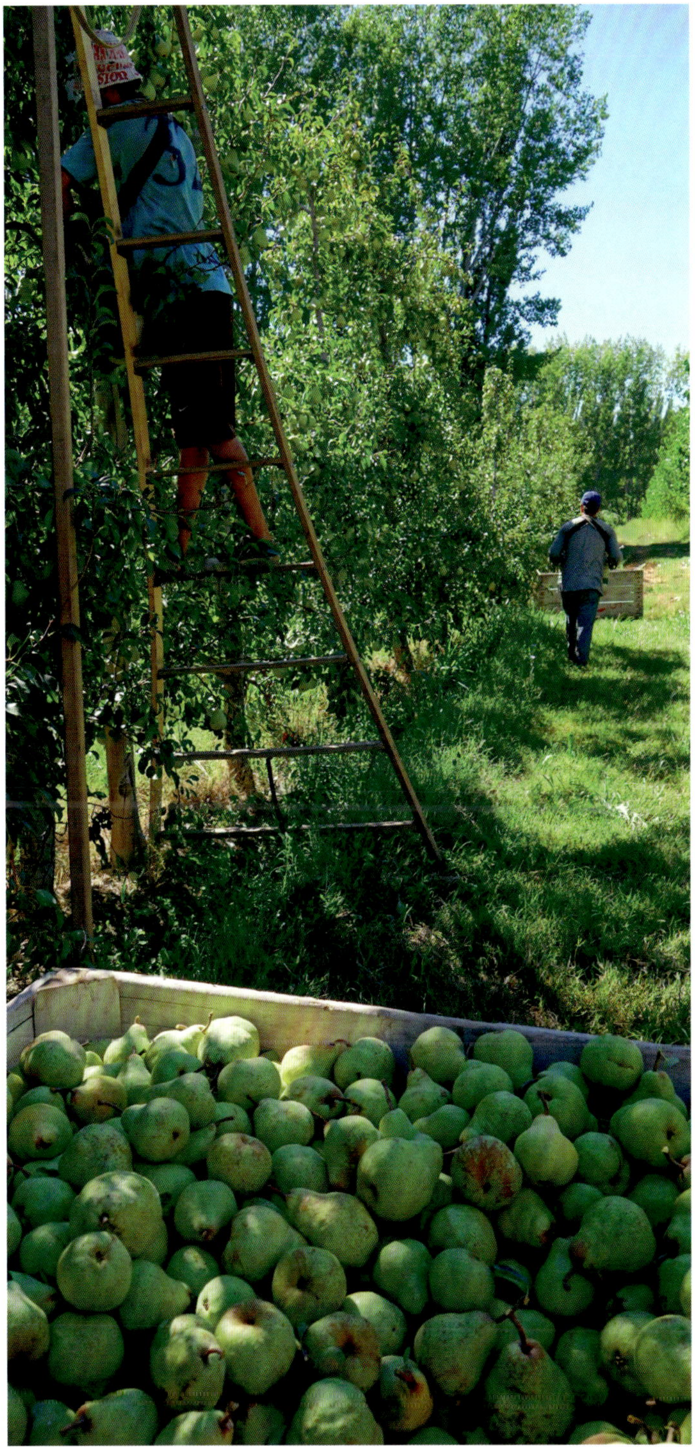

"The Department of General Roca (Alto Valle de Río Negro), has the oldest vineyards which gave rise to the provincial viticulture. With the profound study of the wines' evolution harvest after harvest, with tight quality controls, use of technology, controlled use of oak, and the knowledge of international markets, it has made it possible to present Río Negro as a noble wine region with high acceptance in the Argentine market and internationally. Despite the reduction in acreage, Río Negro has privileged quality grapes for premium wines. We can conclude that northern Patagonia is now a 'boutique region' within Argentina where the wines are already recognized in the most demanding markets worldwide."

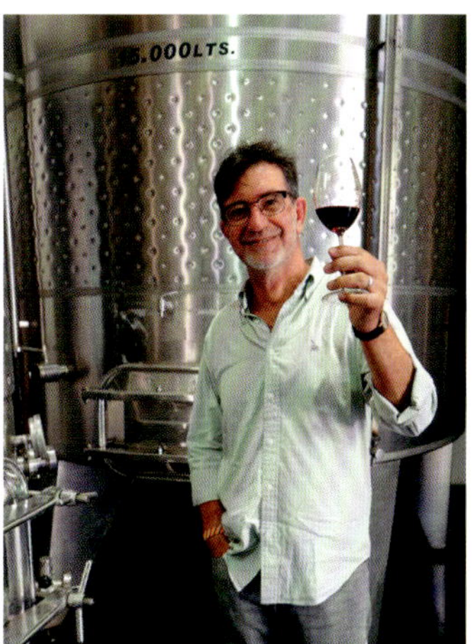

– **Ing. Arg. Carlos Urbano Rota**
Viticulture Directorate of the Ministry of Agriculture

The planting of vineyards and the growth of wineries became prolific, and eventually Río Negro grew to 260 wineries. Río Negro became a huge provider of wine domestically in Argentina. Then came tough competition from Mendoza for volume wine production, and the number of wineries dropped horrifically to almost zero! The farmers who stayed in business replanted their vineyards with pears and apples, as the international opportunities for these fruits boomed. Sadly, many of the vineyards and the wineries were simply abandoned.

Fortunately, Argentina became the No. 1 exporter of pears in the world, particularly Alto Valle, Río Negro, became worldwide recognized for its **Pears**, especially Bartletts (photo left) and **Red Apple** production. The climate, characterized by sunny days, cool nights and dry weather (no rain and no humidity), with access through the valley's irrigation system to unlimited unspoiled water coming from the Andes, helps produce the highest quality fruits, with no use of pesticides. Most particularly their pears have a very clean skin (something other countries can't get) and a unique natural smell, flavor and taste. Simply put... they are super-delicious!

Bodega Humberto Canale, circa 1909, and **Bodega Favretto**, circa 1944, both planted orchards of pears and apples while they persisted with their wine businesses. As a result, they are the only two wineries that are still in existence today. They continue to have prosperous fruit businesses as well.

Today, Río Negro is one of Argentina's up-and-coming wine regions. During the last couple of decades, very smart vintners have been exploring the viticultural potential here, and now there are 20-plus wineries producing extremely high-quality wines. This resurgence has demanded only high-quality wines for the wineries to succeed, and what a treat this is for us!

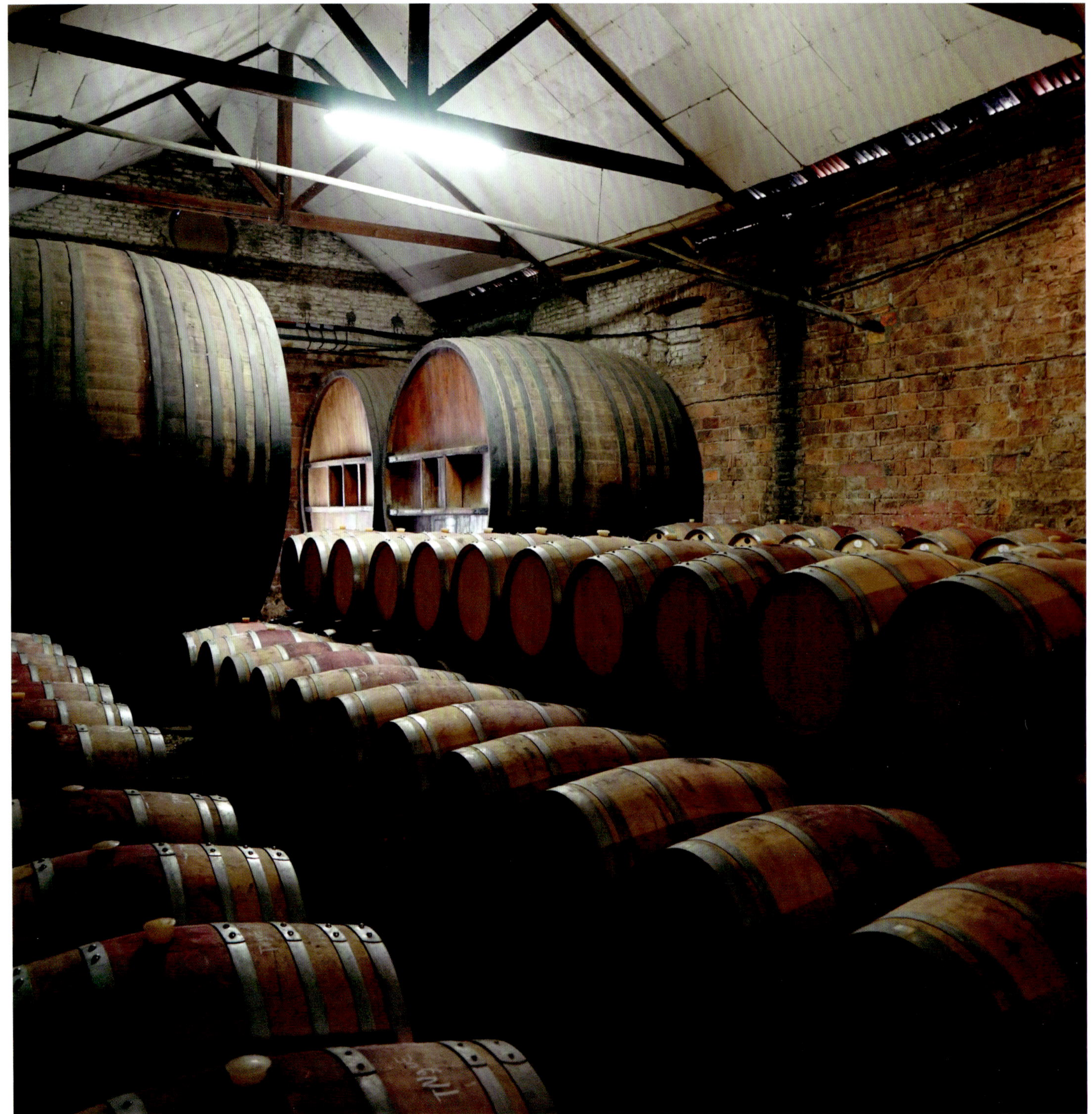

ABOVE, the ancient barrel aging room of Humberto Canale

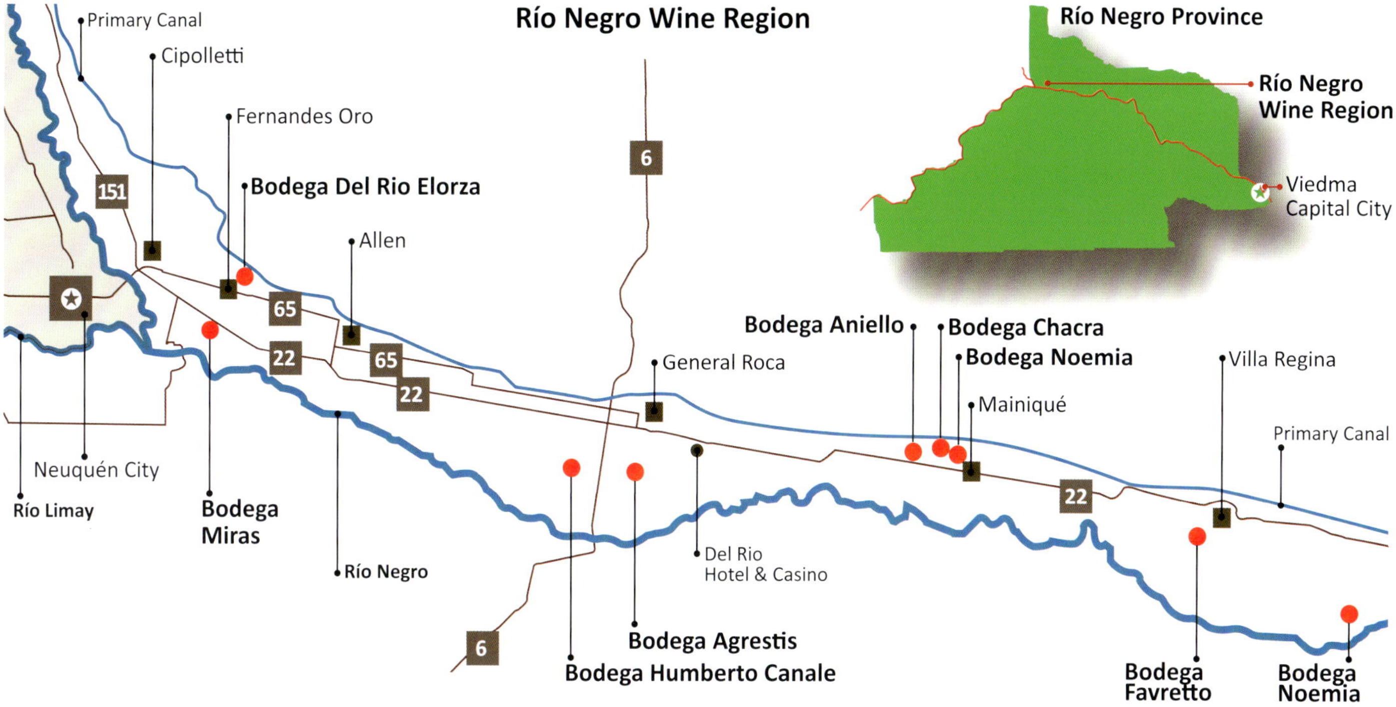

Río Negro Wine Region

Primary Canal
Cipolletti
Fernandes Oro
Bodega Del Rio Elorza
151
6
Allen
65
22
65
22
Neuquén City
Río Limay
Bodega Miras
Río Negro
6
General Roca
Bodega Aniello
Bodega Chacra
Bodega Noemia
Mainiqué
Villa Regina
Primary Canal
22
Del Rio Hotel & Casino
Bodega Agrestis
Bodega Humberto Canale
Bodega Favretto
Bodega Noemia

Río Negro Province
Río Negro Wine Region
Viedma Capital City

The Río Negro Alto Valle is 12 miles wide with the Río Negro river flowing along the southern edge of the valley, and the main canal runs along the north. In between are the numerous vineyards and orchards, with Ruta 22 connecting the cities and town of this wine region.

The Río Negro valley is below the desert plateau elevation, known as the Barda, dug out by the river flowing for millions of years. As the strong winds blow across the desert, the valley below is somewhat sheltered by the prevailing winds, missing the strength as they pass overhead. The thick and tall wind-blocking Alamos trees are still planted around the vineyards and orchards for added protection.

For Argentina, the 800′ elevation on the valley floor here is unusually low for vineyards of the typical high elevations along the Andes Mountains.

As you can see on the map, General Roca is centrally located in the valley, and it is the largest town (population 86,000), offering an ideal location for your hotel stay (other populations are Villa Regina 33,000, Allen 26,000, and Cipolletti 79,000).

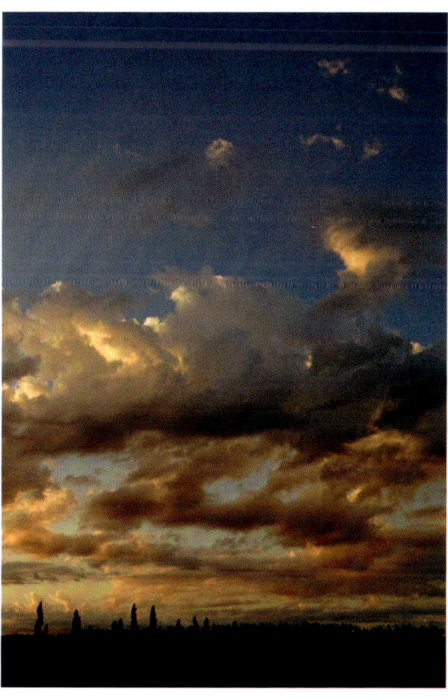

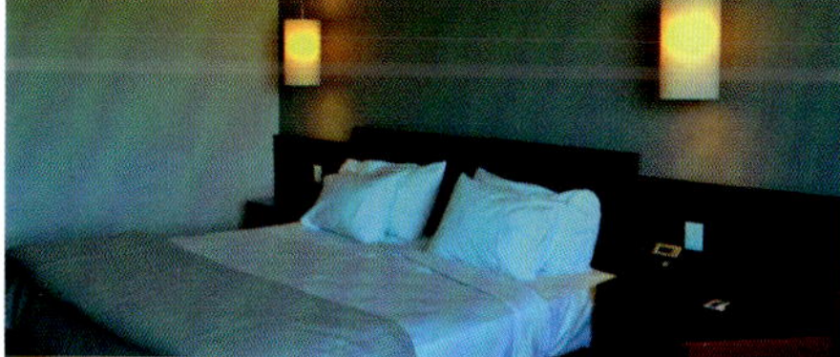

Del Río Hotel & Casino - General Roca

The Del Río is directly located on Ruta 22 in downtown General Roca. This is a new hotel, which is very clean and modern. The rooms are large and spacious, with very comfortable luxuries.

The hotel is completely separate from the casino with its own entrance and restaurant. Breakfast is included and the rates are very good.

They have a gourmet chef for their main restaurant in the casino, which has stage shows in the dining room later in the evening. Early dinners are convenient at their lounge bar, full menu.

011 (+54 298) 443.4188
ReservasRoca@CasinosDelRio.com.ar
CasinosDelRio.com.ar

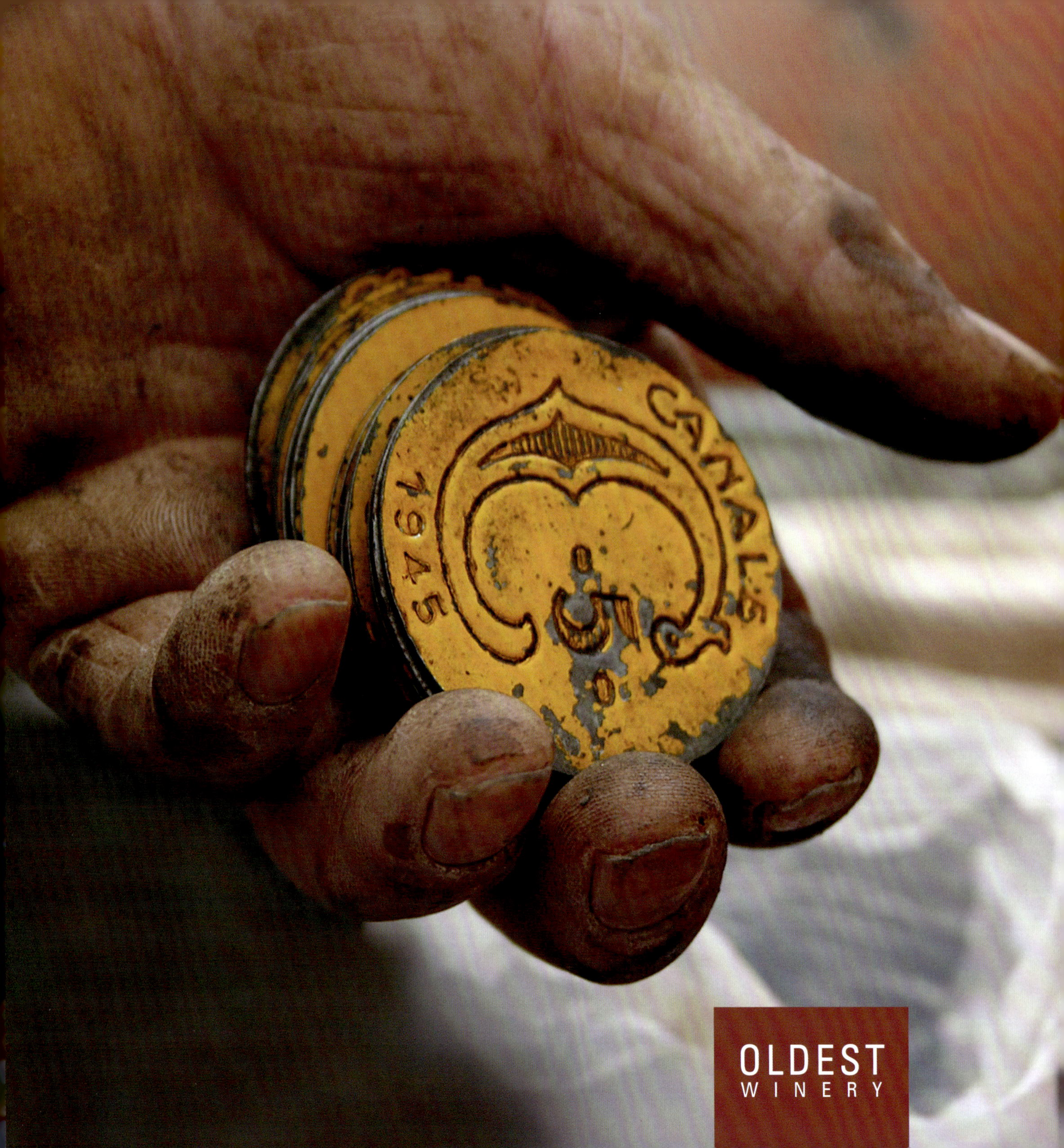
CANALS
1945
OLDEST
WINERY

TEN DECADES, FOUR GENERATIONS, THE LEGACY OF A CENTURY

BODEGA HUMBERTO CANALE

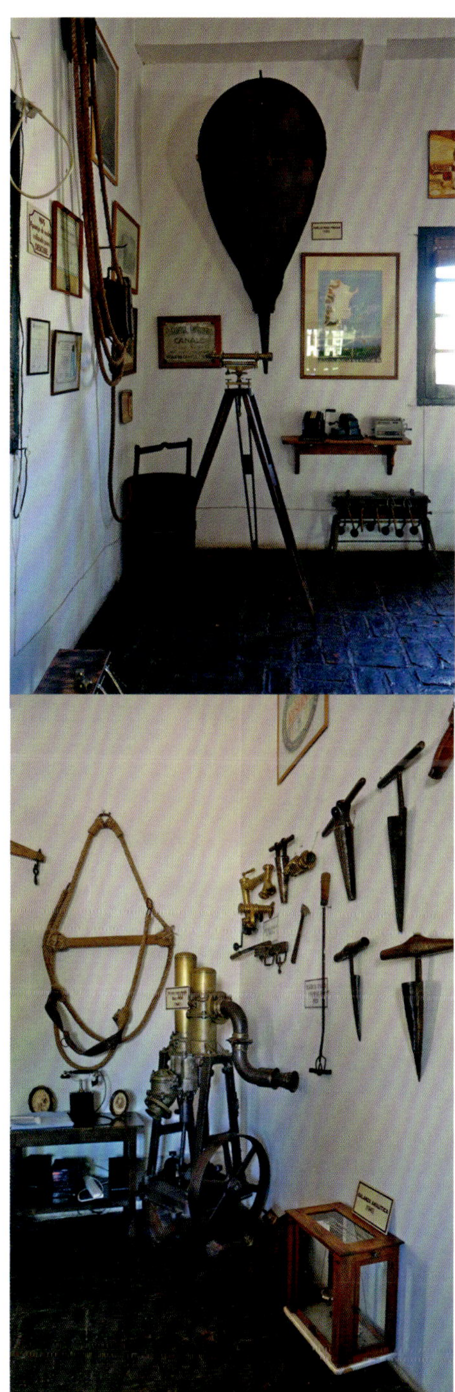

Agricultural engineer (agronomist) Humberto Canale was one of the first on the scene in the late 19th century, assisting in the engineering and development of the canal system from the river. Canale was instrumental in ensuring the size of the main canal was grand enough to provide the quantity of water necessary for the valley's growth over time, and for the numerous and extensive lateral canals which brings the water into the farms.

Humberto Canale was also a visionary entrepreneur and saw the future of Río Negro's agriculture success. In 1909, he started his own winery **Bodega Humberto Canale**, planting 250 acres of vineyards with vine-cuttings he brought over from Bordeaux, France, establishing the first commercial winery in Patagonia. He also planted 250 acres of fruit trees and 500 acres of various other crops. By 1920, Humberto had planted 5,000 acres of vineyards in General Roca, causing a large presence of success and creating a harmonious environment for the attraction and growth of other farmers.

Humberto Canale was part of a long line of Italian immigrants who arrived in Argentina in 1860 from Geneva, Italy. The Canale family was mostly famous for their baked-goods business in Buenos Aires, which was eventually sold to Kraft foods.

Humberto was the only son of the immigrating family who decided to get an advanced education, branch-off from the family's well-established business, to create his own legacy in Patagonia.

On the winery property is a very interesting museum you can visit, showing the history of the family and numerous artifacts of Humberto's farming businesses of the past century (photos left)

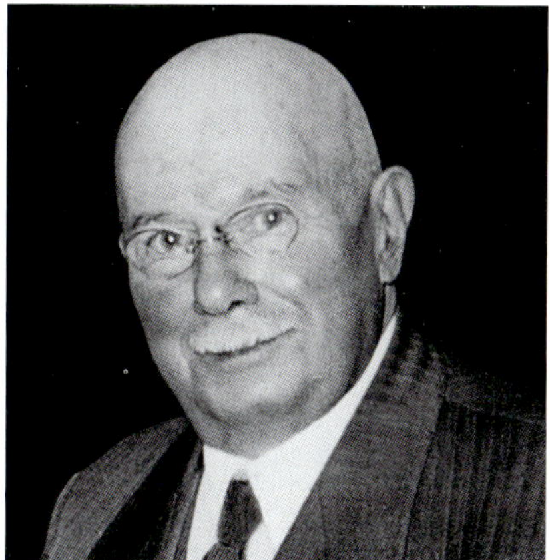

Humberto Canale
(1876-1957)
Visionary & Entrepreneurial Pioneer
of the Patagonian Viticulture

LEFT PAGE, an authentic vintage **1945 Denario**, a yellow token given to pickers after each box of grapes is filled and delivered. For more than a century, Humberto Canale has been giving these coins to their vineyard workers in exchange for bins of hand-harvested grapes.

Denario (Latin Denarius) is an ancient Roman coin that is still used today for counting the boxes that each person has picked during harvest, exchanged at day-end for cash.

Humberto Canale is now making limited edition, hand-crafted wines, from 70-year-old vineyards, to symbolize this tradition. Available in the USA, UK and Japan. Imported by CannonWines.com

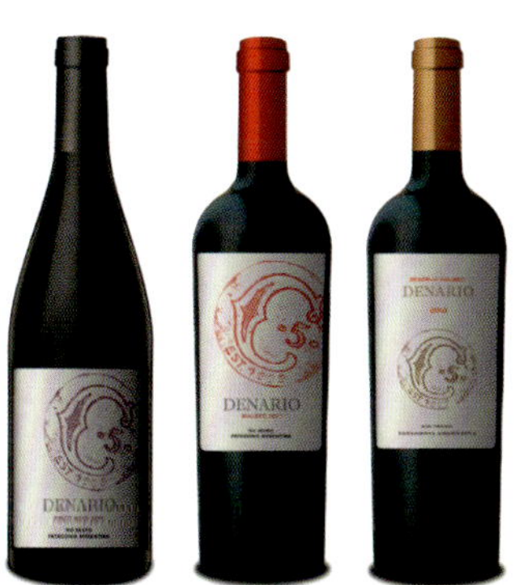

DENARIO - by Humberto Canale
Reserva Malbec • Malbec • Pinto Noir

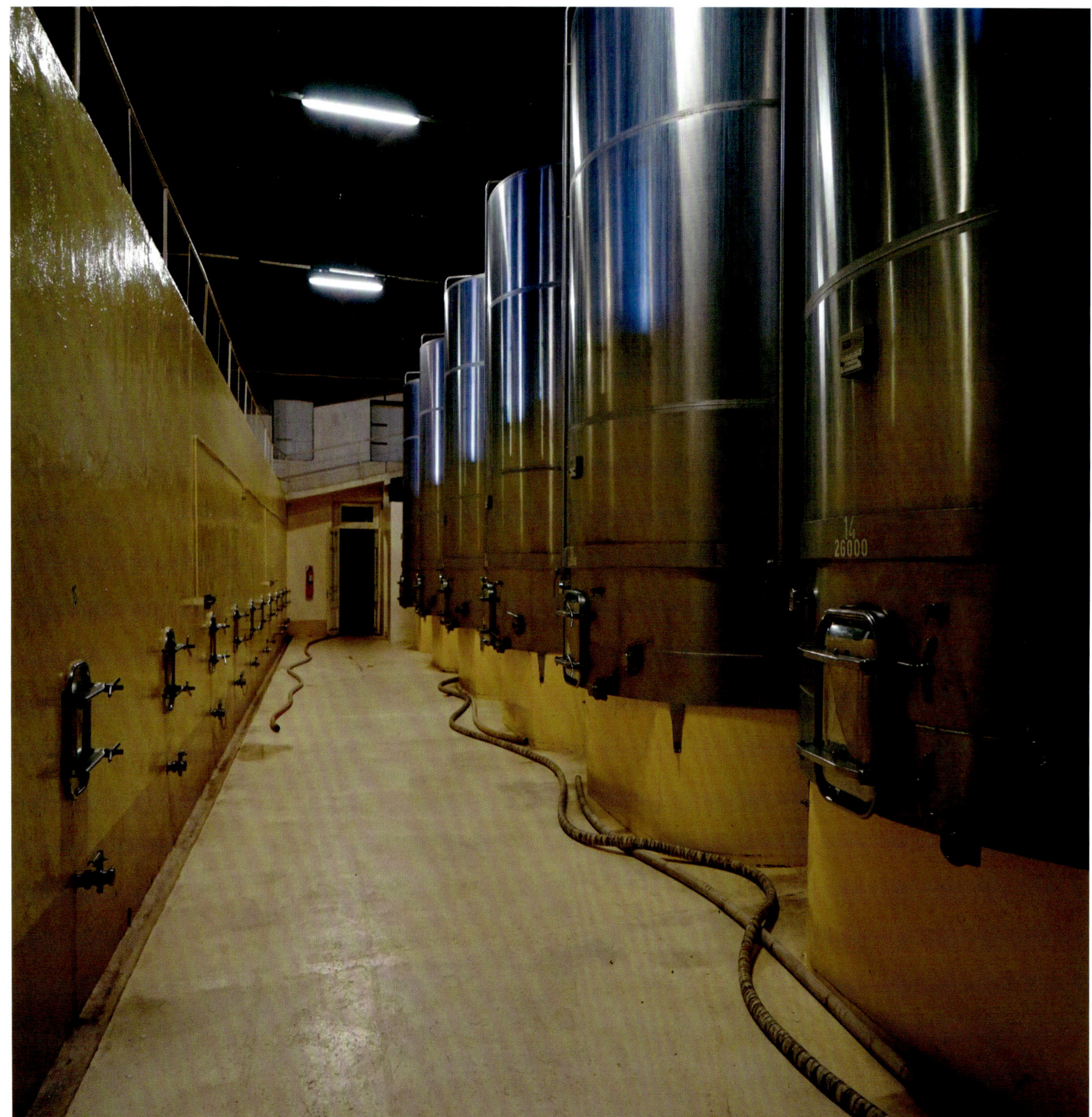

Original concrete wine pools across from new stainless steal tanks, both in full use at Humberto Canale

BEGINNING HERE...

When visiting Río Negro, Humberto Canale is the perfect place to begin. The winery here is huge and has a lot to offer in showing you the full winemaking process in detail. Plus, this will set the stage for you to get to know the Río Negro Alto Valle.

The past century is very much present here in the beautiful colonial-style surroundings. Peruse their on-site museum, walk through the historical vineyards, and see the ancient wine vats and other original equipment... all working alongside the new technology, up-to-date instruments and hardware of modern-day winemaking.

Two-hour guided tours of each stage of the winemaking process are available Tuesdays through Saturdays. This will be an educational experience in both winemaking and the history of this special agricultural region. You will tour through different historical and modern vineyards, see the wine presses, stainless steel tanks, cellars, old oak vats, and the bottling plant. The visit finishes with a wine tasting in the museum.

The winery also offers in-depth training courses (two days, six hours in total) for people who desire a much greater understanding. Available for private individuals and professionals in the restaurant and food industry. Pre-enrollment is required.

Business events can be held at the winery facilities for those companies that would like a unique environment for team-building, training or social events. Their food service, winemaking and tourism departments will custom design a program for both on and off the property activities for your complete trip.

The wines at Canale give you great selection in both grape varietal and price, so you can easily find what you like most. As you can see to the right, they have it all. From the specialties of this terroir of Pinot Noir, Merlot and Sauvignon Blanc to beautiful softer versions of Malbec, Semmilón, Cabernet Franc, and even Cabernet Sauvignon.

Humberto Canale has many different approaches to these wines in the use of oak, age of vineyards, pruning and harvesting, fermentation, and aging. All this adds up to style and quality, and price points that are extremely fair.

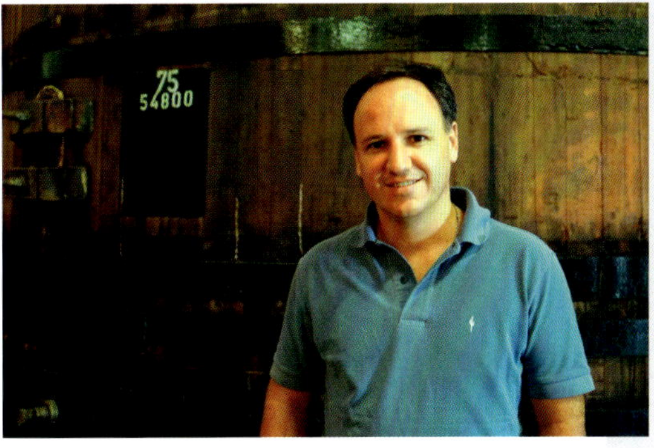

German Barzi Canale
Fourth Generation - Current Director

"Today, in our fourth generation, we are always looking to highlight and communicate our Patagonia identity. We have been blessed with unique climate and soil conditions to produce high-quality wines. We keep pioneering and experimenting with different varieties and elaboration techniques, so as to constantly introduce new products to the market, while expanding our reach to other parts of the world."

"We still believe in the principles that Humberto Canale established over a century ago, respect for our customers, employees, communities, and environment. For the next century, we plan to leverage the experience that we've acquired with over 100 harvest seasons with the ongoing incorporation of the latest technology and know-how, adapting to a rapidly changing world. Preserving and transmitting these values to our future generations is a significant mission for all of us."

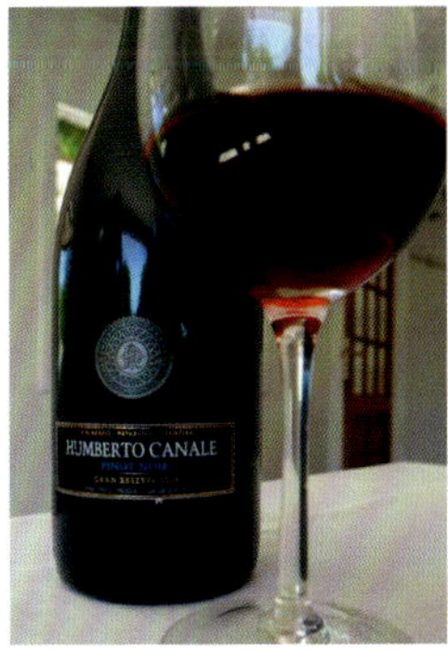

Michael's Favorite Pick
Humberto Canale - Gran Reserva - Pinot Noir

PATAGONIA **RÍO NEGRO** GENERAL ROCA

Winery (Bodega)

BODEGA HUMBERTO CANALE

186 Chacra (4 km south of Ruta 22)
(General Roca, **General Roca,** Río Negro)

011 (+54 298) 443.0415
turismo@BodegaHCanale.com

BodegaHCanale.com

English & Español
2,000,000 bottles produced annually

Total Collection of Wines

Humberto Canale - Centenium
(Merlot, Cabernet Franc, Malbec)

Humberto Canale - Gran Reserva
Pinot Noir • Merlot • Malbec • Cabernet Franc

Humberto Canale - Estate
Pinot Noir • Merlot • Malbec • Cabernet Sauvignon
Cabernet Merlot (50/50) • Sauvignon Blanc
Viognier • Malbec Rosé • Blush (Merlot Rosé)

Intimo Family Reserve
(60% Malbec, 20% Cab Sauv, 20% Cab Franc)

Intimo
Cabernet Sauvignon • Malbec
Cabernet Merlot Malbec (45/45/10)
Sauvignon Banc Semillón (60/40)

Humberto Canale - Extra Brut
(Semillón, Pinot, Sauvignon, Merlot - 50/30/10/10)

Humberto Canale - Black River
Merlot • Malbec • Merlot/Pinot Noir
Sauvignon Blanc • Torrontés

Diego Murillo Varietales
Merlot • Malbec • Torrontés

DENARIO by Humberto Canale
Reserva Malbec • Malbec • Pinot Noir

To get Humberto Canale wines in the USA
Contact Importer New England Wine 203.932.6397
For DENARIO Importer Contact: CannonWines.com

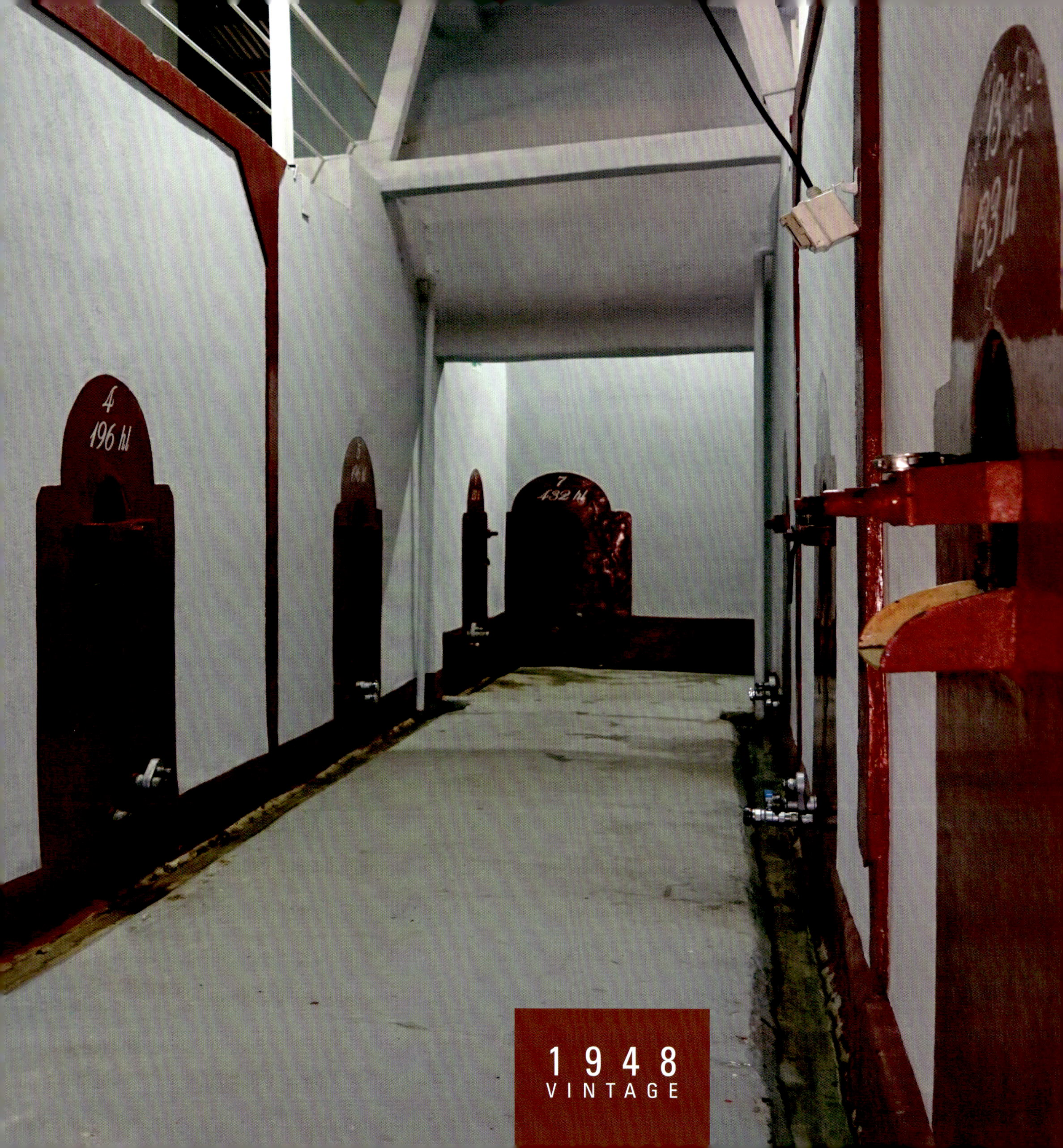

1948
VINTAGE

LIFE IS FOR A GENERATION, A GOOD NAME IS FOREVER

Bodega Favretto is a small hands-on family business, where the family takes pride in the quality of their name as reflected in the quality of their products. They produce quality wines, volume wines, pears, apples and peaches.

They see the birth of the company as the birth of the founder, as synonymous. Ferruccio Favretto was born November 2, 1908 in Pagnano D'Asolo, a small farming community of only 1,000 inhabitants in northeast Italy near Venice. At age 19, Ferruccio hopped on a steam ship to Buenos Aires where he decided to settle down south in Río Negro and to work digging the massive canal system, which has irrigated this farming community ever since.

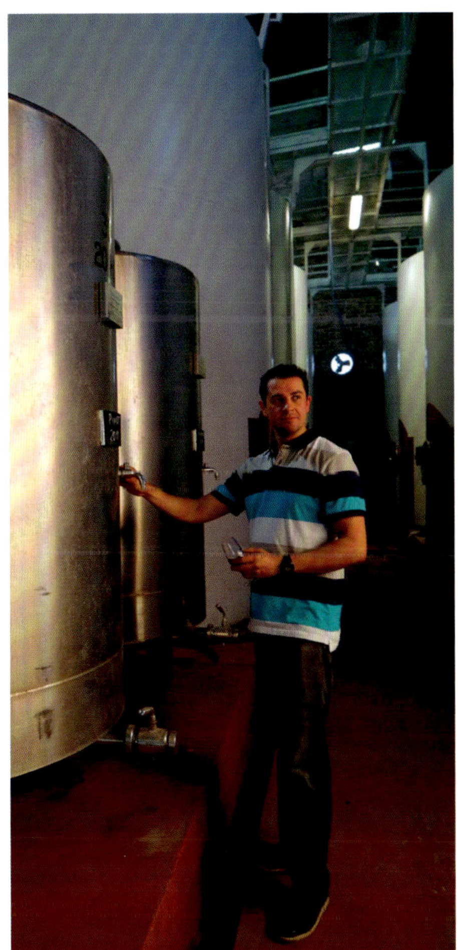

Digging the canal was hard laborious work, so Ferruccio became the town's milkman, and with 20 cows he delivered fresh milk on horseback every morning to his customers. In 1944 Ferruccio started planting vineyards and in 1948 he built the winery to undergo his winemaking business. Planting orchards began in 1980.

Today, third generation grandson Gustavo Favretto (photo below left) and his father make the wines, along with his brother, uncle and mother (who bakes a great light flaky cake, using grapes). This winery has survived three generations of winemaking because it has always produced their **Damajuana Wines**, an old-world glass vessel (photo below), in which Favretto produces "red wine" and "white wine" in five-liter options (the equivalent of five standard size wine bottles) for just US$5. Still today, Favretto provides the community with 500,000 liters of this wine annually.

Visiting the winery is an experience back in time. They still use the same equipment today as they have for over 65 years. Enter the winery of concrete vessels (photo left page) and see the processing machinery of yesterday/today. And what you will find is the hard-working family carrying out another generation of their good name. And enjoy their inviting friendly hospitality.

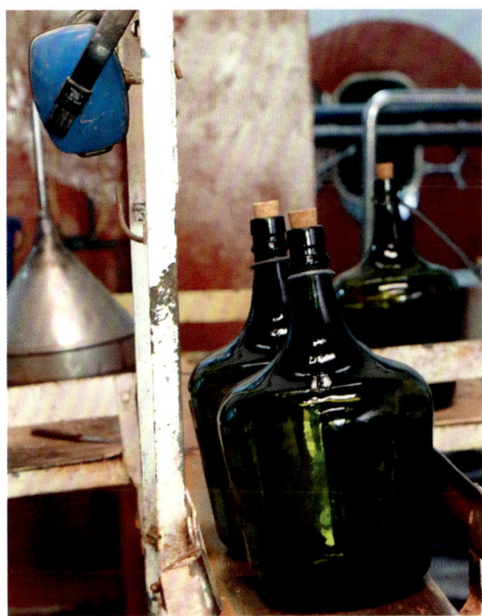

PATAGONIA **RÍO NEGRO** VILLA REGINA

Winery (Bodega)

BODEGA FAVRETTO

Calle Juan XXIII (3 km south of Ruta 22)
(Villa Regina, **General Roca,** Río Negro)

011 (+54 298) 446.1090
consultas@BodegaFavretto.com

BodegaFavretto.com

English, Español & Português
10,000 bottles produced annually

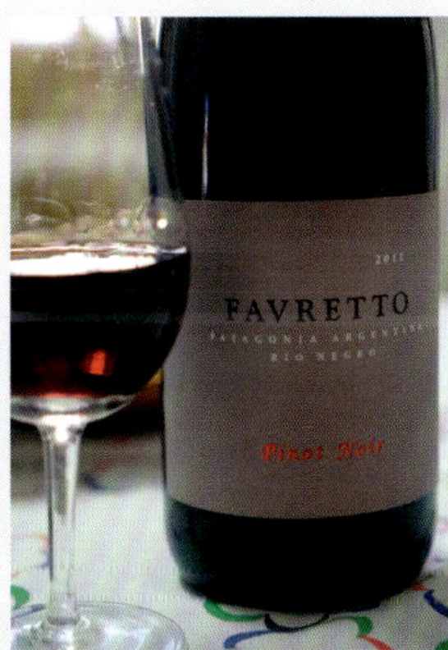

Michael's Favorite Pick
Bodega Favretto - Pinot Noir
(90% Pinot Noir, 10% Merlot)

Total Collection of Wines

Bodega Favretto - Pinot Noir
(90% Pinot Noir, 10% Merlot)

Bodega Favretto - Malbec Gran Corte
(Vintage blend of 70% 2010, 10% 2012, 20% 2013)

Bodega Favretto - Blend de Selección
(60% Cabernet Sauvignon, 30% Malbec, 10% Merlot)

To get Bodega Favretto wines in the USA
Travel to Villa Regina, Río Negro,
for a historical tour and a few bottles

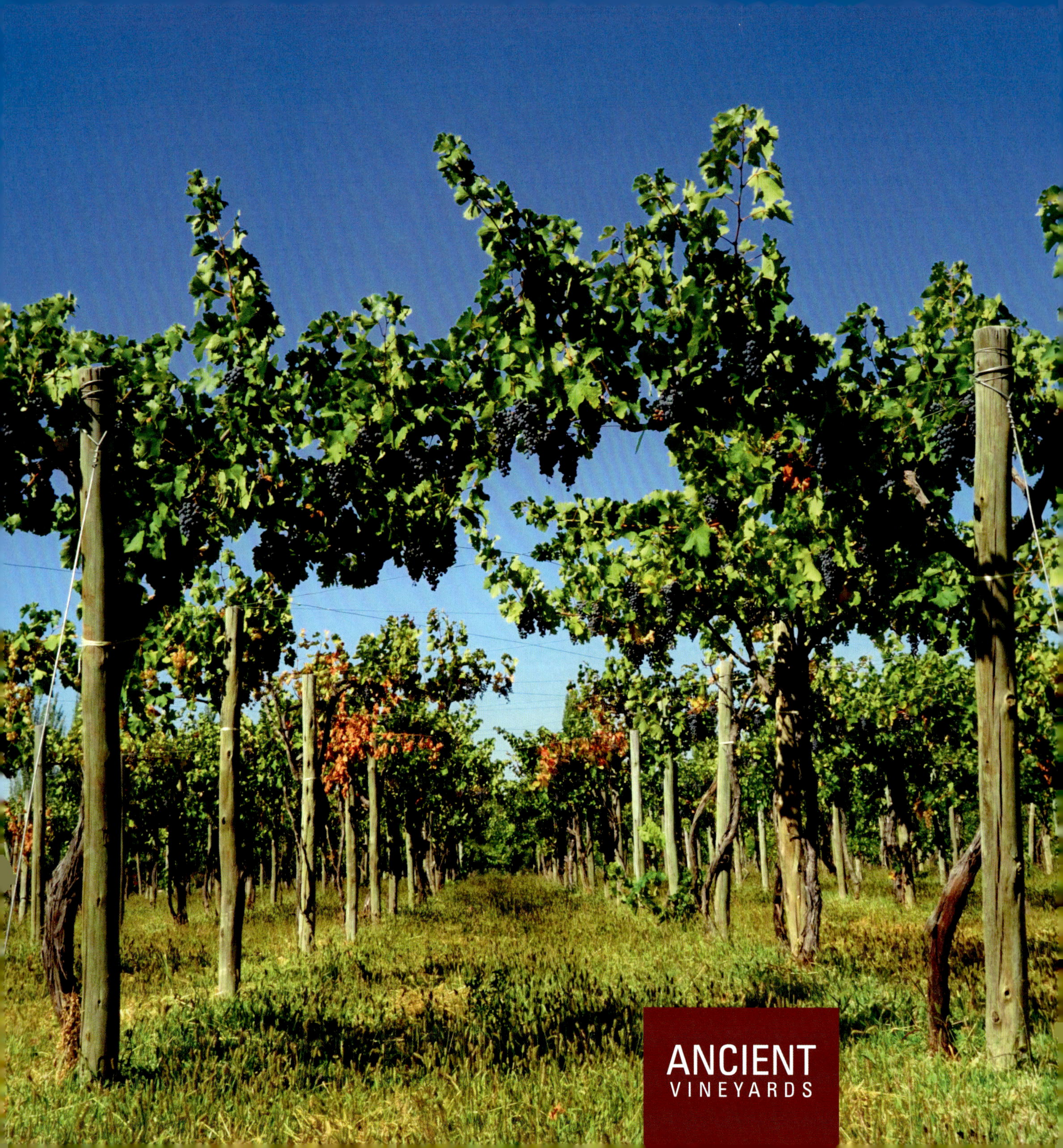
ANCIENT
VINEYARDS

BIODYNAMIC, MACHINELESS, ELEGANT WINES

The inspiration came to find ancient vineyards in Río Negro. *Italian Countess*, Noemía Marone Cinzano, and *Danish Winemaker* Hans Vinding-Diers were on a scouting mission in Río Negro when they discovered old-vine Malbec vineyards planted in 1932. The vines were ungrafted, planted on their rootstock, and sadly left for abandon. They were inspired by the region and the potential of these historic vines, so they purchased the property, where they ultimately built **Bodega Noemía**.

What followed was an extraordinary restoration of the vineyards. This was a true resuscitation to revive the vines from their near-death state. Vinding-Diers used a French method called Massale, selecting the very best vines in the vineyard and propagating them through cuttings. Different from planting clones, Massale selection involves choosing a number of outstanding vines from the vineyard and then propagating new vines from their budwood (strong young shoots bearing buds).

The restoration was conducted all organically and biodynamically, certified through Argencer and Demeter biodynamic standards. Biodynamic agriculture is a method of organic farming that employs a holistic understanding of the agricultural processes, a sustainable agriculture which treats soil fertility, plant growth, and livestock care as ecologically interrelated tasks.

Continuing today, all of Bodega Noemìa's vineyards are farmed biodynamically. They produce their biodynamic preparations exclusively with their own raw materials on their farm, including their own manure and biodynamic composts.

Grapes are all hand-harvested, hand-sorted, hand-de-stemmed, hand-crushed... all gently handled throughout the entire process. The grapes never see a machine! And to further amplify the terroir's signature in the final wines, the fermentation is carried out using only indigenous yeasts naturally occurring in the vineyards.

Everything is hand-made at Noemìa. Even the wine is moved throughout the winery by hand, using only gravity. After fermentation the wine is decanted by gravity into the aging barrels. The bottling is also performed by gravity, and without any filtering. Everything is soft and gentle.

The result is extraordinary wines. My favorite, simply named **Bodega Noemìa**, is a luscious seduction of the most rich and delicate Malbec imaginable. Elegance all the way from this 100% 1932 historic Malbec vineyard!

J. Alberto, named after the Countess's father, is a unique field blend of co-growing, co-harvesting, co-fermenting, and co-aging a single 1955 vineyard of both Malbec and Merlot. The Merlot adds a subtle softness to this wine that you must try.

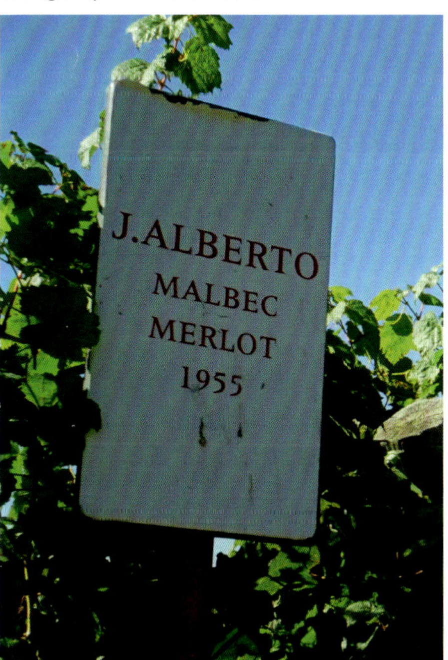

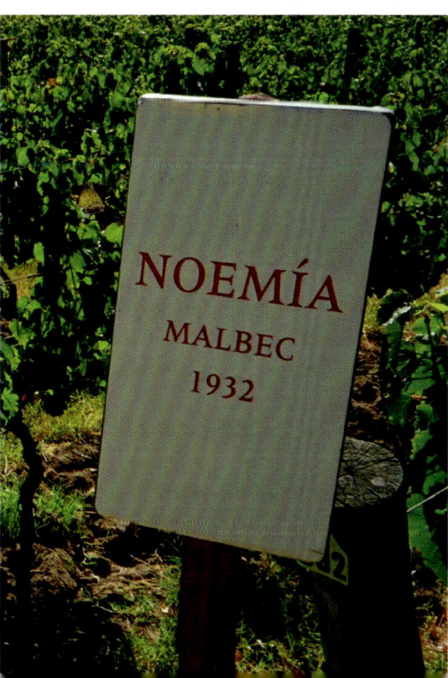

PATAGONIA **RÍO NEGRO** MAINQUÉ
Winery (Bodega)
BODEGA NOEMÍA

1945 Ave Roca (3 km north of Ruta 22)
(Mainqué, **General Roca,** Río Negro)

011 (+54 9 298) 453.0412
comercial@Bodega-Noemia.com.ar

BodegaNoemia.com

Español
110,000 bottles produced annually

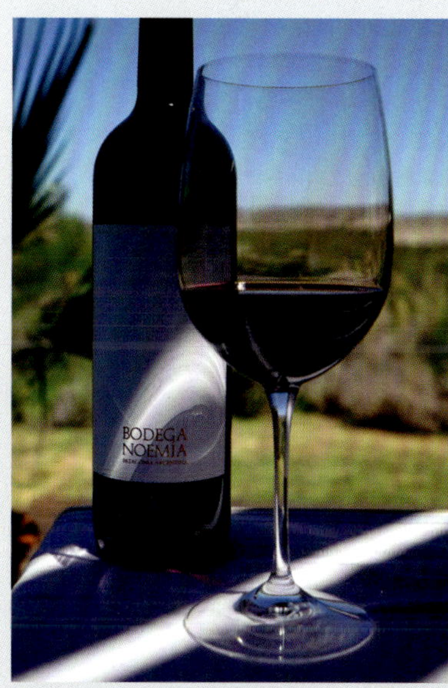

Michael's Favorite Pick
Bodega Noemía (1932 Malbec Vines)

Total Collection of Wines

Bodega Noemía (1932 Malbec Vines)

Noemía #2 (Cabernet Sauvignon & Merlot Blend)

A Lisa (90% Malbec, 10% Merlot)

J. Alberto (95% Malbec, 5% Merlot)
(Co-Grown, Co-Harvested, Co-Fermented, Co-Aged)

To get Bodega Noemía wines in the USA
Contact their Importer at: ViasWine.com

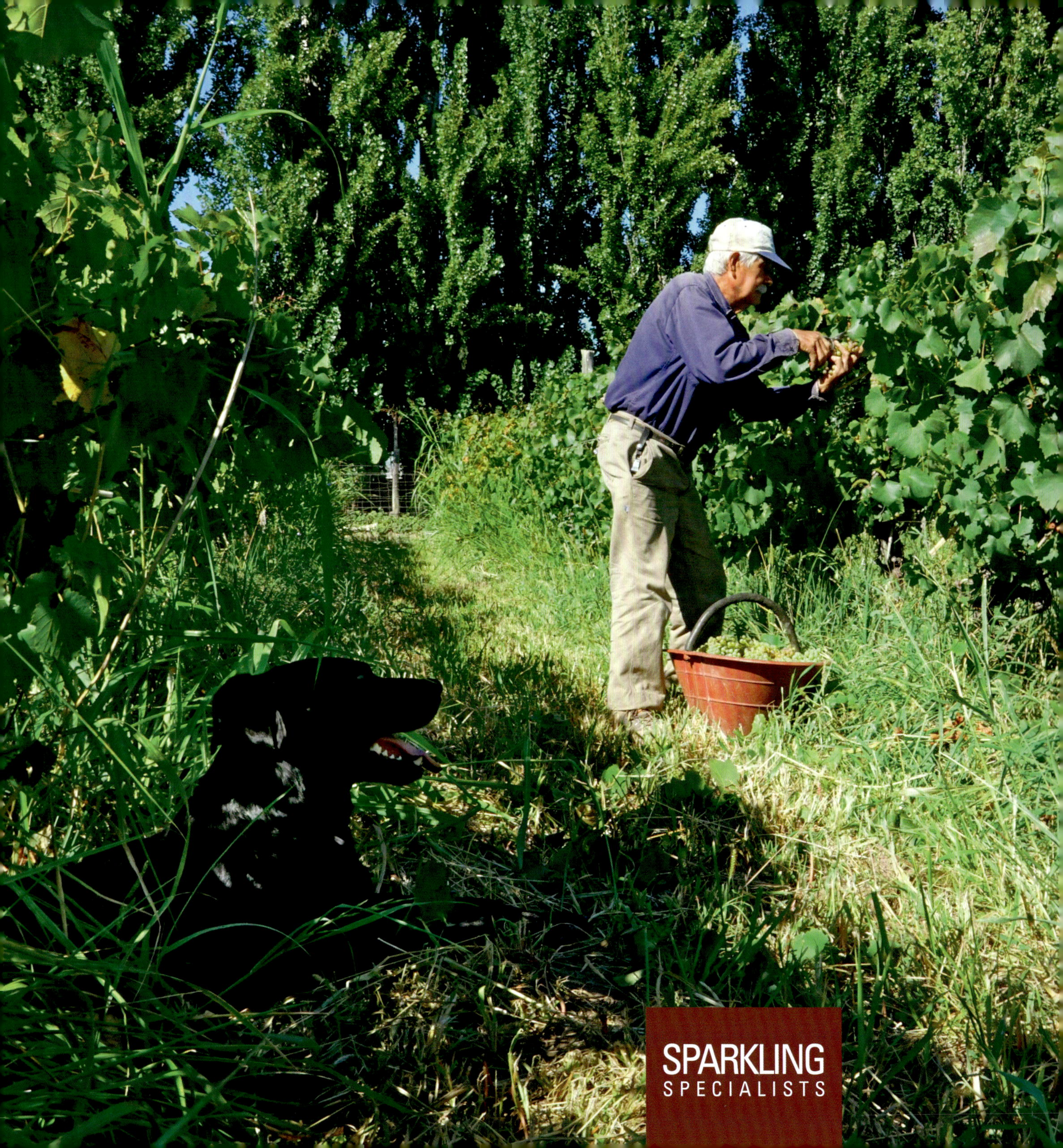
SPARKLING
SPECIALISTS

CHAMPAGNE LOVER?

The focus here at Bodega Agrestis is very straight forward... to make extraordinary sparkling wines in Patagonia. Meticulous effort goes into every step along the way to making their delicate, hand-crafted wines. While they are resemblant of old world French Champagne, they have unique characteristics of the Patagonia terroir which makes them a very special treat.

The winery's founder and agronomist, Norberto Ghirardelli, planted 30 acres of special Pinot Noir and Chardonnay clones he imported from France in 1992. Only these estate-grown hand-harvested grapes are used in their sparkling wines.

Every step in the extensive process of making their sparkling wines is attended to with detail. Every family member is involved. It should not be surprising that Norberto, as an agronomist, places the care of the grapes as the top priority with the concept that the quality is born in the vineyard.

Norberto monitors everything closely, such as... using the irrigation system, conducting proper vineyard management for the individual requirements of each particular varietal, closely observing the vines during their initial spring growth as well as the decisive moment of harvest, measuring their maturity and sugar levels, plus his unique method of hand-picking grapes, which he considers to be one of the most important steps in the pursuit of excellence in his wines.

PHOTO left page, gives you a glimpse into the meticulous attention that is given to harvesting the grapes. Including, the all-important Labrador Love which you can see gracing the vineyard harvest.

Norberto manages the entire journey of the grapes from the vine to the wine in his very own small facility where all fermenting, hand-bottling and hand-corking are taking place, including hand-riddling on traditional pupitres in the traditional Champagne method. The family cultivates everything they make, by hand.

Few people realize that Domaine Chandon (the 250-year-old legacy of French Champagnes) identified Patagonia as the ideal place to produce sparkling wines. After four or five years, Chandon moved to Mendoza for political reasons, leaving the opportunity for Bodega Agrestis and others to prosper in this land.

A VERY SPECIAL AFTERNOON IN THE PARK

The property within the vineyards at Agrestis is a beautiful park setting. Green lawns, mature trees and outdoor furniture to lounge and enjoy the day. A tour at Agrestis includes empanadas and grilled foods to compliment their sparkling wines.

Once in a while, they hold concerts in their park. My suggestion is to get a bottle of their delectable sparkling wines and enjoy a beautiful afternoon amongst the trees in the park.

Essentially, they focus on three sparklings...

Agrestis NG Natural Sparkling is 80% Chardonnay, 20% Pinot Noir. The color is bright yellow with aromas of green apple and banana. The palate is balanced, smooth with a dry-finish characteristic of the natural champagne.

Agrestis NG Rosé Natural is 100% Pinot Noir. This was my favorite! Fruity, without being sweet. A beautiful color with alluring Pinot Noir notes. Sweet on the nose of dried fruits and nuts, a big structured wine of great concentration.

Tenuis Extra Brut Gewürztraminer is their new sparkling of 100% Gewürztraminer (sweet aromatic grape that thrives in cold climates). This is a nice change from Chardonnay and certainly a unique must-try. It is very floral with nice citrus notes.

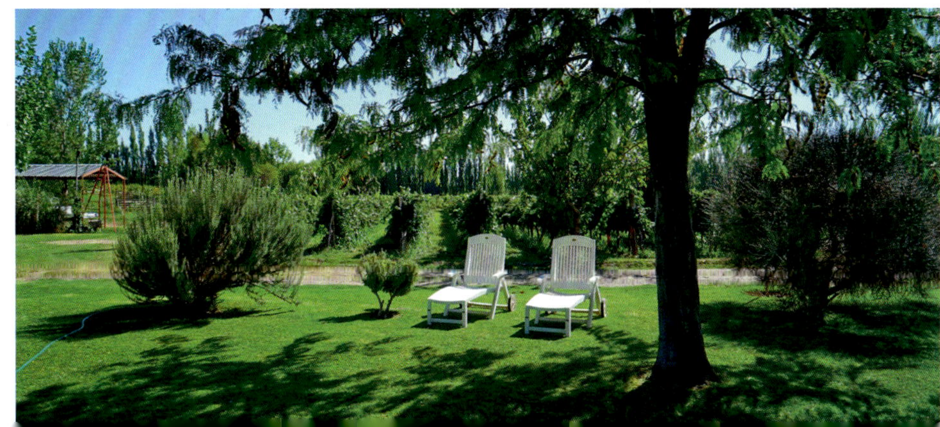

PATAGONIA **RÍO NEGRO** GENERAL ROCA

Winery (Bodega)

BODEGA AGRESTIS

1539 Gobernador Castello
(1.5 km south of Ruta 22)
(General Roca, **General Roca,** Río Negro)

011 (+54 299 15) 429.3284
tursimo@BodegaAgrestis.com.ar

BodegaAgrestis.com.ar

English & Español
20,000 bottles produced annually

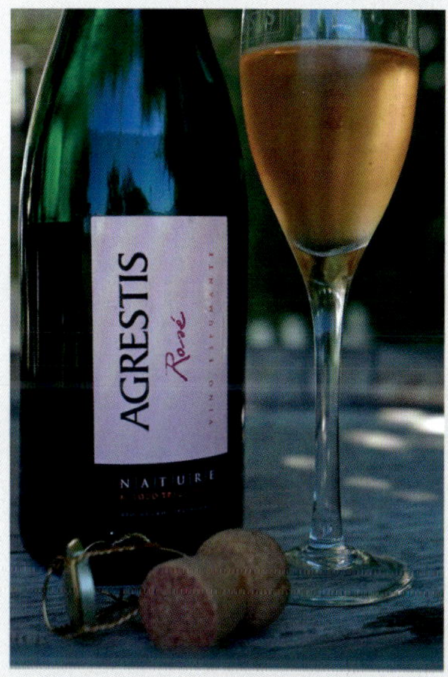

Michael's Favorite Pick
Agrestis NG Rosé Natural

Total Collection of Wines

Agrestis NG Sparkling
(80% Chardonnay, 20% Pinot Noir)

Agrestis NG Rosé Natural
(100% Pinot Noir)

Tenuis Extra Brut Gewürztraminer
(100% Gewürztraminer)

The NG stands for Norberto Ghriadelli

To get Bodega Agrestis wines in the USA
Contact their Importer at: RayaImports.com

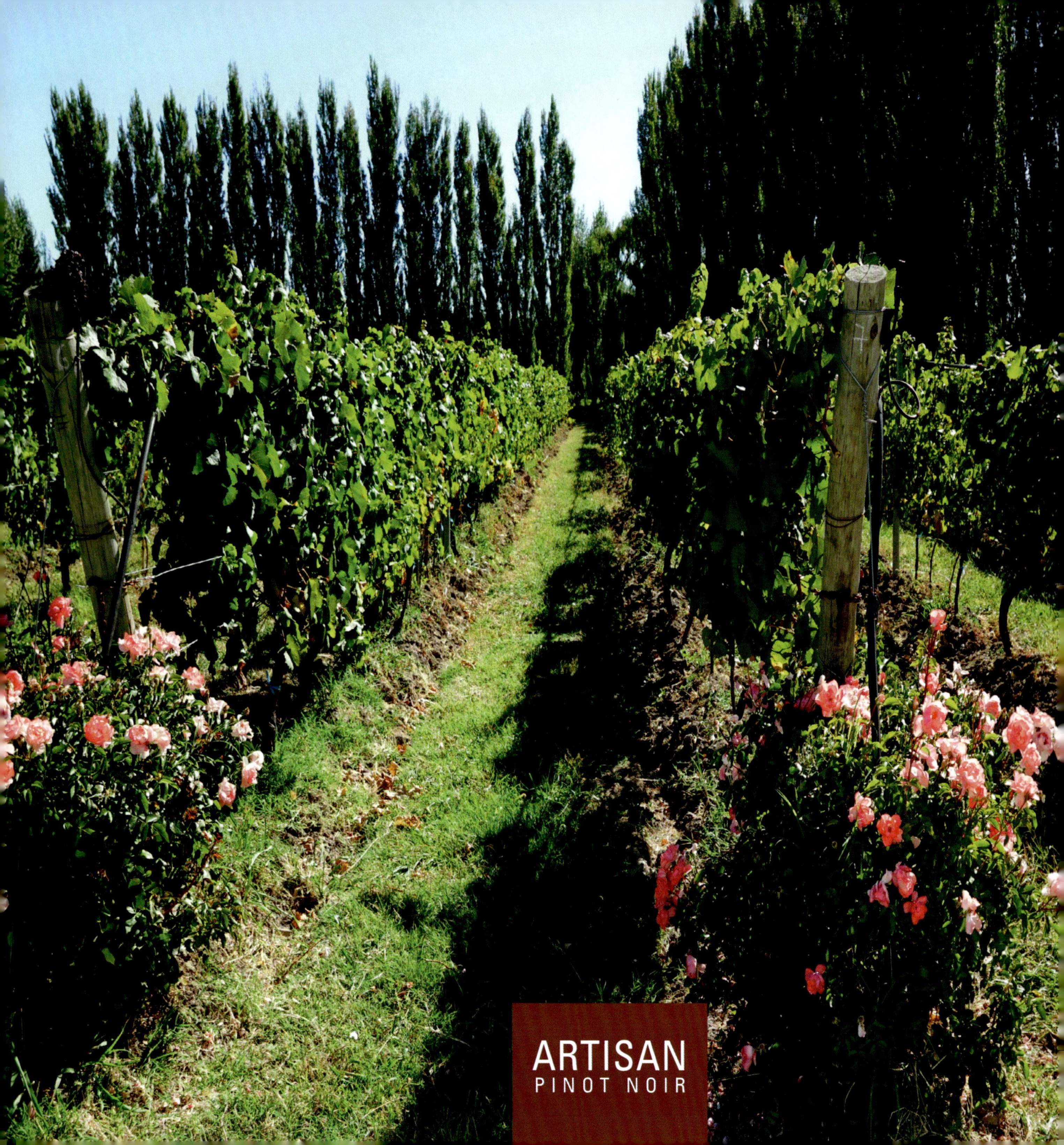

ARTISAN
PINOT NOIR

BIODYNAMIC PASSION FOR EXTREME PINOT NOIR

Let's start with the result... the purest, most delicate, Pinot Noir you can possibly imagine. Bodega Chacra wines have a freshness and pure essence that will delight your palate. They have a delicate lusciousness of raspberries and cherries that I love so much about Pinot Noir. The acidity is very fine. The elegance is at its best!

Chacra wines have the Burgundy elegance with the flavor-richness of California. These wines are receiving the highest ratings among all Pinot Noirs in Argentina. Everything is hand-made here. My favorite, the **Chacra -TREINTA Y DOS- Pinot Noir** from their 1932 vineyards (ergo the name in Spanish) is hand-numbered on each bottle.

Why? The beauty of the wines is a direct reflection of the beauty of the farm. A totally biodynamic environment, and being 100% certified organic and biodynamic, the wines are all natural and unfiltered. The ecosystem within the vineyards is a beautiful place... it's an organic agriculture here that considers the entire vineyard a living organism, promoting all the interdependent flora and fauna to thrive, both above and below ground, including the effects of lunar and seasonal rhythms as well.

Just standing on the property, you feel the aura of this beautiful ecosystem. It is a self-sustaining environment, even for the people, with organic gardens and naturally raised animals.

In 2004, Chacra's founder and visionary, Piero Incisa della Rocchetta, purchased a plot of ancient abandoned vines that had been planted in 1932, naming his first wine *Treinta y Dos* (Spanish for 32) and founding his winery, Bodega Chacra.

Since the acquisition of the 1932 vineyard, Piero continued to purchase other old-vine Pinot Noir vineyards. Next was a vineyard planted in 1955 (calling the wine *Cinquenta y Cinco*), followed by a vineyard planted in 1967 (*Sesanta y Sete* when the wine becomes available). Each of these wines is exclusively single-vineyard Pinot Noir grapes, named after their original planting dates. As old vineyards, they produce small bunches of ultra-concentrated berries that give intensity to their wines.

A fourth wine has also been created and called *Barda* (the Ridge in Spanish). On the ridge of the 1932 vineyard is a 20-year-old, 10-acre plot that provides younger fruit for a different style of their wines.

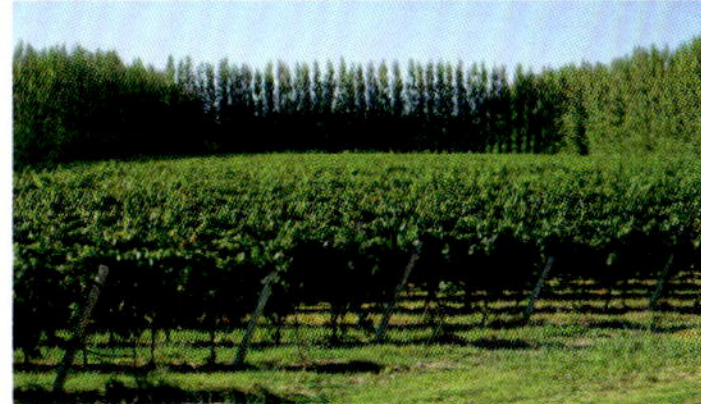

Bodega Chacra Estate Vineyards

Chacra is a local word used to describe a square farm that is equally divided into four smaller squares by canals and is irrigated by gravity. It is bordered by rows of poplar trees that shelter the vines from the strong wind. This wind not only blows away pests and bacteria, it also increases the thickness of the grape skins.

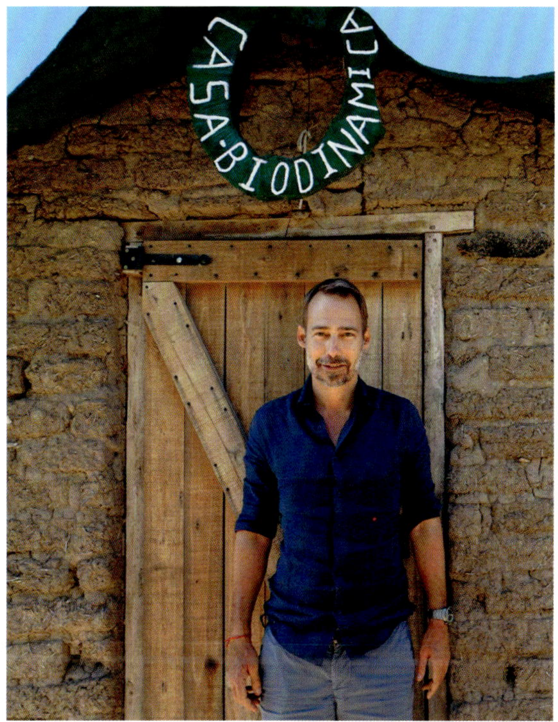

Piero Incisa della Rocchetta
Founder and Managing Director

ABOVE, Piero in front of his hand-built barn, the sanctuary of the biodynamic super-foods which nourish the plants of the farm.

Piero was from the Maremma Wine Region of Tuscany, where he grew up on his family's legendary estate of vineyards and winemaking. He is an Italian noble, a scion of one of Italy's most historically significant families, and the international face of one of Italy's most important wines... Sassicaia.

Piero was cultured in century-old traditions of vineyard management and winemaking, creating his appetite for winemaking, which ultimately inspired a lifelong dream and passion to become a winemaker. He branched out from his Tuscan roots, obtained degrees from several prestigious universities in Switzerland, California and New York, and then headed to South America to produce world-class Pinot Noir in Patagonia.

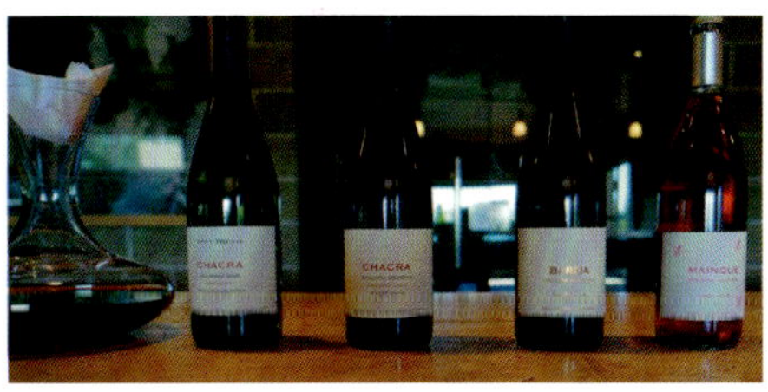

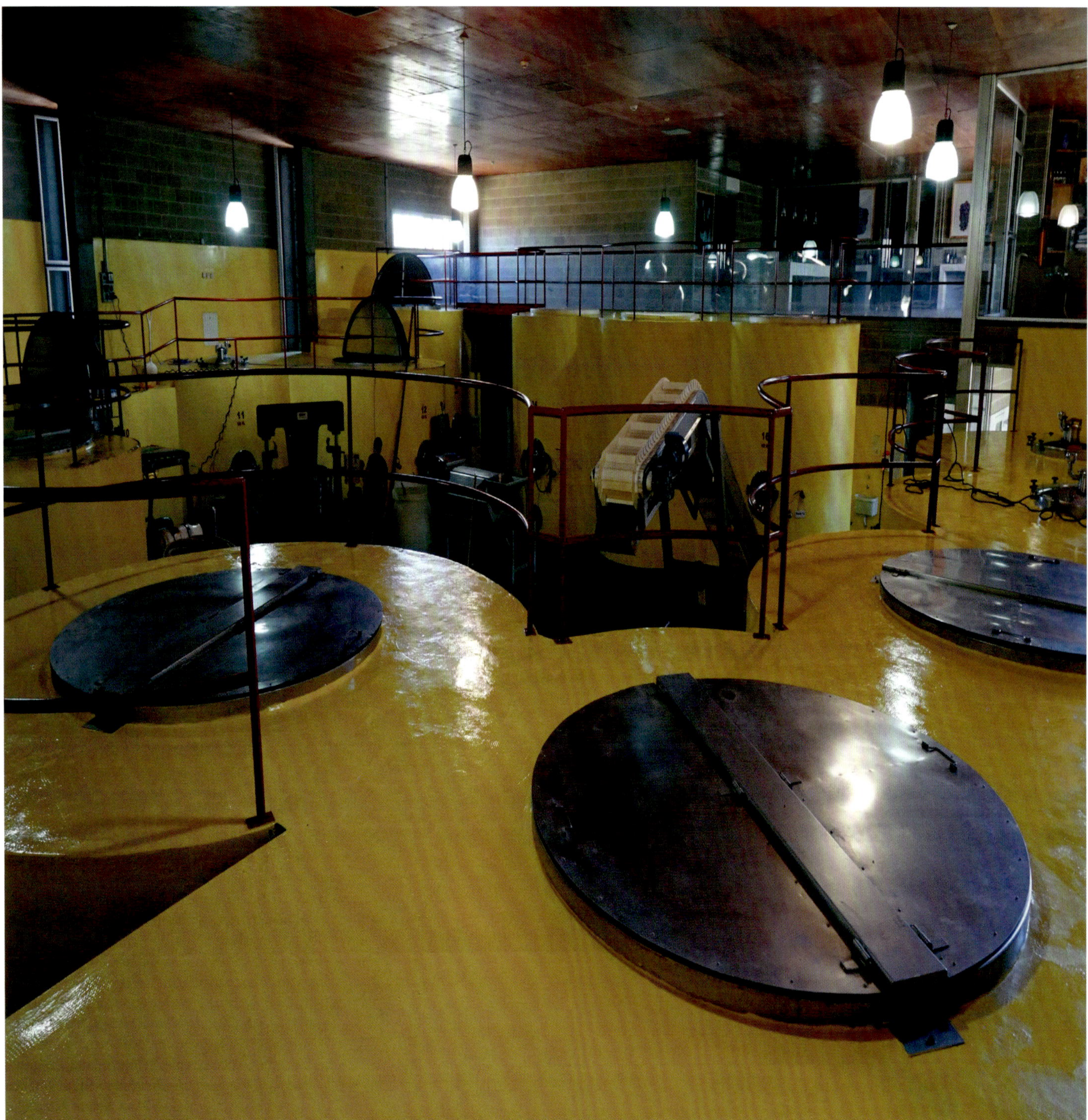

The year after purchasing the 1932 vineyard, Piero Incisa broke ground the next year (2005) on his brand-new and innovative winery. A winery with the expressed purpose of gently and peacefully moving the grapes through the winery for all parts of the delicate harmonious aspects of the wines.

The new winery (photos left page and below) is at the site of the 1932 vineyard. Heusch Architects designed it elegantly simple, a sandstone structure in complete harmony with its desert surroundings, which allow complete control over the winemaking process through gravity.

To fully understand the attention that Piero and his team at Bodega Charca put into the winemaking process, read how they describe what they do to make their wines so very special...

The vineyards of old gnarled Pinot Noir vines, planted on their own rootstocks, are head-trained and produce tiny bunches of small, concentrated berries. The vineyards' pale, dry, porous soils are dominated by gravel and coarse alluvial pebbles with significant limestone content. Irrigation is carried out at most five times during the vine cycle.

A green harvest in January reduces the already small yield, so that at ripe harvest each vine produces at most five small clusters of grapes collectively weighing roughly a pound. The fruit is collected by hand into small boxes in the early morning hours during the first week of March.

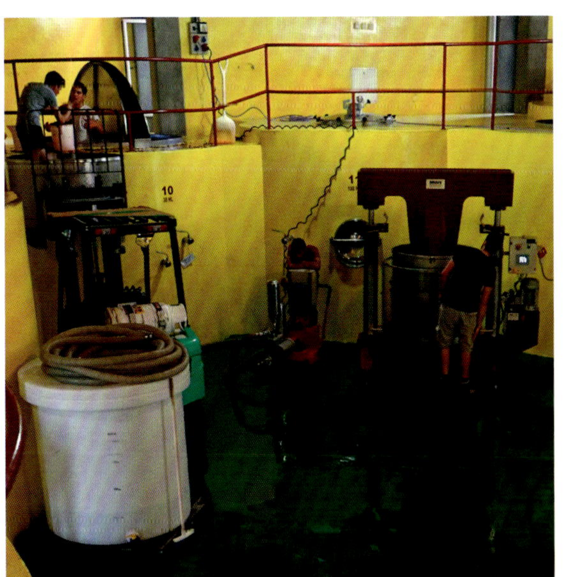

The process of harvesting with these small boxes, each of which holds only eight kilos of grapes, is more tedious than using large containers, but it prevents the fruit on the bottom from being bruised. The grapes are refrigerated on the way to the winery to preserve the freshness of their fruit, and then hand-de-stemmed, sorted and placed in 200-liter cement vats for fermentation.

No mechanization is used at any stage of the production process. The berries are placed whole, without crushing, in the fermentation vat, where the weight of the grapes near the top of the vat crushes some of the grapes at the bottom of the vat. This method, which shares similarities with carbonic maceration, allows the wine to express the subtle, complex and finely textured tannins characteristic of very old vines.

Fermentation is initiated spontaneously by indigenous yeasts, and lasts approximately three weeks at an average temperature of 78.8°F. During fermentation, a layer of carbon dioxide blankets the surface of the cap, which is neither pumped over nor punched down.

Once the alcoholic fermentation is complete, the juice is transferred off the skins into small French oak barrels in the most gentle manner possible, by gravity, without pressing or filtering. Barrels from three different barrel-makers in Burgundy are used, of which only 20% are new. The tight, fine grain of Burgundian oak minimizes oxidation and restrains transfer of oak characteristics to the wine.

Malolactic fermentation begins spontaneously once the wine is in barrel, and is completed in roughly six months. A tiny amount of sulfur is then added to kill any stray yeasts or bacteria, and the wine remains undisturbed on its lees for approximately 12 months in barrel.

Bottling takes place around the first week of June without fining or filtration. The objective is for the oak, the fruit and the nuances of the soil to marry perfectly so that influence of the wood is nearly imperceptible in the wine, and the vine and "terroir" are expressed to their fullest.

PATAGONIA **RÍO NEGRO** MAINQUÉ

Winery (Bodega)

BODEGA CHACRA

1945 Ave Roca (3.5 km north of Ruta 22)
(Mainqué, **General Roca,** Río Negro)

Visitors By Advanced Appointment Only
Write an email to arrange a time
Admin@BodegaChacra.com

BodegaChacra.com

English, Español & Italiano
50,000 bottles produced annually

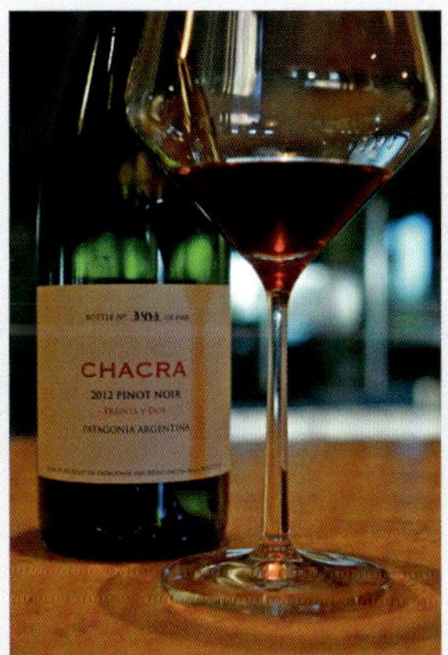

Michael's Favorite Pick
Chacra -TREINTA Y DOS- Pinot Noir

Total Collection of Wines

Chacra -TREINTA Y DOS- Pinot Noir
(1932 Single-Vineyard Wine)

Chacra -CINCUENTA Y CINCO- Pinot Noir
(1955 Single-Vineyard Wine)

BARDA Pinot Noir
(20 Year Old Vines On The Ridge of the 1932 Vineyard)

MAINQUE Pinot Rosé (Pinot Noir)
(In honor of the village Mainqué in which Chacra is located)

To get Bodega Chacra wines in the USA
Contact Importer: GrandCruSelectionsWine.com

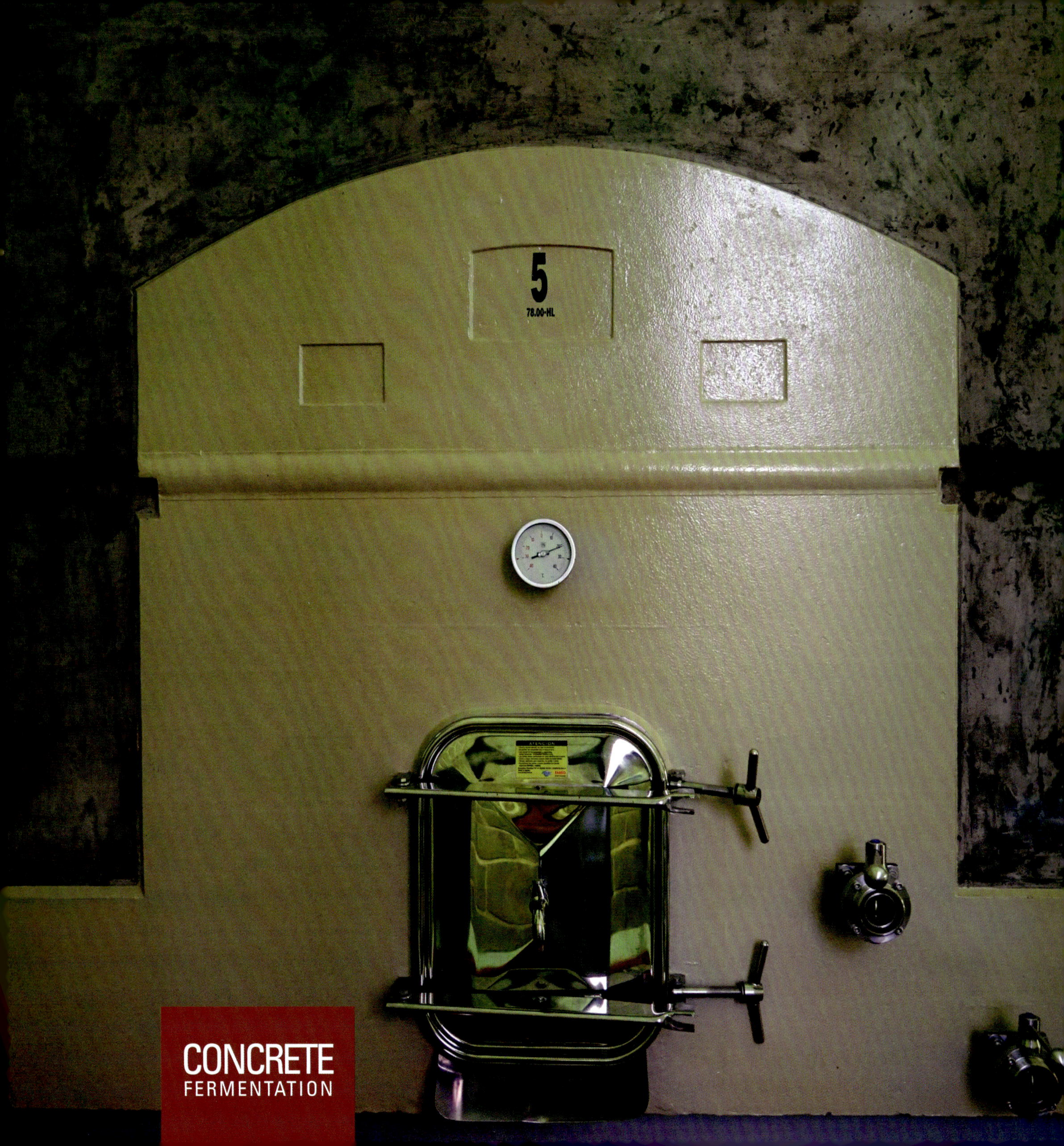

CONCRETE
FERMENTATION

A MAGICAL CHARDONNAY PAIRING WITH SUSHI?

I must confess, I really do not drink Chardonnay. It does not excite me. I am much more of a red wine drinker anyway. That is my taste.

Also my taste is sushi. *Love Sushi!* The challenge with sushi though is that it does not pair well with wine, except saki. So, I usually drink a Japanese beer when I am out for sushi. When I am home with sushi, a French Champaign is delightful.

Until... I met Agustín Lombroni, the winemaker at Bodega Del Rio Elorza, who introduced me to a Chardonnay he makes in raw concrete wine pools (photo left page) and I was captivated. The more I tasted this Chardonnay the more I was craving for sushi... I just knew it would be the perfect pairing. So I brought a couple bottles home with me and headed to a fancy sushi bar.

OK, so the sushi (photos below) was quite the extravagance. So was the Verum Chardonnay. It was the perfect pairing. Just look at the bright fresh yellow color of this wine (photo right). It has very nice acidity, and the nose is floral fruity white peaches. The magic in your mouth is its citrus flavors that begs for sushi. If a white peach could be a citrus or a grapefruit could be a stone fruit, you would have this magic!

The raw concrete is one of Lombroni's secrets. Lombroni consults with Internationally renowned Italian Oenologist Alberto Antonini. Take a peek inside, it is true (photo below). Just raw concrete, without an epoxy sealant typically used in concrete tanks. And no oak, no stainless, 100% fermented and aged in raw concrete wine pools.

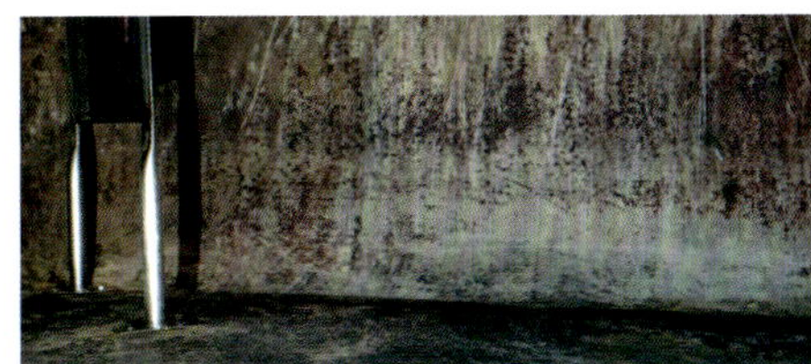

Agustín has a very sensitive palate, and he tells me about his ability to detect plastic in the aftertaste of wine after aging nine months or more in concrete pools with epoxy, while in stainless steel tanks, he detects something more metallic.

With raw concrete, he does not sense this. The wine seems more harmonic, and better expresses its minerality. Because of the slow heat transfer between wine and air, the wine stays at a constant temperature and keeps the fine lees in suspension for longer time, giving more body to the wine.

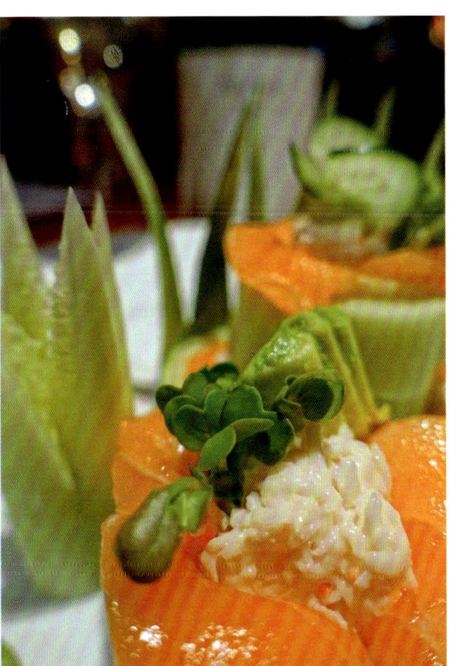

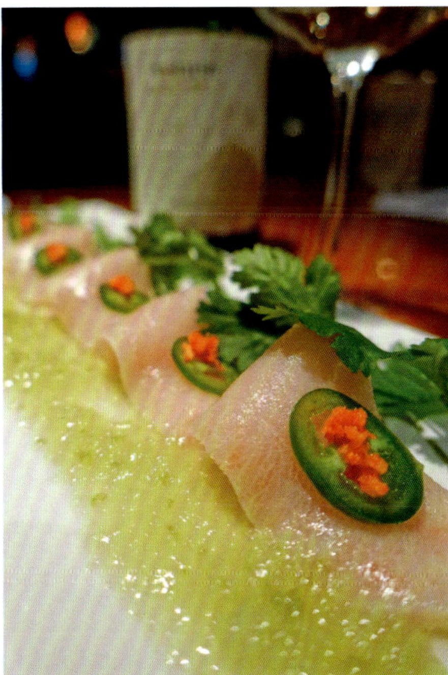

PATAGONIA **RÍO NEGRO** FERNÁNDEZ ORO

Winery (Bodega)

BODEGA DEL RIO ELORZA

1700 Mitre [3 km north of Ruta 65 (old Ruta 22)]
(From Ruta 65 Downtown Fernández Oro, north on Iguazu, east on Primeros Pobladores, north on Mitre, sign on right side of Mitre)
(Fernández Oro, **General Roca,** Río Negro)

011 (+54 299) 507.9957
info@DelRioElorza.com

DelRioElorza.com

English & Español
50,000 bottles produced annually

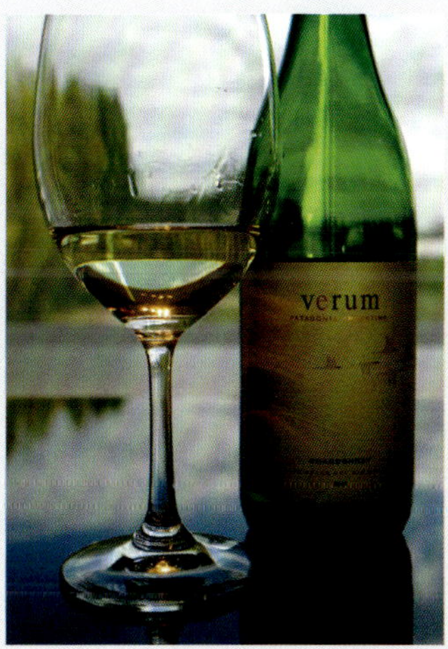

Michael's Favorite Pick
Verum Classic - Chardonnay

Total Collection of Wines

Verum Classic Line
Chardonnay • Sauvignon Blanc
Pinot Noir • Merlot • Malbec
Los Cisnes (Malbec/Merlot Blend)

Verum Reserve Line
Malbec • Merlot • Cabernet Franc

To get Verum wines in the USA
Contact their Importer at: VinoDelSol.com

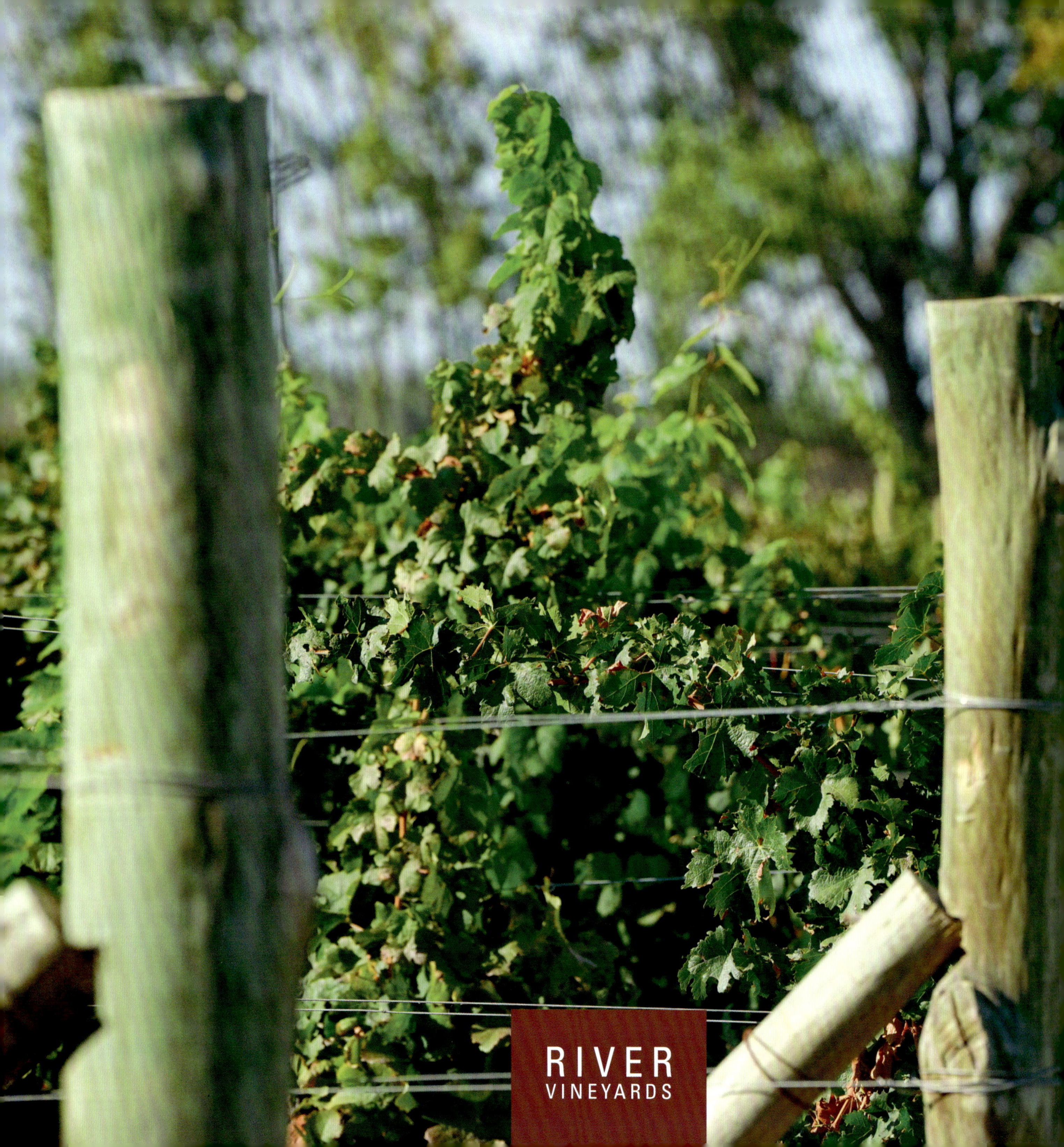
RIVER
VINEYARDS

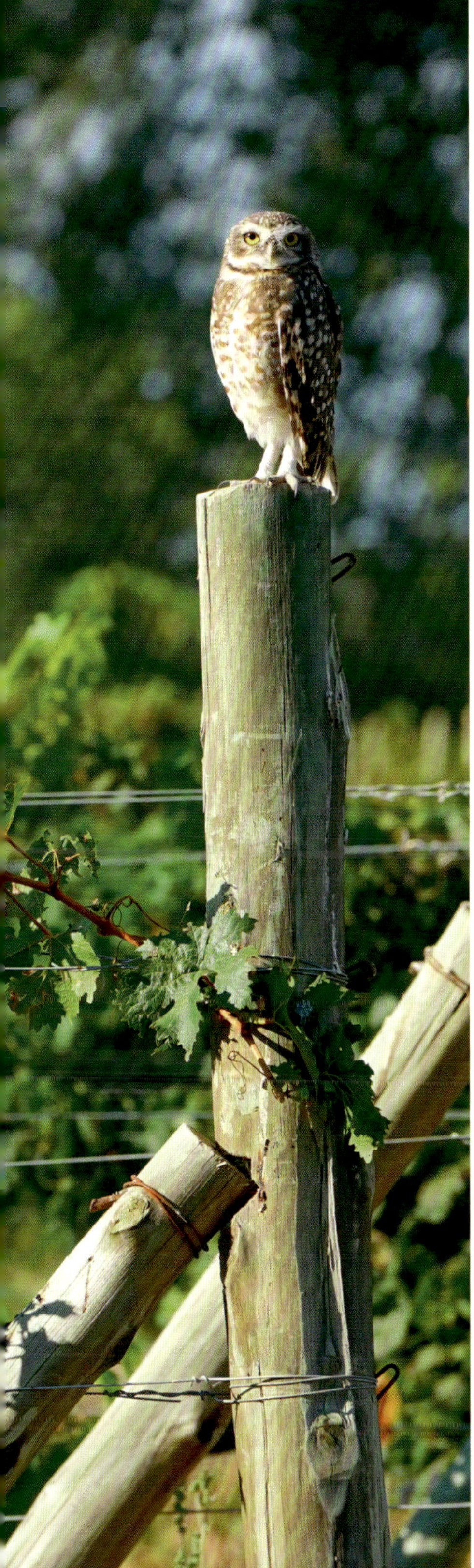

DOWN BY THE RIVERSIDE

As one of the newest wineries in Río Negro, Bodega Aniello has taken a new approach to farming their grapes. They planted vineyards right along the river.

Farming in Río Negro valley was made possible through an elaborate canal system, designed a hundred years ago, feeding farms of all types throughout the valley. Aniello decided to go right to the source of the river for its irrigation; however, the decision was particularly chosen for the unique terroir of river rock and sand that embody the river's edge.

Aniello was started in 2010 when the first parcel was purchased. In the Mainqué district of the Upper Río Negro valley, there is a stunning turn in the river that gives a perfect location for their vines to be planted where the water actually flows directly from the river into the vineyards. This first estate is called *006*, and so is the wine named after the estate that gave its birth. They initially started with Malbec and Merlot, and then added Pinot Noir.

Next, they bought an estate with an old winery originally built in 1927 to be able to provide for the production of their wines. The restoration of the winery was completed in 2015. This estate has old vineyards surrounding the winery, vines planted back in 1932 and 1947. A family of owls has made these vineyards their home (photo left page), and provides protection from varmints who might consider the vines their own plantation.

The old-vine wines, also Malbec and Merlot, carry the name of the winery for its label. Bodega Aniello is a small winery exploring the value of ancient winemaking traditions of Patagonia along with its Italian roots. The owner is committed to sustainable agriculture, and have taken the challenge to migrate from conventional to sustainable farming here.

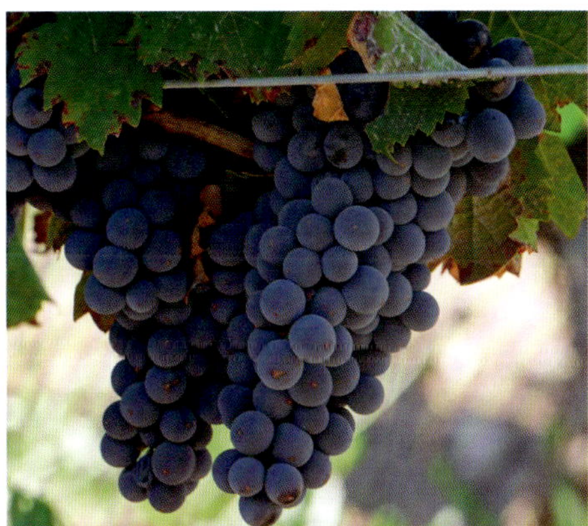

PATAGONIA **RÍO NEGRO** MAINQUÉ

Winery (Bodega)

BODEGA ANIELLO

341 Chacra (2 km north of Ruta 22)
(Mainqué, **General Roca,** Río Negro)

No Phone At Winery
info@BodegaAniello.com.ar

BodegaAniello.com.ar

English & Español
80,000 bottles produced annually

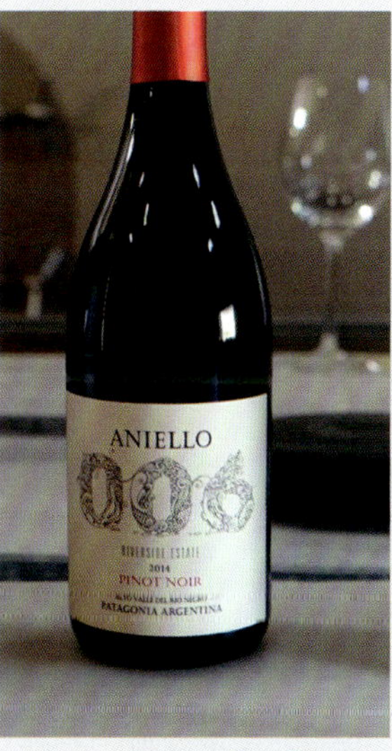

Michael's Favorite Pick
006 Estate - Pinot Noir

Total Collection of Wines

006 Estate - Malbec

006 Estate - Merlot

006 Estate - Pinot Noir

Aniello Malbec

Aniello Merlot

To get Bodega Aniello wines in the USA
Contact their Importer at: MontcalmWines.com

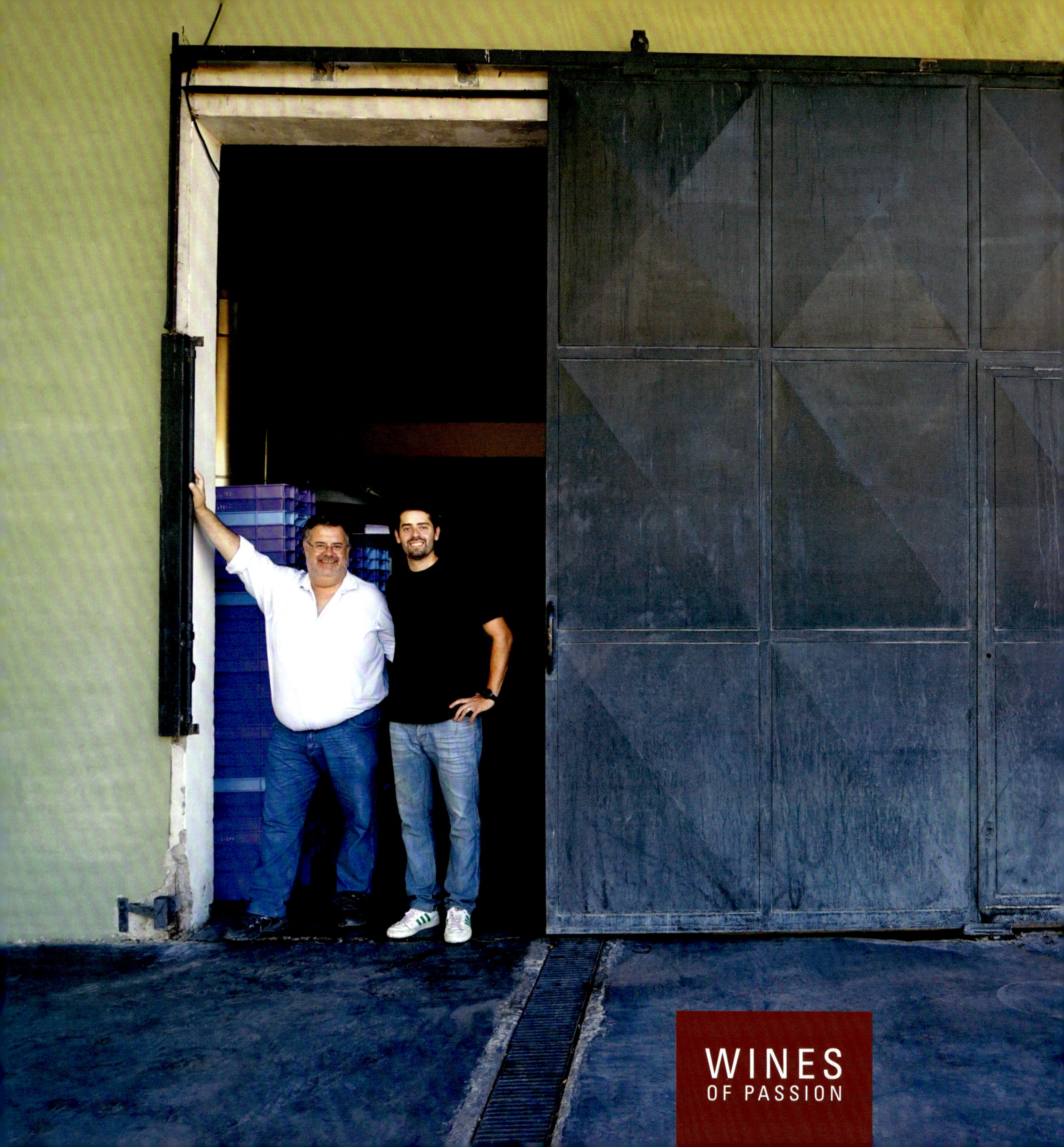
WINES
OF PASSION

THE MARCELO MIRAS SIGNATURE COLLECTION OF WINES

Behind this large grey door (photo left page), inside a building with a disguised name on the wall (from a previous winery tenant "Estepa") is the making of Marcelo Miras's personal collection of wines.

Incognito you might wonder, what is Miras, the truly great winemaker of Patagonia, doing inside this old winery building? He is already Chief Winemaker at Del Fin Del Mundo (Patagonia's largest winery), and is designing wineries and orchestrating the winemaking activities at numerous wineries throughout Patagonia. Whatever he is doing inside this building, it must be extra special, because it bears his signature on every bottle.

Knowing his reputation for remarkable wines throughout Patagonia, it was an easy and curious choice of mine to try his *Miras Reserva Cabernet Franc* at a local Italian restaurant. This experience made me want to see inside the walls of this winery and discover exactly what is going on special at Bodega Miras.

Nobody knows the Río Negro valley better than Miras, as he has been making wine here for nearly 25 years, and knows almost every vineyard, working and abandoned. With 100 years of vine growing and the loss of more than 90% of the wineries in this valley, Marcelo has used his fine-tuned expertise and knowledge to choose the best-of-the-best historic vineyards to make his special wines.

All of the wines are hand-crafted with small batches of excellence, from historic vineyards at various sites throughout the Río Negro valley.

Marcelo's family are all actively involved in the winery, from harvesting, processing and bottling to the marketing of the wines. This is a Miras family business led by his wife Sandra and son Pablo (photos: left page with Marcelo, right, processing freshly harvested grapes, and below, tasting the progress directly from the tank). This is a beautiful family sharing the same love and passion that Marcelo has for creating great wines.

Consider yourself quite lucky if you arrive at the winery on a day that Sandra makes fresh empanadas of various meat fillings (photo below). Totally scrumptious! And pairs perfectly with their *Miras Jovem Malbec Rosé*.

Bodega Miras is the first winery you will encounter when you drive into the Río Negro valley, and also the only winery found directly on the highway (Ruta 22). The only question is whether you want to make this winery your first stop on the way in, or the last winery as you depart.

Vintners throughout Patagonia seek Marcelo's advise on winemaking and he has contributed to the success of most of the wineries in this region... so, this is a special opportunity to taste what a master winemaker would make when he has free reign and puts his name on the bottle.

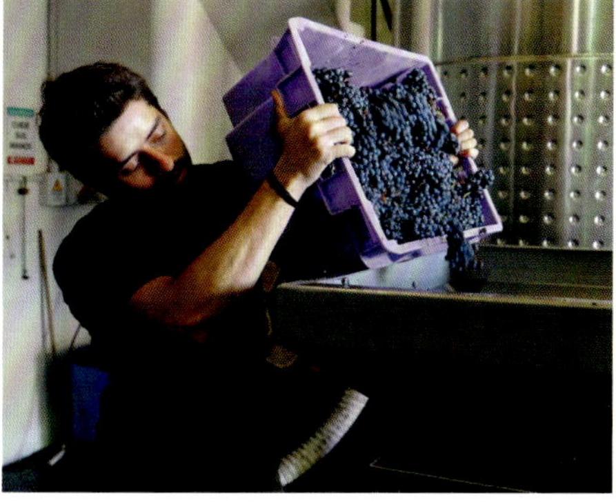

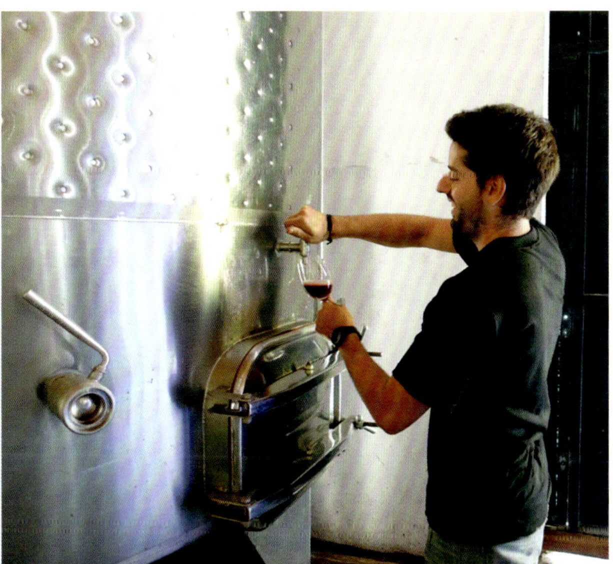

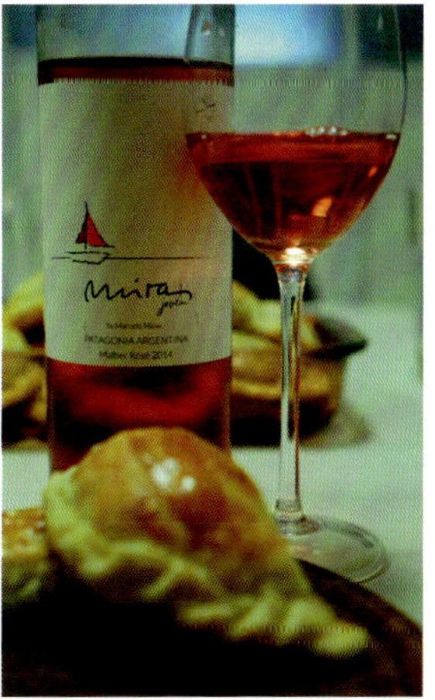

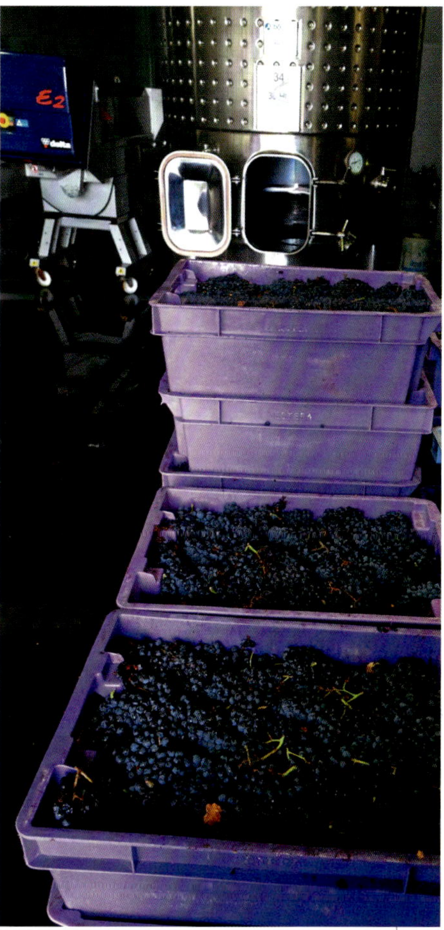

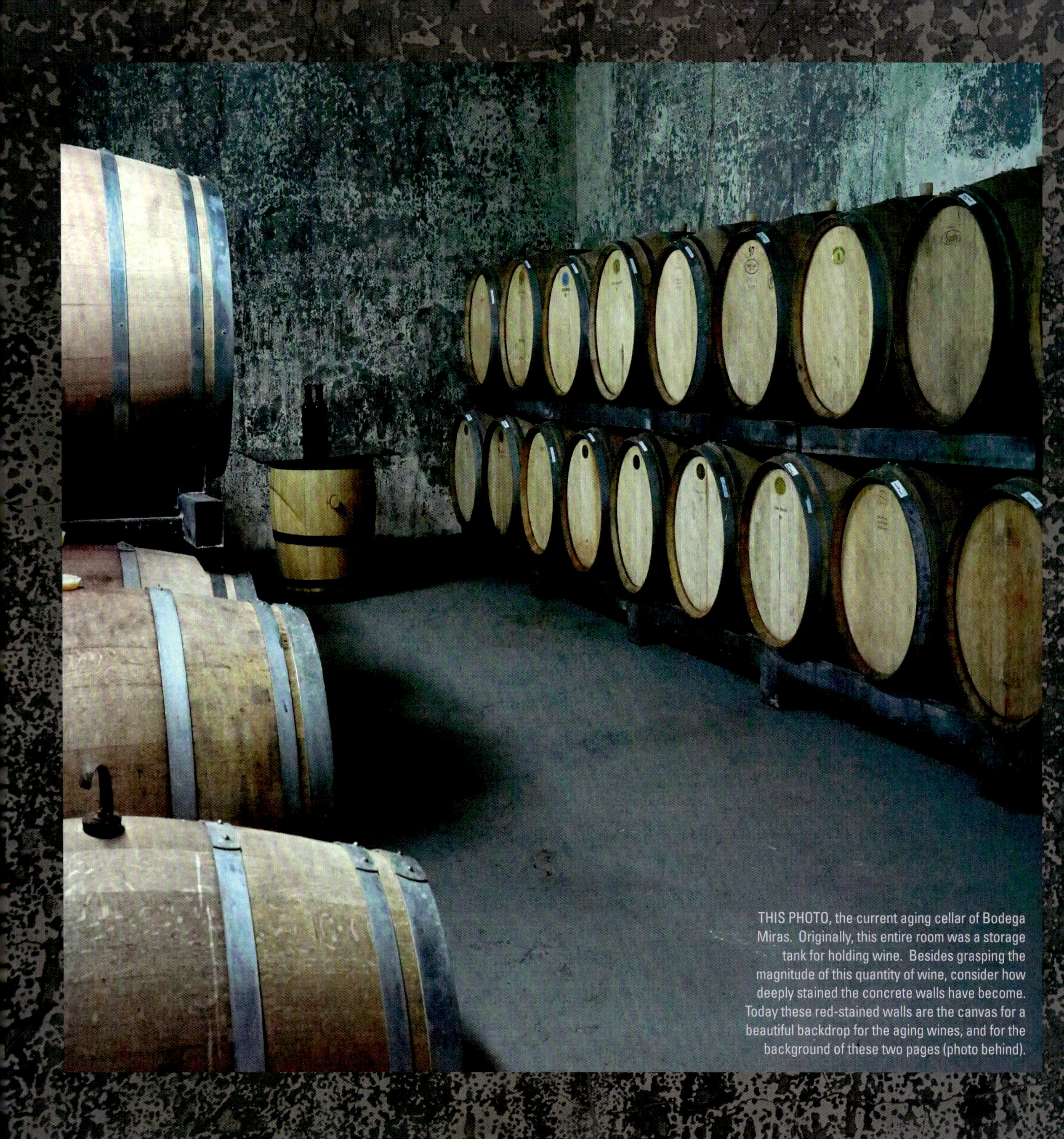

THIS PHOTO, the current aging cellar of Bodega Miras. Originally, this entire room was a storage tank for holding wine. Besides grasping the magnitude of this quantity of wine, consider how deeply stained the concrete walls have become. Today these red-stained walls are the canvas for a beautiful backdrop for the aging wines, and for the background of these two pages (photo behind).

So we began to taste the lineup of wines (photos below), plus a vertical of four Pinot Noirs. All these in an evening of an outdoor Asado of various meats.

Bodega Miras has two styles of wines...

Miras Jovem is their white label wines, which are young, fresh, fruit-forward wines, no oak, and ready to drink immediately.

Miras Reserva is their black label wines. These wines are aged in French and American oak for all the varietials. They are big complex vintages of the very upper echelons of wine. Decant and drinkable now, yet they are fully ageable.

Miras has been experimenting with two rare French varietals... *Semillón* (a white) and *Trousseau* (a red). The Semillón being a unique wine of golden yellow color, honey and citrus aromas, with a nice creamy texture of white fruit flavors in the mouth, and a spicy finish. This is Marcelo's new favorite!

You might know by now that the *Miras Reserva Cabernet Franc* is my wildly happy favorite. If you flew to Patagonia just to buy a case of this wine you would be very happy and thanking me.

I must tell you about the *Miras Reserva Merlot*. He brings back the delightfulness of this grape. The Miras Merlot is so delicate, smooth and full of structure. Miras magically brings out the softness that the Patagonia climate offers to this grape.

Let's get to the Pinot Noir vertical tasting. To get started, fire up the wood and prepare the coals for an *Asado of Lomo*, a pork tenderloin, which is a special cut from the back of the pig. It comes with a layer of fat on one side that cooks away from the hot wood coals. If you prepare the meat the way Marcelo did, simply salt, pepper and lemon, you have yourself a **P**erfect **P**ig & **P**inot **P**airing in the making!

The vertical was the *2012, 2009 and 2005 Miras Reserva Pinto Noir*, and the *2003 Miras Ocio Pinto Noir* (his earlier label).

The *2003 Miras Ocio Pinto Noir* exhibited the magic of its age in smooth, non-fruity earthiness of a 12-year-old wine.

The *2009 Miras Reserva Pinto Noir* was a basket full of raspberries, and truly the professional wine drinker's Pinot Noir!

The Pinot Noirs came after 13 bottles of wine and a mountain of Asado at 1:00am... and yet the perfection of the Pinot & Pig pairing was as if the night had just begun.

Marcelo Miras has mastered the science, as well as the art, of fine winemaking, and he brings the passionate dedication to producing wines at the very highest level of echelons, across all his personal wines and the wines he produces for others (see the full Marcelo Miras profile on pages 306-307).

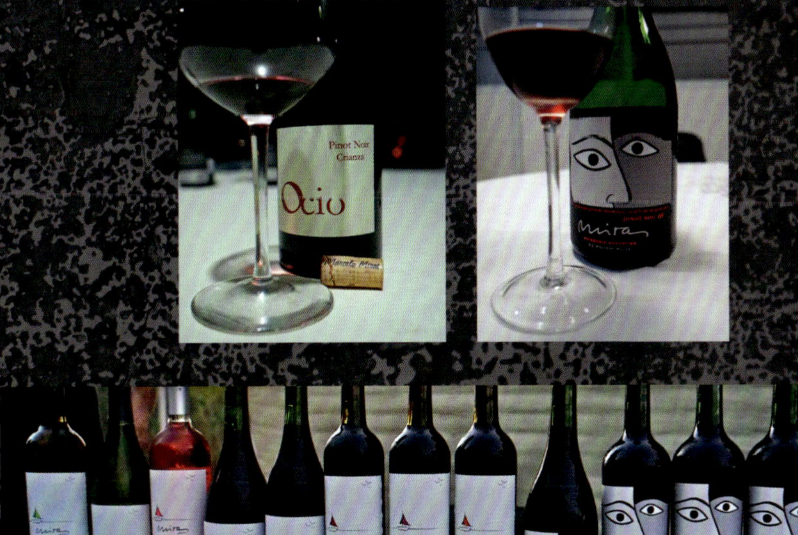

PATAGONIA **RÍO NEGRO** FERNÁNDEZ ORO

Winery (Bodega)

BODEGA MIRAS

1208 Ruta 22 (roadside along Ruta 22)
(15 km from Neuquén, 27 km from General Roca)
(Fernández Oro, **General Roca,** Río Negro)

011 (+54 9 299) 411.0408
info@BodegaMiras.com.ar

BodegaMiras.com.ar

English & Español
30,000 bottles produced annually

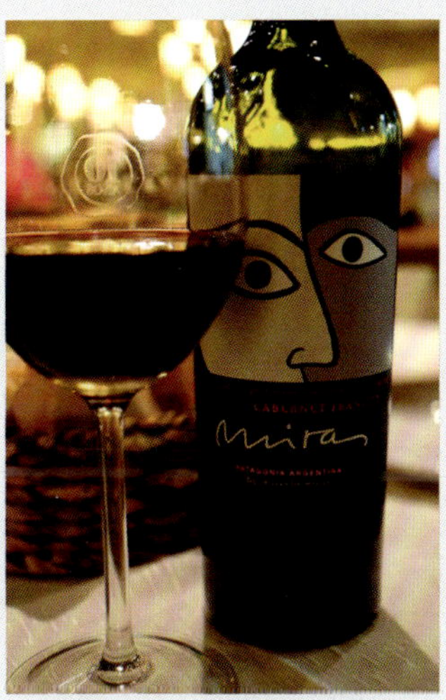

Michael's Favorite Pick
Miras Reserva - Cabernet Franc

Total Collection of Wines

Miras Reserva - Black Label
(Big Oak-Aged Wines of Complex Hierarchy)
Reserva Blend (Malbec, Cab Sauv, Cab Franc, Merlot)
Malbec • Merlot • Cabernet Franc
Pinot Noir • Chardonnay

Miras Jovem - White Label
(Young Fruity Fresh Wines with No Oak-Aging)
Blend (Malbec, Cab Franc, Merlot) • Malbec • Merlot
Pinot Noir • Trousseau Nouveau
Malbec Rosé • Semillón • Chardonnay

To get Miras wines in the USA
Only available at the winery
and well worth the trip to Patagonia

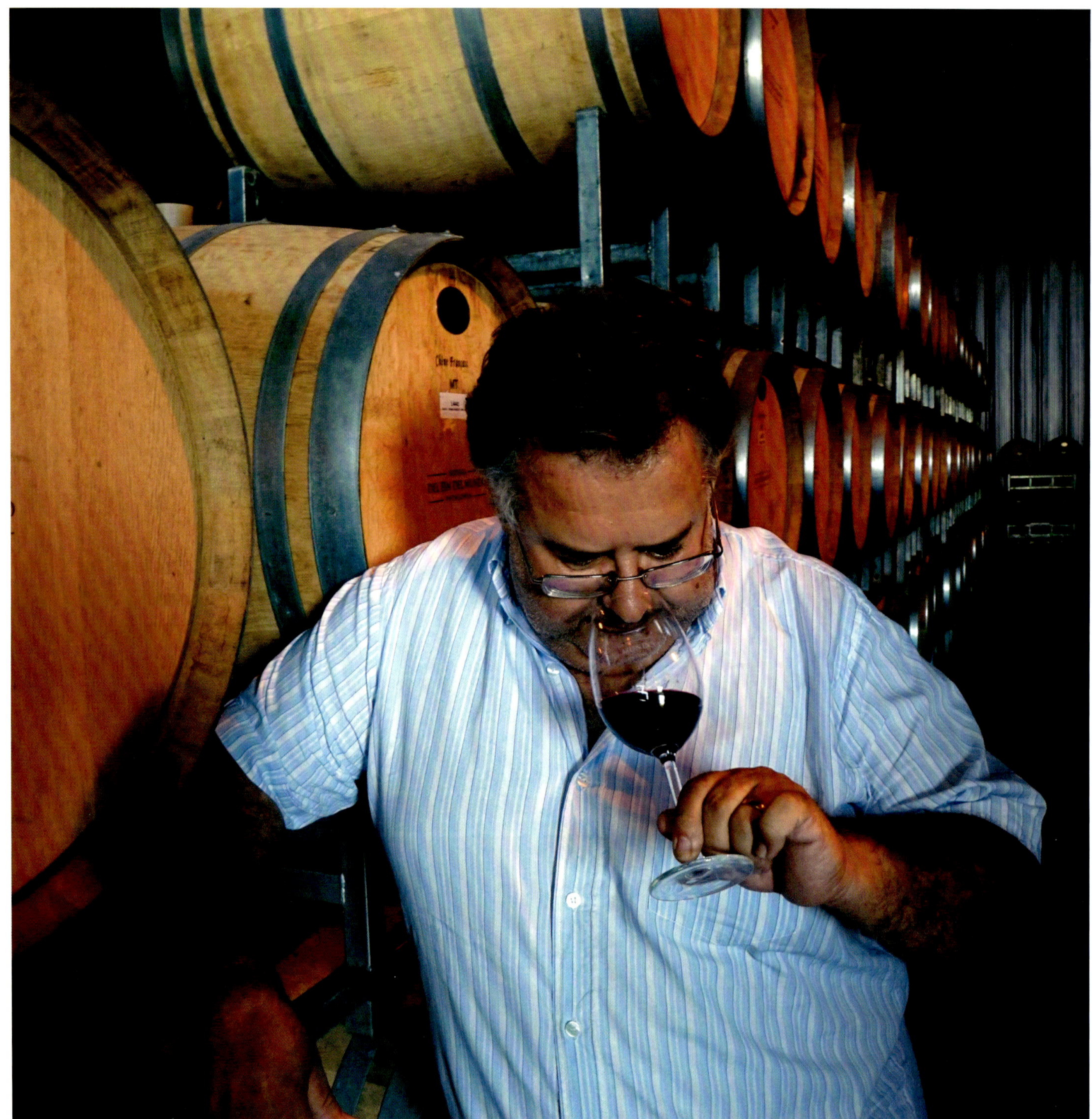

MARCELO MIRAS - WINEMAKER & CONSULTANT

A Legend Behind the Resurgence of the Patagonia Wine Region

Twenty-five years ago, not much was happening in the wine scene in Patagonia. More than 250 wineries had disappeared from Río Negro, leaving, well, just two surviving wineries, Canale and Favretto (reviewed in this book). And, Neuquén as a wine region had not even been dreamt of yet. Things were wine-quiet. Fruit orchards prevailed.

Then in 1990, Marcelo Miras caught the attention of **Humberto Canale's** third generation president **Guillermo Barzi**, who saw a rising star in Marcelo, who started harvesting grapes at age five in San Rafael, Mendoza, received degrees in oenology and frutihortícolas, and then at his first winery job at Vitivinícola Vidaña, he quickly rose to chief winemaker. At age 26, Miras was invited to Patagonia by Barzi, an innovative winemaker himself, to help reinvent the wine industry at Patagonia's largest and oldest winery.

Meanwhile in Mendoza, in 1987 Miras had been introduced to **Raúl de la Mota**, named *best winemaker of the 20th century Argentina*, who instilled in him the value of the French passion for terroir and quality. Interestingly, Marcelo brought his mentor Raúl with him to Humberto Canale and together they began this new era of excellence in winemaking in Patagonia.

Twelve years later, with a new thriving wine industry being born of quality, innovation and excellence in Río Negro, Miras was now being presented with a huge opportunity... to create the world's newest wine region out of the windy desert of barren Neuquén. As sad as it was to leave Canale, Miras embarked on a journey with **Julio Viola** who had the vision and grand dream to create a brand-new wine region.

Accessing the canals from the Neuquén River, planting more than 2,000 acres of vineyards, building an impressive state-of-the-art winery, and developing the most exciting lineup of wines, plus consulting with the famous French winemaker **Michel Rolland**, Marcelo is now at the helm of the largest winery in Patagonia, making over 11 million bottles of wine annually (more than all other wineries in Patagonia combined), and realizing the dream of putting Patagonia back on the map, in a big way, as a wine region which produces high-quality and innovative wines.

Along the way, Miras has had a hand in the success of almost every winery in Patagonia... either hands-on by designing wineries, choosing vineyards, defining vine management, determining harvests, perfecting vinifications, or refining blends. If not directly, Miras has indirectly helped every winery through establishing a new environment conducive for wineries to blossom, and also helped the region to be known for high-quality wines.

Twelve more years as the Chief Winemaker at **Bodega Del Fin Del Mundo** and **Bodega Malma** in Neuquén, Miras decided it is time to put his personal name on the bottle and bring his entire family into his wonderful world of extraordinary winemaking. In 2014, Marcelo took over an abandoned winery building and established **Bodega Miras** where he is now producing two styles of his own wines (see chapter on Bodega Miras).

\- - - -

I often wonder what makes great people great at what they do. Albert Einstein and his theories; Thomas Edison's endless inquisitiveness; William Shakespeare's profound writings... and Marcelo Miras's magic touch with wine. How does one person have such a huge influence on so many wineries, and can even influence an entire wine region into success. Here is my take...

Marcelo grew up with the scent of fermenting wine in his nostrils, and his childhood exposure to fruit fragrances further developed his nose. He surrounded himself with brilliant people innovating wine... De La Mota, Barzi, Viola, and Rolland, to name a few greats. Plus, he obtained the right college education. And, Marcelo is an extremely hard worker, putting in as much as 18 hours a day to perfect his craft.

Others have passion for the end product of delicious wine. For them, winemaking is a recipe that you follow. On the contrary, Marcelo has passion for the process. He does not stop at good, he is constantly thinking about what is going on, and his mind is always thinking in the future. He is creating, passionately, each wine as a unique masterpiece!

Miras knows how to make the kind of wine a vintner or winemaker wants to achieve. He is able to manage the difficulties that come along the way. He claims to practice *Risky Oenology*... that if you try to make wine naturally, the process may fail. He says it is necessary to keep one card up his sleeve to sort things out. His passion and knowledge in the process give him a distinct advantage in producing an extraordinary and predictable outcome.

Every day, Marcelo is inspired by so many wineries, their diverse people and the different wines they want to create. Sometimes it is the magic of Pinot Noir that Patagonia is known, other times it is sparkling wines or creating special qualities in Merlot, or experimenting with unique varietals or winemaking methods. No matter what it may be, Marcelo is passionate about every step towards the ultimate of quality wine.

Marcelo has a great personality, jovial, with a contagious smile perfect for inspiring his winemaking teams. And his family is beautiful. His wife Sandra and their five children play different roles in their family winemaking business.

What is next for Marcelo Miras? Well, he has many experiments going on... innovating new wines and wine techniques, all to create unique and masterful wines of tomorrow. I do know... that he wants to make the ***Best Patagonia Pinot Noir*** ever, ageable for 50 years! Plus, Marcelo's good friend and valued mentor, Raúl de la Mota, told him he must make family wines as his retirement and his family legacy. Whatever is next though, Marcelo has set the stage for a future of greatness, a reputation of quality that all of Patagonia now benefit.

BUENOS AIRES **A FOOD & WINE ADVENTURE**

The Gateway City of Access to Argentina's Wine Regions of Mendoza, Salta and Patagonia

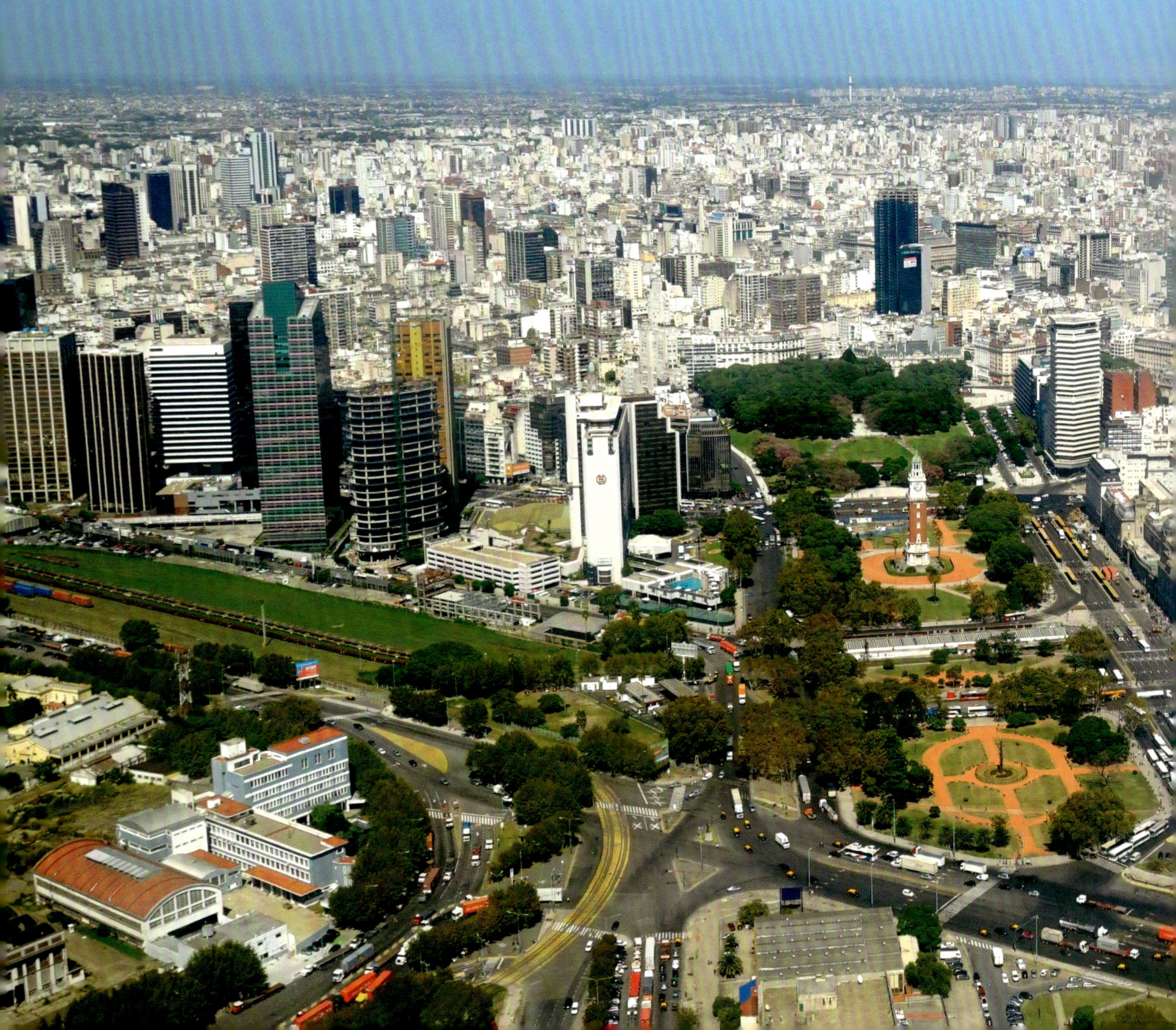

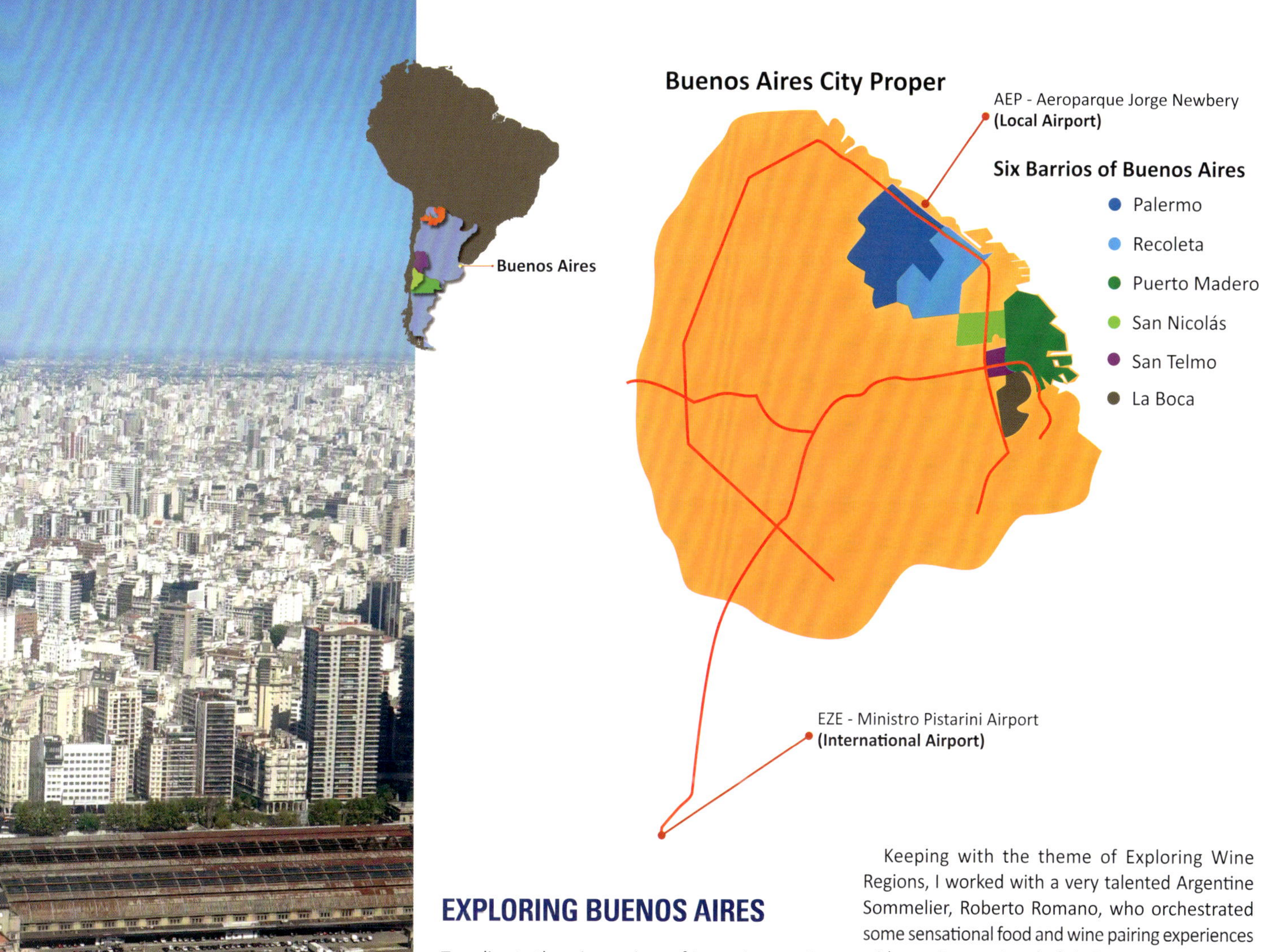

EXPLORING BUENOS AIRES

Traveling to the wine regions of Argentina requires you to fly through either Buenos Aires (photo left page) or Santiago, Chile. There are no direct flights! From Buenos Aires, there are direct flights onto Mendoza, San Rafael, Salta, and Neuquén.

Arriving at the Buenos Aires International Airport (EZE), which is south of the city, you then must transfer (30-90 minutes by taxi depending on traffic) to their domestic airport (AEP) to fly on to the wine regions. The domestic airport is located downtown adjacent to the most exciting part of the city, so why not stay for a few days and enjoy Argentina's big (pop 12.7 million) cosmopolitan capital, known for its European atmosphere, passionate tango, vibrant nightlife, and extraordinary restaurants and chefs.

Keeping with the theme of Exploring Wine Regions, I worked with a very talented Argentine Sommelier, Roberto Romano, who orchestrated some sensational food and wine pairing experiences with very interesting chefs in Buenos Aires. Some were top chefs, the very best chefs of the city. Others were local gems, with creative eclectic styles.

Buenos Aires is a large city made up of 48 Barrios (neighborhoods). All of the food & wine experiences in this book are located within these adjacent Barrios... Recoleta, Palermo, San Telmo, La Boca, Barracas, and Puerto Madero. Each of them is a short taxi ride from Recoleta, which is the Beverly Hills of Buenos Aires, central to many of the city's most interesting and beautiful hotels, including the Algodon Mansion.

OK, now go enjoy *The Paris of South America*... Buenos Aires is waiting for you!

INTERESTING BARRIOS OF BUENOS AIRES

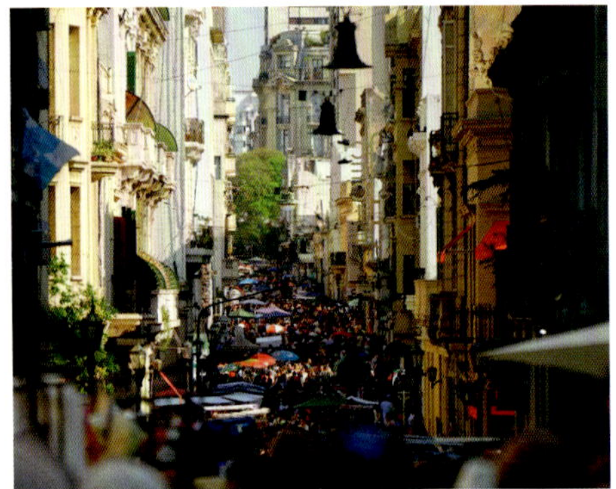

SAN TELMO

The Original Affluent Neighborhood

San Telmo is the oldest barrio of Buenos Aires, and a well-preserved area of the Argentine metropolis, with its colonial buildings. Cafés, restaurants, tango parlors, and shops line the cobblestone streets, often filled with artists and dancers. Every Sunday, there is a 10-block street fair with hundreds of artisans and craft vendors (photo above).

During the 19th century, the installation of gas mains, lighting, sewers, running water and cobblestone streets attracted the growing middle and upper classes. This interest by the well-to-do of Buenos Aires created a construction boom of numerous grand and impressive homes here.

This auspicious era though ended abruptly when yellow fever struck the area in 1871. This epidemic quickly claimed more than 10,000 lives and made its citizens believe that the fever was somehow in the air in the barrio and contagious just by living there, causing a quick and massive exodus.

Tango was born here as the music and dance of the sadness of the era, the closeness of the people, and the bohemian nature of its new attraction of artists. Large homes became tenement housing during a wave of immigration from Europe between 1875 and 1930 to large communities of British, Galician, Italian, and Russian immigrants. San Telmo became the most multicultural neighborhood in Buenos Aires, and is a revival of today.

On the following pages...

- **El Baqueano Cocina** (Restaurant)
- **Sagardi Cocineros Vascos** (Restaurant)

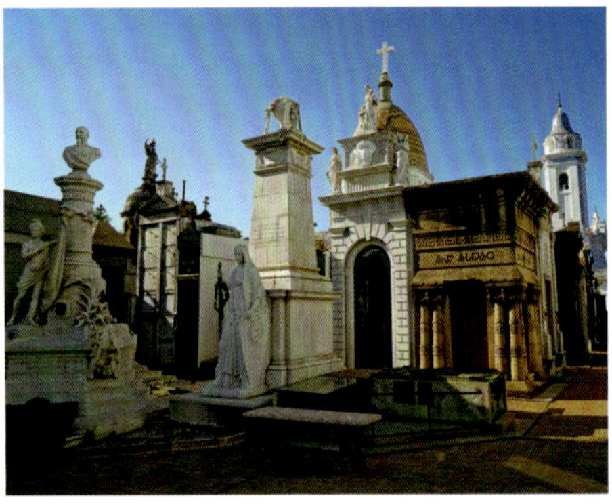

RECOLETA

The Beverly Hills of Buenos Aires

Recoleta is a luxurious downtown residential neighborhood, the most affluent in Buenos Aires, with some of the priciest real estate in the city. It is an area of great historical and architectural interests.

Recoleta is one of the highest points in the city, which attracted wealthy families from San Telmo who escaped the deadly yellow fever outbreak that began in 1871. It was for this reason that the wealthy settled in Recoleta where the height of the terrain reduced the presence of insects that transmitted the diseases.

From that time on, Recoleta has been one of the most stylish and expensive neighborhoods in Buenos Aires, home to private family mansions, foreign embassies and luxury hotels.

The European ambiance comes to life in Recoleta, and helps give Buenos Aires the nickname *The Paris of South America.* It is predominantly French-style architecture here with a great number of Châteaux built imitating those of Paris and the Loire Valley in France, and almost always designed by French architects.

The Recoleta Cemetery (photo above) is a 14-acre site of 4,691 vaults, all above ground, among which 94 have been declared as National Historical Monuments, with the graves of notable people, presidents of Argentina, Nobel Prize winners, and a granddaughter of Napoleon.

On the following pages...

- **Algodon Mansion** (Hotel and Restaurant)
- **Four Seasons Pony Line** (Restaurant)
- **Tarquino Nueva Cocina** (Restaurant)

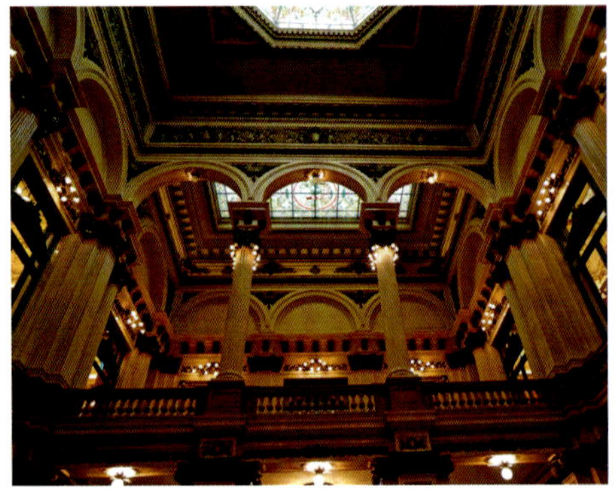

SAN NICOLÁS

Historical Monuments & Theatres

San Nicolás is the barrio of the City of Buenos Aires with most of the city and national government structures and monuments, and also home to much of the Buenos Aires financial sector, including the Buenos Aires Stock Exchange. It is more commonly referred as El Centro (city center).

San Nicolás incorporates most of the Buenos Aires central business district, underscored by the presence of the Argentine Central Bank and National Bank, Argentina's largest bank. It is home to the headquarters of numerous leading Argentine firms, as well as the local offices of a number of international companies, such as Citibank, Deutsche Bank, IBM, Microsoft, and Santander Bank.

There are numerous monuments and important sites to visit here... Palace of Justice, Buenos Aires Metropolitan Cathedral, The Obelisk, Santa Catalina Church, Mirador Massue, St. Nicholas Hostel, Central Bank of Argentina, Post Office Palace, San Martín Cultural Center, Luna Park Stadium, and Galerías Pacífico. San Nicolás has one of the greatest concentrations of theatres and cinemas in the world, with Gran Rex Theatre, Cervantes Theatre and Teatro Colón to name a few.

Teatro Colón is the main opera house in Buenos Aires, ranked third best opera house in the world by National Geographic, and is acoustically considered among the five best concert venues in the world. A massive four-year renovation reopened the theatre in 2010 to a spectacular place to visit (photo above). Other venues are the Berlin's Konzerthaus, Vienna's Musikverein, Amsterdam's Concertgebouw, and Boston's Symphony Hall.

INTERESTING BARRIOS OF BUENOS AIRES

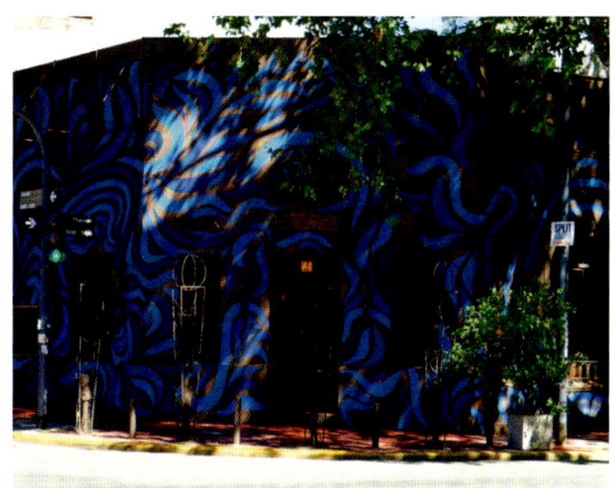

PALERMO

YOUNG, CHIC, NIGHTLIFE... UPSCALE ART SCENE

Palermo is the largest barrio in Buenos Aires with over 225,000 population and divided into seven sub-barrios. Palermo is known for its younger crowd and upscale environment of cafés, shops, restaurants, and a nightlife that goes all night. Tango starting at 3:00 am is a common sight.

Palermo Chico is the wealthiest sub-barrio of strictly residential high-rise luxury condominiums and apartment developments. It's very nice!

Palermo Soho is a small area of Palermo that has been redeveloped into a new trendsetting vogue district of fashion, design, restaurants, bars, and street culture. The atmosphere in many cafés and restaurants strives to be the *alternative*, making this area particularly popular amongst the young, upper-middle-class Argentine as well as the trendy tourists. This area has traditional low-house architecture which have been adapted into boutiques and bars, creating a bohemian feel (photo above). This is a happening spot and the place to get you in touch with the romantic Tangoess lifestyle of Buenos Aires.

Palermo Hollywood got its name as a result of many TV and radio producers moving here in the mid-90s. It is best known for its concentration of restaurants and clubs, such as *Club Atlético Palermo* of British roots founded in 1914 as a social institution where gentlemen of high class met.

On the following pages...

- **Perón Perón** (Restaurant & Bar)
- **Pain et Vin** (Wine Bar & Restaurant)

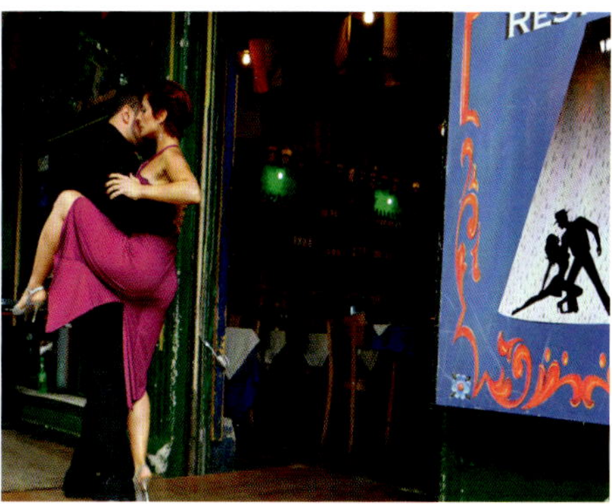

LA BOCA

AUTHENTIC ITALIAN FOOD & ARGENTINE TANGO

La Boca is a barrio of a few blocks of concentrated restaurants with tango dancing among very colorful buildings. Outside this tiny area is not attractive, inside is worth your visit.

La Boca has a strong European flavor, with many of its early settlers being from the Italian city of Genoa. It has always been a center of radical politics, having elected the first socialist member of the Argentine Congress (Alfredo Palacios in 1935) and was home to many demonstrations during the crisis of 2001.

Most interesting was that La Boca actually seceded from Argentina. Imagine this little barrio being its own country! The rebels even raised the Genoese flag, which was immediately torn down personally by then President Julio Argentino Roca.

La Boca is a great destination to visit though. It is filled with colorful houses and the streets are pedestrian only. *The Caminito* is a street museum and traditional alley where tango artists perform and tango-related memorabilia are sold. It gained cultural significance because it inspired the music of the famous tango *Caminito* (1926), composed by Juan de Dios Filiberto, and played in *La Ribera Theatre*, a 650-seat colorful theater funded by the famous Argentine painter Benito Quinquela Martín.

This is a great place to see colorful architecture, watch lots of tango and eat authentic Italian food. Most restaurants, and there are numerous, have outdoor seating on the pedestrian streets with live tango dancers entertaining their guests (photo above). Plus, there are also many tango clubs and Italian taverns.

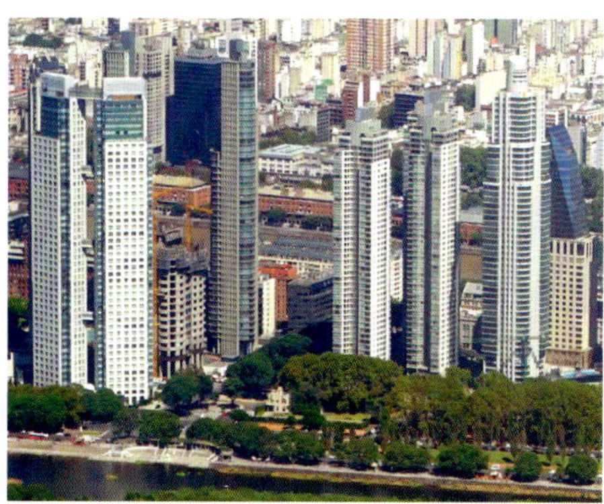

PUERTO MADERO

NEW MODERN SKYLINE OF BUENOS AIRES

Puerto Madero, originally the docking port for large cargo ships of the 1880s, has now been redeveloped into the city's newest neighborhood with a modern high-rise skyline, and upscale shops and restaurants.

Puerto Madero was a 10-year project to build a modern port to accommodate the larger cargo ships of the late 19th century, when Puerto La Boca was no longer able to accommodate due to its shallow riverfront. Not long after the completion of this engineering landmark of its time, the introduction of even larger cargo ships made Puerto Madero obsolete.

As a result, Puerto Madero quickly decayed, becoming one of the city's most degraded areas. It became a slum of abandoned warehouses and large tracts of undeveloped land. In 1989, the joint governing bodies agreed to an urbanization plan which attracted local and foreign investment, and led to a massive regeneration effort, recycling and refurbishing the warehouses into elegant houses, offices, lofts, private universities, luxurious hotels and restaurants.

Puerto Madero has been redeveloped with an international flair, attracting renowned architects who have created Puerto Madero as today's trendiest barrio in Buenos Aires. Led by the opening of the Hilton Buenos Aires towers, dozens of new residential high rises of up to 50 stories have been built including other luxury hotels and office buildings.

On the following pages...

- **Faena Bistro Sur** (Restaurant & Lounge)

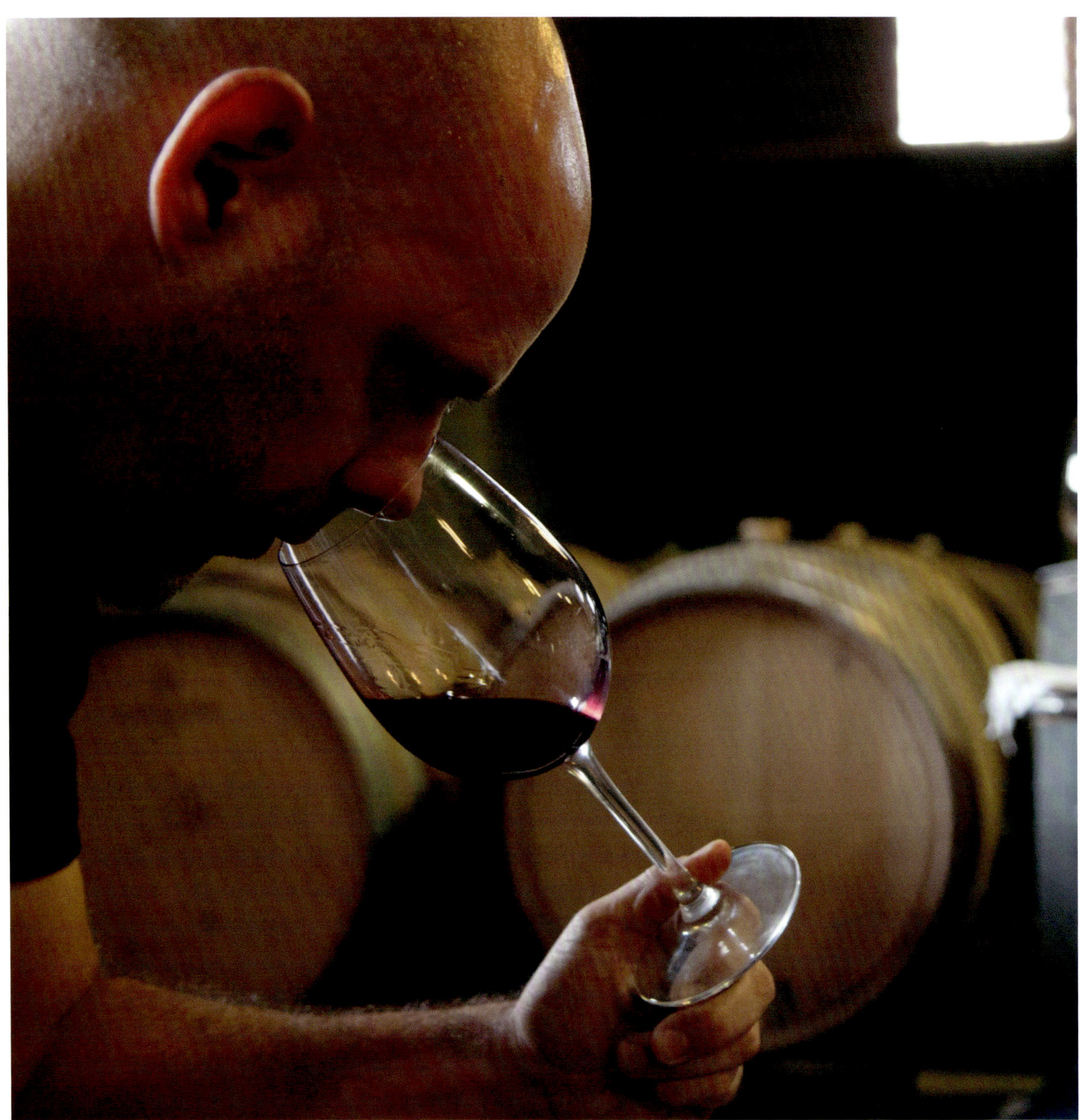

UNUSUALLY CREATIVE CHEFS

Can you imagine exploring restaurants in Buenos Aires, chosen by a Sommelier? Can you imagine having the inside track on some of the most interesting chefs of Buenos Aires? Now you do!

A year ago, I was in Mendoza, specifically Valle de Uco, at *Finca Blousson Vins & Bistró*, a gathering place where people from all over the world come to talk and taste wine. That day, the owners of a luxury resort, a notable winemaker, and an interesting sommelier from Buenos Aires, came to have lunch, conversation and share their passions about wine (see the full story earlier in the book).

This was where I met *Sommelier Roberto Romano* and became fascinated with his unique pursuits from his oenophile skills. We mingled, exchanged ideas and stories, drank spectacular wines... and Roberto invited me to his city to taste the best of Buenos Aires. That was an invitation to explore restaurants chosen by a Sommelier and have the inside track of the interesting chefs of Buenos Aires!

The common thread among all the chefs is that they are all wildly creative and extremely unique characters of the palate. It is worth stopping for a few days in Buenos Aires, extending your wine region adventures, in order to experience these chefs' unique cuisine.

You can drink pizza from a martini glass, eat a politically incorrect capitalist pig, discover a white salmon exclusively from Argentina waters, and dine in the fanciest place, or a hole-in-the-wall with the personal attention of a husband/wife, chef/sommelier team of creative gourmet foods.

Enjoy these writings, you are now connected...

SOMMELIER-DESIGNED WINES

Barroco is not a winery, it is a concept. A concept of choosing unusual opportunities for interesting wines. Think about this... Roberto is not committed to properties filled with vineyards, nor buildings fixed in certain regions, nor expectations of ongoing vintages of the same qualities. Roberto, on the other hand, is unencumbered, free to explore the most interesting wines of his choice.

Picture a Sommelier choosing his most interesting wines to bottle. Roberto tells me that one of the reasons he is a great Sommelier is because he can recall every single wine he has ever tasted, including all its nuances. Now armed with this library of tastes and aromas filling his head, Roberto explores Argentina to find the ultimate wines.

For example... Roberto was wandering through Mendoza, finding himself in a small winery looking at a vat filled with 8,000 liters of Viognier. The winemaker who made this wine became uninterested in this aging wine because he wanted to pursue red wines. The Viognier was fermented in French oak barrels and aged in tank on its lees for a year.

Roberto bought the entire vat, as he should. I brought some of this wine home with me from Argentina. The nose is a floral bouquet that jumps out of the glass. The flavors are rich and fruity, with very pronounced white peach. Nicely balanced acidity too.

As with any of the Barroco Wines, they are available while Roberto has his hands on them, then they will be gone forever. Every wine is its own special acquisition, and Roberto ships worldwide.

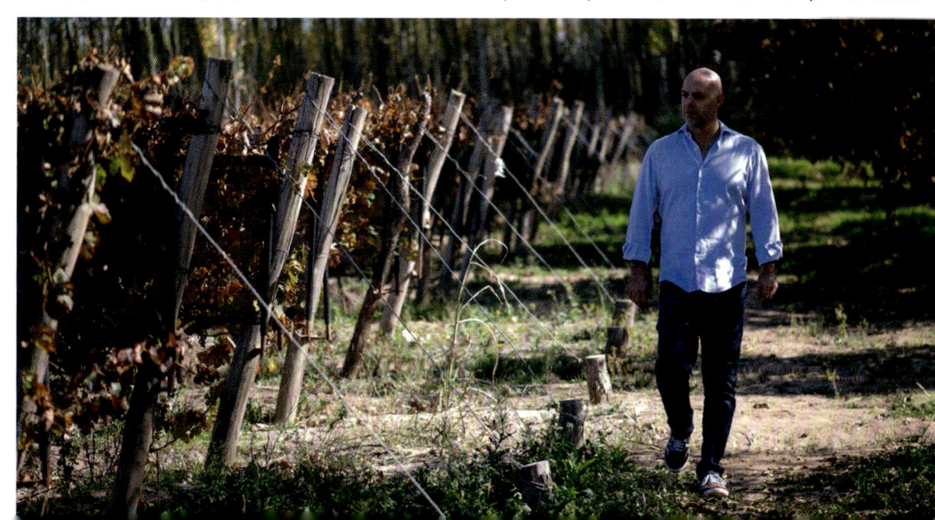

BUENOS AIRES **DOWNTOWN**

Sommelier & Wines

ROBERTO ROMANO

BARROCO WINES

011 (+54 9 116) 864.8779
RobertoRomanoAR@gmail.com
Romano@VinosBarroco.com

RobertoRomanoAR.com.ar
VinosBarroco.com

English, Español & Portugués

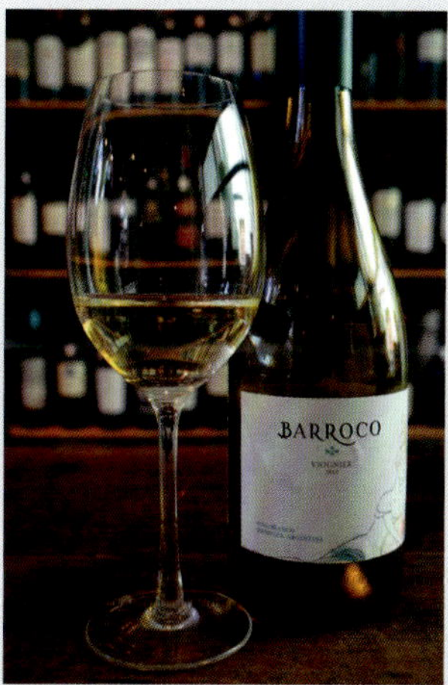

Michael's Favorite Pick
Viognier - *Expression Water*

Total Collection of Wines

Viognier - *Expression Water*

Malbec - *Expression Fire*

Malbec & Cabernet Blend - *Expression Earth*

Syrah & Grenache Rosé - *Expression Air*

Sparkling Pinot Noir - *Expression Aether*

To get Barroco Wines in the USA
He ships worldwide in 6- and 12-bottle cases
Write him at: Romano@VinosBarroco.com

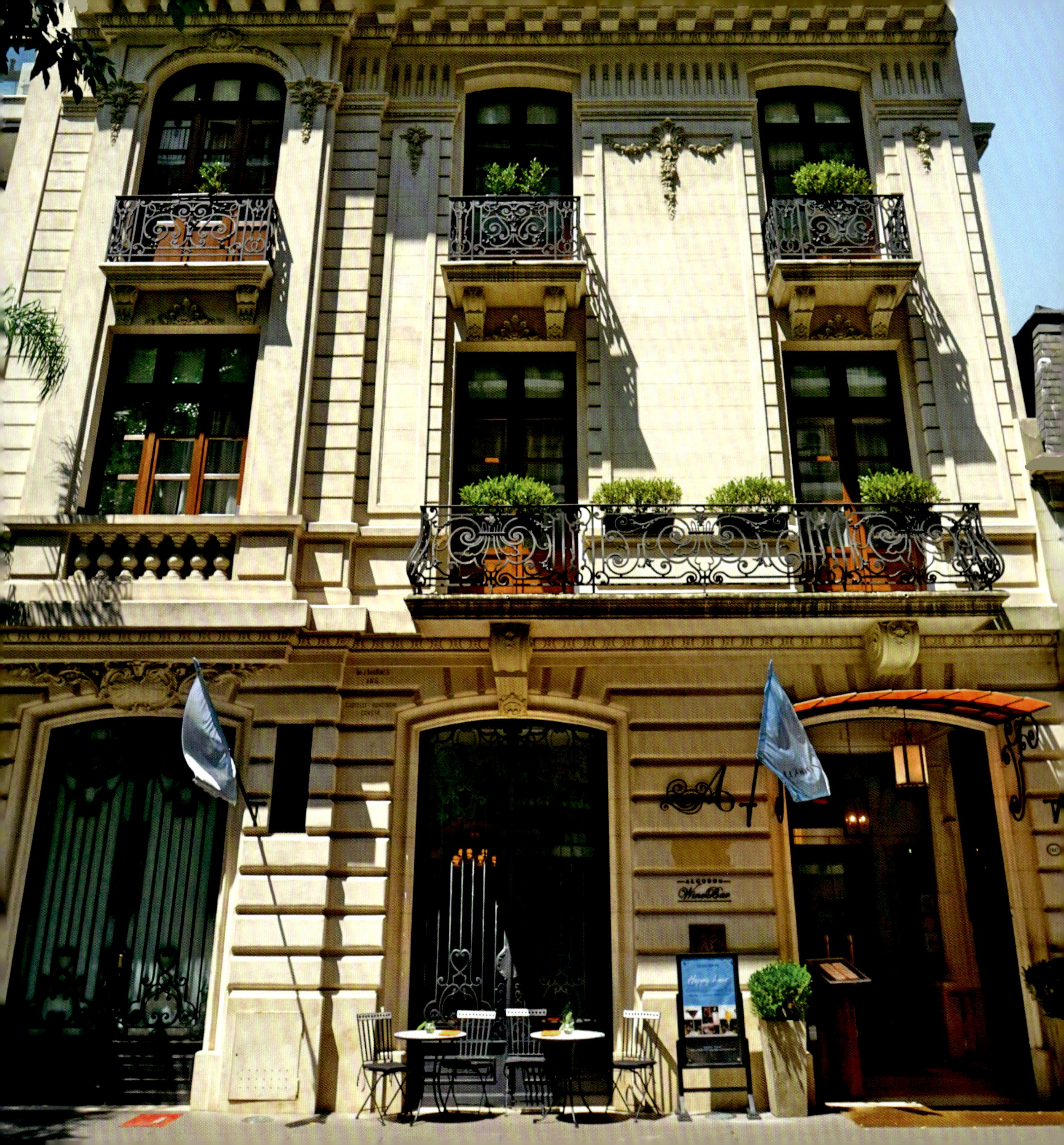
ALGODON
WineBar
Happy hour

PRIVATE MANSION STAYING

Why stay in a hotel, when you can stay in a luxury mansion? **The Algodon Mansion** is more than a five-star Relais & Châteaux hotel, it is a mansion with butler-type service. With only 10 rooms, the personal service here is impeccable, and 24/7. Their focused attention to the finest details is part of the magnificent experiences. It is this excellence that I define as butler-type service.

This 1912 historic mansion has been glamorously restored into a luxury guest property located in the Recoleta neighborhood (the Beverly Hills of Buenos Aires). The Mansion is classic French-style architecture (photo left page) with contemporary elegance and sophistication inside. All the rooms are very large suites with living rooms, bedrooms and gigantic bathrooms.

The **Algodon Wine Estates** is their sister property in San Rafael, Mendoza (with direct flights), where winemaker Mauro Nosenzo makes an impressive lineup of wines. My favorite is his *Algodon Malbec Bonarda Estate Blend.* In addition to the winery, vineyard properties are available to build a home, plus there is a hotel, restaurant, tennis and golf.

The Mansion has a private open-air rooftop terrace sporting a **Rooftop Pool**, **Davidoff Lounge**, and **Le Spa** with steam, sauna and massage pampering.

The **Algodon Wine Bar** has a beautiful ambiance of luxury and style suitable for a romantic evening, a professional meeting or a casual meet-up. And the **Algodon Kitchen** provides full service to the bar if you choose not to dine in their dining room.

Executive Chef, Leandro Zaragoza has a fresh concept of seasonal menus in order to present only the freshest ingredients acquired locally, and from their Algodon Wine Estates plantation (extra virgin olive oil, fresh fruits and vegetables). Zaragoza calls his cuisine **Sophisticated Mendocinean-Style** (Mendoza wine region foods). Such a perfect way to get warmed up for your wine region adventure!

The menu also has been created to pair well with their Algodon Wines. I did a full pairing course and it was a fantastic experience. My highlights were...

- **Filet Mignon** with herb potatoes and topped with red and yellow chopped peppers; paired with *Algodon Estate Bonarda* (aged 14 months in oak).

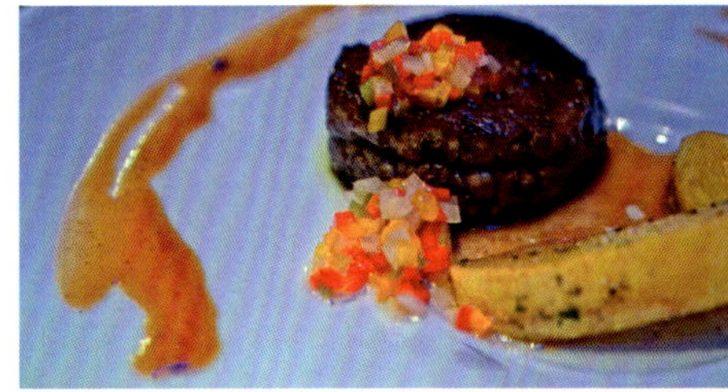

- **BBQ Pork Ribs** with barbeque sauce and potatoes; paired with my favorite *Algodon Malbec Bonarda Estate Blend* (aged 18 months in oak, 70% Malbec).

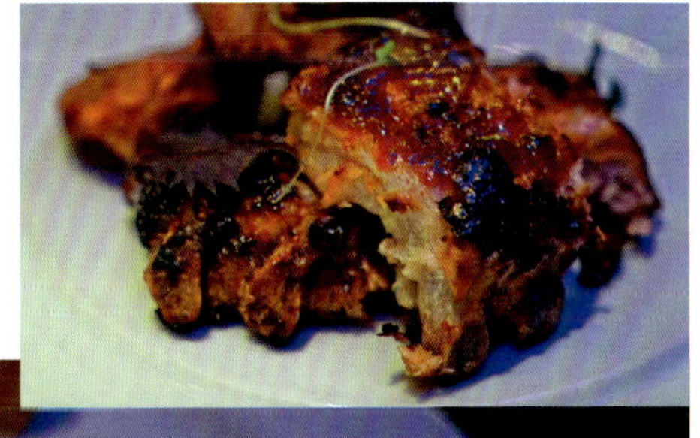

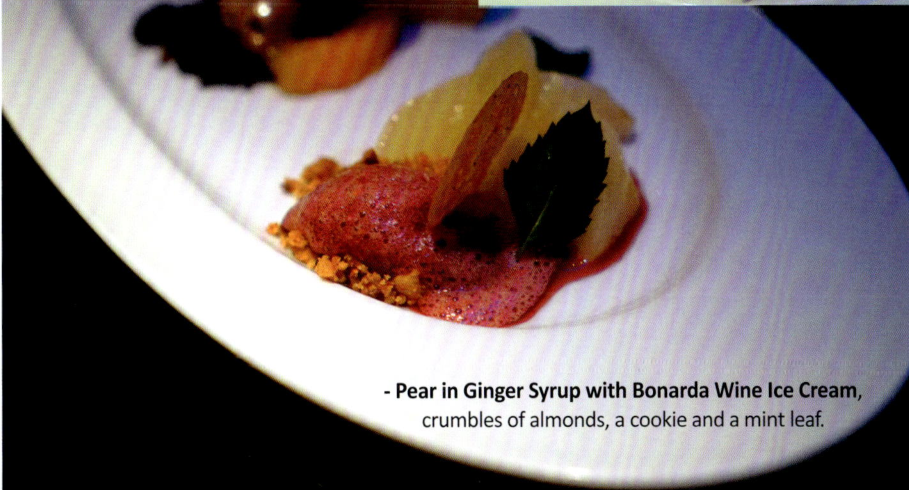

- **Pear in Ginger Syrup with Bonarda Wine Ice Cream,** crumbles of almonds, a cookie and a mint leaf.

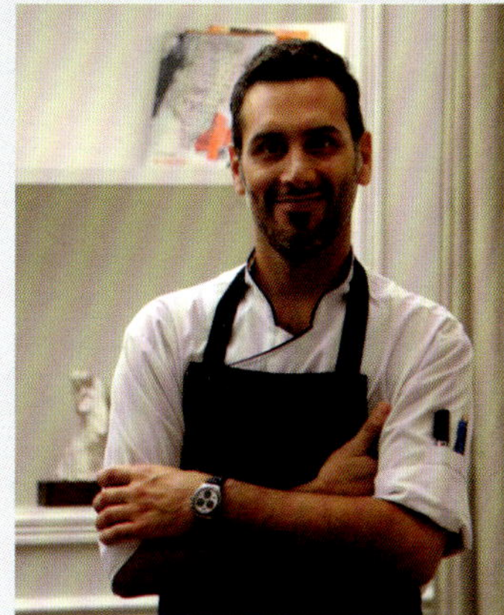

Leandro Zaragoza, Executive Chef
Native - Buenos Aires, Argentina
Studied - Instituto Educativo Argentino

Previous Experiences...
Chef - Four Seasons, Buenos Aires
Chef - Sheraton, Buenos Aires

Hotel and Restaurant Reservations
011 (+54 113) 530.7777
reservations@AlgodonMansion.com

AlgodonMansion.com
1647 Montevideo, Barrio Recoleta

English, Español & Portugués
Hours - 7:30 am - Midnight

Chef Juan Gaffuri

FOUR SEASONS PONY LINE

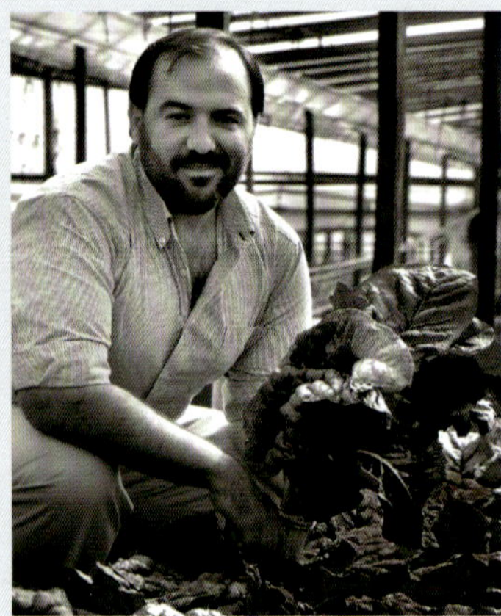

Juan Gaffurl, Executive Chef
Native - Rosario, Argentina
Studied - Grandmother

Previous Experiences...
Chef - Four Seasons Hotels in Egypt, Mexico, Washington DC and San Diego CA, USA
Chef - Park Hyatt, Beunos Aires
Chef - Sheraton Hotel, Buenos Aires

Restaurant Reservations
011 (+54 114) 321.1730
elenaponyline@FourSeasons.com

ElenaPonyLine.com
1086 Posadas, Barrio Recoleta

English & Español
Hours - 11:00 am - 2:00 am

BEST BURGER IN BUENOS AIRES

With all the fancy foods in Buenos Aires, there will be that moment that you just want to have a burger. And the best burger in town is at the Pony Line Lounge at the Four Seasons Hotel in Recoleta.

Executive Chef, Juan Gaffuri, has devised two very exciting Pony Line Signature Burgers. The photo should say it all. I am getting hungry just thinking about it again. Burgers come with a fresh garden salad, and pair perfectly with an ice-cold beer, or a wine by the glass. The Pony Line has a full bar with many interesting specialty drinks as well.

- **THE ORIGINAL** with Lincoln cheese, bacon, crispy onion, pickles, and BBQ sauce (photo below).
- **45-DAY DRY AGED** with brioche, homemade relish, and fresh herb aioli.

In Argentina, **Polo** is a very important sport, as important as soccer, just ask any player! Polo enthusiasts will tell you that the Argentina polo season is the best in the world! Argentina has more players, and higher standards. It is the Mecca for Polo! Six of the seven top handicap (10 goals) players in the world are from Argentina.

Inspired by this exciting and affluent sport, the Pony Line brings on a vibrant after-party in this chic sophisticated lounge at the Four Seasons Hotel. Pull up a table in front of their luxurious leather couches and chairs. A rich environment of casual fare.

Later in the evening, the Pony Line turns into a party with their resident DJ mixing tunes for locals and guests wanting to meet friends and strangers in this spiced up environment.

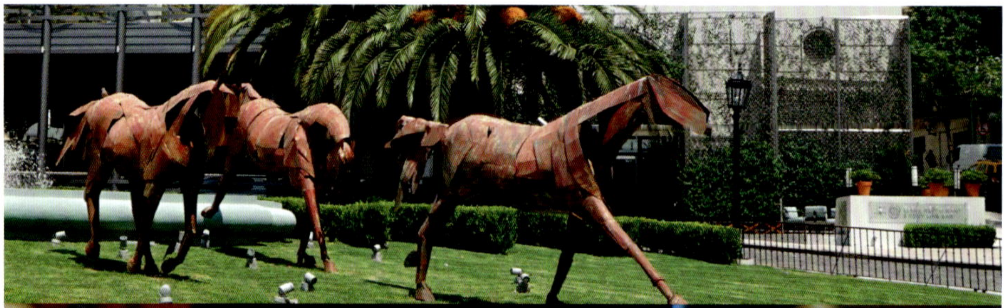

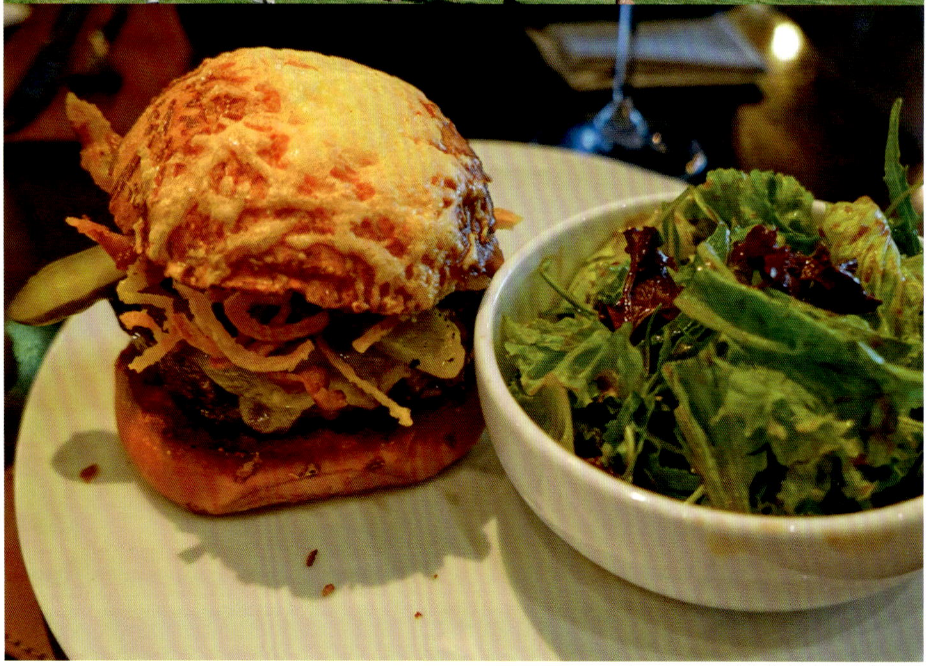

OUTRAGEOUSLY INNOVATIVE!!!

Pizza in a martini glass! Really?

Executive Chef, Dante Liporace, must be the most wildly creative chef imaginable in the world, not just Buenos Aires! In 2008, Dante was just a lone soldier creating his unbelievable concepts, attempting to get the attention of Argentines to a new way of experiencing food. Several years later, he inspired four other chefs in Buenos Aires to take highly innovative approaches to their cooking.

At Tarquino Nueva Cocina, one of the most opulent restaurants in Buenos Aires (appropriately located in the Recoleta neighborhood), Chef Liporace delivers the most outrageous dining experience you will ever encounter!

Dante has received a lot of attention over creating a luxuriously liquid pizza he calls **Provolone Pizza**, a chemistry-perfect, dough-free foamy deliciousness served in a martini glass (photo below)! You can distinctly taste the bread, cheese and meats (salami and sausage) just like a traditional pizza.

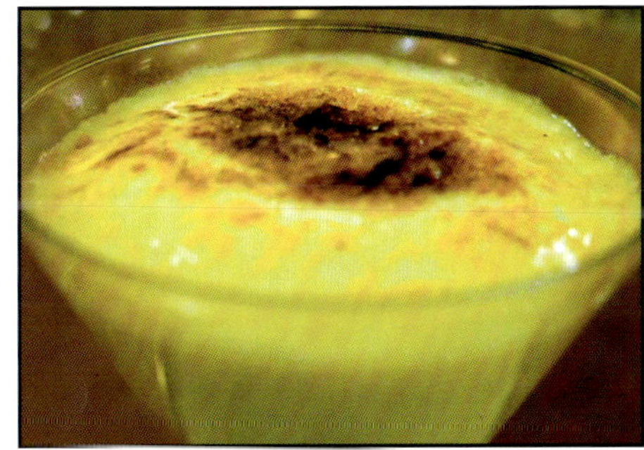

Dante is clearly a molecular gastronomist, a chemist of the culinary arts, energizing his patrons with very bold, unusual and startling techniques. His food is not just eye-catching, I can assure you, the flavors you will experience are scrumptious.

His chemistry includes innovative collaborations with sommeliers too. He created **Tomato and Green Apple Soup** with a floating oyster and slow cooked bacon aside a vanilla ice cream ball (photo below); and paired it with the *Lindaflor Chardonnay*, a very impressive Argentine Chardonnay. To perfect the pairing though, he first coats the inside of the wine glass with lemon juice and fish oil... and then pours the wine into the glass. Seems like an odd thing to do; however it magnifies the pairing quite well.

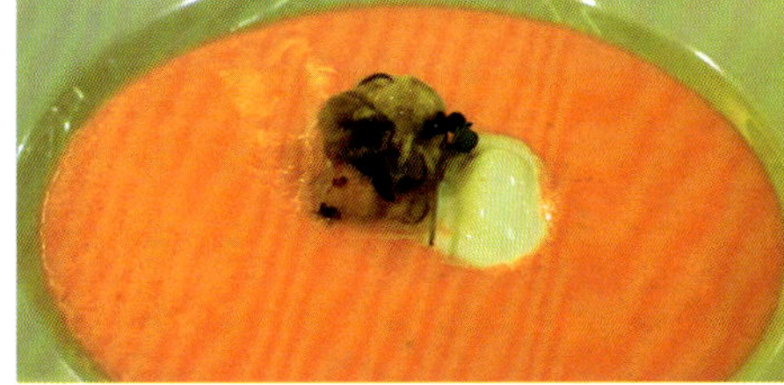

If you would like to experience Argentine beef in Dante style, he has created a 10-course, head-to-toe tasting menu that uses all parts of the cow, called **La Sequencia de la Vaca** (the Cow Sequence).

What will Dante do next? I cannot wait!

Another fascinating and beautifully designed dish is his **Stewed Duck** atop bread pudding, with orange puree and mango ball (photo below).

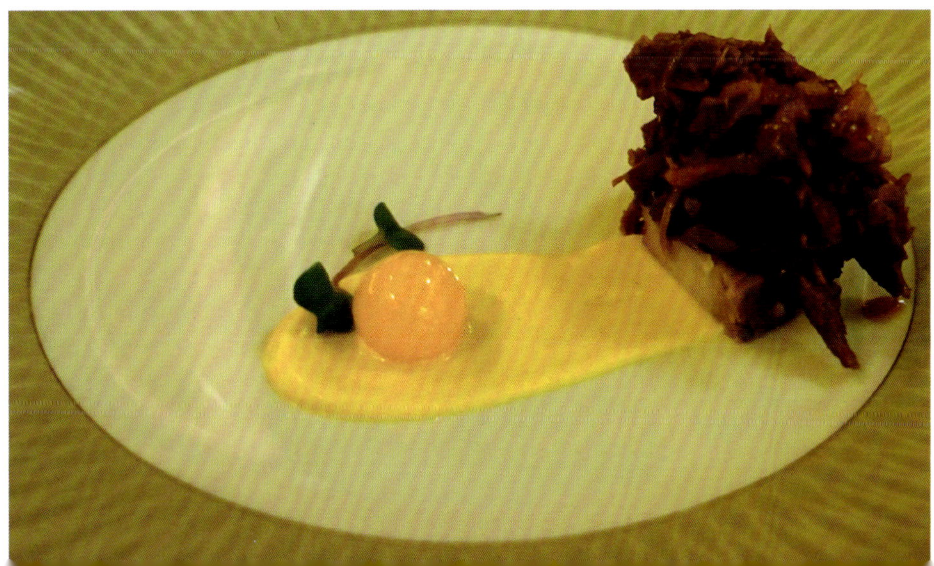

BUENOS AIRES **DOWNTOWN** RECOLETA

Chef Dante Liporace

TARQUINO NUEVA COCINA

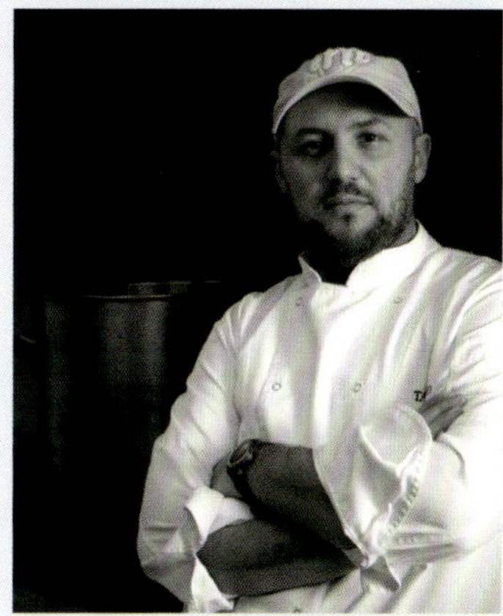

Dante Liporace, Executive Chef
Native - Buenos Aires, Argentina
Studied - Gato Dumas, Buenos Aires

Previous Experiences...
Executive Chef - Moreno Restaurante, Buenos Aires
Executive Chef - Nervous Waters, Argentina
elBulli Restaurante - Roses Catalonia, Spain
(considered the best restaurant in the world)

Apprenticed with Ferran Adrià (elBulli)
(considered one of the best chefs in the world)

Restaurant Reservations
011 (+54 116) 091.2160

TarquinoRestaurante.com.ar
1967 Rodríguez Peña, Barrio Recoleta

English & Español
Hours 12:00 pm - 2:30 pm, and 8:00 pm +

BUENOS AIRES **DOWNTOWN** SAN TELMO

Chef Fernando Rivarola

EL BAQUEANO COCINA

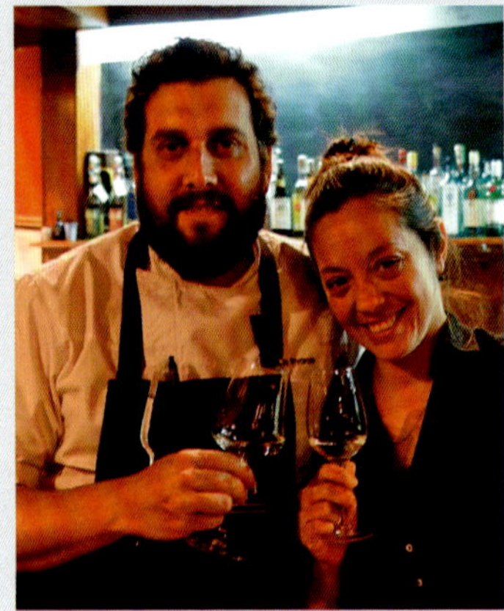

Fernando Rivarola, Executive Chef
Native - Buenos Aires, Argentina
Studied - Sebastian Grimaldi Culinary Institute, Mar del Plata, Argentino

Previous Experiences...
Chef - Restaurant Lera, Castile and Leon, Spain
Apprentice - Chef Jose Luis Lera

Restaurant Reservations
011 (+54 114) 342.0802
ElBaqueanoRestaurante@gmail.com

RestoElBaqueano.com
499 Chile, Barrio San Telmo

English & Español
Hours - 8:00 pm - Midnight

CHEF-SOMMELIER TEAM

Experience extraordinary culinary creativity with ***Executive Chef Fernando Rivarola***, another one of the Top-Five Highly Innovative Chefs of Buenos Aires... teamed with his extremely talented wife, ***Sommelier Gabriela Lafuente***, you have a magic combination at El Baqueano Cocina, their restaurant in the San Telmo barrio.

Not a fancy neighborhood, until you step inside this enchanting restaurant and you are in an isolated world of culinary pleasures. You will experience exotic meats from different parts of Argentina that are created around interesting social statements and paired with top-level Argentine wines.

Fernando and Gabriela live to create the most extraordinary culinary experiences... working together like two scientists, discussing the nuances of each pairing in order to deliver a very unique eight-course tasting menu (only option). This is their all-consuming passion, for all of us to love!

- Cordero Patagónico - Patagonian lamb with goat yogurt and seaweed - expressing the lamb's desire to live at the sea; paired with *Desierto Pampa Malbec* (by Paul Hobbs in Patagonia).

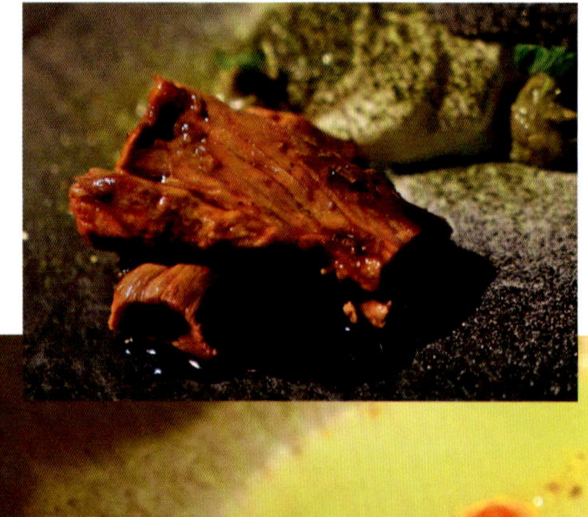

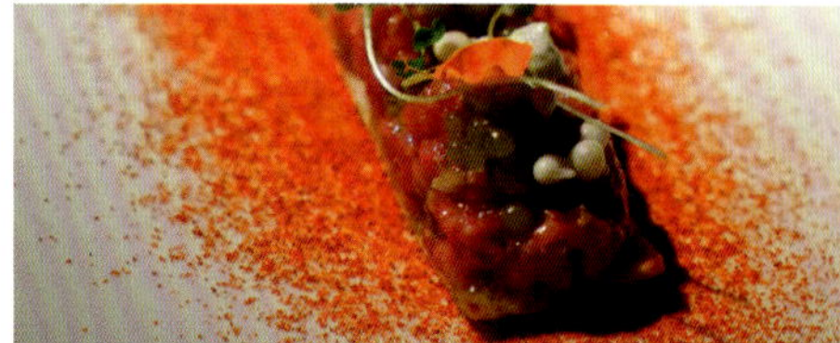

- Crudo de Llama - Raw llama meat with spicy red pepper from Cachi, white puree of capers and white okra balls - the raw expression of the llama being the meat of the north, no cows, no asado; paired with a *Collovatti Torrontés*, La Rioja, Argentina.

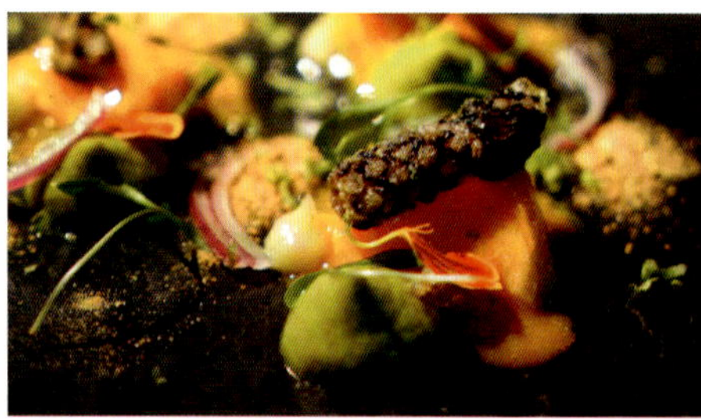

- El Salmón Que Quería Ser Rosado - White salmon seviche, topped with salmon skins, puree of haba beans, tangerine reduction sauce, and dusted with tangerine, orange, lemon, lime, and grapefruit skin dust - expressing the salmon that wants to be pink; paired with *Zorzal Blanc de Cal* (an Eggo Sauvignon Blanc from the rocky limestone of Tupungato).

- Declinación de Tomates Orgánicos Reliquia - A cold fresh soup of concentrated juices from white, yellow and green tomatoes, dried tomato dust, dried beet skins, dried basil seeds, and bread from strained tomato pulp - expressing the 17-year resurgence of seeding new organic tomatoes; paired with *Salentein Brut Rose* (Sparkling Pinot Noir).

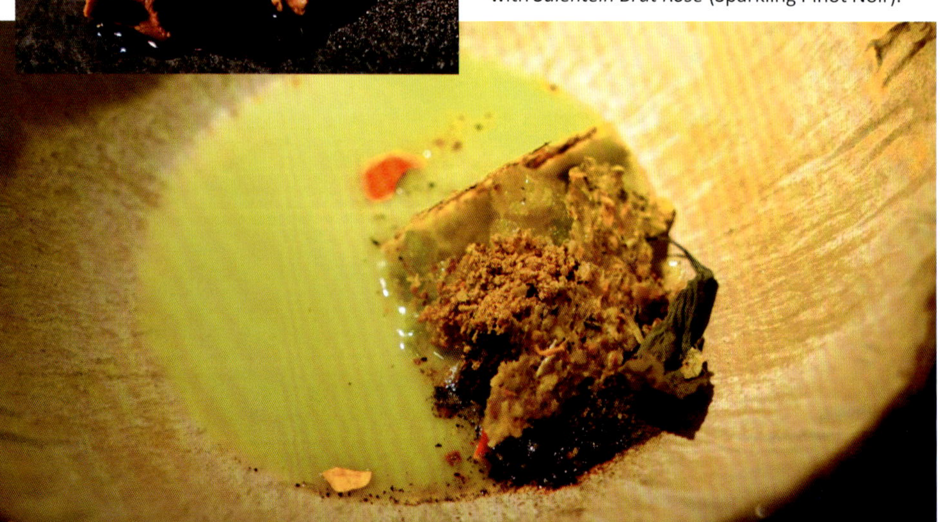

FOOD LOVERS' PARADISE!

Coming directly from the Basque region of Spain, **Executive Chef, Txemi Andrés,** delivers gourmet recipes from this special little area of northeastern Spain and southwestern France.

The Basque society distinguishes itself from these two countries with its own language, culture and delicious foods. The Spanish Basque province capital is San Sebastián, a city of 178,000 people with 2,000 restaurants (a ratio of restaurants to population exceeding any city in the USA).

The Basques love food, and know how good fresh ingredients (painstakingly prepared) can taste. Basques spend more than twice as much of their disposable income on food as we do in the United States, and they spend a greater percentage of their time on cooking and eating too.

Gastronomy is the Basque culture, which brings family and friends together around the kitchen to share this common hedonistic love of life. In 1996, the Sagardi Restaurants started spreading this culinary treasure throughout Spain. Today there are 17 Sagardi Cocineros in Spain plus one in Buenos Aires. Why? Because Sagardi's founder Iñaki Lz de Viñaspre loves Argentina and now lives in Mendoza making wine in La Consulta.

The Basques truly love steak, particularly a T-Bone. And the preparation is just as special...
 - **Half-Sided T-Bone -** a very thick cut of half of an extremely high-grade T-bone steak, crusted thickly with large rock salts (which are removed after cooking), and then grilled over extremely hot wood embers for only five minutes per side (photo below); paired with *Uco Acero Malbec.*

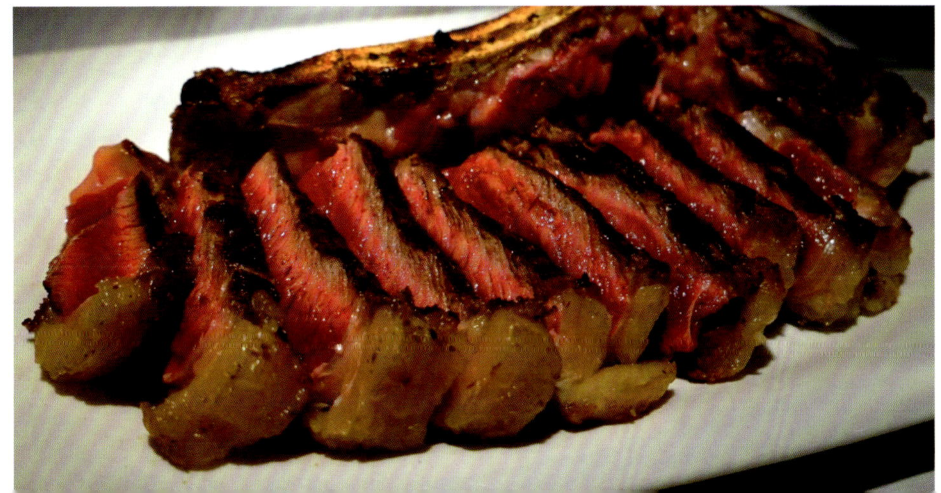

The Basques love seafood and eat four times as much fish as the average Frenchman. Chef Txemi prepares an amazing fish of the day, every day...
 - **Merluza -** a delicate rich white ocean fish from very cold waters, prepared with olive oil, salt, parsley and cider vinegar (photo immediate below); paired with *Uco Acero Malbec.*

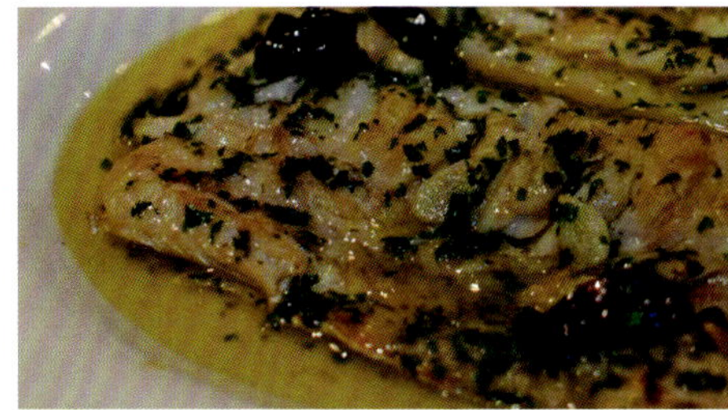

In keeping with traditional Basque cuisine, Sagardi has a large **Pintxos Bar**, the same idea of sitting at a sushi bar, except with different food. Pintxos literally means spike in English. Each small bite is held together with a toothpick spike and comes in a huge variety of 80 constantly evolving seasonal produce and new tendencies (photo below). Enjoyed at all times of a day... breakfast, appetizer, lunch or a casual dinner.

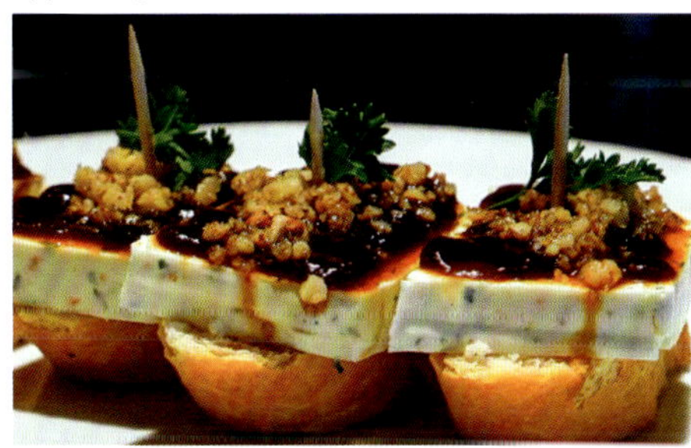

BUENOS AIRES **DOWNTOWN** SAN TELMO

Chef Txemi Andrés Alonso

SAGARDI COCINEROS VASCOS

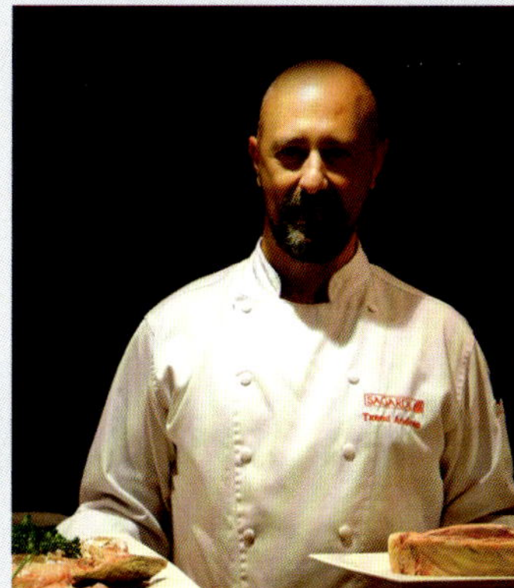

Txemi Andrés, Executive Chef
Native - Bilbao, Basque, Spain
Studied - Escuela de Hosteleria de Leioa

Previous Experiences...
Chef - Sagardi, Taberna Basca Irati, Spain
Owner/Chef - Medina Club, Barcelona, Spain
Chef - Casablanca Hotel Restaurant, Canary Islands
Chef - Almirante Colón Restaurant, Canary Islands

Apprenticed with Master Chef Pepe Rodríguez

Restaurant Reservations
011 (+54 114) 361.2538
reservas@Sagardi.com.ar

Sagardi.com.ar
319 Humberto Primo, Barrio San Telmo

English, Español, Basque & Français
Hours - 1:00 pm - 4:00 pm, 8:00 pm - Midnight

BUENOS AIRES **DOWNTOWN** PALERMO

Chef Gonzalo Alderete Pagés

PERÓN PERÓN RESTO BAR

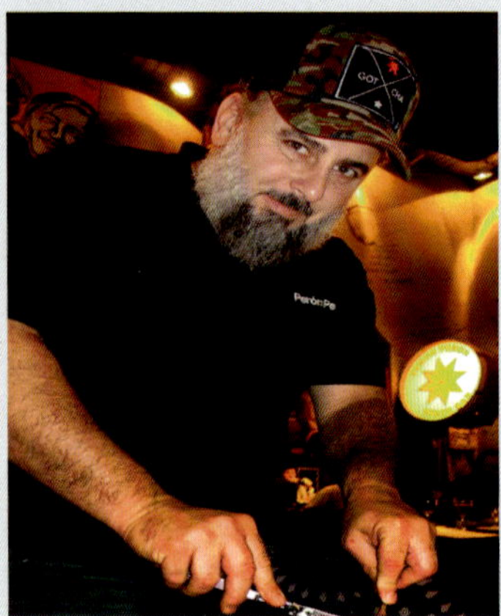

Gonzalo Alderete, Executive Chef

Native - Salta, Argentina

Studied - Self-taught... from books, friends and his grandmother. Started cooking professionally at Perón Perón in 2012 when he co-founded this unique restaurant.

Previous Experience...

- Psychologist (I can just imagie his ex-patients drove him to the crazy concepts of Perón Perón)

Restaurant Reservations
011 (+54 114) 777.6194
peronperonrestobar@gmail.com

Facebook.com/ElPeronPeron
2225 Carranza, Barrio Palermo Hollywood

English & Español
Hours - 6:00 pm - 4:00 am

POLITICALLY INCORRECT CUISINE

Three times elected **Argentine President Juan Perón** and **First Lady Eva "Evita" Perón** were both highly controversial political leaders. This love/hate relationship lives on in *Restaurant Perón Perón* in the Palermo Hollywood barrio... where sarcastic humor plays in favor and against the Perón family.

The atmosphere here is wild and barbaric, filled with memorabilia of all sorts, including a candle-lit memorial of Eva. The graffiti on the walls become works of art (photo top right).

At any moment, music fills the room with *La Marcha Perónista*, the marching national anthem of the Peronist movement. It is customary to sing along (as if I knew the words) with cheers and toasts throughout the restaurant (I could handle that).

The food is rich and homemade, timeless flavors of grandma's love. The menu is designed by ***Executive Chef Gonzalo Alderete*** to poke at the times of the Perónista era. And he is very proud that his all-day and all night slow cooking style has the highest calories of any Palermo restaurant.

The wine list is small; however, with very interesting quality choices from small, hard-to-find wineries. The drinks are much more fun... tasty and politically very incorrect. For example...

- **Long Live F#%king Perón** - *Viva Perón CARAJO!* - Grappa mixed with orange syrup, orange juice and bitters as strong as the People.
- **Shirtless** - *Descamisado* - Justicialista Reserva, a San Juan white wine with oranges and orange syrup. It is (ha ha) fruity and dry, and paired with...
- **Capitalist Pig** - *Bondiola Braden* - The back of the neck of a pig, served with rosemary potatoes, arugula and onion chutney (photo middle right).
- **Served On The Floor** - *Entrana al Parquet* - Perón built free homes with wooden floors for the poor, and these residents would take up and use their wood floors as firewood to cook their meats (Asado!). Here, you can have a skirt steak served on a wooden plank, garnished with your choice.

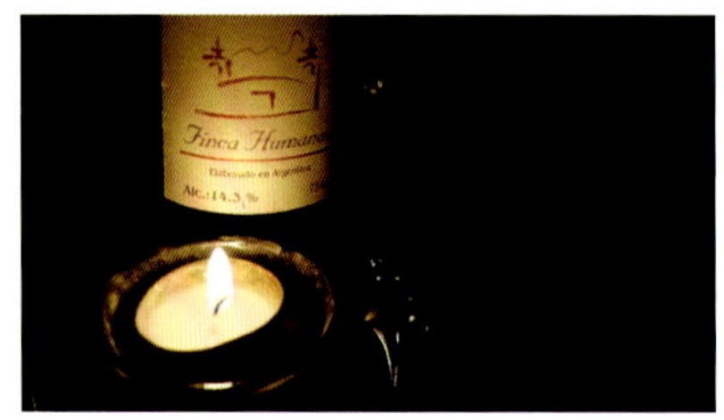

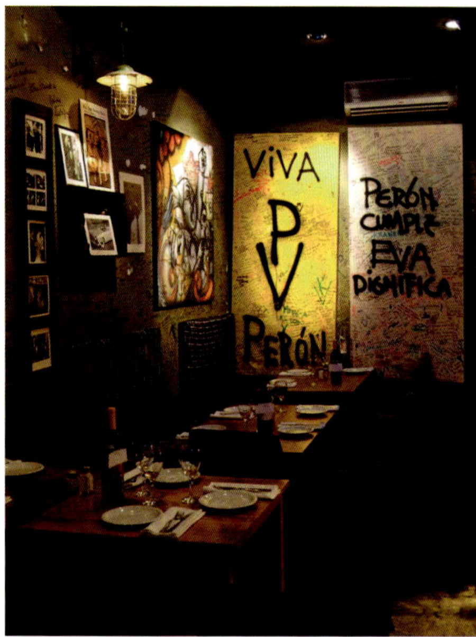

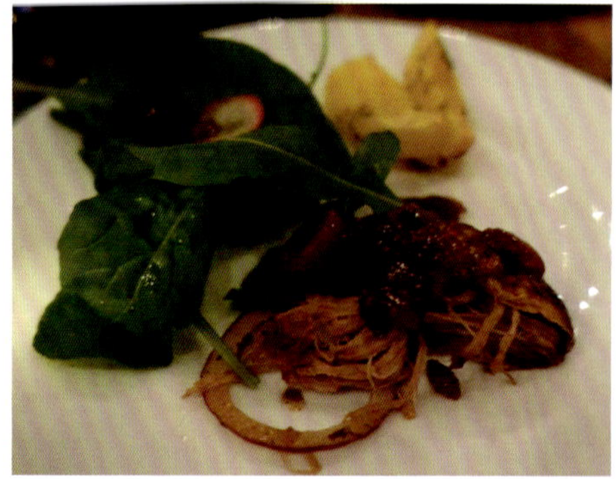

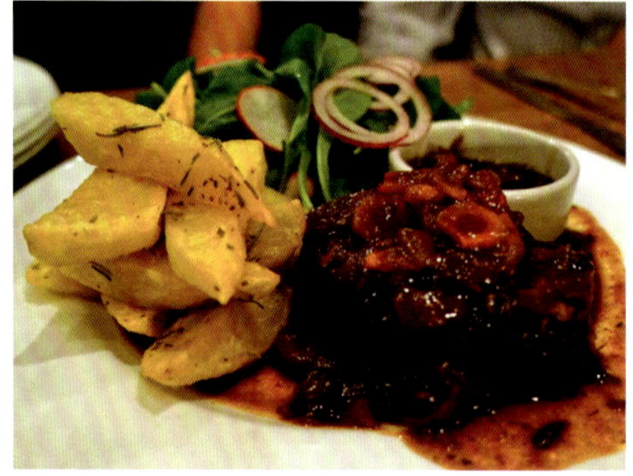

Viva Perón!

BEST WINE LIST IN BUENOS AIRES

Sommelier Eleonora Jezzi Riglos

PAIN ET VIN

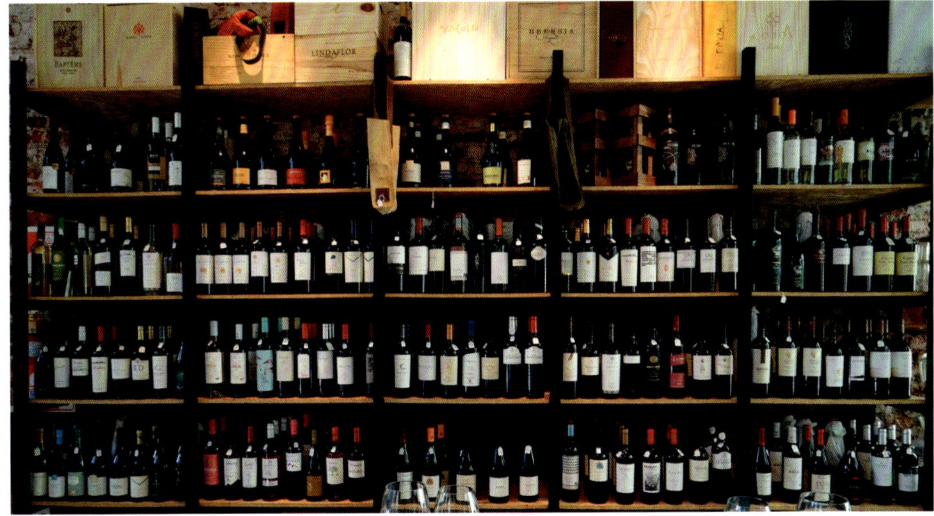

Pain et Vin is a quaint little **Wine Bar and Bakery** in the Palermo Soho barrio that carries the *Who's Who* of Argentine wines. They have at least 200 wines at any one time, and always rotating.

I have devoted 13 weeks to rigorously exploring the wine regions of Argentina. I met some of the most notable winemakers of this country, and tasted nearly 600 bottles of their wines. Needless to say, I now know the wines of Argentina very well... and can tell you that **Sommelier Eleonora Jezzi,** co-owner of Pain et Vin, knows exactly what she is doing in stocking her shelves with the more interesting, most notable and many exclusive, hard-to-find wines of her country.

With wine shop prices, not restaurant markups, you can sit down to enjoy a salad or sandwich, and they will open bottles without a corkage fee. Plus, they serve 10 wines by the glass every day. I know most of the wines on her shelves, and I love them. This is truly the best wine list in Buenos Aires!

Eleonora's husband, also partner in Pain et Vin, is **Israeli Chef Ohad Weiner**, who has become the Master Sourdough Baker providing to many of the hotels and restaurants in Buenos Aires. This Argentine/Israeli love affair rocks the cool casual world of cafés with their top-quality cheeses, gourmet coffees, healthy salads, and scrumptious sandwiches made with Weiner's fresh-baked sourdough breads... made in a special oven he built himself.

- The BLT - A delicious sandwich of thick bacon strips, crispy lettuce and fresh tomatoes, made with Weiner's homemade bread and slathered with aïoli (a Provençal sauce made of garlic, olive oil, egg yolks, and seasonings), photo below right.

- Quinos Salad - A healthy choice of various baby greens and the supergrains of quinoa and lentils, with a generous scoop of goat cheese, photo below left.

- Barroco Viognier - The perfect wine pairing for both dishes... at room temperature was my choice.

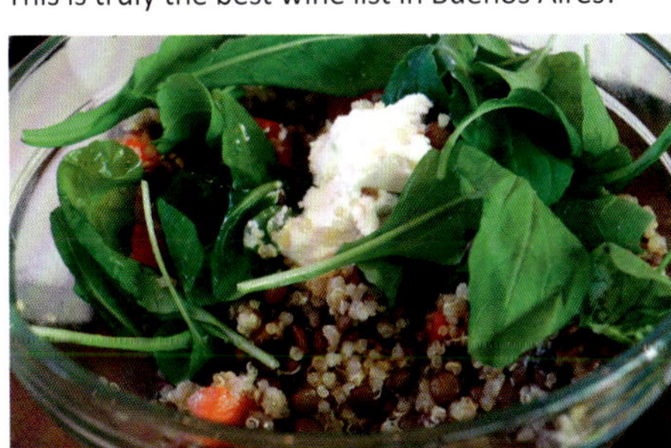

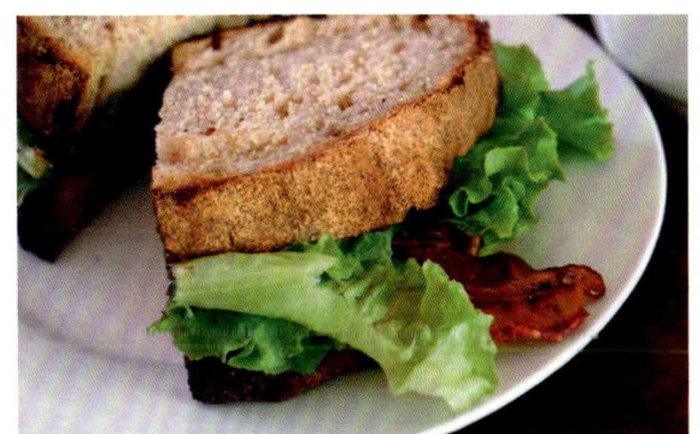

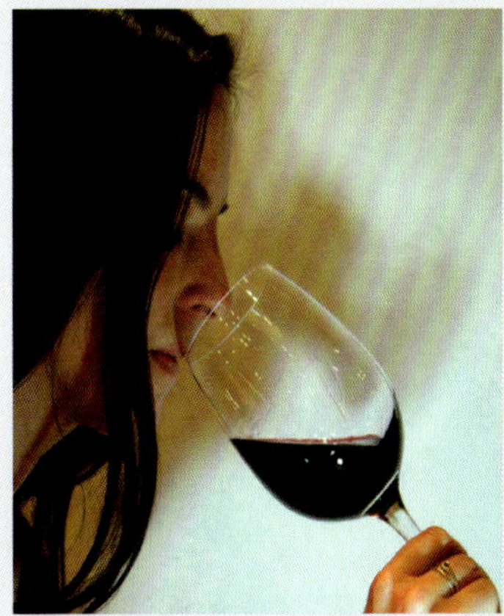

Eleonora Jezzi, Sommelier

Native - Buenos Aires, Argentina

Studied - Sommelier at Colegio de Cocineros Gato Dumas, Bogotá, Colombia

Previous Experiences...

Sommelier - The Wines of Pancho Lavaque, Buenos Aires

Sommelier - Soma Vinos, Buenos Aires

Sommelier - Uva (Grape) Mystic, Buenos Aires

No Reservations Needed

Private Wine Tastings Available

011 (+54 114) 832.5654

info@Pain-Et-Vin.com

5132 Gorriti, Barrio Palermo Soho

English & Español

Hours - 9:00 am - 9:00 pm

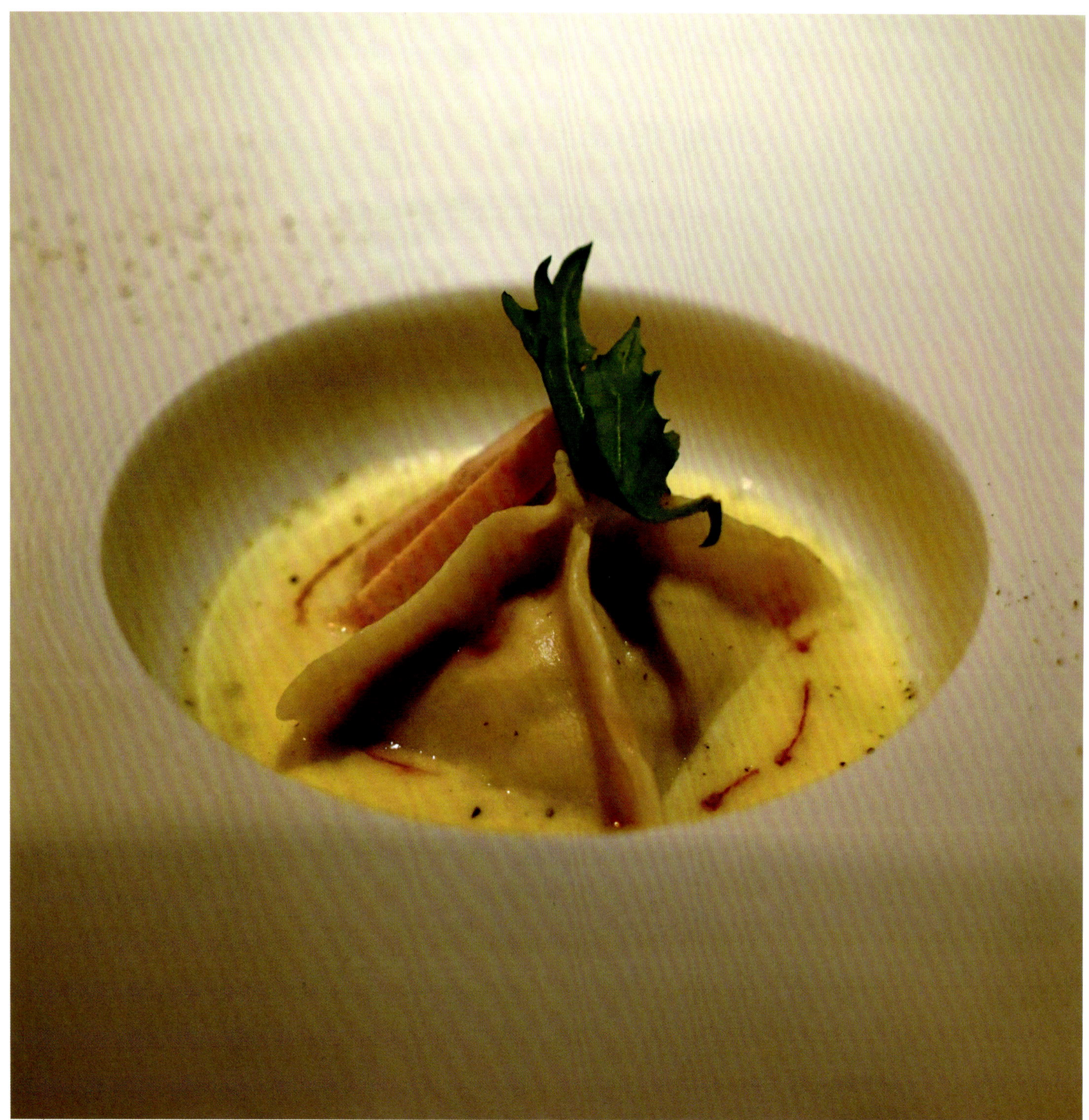

Chef Rodrigo Vazquez

FAENA - BISTRO SUR

THE FAENA EXPERIENCE

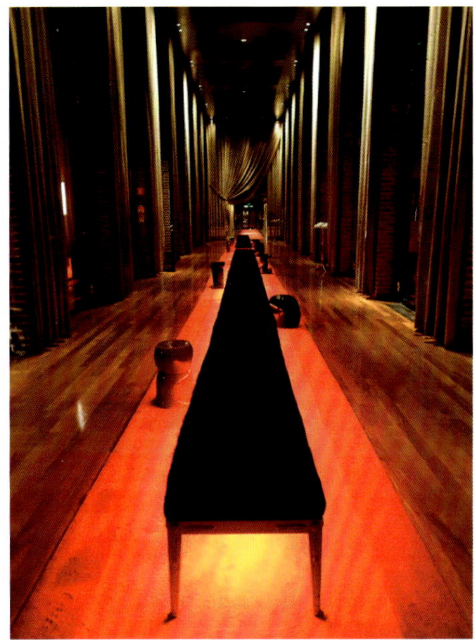

Enter the **Faena Universe** and you will find yourself in another world... a place in the cosmos of ultra-luxury, decadence, creativity, a playground of music, dining, socializing, and passion.

The Faena is a wildly beautiful restoration of an industrial manufacturing building in Puerto Madero transformed into the most unique hotel, restaurant, lounge, pool bar... experience.

Faena's **Bistro Sur** is their chic restaurant in its own atmosphere of the cosmos of all white elegance, a spectacular design of Philippe Starck... with **Executive Chef, Rodrigo Vazquez** creating an equally impressive cuisine.

Rodrigo uses classic regional foods and gives them a modern twist of complicated innovative techniques. A-la-carte is available, however when you have such an inventive chef like Rodrigo, a tasting menu is the way to go. A five- course concept is typically available. I indulged with a 10-course experience of magnificent results. Everything was extraordinary, creative and delectable.

- **Rabbit Ravioli** (photo left page) a confit of rabbit seared in olive oil and served juicy with mascarpone cheese, chopped thyme and lemon skin, topped with fresh ground pepper; paired with the *Chacra Mainque Pinot Noir,* from Río Negro, Patagonia.

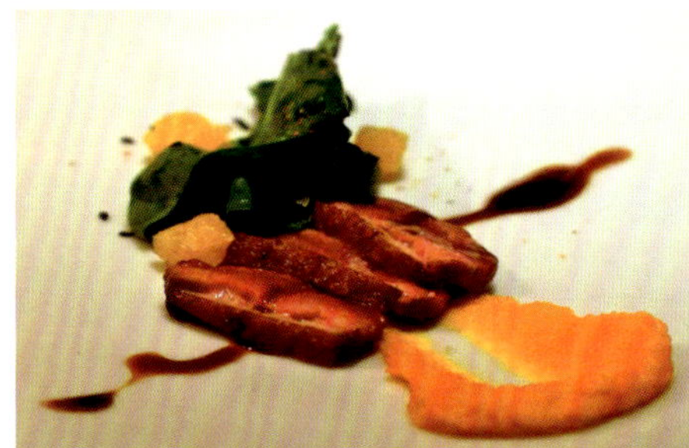

- **Duck Breast** (photo above) served juicy with sautéed bok choy and fresh oranges, and carrot puree (boiled in orange juice); paired with *Julius Caesar - Ave - Imperium Blend (70% Cab Franc, 30% Malbec).* Powerful with black cherries as the name indicates.

- **Octopus & Bay Squid** (photo below) fresh baked octopus leg and fried baby squid, aside a turnip puree with garlic, smoked green pepper dressing and red turnip pickled in vinegar and soy; paired with the *Luigi Bosca Riesling* from Las Compuertas, Mendoza.

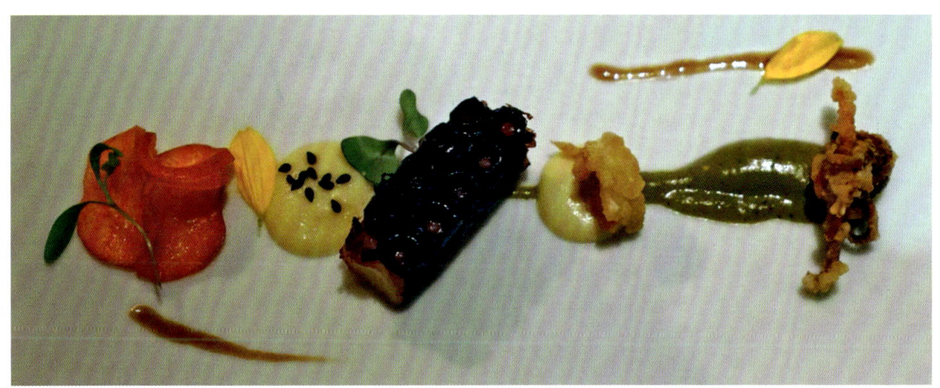

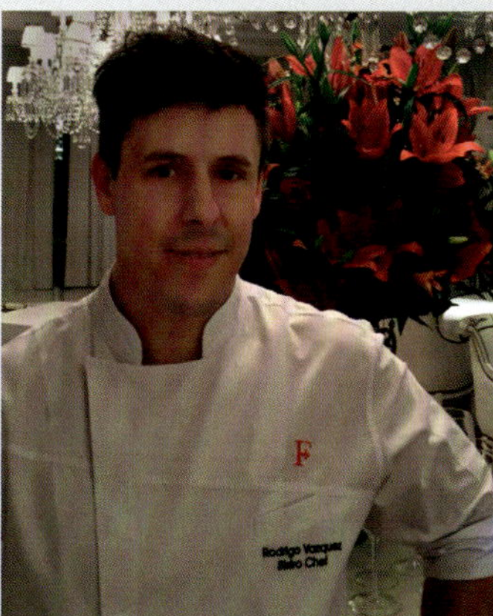

Rodrigo Vazquez, Executive Chef

Native - Buenos Aires

Studied - Argentine Institute of Gastronomy

Inspired by his grandmother's culinary passion

Previous Experience...

Chef - Alvear Palace Hotel, Buenos Aires

World Tour - Seeking new tastes and food cultures...

In Latin America - Mexico, Costa Rica, Panama, Colombia, Perú, Ecuador, Bolivia, Chile, and Uruguay

Also, in Southeast Asia, Europe and New York

Restaurant Reservations

011 (+54 114) 010.9200

ReservasUniverse@Faena.com

Faena.com

445 Martha Salotti, Barrio Puerto Madero

English & Español

Bistro Sur: 8:00 pm to Midnight

The Library Lounge: 10:00 am to 3:00 am

La Catedral (pool lounge): 10:00 am to 3:00 am

El Mercado (casual restaurant): 7:00 am to 2:00 am

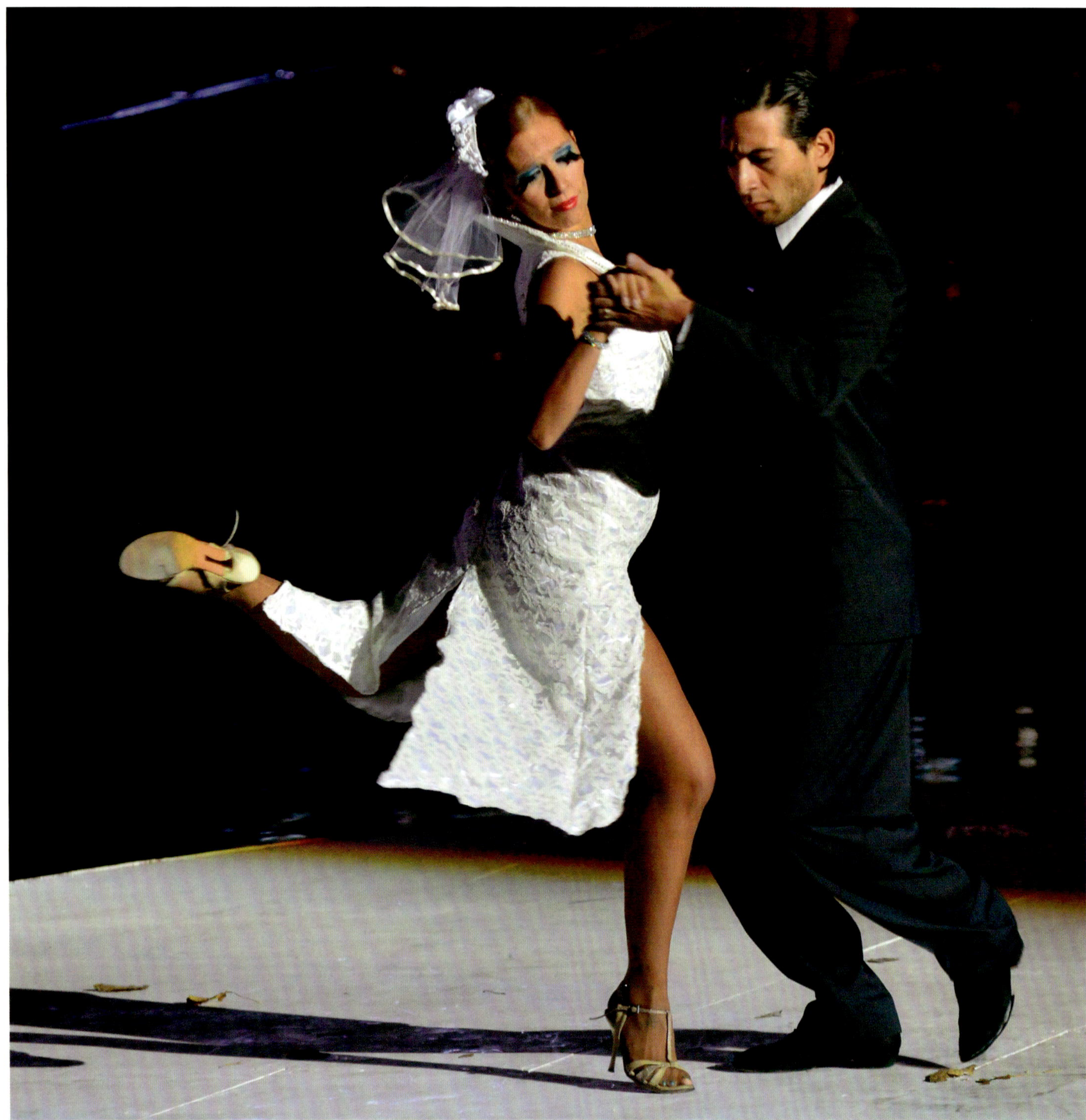

ARGENTINE **TANGO**

The Seductive, Dramatic, Romantic, Sultry Sexy Dance of Buenos Aires

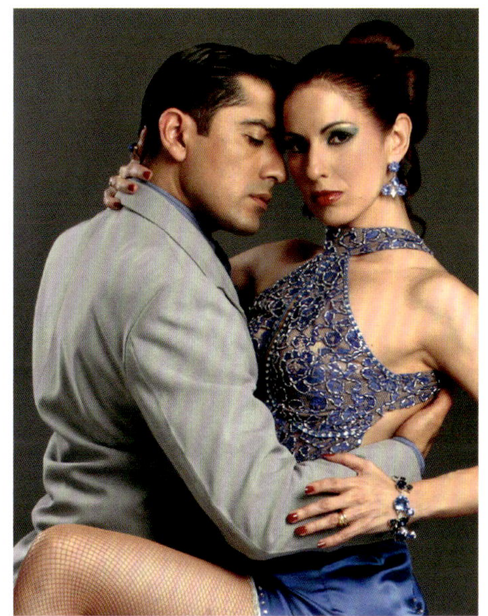

Tango and Argentina are synonymous. It is part of the culture, especially in Buenos Aires. You could say that Buenos Aires is the capital city of Tango for the world. Tango is a passion that lives in the framework of this city, and is expressed in the hearts of the people who live there.

Argentina is known for its luscious Malbec, succulent Asado, arousing Mate, beautiful People, affectionate Culture, and... its ***Very Sexy Tango!***

Tango is a particularly close intimate dance. You are breast-to-breast with your partner. An embrace! Faces touching at times. Bodies moving in a very seductive and provocative manner. I remember one of my instructors explaining to me that to learn Tango I needed to make love to his wife on the dance floor, that Tango is an intimacy of my getting lost in her, feeling her, and the music, all as one. The steps are not formal, and the expression is one of very sensual movements and gestures.

If you are a romantic, this dance is for you.

Oddly, Tango music is actually very sad, and was born in the San Telmo barrio in the late 19th century following yellow fever as the neighborhood regained itself as a working class community of immigrants and artists living commune-style in the vacated buildings. Tango became their expression and created closeness during these hard times.

Tango quickly became popular and spread internationally, particularly in Europe. The leading figure making Tango famous was musician and songwriter Carlos Gardel (bronze sculpture below).

The King of Tango - Carlos Gardel

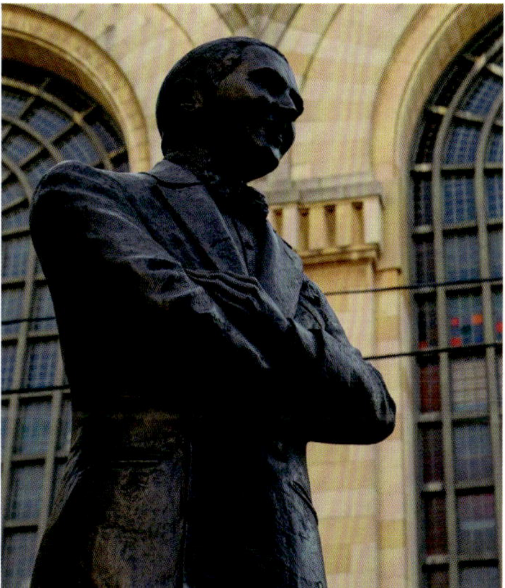

It is not surprising that Tango made its way to Europe, especially France, as Carlos Gardel, the King of Tango, was actually born in Toulouse, France. His unwed mother escaped from this social stigma in France, and brought Carlitos (as she affectionately called him) to Buenos Aires when he was two years old, telling the immigration authorities that she was a widow. It worked.

The French/Argentine singer, songwriter, composer, and actor became the most prominent figure in the history of Tango, and brought Tango back to his birth country. Gardel's baritone voice and the dramatic phrasing of the Tango lyrics made his three-minute Tango recordings masterpieces by the hundreds. Gardel wrote several classic Tangos that mesmerized the world into the love of Tango.

Initially, the prominent people of Buenos Aires disregarded Tango as being unworthy of consideration because it lacked credibility as the music and dance of the poor, from the barrio they used to live prior to the devastation by yellow fever.

The story changed though when France embraced Tango and it became the beautiful dance of *Romantic Paris*. Affluent Recoleta was inspired by and built of Classic French Architecture emulating the French culture. Recoletans made it important to embrace the French society, which was now in love with Tango. This was the turning point for Tango to become part of all social and economic aspects of Argentine society. Today, Tango can be found throughout Buenos Aires, as it would be difficult to be in this city and not to see Tango, just as it would be easy to find shows, restaurants and clubs with Tango dancing every night.

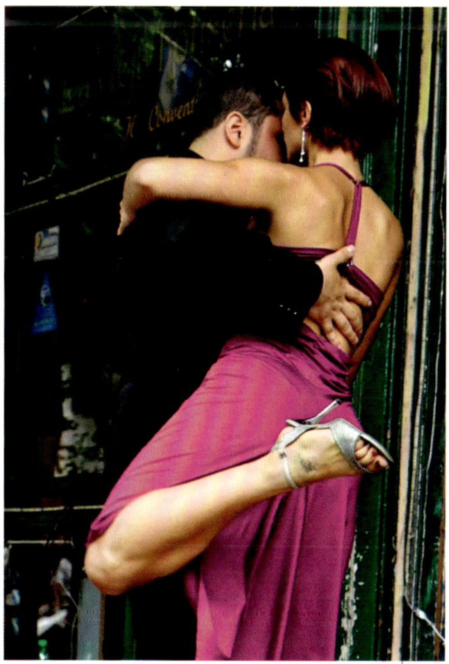

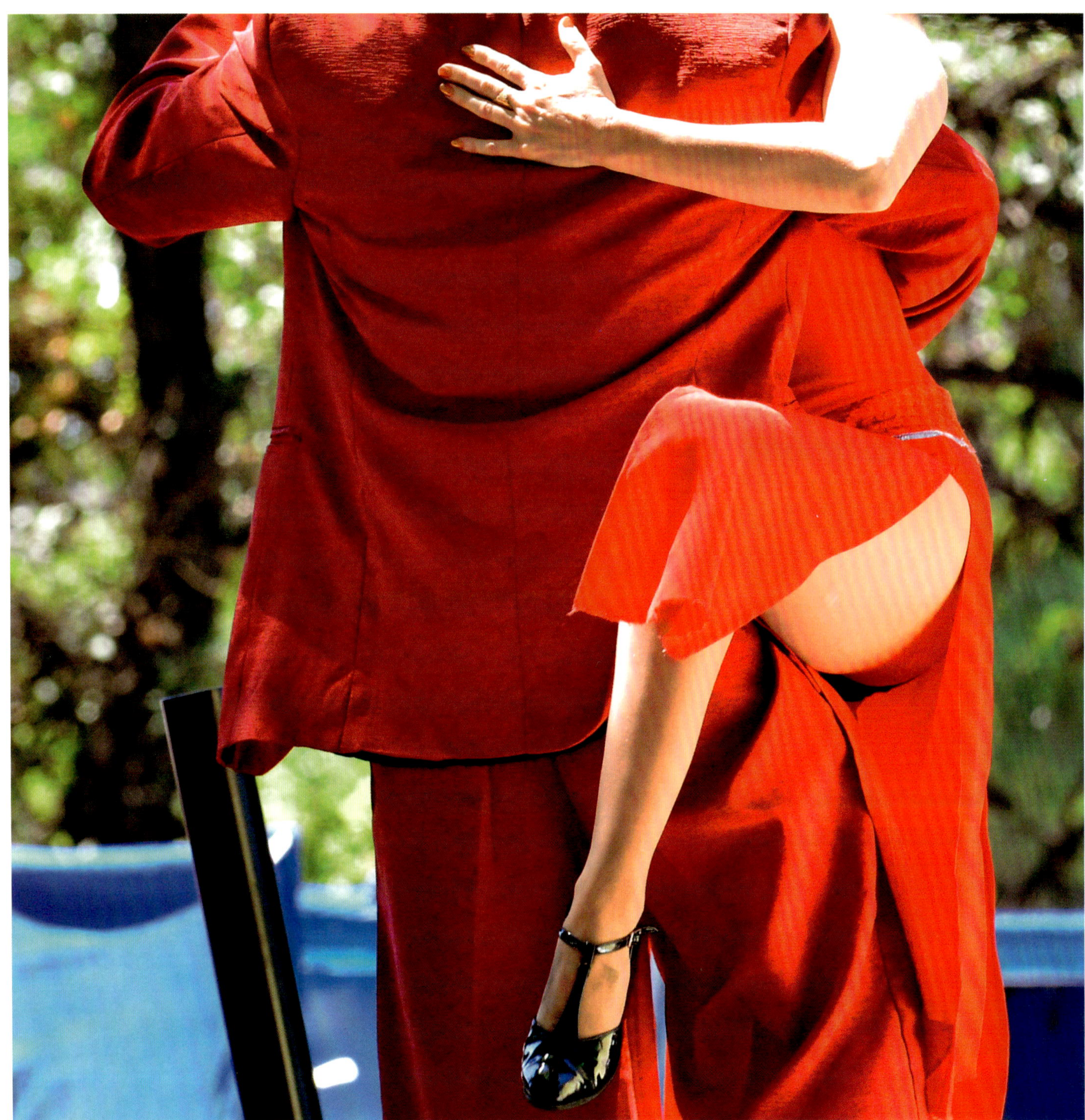

TANGO IN BUENOS AIRES

Tango is everywhere in Buenos Aires. Practically around every corner, in every barrio and there are numerous Tango Clubs throughout the city. And it is important to know that Tango is not very prevalent in the rest of Argentina. So, if you want Tango experiences, Buenos Aires is the happening Tango place!

For me, Tango is so inviting that learning to dance this beautiful sexy art is always a passion when in Argentina. I was fortunate to be able to meet some of the best people to learn the ravishing moves of this Argentine passion. And here I share with you...

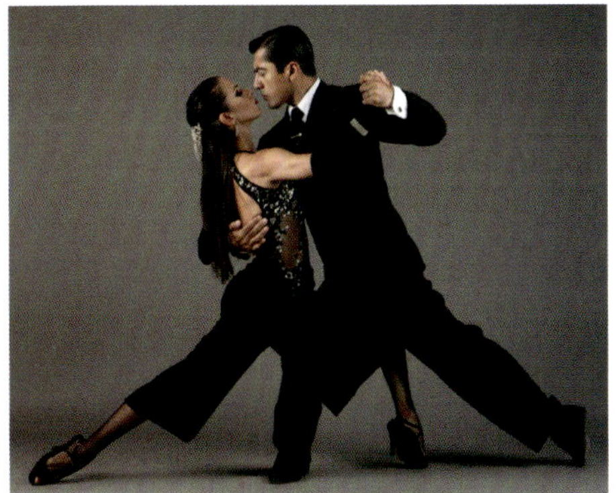

Alejandra Armenti and **Daniel Juárez**
Private and Group Classes (*English & Español*)
011 (+54 114) 720.2924 • info@CorporacionTangos.com
CorporacionTangos.com

Alejandra and Daniel are the ideal combination to learn both the male and female interactions of Tango. And perfect for couples being able to experience the embrace, the movements and the passions of Tango directly, on the dance floor. They are professional Tango dancers who launched the Tango Dance Company in 2003 to teach and perform Tango... and are Directors and Choreographers of Spectacular Tango Shows throughout Buenos Aires.

Naomi Hotta (*English, Español, Français & Japanese*)
Private Lessons & Tango Club Tours
011 (+54 9 115) 863.3578 • NaomiHotTango@gmail.com
NaomiHotTango.com

Naomi is a friend of mine from Los Angeles who started her dance career in Tokyo Japan learning Rhythmic Sports Gymnastics, following Ballroom Dance, Flamenco and Salsa, she got hooked on Tango in 2003. Naomi moved to Buenos Aires in 2004 and has made Tango her life ever since. She is very talented, cultured and a really nice person.

MILONGAS IN BUENOS AIRES

Tango Clubs are known as Milongas... places where people dance Tango. There are numerous Milongas in Buenos Aires. Here are a few for a variety...

Salon Canning
Monday, Tuesday and Friday Nights
Arrive after midnight. Performances begin 1:30 am

La Viruta
Friday and Saturday Nights after 3:00 am
Sunday and Wednesday Nights after 1:30 am

Maldita Milonga
Sunday Nights (more hip music, bar-milonga)

Bendita Milonga
Monday Nights - Orchestra plays from 11:00 pm
Performances begin at Midnight

Outside of Buenos Aires, you will not see the life of Tango in your presence unless there are special events or you seek it out. Vendimia is the harvest festival that occurs every year in all of the wine regions. There are parades on the streets and plenty of Tango dancers to allure and delight you.

TANGO IN DOWNTOWN & MAIPÚ, MENDOZA

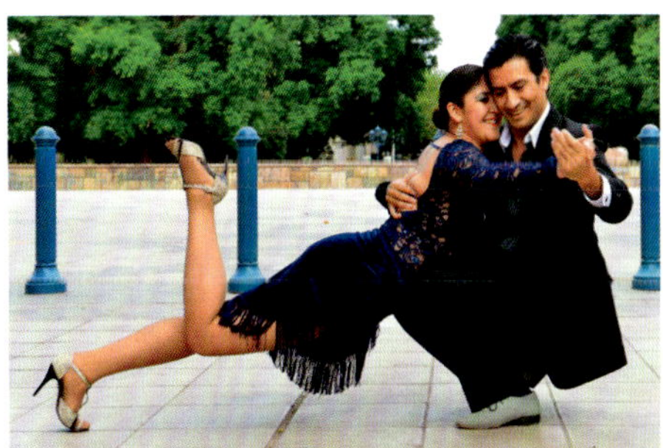

Carola Sosa and **Exequiel Capeda**
Private Lessons (*English & Español*)
011 (+54 261) 481.6749 • MaipuDanza_Tango@hotmail.com.ar
facebook.com/mdtango.compania

Carola and Exequiel are very talented Tango Performers. They are most well know for directing the Maipú Tango Festival every year in June, a two-day festival of musicians and dancers from all over the country. It is considered one of the most important Tango encounters in Argentina.

TANGO IN SAN RAFAEL, MENDOZA

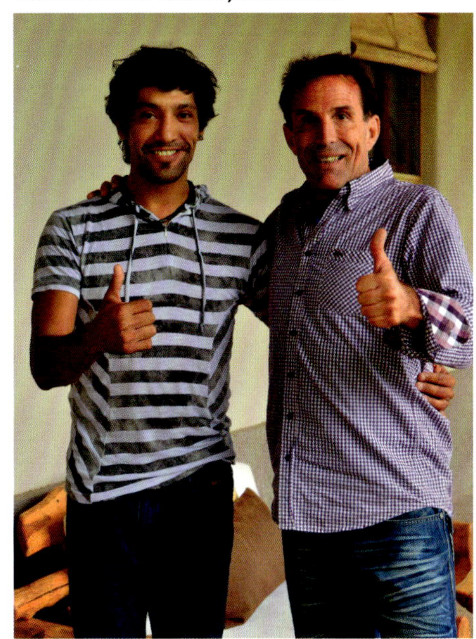

Pablo "Tato" Mardones
Private Lessons (*Español Only*)
011 (+54 260 15) 435.4296 • pablomardones456@gmail.com
facebook.com/ltatitol

Tato is a very special discovery. I had been looking for someone to teach me Tango while in Mendoza. At that time, I did not realize it would be challenging to find an instructor outside of Buenos Aires. Through networking with new Argentine friends, I was finally introduced to Pablo Mardones, known as Tato. He is a genuine friend.

Tato is a professional Tango Performer, not a traditional teacher of Tango. If you contact him and tell him I sent you, he will unveil his talents with you. Be prepared, he does not speak English, but dancing is not about talking anyhow.

His style is not formal. He will show you the basic steps and then move quickly into engaging you in creating your own flow of the dance. Tango has very little to do with regimented steps. It is more about the sensual movement between the bodies, seduced by the music. Tato is in that rhythm.

MILONGA IN SAN RAFAEL, MENDOZA

MTD Aisla Tu Mundo
Performances begin 2:00 am
This is a Private Club, ask Tato to get you in.

SANTIAGO DE CHILE **A DOWNTOWN EXPERIENCE**

The Gateway City to Access Mendoza, Argentina's Primary Wine Region

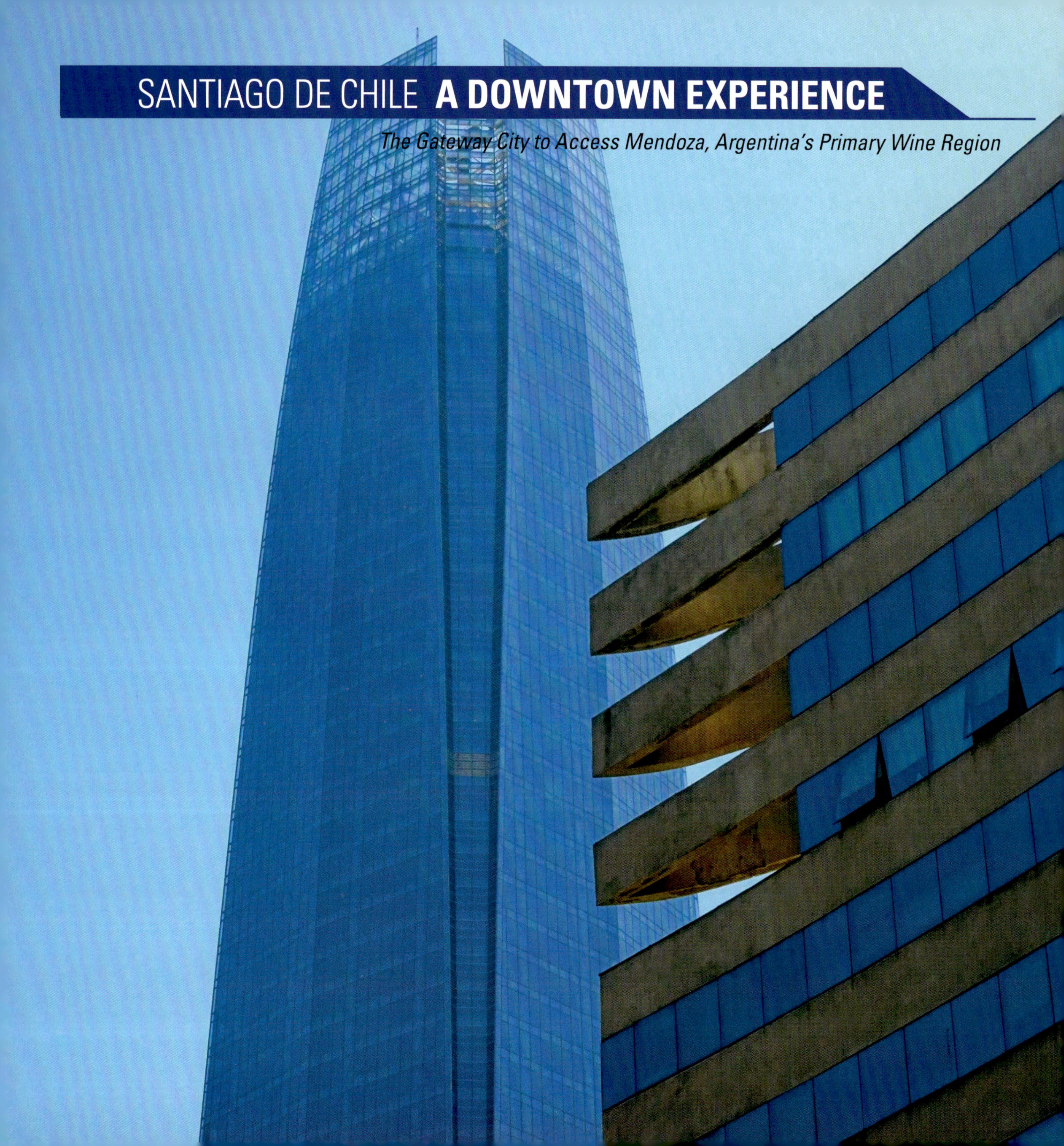

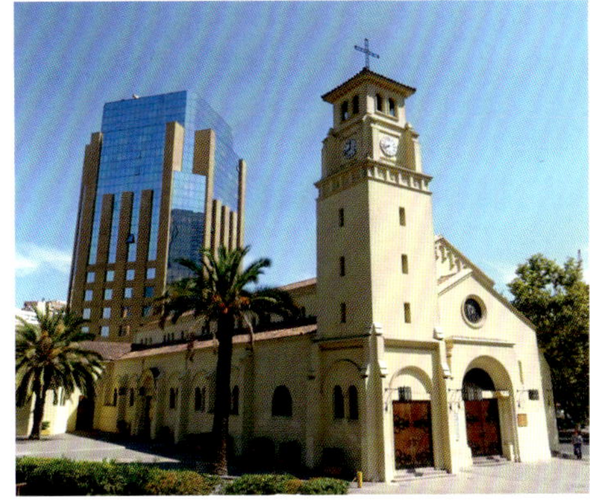

Going to the Argentina Wine Regions requires you to fly through either Buenos Aires (see previous chapter) or Santiago de Chile. There are no direct flights to the wine regions. From Santiago, there are flights onto Mendoza and Buenos Aires. Mendoza is just 100 air miles from Santiago, or 225 winding road miles through the massive Andes Mountain range that separates the two cities (and countries). So, flying over the mountains is really the only efficient option with flights being less than an hour, versus a five-hour drive.

If you choose the Santiago International Airport (SCL), why not stop for a day or two to enjoy this modern Latin American city. There are nearly seven million people in the metro of this modern cosmopolitan capital of Chile.

In 2010, there was an 8.8-magnitude earthquake about 200 miles southwest of Santiago. As a result, the city was rebuilt, and now Santiago has become a skyline with modern high-rise and low-rise buildings.

Chile is a 2,653-mile-long string of land squeezed between the Pacific Ocean and the towering Andes to the west of Argentina. It averages 109 miles wide and is only 40 miles wide at its narrowest point.

Chile also has numerous wine regions, enveloping the same distances south of the equator as Argentina for optimum wine grape growing. Chile is very different though being west of the Andes and having the influence of the Pacific Ocean. The Chilean wine regions are explored in our book ***Exploring Wine Regions - Chile***.

Keeping with the theme of Exploring Wine Regions, I suggest, in the following writings, a culinary experience as you explore the downtown areas of this beautiful city.

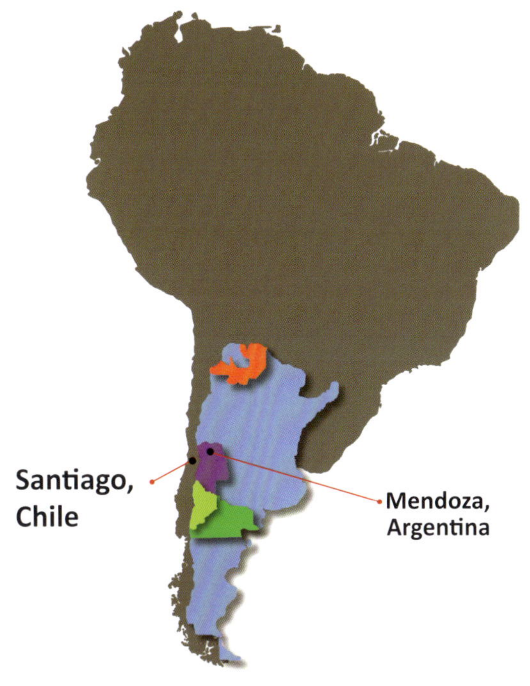

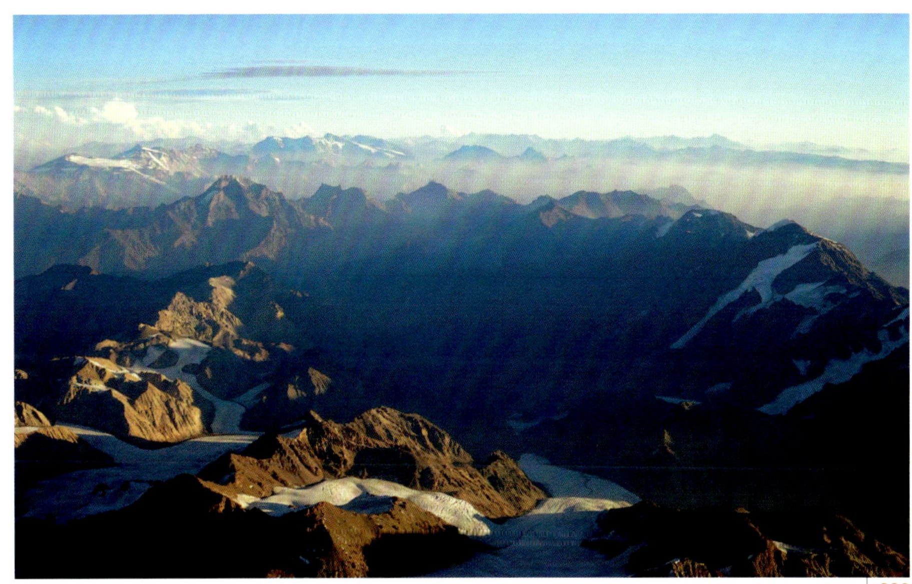

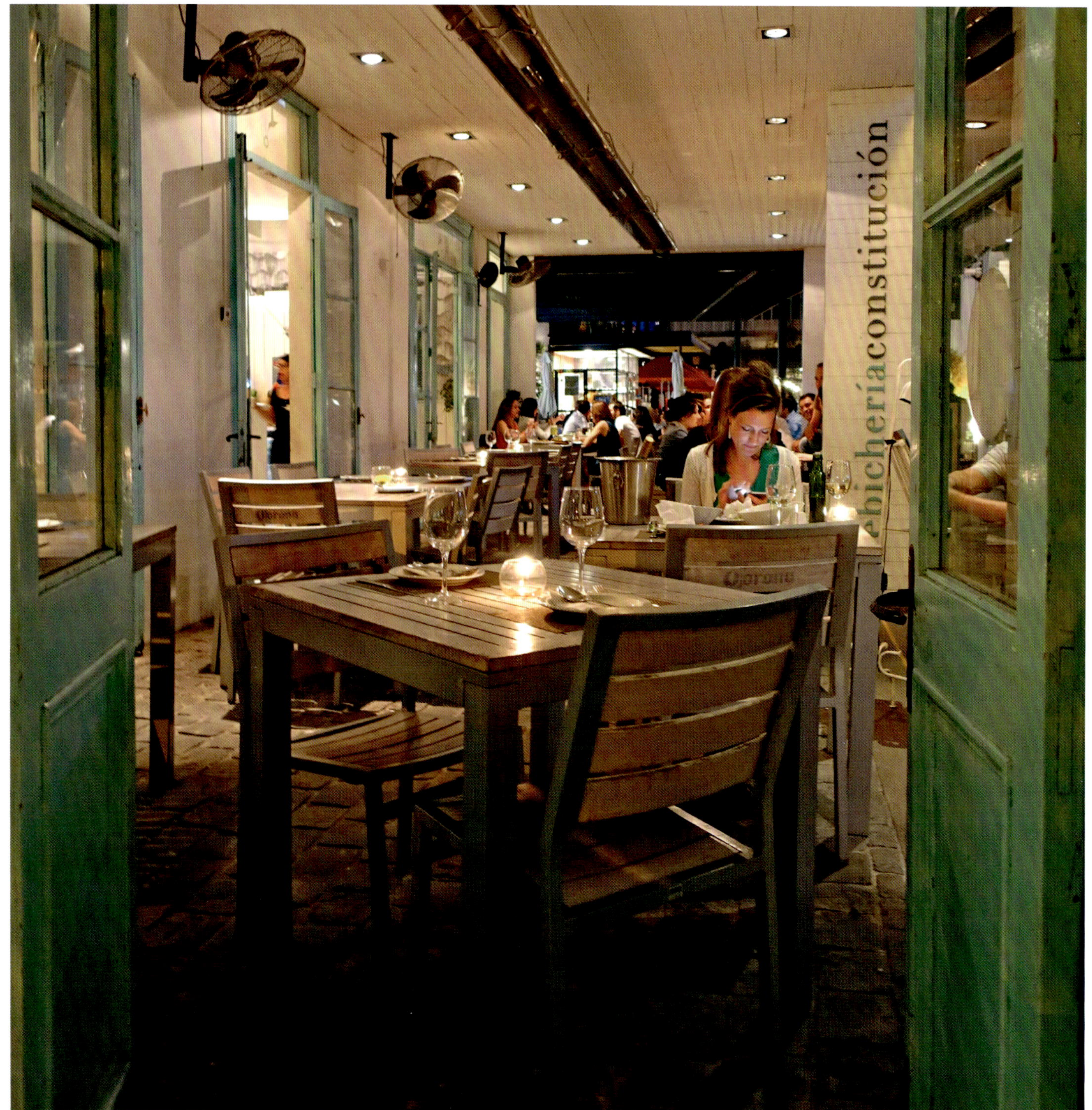

Cebichería Constitución, a ceviche restaurant in Patio Bellavista

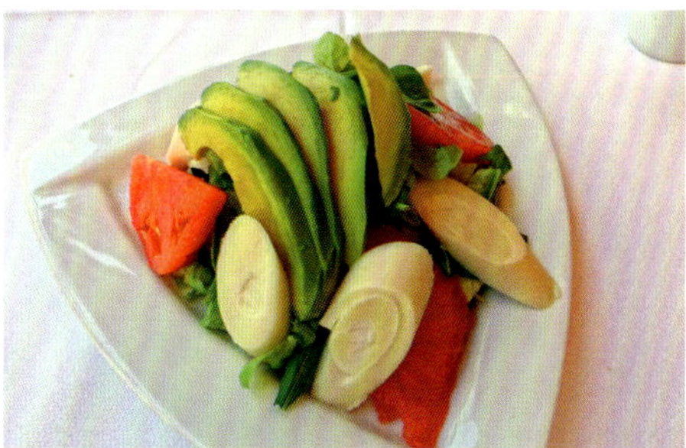

Baby Bamboo and Avocado Salad
Le Due Torri, Restaurante Italiano

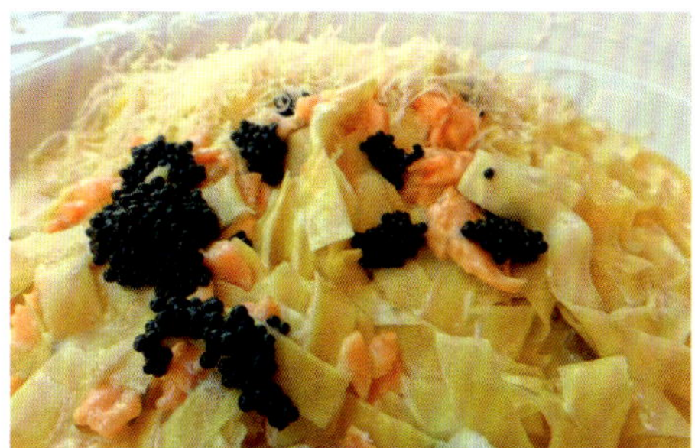

Salmon Pasta topped with Caviar
Le Due Torri, Restaurante Italiano

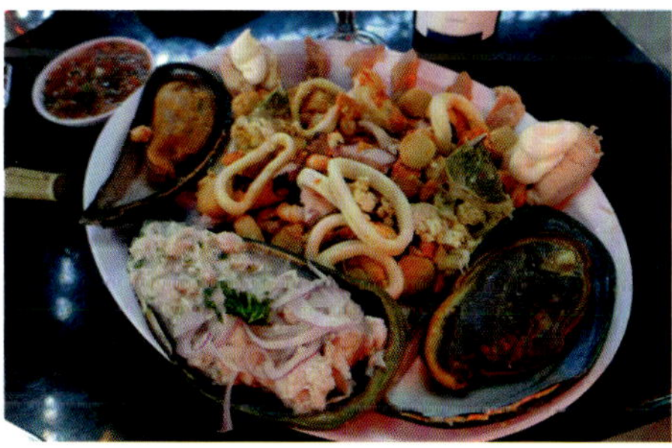

Restaurants in the Mercado Central Seafood Market cook any of the seafood found throughout the Mercado

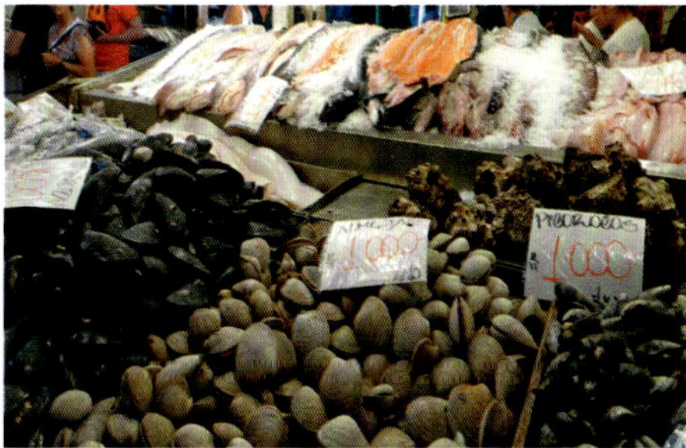

One of numerous seafood vendors at the Grand Mercado Central

HISTORIC & MODERN SANTIAGO

I recommend staying in downtown Santiago and touring the city's historical monuments, buildings and museums dating back to the 14th century... mixed with their new modern architecture, shopping and culinary opportunities.

The **Hop On / Hop Off double-decker buses** tour downtown, giving you extraordinary views of the neighborhoods and making 12 stops that you can hop off and then back on again, unlimited.

Two of these neighborhood (Barrio) stops are particularly inviting for your hotel stay in safe areas.

Barrio Isidora Goyenechea... nicknamed Sanhattan, is the Manhattan of Santiago (acronym) with its NYC-style modern high-rise buildings, including the **Gran Torre Santiago**, 63-story, US$495 million skyscraper completed in 2014 as the tallest building in Latin America (photo previous spread). You will feel at home seeing many U.S. companies, retail and restaurants in this area. The **Le Due Torri** (photos left) is an outstanding Italian culinary experience here. **The Ritz-Carlton** is here too if you want the ultimate of luxury accommodations.

Barrio Bellavista... is a bohemian community of artists and the most touristy of the downtown neighborhoods. This is the former home of famous Chilean poet Pablo Neruda, where his artistic vibe is still felt today. Bellavista is also a college town full of young energy and nightlife everywhere. **Patio Bellavista** is a huge multi-level outdoor historic restoration of the inside of a square block with nearly 100 restaurants and shops, including **Cebichería Constitución**, a ceviche restaurant (photo left page). Across the street is the **Hotel Boutique Tremo**, a boutique hotel recently restored. A nice quiet little place with good prices. Bellavista is adjacent to **Parque Metropolitano**, a massive park with swimming pools, a botanical garden and zoo.

Mercado Central... is the central market for fresh seafood housed in a huge industrial building since 1872. In the center, restaurants cook and serve the fresh caught fish (photos left). On the surrounding streets, you will find vendors of fruits and vegetables of all sorts (photo right).

Historic Center... Plaza de Armas, founded in 1541, contains the National History Museum and neoclassical landmarks.

Hotels & Restaurants

CULINARY EXPERIENCE

Santiago Hop On / Hop Off
011 (+56 22) 820.1000 • ViajesTuristik.com
Every 30 minutes from 9:30 am to 6:00 pm
(US$31 day passes available at each stop)

The Ritz-Carlton, Santiago
011 (+56 22) 470.8500 • RitzCarlton.com/Santiago
15 Calle El Alcalde, Barrio Isidora Goyenechea
sclrz.leads@RitzCarlton.com

Hotel Boutique Tremo
011 (+56 22) 732 4882 • TremoHotel.cl
032 Alberto Reyes, Barrio Bellavista
contacto@TremoHotel.cl

Patio Bellavista
011 (+56 22) 248.9171 • PatioBellavista.cl
Underground Parking - 052 Bellavista (between Constitution and Pio Nono), Barrio Bellavista
Open - 8:00 am to 3:00 am

Cebichería Constitución
011 (+56 22) 248.9171 • Trel.cl
70 Ave Constitución, Patio Bellavista, Barrio Bellavista
Lunch and Dinner - 11:00 am to 12:00 Midnight

Le Due Torri
011 (+56 22) 231.3427 • Trl.cl
2908 Isidora Goyenechea, Barrio Isidora Goyenechea
Lunch 12:30 to 4:00 and Dinner 8:00 to 12:30

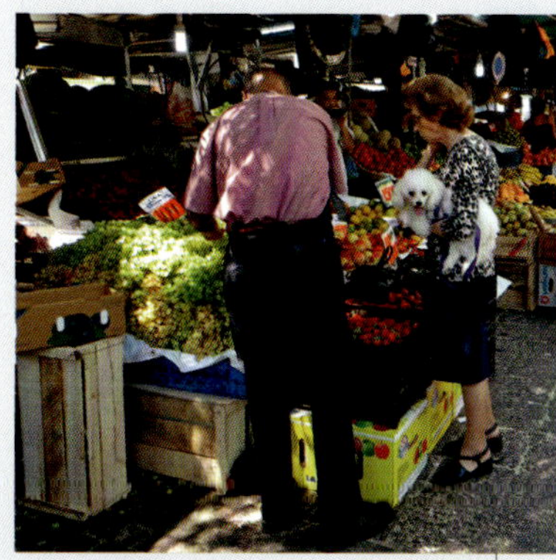

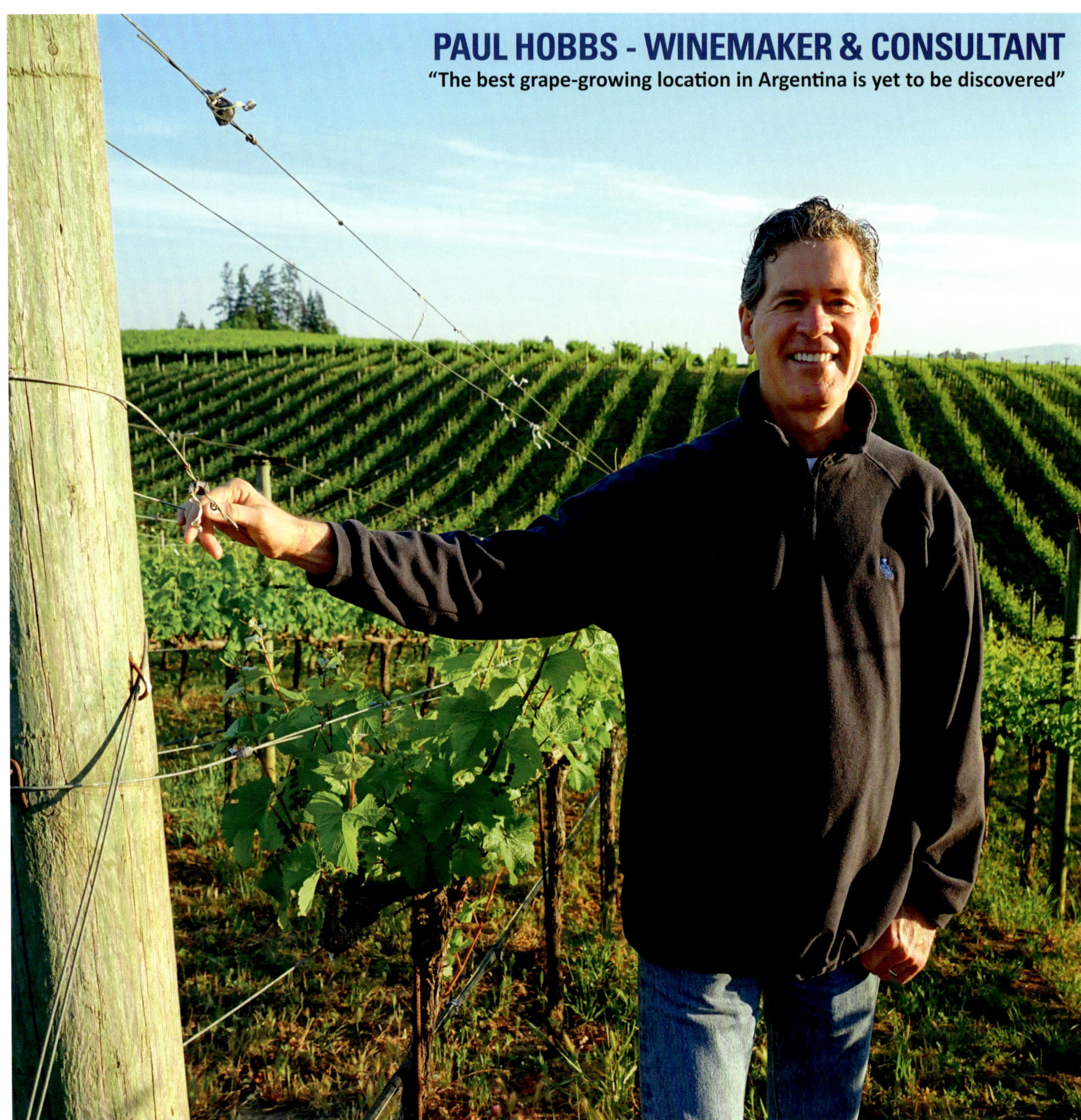
PAUL HOBBS - WINEMAKER & CONSULTANT
"The best grape-growing location in Argentina is yet to be discovered"

MEET THE WINE GURU

As many of you might know, Paul Hobbs is one of the very top wine consultants in the world. He is world renowned as the oenologist to choose if you want to produce extraordinary wines that are notable and distinctive in a class of uncommon quality. And there is proof... perfect 100-point scores for his wines from the esteemed wine critic Robert Parker, who twice named him "***Wine Personality of the Year.***" Forbes Magazine calls Paul Hobbs: ***The Steve Jobs of Wine.*** Today, some 35 winery clients around the world pay Hobbs tens of thousands of dollars every month to engage his precision and passion for the extraordinary.

Why is Paul so good at what he does? I enjoy people who are passionate about the pursuit of quality, and I love to learn what makes them great at what they do. So, I spent time with Paul, getting to know him, and talking with others who know him too. My conclusion is to update Forbe's metaphor to... ***Hobbs is the Bach of Wine.***

Interestingly, Paul Hobbs and Johann Sebastian Bach have a lot in common in orchestrating masterpieces. Although Bach is considered the greatest composer of all time, he never actually invented any new styles or forms of music. Instead, Bach perfected every single piece which existed in his day. Similarly, Hobbs did not invent the grape, instead he has focused on perfecting them. Paul's roots are farming and it is in his blood from childhood. As a farmer, he spends endless hours in the vineyards perfecting the grapes. As with Bach, Hobbs devotes countless more hours than most of his rivals. Paul is up with the sun and works until that very last ray of light hits the vineyards.

Paul is not afraid to get his hands dirty in the vineyards, when other winemakers and consultants don't even want to get their shoes dusty. This reminds me of Mozart and Beethoven who hated to write Fugue (complex contrapuntal compositions interweaving the parts).

Speaking of complexity, winemaking can be as simple as watering grape vines, fermenting the fruit and putting the juice in the bottle. Yet, in order to make extraordinary wine, it takes on a complexity of many moving parts and experimentation to perfect every aspect of the process. Paul is passionate about every nuance of the process. He is meticulous about everything, fanatical about even the little details of cleanliness. Remember Bach's Mass in B Minor? The Sanctus was a six-part chorus with a four-voiced fugue. In the annals of fugal composition, no composer has ever attempted what Bach accomplished, and this piece has been argued by many composers to be the single greatest work of music of all time, in any genre, any style.

Are you seeing the correlation? Do you see the commitment and dedication both these men give to their art as creators of masterpieces? Both men have taken on the intellectual depth of their crafts, mastered the technical demands, experimented with innovations, and worked tirelessly with passion for the results we all enjoy.

It all started with Paul growing up on a farm in upstate New York, driving a tractor at age six, learning from his father the value of working hard and being demanding with what you do. His family lived off the land, so farming success was critical to having food on the table.

Because of his agricultural beginning, Paul's focus and depth of understanding are in the vineyard; meticulous vineyard management followed by very little intrusion into the winemaking process. Paul prefers natural fermentation with native yeasts and a little experimentation thrown in... like fermenting directly in the oak barrels. After graduating from U.C. Davis, Paul began his career with innovative winemaker Robert Mondavi, experimenting with barrel fermentation techniques.

Thanks to Hobbs's early success, Mondavi and Baron Philippe de Rothschild put him in charge of creating their famous American/French Joint venture, Opus One Winery, in Napa Valley.

Years later, while on a trip to Chile, Paul found himself accidentally in Argentina, getting hooked on the Argentine's immense passion for making wine.

Paul was introduced to Nicolás Catena of the Catena Zapata winery in Mendoza, a very successful vintner with volume wines in Argentina (300 million bottles annually). Catena had a dream of making high-quality wines that would get the attention around the world, especially the United States. Catena had a strategy and the immense resources necessary to fulfill this aspiration... and Paul Hobbs was his American expert to help him pull it off.

Hobbs was challenged doing odd things... like to start by making a super-premium white wine in the land of big bold red grapes! Hobbs did it anyhow with a high-scoring attention-getting Chardonnay. He then went on to convince Nicolás that Malbec would be the real success, and he proved it by importing the Catena wines himself to the USA.

Over the next 10 years, Paul and Nicolás were able to change the Argentina wine industry to become the fifth largest wine region in the world, now known for superior quality wines, especially Malbec. Hobbs became the leading advocate for Argentina wines in the USA.

Other winemakers noticed Hobbs's work and the quality of the Catena wines, and wanted his expertise too. Quickly Paul had a consulting business with over 35 winery clients around the world, 10 of which are in Argentina. If you ever stop at one of the following wineries, you will know the consulting quality behind their great wines.

In Mendoza... **Bodegas Salentein (page 138)**, Domaine Bousquet, Riglos, Rutini Wines, Bodega Pasqual Toso, Viniterra, and Vicentin.

In Salta... **El Porvenir de Cafayate (page 222)**

In Patagonia... **Familia Schroeder (page 268)**, and Bodega del Desierto.

Paul also has his own winery in Mendoza, ***Vina Cobos Winery*** in Lujan de Cuyo (photo below), plus his ***Paul Hobbs Winery*** in the famed Russian River AVA of Sonoma County, California (photo left page).

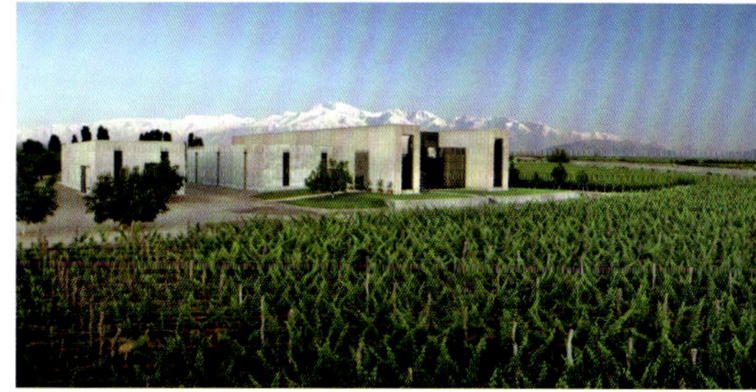

What's next for Paul? Discovering new vineyards! Paul believes that the best grape-growing location in Argentina has yet to be discovered! Paul is highly regarded for his ability to identify exceptional vineyard locations. Recently, he purchased a property in Valle de Uco, Mendoza, in the middle of barren desert midway between Salentein and Casa de Uco (vineyard properties he admires), and has begun planting what might be the next best thing

And the passion for quality thrives on...

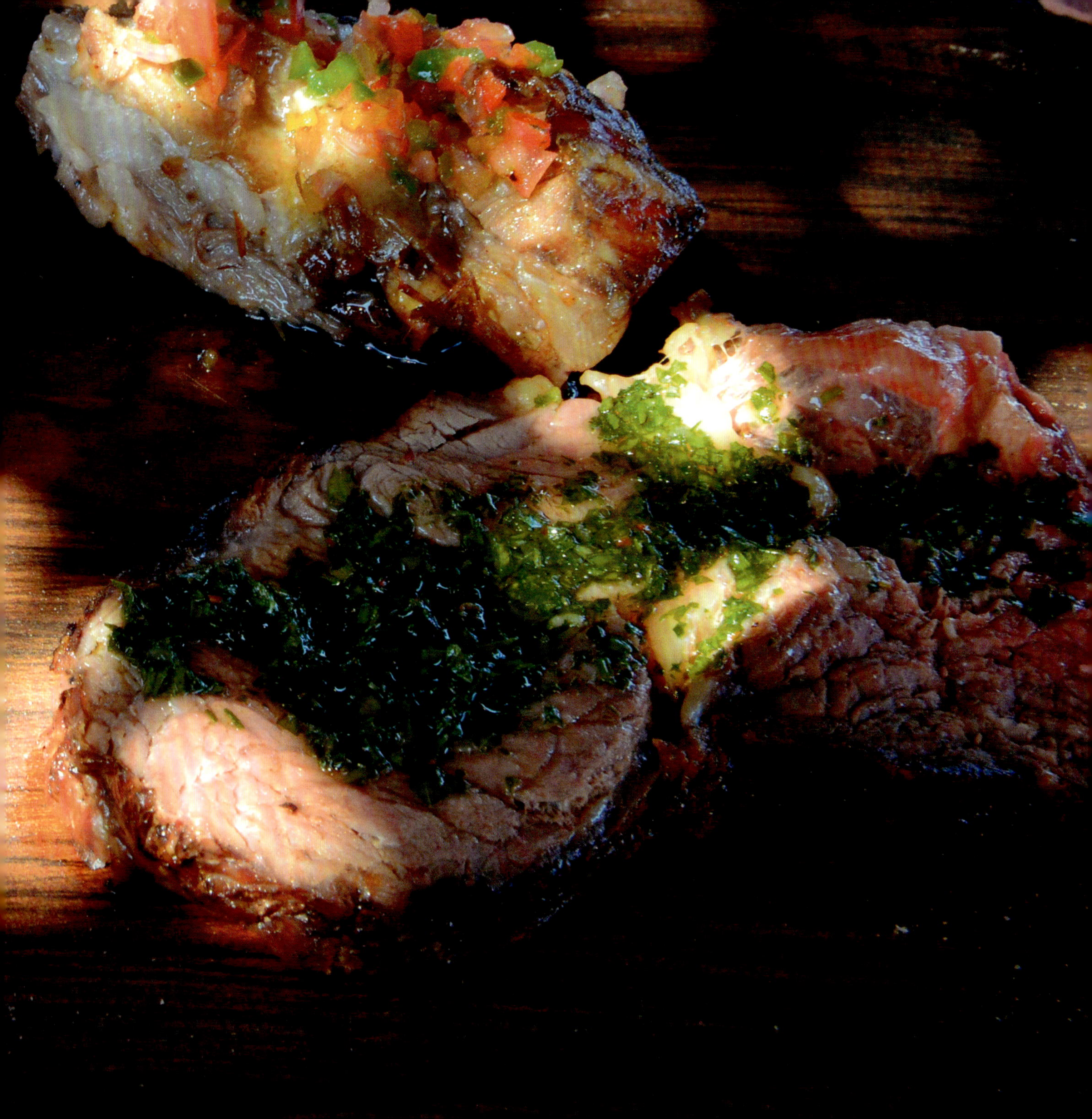

ARGENTINE BEEF **EXTRAORDINARY**

*Once You Have Tasted **Authentic Argentine Asado,** You Will Crave These Flavors Forever...*

And so we have heard, *Argentina's Beef is the best in the world!* This was in the back of my mind, forgotten, and I really did not give much thought to how much better the beef would be when traveling to Argentina... until I took the first bite.

The best way to give you a perspective on how good is this beef; the flavors are so attractive, you will keep eating, and eating, and eating until you are absolutely stuffed full. And then you will continue to eat more, it tastes that good. And you will eat until you hurt. And then you keep eating more...

No wonder a nap in the afternoon is common. And this is just lunch. Dinner is more. I have never eaten as much as I did during the first five weeks I was in Mendoza, and yet I came home losing weight. It's a high-quality, high-protein, low-fat diet. And, I am sure it didn't hurt that I always paired the meat with a Mendoza Malbec, or an Argentine Cabernet.

It did not take me long to figure out why Malbec is their chief wine. It is because beef is the key component of traditional Argentine cuisine, and they pair perfectly! Beef and Malbec are not just a food and a wine in Argentina; it is a cultural treasure, a way of life, a heritage well fermented in all strata of society, with the average Argentine consuming nearly 350 pounds of beef a year. That's practically a pound of beef per day, every day!

With the beef so delicious in Argentina, I was always craving for the next meal. I got to think though... I wonder how could I fit a little baby cow in my suitcase to bring him home? :-)

OK, so why? You have to be asking yourself the same question I was able to ask over and over again, in person... Why is the beef so extraordinarily good? Is it what the cows eat? Is it the species? What is it that makes the beef so amazingly good?

I got answers... lots of answers. And I am convinced it is for the accumulation of quite a few reasons. Here are what I discovered:

LEFT PAGE, Nine-hour **Grilled Rib Eye** topped with fresh chimichurri sauce.

BOTTOM, a **Parrilla,** the classic Argentine barbecue grill found in most backyards and behind most restaurants. To its right, a **Horno de Barro,** an igloo-shaped oven where baking is done; for example, empanadas, potatoes and fresh breads.

RIGHT, a **Vacío,** an interesting cut of beef not often served outside of Argentina. It's a thin cut of meat from the flank of the animal that is characterized by a layer of fat on the outside; however, no fat on the inside.

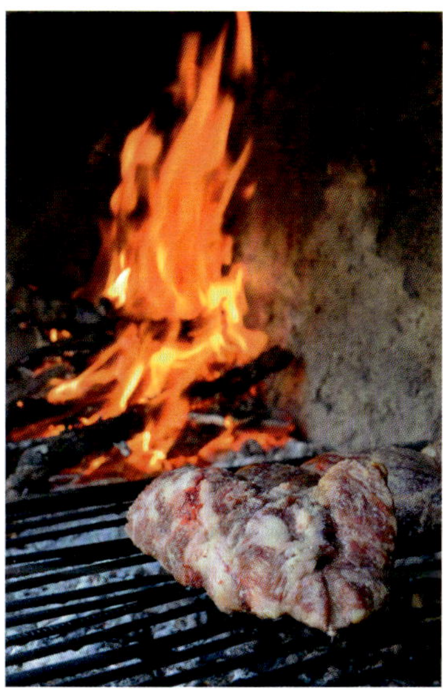

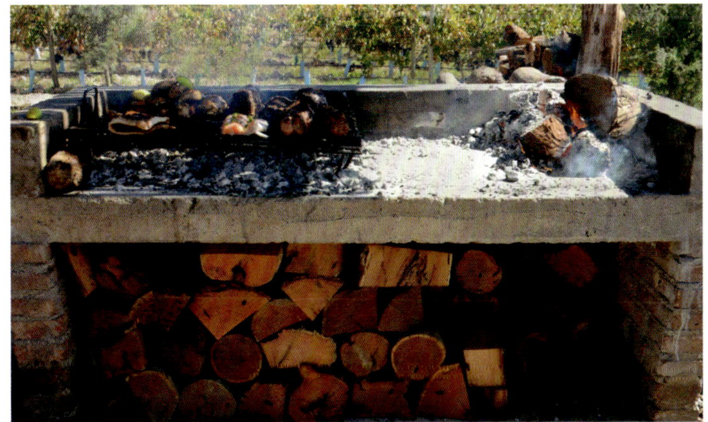

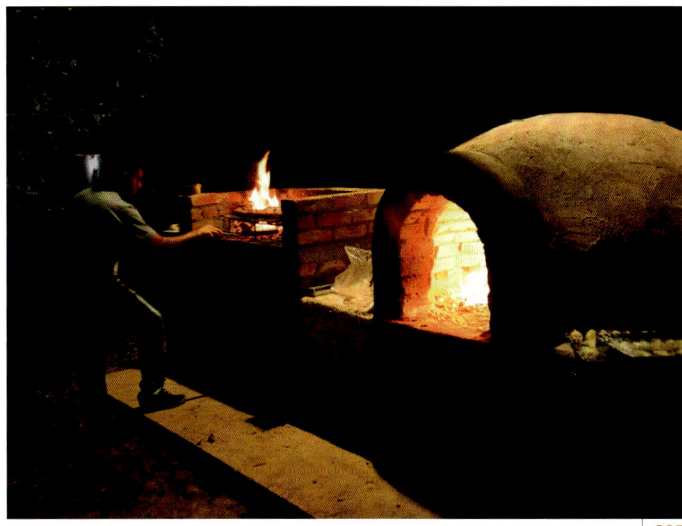

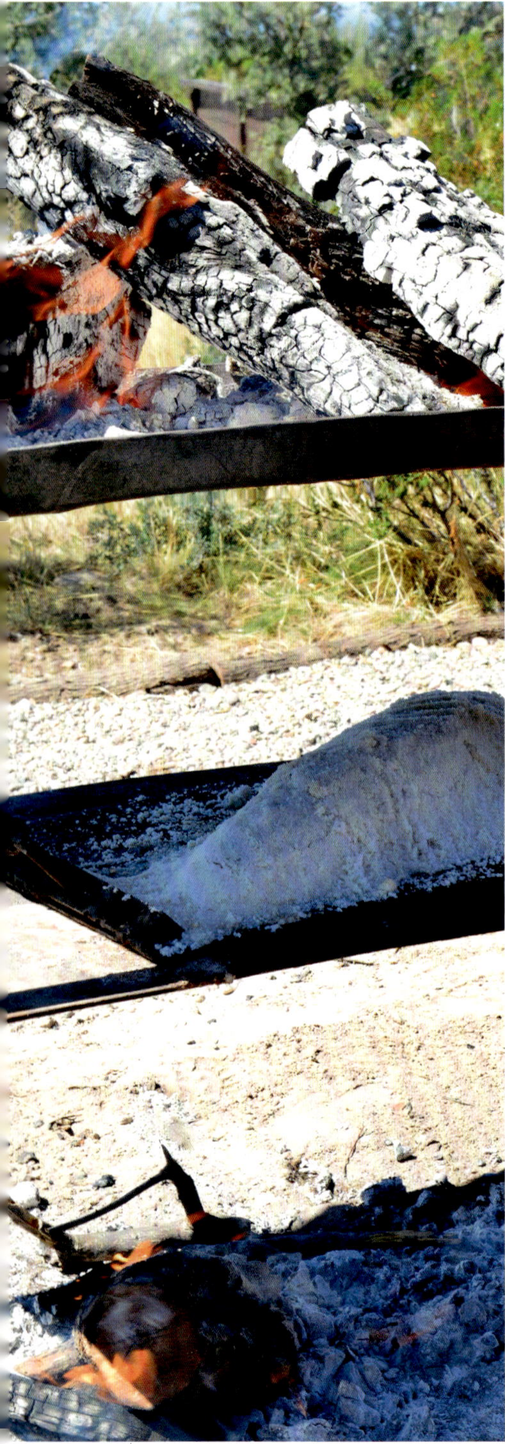
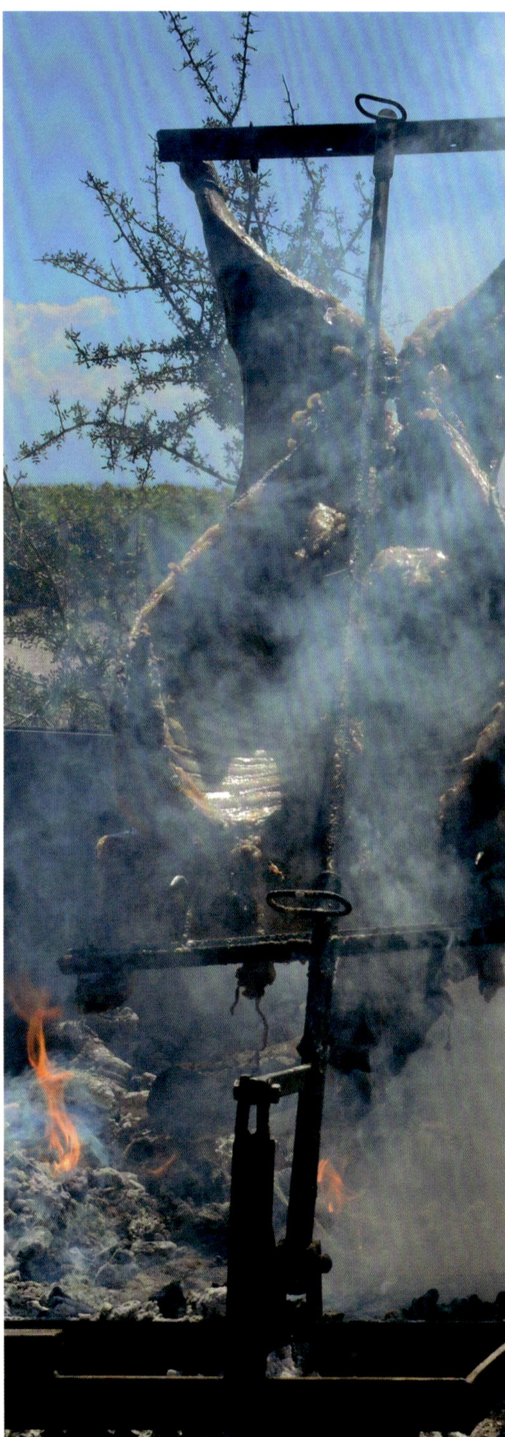
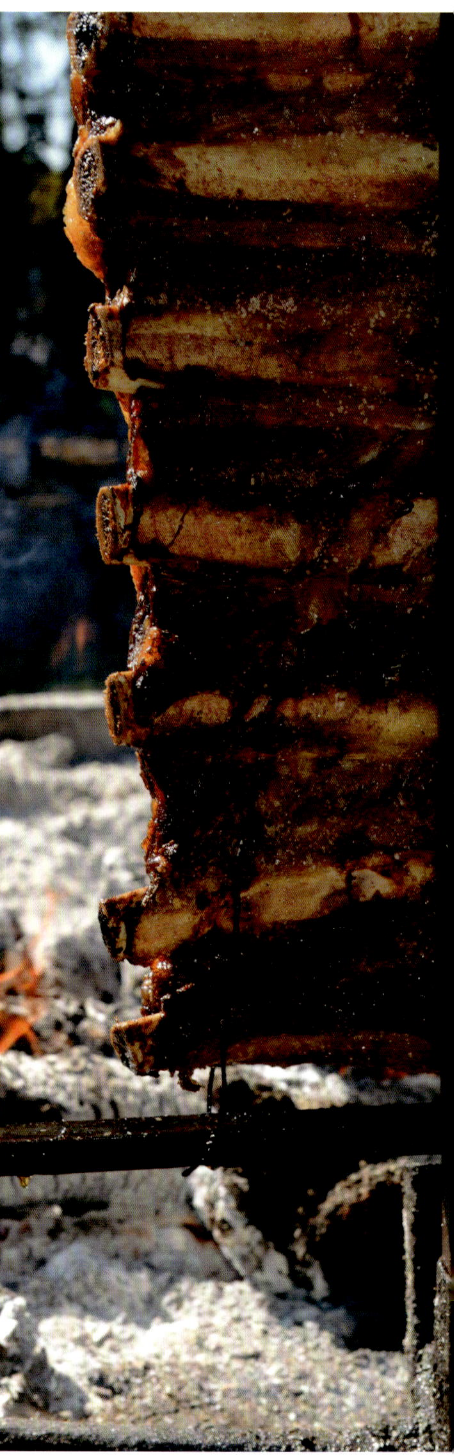

- First, the Argentines start with a great species of cow, Aberdeen Angus, which has a long-standing reputation of quality cattle and their breeding.

- Exercise, diet and living conditions play major roles. The cows wander freely over the vast plains of fertile lowlands to the south of Buenos Aires, dining on rich grasses that thrive in a mild climate. These rich grasses having deep extensive root structures, absorbing the numerous minerals unique to this fertile soil of Argentina, are being consumed in the cows' diet, adding flavors to their meat. Their natural grass diet produces beef that contains less saturated fat, fewer calories, more omega 3 fatty acids, and more vitamin E. These grass-grazing, free-roaming cattle live in natural conditions free from stress, and of course no hormones or antibiotics.

- In Argentina, the butchers cut the cows in a different manner than what we are used to in the United States, Europe, etc. These unique methods of butchering, produce different cuts of beef, creating unique flavors. Also, the Argentines are not into aged-beef, they use fresh cuts of meats.

- Argentines consider grilling an art form, associated with as many dos and don'ts as a religious ritual. The cook who invites you to a barbecue will insist it is his/her impeccable grilling techniques that release the beef's magnificent flavors. This is how it is prepared: slow cooked for hours, outside, using real wood embers (in the wine regions, the wood is oftentimes grape vines).

ASADO PREPARATION PHOTOS, LEFT TO RIGHT
Salt-Encrusted Salmon, cooked above and below racks of burning embers; **Butterflied Lamb** slowly roasting on an open fire; **Beef Ribs** soaking up the natural wood-smoke flavors; a good view of the **Parrilla** and preparing a **Parrillada**, a platter of different types of meats; **Asado**, a culinary tradition in Argentina, is prepared anywhere, even inside the fireplaces of homes and restaurants.

This is the typical religious order...

1. Use a grill that is scrupulously clean.
2. Build a fire with wood.
3. Let the fire burn to embers.
4. As you get hot coals, spread them under the grilling rack.
5. When grill floor is hot, rub the grilling rack with a piece of fat.
6. Salt the meat before cooking. Use only salt to bring out the flavors and juices in the meat. No seasoning, no marinade, and no sauces!
7. Place the meat on the grill and quickly sear the outside by lowering the grill top or increasing amount of embers, then adjust the grill or embers to cook the meat slowly. Keep the meat between four and six inches above the embers.
8. Do not move meat around on the grill; move only embers.
9. Turn meat only once, with tongs; do not puncture with a fork or cut with a knife to check for doneness or you will lose juice and flavor.
10. Serve the moment the meat is cooked.

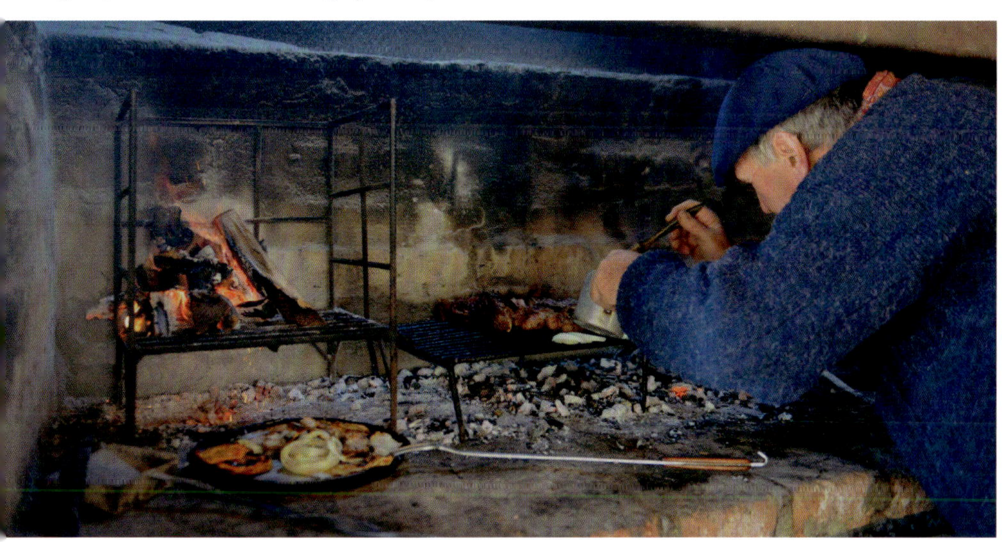

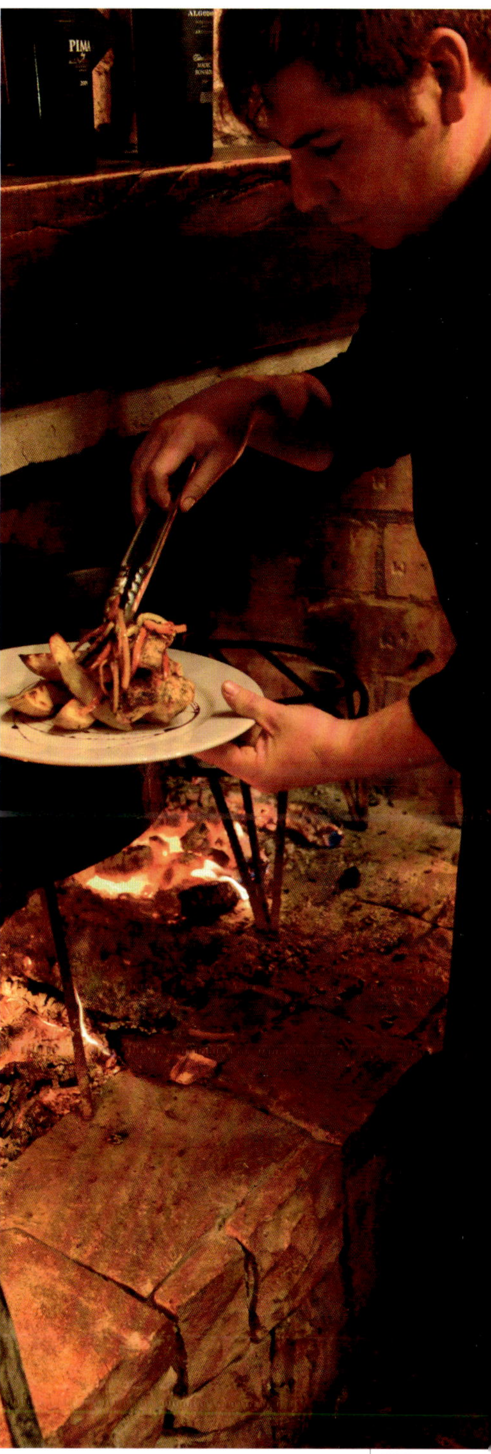

YERBA **MATÉ**

The Strength of Coffee, the Nutrition of Green Tea and the Euphoria of Chocolate

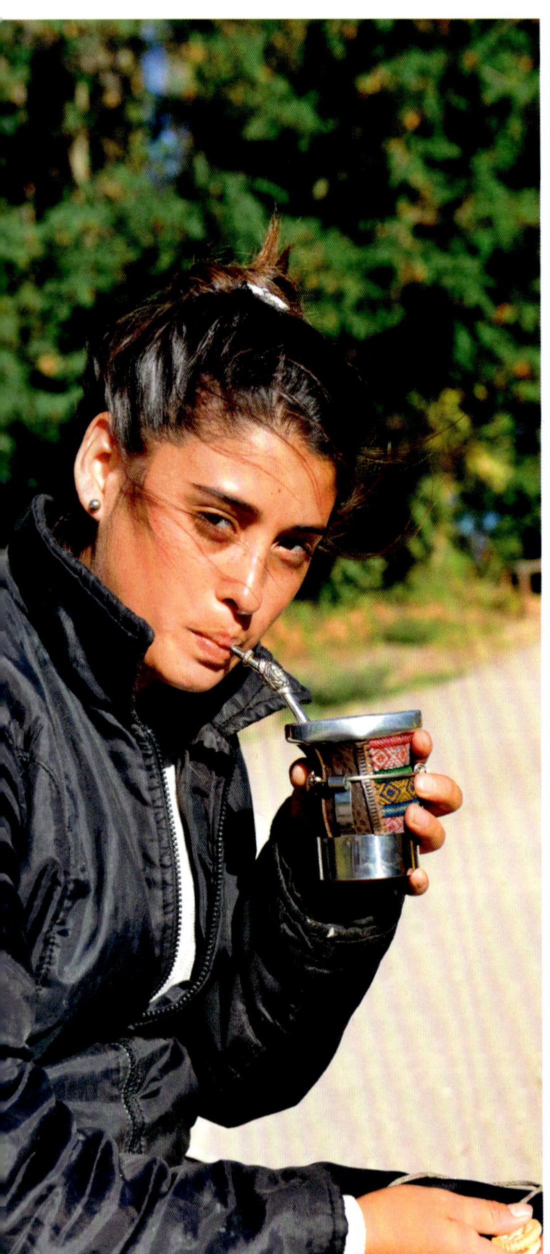

Yerba Maté is Argentina's energizing social drink with huge nutritional health benefits. Directly translated, Yerba Maté means "herb gourd" and is exactly that... an herbal tea drank from a gourd cup.

Yerba Maté was first consumed in the 16th century by the indigenous people of Southern Brazil, Paraguay and Argentina, naturally growing in their Atlantic Rainforests. Today, it is just called Maté, still grown in the same places and is consumed 10 to 1 over coffee in these countries.

Unlike other sources of caffeine, Yerba Maté is both relaxing and stimulating, giving the energy of coffee without the jitters, anxiety or the crash after the high. And speaking of high, it also has the euphoria of chocolate, which stimulates the endorphins in the brain that make you feel very happy.

The nutritional factors of Maté are tremendous! Yerba Maté is a nutrient-rich superfood packed with large doses of antioxidants and polyphenols. It has 196 active compounds, contains 24 important vitamins and minerals, including vitamins A, B, C, E, calcium, iron, potassium, magnesium, magnanese, zinc, and an array of amino acids... making it an important food for disease prevention, a positive well-being and easing the signs of aging.

In addition, research has shown that Maté benefits the immune system, digestive health and stress, reduces the risk of diabetes and hyperglycemia, cholesterol levels, and the risk of heart attack and stroke. In highly concentrated doses, Maté is being used to treat heart disease with its vascular regenerative characteristics. Maté increases the supply of nutrients and oxygen to the heart, increases mental energy and focus, improves mood, and promotes deeper sleep. And it is an appetite suppressant.

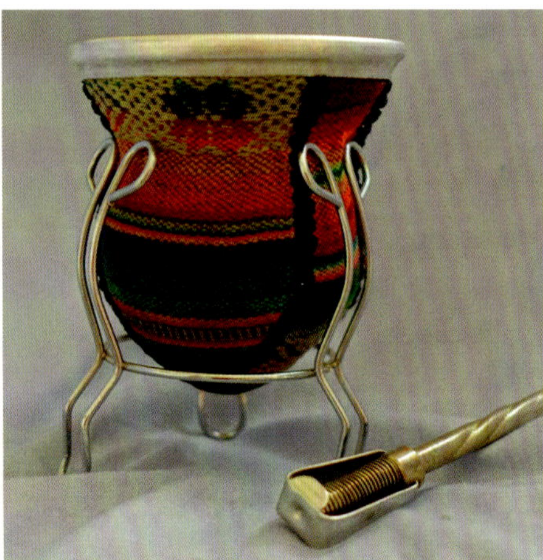

In the United States, you can buy Maté in a health food store. In Argentina, Maté is a social drink that is a part of every day life, even more than what we are used to with the coffee-house craze. The typical Argentine carries around Maté with a gourd cup, a steel straw, and a thermos of hot water. It is consumed at all times of the day. The average Argentine consumes 11 pounds of Maté annually.

Maté has quite a distinct flavor, one that resembles an infusion of herbs and grass. It is believed that the act of drinking Yerba out of the gourd helps one receive the healing properties of the Yerba, while also maintaining its history as being a symbol for friendship and community.

In the same way as people meet for tea or coffee, friends often gather and drink Maté. Sharing Maté is a ritual following customary rules. The gourd is given by the brewer to each person, often in a circle, in turn drinking a few mouthfuls and returns the gourd to the brewer, who refills it and gives it to the next person in clockwise order.

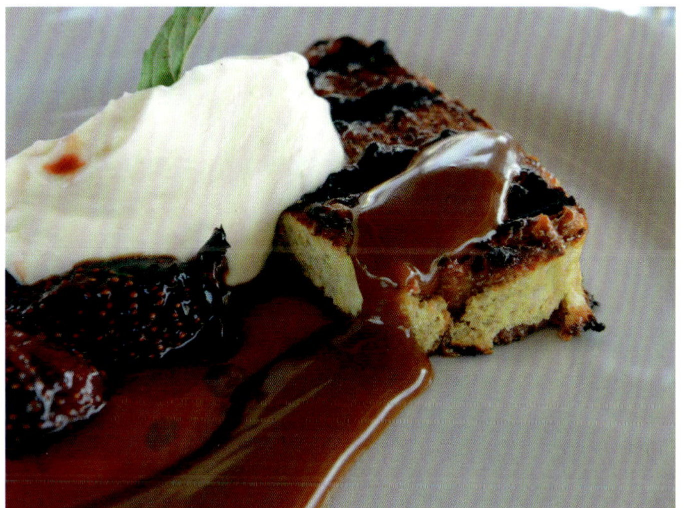

SMILE **DULCE DE LECHE**

The Argentine Confection of National Heritage

Dulce de Leche is a sweet, creamy, sticky confection. Now, while a confectionery is the art of making foods that are rich in sugar and carbohydrates, in Argentina making Dulce de Leche is an art of incorporating this sweet dessert into every meal... a staple for breakfast, lunch, dinner, and a snack anytime.

Dulce de Leche is a confection prepared by slowly heating milk and sugar to create a substance that derives its taste from the Maillard reaction, changing flavor and color. Literally translated, Dulce de Leche means "sweet of milk."

The most basic recipe calls for slowly simmering milk and sugar, stirring almost constantly, for a minimum of three hours... some say the best Dulce de Leche comes from slow stirring all night. And one must wonder does the chef sing or whistle all night, or read a book while stirring... or turn to manufacturers with the automated equipment to maintain the stir?

The San Isidro Labrador company claims their Dulce de Leche is different because their extremely high-quality Jersey cows produce richer, more nutritive milk, which makes their product smoother, creamier, healthier and more balanced than most others.

Dulce de Leche is used to flavor candies and other sweet foods, such as cakes, churros, cookies, waffles, crème caramel (known as flan), and ice creams. It provides the "toffee" part of English Banoffee pie and is also a popular spread on pancakes and toast, while the French confiture de lait is commonly served with fromage blanc.

Hands down, the country best known for its Dulce de Leche is Argentina, where it has been adopted as a national heritage. No country other than Argentina can claim 6.6 pounds annually per capita consumption, and after spending a little bit of time here, it is easy to understand why.... it is everywhere, and at every meal.

Dulce de Leche brings about a smile from those who know. It Is the tawny siren that lures innocents towards the fridge in the middle of the night, eyes glazed and spoon quivering in hand. Now that you are going to Argentina, beware, don't say I didn't warn you!

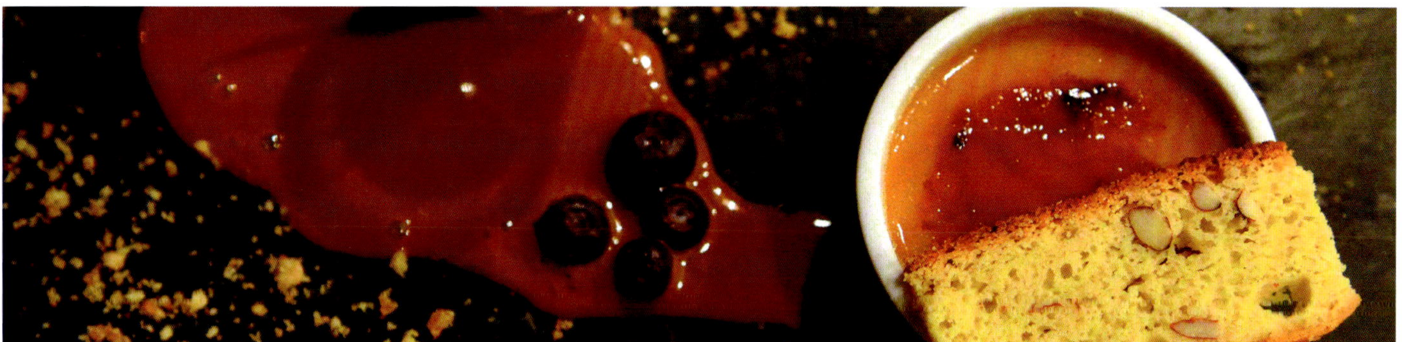

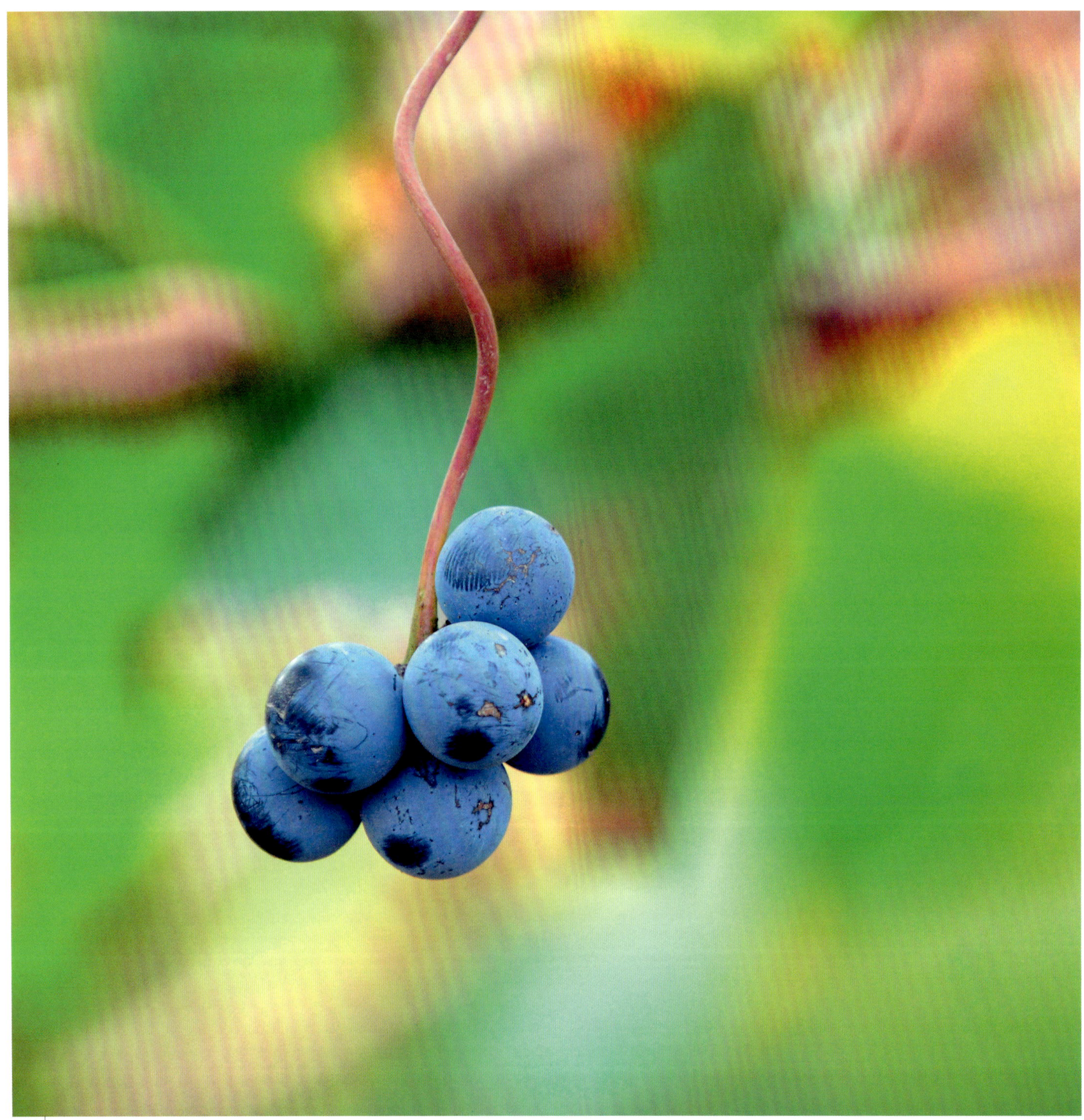

SO, DID I MEET A MALBEC I DIDN'T LIKE?

After three trips with 13 weeks of exploring Argentina's wine regions, I came home with an abundance of knowledge, interesting stories and spectacular photography... and some very special friends I made along the way.

By now you must be wondering, as the opening question begs...

Did I meet a Malbec I did not like?

If I get to go back to Argentina again, then the answer is... *I still do not know!*

As you can see throughout this book, the culinary explorations in Argentina were just as exciting as the wines. With the tremendous diversity of cuisine along with the creative styles in preparing these foods, I was introduced to an abundance of different kinds of wines. The first conclusion from all these is that Argentina is not just about Malbec. While the terroir is magical for growing Malbec, the wine regions actually offer so much more to an expanding palate of winemaking.

To be direct with you though, yes, I did meet a Malbec I did not like, and I hid every bottle from you in this book. As with anything, there are low-, medium- and high-quality versions. Now that my palate has evolved tremendously from this experience, I am able to taste the nuances of qualities like never before. I thoroughly enjoyed meeting different Malbecs from various regions, as each individual place has its own uniqueness to offer. What I enjoyed most was discovering which grapes did best in which environments, and the special nuances derived from each terroir and winemaker.

As we all discovered from my explorations with this book, Argentina is much more than just Malbec. I fell in love with this country... the beautiful people, their hospitable culture, the delicious foods, fantastic weather, and the spectacular wines! And Argentina fell in love with me too. From all three of my journeys that I was in Argentina, the day I departed, the sky was pouring with rain... *Don't Cry For Me Argentina...* I will be back to see you again. Our love affair is everlasting!

What began as a quest for Malbec has become a passion for a country. I hope you soon take this journey and explore the wine regions of Argentina!

Happy Tasting,

Michael C. Higgins, PhD

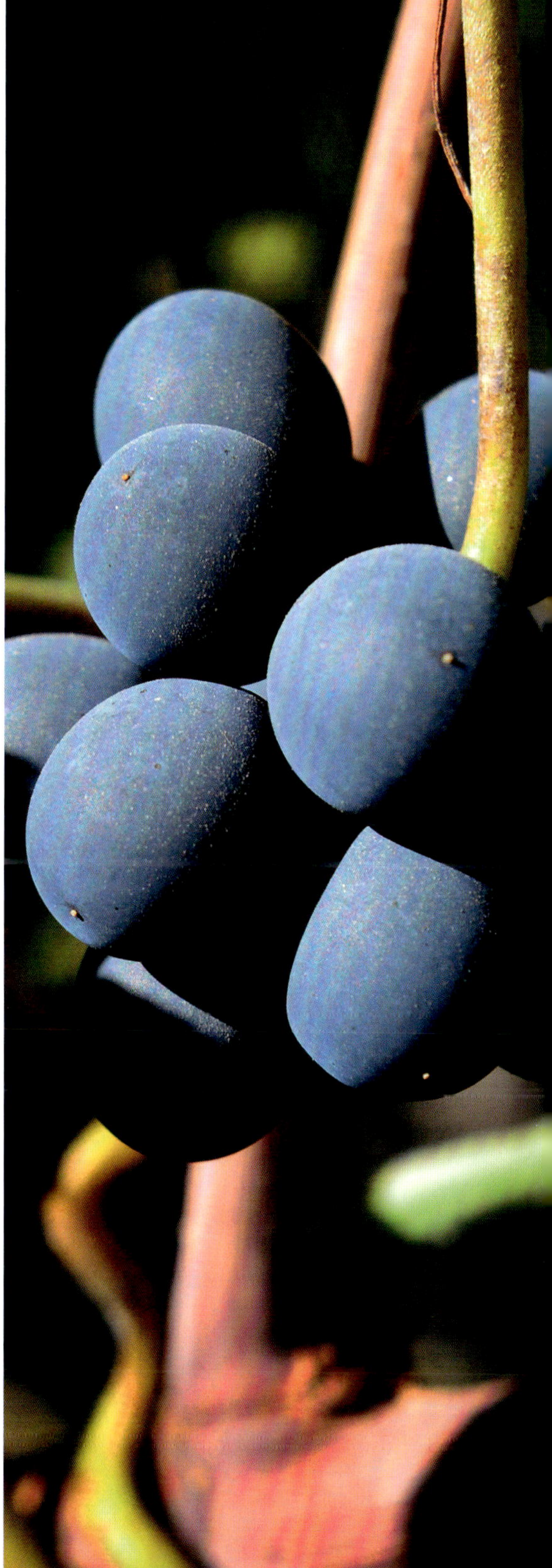

HAIL HALTING TECHNIQUES

Vineyard Netting & Cloud Seeding

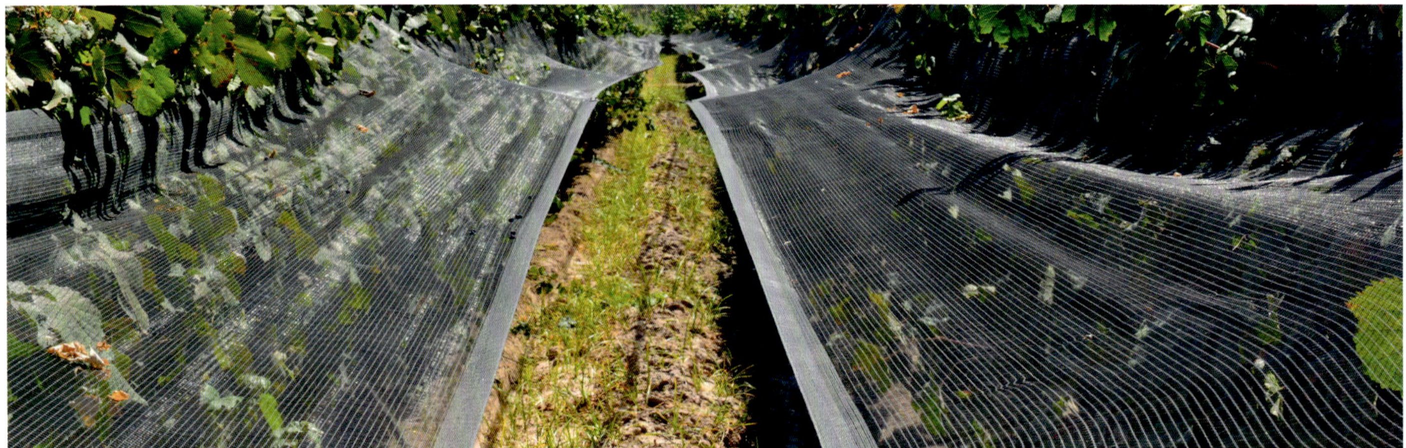

VINEYARD NETTING

See the netting over the grape vines? Are you thinking it is there to protect the grapes from the birds? Think again. Surprisingly, the vineyards do not have the problem of birds eating their grapes like other wine regions.

The netting here is to protect the grapes against hail. From the Andes Mountains come big storms, and some can have large hail. They can occur in the summer and fall harvest time. Picture large hail hitting the grape clusters. Kaboom, the grapes are thrown to the ground and the crop is lost. To protect the grapes from the hard-hitting hail, many of the vintners put up protective netting in the vineyards.

CLOUD SEEDING

Argentina is now using a fascinating concept, *Cloud Seeding*, to reduce the problem of hail damage to their vineyards.

Cloud Seeding is a form of intentional weather modification to change the quantity or type of precipitation that falls from clouds. This is accomplished by dispersing substances into the air that serve as cloud condensation or ice nuclei, which alters the microphysical processes within the clouds.

Simply, a cloud is the development of moisture attaching itself to particles in the air. When the moisture and particles accumulate, we see clouds. When the clouds become voluminous, temperature changes occur creating the up and down drafts that eventually emit rain. When they become massive, these cloud formations develop into thunderstorms and hail storms at their peaks.

Cloud Seeding is the introduction of additional particles into the clouds. Silver is the primary particle used in this process. Airplanes and rockets are the vehicles to penetrate weather and to release the silver into the clouds.

WEATHER ALTERING RESULTS

Cloud Seeding is primarily used to increase precipitation in areas experiencing drought, to reduce the size of hailstones that form in thunderstorms, and to reduce the amount of fog in and around airports.

For many decades, scientists have been experimenting with interfering with cloud development in order to alter weather. There are many reasons to alter weather. One is to induce more weather in dry areas. By flying airplanes into the clouds and depositing particles, cloud formation increases rapidly, and rain occurs. This is particularly helpful for farming when drought conditions occur.

The opposite was used in China to stop weather from raining on the Beijing Olympic Games. By shooting 1,000 rockets filled with silver into a oncoming storm, the Chinese were able to induce the rain to fall sooner, and somewhere else, prior to reaching Beijing.

Cloud Seeding has many commercial applications... dependable and affordable water-supply, inducing snow in ski areas, and helping farmers with increased irrigation and halting hail damage.

HAIL HALTING IN ARGENTINA

Argentina is sending airplanes into the clouds of hail storms in the wine regions of Mendoza, sitting next to the massive Andes Mountain Range. These airplanes are dispersing silver into the clouds of the hail storms making the hail smaller and non-destructive.

Moisture adheres to particles, and the induced silver provides many more particles for the moisture to adhere, resulting in more pieces of hail. With more hail from the same amount of moisture, hail size reduces to small pieces. In other words, as the hail increases in quantity, they multiply into smaller and smaller sizes, which either melt before they reach the ground, or are just too small to cause any crop damage. This makes the vintners and the grapes very happy.

NETTING IN PATAGONIA

In Patagonia, the netting you see is for protecting the grapes from the high velocity winds. Far from the Andes, hail does not reach this area.

IMPORTANT TRAVEL INFORMATION

Important Things You Need To Know Traveling To Argentina

Reciprocity Entrance Fee
If you are traveling with a United States, Canadian or Australian passport, Argentina will hit you up for a Reciprocity Entrance Fee. USA is US$160 for ten years, Canada is US$150 for five years, and Australia is US$100 for one year.

Beware, some airlines will not tell you about this fee until you get to the airport, and then they will not let you board their airplane without proof of fee paid. This proof is a receipt with a bar code for proof of payment. Flying your own airplane should not bear a problem because you can pay the fee at the airport when you arrive.

Prepay the fee here: mirgationes.gov.ar

Two Different Airports in Buenos Aires
There are no direct commercial flights to Mendoza from North America, Europe or pretty much anywhere else except Buenos Aires and Santiago, Chile. If you fly commercial airlines to Buenos Aires, you will land at their international airport, and then have to take a taxi or bus to the domestic airport 20 miles away which can be a long drive through traffic (30-90 minutes by taxi depending on traffic). Santiago, Chile is the preferred airport to get to Mendoza. So close you could almost walk between the two cities if there wasn't a large Andes Mountain range in between.

When traveling to Salta, San Rafael or Patagonia, the route of flight is through Buenos Aires. This subjects you to the double Buenos Aires airports, except LAN Airlines has special arrangements to fly some flights through the domestic airport from Santiago, Chile and then on to Salta, San Rafael or Patagonia, saving you the lengthy transfer. There are also a few flights from Mendoza to Salta, however very infrequent and more expensive. I have researched this extensively and this is your best option.

Argentina Currency (ARS)
The currency in Argentina is the Argentine Peso, known as ARS. Argentina has an exchange rate that fluctuates greatly due to high inflation and government restrictions towards locals converting their ARS to U.S. Dollars. This has created a flourishing black market for their currency. There are two exchange rates in Argentina. There is the official exchange rate at the bank, and a black-market exchange rate that will give you significantly more for your money, ranging from 60% to 80% more. Black-market vendors are readily available for businesses on the streets, and the exchange is with authentic ARS currency. This is not back-alley transactions, some of the black-market bankers have regular offices you can visit.

Telephones & Calling
Dialing International = 011
Argentina Country Code = 54
Mendoza Area Codes = 260, 261, 262
Salta Area Codes = 381, 386, 387
Patagonia Area Codes = 298, 299
Buenos Aires Area Codes = 113, 114, 116
Cell Phone Codes = 9 or 15
(if code is "9" it goes <u>before</u> the area code)
(if code is "15" it goes <u>after</u> the area code)

Example: 011 +54 (260) 555.1212
Cell Example "9": 011 +54 (9) (260) 555.1212
Cell Example "15": 011 +54 (260) (15) 555.1212

If you would like to have cell phone service in Argentina, bring a cell phone which uses a SIM card. For example, Google Nexus phones. Be sure it is unlocked. In Argentina, you can buy a sim-card and then purchase minutes as you go. A cell phone is not necessary though, for my 13 weeks in Argentina, I communicated exclusively via emails and Skype. Internet was available in every place I stayed.

Three Types of Corks
In Argentina, you will find that natural corks are not as commonly used in their bottles as you find elsewhere in the world. You must consider your corks when considering the aging of the wines you purchase.

Natural Corks tend to be found only in their very high-end wines, especially those intended to be for long-term aging.

Agglomerated Corks are what you will see most commonly in Argentine wines. They are made of cork dust and pieces (a by-product of the natural cork production) mixed with glue and formed into the cork shape. They are much cheaper; however, they are rated to be only reliable for short-term aging (one to two years). I have kept bottles using these corks for much longer periods of time (up to five years so far) in my cellar without any problem.

Synthetic Corks, which are made from plastic compounds and designed to look and "pop" like natural corks, are not commonly used here. You will see them from time to time, and these corks are only for short-term use because of the risk of air getting past the plastic and entering the bottle. Synthetic corks are not biodegradable (as are the other two corks) and can be difficult to extract from the bottle.

Different Lunch & Dinner Times
Typical business hours in Argentina are from 10:00am to 1:00pm and then 5:00pm to 9:00pm. Therefore, lunch is from 1:00pm to 5:00pm (big lunch with a nap), and dinner 10:00pm to 1:00am. It is not uncommon for a typical family to sit down for dinner at midnight. So, if you are thinking you might want to have dinner at 7:00pm, think again. Restaurants do not open until 9:00pm and people generally do not start showing up until 10:00pm (remember, they just got off work at 9:00pm).

THE INDEX

Finding Your Way Around Easily

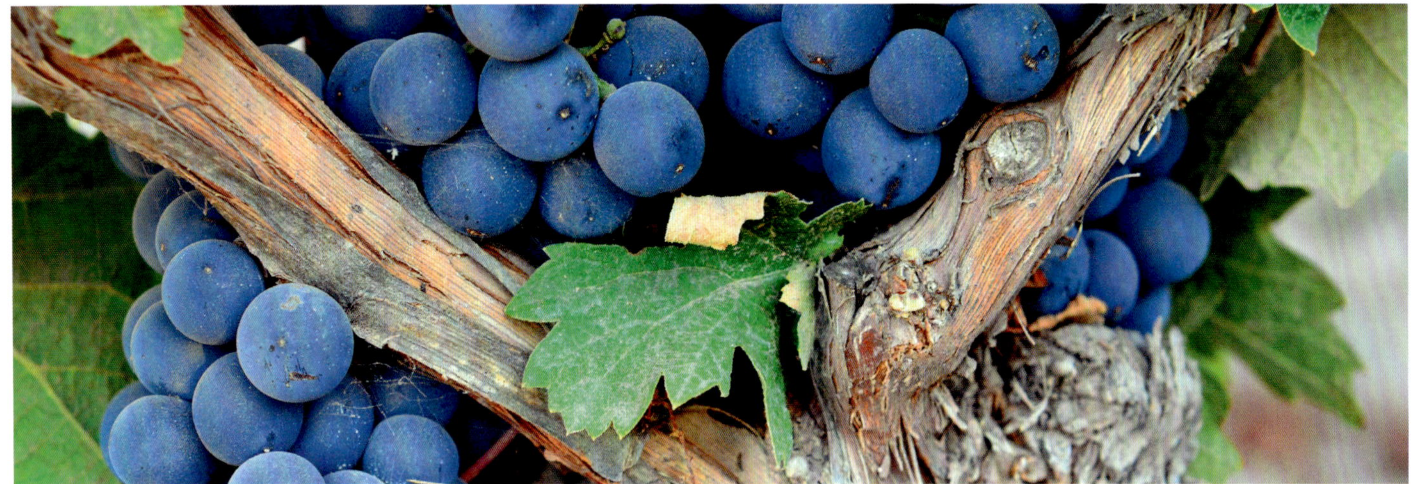

THE INDEX

Finding Your Way Around Easily

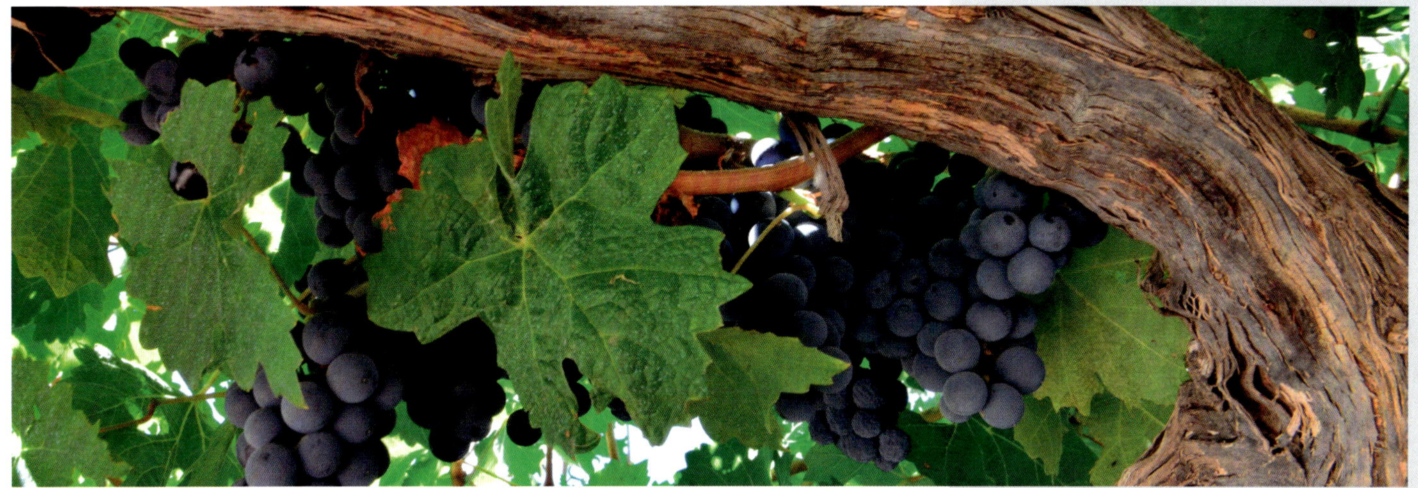

DISCOVER OUR WEBSITE

ExploringWineRegions.com

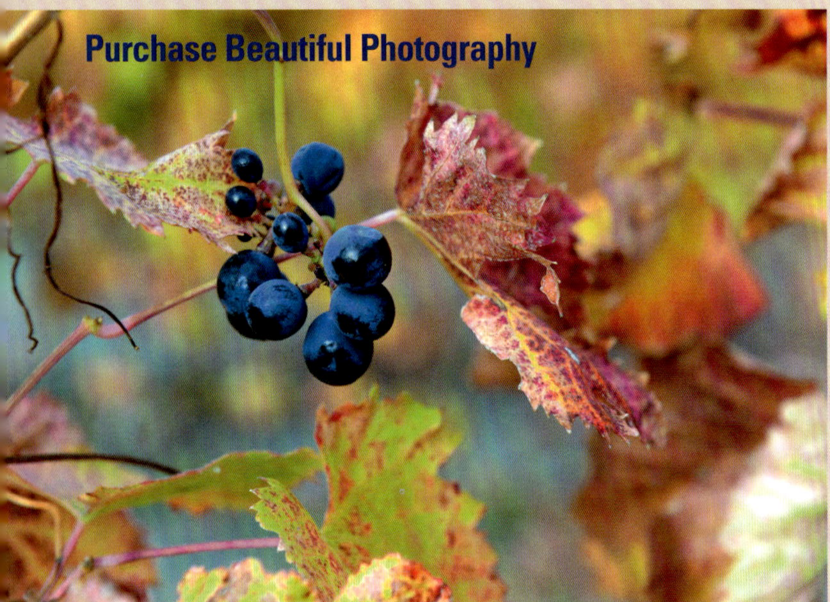

Daily Informational Blogs

Book Discounted Travel to Wine Regions

Digital Travel eBooks & Mobile Apps

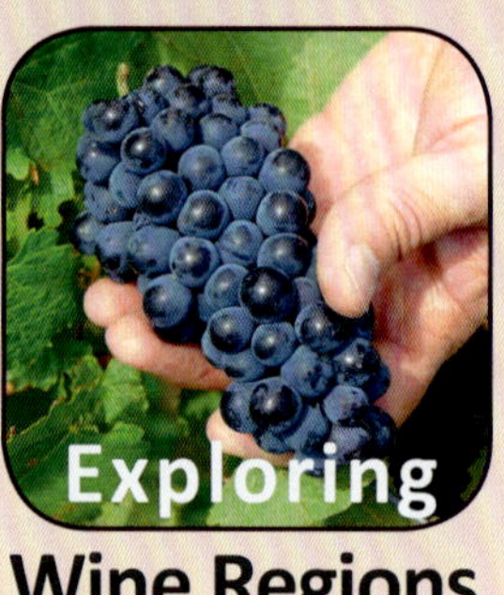

Wine Regions

Find Cool Wine Goodies

Wine Stoppers & Pourers

Exclusive Wine Deals

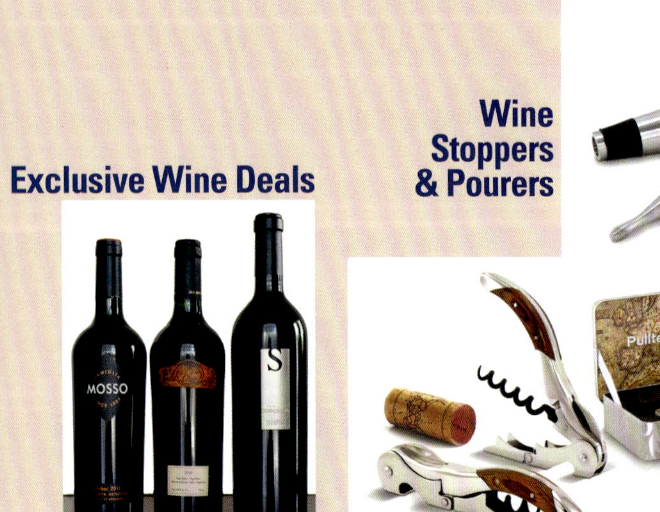

Buy Unique Wines

Natural Wood Corkscrews

Order More Books

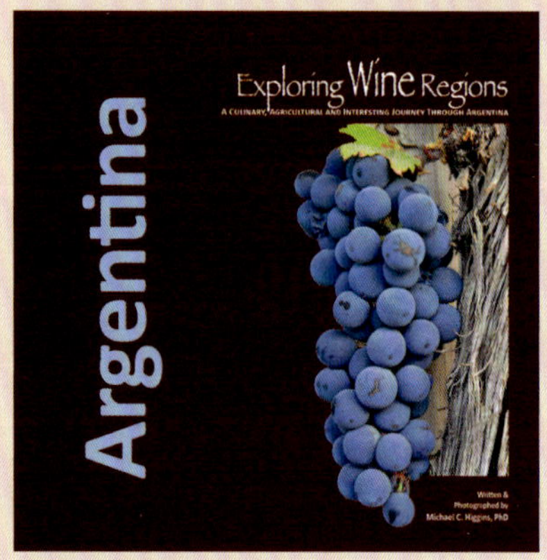

Get Autographed Copies of the Book

Limited-Edition Gift Book in a Designer Box

ExploringWineRegions.com

GET MY EXTRA CHAPTERS - FREE

More Valuable Information to Know

There are more great things to tell you about. As of the printing of this book, I have already written three more chapters to share with you. I will send them to you digitally, at no extra charge, more good stuff to know about exploring wine regions in Argentina.

To get the extra chapters for free...
Send us your: Full Name, Email, Zip Code, and where you purchased this book, to:
Extra@ExploringWineRegions.com

Chapter 1 - How To...
SHIP WINE HOME FROM ARGENTINA... FOR FREE

This is not a list of wineries who will ship for free when you buy their wines. Some wineries will do that though, if you buy enough of their wine. I am referring to how to ship multiple bottles from many different wineries, all for free.

International shipping can be very expensive, especially for wine, because it weighs a lot. Discover my little secret in how to ship dozens of bottles for free. I will also give you important packing tips to protect your precious wines.

Chapter 2 - Is It Possible...
TRAVEL FOR A MONTH WITH ONLY CARRY-ON LUGGAGE

YES! It really is possible to travel for a month with only carry-on luggage. I did it. Three times! Five weeks traveling with just one carry-on suitcase.

This includes not just casual clothes, business clothes and nice evening wear as well. And, for both men and women.

There are numerous techniques to make this all possible. I detailed everything in this extra chapter. I highly suggest you learn the secrets. It will make your travels much more enjoyable and convenient.

Chapter 3 - Discover...
MY TOP-TEN MOST ROMANTIC PLACES IN ARGENTINA

Would you like to know the most magical places to kiss? How about the most romantic dining locations (inside and outside)? How about the best places to cuddle up with your sweetheart?

This chapter is for the lovers of the heart, those with passionate desires. I am insatiable, and never miss discovering those magical romantic settings.

I was there. Took pictures. Indulged. And sharing them all with you.

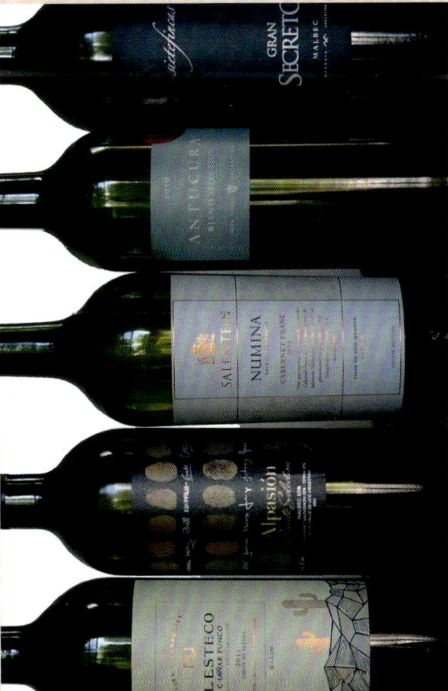

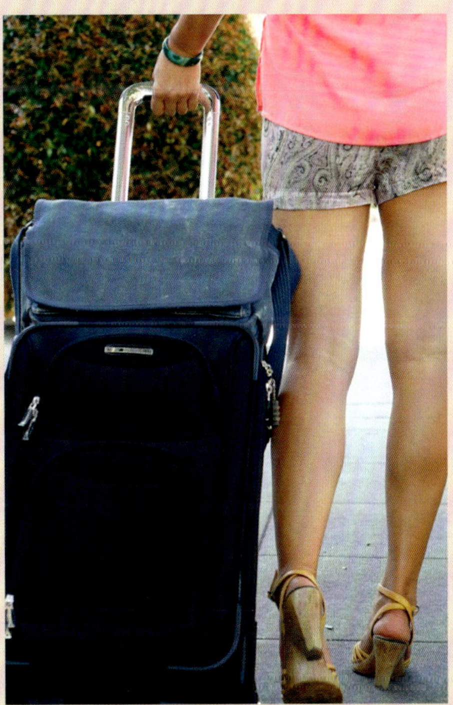

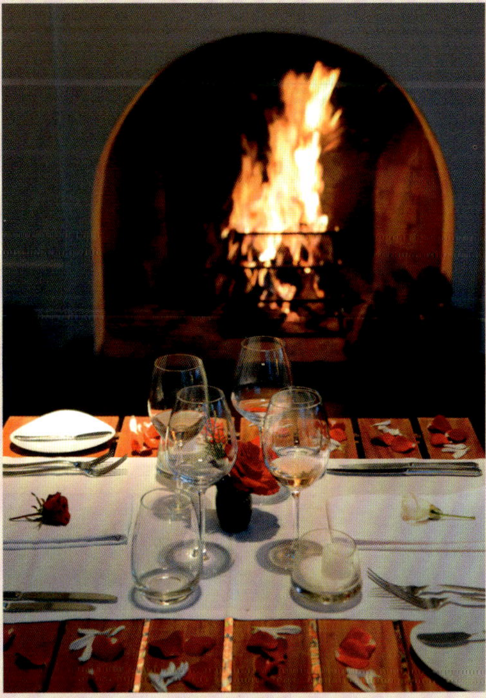

AUTHOR AVAILABLE FOR SPEAKING ENGAGEMENTS AND MORE

Master Storyteller Dr. Michael Higgins, will Entertain and Educate Your Group

The Exploring Wine Regions Team

Michael C. Higgins, PhD
Author & Photographer

Paul Hobbs
The Foreword & Advisor

Li Wu, CPA
Editor & Research Chief

Carol Hansson
Assistant Editor

Deidre Vargas
Administration

Ravi Darira
Web & App Developer

Reach Michael through our website at:
***ExploringWineRegions.com/*contact**
Or call: 626.618.4000

DR. HIGGINS IS THE PERFECT WINE-TOPIC SPEAKER & ENTERTAINER

Michael is a storyteller... as a way of life, just talk to him and then you will know. He wrote this entertaining and educational book of stories exploring the wine regions of Argentina. Taking this storytelling mixed with his immense knowledge of wine and Argentina... you have the recipe for a super-entertaining time with Michael as your keynote speaker or small gathering discussion. Your group can't help but learn interesting information and be totally entertained during his talks.

Remember... Michael engaged numerous leading vintners, winemakers, sommeliers and chefs, plus many other professionals in wine, hospitality and tourism during his 13 weeks in Argentina. This is on top of his 20 years of involvement with wine and travel publishing, and the daily interaction with his love of wine. All these lead to a most knowledgable and interesting discussion from an insider's perspective.

JOIN US...

On a Spectacular Wine Region Adventure

We create over-the-top insider wine tours. These are very small groups, by invitation only, to experience behind-the-scenes, not available to the public, activities. We are connected with the right people to create extraordinary and special activities you just cannot buy. Our excursions are amazing, just read the testimonials on our website. To get on our invite list, send us your name and zipcode to: **JoinUs@ExploringWineRegions.com**

Join Our Supper Club

Dine with Michael, in a very special food & wine pairing educational experience in the privacy of your home (or in a closed-door restaurant). Our Supper Club brings together a top chef with extraordinary wines, all prepared 100% customized for you. You define the experience, and we create the extraordinary. Each hand-picked wine comes with fun and educational stories to entertain you and your guests in your intimate setting.

Hire Michael to Travel with You to a wine region, as he will introduce you to the most interesting people and spectacular wines. By having Michael along, you will be hanging out with the movers and shakers of wine. This is a remarkable experience that can be designed to be your most over-the-top experience ever!

If you want to go travel by yourself instead, **Michael can help you create a customized itinerary** of extraordinary nature.

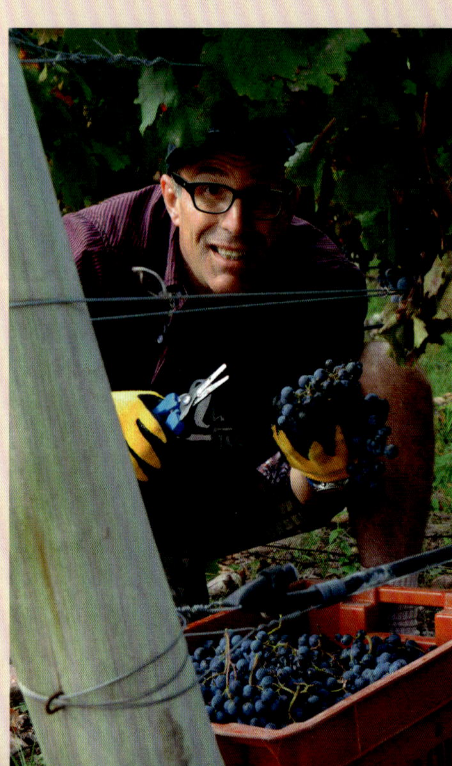

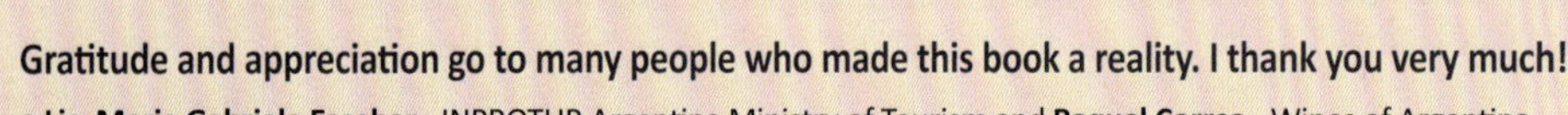

Gratitude and appreciation go to many people who made this book a reality. I thank you very much!

- **Lic. Maria Gabriela Escobar** - INPROTUR Argentina Ministry of Tourism and **Raquel Correa** - Wines of Argentina.
- **Deborah Deandrea** - Valle de Uco Association of Tourism & Wineries and **Marcelo Flores** - Tunuyán Tourism.
- **Alejandra Cardona** - ProSalta Foundation and **Lic. Luciana Zambón** - Salta Ministry of Tourism.
- **Miriam Capasso** - Tourism Patagonia, **Lic. Verónica Linares** - Tourism Patagonia Press Office, and **Marcelo Miras** - Oenologist.
- **Debora Calore** - Neuquén Tourism, **María José Huc** - x4Rumbos, and **Federico Boxaca** - Familia Schroeder.
- **Lic. Carolina Ciliberto** - Río Negro Ministry of Tourism, **Matías Piermarini** - Río Negro Wine Tourism, **Sofia Figueroa** - Río Negro Tourism, and **Ing. Arg. Carlos Urbano Rota** - Río Negro Ministry of Agriculture.
- **Lauren Beebe** - Algodon Group, **Roberto Boriero** - La Cima Tourism, **Lucas Paracha** - Arakur Ushuaia, **Leonard Gelfand** - Gelfand Vineyards, **Karen MacNeil** - The Wine Bible, **Shelbi Herring** - Copa Fina Wine Imports, **Betty Reinke** - Main Street Books, **Aimee Higgins** - Advisor, **Santiago Achaval** - Achaval-Ferrer Winery, and **Roberto Romano** - Sommelier.

GET THE BOOK'S APPS

Wine Region Apps for both Apple and Android Devices

Free Easy Access to Our Website...
APP - ExploringWineRegions.com

This App gives you direct access to our website from your phone or tablet, without you having to open your browser or type in our web address. With just one click, you get quick and easy access to all the many great things on our website.

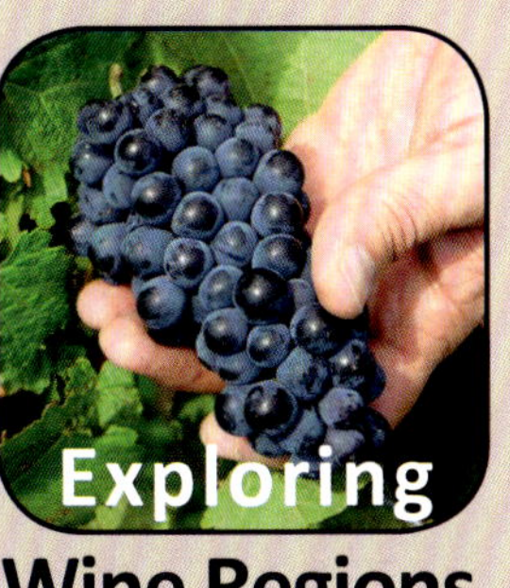

Wine Regions

eBook Digital Version of the Book...
APP - EWR Argentina

This App is an eBook version of the ***Exploring Wine Regions*** - Argentina book. You may not want to travel with the printed book, so we have created this mobile eBook for you to have everything in the book at your fingertips whereever you go. No Internet needed once you download the App.

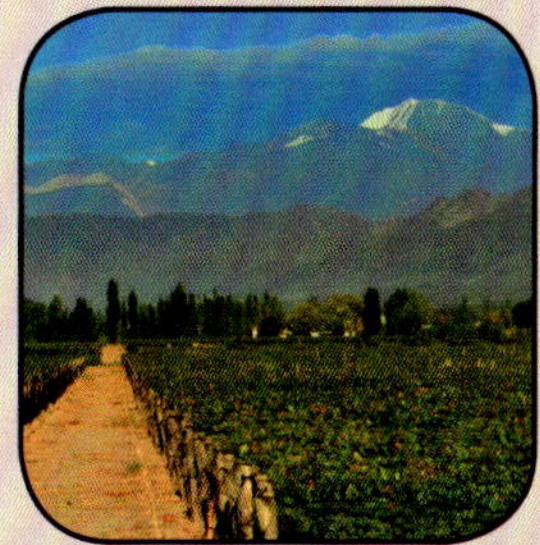

EWR Argentina

Both Apps available in the **iTunes App Store** and **Google Play Store**

Get Special Wine Packs & Deals

In my Wine Regions travel, I come across wines that get my attention, that I want to take home and put in my own personal cellar. In Argentina alone, I tasted 583 bottles of wine (that I can remember), and when something stands out, I make a note of it. I savor the experience.

Sometimes the wines I discover are extraordinary because they have unique flavors distinctive to their terroir, or the winemaker is up to something surprising, or my in-depth knowledge of the region allows me to identify the best wines ideal to the environment. Other times I simply find deals for amazing quality wines; and this happens often. And some other times I am getting the insider track of what is coming up to be great.

With these relationships and special intel, I have organized my unique wine finds, and packaged them at great prices. I have **Featured Wineries** with special offers I have arranged from my personal relationships. Go to our website and see the current offerings.

Scan this QR code to go directly to the wine section of our website, or type the link below in your browser.

ExploringWineRegions.com/**wine**

Book Discounted Travel to the Wine Regions

Is it time to explore the wine regions? Ah yes, it is always time! Simply create an interesting itinerary from my book... there are so many exciting choices (or contact me for a customized itinerary to meet your specific desires), and then go to my website to book your trip.

A search engine is in place on my website for you to find the right airline, the perfect wine region lodge/hotel/resort and a car rental at the lowest online discounted rates.

Powered by Priceline.com, this search engine gives you access to the best possible pricing for wine region trips. Priceline has also created special package deals available through our website. And, everything is supported by their world-class customer service.

Scan this QR code to go directly to the travel booking section of our website, or type the link below in your browser.

ExploringWineRegions.com/**travel**

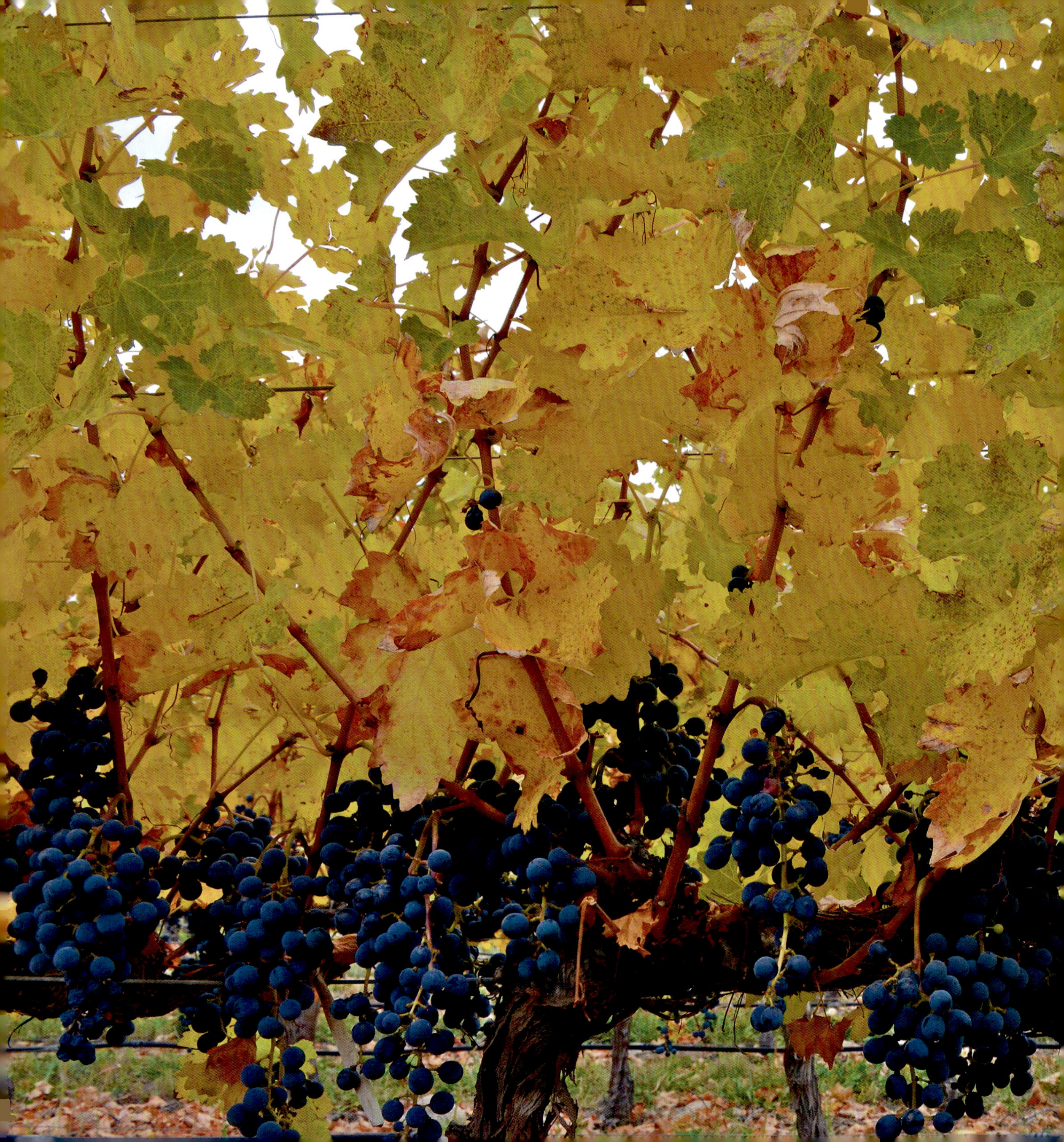

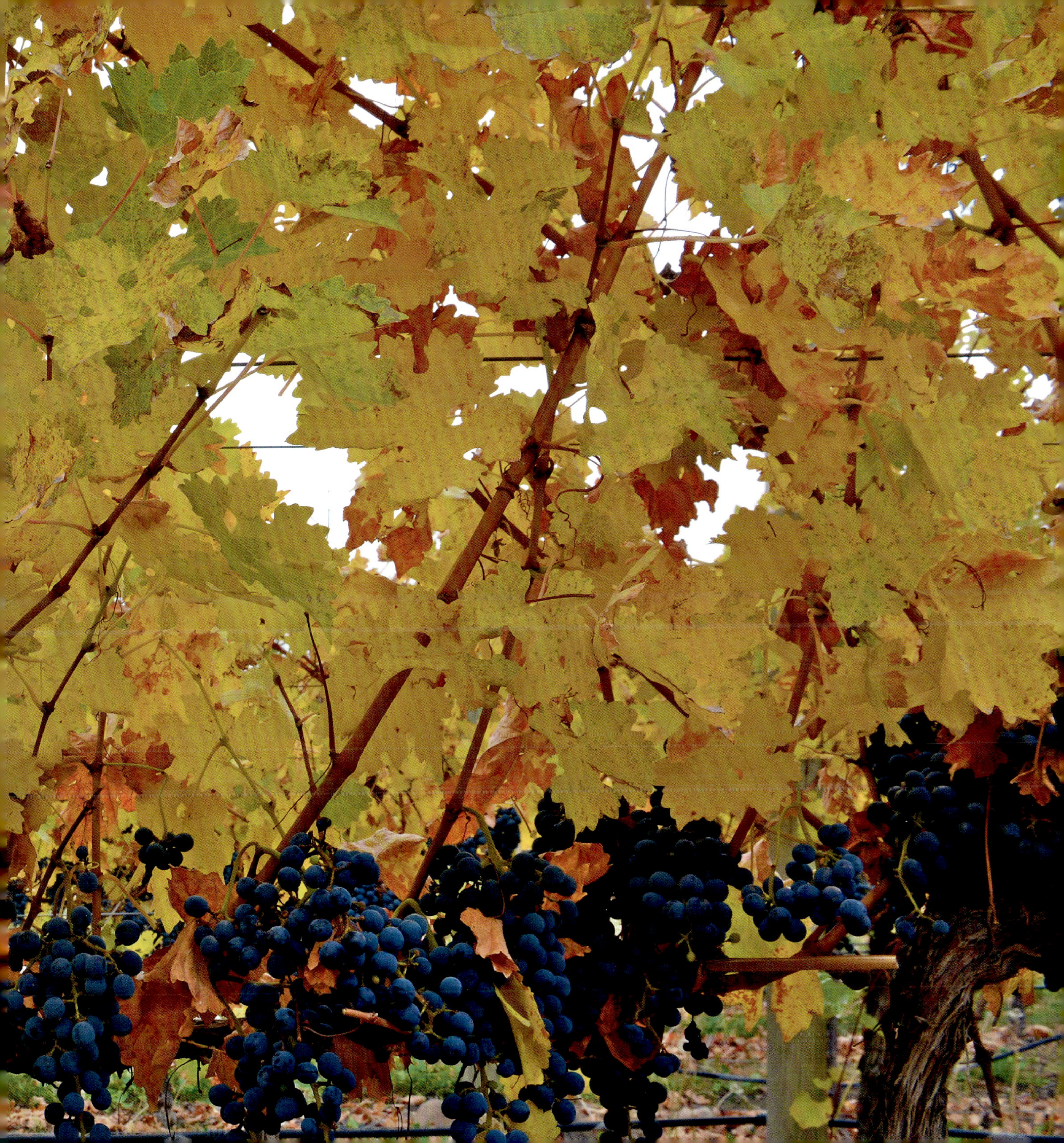

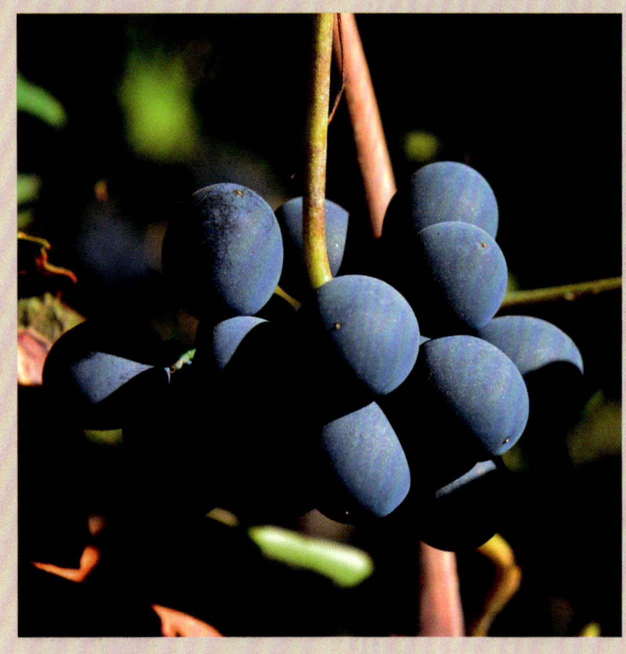